A Tahitian and English Dictionary, With Introductory Remarks on the Polynesian Language, and a Short Grammar of the Tahitian Dialect

Cne Mardy.

Artemise

17 août 1852.

donné à Mr Jules Remy
le 18 Octobre 1854 à Honolulu

A

TAHITIAN AND ENGLISH

DICTIONARY,

WITH

INTRODUCTORY REMARKS

ON THE

POLYNESIAN LANGUAGE,

AND A

SHORT GRAMMAR

OF THE

TAHITIAN DIALECT:

WITH AN APPENDIX

CONTAINING A LIST OF FOREIGN WORDS USED IN THE TAHITIAN BIBLE, IN COMMERCE, ETC., WITH THE SOURCES FROM WHENCE THEY HAVE BEEN DERIVED.

TAHITI:
PRINTED AT THE LONDON MISSIONARY SOCIETY'S PRESS.

1851.

INTRODUCTORY REMARKS

ON THE

POLYNESIAN LANGUAGE.

THE inhabitants of most of the numerous Islands of the South Sea, called by modern Geographers by the general name of *Polynesia*, have one common Language, which for that reason may be called the *Polynesian*; it prevails also over a considerable part of *Australasia*, yet it has apparently no affinity with the languages or dialects of the major part of the Australasians.

The Polynesian, whether it may be considered as a primitive or mother tongue itself, or a sister of the *Malay*, derived from one common parent, is undoubtedly of great antiquity, the people that speak it being, it is probable, separated for ages from the rest of the world, having no intercourse with any other nation, and thinking till lately, that they themselves were the only people in existence.

And while, as the Language of a rude and uncivilized people, it has, as might be expected, many deficiencies, when compared with the highly cultivated and polished languages of Europe, it has, at the same time, in some respects, a force, a simplicity, and precision, as in the instance of the personal pronouns, that may perhaps be superior to them all.

Its resemblance to the Hebrew in the conjugation of the Verbs, and in many of its primitive words, could easily be shown; many words seem to have truly Hebrew roots, such as *mate*, death, *mara* or *maramara*, bitter, *rapaau* to heal, *pae*, side, &c.

As the Polynesian prevails over such a vast tract of the South Pacific Ocean, and is spoken by people for the most part inhabiting small detached islands, having little or no intercourse with each other, it has a great variety of dialects, yet not so different, but they all may easily be known to belong to one common language.

Of these Dialects, the principal are, the *Samoan*, the *Hawaiian*, or that of the Sandwich Islands, the *Marquesan*, that of *New Zealand*, the *Tongatabuan*, or that of the Friendly islanders, and the *Tahitian*. The others, so far as they are known, bear more or less affinity, some to one, and some to another of these.

There is, in the Polynesian Language, a great number of radical or primitive words, that seem to prevail through all the dialects, having nearly the same pronunciation, and the same ideas affixed to them; such as *mate*, death; *vai*, water; *ua*, rain; *fenua*, land; *tai*, the sea; *uta*, the shore; *metua*, a parent; *Atua*, God, &c.

Other words, such as the numerals, the personal and possessive pronouns, are nearly the same in all the groups, and probably the same may be said of the use of the adjectives, and of the conjugation of verbs.

Many words, however, appear very different, when they are not so in reality, because in some dialects the first syllable of a word is dropped or exchanged; as, *t* for *k*, *h* for *f*, *n* for *ng*, *l* for *r*, or the contrary, as the word *man* in the *Hawaiian*, is *kanaka*; as also in *Parata* or one dialect of the *Paumotu* people, in the *Marquesan* it is *anata*, in the *Tongatabuan*, *tangata*, as also at *New Zealand* and *Samoa*, and in the *Fijiian* dialect, it is *tomota*, and in the Tahitian, *taata*. *Ika* is the general word for *fish* in the different dialects, but *ia* in Tahitian, also *buaka* for a hog, but *puaa* in Tahitian. *Ra* is the general word for the sun, but at the Marquesas, *a*, and the Friendly islands, *la*. *Ariki* and *aiki* are the general words for a king or principal chief, in Tahitian, it is *arii*.

Of the above dialects, those that bear the greatest resemblance to each other are the Hawaiian, the Marquesan, and that of New Zealand; the Tahitian comes next, and differs chiefly from them in abridging the words, and dropping a great number of consonants, and in discarding entirely the nasal *ng*, the *g*, and *k*.

The Tongatabuan dialect differs from them all in many respects, it substitutes the *l* for the *r*, and uses the *j* consonant, which the other dialects never do, it has strong aspirates resembling the Greek *chi*, or the ancient British *ch*, and has a great number of words unknown in the other dialects of the Polynesian language, but they may probably be traced to the dialects used at the Fijis, New Caledonia, and the Marian or Ladrone islands; there seems to be nothing in the dialect of the Friendly islanders to support the conjecture that the New Zealanders are *their* descendants.

The *Fijiians* are undoubtedly a different race of people from the Friendly islanders, and apparently from all that speak the Polynesian language; and though their language is partly Polynesian, they have a great many words that indicate a different origin. The words *Kaluo*, God; *Leva*, a woman, *Siego*, the Sun, *tolatola*, a shoulder, *sala*, a leg, &c., seem to have no affinity with the true Polynesian, though they may have with some of the Malay dialects; *bulam* or *bulan*, the words used by the Fijians for the moon, are also used by the Malays.

Before these introductory remarks are closed. it will be well to point out the general modes adopted by the Tahitians of transmitting historical facts, previous to the introduction of letters among them.

They had several methods by which they secured that object, and the first that may be mentioned, was, the history of their gods. This was called in the native language, "Rohu Atua" In their accounts, gods and men were so blended together, that it is impossible to distinguish, in many cases, the one from the other.

Taaroa, was considered by them as self existent, and the creator of all things, and as such, they presented to him the first fruits of their lands.

Taaroa first created the family of the gods, who dwelt with him in the "Po," or region of darkness. He next created a secondary class of deities, to superintend the affairs of this world.

These were said to be made from a log of Aito, cut up into chips, and each chip was converted into a secondary deity.

The first man and woman, descended from Taaroa by his daughter "Hina" She is said to be now in the moon.

The Rohu Atua gives the following account of the titular god and royal family of Huahine.

Tutapu and his wife dwelt on a land called Puatiiiura. They had an only daughter, Hotuhiva. No husband was to be found for her on her own land. Her parents, however, were very anxious she should obtain one, and therefore put her in a drum, called Taihi, under the care of Tane and the god or idol Taputura, and sent her to sea. After sailing about for some time, they landed at Manunu on Huahine; which name signifies "cramped."

The spot was formerly called "Toerauroa."

Tane became the titular god of Huahine. The young lady, Hotuhiva, was married to a chief named Teaonuimaruia. They had two sons, Tina, and Hena, and they are considered to be the ancestors of the present chiefs.

Another method was the "aufau fetii," i. e. family genealogies. The sovereign Chiefs paid more attention to this subject than persons of the lower orders did. Their accounts extend much farther back, and are more correct than those of the latter class.

On the supposed validity of these genealogies, the Chiefs found their claims to supreme authority; and the land proprietors their claim to their patrimonial possessions. Parents, therefore, are very careful to teach their children the aufau fetii, that they may trace back their ancestors as far as possible. When a dispute arises respecting land, each party repeats the list of his ancestors who have been proprietors of the said land, and the person who can trace farthest back into past ages, and give the most consistent account of his pedigree, is allowed to have just claim to the disputed land.

All such genealogies were committed to memory; and when reference was made to them in land disputes, the parties trusted entirely to it, and do so, in most cases, at the present time; some few only having written them. The Sovereign chiefs were, as every thing belonging to them was, moa (sacred), and few besides themselves, were acquainted with them.

Legendary tales formed another method which they adopted of transmitting historical facts from generation to generation, and some of these were highly wrought in hyperbolical language, to give to the individuals of whom they were related, and to their descendants, a claim to the reverence due to a divine nature.

Giving peculiar designations to their wars, victories, and individuals, was another custom practised to memorialise past events.

There has been a great aptness among these islanders from time immemorial, in selecting terms for such a purpose.

A destructive sea fight near an island on the reef of Raiatea, is designated "Te tamai i te hoo roto;" and the mention of that term to the old men who were engaged in it, calls to mind the awful scenes and conflicts which then took place, and which were witnessed by them.

Another conflict between the Poraporans, and the islanders of Raiatea, and Huahine, is called "te tamai huri aua;" this term reminds the Poraporans of the greatest state of humiliation they had experienced for many years; as their fastness was almost taken, and themselves were compelled to sue for peace and liberty.

Another method of commemorating individual circumstances, as well as public events, was that of taking new names, which has long been very common, and is still practised. These circumstances are, accidents, sickness, deaths, &c. A father takes the name "avae mai," (diseased foot) because his child, or some other member of the family, had been suffering from a bad foot. Another is called "Iriti," because some person of the family died of convulsions. Another is named Piha-ati, from the circumstance of a relative having been buried in a coffin made of the ati. The name Pomare, was given to him upon the same principle, illustrated by the foregoing circumstances. Po, signifies night, and Mare, coughing; and as the sovereign had had a severe *night* of *coughing*, he adopted the name.

The last mode that shall be mentioned is their Pehes, or songs.

Such a practice of transmitting historical circumstances to posterity, common to all unlettered countries, was frequently adopted by the inhabitants of the Society and Georgian islands. These pehes were of a national, domestic, and individual character.

The inhabitants of one island would set forth the peculiar character, and convey their own ideas of the inhabitants of a neighbouring island. Some circumstance which occurred in the wars, would often form the foundation of a pehe.

Parties on the same island composed pehes respecting their fellow islanders. These refer to some disagreement between themselves; and also to any particular line of conduct pursued by certain individuals.

To such an extent was the practice adopted, that there are pehes respecting almost every district, piece of land, and family.

After the arrival of the Missionaries, much labour was spent during the first years of their residence in the islands, collecting materials for a dictionary, which was eventually drawn up with considerable care, and sent home to England to be printed, by the Directors of the London Missionary Society; but as the Missionaries were not, at that period, fully agreed among themselves as to the orthography, the Directors recommended delay in order to consider what alteration of that kind might be thought advisable. The present work was arranged by the Rev. John Davies, of Papara, and was ready for the press upwards of twelve years ago, and part of it was then actually published by the Rev. D. Darling, at Bunaauïa, but deficiency of type, and other unavoidable circumstances, interrupted the progress of the work.

The following short grammar is a second edition of the one which was published in 1823, with corrections and additions.

A

SHORT GRAMMAR

OF THE

TAHITIAN DIALECT.

THE TAHITIAN ALPHABET.

LETTERS.	NAMES.	SOUNDS OF PRONUNCIATION.
A a	ah	as a in Father.
E e	e	as a in Fate.
F f	fa	as f in Farm.
H h	he	as h in Heaven.
I i	i	as e in Me.
M m	mo	as m in Mote.
N u	nu	as n in Noon.
O o	o	as o in Go.
P p	p	as p in Pat.
R r	ro	as r in Rode.
T t	t	as t in Time.
U u	u	as u in Rule.
V v	v	as v in Veer.

The above letters represent what are termed *native* sounds. The remaining letters are foreign sounds, and are pronounced as follows:

B	pronounced as p.
D, G, K, S, Z	pronounced as t.
L	pronounced as r.
W	pronounced as ua.
Ph	pronounced as f.

The Tahitian dialect abounding in vowels, and discarding every hard consonant, it is very difficult for the Tahitians to pronounce such consonants as occur not in any of their own words; yet there seems to be a necessity of introducing the above supplementary letters for the sake of proper names and foreign words. Several of them are used in the other dialects.

Some of the Tahitian consonants are often exchanged, as *f* for *h*, and *h* for *f*, in a considerable number of verbs, when the prefixes *faa* or *haa* occur. The *h* is invariably pronounced with the aspirate, though frequently so softly, as not to be perceived by foreigners, unless peculiar attention be paid to it. Sometimes the *r* and the *n* seem to be exchanged, as *ramu, namu,* but what is most remarkable in the pronunciation of the Tahitian consonants, is, the universal practice of confounding *b and p, d* and *t,* and it is a fact, that scarce a Tahitian can be found, who is able to distinguish between them. In spelling or pronouncing the letters singly, they run all the *ps* into *b*, and all the *ts* into *d;* but in speaking, they immediately turn most of them into *p* and *t*, and there is hardly a Tahitian word, in which it can be said, that *b* and *d* are universally used. These two letters *b* and *d* have, therefore, been rejected from the Tahitian Alphabet. Some few words in the dictionary commencing with *b*, will be again found under the letter *p*.

OF THE VOWELS.

The common sound of the Vowels is that which is exemplified above; but there are many instances where the same sounds in *quality*, are different in *quantity*, being much longer in some words, where the vowels ought to be marked with a circumflex, thus; â, ê, î, ô, û. In some few instances the vowel *a* is pronounced very short, as in *tapono*, a shoulder, *tata*, to bale, *tatou*, to count, *parau*, speech, &c., which might be marked thus; tàpono, tàtà, tàtau, &c. In some few others, it seems to have the sound of *a* in the English word liar, as, *pape*, water, *vave*, soon, and the future adverb *ia*.

DIPTHONGS.

The Tahitian dipthongs are all of that character which is termed proper; as each vowel has its own distinct sound.

SYLLABLES.

In the formation of Tahitian words, the consonants must be invariably separated by one or more vowels. And when Tahitians write, or pronounce Foreign words, they always insert vowels between the consonants. Every syllable is invariably terminated with a vowel.

WORDS

The words in Tahitian, as in English, may be divided into nine different sorts, viz.: the article, the noun, the adjective, the pronoun, the verb, the adverb, the preposition, the conjunction, and the interjection.

OF THE ARTICLE.

If the Article be considered as an "index to the noun, to limit and designate its signification," the following appear to be used in Tahitian as articles: a, te, o, na, mau, tau, pue, hui, te hoe, e tahi, and ma or maa.

1. *E* and *te* are commonly (not always,) what *a*, or *an* and *the* are in English, viz, indefinite and definite articles, as in the following examples;

e taata, a man,	te taata, the man.
e manu, a bird,	te manu, the bird.
e fare, a house.	te fare, the house.
e pure, a prayer.	te pure, the prayer.
e tahua, a priest,	te tahua, the priest.

Sometimes the article *te* is prefixed to proper names; as Te maharo, Te mehameha, &c., apparently to ease the pronunciation; and at other times it is placed before nouns, where no article would be used in English, as *te Atua*, which ought to be translated *God*, and not, the God.

Sometimes it seems to be rather emphatic than definite, as when Captan Wallis visited Tahiti in 1767, some of the old people in relating the circumstance, and the consternation the inhabitants were in on seeing the ship, &c., say "tao aera ratou, e ere outou *te taata*.' they thought that you were not *men* but gods, or some superior beings.

2. The *o* is supposed to have the nature of an article, as it is prefixed as an index to the pronoun when in the nominative case, as o vau, o oe, o oia, o maua, &c., as also to proper names of persons and places; as o Pomare, o Tu, o Tea, &c., o Moorea, o Huahine, o Raiatea, o Tahiti, &c.; some, however, suppose it to be the sign of the nominative case. Not understanding this, strangers have often made it a part of the name itself, as *Otahiti;* but there is no more propriety in writing Otahiti for the name of the Island, than there would be in writing Oengland and Ofrance, for England and France.

3. The words *te hoe* and *e tahi* are used in Tahitian exactly in the same way as the French *article of unity*, viz.; when *un* or *une* is used, they are prefixed to nouns to signify *one thing* in a vague sense, as the French say, *une pomme*, an apple, *une heure*, an hour, so the Tahitians would say, *te hoe vi, te hoe hora*, any one, but only one in a vague sense.

When the noun will not admit of individuality, as wind, water, earth, &c. *ma* or *maa* is prefixed, as *maa pape*, some water, *maa matai*, some wind, *&c.* and often the article of unity is also used; as, homai *e tahi* or *te hoe maa pape*, give me some little water.

4. The words *na, mau, tau, pue*, and *hui*, are prefixed to nouns, to denote plurality in such nouns, and to limit and restrict in a manner, well known to the natives, but not easily attained by a foreigner.

Na is prefixed to nouns to denote, in general, a small plurality, two or three, or a small number, as *na* metua, parents, both father and mother; *na* taata, the men, two or three, or a few; but sometimes it may denote a great number, when it is uncertain.

Mau seems to be an unlimited plural, as *mau* taata, men, any number; *mau* metua, parents, without limiting the number.

Tau seems to be used to denote a small indefinite plurality in the noun, as "aita rea *tau* taata rii," but few men, two or three, or a small number; yet it does not seem to be used exactly as synonymous with *na*. The words *pue* and *hui* are also prefixed to certain collective nouns, and mark no definite plurality; as, *pue arii*, the royal family or principal chiefs, *pue raatira*, the subordinate chiefs collectively, *hui arii*, and *hui raatira*, appear to have nearly the same meaning as pue arii and raatira; but *pue taata* seems to be an exception, as being more limited; *hui hoa*, is also used for friends, denoting a number of them without limiting it.

OF NOUNS.

Nouns have two numbers, the singular and plural, or, perhaps more properly, the Tahitian nouns, when not in the singular number, have a plurality limited or unlimited, as determined by the articles mentioned above, viz., *na*, *mau*, *tau*, *pue*, and *hui*, which are prefixed to the various nouns, for there is nothing *commonly* in the noun itself, to signify either number or gender. Sometimes the plurality of the noun is signified by the adjective following it, as *puaa maitatai*, good hogs.

Na prefixed to a noun denotes a limited plurality, as;

Iä, fish, na iä, two, or a few fishes.
Ofai, stone, na ofai, stones, two or more.
Pepe, a butterfly, na pepe, butterflies, two or more.
Rao, a fly, na rao, flies, two or more, but limited.

The unlimited plurals are formed by prefixing mau to the noun, as;

Atua,	God,	mau Atua,	Gods.
Varua,	Spirit,	mau Varua,	Spirits.
Fatu,	Lord,	mau Fatu,	Lords.

Arii,	King,	mau Arii,	Kings.
Haavâ,	Judge,	mau Haavâ,	Judges.
Fetia,	Star,	mau Fetia,	Stars.
Fenua,	Country,	mau Fenua,	Countries.

OF GENDER.

The gender is distinguished, either by different words, or by adding *tane* or *vahine ; oni* or *ufa*, to the noun, as follows;

Paha, a boar,	Matiaa, or maiaa, a dam or sow.
Tuane, a brother of a sister,	Tuahine, a sister of a brother.
Tamaroa, a boy,	Tamahine, or potii, a girl.
Tane, a male,	Vahine, a female of womankind.
Oni, a male, of beasts,	Ufa, a female of beasts.

Most of the nouns have no gender, and may be considered as neutral, or common, when not determined by the connexion, or by *tane* or *Vahine*. *oni* or *ufa*, being added to the noun; as, *metua*, a parent, male or female; but to determine which, *tane* or *vahine* must be added; thus, *metua tane*, a father, or male parent, *metua vahine*, a mother or female parent, *metua hovai*, a parent in law, *metua hovai* tane, a father in law, *metua hovai* vahine, a mother in law, *hunoa*, a child in law, *hunoa tàne*, a son in law, *hunoa vahine*, a daughter in law. *Puaa* is a common noun, and means any one of the swine kind, but *puaa oni*, is a male of the swine, and *puaa ufa*, a female or sow. So *manu*, a bird, is in itself a common noun, and so is *iă* a fish, *raau*, a tree or plant, but when a tree or plant is to be distinguished as male or female, tane or vahine is added, as *ninita tane*, the male papaw tree; *ninita vahine*, the female papaw. *Moora* is any of the duck or goose kind, and so is *moa*, any of the domestic fowl kind, and to distinguish cock and hen, goose and gander, duck and drake; *oni* or *ufa*, must be used.

OF CASE.

If by case be understood the different endings of the noun, the Tahitian nouns have no cases, that is, nothing in the noun itself to distinguish its case. It has been said that English nouns have but one variation of case, viz.: the genitive or possessive, and therefore English cases of nouns are distinguished by the prepositions, to, for, with, from, by, &c., and by the same means the Tahitian cases of a noun may be distinguished, viz., by the little words *a, na, o, no, te, i, e,* and *ia.*

EXAMPLES.

Haavâ, a judge.

SINGULAR.

Nom. Te haavâ, the judge.
Gen. No te haavâ, of or belonging to the judge.
Dat. I te haavâ, to the judge.
Acc. I te haavâ, the judge.
Voc. E te haavâ e, o judge.
Abl. E, i, or na, te haavâ, by the judge.

PLURAL.

N. Te mau haavâ, the judges.
G. No te mau haavâ, of or belonging to the judges.
D, I te mau haavâ, to the judges.
A. I te mau haavâ, the judges.
V. E te mau haavâ e, o judges.
Ab. E, i, or na, te mau haavâ, by the judges.

Substitutive pronoun, mea, such an one.

SINGULAR.

N. O mea, such an one.
G. No mea, of such an one.
D, Ia mea, to such an one.
A. Ia mea, such an one.
V. E mea e, o such an one.
Ab. E, ia, or na, mea, by such an one.

OF THE ADJECTIVE.

The adjective is commonly placed after the noun to express its quality; as, taata *maitai*, a *good* man, Atua *mana*, a *powerful* God, raau *maoro*, a *long* tree, te rai *teitei*, the *lofty* sky, te ofai *teimaha*, the *heavy* stone, parau *paari*, *wise* speech.

In some few instances the Tahitian adjectives correspond in number with the nouns to which they belong, as:

SINGULAR.	PLURAL.
E taata maitai, a good man,	E taata maitatai. good men.
E taata ino, a bad man,	E taata iino, bad men.
E raau rahi, a large tree,	E raau rarahi, large trees.

The word *mau* might be inserted; as, *mau* taata maitatai, good men.

There is nothing in the adjective itself to denote comparison, or degrees of qualities, this is done by the aid of particles, *i*, *ae*, *atu*, *hau*, *roa*, *ino*, and *e*, as:

E mea maitai, a good thing.
E mea maitai *ae*, a better thing in a small degree.
E mea ino, a bad thing.
E mea ino *ae*, a worse thing, or a little worse.
Teitei, high, teitei *ae*, a little higher.
Rahi, great, rahi *ae*, a little greater.
Rahi *atu*, great beyond the thing compared.
Rahi *roa*, very great.
Rahi roa *atu*, greater still, or beyond.
Rahi roa *ino* atu, immoderately great.

Sometimes the word *hau* is used when two things are compared; as, o tei *hau* ïa i te rahi, that *outstretches*, or outdoeth in greatness. Hau *atu* is also used, when it is still greater, as:

E mea maoro, a long thing.
Ua *hau* teie i te maoro, this is longer.
Ua hau *atu* hoi teie, this is still longer.
Ua hau *e* atu teie, this is much longer than any of them.

Another way of comparing is by placing the adjective before the noun that is to be compared with another, and inserting the preposition *i* or *ia* between those two; as, e rahi teie *i* tera, this is great to that, or e iti teie *i* tera, this is little to that. E rahi Tahiti *i* Moorea, Tahiti is great to Moorea; e rahi atu Beretane, Britain is great beyond Tahiti; e rahi roa 'tu America, America is great beyond them all.

Sometimes an accumulation of epithets is used to magnify the greatness, or signify the littleness of an object; as, E mea ino rahi roa tu, a thing *exceedingly* bad,

E mea iti haihai roa, a thing *exceedingly* little.

OF THE PRONOUNS

The personal pronouns are used in the Tahitian with peculiar precision, they are of three sorts, singular, dual, and plural.

SINGULAR PRONOUNS.

1st. Person, O Vau, I.
2d. Person, O oe, Thou.
3d. Person, O oia, He, She, or it.

O mea is also often used as a substantive pronoun in the 3d. person singular, answering to *such an one.*

DUAL PRONOUNS.

1. { O Taua, Thou and I, or we two.
   { O Maua, He and I, or I the speaker, and another.
2. O Orua, Ye two.
3. O Raua, They, two persons spoken of.

PLURAL PRONOUNS.

1. { O Tatou, ye and I, or we and you, and our party.
   { O Matou, we, three or more.
2. O Outou, you or ye, three or more.
3. O Ratou, they, three or more.

Vera is also a plural indefinite pronoun of the third person. It is commonly used in speaking of persons in their presence, and may be either dual or plural.

The pronouns have no distinction of gender, but the cases are distinguished as follows:

SINGULAR.

N. O Vau, I.
G. Na'u, no'u, mine.
D. Ia'u, to me.
A. Ia'u, Me
Ab. Ia, na, or e au, by me.

DUAL.

N. { O taua, Thou and I, or we two.
O maua, He and I.

G. { Na taua, no taua, Ours, two.
Na maua, no maua, His and mine.

D. & A. { Ia taua, us two, to us, &c.
Ia maua, him and me, to him and me.

Ab. { Ia, na, or e taua, by us two.
Ia. na, or e maua, by him and me.

N. O orua, ye two.
G. Na orua, no orua, belonging to you two.
D. & A. Ia orua, ye two, to you two, &c.
Ab. Ia, na, or e orua, by you two.

N. O raua, they two.
G. Na raua, no raua, theirs, two.
D. & A. Ia raua, them two, to them.
Ab. Ia, na, or e raua, by them.

PLURALS.

N. { O tatou, ye and I.
O matou, we three or more.

G. { Na tatou, no tatou, ours, ye and I.
Na matou, no matou, ours three or more.

D. & A. { Ia tatou, to us and party.
Ia matou, us three or more, to us,

Ab. { Ia, na, or e tatou, by us and party.
Ia, na, or e matou, by us three or more.

N. O outou, you or ye, three or more.
G. Na outou, yours, three or more.
D. & A. Ia outou, you three or more, to you, &c.
Ab. Ia, na, or e outou, by you three or more, &c.

N. O ratou, they, three, or more.
G. Na ratou, no ratou, theirs, three or more.
D. & A. Ia ratou, them, three or more, to them, &c.
Ab. Ia, na, or e ratou, by them, three or more.

THE INDEFINITE PLURAL, *Verâ.*

N. O verâ, they.
G. Na verâ, no verâ, theirs.
D. & A. Ia verâ, them, to them, &c.
Ab. Ia, na, or e verâ, by them.

POSSESSIVE PRONOUNS.

SINGULAR.

1st. person, Na'u, no'u, ta'u, to'u, a'u, o'u, mine.
2d. person, Na oe, no oe, ta oe, to oe, a oe, o oe, thy, thine.
3d. person, Na'na, no'na, ta'na, to'na, a'na, o'na, his, hers, its.

As *ana* and *ona* appear to be both used as pronouns of the 3d. person singular, so it appears also that the possessives, na'na, no'na, ta'na, to'na, a'na, o'na, and the objective ia'na, are contractions of na ana, no ona, ta ana, to ona, a ana, o ona, ia ana or ia ona.

Sometimes the possessive pronouns of the singular, differ from the above, and may be called *neuter* or universal possessives, as they regard not the difference of *na* and *no*, as,

1st. person, Tau, my, (rather than mine.)
2d. person, To, thy.
3d. person, Tana, (pronounced short) his, hers, its.

Sometimes another deviation from the common rule occurs, viz; substituting the possessive of the first person singalar, for the second, omitting the apostrophe only; as, tau, tou, nau, nou, au, ou, for ta oe, to oe, na oe, no oe, &c. It seems to be a complimentary form, like the English *you* for *thou*.

DUAL.

1st. person. Na taua, no taua, ta taua, to taua, a taua, o taua, Ours, (two) myself and another I am speaking to.

Na maua, no maua, ta maua, to maua, a maua, o maua, mine and his or hers.

2d. person. Na orua, no orua, ta orua, to orua, a orua, o orua, belonging to you two.

3d. person. Na raua, no raua, ta raua, to raua, a raua, o raua, theirs (two) that I am speaking of.

PLURAL.

1st. person. Na tatou, no tatou, ta tatou, to tatou, a tatou, o tatou, Ours, I or we, and the party addressed.

Na matou, no matou, ta matou, to matou, a matou, o matou. Ours, three or more.

2d. person. Na outou, no outou, ta outou, to outou, a outou, Yours, three or more.

3d. person. Na ratou, no ratou, ta ratou, to ratou, a ratou, o ratou, Theirs, three or more.

There are distinctions as to the use of *na*, *ta*, and *a*, and of *no*, *to*, and *o*, the following are examples; *Na* vai te maa? whose is the food? *Na* mea, it belongs to such a one. Parau *na* te Atua, the word of God. Te oe *na* Golia, the sword of Goliath. Tamaiti *na* te arii, the king's son. Fare *no* te Atua, the house of God. Fenua *no* Iseraela, the land of Israel. Te Atua *no* te rai, the God of heaven. *Ta'na* maa, his food; *to'na* ahu; his cloth; *ta'na* parau, his word; *to'na* reo, his voice; aita *a'na* maa, he has no food; aita *o'na* ahu, he has no garments, aita *o'na* manao, he has no thoughts, &c.

RELATIVE PRONOUNS.

The relative pronous are *tei, o tei, na'na, eaha, vai, taua, teihea,* and *tei reira,* answering to who, which, that and what; as, E ao to'na *o tei* matau ia Iehova, Blessed is he *who* feareth the Lord. Te taata *na'na* te hara ra, the man *whose* the sin is. Oia te taua mau ra, *o tei* haapao maitai mai i te ati raa ra, he is a true friend, *who* is faithful in adversity. *Taua* mea i parau hia ra, the thing *that* was spoken of. *Taua* taata ra, *that* man. E ere ra to *tei reira* fenua anae ra, "and not for that nation only" John, xi. 52. *Aha* or *eaha, vai,* and *teihea* are used interrogatively only; as, *E aha* taua mea ra? What is that thing? *Eaha* tena? *What* is that (by you.) *Eaha* te Atua? E Varua. *What* is God? A Spirit. *O vai* te haere? *Who* goes? Na *vai* te taoa? *Whose* propery? or to whom does it belong. Tei ia *vai* te taoa? With *whom* is the property? *Teihea* te huru? *What* is its likeness? *Teihea* te maitai, *teie* anei, e *tera* anei? *Which* is the best, this or that? *Vai,* is commonly applied to persons, and *eaha* to things, as who and which are used in English. *Vai* is thus declined;

N. O vai? Who?
G. Na vai? no vai? Whose?
D. & A. Ia vai, Whom? to whom?
Ab. E, Ia, or na vai? by whom?

DEMONSTRATIVE PRONOUNS.

The demonstrative pronouns are, *teie, teie nei, eie, eie nei,* referring to a thing, or things at hand, and *tera, era, tena, ena,* to things at a distance. *Teie,* seems to answer exactly to the French *ceci,* this, and *teie nei,* to *celui ci* and *celle ci,* this here close at hand; but sometimes the *t* is dropped, and *eie* or *eie nei* used, as, *teie* taata, *this* man, *teie nei* vahine, *this* woman here, I naha *eie* pue o' epiti, "behold here are (or these) two swords." Luke xxii, 38. Epiti *eie,* these two, or two these, (literally) i *eie nei pue* mahana, these days (ces jours ci.) Luke xxiv, 18.

Teie nei mau mea, *these* things here. *Tera,* that at a distance, as *celui la* and celle la, that there; *tera* mau mea, those things at a distance, *ceux la* and *celles la*. *Tera* taata, *that* man at a distance, *tera* mau taata, *those* men, as if pointed out at a distance.

Tena is also *that* at a distance, but it differs from *tera* in being addressed to the person or persons at the place where the thing pointed at is, or is supposed to be, the *na* is sometimes added; as *tena na* mau mea, *those* things at the place, or near the place of the person addressed. *Outou na, you there*, that I am speaking to.

Taua, its contractive *aua*, and *ia* are also often used as demonstrative pronouns, when *taua* or *aua* are used, they ought to be followed by *ra, nei*, or *na*, in some part of the same sentence; as, *taua* peropheta *ra*, that prophet expected, or spoken of. *Taua* mea *nei*, that thing *here* mentioned or understood. *Taua* taata i parau hia *ra*, *that* man spoken of. *Taua* taata *na*, *that* man before mentioned. *Ia*, is used often as a demonstrative, as Oia *ia*, *that* is it, or it is *that*, O vau *ia*, I am *that*, or I am *he* or *it*. The *ia* by a peculiar idiom of the Tahitians is often used as a demonstrative, where no such word would be used in English; as, "E peropheta ia oia," he is a prophet. John ix. 17. "Na'u *ia* ratou i tiai i to ioa na." I kept them in thy name. John xvii, 12.

There are other words sometimes used as *indefinite* pronouns, viz. *e tahi, ve tahi, fanu, too fanu, te hoe pae, e tahi pae, &c.*, as, Te paraparau ra *etahi pae*, te haapii raa *ve tahi*, te parahi noa ra *te hoe pae*, te papai raa te rahi; *some* are conversing, *others* are learning, *some* are sitting idle, but most are writing. E *fanu* ia, *some* fish. E *toofanu* mau Pharisea, *some* of the Pharisees.

The Tahitian personal and possessive pronouns are often made emphatic by affixing or adding to them the particle *iho*, answering to the English *self*. It implies not only emphasis but opposition also, as na'na *iho* i parau, he spoke of it him*self*. Na'na *iho* i hamani, he made it him*self*, without the assistance of another. This particle always identifies the person, time, place, or thing, spoken of.

PERSONS SINGULAR.

Nom. O vau iho, myself.
O oe iho, thyself.
O oia iho, himself, herself, itself.

PERSONS DUAL.

Nom. O taua iho, Thou and I ourselves.
O maua iho, He and I ourselves.
O orua iho, You two yourselves.
O raua iho, They two, themselves.

PERSONS PLURAL.

O tatou iho, ourselves, I or we speaking and another, and so of matou iho, outou iho, ratou iho.

Gen. Na'u iho, no'u iho, ta'u iho, to'u iho, a'u iho, o'u iho, mine myself, not another's; and so of
Na oe iho, no oe iho, ta oe iho, to oe iho, a oe iho, o oe iho.
Na'na iho, no'na iho, ta'na iho, to'na iho, &c.
Na taua iho, no taua iho, ta taua iho, &c.
Na matou iho, no matou iho, &c.
Na outou iho, &c. Na tatou iho, &c.

D. & A. Ia'u iho, myself, to myself.
Ia oe iho, thyself, to thyself.
Ia'na iho, himself, to himself.
And so of all the following:
Ia taua iho, ia maua iho, ia orua iho, &c.
Ia tatou iho, ia matou iho, ia outou iho, &c.
Ab. N'au iho, &c., by me, &c.

OF VERBS.

The Verbs in Tahitian are of three sorts, active, passive, and neuter. A verb active is such as *hinaaro*, to *love*, *amu*, to *eat*; as, te *hinaaro* nei au i te parau maitai, I *love* the good word. Te *amu* nei au i te maa, I *eat* the food.

A Verb passive is commonly known by the particle *hia* being added to it, as hinaaro *hia*, *loved*, e mea *hiaaro hia* e au te parau maitai, the good word is *loved* by me. The verb neuter is such as *noho*, to sit, *tia*, to stand, it declares the being, state, or condition, of the person or thing mentioned; as, *pohe*, to be sick or dead, te *ara* ra oia, he is *awake*; te *taoto* ra, he is *asleep*.

But besides being distinguished as active, passive, and neuter, most Tahitian verbs have a *causative active*, and a *causative passive* form, resembling the Hebrew conjugation termed *Hiphil*, and its passive *Huphal*. All the regular active verbs may therefore be conjugated four different ways, as, for example; *ite*, to know; *faaite*, to *cause* knowledge, or make known; *ite hia*, known; *faaite hia*, to *cause* to be known.

The *causative* form of the verb is denoted by prefixing *faa*, *haa* or *ta*, to the verb; the passive by adding the particle *hia*, or in some instances the *a*; the causative passive by prefixing *faa*, *haa*, or *ta*, and affixing the *hia*; as, *faa* ora *hia*, *faa* amu *hia*, *haa* mau *hia*, &c.

The neuter verbs, and most, if not all the nouns, may be turned into causative active verbs by prefixing the *faa*, *haa*, or *ta*, and into the causative passive by adding the *hia*; as, *mate*, to be dead, *haa* mate, to cause death, *haa* mate *hia*, to be caused to be killed or slain, or to be *caused* to be in a state of *mate*, or death. E *vaa*, a canoe, *haa* vaa, to get a canoe, (or literally to cause a canoe,) *haa* vaa hia, to cause a canoe to be *obtained*.

The Verbs have three persons, the singular, vau, oe, oia, ana or ona; the dual, taua, maua, orua, raua; and the plural, tatou, matou, outou, and ratou, besides the indefinite *vera*, and the substitutive *mea*.

The verbs have the following modes or moods; the Indicative, te *parau* nei, *speaks* here; the Imperative, a *parau*, *speak*, or do speak; and the Subjunctive, ahiri *parau*, e parau atu vau, had I any thing to speak, I would speak. There are four tenses or times, in which the verb speaks; viz., the present; as, te papai nei au, I write, or am now writing; the imperfect, te papai ra vau, I was (then) writing, the perfect, i papai na vau, I wrote or have written, the future, e papai au, I shall or will write. These four tenses have commonly these marks, the present is denoted by prefixing *te* to the verb, and inserting *nei* between it and the pronoun; the imperfect by prefixing the *te*, and inserting the *ra* instead of the *nei*; the perfect by prefixing an *i* to the verb, and adding the *na*; the future by prefixing the *e*.

Should it be thought more convenient or regular to reduce the conjugations to two, then the first would be the verb active; as, *hinaaro* to love, and its passive hinaaro*hia*, loved; and its second conjugation would be, *faa* hinaaro, to *cause* to love, and its passive, faa hinaaro *hia*, caused to be loved. But inconveniences would attend this method in respect of neuter verbs, &c.; as, manao, haamanao, manao hia, &c.

The *nei* and the *ra* are marks of *locality* as well as of time, as for example; te papai *nei* oia, he writes here at this place, and te papai *ra* oia, he writes or is writing *there*, at that place, but the tense is the present.

E HAAPII TO TEACH. (VERB ACTIVE)

INDICATIVE MOOD.—*Present Tense.*

1 pers, sing. Te haapii nei au, I teach,
2 - - - - - Te haapii nei oe, Thou teachest.
3 - - - - - Te haapii nei oia, He she, or it teaches.
1 dual, { Te haapii nei taua, I and thou teach.
Te haapii nei maua, I and he teach. }
2 - - - - - Te haapii nei orua, You two teach.
3 - - - - - Te haapii nei raua, They two teach.
1 plural, { Te haapii nei tatou, I or we and party addressed, teach.
Te haapii nei matou, We 3 or more, teach. }
2 - - - - - Te haapii nei outou, You 3 or more, teach.
3 - - - - - Te haapii nei ratou, They 3 or more, teach.

Imperfect Tense.

1 sing. Te haapii ra vau, I taught or did then teach.
2 - - - Te haapii ra oe, Thou taughtest or did then teach.

3 - - - Te haapii ra oia, He she or it taught or did then teach.
Dual, Te haapii ra taua, maua, orua, raua, etc.
Plural Te haapii ra tatou, matou, outou, ratou, etc.

Perfect Tense.

1 pers. sing. I haapii na vau, I have taught.
2 - - - - - I haapii na oe, Thou hast taught.
3 - - - - - I haapii na oia, He she or it has taught.
Pers. dual. - I haapii na taua, maua, orua, raua, etc.
Pers. plural, I haapii na tatou, matou, outou, etc.

Future Tense.

1 pers. sing. E haapii au, I will or shall teach.
2 - - - - - E haapii oe, Thou wilt or shalt teach.
3 - - - - - E haapii oia, He, she or it will or shall teach.
Pers. dual. - E haapii taua, maua, orua, raua, etc.
Pers. plural. E haapii tatou, matou, outou, ratou, etc.

IMPERATIVE MOOD.

2 pers. sing. A haapii oe, teach thou, or do thou teach.
3 - - - - - E haapii oia, let him or her teach.
2 pers. dual. A haapii orua, teach you two, or do you, etc.
3 - - - - - E haapii raua, let them two teach.
2 pers. plural. A haapii outou, teach you three or more.
3 - - - - - E haapii ratou, let them 3 or more, teach.

SUBJUNCTIVE MOOD.

Present Tense.

The present tense of the subjunctive is usually the same as the indicative, the condition being implied and understood from the connection, as follows:

1 sing. Te haapii nei au, If I teach or am teaching.
2 - - Te haapii nei oe, If thou teach, or art teaching.
3 - - Te haapii nei oia, If he, she, or it teach, etc.
Dual. Te haapii nei taua, maua, orua, etc.
Plural. Te haapii nei tatou, matou, outou, etc.

Sometimes the conditional conjunction *Ahiri*, if, is prefixed to the verb, and the tense appears to be the present imperfect, as:

1 sing. Ahiri te haapii nei au, If I were now teaching or were now to teach.
2 - - Ahiri te haapii nei oe, If thou wert now teaching, or wert now to teach.

3 - - Ahiri te haapii nei oia, If he were now teaching, or were he now to teach.

And the same in all the duals and plurals.

Imperfect Tense.

1 sing. Ahiri te haapii ra vau, If I were then teaching.
2 - - Ahiri te haapii ra oe, If thou taught or wert then teaching.
3 - - Ahiri te haapii ra oia, If he, she or it taught, or were then teaching.

And the same of all the duals and plurals.

Perfect Tense.

1 sing. I haapii na vau, If I have taught.
2 - - I haapii na oe, If thou have taught.
3 - - I haapii na oia, If he, she, or it have taught.

The same of the duals and plurals.

Future Tense.

1 sing. E haapii au ra, If I shall or will teach.
2 - - E haapii oe ra, If thou shalt or wilt teach.
3 - - E haapii oia ra, If he or she shall or will teach.

The same of the duals, and plurals.

It is also common to prefix *ia* to the verb when in the future of the subjunctive; as,

1 sing. Ia haapii au, If I will or shall teach.
2 - - Ia haapii oe, If thou wilt or shalt teach.
3 - - Ia haapii oia, If he or she will or shall teach.

And the same of the duals, and plurals.

Or thus, Ia haapii au ra, oe ra, oia ra, etc.

HAAPII HIA, TO BE TAUGHT. (VERB PASSIVE)

INDICATIVE MOOD.—*Present Tense.*

1 sing. Te haapii hia nei vau, I am taught.
2 - - Te haapii hia nei oe, Thou art taught.
3 - - Te haapii hia nei oia, He or she is taught.

The same of the duals, taua, maua, etc.

And of the plurals tatou, matou, etc.

Imperfect Tense.

1 sing. Te haapii hia ra vau, I was (then) taught.
2 - - Te haapii hia ra oe, Thou wast taught.
3 - - Te haapii hia ra oia, He or she was taught.

The same of the duals and plurals.

Perfect Tense.

1 sing. I haapii hia na vau, I have been taught.
2 - I haapii hia na oe, Thou hast been taught.
3 - - I haapii hia na oia, He or she has been taught.
The same of the duals and plurals.

Future Tense.

1 sing. E haapii hia vau, I shall or will be taught.
2 - - E haapi hia oe, Thou shalt or wilt be taught.
3 - - E haapii hia oia, He or she, shall or will be taught.
The same of the duals and plurals.

IMPERATIVE MOOD.

The passive verb is often used imperatively, as *haapii hia*, when the subject or person is not mentioned but understood, it is generally, however, so used when the adverbs of prohibition *eiaha*, or *auaa*, precede; as, eiaha e haapii hia, let (him, her or it, understood) not be taught, auaa e parau hia tu, let (the person understood) not be addressed or spoken to.

The imperative of passive verbs is very often expressed by way of wishing or intreating, and is much used in prayers or supplicatory addresses; as,

1 sing. Ia haapii hia vau, may I or let me be taught.
2 - - Ia haapii hia oe, mayest thou, or be thou taught.
3 - - Ia haapii hia oia, may he or she be taught.
The same of the duals and plurals.

SUBJUNCTIVE MOOD —*Present Tense.*

1 sing. Te haapii hia nei au, If I be taught.
2 - - Te haapii hia nei oe, If thou be taught.
3 - - Te haapii hia nei oia, If he or she be taught.
The same of the duals and plurals.

The condition of this tense is commonly understood by the connection, or tone of voice, so as not to be mistaken.

This tense is also often used like the present and perfect, without expressing the condition; as,

E haapii hia vau, oe, oia, taua, maua, &c., tatou, &c.

Imperfect Tense.

1 s. Ahiri te haapii hia ra vau, If I were then taught.
2—Ahiri te haapii hia ra oe, If thou wert then taught.
3—Ahiri te haapii hia ra oia, If he or she were then taught.
The same of the duals and plurals.

Perfect Tense.

1 sing. I haapii hia na vau, If I have been taught.
2 - - I haapii hia na oe, If thou have been taught.
3 - - I haapii hia na oia, If he or she have been taught.
The same of the duals and plurals.

Future Tense.

1 sing. Ia haapii hia vau, If I shall or will be taught.
2 - - Ia haapii hia oe, If thou wilt or shalt be taught.
3 - - Ia haapii hia oia, If he or she will or shall be taught.
The same of the duals and plurals.

TAOTO, (or moe) to sleep, (Verb neuter.)

INDICATIVE MOOD.—*Present Tense.*

1 sing. Te taoto nei au, I sleep.
2 - - Te taoto nei oe, Thou sleepest.
3 - - Te taoto nei oia, He, she, or it sleeps.
The same of the duals and plurals,

Imperfect Tense.

1 sing. Te taoto ra vau, I slept, or was then asleep.
2 - - Te taoto ra oe, Thou didst sleep, or wast then asleep.
3 - - Te taoto ra oia, He she or it slept, or was then [asleep.
The same of the duals and plurals.

Perfect Tense.

1 sing. I taoto na vau, I have slept.
2 - - I taoto na oe, Thou hast slept.
3 - - I taoto na oia, He she, or it has slept.
The same of the duals and plurals.

Future Tense.

1 sing. E taoto vau, I will or shall sleep.
2 - - E taoto oe, Thou wilt or shalt sleep.
3 - - E taoto oia, He she or it will or shall sleep.
The same of the duals and plurals.

IMPERATIVE MOOD.

2 sing. A taoto oe, sleep thou, or do thou sleep.
3 - - - E taoto oia, let him or her sleep.
2 dual. A taoto orua, sleep you two.
3 - - - E taoto raua, let them (two) sleep.
2 plural A taoto outou, sleep you, three or more.
3 - - - E taoto ratou, let them (three or more) sleep.

Sometimes in the imperative the pronoun is omitted, but understood from the circumstances; as, A taoto na, sleep. the *na* being often added to the verb.

SUBJUNCTIVE MOOD.—*Present Tense.*

1 sing. Ahiri te taoto nei au, If I be asleep.
2 - - Ahiri te taoto nei oe, If thou be asleep.
3 - - Ahiri te taoto nei oia, If he or she be asleep.
The same of the duals and plurals.

Imperfect Tense.

1 sing. Ahiri te taoto ra vau, If I were asleep, or was then asleep.
2 - - Ahiri te taoto ra oe, If thou wert asleep, or wast then asleep.
3 - - Ahiri te taoto ra oia, If he, or she were asleep, or was then asleep.
The same of the duals and plurals.

Perfect Tense.

1 sing. I taoto na vau, If I have slept.
2 - - I taoto na oe, If thou have slept.
3 - - I taoto na oia, If he, she or it have slept,
The same of the duals and plurals.

Future Tense.

1 sing. Ia taoto vau, If I will or shall sleep.
2 - - Ia taoto oe, If thou wilt or shalt sleep.
3 - - Ia taoto oia, If he, she or it will or shall sleep.

The same of the duals and plurals.

Or it may be thus expressed, ahiri, vau, oe, oia, taua, &c , e taoto, or ahiri e taoto vau, oe &c., or else without the condition expressed thus, E taoto vau ra, if, or should I sleep, and so of the other pronouns.

The *Infinitive* of the foregoing verbs, is merely the verb itself, as, *haapii, haapii hia,* and *taoto,* or thus by prefixing an *e*, E haapii, to teach, E haapii hia to be taught, and E taoto, or e moe, to sleep.

As to what is termed a *Participle,* there is in Tahitian nothing, apparently, that is sufficient to denominate it a different part of speech or even a different modification of the verb, except it be in the words *taiha,* and *otoha,* crying or saluting; but they appear to be nouns, and so are *hamaniraa hia,* the time or place of making, *purauraa hia,* the time or place of speaking, *faaoraraa hia,* the healing, or time or place of healing, &c.

An example of a regular Tahitian Verb in all its conjugations, moods and tenses.

MAU, to hold.—First Conjugation.

INDICATIVE MOOD.—*Present Tense.*

1 sing. Te mau nei au, I hold.
2 - - Te mau nei oe, Thou holdest.
3 - - Te mau nei oia, He or she holds.
p. dual. Te mau nei taua, maua, orua, raua.
p. plur. Te mau nei tatou, matou etc.

Imperfect Tense.

1 sing. Te mau ra vau, I held, or did then hold.
2 - - Te mau ra oe, Thou heldest or didst then hold.
3. - - Te mau ra oia, he or she held.

Perfect Tense.

1 sing. I mau na vau, I have held.
2 - - I mau na oe, Thou hast held.
3 - - I mau na oia, He or she has held.
The same of the duals and plurals.

Future Tense.

1 sing. E mau au, I will or shall hold.
2 - - E mau oe, Thou wilt or shalt hold
3 - - E mau oia, He or she will or shall hold.
The same of the duals and plurals.

IMPERATIVE MOOD.

2 sing, Mau oe, hold thou, or do thou hold.
3 - - - Mau oia, Let him or her hold.
1 dual. Mau taua, hold thou and I.
2 - - - Mau orua, do you two hold.
3 - - - Mau raua, let them two hold.
1 plural. Mau tatou, let us, three or more, hold.
2 - - - Mau outou, hold you, three or more.
3 - - - Mau ratou, let them, three or more, hold.

Subjunctive Mood.—*Present Tense.*

1 sing. Te mau nei au, If I hold.
2 - - Te mau nei oe, If thou hold.
3 - - Te mau nei oia, If he or she hold.
The same of the duals and plurals.

Imperfect Tense.

1 s. Ahiri te mau ra vau, If I held or did then hold.
2 - Ahiri te mau ra oe, If thou held or didst then hold.
3 - Ahiri te mau ra oia, If he or she held.
The same of the duals and plurals.

Perfect Tense.

1 sing. I mau na vau, If I have held.
2 - - I mau na oe, If thou have held.
3 - - I mau na oia, If he or she have held.
The same of the duals and plurals.

Future Tense.

1 sing. E mau au ra, If I will or shall hold.
2 - - E mau oe ra, If thou wilt or shalt hold.
3 - - E mau oia ra, If he or she will or shall hold.
The same of the duals and plurals.

Or it may be expressed thus, Ia mau au, Ia mau oe, Ia mau oia, taua, maua, &c., commonly adding the ra.

2d. Conjugation, HAAMAU, causing to hold.

Indicative Mood.—*Present Tense.*

1 s. Te haamau nei au, I cause to hold, or do cause to hold.
2 - Te haamau nei oe, Thou causest to hold.
3 - Te haamau nei oia, He or she causes to hold.
The same of the duals and plurals.

Imperfect Tense.

1 sing. Te haamau ra vau, I (then) caused to hold.
2 - - Te haamau ra oe, Thou causedst to hold.
3 - - Te haamau ra oia, He or she caused to hold.
The same of the duals and plurals.

Perfect Tense.

1 sing, I haamau na vau, I have caused to hold.
2 - - I haamau na oe, Thou hast caused to hold.
3 - - I haamau na oia, He or she has caused to hold.
The same of the duals and plurals.

Future Tense.

1 s. E haamau au, I will or shall cause to hold.
2 - E haamau oe, Thou wilt or shalt cause to hold.
3 - E haamau oia, He or she will or shall cause to hold.
The same of the duals and plurals.

IMPERATIVE MOOD.

2 s. A haamau na oe, cause thou to hold.
3 - - E haamau oia, let him or her cause to hold.
1 dual E haamau taua, do you and I cause to hold.
2 - - A haamau na orua, let you two cause to hold.
3 - - E haamau raua, let them two cause to hold.
1 plur E haamau tatou, let us 3, or more, cause to hold.
2 - - E haamau outou, let you 3, or more, cause to hold.
3 - - E haamau ratou, let them 3, or more, cause to hold.

SUBJUNCTIVE MOOD.—*Present Tense.*

1 sing. Te haamau nei au, If I cause to hold.
2 - - Te haamau nei oe, If thou cause to hold.
3 - - Te haamau nei oia, If he or she cause to hold.
The same of the duals and plurals.

Imperfect Tense.

1 sing. Ahiri te haamau ra vau, If I then caused to hold.
2 - - Ahiri te haamau ra oe, If thou didst cause to hold.
3 - Ahiri te haamau ra oia, If he or she caused to hold.
The same of the duals and plurals.

Perfect Tense.

1 sing. I haamau na vau, If I have caused to hold.
2 - - I haamau na oe, If thou have caused to hold.
3 - - I haamau na oia, If he or she have caused to hold.
The same of the duals and plurals.

Future Tense.

1 sing. Ia haamau au, If I will or shall cause to hold.
2 - - Ia haamau oe, If thou wilt or shalt cause to hold.
3 - - Ia haamau oia, If he or she will or shall cause to hold.
The same of the duals and plurals.

MAU HIA, to be held.—3d. Conjugation.

INDICATIVE MOOD.—*Present Tense.*

1 sing. Te mau hia nei au, I am held.
2 - - Te mau hia nei oe, Thou art held.
3 - - Te mau hia nei oia, He or she is held.
The same of the dual and plurals.

Imperfect Tense.

1 sing. Te mau hia ra vau, I was (then) held.
2 - - Te mau hia ra oe, Thou wast held.
3. - - Te mau hia ra oia, he or she was held.
The same of the duals and plurals.

Perfect Tense.

1 sing. I mau hia na vau, I have been held.
2 - - I mau hia na oe, Thou hast been held.
3 - - I mau hia na oia, He or she has been held.
The same of the duals and plurals.

Future Tense.

1 sing. E mau hia vau, I will or shall be held.
2 - - E mau hia oe, Thou wilt or shalt be held
3 - - E mau hia oia, He or she will or shall be held.
The same of the duals and plurals.

IMPERATIVE MOOD.

1 sing. Ia mau hia vau, may I or let me be held.
2 - - Ia mau hia oe, mayest thou, or be thou held.
3 - - Ia mau hia oia, may he or she be held.
The same of the duals and plurals.

SUBJUNCTIVE MOOD.—*Present Tense.*

1 sing. Te mau hia nei au, If I be held.
2 - - Te mau hia nei oe, If thou be held.
3 - - Te mau hia nei oia, If he or she be held.
The same of the duals and plurals.

Imperfect Tense.

1 sing. Te mau hia ra vau, If I were or was then held.
2 - - Te mau hia ra oe, If thou wert held.
3 - - Te mau hia ra oia, If he or she were held.
The same of the duals and plurals.

Perfect Tense.

1 sing. I mau hia na vau, If I have been held.
2 - - I mau hia na oe, If thou have been held.

3 - - I mau hia na oia, If he or she have been held.
The same of the duals and plurals.

Future Tense.

1 sing. Ia mau hia vau, If I will or shall be held.
2 - - Ia mau hia oe, If thou wilt or shalt be held.
3 - - Ia mau hia oia, If he or she will or shall be held.
The same of the duals and plurals.

4th. Conjugation, HAAMAU HIA, causing to be held.

INDICATIVE MOOD.—*Present Tense.*

1 sing. Te haamau hia nei au, I am caused to be held.
2 - - Te haamau hia nei oe, Thou art caused to be held.
3 - - Te haamau hia nei oia, He or she is caused to be [held.
The same of the duals and plurals.

Imperfect Tense.

1 s. Te haamau hia ra vau, I was then caused to be held.
2 - Te haamau hia ra oe, Thou wast caused to be held.
3 - Te haamau hia ra oia, He or she was caused to be held.
The same of the duals and plurals.

Perfect Tense.

1 s. I haamau hia na vau, I have been caused to be held.
2 - I haamau hia na oe, Thou hast been caused to be held.
3 - I haamau hia na oia, He or she has been caused to be [held.
The same of the duals and plurals.

Future Tense.

1 s. E haamau hia vau, I will or shall be caused to be held.
2 - E haamau hia oe, Thou wilt or shalt be caused to be held.
3 - E haamau hia oia, He or she will or shall be caused to [be held.
The same of the duals and plurals.

IMPERATIVE MOOD.

1 s. Ia haamau hia vau, may I be caused to be held.
2 - Ia haamau hia oe, mayest thou be caused to be held.
3 - Ia haamau hia oia, may he or she be caused to be held.
The same of the duals and plurals.

SUBJUNCTIVE MOOD.—*Present Tense.*

1 s. Te haamau hia nei au, If I be caused to be held.
2 - Te haamau hia nei oe, If thou be caused to be held.
3 - Te haamau hia nei oia, If he or she be caused to be held.
The same of the duals and plurals.

Imperfect Tense.

1 s. Te haamau hia ra vau, If I was then or were caused to be held.
2 - Te haamau hia ra oe, If thou wert caused to be held.
3 - Te haamau hia ra oia, If he or she were caused to be held.
The same of the duals and plurals.

Perfect Tense.

1 s. I haamau hia na vau, If I have been caused to be held.
2 - I haamau hia na oe, If thou have been caused to be held.
3 - I haamau hia na oia, If he or she have been caused to be held.
The same of the duals and plurals.

Future Tense.

1 s. Ia haamau hia vau, If I will or shall be caused to be held.
2 - Ia haamau hia oe, If thou wilt or shalt be caused to be held.
3 Ia haamau hia oia, If he or she will or shall be caused to be held.
The same of the duals and plurals.

The above is the conjugation of a regular verb in its various modes, times, and significations; but there are in Tahitian, as in other languages, anomalous verbs of various kinds. Some are irregular in their form, others in their significations, or applications, as they are now used by the natives, such as *ani* to ask, *faa ani*, to give away.

Some are often used as auxiliaries to other verbs, and sometimes as principal verbs themselves, as *pau*, which commonly accompanies another principal passive verb; as, Ua *pau* i te *amu hia*, it is eaten, or *consumed* by eating, sometimes it is used alone, signifying consumed, vanquished, or conquered.

Ua, is a particle of very frequent use, and may be considered as an *affirmation* or auxiliary verb of being, but not a distinctive mark of tense. It is prefixed to verbs to signify, that the action expressed by the verb has taken place, or is now existing, or shall exist or take place in connection with some act or circumstance, mentioned or implied, as for instance, "A vavahi na teienei nao, e *ua* rui toru anae *ua* tia faahou ïa ia'u. John ii. 19.

It is moreover used as a prefix to all kinds of adjectives *affirming* the present existence of the quality mentioned, and strongly *implying* its former absence, or the want of; as,

Ua ino, it is (now) bad,	Ua meumeu, it is thick.
Ua maitai, it is now good,	Ua rairai, it is thin.
Ua poto, it is short,	Ua ereere, it is black.
Ua roa, it is long,	Ua teatea, it is white.
Ua teitei, it is high,	Ua rearea, it is yellow.
Ua haahaa, it is low,	Ua uraura, it is red.

Most nouns may be turned into different kinds of verbs in the following manner;

Nouns.	*Verbs Active.*	*Verbs Passive.*
Aho,	faa aho	aho hia.
Amaa	faa amaa	amaa hia.
Amae	faa amae	amae hia.
Anae	faa anae	anae hia.
Ete	faa ete	ete hia.
Ioa	faa ioa	ioa hia.
Fata	faa fata	fata hia.
Fare	faa fare	fare hia.
Pape	tapape	pape hia.
Manao	haamanao	manao hia.

Adjectives are turned into Verbs thus:

Adjectives,	*Verbs Active,*	*Verbs of the 4th conjug.*
Aano	faa aano	faa aano hia.
I	faa i	faa i hia.
Iti	faa iti	faa iti hia.
Itoito	faa itoito	faa itoito hia.
Fatata	faa fatata	faa fatata hia.
Maitai	haamaitai	haa maitai hia.
Nehenehe	faanehenehe	faa nehenehe hia.

Verbs neuter.	*Verbs active.*	*Verbs of the 4th conjug.*
Ara	faa ara	faa ara hia.
Ata	faa ata	faa ata hia.
Moe	haamoe	haamoe hia.
Noho	faa noho	faanoho hia.
Taoto	faa taoto	faataoto hia.
Vare	haavare	haavare hia.

Some words are used as nouns and verbs neuter without any alteration but in the 2d. and 4th conj., thus;

Nouns.	*Verbs neuter.*	*V. of the 2d.*	*V. of the 4th conj.*
Ora	ora	faaora	faaora hia.
Mate	mate	haamate	haamate hia.
Pohe	pohe	haapohe	haapohe hia.
Ea	ea	faaea	faaea hia.
Oto	oto	faaoto	faaotohia.

But besides the above mentioned distinctions of the verbs, there are others of *reduplication*, not yet taken notice of, and those of various forms.

Some appear to have *a duality* of number, although not always perhaps definite, such as *popohe, hohore, rereva, apipiti*, &c. Others, signifying a repetition of the action have the whole verb doubled, as *hiohio, revareva*, &c.

But the greatest number in repeating the verb, drop a syllable or a letter, some in the first, as *hahaere, paraparau, horohoroi, hohoe*, &c., others in the last part of the compound; as, *opanipani, patiatia, amuimui, manaonao, faarooroo, apoopoo, faaiteite, faatiatia, tipaopao, aroharoha, vaiihoiho*, &c., others differ from all these in their form or application, as, *pararahi, parahirahi, pararau*, &c.

The following is a list of them:

Horo, to run, *hohoro*, when two persons run together.

Hoo, to barter, buy or sell, *hohoo*, when two persons do so.

Pou, to descend or come down, *popou*, when two persons descend together.

Pohe, to die, (*mate* is the common and old Polynesian word,) *popohe*, when two persons die together, hoe a *popohe* raa.

Reva, to go or depart, *rereva*, when two persons go together.

The greatest number, however, of the *reduplicates*, have no mark of number, but denote a repetition of the action, as in the following examples:

Amaha, to split or open, *amahamaha*, to do so repeatedly.

Amui, to associate, *amuimui*, to do so repeatedly.

Apoo, to meet or assemble for some business, *apoopoo*, to do so repeatedly.

Aroha, to pity, love or compassionate, *aroharoha*, to do so repeatedly.

Faaroo, to hear, *faarooroo*, to listen or hearken repeatedly, or hear repeated conversations.

Faaite, to make known, *faaiteite*, to make known repeatedly or by little and little.

Faatia, to relate or rehearse, *faatiatia*, to do so repeatedly, by taking by little any subject of discourse.

Feruri, to reason, or exercise the judgment, *feruriruri*, to do so repeatedly.

Haapii to teach, *haapiipii*, to do so repeatedly.

Hio, to look, *hiohio*, to act the spy by looking or prying into things repeatedly.

Haere, to go or move, *hahaere*, to repeat the motion.

Hopoi, to carry or convey, *hopohopoi*, to carry or convey repeatedly.

Huti, to pull or pluck, *hutihuti*, to pluck repeatedly, as the feathers of a fowl.

Haavare, to deceive, *haavarevare*, to cause repeated deceptions.

Horoi, to wash, *horohoroi*, to wash repeatedly.

Hoe, to paddle or row, *hohoe*, to do so repeatedly.

Mahemo, slipped off, *mahemohemo*, did so repeatedly.

Matara, loosened or got free, *mataratara*, a repetition of the same.

Manao, to think, *manaonao*, to exercise thoughts with anxiety or concern.

Ofati, to break, *ofatifati*, to do so repeatedly.

O oti, to cut, *otioti*, to repeat the action.

Opani, to shut as a door, *opanipani*, to repeat the same.

Patia, to strike, thrust or pierce, *patiatia*, to repeat the action.

Parahi, to dwell or abide, *pararahi*, to dwell or abide, applied to two persons; *parahirahi*, to abide occasionally or for a little while. "No *parahirahi* ae i o outou." John, vii. 33.

Parau, to speak, *pararau*, applied to two conversing together, *paraparau*, to converse repeatedly. *Paraparau raa*, a conference or meeting for speaking.

Rave, to take or receive, *raverave*, to take in hand repeatedly, as a person waiting at table.

Tipao, to mark, *tipaopao*, to do so repeatedly.

Ui, to ask or inquire, *uiui,* to make repeated inquiries.
Utaru, to dig the ground, *utarutaru,* to do so repeatedly.
Vaiiho, to leave, *vaiihoiho,* to leave frequently.

OF ADVERBS.

There are in Tahitian, as in other languages, a great variety of adverbs, the principal of which are adverbs of time, place, order, quantity, quality, affirmation, negation, interrogation, comparison, doubting, indication, restriction, and prohibition.

Of Time.

Time present. *Teie* and *teinei,* now or this present instant, *nei* here, or this present instant.

Time past: *Nauanei,* to day (past); *nanahi,* yesterday, *ia,* when, *i nafea,* when connected with an interrogation, time past; *aenei,* signifying the action past, or gone by; *ra* and *aera* have a similar meaning; *hou,* late or lately, as, *hou aenei,* or hou *iho nei,* lately, past, but not long ago; *mutaa aenei, mutaa iho,* and *mutaa iho ra,* formerly.

Time to come: *Aunei,* or *auanei,* to day, (to come) and sometimes it signifies that an action will shortly take place; *aria,* presently; *ariana,* by and by or shortly; *ia roovauae,* in a little while or shortly; *ia roaroa iti ae,* in a little time or presently; *ia,* when, future; *ananahi,* or *apopo,* to-morrow.

Time indefinite: *Pinepine,* often; *roauiho,* applied to an action often repeated; *mahia,* as, *eita mahia,* soon or quickly, *vave,* soon; *vavevave,* very soon, or speedily; *reira,* then.

Of Place.

Nei, here; *ae,* a little aside, or a small distance higher or lower, or farther off, *iho,* also determines the place of the action, similar to *ae*; *aera* and *ra,* signify distance aside; *na,* denotes the place where the person addressed is, and is opposed to *nei*; as, *i o na,* yonder with you; and *i o nei,* here with me; *atu,* and *atura,* denote the action to be passing from the speaker or agent, or the place understood; *mai, maira* and *mai nei,* the reverse, the aspect of the action being *towards* the person or place understood; *reira,* there, *reiraiho,* there at that very place.

The following are also used as adverbs, *i nia*, above; *i raro*, below; *i roto*, within; *i rapae*, or *i vaho*, out, without; as, *haere i nia*, go above; *haere i raro*, go below, &c.

Of Order.

Matamua or *matamehai*, first in order or foremost; *muri iho* or *muri ue*, that which comes close behind or afterwards; *na*, as oe *na*, thou *first* in order; mata *na* i te papai teienei, write this *first*. Teihea te papai *na*? Which shall be written *first*? Teie *na*, this *first*.

Of Quantity.

Atira, enough, or (there is) a sufficiency; *ariirea*, a little or small quantity; *rahi*, much; *e rahi*, too much; *iti*, little; *e iti*, too little; *noinoi*, little or small; *haihai*, very little; as, *e mea iti haihai roa*, a very little thing; *e raverahi*, many; *aita rea*, few.

Of Quality.

Tia, right or straight; *hape*, wrong; *ino*, ill; *maitai*, well; *teoteo*, proud, or proudly; *neheneh*e, orderly or in good condition; *purotu*, comely; these, and many other adjectives seem to be used adverbially.

Of Affirmation.

E, yea, or yes; *oia*, yes; *ia*, truly so, or truly it is it, or that; *oia mau*, truly so; *parau mau*, or *taru mau*, truth, or the very truth.

Of Negation.

Aore, *aima*, *aina*, *aipa*, *aita*, nay, nor, not; *aita roa*, not at all, or by no means; (time past,) *e ere*, *e ore*, *e ete*, no, not; (time present), *e ore*, *eita*, *eima*, *eina*, the same negatives, with respect to what is future. The time of these adverbs is most exactly observed by the Tahitians.

Of Interrogations.

Eaha or *aha*? What? and sometimes why; as, *Eaha i* ore ai? Why not? No te aha? for what reason or cause? *E hia*? how many? applied to things. Toohia? how many? applied to persons. Nahea? how? or which way? *Eihea*? Where? or at what place? a thing or a person is to be. *Teihea*? Where? when the inquiry is about the place where a person or thing is supposed to be. *Ahea* or *afea*? When? (future); *na-*

hea and *nafea* when? time past, but the *i* is often prefixed, as, *i nafea*, when? *i nanahi*, yesterday.

Of Comparison.

Mai, like unto, *mai* ia'na te huru, like unto him; *te huru a te huru*, of one likeness. *Mai* ia'na te rahi, of one size or bigness with him; *mai* te reira, as that is; *Mai ore mai ora*, likely to be lost, or scarcely saved, but this is a peculiar Tahitian phrase that can hardly be Englished. *Mai ore mai noaa* te boti ia matou. Acts. xxvii. 16.

Of Doubting or Contingency.

Paha, perhaps; *peneiae*, probably, or it may be; *tia* or *tia ae*, peradventure, or it may be.

Of Indication.

Ahio na! lo! behold or take notice; *na* (without an aspirate) see here; *i naha*! behold with attention.

Of Restriction.

Anae, only; as, oia *anae*, he only; *otahi* or *hoe*, only, as tamaiti *otahi*, only son, or tamaiti *hoe* ra.

Of Prohibition.

Eiaha, not, *do not*, imperatively, as *Eiaha* e eia, *do not* steal. *Eiaha* e taparahi i te taata, *do not* commit murder. *Auaa* is used in the same way, as *auaa* haere, do not go.

The above are the principal adverbs in common use, but there are many more belonging to some of the above classes, and others, that may not strictly come under any of them.

OF PREPOSITIONS.

A great number of words appear to be used sometimes as adverbs, and sometimes as prepositions, the principal prepositions are the following;

Na, by, *na* te Atua i hamani i te taata, man was made *by* God.

E, by, e mea hamani hia *e* ana, a thing made *by* him.

Na, for, *na* outou, *for* you, *Na* vai? *for* whom?

No, of, *no* te taata, *of* man. *No* te Atua, of God.

Ia, to, hopoi atu *ia mea*, take it to such an one.

Tei nia, above, *tei nia* tei te rai, *above* in the sky.

Tei raro, below, *tei raro* tei te moana, *below* in the deep.
Tei roto, in, within, *tei roto* i te fare, *in* the house.
Tei vaho, or *tei rapae*, outside, without, opposite to *tei roto*.
I, to or at, *i uta, at a place* inland, e pure te Atua, pray *to* God.
Ma, with, *ma te aau atoa*.
Mua, before; *muri*, behind.
Ia, till; until, e tiai atu vau e *ia* tae mai oia ra. I will wait *till* he comes. *Roto* and *rotopu*, among.
Iho, close by, by the side of. *Fatata*, nigh or near.
Piha'e, and *pihaiho*, lying by the side of.

Also the signs of the cases of nouns, and the genitive and accusative of pronouns, are signified, for the most part, by the prepositions, *i, ia, na, no, ta, to*, and *a*, and *o*, as mentioned before. *Ti*, or *tei*, answers to *in*, but is commonly prefixed to *roto*, or *rapae*; as, tei roto, tei rapae; sometimes otherwise; as, *tei* te pahi, *in* the ship; *tei* te fare, *in* the house.

OF CONJUNCTIONS.

The usual words in Tahitian to join sentences, or different parts of a sentence together, are the following; *e, toa*, or *atoa, hoi, area, oi, ra, a* and *ma*.

E is a copulative conjunction, answering to *and*; as, to rui *e* te ao, day *and* night; tane *e* te *vahine*, husband *and* wife. *Toa, atoa*, and *hoi*, answer to *also*, and *likewise*, as, haere *atoa* matou, we *also* go, haere *atoa* outou, go ye *likewise*. Na te Atua i hamani te rai, *e* to te rai *atoa* ra, nana *hoi* i hamani te fenua *e* te moana, God made the sky *and* the things *also* therein contained, the land *also, and* the deep. *I*, also, often serves as a copulative conjunction where no English word can be found to answer it.

Ma, seems likewise to be a true Polynesian copulative, although lost in the Tahitian dialect, except in counting; as, ahuru *ma* toru, ten *and* three; e piti ahuru *ma* pae, twenty *and* five.

The disjunctives are; *area, e* and *rá*, as in the following examples; eiaha tei reira, *area* teie, not that *but* this; or thus, eiaha ïa, teie *rá*, not that, but this; teie anei, e tera? this *or* that? The following are conjunctions of various kinds; *ia*, if; *ahiri*, if; *oi*, lest, or that it may not; *a* has the same meaning, e ara *a* pohe, take care *lest* (you) die; also *o te*, as, *o te* pohe hoi, lest (he) should die. *I te mea*,-*no te mea*, *noa*, *noa 'tu*, *noa iho*, these are conditional or inferential conjunctions answering to *therefore*, *because*, *although*, &c. "*rave noa a* oia i te semeio i raverahi i mua i to ratou aro, aore a ratou i faaroo ia'na. John xii. 37.

OF INTERJECTIONS.

There are various kinds of interjections, expressive of the feelings or sudden emotions of the mind; as,

Aue! of surprise, wonder, or astonishment. *Aue*! alas! of pain, grief or sorrow. *A*! of sudden indignation or disappointment. *A*! (pronounced differently) on a sudden discovery of something unlooked for. *Aha*! of sudden displeasure or vexation. *Ahe*! of surprise or affectionate concern about something that cannot be helped, as the death of a person. *Aue te piri e*! of wonder and surprise. *Aue te poupou e*! of admiration or wonder. *Haio* of disgust and contempt. *Hee*! of displeasure and vexation. *Uhu*! of disappointment in something that occurred. *Aitoa*! expressive of satisfaction as to some event that has taken place, as well fitting some previous cause or circumstance, or the state of the speaker's mind. *Manava*! of greeting or welcome to visitors. *Io nei oe*! of parting, as adieu, literally, thou be here. *Aita*, and *aore*, although generally adverbs of negation, yet are often used as interjections of wonder or surprise, aita te mahana! how hot it is! aita te toteoe! how cold it is! aita te rave ata e! how difficult to manage!

OF SYNTAX.

The rules of syntax are usually comprised under those of *concord* or agreement of words, and those of *government* or dependence of words; many of the English rules of concord and government will not apply to the Tahitian dialect, but the following observations may be of some use.

The Nominative Case and the Verb.

There is nothing inherent in the verb, (a few of the *reduplicates* only excepted) to signify persons numbers nor gender, and consequently the rules about their concord or agreement with the verb have no place in *Tahitian.*

The nominative case commonly *follows* the verb, and may be easily known by putting the questions O vai ? and eaha? who ? why? which ? what ? as, *Te tere ra te rá,* the sun proceeds on its course. *Eaha te tere?* What proceeds ? *Te rá,* the sun. *Te maue ra te manu,* the bird flies. *Eaha te maue?* What is it that flies ? *Te manu,* the bird. *Haere atura Iesu i Ierusalema,* Jesus went to Jerusalem. *O vai te haere i Ierusalema?* who went to Jerusalem ? the answer must be *Jesus* which is the nominative. But there are instances of the nominative being placed before the verb ; as, *O vau te haere,* I go, or it is I that go. In this construction the *te* must be inserted between the pronoun and the verb; it also implies an opposition ; as, It is I who go, not another. Also when a negative is used ; as, Eita vau e tae, I will not go ; or when an offer is made ; as, O vau nei te haere. I will go.

When two nouns, signifying the same thing, are in apposition, *ra* must invariably be placed between them ; as,

O te Arii *ra,* O Pomare, tei papai.
The Queen, Pomare, who will write.

The omission of the *ra* would place the word "arii" in the genitive, and the sense would be the chief of the queen Pomare.

When two or more nouns or pronouns follow the same verb, the first only has the sign of the accusative case,

E parau atu ia Ioane, ratou, o Petero, e Paulo, ma.

Substantive and Adjective.

The Substantives in general, have no gender, or note of plurality in themselves, yet some of the adjectives have, and ought to agree with the substantives when they are preceded by the plural articles; as, *te mau raau rarahi ra,* the great trees, *mau puaa iino,* bad hogs, *mau taata maitatai,* good men; *tau tamarii tamaroa iino,* some bad boys.

It is also a general rule that the adjective ought to follow the substantive; as E Atua *mana*, mighty God, and not precede it as in English. Substantives are also often implied, but not expressed; as, *maua* ïa, or *te maua*, ignorant, or the ignorant or unskilful, but the word *taata* or *man* is understood.

The Antecedent and the Relative.

The relatives are not affected by number or gender, they are often nominatives to the following verbs; as, te Atua *o tei* faa ora ia'u, the God who preserves me. *Taua*, which agrees with any sort of antecedent, ought always to be followed by either *ra*, *nei* or *na*, in some part of the sentence; as, *taua* taata ra, that man, before spoken of, *taua* peu nei, this custom mentioned or understood; see more on this subject under the relative pronouns.

Of Government.

One word governs another, when it causes it to be in some case or mood.

One substantive governs another; as, *To te Atua ra aroha*, God's pity or compassion; *Tu te arii ra parau*, the king's speech. Interrogative phrases or sentences, ought to be answered according to the interrogation; as, Na vai tera ra mea? Na'u, whose is that thing? Mine. Te aha nei oe? Te ohipa nei au; What doest thou here? I am at work here.

A verb active governs words in the dative or accusative cases; as, *te parau maira ia'u*, speaks to me, *te haapii mai nei ia'u*, teaches me, *te faaite atura ia'na*, makes known to him.

PRAXIS.

Ioane, xiv., 15. Ua hinaaro outou ia'u ra, e haapao i ta'u parau.

Ua, a particle of affirmation affixed to verbs, and adjectives affirming the existence of the action or quality to which it is prefixed.

Hinaaro, love, verb active 2*d* pers. plural, subj. mood, present tense, implying a condition, *if* you love.

Outou, pronoun, 2*d*. person plural, nominative case, you.

Ia'u, pron. 1st. person, singular, acc. case, *me*.

Ra, a particle or adverb of time or place.
E, a sign of the tense of the following verb.
Haapao, verb active, imperative mood, *regard* or *keep*, agreeing with its nominative, *outou*.
I, a prep. or particle of connection, sometimes answering to *to*, and often apparently an expletive.
Ta'u, pronoun. 1*st*. person singular, gen. case, *my*.
Parau, a common subst. sing. number, acc. case, word, speech or command, agreeing with ta'u, *my*.

Ioane, x. 14. O vau te tiai mamoe maitai ra, ua ite au i ta'u iho, e ua ite hia vau e raton.

O, an article prefixed to pronouns and proper names, when in the nominative case.
Vau, pronoun, 1*st*. person singular, nominative case, I.
Te, the definite article, *the*.
Tiaimamoe, a compound noun, sing. number, nom. case, signifying a shepherd, from *tiai*, to keep, and *mamoe*, sheep.
Maitai, an adj. positive degree, singular number, agreeing with tiaimamoe, *good*.
Ra, a particle of emphasis, denoting the shepherd *noted* as good.
Ua, a particle of affirmation prefixed to a verb as mentioned before.
Ite, verb active 1*st*. person singular, Indic. mood, perfect tense, of *to know*.
Au, pronoun, 1*st*. person sing. nom. case, agreeing with ite, and contracted from vau, I.
I, a prep. or particle of connection, as before.
Ta'u iho, an emphatic pronoun, gen. case. a compound of *ta'u* mine, and *iho* self, belonging to myself.
E, a copulative conjunction, *and*.
Ua, a particle of affirmation as before.
Ite hia, the passive of *ite*, to know, 1*st*. pers. sing. Indic. mood, perfect tense, and agreeing with *vau*.
Vau, pronoun, 1*st*. person singular, nom. case, agreeing with *ite hia*.
E, prep. by, denoting the connection between the agent and the object.

Ratou, pronoun, 3*d*. person, plur. acc. case, agreeing with *ta'u iho*.

Ioane, i. 29. Ahio na i te Arenio a te Atua, o te hopoi ê atu i te hara o te ao.

Ahio na, an adverb of indication, behold, take notice, a compound of *hio*, to see, and *na* an adverb of place.

I, a prep. as mentioned before.

Te, the definite article, prefixed to arenio.

Arenio, a common noun, sing. number, nominative case, modified from the Greek *Arnion*, a lamb.

A, the preposition *of*, denoting the genitive case.

Te, an article prefixed to the noun *Atua*, but not definite.

Atua, a common noun, 3*d* person, sing. number, gen. case, *God*.

O te, or *o tei*, relative pronoun, nom. case, *that*, or *which*, agreeing with arenio, its antecedent.

Hopoi, verb active Indic. mood, present tense, 3d. pers. *taketh*, or *conveyeth*, agreeing with its nom., *o tei*.

E, an adverb of place followed by *atu*. from, away, or away from.

I, a prep. or particle of connection as before.

Te, the definite article.

Hara, common noun, 3*d*. person, singular number, acc. case, *sin*.

O, a preposition, a sign of the genitive case, *of*.

Te, definite article, *the*.

Ao, common noun, 3*d*. person, singular number, genitive case, *world*.

END OF THE GRAMMAR.

TAHITI:
PRINTED AT THE LONDON MISSIONARY SOCIETY'S PRESS.

1851.

A

TAHITIAN AND ENGLISH

DICTIONARY.

A, THE first letter of the alphabet and the most frequent in use of all the Tahitian vowels. Its genuine pronunciation is that of the English *a* in the words *lad*, *am*, *an*, &c. and when marked with a circumflex, thus, â, the same sound in quality but longer in quantity. In some few words it sounds very short, as in the first syllables of *navai*, *pape*, *tatâ*, *&c.*

A, *s.* the name of the alphabet; the name of a certain feast where presents were given

—*s.* the inclosure of a house, made of cocoa-nut leaves; a sort of sliding door made of bamboo; the skeleton of an animal

—*a prefix* to verbs, denoting the imperative mood, as *a-horo*, run, do run; also to show that the action or event is about taking place, as *teie au a pohe*, I am going to die. Sometimes it is so prefixed when preceded by an adverb of negation, as *ore aite*, not knowing; *ore ahinaaro*, not having a desire

A, *a prefix* to adjectives of counting with referernce to past time, as *atahi*, one, *arua*, two; while *e* is prefixed in the future, as *etahi*, *erua*; and it is to be noted whether *a* or *e* is in the query, for the answer must correspond

—*an affix* to verbs to signify they are used as nouns, as *hopoi*, to carry or convey, *hopoia*, the thing carried or conveyed, a burden

—*an affix* by means of which a verb active is changed into a passive form, as,—

Rave, to take, *ravea*, taken.
Ite, to know, *itea*, known.

See *hia*

A, *s.* the state of combustion or quality of burning well

—*v.n.* to be in a burning state

—*a.* prepared, as food by roasting, boiling, baking, &c. the opposite to *ota*, raw

A, *s* a method of catching men, beasts, or fishes, by a long reach or sweep

—*v. a.* to sweep by forming a long reach in order to surround and catch men, beasts, &c.

A, *verb aux.* denoting the continuance of the action or of the things mentioned. It commonly follows the verb, as *ia vai a*, let it remain or continue; but often an adverb intervenes, as *te parau noa nei a*, continues to speak
—*v. a.* to have or possess; see *na*, *ta*, and *to*

A, *conj.* lest, for fear that, as *e ara ia oe u pohe*, beware lest thou die, nevertheless, notwithstanding
—*ad.* when, as *i popohe maua, pohe apipiti, a pohe au, a pohe oia*, we were both ill together, when he was ill, I was also ill
—*prep.* belonging to; see *na*, *ta*, *no*, and *to*

A! *interj* of surprise and disappointment, ah! it is gone! or, it is lost!

Aa, *s.* [*aka*, *kaka*,] the root or roots of any tree or plant; hold, right, support; footing or settlement in a country

Aa, *s.* the fibrous substance that grows on the cocoa nut tree; the husk or covering on the young branches of the bread-fruit tree; the integuments inclosing the sugar-cane, bamboo, hoi, &c; the scarf on the skin of a new born infant or other young animals; the skin inside of animals to which the fat about the kidneys adheres; a sieve, or strainer, such as is used for the *pia* or arrowroot

Aa, *s* a provocation, insult, jeer, taunt; a provoker, banterer
—*v.a.* to provoke, banter, insult
—*a* jocular, given to jest

Aa, *s.* the name of a bird of the paroquet kind, or small parrot; there are two sorts, the one called *aa taevao*, which has fine red feathers, the other, *aa mahu*, has no red feathers

Aa, *v. n.* to be thoroughly awake after sleep; to be done, or over done, as dressed food, to be in a state of burning fiercely; to be burning as a plurality of fires [breadth

Aa, *v. a.* to measure length or

Aaa, *s.* the state of agitation which the water is in by reason of the wind; the state of the mind when agitated by fear
—*a.* timorous, agitated
—*v. n.* to be agitated, as the water by a current of air, while there is a general calm, or as the mind by rumours of war or imaginary apparitions

Aaa, *s.* the stringy substance in any kind of food or vegetable, also in native cloth that is not well worked

Aaa, *v a.* to insult or provoke

Aaaa, *int* of laughter or ridicule

Aabu, *s.* the shell of fish, nuts, and seeds
—*v. a.* to hold out any cup or concave vessel to receive any thing, to make or put any thing in a concave form to receive food or other things

Aahi, *s* the fish called albicore; it agrees with the mackarel, but is much larger. The young ones are called *aahi pere-pererau;* the next size, *aahi tumu;* the next, *aahi mapepe;* the next, *aahi vere*, the largest of all, *aahi araroa*. There are also varieties of the aahi, as, *o ouri*, *raura*, *papahi*, &c.

Aahi, *s.* a rag or torn piece of cloth; a wick for a lamp

Aahiata, *s.* the dawn of the day

Aahipatao, *s.* a wary albicore that will not be hooked;—*figuratively*, a person that cannot be imposed on

Aahitiamatau, *s.* an albicore that has been hooked and has escaped; a person who after having been imposed upon has recovered himself

Aahu, *s.* a piece of cloth; cloth in general

Aahu, *s.* a bite; a signal given by biting the lips or gnashing with the teeth

—*v. a.* to bite or nip; to bite or gnash with the teeth as a signal for some violence, mischief, or murder

Aahu, *s.* a spasmodic disease of the bowels; colic

Aai, *s.* a glutton; see *aamu* and *aiai maa*

—*a* gluttonous, voracious, corroding

Aai, *s.* a tale or fabulous relation

Aaia, *s.* a species of mountain-plantain; the name of a shrub

Aaia, *s.* the name of a star; see *aiaia*

Aaia, *s.* abortive fruit; see *aiore*

—*a.* unripe, abortive, as fruit; impure, having animalcules, as standing water

Aaia, *s.* pleasurable sensations of the heart

Aaihere, *s* weeds, underwood, bushes when numerous

—*a* wild, uncultivated, full of weeds

Aaina, *v.n.* to be delighted; see *aaia*

Aainu, *s* bait for fish, see *arainu*, an inducement to do a thing

Aaina, *s.* the name of a small crab common on the sea shore

Aama, *v.n.* to be burning bright and vehement, as a large fire; see *aa*

—*a.* bright, shining; clear as a lamp or fire burning

Aamau, *s.* twenty fathoms in length

Aamau, *s.* a permanent resident; see *aa*

*Aamu, *s.* a tale or story; see *aai*

*Aamu, *s* a glutton; see *aiaimaa*

—*a.* voracious, gluttonous; corroding. spreading, increasing as rust or disease

Aana, *a* accumulative, increasingly heaping up, or adding one thing to another, as *mai aana*, a disease in which successive relapses happen, and supposed formerly to be in consequence of new transgressions against the gods; *parau aana*, words increased by additions so as to become a crime; *hara aana*, an aggravated crime

Aani, *a* given to *ani* or begging

Aano, *s.* breadth, extent, extensiveness

—*a.* broad, wide, extensive; see *apu*

—*v. n.* to extend, reach unto; extending

Aano, *s* sperm or seed of certain fishes; the red berries of the *hauou* or *pua* tree; seeds of gourds, pumpkins, melons, and cucumbers; a cocoa nut water-bottle

Aao, *s.* thin or wasted state of a person by some disease

—*a.* thin; wasted by disease

Aaoa, *s.* the crowing of a cock

Aaoa, *v. a.* to introduce quite an irrelevant or foreign subject into a meeting for discussion

Aaoaoa, *v. n.* to be making a confused noise, as the people at the breaking up of a meeting

—*s.* foolish, incoherent talk; a foolish person

—*v.n.* to talk foolishly and incoherently

Aaoa raa moa, *s.* cock-crowing

Aaone, *s.* large bundles of coarse or unfinished native cloth prepared for a public presentation to the king or principal chief; also the food and other things so presented

Aapiti, *a.* united or doubled; having two sources, as the wind blowing from two different quarters and causing a cross sea

Aapo, *v.a.* to apprehend, catch, or understand a thing quickly

—*a.* apt to understand

Aapu, *v. a.* to take up with the hand

Aara, *s.* [*aula,*] the sweet or fragrant scent of herbs

—*a.* sweet; odoriferous as herbs

Aararû, *s.* the name of a small beetle

—*a.* unripe as the gourd or *hue*

Aarau, *a.* unripe as *aararu*

Aarauaua, *s.* a sort of beetle found among the grass covering the floors of native houses

Aare, *s.* the name of a small shell fish

Aari, *s.* the same as the *nono*

Aari, *a.* irregular; applied to a rope, a tree, or any thing that is narrow and thin in the middle, or slender in one place and thick in another

Aaria, *s.* the part of the face that covers the cheek bone

Aaro, *v. a.* to excavate; to scoop or scrape out

—*s.* the person that scoops; the scoop or ladle by which any thing is scooped or scraped out

Aaru, *s.* a new born infant; see *aruaru*

Aata, *s.* the young shoots of taro; see *moo* and *muoo*; stems of plants or leaves

Aata, *v n.* the dual or plural of to laugh; to laugh repeatedly

—*a.* laughing; much given to laughter

Aataina, *s.* the strong desire or longing of the heart

—*v. n.* to have a strong desire or longing; to have gratification

Aatea, *s.* the name of a species of taro; a fish so called

Aati, *s.* the name of a strong native cloth made of the bark of the bread-fruit tree

Aati, *a.* two in numbering

—*s.* a couple

Aati, *v.a.* to bite, gnaw, or tear with the teeth

—*s.* the bite of a thing; the biter

Aatiaute, *s.* cloth made of *aute* bark

Aau, *s.* [*ngakau, na'au,*] the bowels or intestines—*fig.* the heart or mind; the affections; the conscience; courage or spirit

Aau, *s.* the handle of a tool; the stalk of fruit; the stones and rubbish filled up in the wall of a *marae*

—*s.* the name of a species of the parrot fish

Aau, *s.* the reef of coral rock; *aau piti*, a double reef

Aauanei, *ad.* of time to come; to-day; shortly

Aauaua, *s.* rubbish collected by water

Aauhaoaoa, *s.* a reef that is full of chasms

Aaumairohe, *s.* the quality of one who earnestly desires the other sex, or excessively covets property

Aaunu, *s.* bait for fish; see *arounu*

Aaupiti, *s.* a double mind

—*a.* double minded, undecided; having two stems, as a plant or tree,—*fig.* a person whose father belongs to one country and his mother to another is called *taata aaupiti*

Aauputaporeho, see *aaumairohe*

Aautuaa, *s.* a shameless person, one that is obscene; obscenity; indecency

Aautuai, *s.* a person always thinking of food

Aauraeva, *s.* a person of great hospitality, who denies himself to gratify others

Aavai, *s.* a shower or sudden squall

Aavao, *s.* the name of a paroquet that frequents the interior of the island; the same as *aataevao*; see *aa*—*fig.* a landsman not accustomed to the sea; see *vao* and *taevao*

Aave, *v.a.* to stretch the sling over the shoulder in slinging stones; see *maa*

Aavere, *s.* the name of a bold fish with a long snout—*fig.* a courageous warrior who prefers the front of the battle; a fast sailing canoe

Abobo, *ad.* to-morrow; see *apopo* and *ananahi*

Abu, *s.* the shell of a nut, gourd, or fish; a concave or hollow, as *abu rima*, the hollow of the hand, *abu roro* or *abu upoo*, the skull; a fraternity or family, as *abu arii*, the royal family, *abu atua*, the race of gods, the first is the abu

Abu, *s.* the name of an idolatrous prayer

Abu, *s.* the name of a small tree or shrub; the bark of its roots is used for tanning and colouring native cloth; see *hiri*

Abu, *s.* the fierce and savage quality of pigs or fishes, shown by their running at and biting each other

—*v. a.* to dart or fly at each other, as pigs or fishes; to fall upon each other, as dogs when eating

—*a.* fierce, envious, mischievous

Abu, *a.* wide or broad, as cloth; see *aano*

Abua, *s.* the shaft of a fish spear; see *amuri*

Abua, *s.* a certain *upu* or prayer rehearsed by the sorcerers with the intention of procuring the death of a thief

Abuabu, *v. a.* to dart and bite repeatedly, as fishes, pigs, or dogs; plural of *abu*

Abuabu, *s.* flexibility, pliancy

Abuabua, *s.* a species of bread-fruit; a sapling; a rod or string carried in the hand

—*a.* raw, not properly dressed, as food

Abufera, *v. n.* to withdraw and not interfere in a game, such as *timo raa*, cockfighting, &c.

Abura, *s* a species of mountain taro; see *taro*

Aburu, *a.* tough and old, as the husk of a cocoa-nut

Aburuburu, *s.* rottenness, decay

—*a.* rotten, decayed

Abuta, *v. n.* to appear or be perceptible, as the sun through little openings in the clouds

Abutabuta, *a.* having many holes or openings

—*v n.* having patches or being in patches

Adu, *ad. & prep.* from, beside, more;—from, with reference to the place of a thing, as *haere adu*, go from, in opposition to *mai* or *maira*, towards the place of the thing mentioned or understood, or that of the speaker;—beside, as *aita adu*, none beside; in comparing, it signifies greater, further beyond, as, *rahi*, great, *rahi adu*, greater; *eaha adu?* what more or beyond? see *atu*

Adura, *ad. & prep.* [from *adu* and *ra*,] having a reference to either time or place; see *atura*

Ae, *s.* the name of a sweet-scented plant, used for the sweet *monoi* or native oil

Ae, *v. a. & v n.* [*ake*,] to ascend, climb, mount up; see *paiuma*

—*s* a climber; one who climbs a tree or a hill

—*v.n.* to touch the ground, as a boat or ship

Ae, *s.* the slain in battle that were taken to the *marae* and offered, also other sacrifices to the gods, such as fish; the act of offering; the first beating of the drum at a religious ceremony

Ae, *ad.* yes, yea, in answer to a query or a request, but implying cordiality or indifference according to the tone of the voice. As an adverb of place, there, near at hand, as *tera ae*, that near or just by; *io ae*, a little that way; *nia ae*, a little above; *raro ae*, a little below. In comparing qualities or adjectives, it implies a small degree less or more, as, *ino*, bad, *ino ae*, a little worse; *maitai*, good, *maitai ae*, something better. It is often accompanied with *iti*, little, as, *maoro*, long, *maoro iti ae*, a little longer, not much

—*inter.* of surprise or disappointment; alas!

Aea, *s.* the fibrous roots or stalks of the plant *atuaea*, used for small fishing lines, the joining place of two nets; a new net when first used; the concave part of a crooked piece of timber; an introductory present or peace offering to the gods; an intreaty for peace, *aea tamai* was a human sacrifice previous to the commencement of a war

Aeae, *s.* the name of a tree used only for fuel

Aeae, *v. a.* to carry or convey, to defend the remainder of an army; to succour in distress

Aeae, *s.* the end, design, or object of pursuit, as in the phrase, *ua pu te aeae*, have fully attained the object of pursuit

Aeae, *s.* the state of being out of breath

—*v. n.* breathless; breathing laboriously and quickly

Aeaea, *v.n.* to be exhausted and breathless

Aeaea, *interj* a cry of the *arioi*

Aeaeo, *a.* sallow, sickly, pale by disease

Aebu, *s.* a cup; a cocoa-nut used for a cup

Aeha, *a.* [*aha*, *afa*,] four in counting

Aehaa, *s.* the great sea or deep reaching to the bounds of the horizon; difficulty, danger

Aehai, *s.* a very long distance

—*a.* distant, above or below; difficult to reach

Aehai mata pupure, *s.* a warrior of a terrific aspect

Aeho, *s.* a reed

Aehuehu, *a.* troubled, disturbed, as the mind

—*s.* agitation, disturbance of the mind

Aena, *ad.* a little after, a little aside: see *ae*

Aenei, *ad & aux. v.* sometimes answering to have, has or hath, implying the action to be past, or just gone by, as, *ahia aenei?* how many past or gone by? *ua reva aenei*, just gone; *ua pohe aenei oia*, he died or hath died

Aeo, *s.* a child that is weak and sickly

—*a.* weak, as a child; sickly; peevish; childish

Aeo, *interj.* of contempt or disgust; ah!

Aepa, *s.* the name of a certain prayer; *aepa arii*, a prayer for or on account of the king

Aepau, *s.* the last dying breath; a bequest of a father to his son; wisdom or learning obtained by a son from his father

Aera, *ad.* of time and place; a compound of *ae* and *ra* signifying then or there, or a little aside, according to the circumstances of time and place; see *mai*, *maira*, *tu*, and *atu*

Aere, *s.* a collection or abundance of fish or animals

Aere, *s.* a thick dense forest; the name of a tree of the bark of which native cloth is made

Aere, *s.* a large or extensive bog that cannot be passed; the expanse of sea or firmament whose termination cannot be seen; the unknown state after death; any thing that cannot be found by searching

Aereere, *s.* a bog encrusted with the plant *mapua* and vibrating from unsoundness when trod upon; commotion, agitation, disorder in an army

—*v. n.* to shake or vibrate, as the surface of a bog, or the ground on the fall of some heavy thing; to be agitated or in commotion, as the mind on hearing bad tidings

Aeri, *s.* a hole, such as that of a land crab or of the *varo*; a hole wider at the bottom than the top

Aero, *s.* the tail of quadrupeds, or of the sting-ray and some other fishes; the after-part of some business or conversation; the penis

Aerofai, *s.* the name of a medical plant, called also, *puarau*

Aerorau, *s.* the name of a god; the south-west wind; the fabulous *moo* or lizard, said to have many tails; a person with a numerous retinue

Aerouri, *s.* the name of a mountain plant, (the buckshorn,) called also, *rima rima tafai*

Aeto, *s.* [*aetos*, Gr] the eagle

✓Aetoerau, *s.* a gentle and agreeable westerly wind; a soothing and pleasing state of the mind

Afa, *s* a crack, split, rent, or fissure; a schism or division

—*v. n.* to crack or split; to break or burst, as an abscess; to divide or split in parties. *Ua afa te vai*, is an expression signifying the commencement of hostilities

Afaa, *s.* a large pit or hole, such as a *mahi* pit

Afàfà, *a.* torn or rent in many places; much divided, or having many parties

Afai, *s.* a bearer or carrier of burdens

—*v a.* to carry, bring, or take a thing; to restore the captives of a conquered place, or those who had been banished. *Afai ioa* and *afai parau* are names for a tale-bearer

Afaia, *s.* that which is burdensome, or difficult to manage; a great concern or burden

Afafai, *s.* strength or ability to carry a great burden

—*v. a.* to carry or convey repeatedly; to try the weight of a thing in order to carry it if not too heavy

Afara, *s.* a species of a mountain plantain

—*s* a species of bread-fruit

Afarefare, *v. n.* to hang over, as a wave when ready to break, or as a rock or precipice

Afaru, *s.* a water-bottle or calabash; a sort of ill savoured sauce, used chiefly by old women

*Afata, *s.* a chest, box, coop, raft, or scaffold

Afea, *ad.* when, will, or shall, used only interrogatively and in the future

Afeafe, *s.* height; as *afeafe o te ra*, altitude of the sun

—*a.* long or tall, distant; extended

Afene, *a.* six in counting; see *ahene* and *aono*

Afera, *ad.* ever; ever after; as *afera noatu*, ever, or for ever from this time

Aferefere, *s.* a strong and voracious appetite by reason of which a person will eat any kind of food

—*a.* empty, as the bowels from hunger or the operation of medicine

Afifi, *s.* the name of a medicinal plant

—*s.* a species of banana; a bundle of bread-fruit or cocoanuts tied together

Afii, *s.* the head of a beast, bird, or fish, but not of a man, except by way of contempt

Aha, *s* [*kaha*,] sinnet made of cocoa nut-husk

—*s.* the first enemy slain in battle was called *aha*, because, when obtained, a piece of *aha* was tied to him, he was then taken to a *marae*, and prayers were made over him for further success in the war; and those prayers and ceremonies were called *aha taata*

Aha, *s.* the name of a fish, of which there are varieties, as *aha moe, aha maraurau.* &c.

Aha, *s.* the operation of the *tii*, by which the sorcerer was supposed to cause the death of a person, such were said to be *aha hia*, devoted to destruction

Aha, *s.* the ceremony of presenting at the *marae* a piece of *aha* by a fleet of canoes after their landing as an acknowledgment of the protection of the gods, and prayers were made with an offering of a pig, or of a plantain in the absence of a pig

Aha, *pron. interrogative, aha* or *e aha?* what? *no te aha?* for what? or to what purpose? *e aha atu?* what more or beside? *aha hoi?* what else? *aha iho a?* what besides? *e aha tena?* what is that? (near the person addressed;) *e aha tera?* what is that? (at a distance;) *e aha teie?* what is this? (close by)

—*ad.* how? or why? as *e aha e tia'i?* how can it be? *e aha vau e riri ai?* why should I be angry? *e aha e ore ai?* why not?

Ahà, *s.* a crack, a fissure; see *afà*

—*v.n.* to crack, split open

Ahaa, *s.* a hole or large pit; see *afaa*

Ahaa, *interj.* of fondness on meeting a friend

Ahaaha, *s.* the name of a fish remarkable for its rapidity in swimming

Ahaaha, *s.* rapidity, swiftness; a swift pursuer

Ahaaha, *v. a.* to pursue, as a warrior his enemy

Ahaaha, *a.* neat, smart, of genteel carriage

Ahaaha, *a.* cadaverous, as a dead animal

Ahae, *a.* rent, torn; see *mahae*

—*v n.* to be torn or rent

Ahaeahae, *a.* gentle

Ahaehae, *a.* torn or rent in many places

Ahafirituatua, *s.* a disturber of the peace

Ahafirituatua, *ad.* awkwardly, slovenly done

Ahaha, *v. n.* to boast or vaunt; to exalt one's self

Ahâhâ, *a.* having many cracks or rents; see *afâfâ*

Ahahoi, *interj.* a term of adulation used by *arioīs*

Ahamatarau, *s.* a seditious disturber of the peace

Ahamatatini, *s.* an incendiary; a breeder of mischief

Ahata, *s.* a box or chest; see *pafata*

Ahatahatai, *s.* a piece of sinnet used as a charm on board a canoe when preparing for sea

Ahataina, *s.* a bustling, hurrying person

—*v.n.* to be in a bustle or hurry

Ahataina, *a.* tough, as the sinnet of the *toere*, drum—*fig.* stubborn, obstinate, not giving way

Ahatatai, *s.* the sinnet fastening or tying the barbs at the end of a fish spear

Ahatea, *s* the name of a tree used for the keels of boats; see *mara uri*

*Ahatia, *s.* the name of a certain prayer to the gods, formerly *ahatu*

Ahavai, *s.* black sinnet, made strong and coloured in the mire of some bog—*fig* a handy, strong, and active person

Ahê, *interj.* of surprise, as ah! alas! so let it be! it cannot be helped!

Ahe, *ad.* afterwards, as *ahe i muri iho*

Ahea, *ad.* when? future; see *afea*

Aheahe, *s.* emptiness

—*a.* empty, as the stomach

Ahee, *s.* a verse or paragraph of a funeral dirge; see *pehe, tui,* and *avei*

Aheehee, *v. n.* to ebb, as the sea; see *pahee*

Ahehe, *s.* a rustling noise

—*v. n.* to make a rustling noise, as the wind or rain among dry leaves

*Ahema, *ad.* when, as *afea*

Ahera, *ad.* ever; for ever henceforward

Aheu, *s.* the name of a delicious sort of fish, called, when young, *pauuara,* when half-grown, *marava,* and when 15 or 16 inches long it is *aheu*

Ahi, *s.* [*afi, a'i; api,* Malay;] fire; see *auahi*

Ahi, *s.* [*afi; asi,* Fiji; *buahi,* Marq.] the sandal wood

Ahi, *s.* a flint; a gun-flint

Ahi, *s.* a species of cockle

Ahi, *v. n.* to sit or brood as a hen; cover, overshadow

Ahî, *interj.* of surprise or disappointment

Ahia, *ad.* how many? when inquiring of things in the past time, *ehia?* in the future; *a toohia* and *etoohia* when inquiring about persons

Ahia, *s.* [*ahika, kainga, ohia,*] the native red apple, called also *Eugenia Malauensis*

Ahiahi, *s.* the evening

Ahiahi, *s.* a wound; scars of a warrior; bruises

—*a.* wounded, bruised; shy, as a fish that has been disturbed and will not bite

Ahiahi rumaruma, *s.* a dark and cloudy evening—*fig.* an angry person

Ahifa, *s.* a sort of coral that will irritate the skin when handled

Ahîhî, *v. anomalous,* to join or unite with; used with a negative, *eita oia e ahihi mai,* he will not join.

Ahimaa, *s.* a batch of food; the native oven with its contents, from *ahi,* fire, and *maa,* food

Ahina, *s.* a grey head; a contemptuous name for a grey headed person; see *hinahina*

Ahinamuri, *v. imp.* a wish expressed by the managers of a canoe that it may speed its its way

Ahinavai, *s.* a white haze, mist, or fog, which prevents the discovery of objects; distance that makes objects imperceptible

Ahio, *s.* a certain mode of speech used by the king or herald in making peace

Ahipa, *v. n.* to look at or behold an object

Ahipihapiha, *s.* water made to boil by putting hot stones into it

Ahipihepihe, *s.* a remarkable remedy to cure langour or weakness, frequently used by Tahitian women, who have lately lien-in, and by persons of both sexes in chronic dis orders; perspiration excited by the steam of plants, such as the *mapua* or wild mint, and hot stones, and when the perspiration is most copious, the person comes out and plunges into a river to bathe

Ahiri, *conj.* if, had it been, were it so; *ahiri e e parau mau ra*, had it been truth

Ahiri, *v. anom.* and used imperatively; repeat, go on, speak out, addressed to a person speaking or about to speak

Ahiria, *a.* overtopped or shaded, as a small tree under a great one

Ahiripa, *s.* a great destruction or calamity

Ahiro, *s.* a method of fishing for the fish *moi*

Ahitaa, *s.* the flank of a pig; a particular fleshy part of a turtle; the two sides of a seine or fishing net next to its belly

Ahitahuna, *s.* a fire kindled secretly to dress food

Ahitao, *s.* an oven fire; fire as a signal; the name of a prayer and ceremony before a cock fight

Ahitarahu, *s.* a fire kindled in the interior of the island to dress food during such times as the whole coast was sacred and no fire allowed to be kindled

Ahitea, *s.* a firebrand tied to the end of an arrow and shot over a river or other water towards a person on the other side

Ahitopi, *a.* brisk, vigorous —*s.* a vigorous person

Ahitu, *a.* [*ahiku, fitu, itu,*] seven in counting

Ahitu, *s.* a term in use in the amusement or exercise of arms called *turaau*

Ahitu, *s.* the assistants of a canoe builder

Ahitu, *s.* a company of idolatrous priests, a sort of Nazarites, residing in a sacred house in a *marae*, and observing peculiar customs, such as not shaving, not cutting the hair, &c.

Ahitutariaroa, *s.* an attendant or servant of the god *Oro*

Ahitutu, *s.* the name of an odoriferous tree used for perfume, and its charcoal for a sort of ink to mark the skin with; see *tatau*

Ahitututu, *s.* a name given to a disagreeable odour, or smell of greasy substances burning

Ahitutututu, *s.* the same as *ahitututu*

Ahivamuri, *s.* the lower part of the stern of a canoe

Aho, *s.* the rafter of a house; thread, cord, twine

Aho, *s.* the breath of animals; *e huti te aho*, to breathe or draw the breath

Aho, *s.* a certain stone set up in a *marae* where the priest set up his *tapaau*, or cocoa nut leaves twisted so as rudely to represent a man

Ahoa, *s.* a prayer made at the time of clearing a *marae* of weeds and rubbish

Ahoa, *s.* the presentation of the first-fruits to a god, or to the king

Ahoa, *s.* small notches in the edge of a tool [*uruhoa*
Ahoa, *s.* the headache; see
Ahoaho, *s.* trouble, perplexity, calamity [plexed
—*v. n.* to be troubled or per-
—*a.* troubled; distant for convenience, such as wood and water, a place where such is not at hand is *vahi ahoaho*
Ahoahoa, *s.* the headache; a pain with a continual din in the head; see *hoa* and *uruhoa*
Ahoahoa huri fenua, *s.* a tempest, a hurricane
Ahoea, *s.* a war-term for a company or a party in reserve
Ahoehoe, *v. n.* to bend down, as the branches of a tree
Ahomaoro, *s.* long breath, long life; perseverance
Ahomure, *s.* short breath; want of perseverance
Ahonui, *s.* perseverance, patience
Ahopapaa, *a.* successful, as in fishing
Ahopau, *s.* shortness of breath; the asthma
Ahopau, *s.* a person that escapes from the midst of a battle
Ahopoto, *s.* the same as *ahomure*
Ahore, *a.* stripped or barked, as a young tree
Ahore, *s.* the name of a small, spotted fish
Ahoro, *s.* the name of a small crab; the name of a small red and white fish
Ahoro, *s.* the end of a woman's girdle that hangs before
Ahoro, *s.* a piece of wood to repair the keel of a canoe
Ahoro, *s.* straightness
—*v. n.* to be straight
Ahoro, *s.* the dilapidation of a *marae*, of a house, or of a wall; a party that runs from a battle
Ahorohoro, *v. n.* to be crumbling or sliding down, as the earth on the side of a mountain; to run, as a multitude of persons
Ahoru, *s.* the abatement of a disease or of anger
—*v. n.* to abate or cease
Ahoru, *a.* pliant, as a plank or piece of wood that has a slender place and bends when trod upon
—*v. n.* to be bending up and down
Ahoruhoru, *v. n.* to be empty and hollow, as a bag, to be empty as the stomach; to be in fear or dismay
Ahu, *s* [*kahu*,] cloth and garments of all descriptions
Ahu, *s.* heat; feverish heat of the body
Ahu, *v n* to be burnt or scalded, as the words *a* and *ama* cannot be applied to the human body, according to the native notion, but by way of a curse or evil wish connected with cannibalism
Ahu, *v. a.* to throw up or huddle together a heap of things; to pile up stones or throw up earth, as for a fortification; to put up the wall of a *marae*, to make an inclosure to catch fish in shallow places
Ahu, *v a.* to scoop, lade, or shovel; to take up any thing with a vessel or a ladle
Ahua, *s.* a place in the sea so filled with coral as not to admit the passage of a canoe

Ahua, *s.* a piece of wood made use of to fasten the tops of the rafters above the ridge piece in a native house

Ahua, *s.* the blossom of the sugar cane

Ahua, *s.* a curse or imprecation

—*v. a.* to curse

Ahua, *s.* a person that waits on the sick

—*v. a.* to nurse a person; to wait on the sick

Ahuahu, *s.* the heat of the sun or of clothes

—*a.* hot, sultry, not airy

Ahuahu, *s.* a small inclosure to catch fish; a ladle or any thing to bale with

—*v. a.* to lade or bale out water

Ahuahu, *s.* a rasp or rubber made of coral

Ahuahurua, *s.* two parties that have engaged in war, but neither of them prevailed

Ahuapi, *s.* cloth doubled and pasted together; a quilt

Ahuarii, *s.* a raised pavement in a *marae* on which the king was placed and inaugurated with various ceremonies; the persons that invested the king with authority

Ahuàtai, *s.* a certain prayer and ceremony formerly used when war or sickness prevailed; a model of a canoe was made, fitted up, and sent to sea with the supposed sins and sickness on board

Ahuavaha, *s.* one that promises fair, but does not perform

—*v. a.* to deceive by fair speeches

Ahuehue, *s.* confusion, alarm, on account of being unprepared

—*v. n.* to be in confusion or alarm

Ahuena, *s.* property or other things heaped together

Ahufara, *s.* a very fine mat made of *atu* leaves

Ahuhe, *s.* quickness of growth in plants, &c.

—*a.* quick or forward in growth

—*v. n.* to grow or shoot up quickly

Ahui, *v. a.* to collect various articles of property into one place

Ahui, *v. a.* to lift or throw up the rod when a fish bites

Ahuiavae, *s.* footsteps or track

Ahuihui, *v. a.* to join together, as a number of persons in some work; to collect things together, and that repeatedly

Ahuihui, *v. n.* to perceive distinctly; see *mahuihui*

Ahuina, *v. a.* to lift up the rod as a fisherman

Ahumamau, *s.* a garment constantly worn

Ahumaua, *s.* a fortress in the mountains, prayers and ceremonies on the mountains

Ahupapaa, *s.* an inclosure for fish; the wall of a new *marae*, or commencement of a *marae* where there was none before

Ahupara, *s.* a good sort of native cloth

Ahupare, *s.* a fortress in time of war

Ahupâu, or Ahupaau, *s.* an inferior sort of cloth

Ahura, *s.* a sort of slug or sea-snail

Ahura, *s.* a fisherman's prayer; see *hura*

Ahura ouma, *v. a.* to throw up the small fish or fry called *ouma*, and used for a bait

Ahuru, *s.* the name of a fish
Ahuru, *s.* the rotten or decayed state of things
Ahuru, [*angahuru*, *angafulu*, *anauru*, *onohuu*; *pulu* or *sa pulu*, Malay; *sangafulu*, New Guinea; *fulu*, Mad; *pulu*, Tagalis of Manilla; *pulu*, Javanese;] the *adj.* ten
Ahuruhuru, *s.* the young of the fish *ahuru*
Ahuruhuru, *s.* a certain ceremony formerly used by way of augury; killing and inspecting the bowels, &c., of a hog, to find out the event of a war about to commence
Ahuruhurua, *s.* the rough-looking state of a thing
—*a.* illfavoured, ugly, filthy
Ahutae, *s.* a wall or pavement that is equal everywhere
Ahutai, *s.* a party that takes refuge in canoes at sea or on the reef in time of war
Ahuta'i, *s.* presents of cloth, &c., given to chiefs and other visitors; presents given on the death or funeral of a person, called also *ahu oto;* see *ta'i*, *oto*, and *otohaa*
Ahutapae, *s.* one that is a new comer, not belonging to the place; one that joins in a work after it is partly done; a new *marae* derived from an old one
Ahutii, *s.* cloth made by parties severally belonging to a *tii;* see *tii*
Ahutiitii, *s.* appendages to a *marae*, such as *unu*, *tapau*, *fata rau*, *&c.*, which see
Ahuvai, *s* a bringer-up of another's children; the children brought up by a stranger
Ai, *v. a.* [*kai*; *kani*, Fiji; *inakanan*, Malay,] to eat
A'i, *s.* [*kaki*,] the neck of man, beast, or bird
Ai, *interj.* of disapprobation, ah! sometimes it is pronounced long, âî!
Ai, *v. a.* [*ahi*] to copulate, applied to both sexes
Ai, *ad* or *verbal directive*, the word seems to be idiomatic, and to have no exact correspondent word in English. Sometimes it answers to will or shall, as, *afea e oti ai?* when will or shall it be finished? *ananahi e oti ai*, it will be finished to-morrow. It is often connected with a query, and the reason demanded or given, as, *e aha i ore ai?* why not? *ore a ite i ore ai?* because of ignorance it was not (done or accomplished being understood,) *eaha te mea e pohe ai te taata?* what is the reason of man's death? *o te hara te mea e pohe ai?* sin is the cause
Ai, *s.* a technical play-term, ten *ai* are equal to a *re;* see *re*
Aî, *s.* a longing desire for fish
Aia, *s.* a country or place where one makes his abode; an inheritance or portion of land
Aia, *v.n.* to take refuge as those who have lost their land in time of war
Aia, *s.* the open state of a flower
—*v. n.* to open as a flower or blossom; see *uaa*
—*a.* open as a flower; contemptible
Aiaai, *s.* a crime or fault

Aiaha, *s.* a young and courageous warrior

Aiahoto, *s.* the same as *aiaha*

Aiahu, *s.* one that eats on the high and privileged place in a *marae*; see *ahu*

—*v.a.* to eat food upon the *ahu* or high place

Aiahu, *v.a.* to vaunt in an ostentatious manner

Aiahû, *s.* a by-stander at a wrestling time who seizes on one of the parties

Aiai, *s.* a species of the *pandanus*, called also *fara vao*

Aiai, *v.a.* to eat a little repeatedly; see *amuamu*

Aiai, *s.* clearness, fairness

—*a.* fair, clear, unsoiled, white, comely

Aiaia, *v.n.* to be emitting a putrid smell

Aiaia, *s.* some supposed crime

Aiaiahu, *v.a.* to vaunt, to crow over a person

Aiaia maa, *v. n.* to be eager after food

—*s.* one that leaves a place of scarcity for a place where there is abundance of food

Aiaiaoa, *s.* cloth made of the bark of the fibrous roots of the *aoa* tree

Aiaiaoa, *s.* the name of a small sea-eel

Aiaifaa, *v.a.* to eat in the time of certain prayers without regarding the prohibitions of the chiefs, a crime often punished with death

Aiaifaa, *v.a.* to eat improper things, as pregnant women do

Aiaihaa, *v.n.* to be of an ungovernable appetite; to covet every thing

—*v.a.* to eat voraciously

Aiana, *s.* a miser, one very parsimonious

Aiani, *s.* a shameless beggar

*Aiao, *s.* the foot; see *maiao* and *avae*

Aiao, *a.* of a pleasant mien

Aiapuu, *s.* one who avenges the defeat of a wrestler; one that makes good a failure

—*v.a.* to avenge, to make good a former failure; see *taiapuu*

Aiari, *s.* one who follows a chief from attachment, or for his own advantage

Aiaro, *v.a.* to surround a board or eating place, and eat face to face

Aiaru, *s.* the ghost of a dead relation which was supposed to come to the living and inflict sickness or death

—*v.a.* to inflict sickness or death on a person

Aiaruru, *v. a.* to eat or do a thing in a body

Aiata, *v.a.* to eat another's food, or take his property, without leave or consent; to eat, as a dog, whatever might come in his way

Aiato, *v. a.* to extirpate or consume utterly

Aiatupuna, *s.* land possessed by inheritance

Aiava, *v.n.* to rise in the throat as sorts of food

Aibu, *s.* a cup; see *aebu*, *aipu*, and *aua*

Aie, *s.* a species of hard wood that grows on some low islands; a species of *tatau* or skin-marks on the loins and posteriors

Aiea, *v.a.* to act in a deadly manner, as was done, according to the notions of former times, by the ghost of the dead upon the living

Aifatu, *s.* a stranger that becomes the domestic of a chief and works for him
—*v. a.* to attach one's self to a chief and work for him
Aifenua, *s.* a person that covets and takes possession of another man's land
—*v. a.* to take possession of the land of another, from *ai*, to eat, and *fenua*, land
—*a.* covetous of another's land
Aiha, *s.* rubbish brought down to the sea by a great fall of rain
Aiha, *s.* the cord which passes through the pearl fish-hook; the upper and under ropes of a fishing net
Aiha, *s.* heat, sultriness; vexation
—*a.* warm, close and sultry
—*v. n.* to be vexed by importunity
Aihamu, *v. a.* to eat voraciously the leavings of others; to press to the food before others
Aihamumu, *s.* a person who continually imposes upon another by eating his food, &c.
—*v. a.* to devour another's food; to beg another's property till it is all expended
Aiharuma, *s.* a pilferer of food or other things
—*v. a.* to seize upon food as cats and dogs do; to pilfer the food of others
Aihau, *v. n.* to enjoy peace and tranquillity
Aihere, *s.* weeds, rubbish, uncultivated land
Aihuaa, *s.* a person acquainted with genealogies; a genealogical series
Aihuaraau, *s.* a coloniser, or possessor of land taken by conquest
Aihuaraau, *v. a.* to possess land taken by conquest
Aiio, *s.* a disease that breaks out in continual ulcers; domestic broils, internal commotions of a country, a company to commit some evil deed
Aima, *ad.* [*auma*,] no, not, with reference to the past, *eima* is the future; it is commonly pronounced and accompanied with putting the tip of the tongue between the lips, and frequently the negative is signified by that action alone without a word spoken; see *aina*, *aita*, and *aore*
Aimama, *s.* a person that always remains at home and lives with his or her parents to adult age
—*v. a.* to eat food chewed by the mother
Aimamau, *s.* a consumer of food
—*v. a.* to consume the food; to grasp the whole
Aimâtua, *v. a.* to eat with old men only, on account of war or some approaching ceremony
Aimaunu, *v. a.* to nibble, as fish do the bait
Aimaure, *v. a.* to collect and eat fruits and roots before they are ripe
Aimautu, *v. a.* to eat secretly, covering the mouth with the hand
Aina, *ad.* no, not; used as *aima* and *aore*
Aina, *s.* land, country, but the word is obsolete at Tahiti; see *fenua*

Aina, *s.* the skin of the armpits or of the groin, when of a dark colour.

Ainanu, *s.* a constellation consisting of the two stars, *Pipiri* and *Rehia.* According to a Tahitian tradition, they were a boy and a girl left at home while the parents were fishing: the children waited, expecting the fish, with half a breadfruit in the hand of each of them. The parents arrived with the fish, and the children, pretending to be asleep, were not called, and the fish were eaten, the children being *ainanu*, displeased, flew upon the top of the house, and from thence to the sky, where the boy, *Pipiri*, and the girl, *Rehia*, became the two stars forming the constellation *Ainanu*

Ainanu, *s* displeasure or sullenness on account of food or deprivation of a proper share; the feeling of not being duly considered as to food and other things.

—*v. n.* to be displeased on account of food or of being deprived of a due share.

Aiô, *v. a.* to eat what was intended for an *ô* or present.

Aioio, *s* a changeable person.

—*a* changeable, unsettled, as the wind or the mind

Aioio, *interj.* a cry of the *ai ioi.*

Aioio, *a.* crooked or twisting, as a tree.

Aiora, *v. a.* to inflict disorder or death, as the spirits of the dead were formerly supposed to do upon living relations; see *aiea*

Aiore, *s.* an abortive; see *aupara* and *mamaia.*

—*a.* abortive, fallen off, as fruit not ripe.

Aiori, *s.* a species of mountain-plantain.

Aiori, *s.* a species of the *fee* or cuttle fish.

Aiori, *s* a name given to some of the shark's teeth.

Aiota, *s.* rareness, rawness; of undressed food; something disagreeable introduced by a good speech.

—*a.* rare, not sufficiently dressed, as food.

Aipa, *ad.* no, not, as *aima* and *aita.*

Aipâ, *s.* a hog sacrificed to *Teari vahine*, literally, the queen, but meaning some god or goddess; this was at the conclusion of certain prayers, after which the people might eat.

Aipai, *s* sodomy.

—*v. a.* to commit sodomy; see *paia* and *mahû.*

Aipârita, *s* a person that eats in haste.

—*v a.* to eat with unusual hurry.

Aipue, *s.* a play term; the first in the diversion of *timo raa, patia raa fa, &c.*

Airà, *s.* a fishing rod; see *matira.*

Airahu, *v. a.* to eat at the taking off of a restriction.

Airahui, *v. a.* to eat what is forbidden, see *rahui*

—*s.* one that eats what is prohibited.

Airahurahu, *s* the same as *airahui.*

Airaua, *s.* one of the names of the *po*, viz hades or the dark unknown state of the dead.

Airaua, *a.* bedridden; ill, as a bedridden person.

Airaurau, *v. a.* to eat by picking bits off from the sides, edges, or outside parts of a baked pig.

Aireire, *s.* the remainder, or little that was left; used with a negative, *aita aireire*, no remainder, none left.

Airôa, *s.* that which is difficult to attain, or come up to, or excel in, as in various games.

Airohe, *s.* the name of a small tyger shell.

Airoiro, *s.* small maggots; see *iro* and *tua;* small fibrous roots of plants.

—*a.* maggoty; having small fibrous roots.

Airuma, *v. a.* to eat sullenly and unsocially, neither regarding those who are near, nor offering them any thing.

Aita, *ad. of negation, past time,* no, not; see *aore.*

Aitâ, *interj.* of wonder or surprise, as *aitâ te marô!* how obstinate! *aitâ te mahana!* how hot the sun!

Aitaa, *s.* a man of another district or country, who, by marriage, becomes an inheritor of land.

Aitaha, *s.* a man that catches many and large fishes, but appropriates them all to himself, not regarding the custom of sending some to the king or chief of the place.

—*v. a.* to eat fish without paying the usual tribute.

Aitahaa, *s.* a person destitute of shame and modesty, that would come and eat naked without regarding the presence of others.

Aitairi, *v. a.* to eat hastily and indecently, tearing the food like a dog.

Aitairiiri, *v. a.* to eat by tearing repeatedly like a dog, and looked upon as a bad omen.

Aitamai, *s.* one that excites to war or contention.

—*v. a.* to excite to war or disturbance.

Aitarahu, *s.* a debtor; see *tarahu.*

Aitaua, *s.* one that avenges the wrong or disgrace of his friend or relation; a country that redeems its character by conquering its conquerors; an avenger of murder, &c.

—*v. a.* to avenge the wrong of a friend or relation.

Aitauae, *s.* a play term in the *timo raa;* also *aitaoae* and *aitauai*, the same as *aipue.*

Aitea, *s.* the first fish caught by the method called *auaho;* the first slain enemy whose body was obtained in time of war.

Aito, *s.* the iron wood, called also *toa* and *amuito.*

Aito *s.* a warrior, hero, conqueror, military man.

—*a.* mischievous, fierce, warlike.

Aitoa, *interj.* denoting satisfaction on account of something disastrous that has happened to another. *Aitoa!* ah! it served him right; he well deserved it!

Aitoa, *s.* the beginning of some words used as a charm; when a person happened to have a fish-bone sticking in the throat, the priest or some other person would say, *aitoa, aitoa, oe i raoa;* see *raoa.*

Aitomoua, *s.* the name of a tree that grows in the mountains, and different from the common *aito* or *toa* tree.

Aitu, *s.* a god or goddess; see *atua.*

Aituhituhi, *a.* given to cursing and swearing.

—*v. a.* to curse, or imprecate evil, and that repeatedly; see *tuhi.*

Aiû, [*ai*, to eat, and *u*, milk,] *s.* a sucking child; an affectionate term for a young person.

Aiuiu, *s.* the great length of the time of a journey; the long breath of a diver.

—*a.* of long continuance, as a journey; long-breathed, as a diver.

Aiva, *a.* [*aiwa, iva, iwa*] nine in counting.

Aivaiva, *a.* great; abundant; large in quantity.

Aivanâ, *a.* learned; well skilled in language, prayers, and heathen ceremonies.

Aivao, *s.* the name of a species of banana.

Aivi, *s.* any ridge of low hills stretching to the mountains.

Ama, *s.* the outrigger of a single canoe; the *paeama* is the left side and is the woman's side; the right is called *pae atea* and is the man's side.

Ama, *s.* the state of being well dressed or cooked, as food; the state of burning well.

—*a.* done or cooked, as food, by boiling, baking, or roasting; see *a.*

—*v. n.* to be in the state of being well cooked as food, or well burnt as stones, &c.

Amaa, *s.* a branch of a tree or plant; the small branches of the bark of which cloth is made; a branch or division of a subject; the head of a sermon.

Amaamaa, *s.* small twigs or branches, see *ara, peapea,* and *rara.*

Amae, *s.* the name of a tree, the wood of which is hard and durable, the leaves were called *rau ava* and used about the sacrifices and various ceremonies, and the tree for that reason was generally planted in the *marae;* see *miro.*

Amafatu, *s.* female attendants on the chiefs; cleverness, skilfulness, ingenuity.

—*a.* clever, skilful, ingenious.

Amaha, *s.* a crack, fissure, opening.

—*a.* cracked, having openings; see *afa.*

Amahamaha, *a.* having many cracks or openings; split in many places; see *afafa.*

Amahatu, *a.* clever, as *amafatu.*

Amahi, *s.* a small fresh water fish, see *oopu.*

Amama, *s.* the name of a certain sweet scented native oil; see *monoi.*

Amara, *s.* the name of a sort of plantain; the first length or row of thatch on a native house when thatching; the first stone laid in the wall of a *marae.*

Amara, *s.* a restriction in regard to food while a canoe, called *vaa amara,* was building, or in preparation, for the use of the king.

Amara, *s.* varieties of the *po reho*, or tyger shell, of which there are, *amara pu fenua*, and *amara iri to patu*, and subdivisions, as *totoe*, *taupo-uru*, *amihi*, *nena*, *aauru*, *roru*, *ovare*, *pai*, &c.

Amaratifai, *s.* an old canoe patched with a piece of sacred wood from a *marae*, and when the king had touched it, or gone on it, it was offered to a god.

Amata auahi, *s.* the first small sticks put together in kindling a fire—*fig.* the beginnings of contention or of war

Amaua, *a.* ignorant, unskilful; see *mauo*.

Amaura, *s.* the name of a mountain tree.

Amaura, *s.* an ignoramus; a contemptuous name for one ignorant of the arts among the natives; awkwardness, ignorance.

Amea, *s.* a branch or bough; the division of a discourse; see *amaa*.

Ami, *s.* the spawn of crabs, lobsters, &c.

Ami, *v. n.* to be at the point of being dried up, as the bed of a river.

Amia, *s.* the name of a medicinal plant.

Amiami, *s* fear, dread of mind, see *faaamiami*.

—*v. n.* to wink with the eyes, as a person apprehensive of a blow; to move the lips quickly, as one out of breath, or a dying person; to pant, as fish taken out of the water; to be in dread or fear, to apprehend danger.

Amiami, *s.* the lid or valve that covers the mouth of crabs

Amiami, *s.* the name of a medicinal plant.

Amihi, *s.* a sort of tyger-shell.

Amiimii, *a.* curled, as hair or wool; cross grained, as a piece of timber.

—*s* the cross or curled state of timber, &c.

Amina, *v. n.* to crave the food that others are eating; to have an unsatisfied desire.

Aminamina, *v. n.* to desire repeatedly what others are eating or enjoying.

Amio, *a.* unsettled, changeable.

Amio, *s* the continued odour of a thing.

—*v. n.* to continue to send forth scent, either good or bad.

Amiomio, *v. n.* to change repeatedly, as the wind.

Amioparai, *s.* the name of a certain mode in the exercise of arms called *tu raau*; a technical war term.

—*v. n.* to retire from the face of the enemy, come round by a circuitous road, rally again, and renew the fight The term is derived from the manner of the fish *parai*.

Amo, *s.* the wink of the eye; a sign made by winking.

—*v n.* to wink, to make a sign by winking; to flash, as lightning when small and frequent.

Amo, *v. a.* to carry on the back. [or shoulder.

Amoa, *s.* a species of fern; there are two sorts, white and black, which are used as medicine for the navel string of infants when newly cut.

Amoa, *s.* the name of a certain feast, when prayers were made, and certain ceremonies used, for the purpose of removing various restrictions in regard to the children of the chiefs and others, who, before the performance of the *amoa*, were reckoned sacred.

Amoamo, *v.n.* to wink repeatedly; to twinkle as the stars.

—*s.* the twinkling of the stars; the winking of the eyes.

Amoamoa, *a.* ill; sallow; of sickly appearance.

Amoamo apipiti, *s* a sign by winking mutually, as two persons of different sexes.

—*v.n.* to wink at each other, as two persons.

Amoamo rua, *v.n.* to approach each other, as two armies.

Amoo, *s.* the name of a certain prayer used in the *marae* before war, and on some other occasions.

Amoomoo, *a.* ill; the same as *amoamoa.*

Amoraa mata, *s* the winking of the eye; a moment, a second.

Amou, *s.* the top end of a tree or plant; the handle of a spear; see *omou.*

Amu, *s.* an eater; the person or thing that eats.

—*v.a.* to eat; see *ai.*

Amuamu, *v. a.* to eat a little repeatedly, as a sick person beginning to recover; see *aiai.*

Amuamu, *v.a* to mock, deride, call ill names.

Amuamu, *v. n.* to grumble, murmur.

Amuhau, *v. n.* to enjoy peace, or the fruits of peace.

Amuhau, *s.* the person or persons who live upon the land which had been conquered; such as enjoy the fruits of peace; see *hau.*

Amui, *s.* four cocoa-nuts tied together cross-wise; a cluster or bunch of fruit.

Amui, *v.a.* to add, collect, put together.

—*v.n.* to associate or join together for some good or bad purpose; to be so joined.

Amui, *a.* productive, as bread-fruit, cocoa-nuts, &c.

Amuimui, *v.a.* to add together repeatedly.

—*v.n.* to join or associate together repeatedly.

Amui raa, *s.* the time or place of collecting, joining, or associating together, addition; an assembly or congregation.

Amuito, *s.* a modern name for the *toa* tree.

Amuo, *s.* the name of a prayer; see *amoo.*

Amuri, *s* the handle of a spear.

Amuri, *ad. & prep.* hereafter; behind; see *muri.*

Amutarahu, *s* a debtor; see *aitarahu.*

Amuto, *s* the same as *amuito, toa*, and *aito.*

Ana, *s.* a cave or cavern; a piece of rough coral used as a grater; the name of a star.

—*v.a.* to rasp or grate, such as the kernel of the cocoa-nut by a piece of coral called *ana.*

Ana, *pron. 3rd person sing.* he, she, or it.

—*poss. pron.* [from *a ana*,] of or belonging to him, her, or it; see *a.*

Ana, *ad.* or *aux. v.* when in the imperative, or when the verb is by way of entreaty, but commonly contracted into *a* or *na;* see *na.*

Anaana, *s.* brightness, shining, lustre.

—*a*, bright, shining, splendid.

Anaana, *s.* small pieces of coral or shells thrown upon the shore by the sea.

Anaana, *a.* indented with small holes, as the coral rocks in the sea; tapering or going in towards the bottom; see *tapere.*

Anaanaea, *a.* revived, recruited, refreshed.

—*v n.* to be revived or recovered, as a sick person; to be refreshed, as a hungry or faint person; to be recruited, as an army.

Anaanatae, *s.* strong desire after an object; the going out of affection.

—*v.n.* to desire ardently.

Anaanateuramea, *s.* the name of a noted savage of old, according to Tahitian tradition; and is sometimes applied to a cruel, savage, mischief-making man.

Anaanaumupo, *s.* the brightness of a night oven—*fig.* a man of a fair speech whose words are not to be trusted.

Anae, *a.* [*anake, nake,*] all; every; only.

—*ad.* together; at once; entirely.

Anae, *s.* anxiety, thoughtfulness.

—*v.n.* to be anxious, thoughtful, grieving.

Anae, *s.* the name of a fish, the mullet.

Anaemoeoho, *s.* the name of a fish; see *orie.*

Anaenae, *v n.* to be repeatedly exercising anxious thoughts, so as to destroy sleep; to be repeatedly disturbed in sleep by some uneasiness of body or mind.

Anafero, *a.* gluttonous, libidinous.

Anahero, *a.* the same as *anafero.*

Anahoa, *s.* a strong wind from the south west.

Anaî, *s.* frugality, economy, carefulness.

Anai, *s.* a row, or layer; see *nanai.*

Anî, *s.* frugally, carefully; cunningly, craftily.

—*a.* clever; skilful; cunning; stingy.

Ananahi, *s.* to-morrow, or yesterday, according to the way it is mentioned; if the preposition *i* is before it, it signifies yesterday, otherwise, to-morrow; see *abobo* and *nanahi.*

Ananahi atura, *s.* the day after to-morrow; or, if preceded by an *i*, the day before yesterday.

Anani, *s.* [*orange*, Eng.] the orange tree and fruit; see *arani.*

Anaohiu, *s.* the end of the coral grater used to scrape the cocoa-nut; a sauce made of cocoa-nut well scraped and made fine.

Anaouru, *s.* the same as *anaohiu.*

Anapa, *s.* a flash of lightning, the flashing of lightning.

Anapa, *v n.* to flash, as lightning or gunpowder.

Anapanapa, *v. n.* to flash repeatedly, as lightning.

Anapape, *s.* a river; the bed of a river; see *anavai.*

Anatiai ahu, *s.* an ill favoured, over grown person; a sentinel set to watch over a fortified place in a cave; see *ahu.*

Anau, *s.* grief of parents for their children, or of children for their parents.

—*v.n.* to grieve, as a parent for his child, or the child for his parent.

Anauru, *s.* a strong, boisterous wind.

Anavai, *s* a river; the bed of a river; see *anapape.*

Anave, *s.* breath; a line, cord, thread; perseverance; longevity; see *aho.*

Anave, *s.* a certain mode of tying a bunch of *uru.*

Anavenave, *a.* addicted to get food at another person's house.

Aneane, *a.* clear, as a fine and cloudless atmosphere;—*fig.* fair and deceptive, as the speech of a hypocrite.

Anee, *s.* ductility; the quality of extension.

—*v. n.* to spread, or extend, as a thing beaten with a hammer or mallet; to slip out, as a wedge.

—*a.* ductile, malleable.

Anehepiro, *s.* a person that monopolises different kinds of fish.

—*v. n.* to be longing for fish, as a sick person.

Anei, *v. of being,* answering to is or are, but used only interrogatively, as, *oia anei?* is it so? or, is it that?

Anei, *s.* the name of an odoriferous shrub.

Ani, *s.* a request, petition; also the petitioner, asker, or beggar.

—*v. a.* to ask, petition, beg, &c.

—*a.* addicted to begging or asking.

Ania, *s.* superficiality; shallowness; the quality of being merely on the surface.

—*a* superficial, slight, shallow, unfounded.

—*ad.* superficially, slightly.

Aniao, *s.* the foot; tract; footstep; see *avae.*

Anini, *s.* giddiness; a sense of turning in the head.

—*v. n.* to be giddy or dizzy.

—*a.* giddy.

Aninia, *s.* a great degree of giddiness or dizziness in the head.

—*v. n.* to be very giddy or dizzy; having a sense of circular motion.

—*a.* giddy, dizzy.

Aniuea, *s.* a species of taro with very hard, deep, and strong roots.

Anivaniva, *s.* a great degree of giddiness or vertigo; called also *aniniva.*

—*v. n.* to be moving in a zigzag course, as an arrow, or lightning.

Ano, *s.* the desolate state of a country, or of a house, for want of inhabitants.

—*a.* desolate, as a house or land.

Anoa, *s.* shape or appearance of the land as to mountains, vallies, capes, shores, &c.

—*a.* distant; lost in distance, as the sun in setting, a ship when lost to sight, &c.

Anoano, *s.* the height of a place; awe; that which causes bashfulness.

—*a* high or distant, so that an object cannot be clearly discerned; terrible or frightful because of height; fearful or bashful in entering into a company.

Anoano, *s.* the seeds of gourds, melons, cucumbers, &c.; see *huero.*

Anoano, *s.* a cocoa-nut water-bottle.

Anoano, *s.* the name of one of the modes of attack, in the exercise of arms called *turaau* or *tiaraau.*

Anoanomarie, *s.* a wise person; one who can solve difficulties.

Anoanomatie, *s.* a native of a a place where his ancestors were before him; a wise person, as *anoanomarie.*

—*a.* clever; wise; intelligent.

Anoanotupu, *s.* a native of a place, or a permanent resident; see *iho tupu.*

Anoaurî, *s.* the steady gaze of a dog at his master; one that will not flinch; a steady friend

Anoe, *s.* the desire to see, hear, or eat.

—*v n.* to have an abiding pleasure in seeing, hearing or eating.

Anoenoe, *v n.* to have continued pleasure in hearing, seeing, &c. so as not to be tired.

Anohi, *s* a fish hook; the point of a fish hook.

Anoi, *s.* a compound; a mixture

—*v.a.* to mix together different ingredients.

Anoi, *a.* mixed, compounded.

Anoinoi. Anonmoni, *v.a.* to mix repeatedly.

Anoparau, *s.* one that can advise, having knowledge of men and things.

Anotaro, *s.* a season.

Anotau, *s.* a season; see *tau* and *matahiti.*

Anotupu, *s.* an inhabitant, a resident.

Anu, *s.* coldness; see *maariri.*

—*a.* cold, see *toetoe.*

Anua, *s.* the name of a tree of hard wood.

Anua, *ad.* superficially; slightly.

Anuanu, *a.* cold, chilly; see *maariri.*

Anuanua, Anuenue, *s.* the rainbow.

Anuanua, *s.* the external part of the root *hoi.*

Anuhe, *s.* the common fern in the mountains; also wire from its supposed resemblance to some fern stalks.

Anuhenuhe, *s.* the apparent greatness of a thing, when not great in reality

—*a.* great in appearance only.

Ao. *s* day; the light; the natural day; bright clouds of the sky.

Ao, *s.* Heaven; blessedness; happiness; the state of the blessed.

Ao. *s* the good reign of a prince; a hospitable man.

Ao, *s* the present life. *te ao nei,* means the present world, the present state of existence.

Ao, *s* the opening buds of trees; the white heart of cabbage, taro &c, the first that comes off in straining liquors, such as the *ava, &c.*

Ao, *s* the name of a large spotted sea bird.

Ao, *s*. the heart of a bundle of cloth; the king who is the head and heart of the country.

Ao, *s*. the grooves of the cloth mallet; also the marks of the grooves in the cloth.

Ao, *s* the part of an arrow that is taken hold of on putting it on the string.

Ao, *s*. the inside bark used for cloth making.

Ao, *s*. the fat of turtles, fowls, and fishes.

Ao, *s*. the name of a ceremony previous to that of the *tihi*; see *tihi*.

Ao, *s*. braided human hair; the string that fastens the *fa* or butt at which men throw their spears.

Ao, *s*. the food that is turned over at random to visitors at certain feasts.

Ao, *s*. the chief or first part of things; the first enjoyment.

Ao, *s*. one of the ropes fastened to a sail.

Ao, *s*. a spy that comes upon a party at night to see what they are doing.

Ao, *s*. the sides of a square; an angle.

Ao *v.a.* to rip up the bark of small branches for cloth making.

Ao, *v. a.* to press the liquid out of the *mou* or strainer, such as that of the *ava*, the *pia*, or cocoa nut kernel

Ao. *v. n* to peep as an eel out of its hole; to appear again, as a lost fugitive.

A'o *s*. [*ako*,] counsel, warning, advice. reproof.

A'o, *v. a* [*ako*, *onai*.] to counsel, advise, warn, reprove, exhort, preach.

— *s* a counsellor, adviser, exhorter, preacher.

Aoa, *s*. the name of a tree, called also *ora* and *ore*, and of the bark of which cloth is made, called by the same names. Tradition says that the tree first grew in the moon, from whence the seed was brought to the earth by a bird.

—*s*. the name of a species of bread fruit.

—*s*. the name of a medicinal plant; see *putorea*; also a species of coral.

—*s*. a play term of the *apere raa*.

—*a*. well peopled, having many [houses.

Aoa, *v. n*. to bark or howl, as a dog.

—*s*. the howling of dogs.

Aoahe, *v. n*. to look well to one's self.

Aoaia, *v. a*. to collect food and other things with care.

Aoaia, *s*. the unabated pleasure of a fisherman.

Aoao, *s*. [*kaokao*,] the ribs.

Aoao, *s*. slimness, length and well shapedness

— *a*. slim, tall, well shaped.

Aoaoa, *a*. rambling, unsettled; also silly, or delirious.

—*v. n* to be delirious, or roving; also to be foolish or silly.

—*s*. the indistinct noise made by a number of persons at a distance.

Aoaoaehaa, *s*. narrowness, or confined state when applied to land.

Aoaoaehaa, *a.* narrow, as a tract of land between a mountain and the sea.

Aoaomaraia, *s.* the name of a person called the *father of fire*, because he was the first discoverer of the art of procuring fire by friction; before his time the people eat their food raw; see *Mahuie.*

Aoaopeapea, *s.* the name of a *tii* to which prayers were addressed by conjurors.

Aoaotahi, *s* a broad rib bone; an intrepid warrior.

Aoareva, *s.* the large or coarse grooves of the *ie* or cloth beating mallet.

Aofa, *s.* a species of plantain.

Aofaofa, *s.* the straight and tall growth of persons, or of trees.

—*a.* straight and high, applied to a good looking tree; slim and tall when applied to persons.

Aofeofe, *a.* the same as *aofaofa.*

Aoha, *s.* the same as *aofa.*

—*v. n.* to lean or bend down as a fence, or the branch of a tree.

Aoheohe, *a.* long and slender as trees; see *aofaofa.*

Aoi, *v. a* to move a thing a little; to shake, as the wind does a tree; see *arori.*

Aoioi, *v. a.* to move or shake a thing repeatedly.

—*v. n.* to be moving repeatedly as a tree shaken by the wind.

Aoioi, *s.* the shaking or repeated moving of any thing.

—*a.* shaken, moveable.

Aorai, *s* a name formerly given to the king's house.

Aore, *ad* [*akore, ao'e, aohe, aole, kaore, kare,*] no, not, with reference to the past; see *aita.*

Aorereva, *s.* a species of native cloth.

Aorereva noa, *s.* flying clouds; unsettledness of residence.

—*a.* unsettled.

Aoroa, *s* the firmament or heaven; called also *moana roa*, and said to be the residence of the god *Tane.*

Aoti, *s.* a pair of scissors; a person that cuts hair.

—*v. a.* to cut or crop with scissors.

—*a.* dressed or polled; see *paoti.*

Apa, *s.* a fish hook with two feathers fixed to it for catching some sorts of fish; also a young bird.

—*s.* the lining of a garment.

—*v. a.* to join together two pieces of the tyger shell to make an instrument to catch the *fee* or cuttle fish.

—*v. a.* to dart a reed so as to slide along the ground.

Apà, *s.* a mode of using the hands in a native dance.

—*s.* an enclosure, where the young king or infant son of a chief was put to sleep.

—*s* a person that eat restricted food, and yet could not be hurt by the arts of the sorcerers. The principal god of the *apá* was *Roa*, to whom prayers were addressed, full of imprecations and curses on the sorcerer and his family.

Apaa, *s* the name of a fishhook made of scaly pearl shell.

Apaa, *s.* the blossom of the *tiare* when fully open; also an idol made of sacred cloth and birds feathers.

Apaa, *s.* a sort of thick cloth made by men, (not by women as usual,) of the *aute* bark, and worked by night, to be sacred to the gods, and was used to cover them during certain ceremonies.

Apaahoe, *v. n.* to be joined or united in one, to be in league.

Apaahui noa, *s.* a stranger or foreigner.

Apaapaa, *s* chips, splinters; also some thing reported or known in an indirect way, not properly authenticated.

Apaapa, *s* one side of a thing when divided through the middle, as the carcase of a beast or fish, the side of a house, &c.

—*s.* birds of all sorts; see *manu.*

—*v. n.* to flap as a sail, or as the wings of a bird.

—*s.* a seat in a canoe.

Apaapa, *s.* the name of the seventh of the Tahitian moons or months.

Apaapañai, *s.* the name of a small fish with very wide fins; *fig.* an ostentatious person.

Apaapia, *s.* a ceremony used in making peace between contending parties; a piece of cloth was laid down by one party, and if the terms of agreement were approved, the other party laid another upon it; if not, it was torn, and war followed; see *manufaite.*

Apaariaria, *s.* the name of a beautiful cloth made of the *aute* bark; see *aute.*

Apae, *a.* five in counting; see *arima.*

Apae, *s.* a roost or perch for fowls.

—*v. n.* to roost as a fowl.

—*s.* the restoring of a chief to his possessions; the party that restored him.

Apai, *s.* the name of a certain game; the player at the game *apai.*

—*v. a.* to play with bat and ball at the game *apai;* to carry or convey on the wing.

—*v. a.* to string together the *raoere* or leaves used as a fishing net; to take off the husk of a cocoa-nut.

—*s.* a stringer of cocoa nut leaves.

Apâpâ, *s.* a parcel of *aute*, or the bark called *pouru*, laid out by the women for cloth making.

—*v a.* to put the bark of the *aute* or of the bread fruit branches in layers in preparation for cloth making.

Apapafara, *a.* hasty in speech as when angry.

Apapavai, *a* smooth, still, unruffled, as the surface of the water in a calm; smooth and unruffled in temper; smooth and fair.

Apape, *s* the name of a tree used for boat building; the leaves are like those of the ash; see *avai*; the name also of a shrub.

—*s.* a sort of scented cloth; called also *vaivai.*

—*v. a.* to use the leaves of the shrub *apape* for scenting cloth.

Apara, *s.* a name given to *pia* and other things when collected together, from a strange notion, formerly entertained, that they would vanish away if called by their proper names.

Aparai, *s.* an enclosure for an infant, the son of a king or a principal chief, who was sacred till certain ceremonies had been performed; also a temporary *marae*.

—*a.* clear, cloudless, applied to the sky.

Aparau, *s.* a person or speech that causes laughter.

—*v. n.* to be jocular or jesting

Apari, *a.* rocky, dangerous to pass on account of rocks, or broken coral reefs.

Aparima, *s* a teacher, or regulator of the *ori* or Tahitian dance; see *faatia*.

Aparipari, *a.* rocky, full of broken corals.

Aparu, *s.* the name of a species of *ope*, [*arum costatum*,] less acrid than some other kinds

—*s.* a sort of fish hook.

—*s.* a consultation of the chiefs about peace or war, or the best measures to be adopted.

Aparuparu, *s.* the consultation of chiefs; called also *aparuparu roa*, and *uparu ruaroa*.

—*s.* the name of a fish-hook.

Apata, *s* a thicket or wood that is hardly penetrable; a cluster of branching coral in the sea.

Apatahi, *v. n.* to cast a side glance at a person on account of displeasure or of shame.

—*a.* one sided, as a certain flower is said to be, *tiare apatahi*, see *tiare*.

Apatoa, *s.* the north.

Apatoerau, *s.* the south,

Ape, *s* [*kape*,] the *arum costatum*, of which there are several varieties.

—*s* the act of flinching from danger, or of avoiding the consequence of an argument.

—*v. n.* to flinch, so as to avoid a blow.

Apea, *s.* a twig, or a branch.

Apeape, *v. n.* to flinch repeatedly.

Apeau, *s.* a lean sort of turtle.

Apeau, *a.* shy, ashamed.

Apeapea, *s.* small twigs or branches.

Apee, *s.* the name of a small fish that follows a large one.

Apeepee, *s* the name of a game among children.

—*v. a.* to make feathers to fly, a children's game.

Apehava, *s.* a large over grown *ope*, under the shade of which people sometimes eased themselves, it was therefore abominated and not eaten, a lazy worthless person so called by way of contempt.

Apepe, *v. a.* to add to one's own the food or property of another.

Apepe, *s.* a piece put on a sail when torn. [*tapepe*.

—*v. a.* to patch or piece, see

Apepe, *v. a.* to do something beside, or not to the purpose, to be seeking more than one's own.

Apepepepe, *v. a.* to heap one thing upon another.

—*v. n.* to roll as one wave upon another.

Apere, *s.* the reed thrown or darted in the game called *aperea*; the person that throws the reed.

Apere, *v. a* to play the game of *apere.*

Aperea, *s.* the name of a certain game.

Apeta, *s.* the name of a war canoe.

Apetahi, *v. n.* to look aside, or askance.

Apetai, *s.* the name of a sea eel that is not eatable.

Apeu, *s.* the inside of a bow towards its ends.

Apeu, *s.* a mode of fishing for the *iihi* fish.

Api, *s.* folds of cloth pasted together; the leaves of a book; the bi alve shells of fish; a part of a canoe.

Api, *s.* a small spotted fish.

Api, *v. n.* to be full, occupied, closed up.

—*a.* filled, occupied as a place.

Api, *v. a.* to confederate together, as different parties; to join, as the sub-divisions of a fleet of war canoes.

Apî, *a.* young, recent, late; see *hou.*

Apia, *a.* closed, as the oyster or *pahua* shells.

Apiapi, *s* narrowness, confinedness of a place or of the mind; straightness, difficulty as to choice.

Apiapi, *a.* filled, occupied; narrow.

Apiapi, *s.* a cloth, dyed and perfumed with certain plants.

Apiparau, *s.* the valve that joins the pearl oyster shell.

Apihuoi, *s.* a mode of attack in war when a party is kept in reserve; a vagrant and worthless person.

Apipiti, *ad.* together, altogether, by parties joining together.

Apiri, *s.* the name of a small tree that grows on high ground.

Apiri, *s.* a species of banana; also the name of a fresh water fish, a sort of *oopu.*

Apiti, *s.* a couple, or two joined together.

—*a* two in counting; see *epiti* and *erua.*

Apiti, *v. a.* to join or unite with another.

—*v. n.* to have two sources, applied to the wind when coming from two different quarters.

Apitia, *v. n.* to be in a joining state, as two trees growing jointly; two parties in one.

Apitipiti, *v. n.* to couple or join things together repeatedly; the plural of *apiti.*

Apito, *s.* a party joined hand in hand; the act of joining things together.

—*v. a.* to join things together; join hand in hand.

Apiu, *s.* the leaves that are first put on the food in covering it up in the native oven.

Apo, *s.* the act of catching a thing thrown to a person; the person who so catches a thing.

—*v. a.* to catch a thing thrown to a person.

Apo, *s.* a hollow place in a rock.

—*a.* hollow, as the belly of a hungry person.

Apoa, *s.* the score on the lower end of the rafters of a native house; the end of the outrigger that joins the canoe.

—*s.* a war-term applied to that part of the army that is behind the *viri,* or those in the van.

Apoahu, *s.* the name of a species of bread fruit, called also *arave.*

Apoapo, *v. a.* to catch repeatedly things thrown at a person.

—*v. n.* to contract the abdomen.

Apoi, *s.* the inner or curved part of a bow, or of any crooked thing.

Apoo, *s.* a pit, hole, grave, aperture; see *rua.*

—*s.* a council, or meeting for consultation.

—*v. n.* to meet, or assemble together for consultation.

Apooaahi, *s.* the place where people fish for the *aahi;* see *aahi.*

Apooihu, *s.* the nostrils; see *ihu.*

Apoomatai, *s.* the source of the wind, or the quarter from which it blows.

Apoopoo, *v. n.* to be consulting secretly about a person, and speaking ill of him behind his back.

Apoopuaa, *s.* a place frequented by hogs.

Apooraa, *s.* a council or assembly convened; a meeting; the time or place of meeting.

Apopo, *s.* and *ad.* to morrow; see *ananahi.*

Aporo, *s.* the small fruit at the end of a bunch.

Apou, *s.* the inside of a bow.

Apu, *s.* the shell of seeds, nuts, and fish.

Apu, *s.* width, breadth; see *aano.*

—*a.* wide, broad.

Apu, *v. a.* to dart or fall fiercely on each other as hogs and dogs when eating, or as certain fishes. add a hu

Apua, *s.* the handle of a spear; see *amuri.*

Apua, *s* a prayer used by sorcerers.

Apua, *s.* a string of *tiare* flowers tied about the head by the women.

Apuapu, *s.* a large species of the *ti,* or the *Dracæna terminalis.*

Apuapu, *s.* pliancy, flexibility.

—*a.* pliable, flexible; thin or slender as a cup, or the bottom of a canoe, or something that is hollow.

Apuaria, *s.* sultry; scorching, as the heat of the sun.

Apuaroa, *s.* an agreeable, slight breeze of wind.

Apufera, *v. n.* to withdraw, a play-term.

Apumaa, *s.* a hospitable person.

—*a.* hospitable, generous with food.

Apumata, *s.* the socket of the eye.

Apuô, *interj.* a cry on the discovery of a ship or a large canoe, *apuô! apuô!*

Apupape, *s.* the brains of a beast.

Apupipape, *s.* the brains of a beast, but not of a man, except by way of contempt.

Apupivai, *s.* the same as *apupape.*

Apura, *s.* a species of *taro;* see *mapura.*

Apurima, *s.* the hollow of the hand.

Apurima ore, *s.* an empty hand; a term used in the game *tuutuupiri;*—*fig.* a person who has disappointed another's expectation.

Apuroro, *s* the human skull

Apurua, *s* a term applied to relations by marriage, a parent of the party married becomes the *apurua* to the parent of the other party that is married.

Aputa, *v. n.* to pierce through or enter, as light through small openings; to enter the mind as perceptions of things.

Aputaputa, *v. n.* having been pierced repeatedly.

—*a.* having several light spots or patches, as the white feathers in a dark bird; full of holes or of patches.

Apuu, *s.* prominent risings on the top of the hills; see *puu*

—*s* the short risings of the waves of the sea.

Apuvai, *s.* the brains of a beast.

Ara, *s.* a road or path; see *ea*

Ara, *s* small twigs or branches; see *peapea.*

Ara, *v. n.* to awake; to be watchful.

—*a* awake; wakeful; watchful

Ara, *s.* the skin on the back of the shark.

Ara, *v. n.* to come to notice; to transpire; to be mentioned or divulged.

Arâ, *s.* a species of hard black stone.

Ara, *v. a.* to importune the gods, and make much of them by presents, &c., to gain their countenance in war.

Araa, *s* a messenger sent before a chief and company to give information of their approach; or to give notice of the approach of some feast or religious ceremony.

Araa, *s* the small fry of fish, used as bait for the large ones

Arâa, *v. n.* to be raised or lightened, as a vessel in the water. or as a thing that was sunk; to be raised to prosperity from a degraded state.

Ara aau. *v n.* to remain sleepless at night

Ara aau, *s* the middle or highest part of the coral reef, where people walk and stand to fish.

Araaha, *s.* a part of a canoe sewn together with *aha* or sinnet.

Araara, *s.* the glaring of the eyes of animals.

—*a.* sparkling glaring shining.

Araara, *s.* the face or eyes; the first beginning of a thing; the edge of a tool; see *mata.*

Arâarâa, *v. n.* to be convalescent; to be raised from depression by some unexpected good news.

Araaraaivao, *s.* an inhabitant of the upper vallies; a wild or untamed animal

—*a* wild, untamed, unaccustomed to the sea side, as an inhabitant of the interior of the country

Araaravî, *s.* the name of a fish, which when full grown is called *hinoa.*

Arauravî, *v. n* to be brought under, cowed, or conquered; see *rí.*

Araatia, *s.* the out posts of a house

Araau, *s* the current of water between rocks

Araau *s* a longing desire to go, or to obtain some object.

Araau, v n to be employed in telling tales at night, or in other talk, so as not to sleep.
Araavero, s a store laid up for exigencies.
Araburabu, v n. to swing up and down, as a long pole when carried on the shoulder.
Arae, s a small variegated fish.
Araea, s. [*alaea*,] red earth; bricks; red crockery ware; reddish colours
Araea, v. n to be almost suffocated in eating voraciously.
Araeri, s an oblong basket made of cocoa nut leaves.
Arafaa, s. a fish trap.
Arafati, s small branches broken off by the wind; see *ara* and *fati*.
Arafene, s. the elephant fish, modified from the English word *elephant*.
Arafenua, s. a name given to a high wind from the westward
Araharaha, s. a fish, called also *paraharaha*.
Araharaha, s a road with many turnings.
Arahea, s a partial calm, when there is wind at a distance on both sides.
Arahi, a. much or many; see *nui*.
Arahi, v. n. to dwell, sit, abide; see *noho*.
Arahiu, s. the uppermost extremity of a tree; also the point or small end of an instrument.
Arahapehape, s. a war term signifying the small remainder of a party that continued to fight when most had fled
Arahoua, s. a part of a canoe that is bored for tying with sinnet; a decrepit old person.
Arahu, s coal; charcoal; the remains of any thing burnt but not reduced to ashes.
Arâhuepini, s. a very hard stone; see *arâ*.
Arahuepini, s. a heavy blow from a boxer; an athletic, clever fellow; one that is dextrous and unwearied, and will not be moved or give way; a close, stingy fellow.
—*a*. stingy; ill looking.
Arahura, s a war term signifying a party that skirmishes in the front of the main army.
Arahurahu, s. a small black marine bird.
—*a*. blackish; of a dark colour.
Arai, s. an interposer, mediator; an obstruction.
—*v a*. to interpose, mediate, obstruct.
'Arai, s pearl shell brought from a certain place in the small islands to the eastward of Tahiti, called *Arai*, hence the name; a pearl fishing hook.
Araia, s a species of stuff, black-coloured cloth.
Araia, s the liver: see *paraia*.
Araia, s a person's own place of birth.
Arâia, s. the middle of the space between two islands; see *aua*; the place or boundary from which fish or birds return to their usual haunts.
Araihupehupe, s a certain part of the native female dress called *tihi*; see *tihi*.
Araimoana, s. a bunch of red feathers fixed in the body of the *too* or image representing one of the gods
Arainu, s. bait for fish.

Araiore, *s.* the ridge pole of a house.

Araiore, *s.* a war term, signifying a certain mode of attack not expected by the enemy.

Araireva, *s.* a great perpendicular height; a great depth; a great distance at sea.

Arairi, *s.* a sort of basket; see *arapapa.*

Aramaehae, *s.* a mode of seizing or of holding the spear; see *araiore.*

Aramihi, *s.* the name of a small edible crab.

Aramii, *v. n.* to be displeased, to feel pain from ungratified desire.

Aramii, *a.* angry, displeased.
—*ad.* niggardly.

Aramoe, *s.* forgetfulness.

Aramoe, *a.* lost, forgotten; see *moe.*

Aramoi, *s.* & *a.* the same as *aramoe.*

Aramoina, *a.* forgotten, lost; see *moe.*

Aramoomoo, *s.* a sort of an edible crab.

Aramuamua, *s* the same as *aramoomoo*

Arani, *s.* [*alani.*] from the English, orange, the tree and fruit; see *anani.*

Aranoa, *s.* the common road, in distinction from that of the *marae* or sacred place.

Aranua, *s.* the name of a small odoriferous shrub that grows in the mountains.

Aranui, *s.* [*alanui,*] the great or public road.

Araoa. *s.* the side plank of a canoe.

Araoa, *s.* the throat; see *arapoa.*

Araoa, *s.* the eye socket.

Araoe. *s.* one species of the red fish *iihi*

Araooti, *s* a war term, see *aratipi.*

Araoumia, *s* a mode of wrestling.

Araouma, *s.* a road over the breast; a term applied to some viscious actions among the natives.

Arapa, *s.* a sort of basket.

Arapae *s.* a slanting or crooked road along the rocks.

Arapai, *s.* the wall plate, or the piece on which the rafters lodge; called also *apai* and *iope.*

Arapaia, *s* the liver; see *paraia.*

Arapapa, *s.* the name of a basket.

Arapepe, *s.* the name of a small fish; called also *pereaiai.*

Arapepe, *s.* a small axe or tomahawk; the name of a basket, the same as *arapapa.*

Arapoa, *s.* the throat.

Arapoa, *s.* the bend of the leg; a part of a spear; see *atai.*

Arapoa, *s.* gluttony, voraciousness
—*a.* gluttonous, voracious; see *aai.*

Arapofai, *v. a.* to instigate the people to warlike exploits, and that repeatedly There was also a certain prayer used for the *arapofai.*
—*s.* a seditious person.

Arapofaifai, *v. a.* to repeatedly stir up the people to warlike actions.

Arapuo, *s* the line of pith, or heart of a tree; see *puo.*

Ararâ, *a.* hoarse, through calling or much speaking.
—*s.* hoarseness.

Ararà, *v. n.* to become hoarse through calling, or much speaking.
—*adv.* hoarsely.

Arara, *s.* a name given to the most common and lively sort of lizard; see *moo.*

Arara, *s.* the ascent of an arrow.
—*v. n.* to be diverging upward from the intended course, applied to an arrow.

Ararahoa, *v. n.* to have the head-ache; to be weary of something disagreeable.

Arare, *a.* indistinct, as the voice of a person just roused from sleep.

Araroa, *s.* the largest sort of the [albicore.

Araroa, *s.* the first hog taken to the king on taking off a restriction; the first of fish caught by a new fishing canoe.

Araroa, *s.* a long road; a certain kind of *monoi* or sweet scented oil, the ingredients of which were fetched from a distance.

Arataata, *s.* a plank laid fore and aft of a canoe along the side; the seats where the rowers sit in a boat; the highest part of the coral reef where people walk.

Aratai, *s.* [*alakai,*] a leader, guide, conductor.
—*v. a.* to lead, guide, conduct; see *faa aratai.*

Arataio, *s.* the name of a fish.

Arataiò, *s.* a path over a ledge of rocks.

Arataua, *s.* the name of a fish; the same as *arataio.*

Arataua, *s.* the *taua* or friend, having been made use of as the means of procuring some good.

Aratàumi, *s.* the number of marks of the breast-plates, called *taumi*, marked on the skin.

Arataura, *s.* a rope ladder; a rope to climb by; one placed as a guide for a blind person.

Aràtavai, *s.* a round, hard, and smooth pebble, found in water courses, and used by slingers.

Aratea, *a.* pale, as the countenance through fear.

Arateità, *s.* rubbish drifted from the land into the sea, and remaining in a long row between the reef and the shore, and resembling another reef; also the body of a net when the fisherman pulls each end near together; one who excites to vigilance and courage.

Aratia, *s.* a road, a path-way; see *ara.*

Aratiapapau, *s.* a fordable place at the mouth of rivers.

Aratio, *s.* a passage near the shore abounding with the sharp *tio* or oyster shells, and dangerous to the naked feet.

Aratipi, *s.* a war term, signifying that a party is to be placed so as to take advantage of the enemy, either in coming behind or in the flank; see *araooti.*

Aratò, *s.* the person that pulls or drags any thing.
—*v. a.* to pull, or drag along the ground; to bring by violence.
—*v. n.* to be trailing, as a long garment along the ground.

Aratu, *s.* a road or path; see *ea, ara, &c.*

Aratua, *s.* the name of a cutaneous disease of the back; also small maggots or worms.

Aratuaririi, *s.* disagreeable, as a road; a long unpleasant journey; or a tedious piece of work.

—*a.* long, tedious, disagreeable as a road, or work with little prospect of finishing it.

Aratutia, *s.* a road, so called when two persons meet on it.

Aratutu, *a.* surfeiting, applied to food.

Araû, *a.* unripe, or not full grown, as a gourd or calabash.

Arau, *s.* the two wings of a large fishing net, the middle is called *tahe*; also a mode of fishing.

Arau, *a.* long, crooked, and bad, as a tree; long as a wave of the sea; see *araurau.*

Araua, *s.* a good pilot, who knows well how to manage a boat or a canoe in dangerous and difficult places.

Araua, *a.* rough, unpolished, as a piece of hewn timber; having breaks and notches as the edge of a tool; see *nihoniho.*

Araunu, *s.* bait for fish; see *arainu.*

Araurau, *s.* a long wave of the sea.

Arauru, *s* the beginning of a subject; the top end or extremity; a slight or partial relation of a matter.

Arava, *s.* a bunch of long red feathers, sacred to the gods; see *ura.*

Arava, *s.* a stripe, or contusion; see *irava.*

Arava, *s.* the larger sort of cuttle fish; a large species of the star fish, with four long and four short rays.

Arava, *s.* a subdivision of inferior chiefs under a superior.

Arava, *a.* fair, beautiful, white.

Aravaa, *s.* a passage for a canoe or boat through the reefs and shallows.

Aravaitaio, *a.* of a graceful figure or mein; fair, as a corps that appears as if still alive.

Aravao, *s.* a person that resides in the upper vallies; see *taevao.*

Aravarava, *s.* stripes or lashes on the skin.

Aravei, *s.* a species of large bread-fruit.

Aravî, *s.* the subdued, or depressed state of a party, person, or animal.

—*a.* subdued, depressed.

—*v. n.* to be in a depressed state; to be in fear; to become thin by disease.

Aravî, *a.* unequal, as the strands of a rope.

Aravihi, *s.* ingenuity, knowledge, skill.

—*a.* ingeneous, skilful, cunning.

Are, *s.* [*ale,*] a wave or billow of the sea.

Area, *conj.* but, but as for, as when, as for instance.

Area, *s.* the space between two objects.

Area, *adv.* presently, by and by; see *aria.*

Area, *s.* the resistance that food or drink meets with so as to cause its return by the nostrils.

Area, *v. n.* to return as drink by the nostrils.

Area, *verb anomalous*, to suppose, conclude, expect with reference to the past, as *area ra vau*, I thought, supposed, or expected so and so; see *atia ra*.

Areare, *s* sickness, qualmishness of the stomach as in sea-sickness, or loathing food, also perturbation of mind.

—*v. n.* to be sick or qualmish

Areâre, *a.* thin, worn out, as the bottom of a canoe; nearly cut through as a tree; nearly worn out; also difficult of access, as a thing on the summit of a high rock.

Arearea, *v. n.* to be diverted or pleased by company.

—*a.* cheerful, gay, through the presence of company.

Arearea, *s.* the spaces between the knots on the sugar cane, bamboo, reeds. &c.

Arearea, *s* a stranger.

Arefatumoana, *s.* a heavy rolling swell of the sea.

Areho, *s.* a sort of shelled snail found among the bushes.

Arehu, *s.* the name of the third Tahitian month; sometimes called *iarehu* or *o iarehu*.

Arehu, *s* darkness. gloominess of the evening

Arehurehu. *s* duskiness. increasing darkness of the evening.

Arematua, *s.* a wave that has been long in forming.

Aremu, *s.* the lower part of the spine.

Arepu, *v. a.* to disturb the water as fish do in swimming; to cause commotion.

Arepurepu, *v. a.* to disturb repeatedly.

—*v. n.* to be repeatedly in agitation; to be disturbed as people by news of war, &c.

'Arerarera, *s.* the faultering state of the voice.

—*v. n* to faulter or stammer, as a sick person, or one in sleep.

—*a.* faultering, stammering.

—*adv.* faulteringly.

Arere, *s.* a messenger; one appointed as the king's messenger; see *vea, tuutuuvea.*

Arero, *s.* [*alelo, elelo, e'eo,*] the tongue.

Arero, *s.* the king's sacred and royal girdle or *maro*, to which the names *Hihiopea, Tauuhauiti, Hanea*, and *Haoa* were given; these were the names of the tongues, or pendant parts; and *Terai puatata* was a name of the whole *maro*, which was used at the coronation.

Arero, *s.* any small slip of cloth; the pendant parts of a *maro* or girdle.

Aretea. *s.* the white waves of an agitated sea.

Aretu, *s.* a species of grass; see [*nonoha*

Areu, *s* a piece of cloth worn about the loins; see *pareu.*

Areue, *s* a wave that breaks over a canoe or a boat.

Areva, *s.* a species of lizard with a branching or divided tail

Areva, *s.* the male, or the larger species of the *totara*, or hedge hog fish.

Areva, *s.* a species of the sandal wood; also any wood that splits easily.

Areva, *s.* a sort of thin white native cloth, with long stripes from the coarse side of the mallet.

Areva, *s.* the name of one of the spears, or sticks, used in the exercise of arms called *turoau.*

Arevareva, *s.* scales on the skins of the great *ava* drinkers.

Arevareva, *s.* the name of a large spotted bird, said formerly to be inspired at times by the god *Manuteaa*; see *oovea.*

Arevareva, *s.* the name of a cutaneous disease.

Ari, *s.* the boundless deep; a bog of an unknown depth; any thing boundless in depth, height, or extent; also applied to the emptiness of the body.

Ari, *a.* empty, as the stomach; waste, as the land forsaken by its inhabitants, frightful, as a place in battle.

Ari, *s.* the tribute paid to the king, or a principal chief; the advantages obtained by marriage, or otherwise, such as land, property, influence, or government.

Ari, *s.* a wave or billow; see *are* and *aru.*

Ari, *v. a.* to scoop out the earth from a hole with both hands.

Aria, *s.* the space between objects; the parts between the knots of sugar cane, bamboo, &c.

Aria, *s.* the penis of animals.

Aria, *s.* a spot, or small blemish in a thing. [see *iti.*

Aria, *v. a.* to gripe, pinch;

Aria, *adv.* [*alia,*] shortly, presently, by and by.

Aria ana, *adv.* shortly, in a little time.

Aria aena, *adv.* after a little while, shortly.

Aria'na, *adv.* a contraction of *aria ana.*

Ariari, *s.* clearness, transparency.

—*a.* clear, fair, transparent; see *aiai.*

Ariari, *s* the thinness or worn out state of a thing.

—*a.* thin or small in some places.

Arihi, *s.* the ropes that are fixed to a fishing net, the upper one to which the *raai* or corks are fixed, is called *arihi i nia,* and that to which the stones are fixed is called *arihi i raro. Fig*, the word was extensively used, *arihi i nia,* were prayers made in time of war called by the names, *Paepaetuairi, Tefaatainuu, Tiataahiarepo, Tumuriri, Teeaea,* and *Hamoiterai.* The *arihi i raro* were those that stirred up the people to vigilance and activity, the chief priests, and other leading chiefs.

Arii, *s.* [*ariki, aiki, alii, eiki, hahaiki agi,*] a head or principal chief, a king; see *rai.*

Arii, *s.* a small quantity or trifle; see *rii.*

Ariiae, *s.* a small quantity.

—*v.* let it be small.

Ariihuaamanu, *s.* a bunch of red feathers that were to represent the king at certain ceremonies.

Ariirea, *s.* a small or moderate quantity.

Ariitahua amanu, *s.* the same as *aruhua amanu.*

Aritapiripiri, *s* the name of a god that could, it was said, heal all diseases, and perform other wonders.

Aritapotu ura, *s.* the name of another Tahitian god.

Arima, *a.* [*alima, ima,*] five; see *rima.*

Ario, *s* [Greek, *argyrion;* British, *arian;* French, *argent;*] silver; see *moni.*

Arioi, *s.* a certain fraternity of players, that travelled through the islands, and observed peculiar customs; see *taio* and *taua.*

Aripiripi, *s.* slenderness, weakness through being slender.
—*a.* weak, slender, swagging.
—*v. n.* to tremble through weakness; to swag as a sail.

Aripo, *v. n.* to be whirled about by the wind.

Ariporipo, *v. n.* to be whirled about repeatedly.

Aripuripu, *adv.* hobblingly, as in walking.

Ariri, *s.* the name of a small shell fish.

Arita, *s.* the fibrous root of the plant *faiapepe;* see *ieie.*

Arita, *s.* the name of a basket.

Aritu, *s.* a person who seizes his prey in time of war.

Ariva, *s.* the slender state of a board, or piece of timber.
— *a.* slender, thin.

Arivariva, *a.* having many slender places.

Arivariva, *s.* the name of a small fish that wriggles like an eel.

Arivariva, *v. n.* to wriggle like an eel.

Aro, *s.* [*alo, a'o,*] the front, face, presence of a person.

Aro, *v. n.* [*ngaro, na'o,*] to be lost or forgotten; to be unknown, never known or understood.
— *a.* lost, forgotten, unknown.

Aro, *v. a.* to wage war, to fight as two armies.

Aroâ, *s.* a road or street; the smoothest and best side of a piece of timber, leaves, cloth, or any thing that has a difference in the surface; see *taoâ;* the space between two canoes.

Aroa, *a.* kind, hospitable to visitors.

Aroa, *s.* the ridge of a hill or mountain; an interior ridge; the view taken of a subject or of certain customs.

Aroaro, *s.* indistinctness, mysteriousness.
—*a.* dark, mysterious; lonesome, desolate.

Aroaro, *s.* the lining of a garment.

Aroaroa, *a.* dusky, dark, indistinct.

Aroe, *s.* a small bowl in the shape of a canoe.

Aroeroe, *a.* slender, without branches
—*v. n.* growing long and weak on account of shade.

Aroeroe, *s.* the name of a worm found in decayed wood.

Aroeroe, *a.* indistinct, as the vision of a person that had been looking at the sun, or some shining body.

Aroha, *s.* [*aloha, aoha, aroa,*] compassion, pity, sympathy, love, affection.

Aroha, *v. a.* to have pity or compassion; to shew mercy, love, sympathy.
—*a.* pitiable, as *tanta aroha*, a pitiable man, or one who is an object of compassion.
Aroharoha, *v. a.* to repeatedly commiserate.
Aroharoha, *a. of comparison*, as *aroharoha ae tei mutaaiho*, it was not comparable to the former, (an idiomatical expression.)
Aroha tae, *s* empty sympathy.
Arohi, *v. anomalous*, a word of excitement to be brisk, active, vigilant.
Aroine, *s.* the sea between the reef and shore.
Aroire, *s.* a path way along the reef.
Aromanava, *s.* a term of endearment used in a *pehe* or ditty for children.
Aromoi, *v. n.* to forget; see *aro* and *moi*.
Aromoina, *v.n* to be forgotten; see *aramoina*.
Aronee, *v. a.* to draw near to an enemy by crawling along the ground to fight, from *aro*, to fight, and *nee*, to crawl.
Aropa, *s.* a mistake, error, misstep; the loss of something by turning aside.
—*v. n.* to turn about, or look another way.
Aroparopa, *v. n.* to turn aside repeatedly.
Aroparopa, *adv.* staggeringly, irregularly.
Aropito, *v. a.* to prepare for fighting, but in approaching the enemy to join hands together.
Aroraa, *s.* a battle; the time or place of fighting.
Aroreva, *s.* the name of a stone adze formerly in use.
Arori, *s.* a movement.
—*v n.* to be moving, or shaking; to stagger.
Arorirori, *v n.* to be repeatedly moving or shaking.
Arorua, *s.* [*arorua*,] a single combat.
—*v. n.* to face each other as two combatants.
Aroro, *s.* a rope used as a stay to the mast of a sailing canoe.
Aroro, *v. n.* to be lost to view, as a star that was a guide at sea; lost as a word or sentence that is obsolete; to be extinct as a family.
Arorua, *s* a second in a combat; a friend or beloved child; called also *aropiti*.
Arotahi, *v a.* to fight in a compact body, when the whole meet fairly together.
Arotapupu, *s.* a skirmishing fight, a fight at random.
Arotarere, *v. a.* to cast away a friend or companion, without any concern.
Arotavae ureroa, *s.* a disgraceful combat.
Arote, *s* [Gr. *arotron*, Lat. *aratrum*,] the plough.
Aroti, *v. anom.* be vigilant; see *arohi*.
Arotira, *s.* a certain ceremony performed at the *marae*, with prayers, previous to a voyage.
Aroviri, *s.* the advanced party in war; the van of an army.
Aru, *s* a wave or billow when two or three break together on the coral reef.
Aru, *s.* a forest, a thicket of wood.

Aru, *s* an elderly person, when the skin becomes wrinkled.

Aru, *s.* a large fishing net, ten fathoms long; the line or rope of a fisherman when coiled together; a fisherman's prayer.

Aru, *s.* the joyful exultation of a voyager; also a false accusation.

Aru, *s* the extinction or ceasing of desire.

Arua, *a.* [*alua, ua, aua,*] two; see *rua.*

Arua, *s.* a hole or pit; see *rua.*

Aruà, *s.* consternation and regret at the loss of a person in war.

Aruaru, *s.* a new-born infant.

—*a* infantile, childish.

Aruaru, *s.* a pursuer, a huntsman.

—*v. a.* to hunt, pursue; see *auau.*

Aruaru, *s.* a species of coral; also a rasp made of it, to rasp canoes.

Aruaruà, *s.* consternation on account of repeated defeats in war.

—*v. n.* to be heavy through age or infirmity; to have lost usual energy.

—*v. n.* to be in commotion, as the sea after a storm.

—*a* uneven, as a country full of hills and vallies; jaggy, ragged.

Aruaru porepore, *s* eager pursuit of property.

Aruarui, *s.* sudden alarm of war in the night; called also *aruapo*

Arue, *v. a.* to praise, commend, [or laud.

Arue, *s.* the noise made by calling aloud, and thereby causing an echo.

Arue, *s* praise, commendation.

Arueroa, *s.* the south west wind.

Aruerue, *s.* the noise made by calling aloud, and thereby causing a repeated echo.

—*v. n.* to be reverberating, as the echo of some loud noise in the top of the vallies; to be agitating, applied to water.

Arufaahema, *s.* deception by fair words, while a plot of destruction has been planned.

Arufaaî, *s.* a swelling sea, rising on both sides of a canoe or boat.

Arufaaipaea, *s.* words of conciliation, without sincerity.

Arufaatiapapau, *s.* a wave that breaks unexpectedly.

Arufetoitoi, *s.* a cross sea, or confluence of waves breaking at once.

Aruhao, *s.* a sea that breaks out of its usual course.

Aruhe, *s.* a fresh water fish, a species of *oopu.*

Aruhi, *s* a thing in its weak state; a bird just hatched; a weak inefficient person.

Aruhiri, *s* a wave that curls and breaks.

Arui, *s.* night; see *rui* and *po.*

Arumahora, *s.* a long swelling sea that does not break.

Arumaruma, *a* dark, cloudy.

Arumata, *s.* the inside covering of the eye.

Arumatara, *s.* a clear and open [sea.

Aruonaona, *s* a sea that rises continually.

Arupapai tohe, *s.* a sea that rises behind,—*fig* a slander behind one's back.

Arupare, *s.* a temporary house or shed; a prayer used by fishermen.

Arupopore. *v. a.* to pursue with eagerness

Arupue. *v. a.* to take at random what belongs to others

Arupapure, *s.* a foaming sea.

Arure, *s.* food beaten into a pulp; see *popoi.*

Aruri, *a.* left, in opposition to right.

Aruri, *adv.* indistinctly, as *fa roo aruri,* to hear or perceive indistinctly.

Aruriri, *s.* a sea that in breaking sends up its sprays towards the clouds.

Aruriruri, *s.* a rumour, an indistinct report, not well defined.

Arurorirori, *s.* a very strong and heavy surf, which cannot be passed.

Aruru, *s.* a species of the cavally fish.

Aruru, *adv.* together or collectively.

Arutahopu, *s.* a sea that breaks and falls before a person, or at his feet.

Arutapoipoi, *s.* a sea in continued succession; called also *arutamunamuna.*

Arutataino, *s.* a wave that fills a canoe or a boat and sinks it; called also *arufauee.*

Arutiatiafeau, *s.* a wave that covers a person, and takes away his breath; called also *arueehi.*

Arutiraoiraoi, *s.* a contending sea; *fig.* conflicting of interests.

Aruta, *v. a.* to seize food before it is served out.

—*s.* the act of so seizing food

Arutaruta, *v. a.* to seize food repeatedly before it is served out.

Arutuatea, *s.* a heavy sea that can be seen and prepared for.

Ata, *s.* a cloud, a shadow.

Ata, *s.* a certain prayer at a *marae*; the shaded or ornamented part of a mat called *vane.*

Ata, *s.* stalks of leaves, flowers, and fruits; the tops of the *umara, taro, &c.*

Ata, *s.* [*kata,*] laughter.

—*v. n.* to laugh.

Ata, *s.* the twilight; see *aahiata.*

Ata, *s.* a messenger sent before a chief.

Ata, *s.* a bait thrown to fish.

Atâ, *a.* unwilling, unapt, as *faaroo atâ,* unwilling to hear or obey; *haapu atâ,* unapt to learn; it also signifies a negative like the English less, as *haapao,* to regard, *haapao atâ,* regardless; also durable, as *mea vaiho atâ,* a durable thing, or thing of a long continuance; also difficult to get or attain, as *e mea noaa atâ,* a thing difficult to get.

Ataa, *a.* split, much divided; see *paatoa.*

—*v. n.* rent asunder.

Ataata, *v. n.* to laugh repeatedly; to laugh together as a company.

Ataâta, *a.* shocking, disgusting.

—*v. n.* to be shocked or disgusted.

Ataata, *a.* laughable, contemptible.

Ataataa, *s.* withdrawment; disengagedness

—*v. n.* to withdraw; to be disengaged.

Ataata raa, *s.* an object of contempt.

Ataata roa, *s.* a heavy and continued rain.

Ataata roroa, *s.* the same as *ataata roa.*

Ataava, *s.* a shoot of the *ava* plant; *fig.* a worthless person.

Atae, *s.* a deciduous tree bearing scarlet flowers.

Atae, *interj.* a word used in various exclamations of wonder, surprise, affection, disgust, according to the nature of the subject, and the tone of voice; as *atae ae! atae hoi! atae ai hoi! atae hoi e! atae ai i teie! atae atu ai i te mea ra!*

Atae ra, *interj.* of sympathy on the visit of a friend.

Ataetai, *s.* the name of a white bird; also nimbleness.

Ataetai, *a.* nimble of foot.

Ataha, *v. n.* to turn aside.

Atahataha, *a.* narrow, as the border of low land between the mountains and the sea shore.

Atahe, *s.* the name of a small tree of hard wood; also one of the methods of using the spear in the exercise of *turaau.*

Atahi, *a.* [*akahi, ata'i, taha,*] one in counting.

Atahira, *s.* a dirge or song; a word used at the beginning of a song.

Atai, *s.* a species of fern.

Atai, *s.* the head of a spear.

Ataivaha, *a.* obstinate; a play-term used by archers.

Atama, *s.* affection for a child.

Atama, *s.* [*akamai,*] wisdom, intelligence; an intelligent person.

—*a.* wise, intelligent.

Ataniho, *s.* a smile.

—*v. n* to smile.

—*a* smiling.

Ataniho, *s.* a deceitful smile.

Ataooti, *s.* cuttings of the *ava* plant; also a native of a place.

Ataore, *s.* senseless laughter.

Atapaoho, *s.* laughter, loud laughter.

Atara, *s.* a species of bread fruit.

Atara, *s.* the name of a fish.

Ataraioio, *a.* handsome, of a graceful mein.

Atari, *s.* a bunch of cocoa-nuts, or plantains.

Atari, *a.* unstable, moveable.

Ataritari, *v. n.* to be unsteady, changeable.

Ataritari, *a.* unstable, unsteady in words or actions.

Ataritari, *v. a.* to tie up bundles of bread-fruit, &c., repeatedly.

Ataro, *a.* right, not left; see *atau.*

Atata, *s.* the name of a small [fish.

Atatia, *s.* running water; a rill that never dries.

—*a.* running, applied to water.

Atatiitii, *s.* the great morning clouds; any thing of imposing appearance, or gorgeously decorated, though of little consequence.

Atatu, *s.* the state of being agitated.

—*v. n* to be in disorder or agitation.

Atatutatu, *v. n.* to be repeatedly agitated and thrown into confusion, or consternation of mind.

—*a.* agitating.

Ataturuinoa, *s.* one who runs off suddenly to join another party.

Ataturuirua, *s.* clouds going two different ways; a treacherous person that will take to either party, as it suits him.

Atau, *a.* right, in opposition to left, as *rimaatau,* right hand; see *aui.*

Atavai, *s.* small streams of water.

Atavai, *a.* pretty, elegant.

Atavai, *s.* adoption; see *tavai.*

Atave, *s.* a cluster of fruit; see *atari.*

Ate, *s* the liver of animals; see *paraia.*

Ate, *s.* the calf of the leg.

Atea, *s.* openness, clearness, distinctness.

—*a.* clear, having no obstruction, no obscurity.

—Atea, *a.* distant, far off; also beforehand.

Ateate, *s.* purity, clearness, as of water or any liquid.

—*a.* clear, as the countenance; free from deceit; sincere.

Ateau, *s.* part of the liver to which the gall-bladder is attached; *fig.* a person of boldness and courage.

Ateau, *s.* a war term signifying chiefs, warriors, leading or principal men.

Ateau, *a.* courageous, fearless

Atehuhu, *a.* fierce, daring.

Atere, *v. n.* to spread; see *anee.*

Aterima, *s.* the thick part of the arm.

Ateroa, *s.* the milt or spleen.

Atete, *s.* a rattling noise of things striking together.

—*v. n.* to rattle or tinkle; to chatter as the teeth through cold.

Atetetete, *v. n.* to tinkle or make noise repeatedly; to chatter with the teeth.

Ateuteu, *v. n.* to sprout, or spring up, as vegetables; see *oteu, oteuteu*

Ateuteu, *v a.* to affect the mind slightly by a report, threat, or relation.

Ati, *s.* the *tamanu* tree; see *tamanu.*

Ati, *s.* a faithful friend that will cleave to a man in distress.

Ati, *s.* a strait, trial, difficulty.

Ati, *s.* a haul of fishes.

Ati, *v. a.* [*ngati,*] to cleave or adhere to a person; to join.

Ati, *v. a.* [*aki,*] to bite with the teeth, to sting.

Ati, *v. n.* to be enclosed or entangled; see *puni.*

Ati, *s.* a name applied to the bird *otaha* when of one colour, *ati*, or *otaha ati.*

Ati, *a patronymic prefix* pointing out the name of the parent or ancestor with the descendants, as *Ati Iuda,* the descendants of (their father) Judah.

Atia, *a.* enough; see *atia.*

Atia, *s.* a fence; see *patia.*

—*v. a.* to put up a fence.

Atiara, *v. anomalous,* thought, supposed, or expected; see *area.*

Atiati, *s.* a species of grass bearing a troublesome bur; also a foreign plant brought to the island; see *piripiri.*

Atiatia, *s* the name of a small black and spotted fish.

Atiau, *s.* a term used by fishermen when the *au* or current prevents their sweep.

Atiauru, *s.* a mode of fencing with spears in the exercise called *turaau.*

Atihuta, *s.* the name of a fierce fish, said to pierce and bite its prey, and then to give notice to the shark.

Atii, *s.* the name of a fresh water fish of the eel kind.

Atiie, *s.* the name of an eel full of bones.

Atiitii, *v. a.* to beat small scraps of cloth with the cloth mallet, as little girls do.

Atipa, *s* the name of a fish.

Atipari, *v. a.* to return, hasten back.

Atipi, *s.* a piece of coral.

Atipi, *a* flat and broad, applied to a stone.

Atipi, *v. a.* to skim a stone along the water.

—*s.* the person who throws the stone.

Atipuni, *v. n.* to be enclosed, or in a besieged state; see *puni.*

Atira, *a.* enough.

Atire, *a.* the same as *atira* and *atia.*

Atiretire, *s.* a remainder; the little that was left.

Atita, *s.* agitation.

—*v. n.* to be agitated by bad news, by fear, or anger.

Atitatita, *v. n.* to be repeatedly agitated.

Atiti, *s.* a flat stone thrown along the surface of the water; see *atipi.*

Atîtî, *a.* firm; well tied or secured.

Atiti, *s.* the broken stalks of the yam, which are traced in order to find the root in the ground.

Atiti. *s.* rudiments or elements of knowledge.

Atitia, *adv.* all around; for every one.

Atitipau, *s.* a person of general information.

Atiu, *s* a young cocoa-nut just formed; the name of a play.

Atiuaea, *s.* the name of a yellow running plant; see *aea*; a swoon or syncope, as in swooning there is sometimes a sensation of the eyes resembling the appearance of the *atiuaea.*

Ato, *s.* a thatcher, a plucker of leaves or flowers.

Ato, *s.* the art of thatching houses.

Ato, *v. a.* to thatch; to rip or pluck off; to pluck leaves or flowers; see *pofai.*

Ato, *v. n.* to be nodding through drowsiness.

Atoa, *passive of the verb ato,* and applied metaphorically, to be taken off by death, as *aore roa te hoe i atoa,* not one has been taken off by death.

Atoa, *a.* [*katoa,*] all, every one, every thing.

Atoa, *adv.* also, too, likewise.

Atoa, *s* a tempestuous wind.

Atoa, *a.* fearless, athletic.

Atoa, *a.* rocky; see *toa.*

Atoatoa, *a.* full of rocks.

Atoatoa, *s* a tempestuous wind; also wind in strong contrary currents.

Atoatoa, *s.* the name of a fish.

Atoatoa, *s.* the seed of certain trees such as the *tamanu,* and the gourd; the seed of fishes; testicles of animals.

Atoauru, *v a.* to break off small twigs, or the ends of branches; *fig.* to have but a superficial knowledge of a thing or fact, and yet making much of it.

Atohatoha, *s.* a pleasing or satisfactory feeling of the mind
—*a.* pleasing, agreeable.
Atohei, *s.* a gatherer of flowers for a garland.
—*v. a.* to pluck and gather flowers for a *hei* or garland.
Atoi, *s.* the state of fruit when nearly ripe.
Atore, *s.* the person who embowels an animal; the knife used for that purpose.
—*v. a.* to take out the entrils.
Atori, *v. n.* see *mautori.*
Atori, *a.* devoted for the use of the gods.
Atoritori, *a.* devoted repeatedly, as food, &c.
Atoro, *s.* a sweet scented herb, hence the expression, *mai te atoro ra,* as the *atoro,* (in sweet odour.)
Atoroiore, *s.* the long pole that is laid between the upper ends of the ratters above the ridge pole, in a native house; called also *atoro toro iore.*
Atoronai, *s.* a tree of hard wood, and bearing small berries.
Atoroirai, *s.* the name of an active god.
Atororai, *v. n.* to ascend towards the sky.
—*a.* strong and active.
Atororoiroi, *a.* smooth, fallen, as the sea
Atoru, *a.* [*akolu, atolu, ato'u,*] three.
Atoti, *s.* a species of small black fish; it is of a strong smell when roasted; and is noted for destroying the shark; there are two sorts, the *atoti poa,* and the *atoti puahi.*
Atoto, *s.* a small gummy shrub.

Atu, *s.* [*aku,*] the name of a fish, the same as the *auhopu*
Atu, *s.* a species of the *Pandanus,* the leaves of which are used for making hats and fine mats; see *moea.*
Atu, *adv.* or *verbal directive* and *prep.* from, beside, more, see *tu* and *adu.*
Atua, [*Akua, Okua,*] God, the general name for a Diety; see *Aitu.*
Atuahâra, *s.* a god that was supposed to enter into a person by means of a curse, and in consequence, he was said to be *atuahâra hia.*
Atuaooa, *s.* the name of one of the gods.
Atuatu, *s.* state of a house well furnished, or a country well stocked.
Atuatu, *s.* a person that is active in getting things complete about him.
—*a.* neat, well furnished, in good order.
Atuhee, *s.* the name of a fish.
Atuhee, *s.* a handsome woman; a woman that is clever, ingenious.
Atuhee, *s.* a stranger or foreigner.
Atumotu, *s.* a land without a hill or a mountain.
Atupaparimi, *s.* the bottom of the great sea, the foundation of the earth.
Ature, *s.* [*akule,*] the young of the *ofee* fish.
Aturi, *s.* a running plant of a sour taste, like sorrel
Atute, *s.* the name of a fish.
Aturu, *s.* a prop, a support, see *paturu.*
Atutoa, *s.* an incendiary; also a boasting heedless person.

Atutu, *s.* a stir, noise; commotion caused by reports of war, &c.

Atututu, *v. n.* to be repeatedly agitated by reports of war, or by the near approach of visitors of quality.

Au, *pron.* [*aku*, *ku*, Malay *aku* and *ku*,] I, the first person singular; see *vau*.

Au, *s.* a current, or stream; smoke, vapour.

Au, *s.* a needle; the gall of animals.

Au, *s.* a dangerous fish with a long snout, like the sword fish.

Au, *s.* a stone put in the *marae* to avert some evil that was feared; also rubbish.

Au, *s.* a stone sent to the chiefs to require a human sacrifice.

Au, *s.* the name of a mountain tree of sweet odour.

Au, *s.* the hottest part of a battle.

Au, *s.* a sort of sea snail.

Au, *v. n.* [*hau*, *kaukau*,] to swim in the water; to move.

Au, *v. n.* to rise as a star.

Au. *v. n.* to be melting with fear; see *puaa au*.

Au, *v a.* to fit, to agree.

Au, *v. a.* to sew with a needle.

Au, *v. a.* to pursue; see *auau*.

Au, *v. a.* to scrape together or heap up rubbish.

Au, *a prefix* to several nouns, as *au taeae*, *au tahua*, *au fenua*, *&c.*

Au, *poss pron.* my, mine.

A'u, *poss. pron.*] a contraction of *a au*; see *ta'u* or *taau*; my, or mine.

Au, *a.* meet, fit, agreeable, suitable.

—*s.* fitness, suitability, agreement.

Aua, *s.* a cup, dish, plate; see *aipu*.

Aua, *s.* a fence or enclosure; a field.

—*v. a.* to put up a fence, to enclose a place; see *patia* or *pa*.

Aua, *s.* the name of a tree; see *autaraa*.

Aua, *s.* the name of a fresh water fish.

Aua, *s.* chips from a sacred canoe, or of a *too* representing a god.

Aua, *a.* ceased to bear offspring.

—*s.* a woman or an animal that has ceased to bear offspring; see *tiipa*.

Aua, *s.* an unsightly place of rubbish.

Auaa, *adv.* and *conj.* [*auraa*, *auraha*,] not; do not, imperatively; see *eiaha*; unless, but for that; save that.

Auae, *s.* the inner part of the lower jaw.

Auaerea, *s.* a vain prodigal; one that depreciates the goodness of another; one that pretends ignorance of what is well known to him.

—*a.* impertinent, shameless, proud.

Auafà, *s.* a bursted gall;—*fig.* a daring fellow that is void of fear.

Auafà ore, *s.* a person of a bashful timid disposition.

Auaha, *s.* a fishing term for a large haul of fishes.

Auahi, *s.* [*ahi*, *afi*, *a'i*, Malay *api*,] fire.

Auahi, *s.* a shepherd, a feeder of hogs or other animals.

Auahi ta raufau, *s.* food cooked

for the goddess *Toimata*, baked early in the morning, and put on the *fata* or alter.

—Auaho, *s.* a mode of fishing with a hook and long line; the person who so fishes.

—*v. a.* to fish with a hook and long line.

Auaho, *s.* a person not affected with shame, or who is not bashful in public.

Auahori, *s.* a wandering fish; see *aua* and *hori*, —*fig.* an unsettled person.

Auai, *s.* a piece of soft wood on which the point of another piece called *aurima* is rubbed, to procure fire by friction.

Auanei, *adv.* to day, (to come;) also presently, shortly, by and by.

Auariiroa, *s.* one of the trees said by tradition to be destined to hold up the sky; the leaves resemble those of of the oak; see *autaraa.*

Auataetae, *s.* a person that wastes away and appears of a yellow complexion; the name is borrowed from the fish *aua*, which is sometimes affected by the heat of the sun on the fresh water, so that it becomes yellow and dies; see *aua.*

Auatamino, *s.* an unsettled wandering person; the name is from the habit of the fish *aua.*

Auataroto, *s.* *aua* of the lake; applied to a person that settles in some evil habit.

Auati, *s.* a piece of wood used for friction; see *auai.*

Auatitai, *s.* a piece of wood that has been wetted or soaked in salt water, consequently no fire can be procured from it by friction; —*fig.* a person that can bear much without being angry, or having his passions stirred.

Auau. *s.* the gall of the fish *au.*

Auau, *s.* a person that pursues a man or beast; see *aruaru.*

—*v. a.* to hunt or pursue.

Auau, *v n.* to chew food.

Auau, *v. n.* to gnash the teeth; to stammer in speaking.

Auaua, *adv.* slovenly done, applied to the work of women in cloth making.

Auau mahana, *adv.* speedily, hastily.

Auauavae, *s.* a follower of the foot; one that is obsequious as an attendant or servant; also what a person may obtain as the effect of a journey, or meeting with, or following a chief.

Auaveru, *s.* the name of a fish.

Aue, *interj.* [*auwe*,] of grief, alas! oh! sometimes an exclamation of wonder or surprise.

Aue, *s.* noise, tumult.

—*v. n.* to clamour, make a noise.

Auea, *s.* a healer of those possessed by a *tu*; the name of a prayer by the *apa.*

Aueha, *s* one of the instruments with which a net is made.

Aueha, *s* the spaces between the meshes of a net; also a name given to an old man.

Auete, *s.* the name of a certain feast, when the men used to eat together some sacred food.

Aueue, *v. n.* to shake; to be agitated.

—*s.* agitation of mind; disturbance.

Auene, *a.* moveable
Aufaere, *v. n.* to swim unskilfully, not having learned.
Aufarere, *a.* friendless, cast away.
Aufatu, *v. a.* to lay the hand or arm across the brow; to lay fire-wood cross wise.
Aufa, *s.* the name of the larger *totara* or hedge hog fish.
Aufau, *s.* [*auhau*,] a tribute or tax; contribution.
—*v. a.* to pay a tax or tribute; to contribute property for any purpose.
Aufau, *s.* the handle or helve of a tool.
—*v. a.* to helve or put a handle to a tool.
Aufau fetii, *s.* the genealogy of a family. *Aufau atua*, the genealogy of the gods
—*v. a.* to search or trace the genealogies of a family, and its various relations.
Aufenua, *s.* the permanent residents of a place.
Aufenua, *s.* the name of a plant.
Auha, *s.* rubbish washed down by torrents from the vallies and mountains.
Auhâ, *s.* an aged person.
Auhâ, *s.* thirst.
—*a.* thirsty, overcome with heat.
Auhaa, *s.* a part of the apparatus of a conjuror.
Auhaa, *s.* the female genitals.
Auhala, *s.* the piece of wood held in the left hand to form the meshes of a net.
Auhoe, *s.* inspired attendants on a god or on a chief, who row the canoe of that god or chief
Auhopu, *s.* a modern name of the *atu* fish; see *atu*.
Auhune, *s.* harvest, or season of plenty. [as food, &c.
Auhuu, *a.* abundant. plenteous.
Aui, *s.* fish. fowl, or pig presented by the people with bread fruit, *taro*, or other food.
Aui, *s.* a swelling, or an abscess in the groin
Aui, *a.* left, in opposition to right, as *rima aui*, left hand; see *maui* and *atau*.
Auira, *s.* a long line of fires kindled along the beach, at night, to make a show.
Auiru, *s.* a mode of placing fuel or fire-wood; see *fatui*.
Auiui, *adv.* anciently, *mai tahito auiui mai â*, of old, anciently, or from of old time even to this.
Aumaha, *s.* sultriness; see *auha*.
—*a.* sultry, close, warm.
Aumai, *s.* abiding grief; longing; earnest desire.
—*v. n* to be grieving, longing, desiring earnestly; also to deny one's self for the service of another.
Aumaire, *a.* deeply indented, as the leaves of the bread fruit called *maire*, *pia*, *umara*. &c.
Aumama. *v. a* to chew food for a child.
Aumâmâ, *a.* light footed· nimble.
—*adv* sprightly
Aumanava, *s.* the hair of the bosom; thoughts or affections of the heart.
Aumanava, *s.* a bosom friend: called also *roto manava*
Aumaote, *s.* one who enters into another's labour, and gets the applause of the work, though another had done it.

Aumaoti, *s.* a stirrer up of contention.

Aumata, *s* a reciprocal look; a thing that is agreeable to the eye; from *au* and *mata.*

Aumata, *v. n.* to be looking with joy on an object.

Aumauiui, *s.* sympathy with another's grief.

Aumea, *s.* the gills of fishes; see *raumea.*

Aumihi, *s.* grief, pity, compassion; see *mihi*

Aumii, *s.* a strong or eager desire after things.

—*v. n* to be eager after many or different things.

Aumiimii, *v. n.* to desire repeatedly the possession of the things sought after.

Aumiti, *s.* smacking with the mouth as a sign of pleasure on account of things seen or heard.

—*v. n.* to be smacking with the lips; to be pleased in hearing or seeing.

Aumitimiti, *v. n.* to be smacking repeatedly with the lips.

Aumoa, *s.* a low fence enclosing a court in front of the native houses.

Aumoana, *s* a stick held in a defensive position in the exercise called *tuiaau.*

Aumoana, *s.* a fishing term

Aumoana, *s.* a good swimmer.

Aumunamuna, *s.* a whisper.

—*v. n.* to whisper.

Auna, *v. n.* to think or muse as a person that cannot sleep

Auna, *v. n.* to hope for, or expect something desirable.

Aunauna. *v. n* to be repeatedly thinking or musing; to be alarmed

Aunauna, *s.* alarm.

Aunati, *v. a.* a term used imperatively, as, be brisk, seize him; also *anuti.*

Aunati, *s* a piece of wood used for friction.

Aunee, *v. n.* to bend oneself and creep to avoid being seen.

Aununu, *s.* the sixth of the Tahitian lunar months.

Aunuu, *adv.* gently, leisurely in working

Auô, *s.* a careless mode of calling upon a person.

—*v. a* to call; see *tuoro.*

Auoaro, *v. n* to swim with the face downward.

Auono, *s.* a large fleet; or a company of travellers.

Auotua, *v. n.* to swim on the back.

Aupâ, *s.* the name of a tree of hard wood.

Aupaa, *s.* the old or under leaves of a plant.

Aupâpâ, *s.* the flatness of the roof of a house, or of a tree that grows flat.

—*a.* flat as the roof of a house; flat and broad as the top of a tree.

Aupapa, *s.* a small fish.

Aupape, *s.* a square bed of *taro;* a division in a *taro* ground.

Aupape, *s.* the plantain stalks used in a native oven to prevent food from burning.

Aupape, *s.* a figurative expression to signify a person that smoothes over a thing, or softens it to prevent irritation.

Aupara, *s.* unripe fruit that falls from a tree: see *aaiore.*

Aupari, *v. a.* to hew off the rough part of a piece of timber.

Aupari, *v. a.* to reach out the hand and grasp at a thing for safety.

Aupari, *v. n.* to grope as a blind man; to be vexed at a disappointment.

Aupari, *v. a.* to accuse a person falsely.

Aupariparì, *plural* of *aupari.*

Auperu, *s.* a piece of cloth folded up; the chief part of a mess of food; see *inai.*

Auperu, *v. a.* to fold up cloth; to tie up or fold food in leaves to be baked in the native oven; see *vehi.*

Aupiipii, *s.* a line or succession, as of canoes in a fleet.

Aupiipii, *v. n.* to follow in a train.

Aupiipii, *s.* a sailing term, signifying to sail by the wind.

Aupori, *v. a.* to make much of a person or of property.

Auporipori, *v. a.* to make much of a thing or person, with a repetition of the action.

Aupupu, *v. n.* to be in succession as the stars in rising; to assemble together in one body for defence, or mutual protection.

Aupuru, *v. a.* to treat with kindness and love; to feed or nourish.

Aura, *v. a.* to chop in a rough manner; to break off the branches of a tree or plant in a rough way.

—*a.* roughly chopped or broken off.

Auraa, *s.* fitness, agreement; also the meaning or signification of a word or thing.

Auraa, *adv.* [*auraka*], not, do not; see *auaa.*

Aurai, *s.* a bed of *taro;* see *aupape.*

Aurai, *s.* a mode of fishing.

Aurara, *v. n.* to be idle and moving about; see *ori.*

Aurara, *a.* avaricious.

Auraro, *v. n.* to yield, to be subject to another; to regard the interests and commands of another. +

Auraro, *a.* yielding, submissive.

Auraro, *s.* subjection, submission.

Aurau, *a.* unstable, fluctuating.

Auraura, *s.* a small leaping fly found by the sea shore.

Auraura, *s.* the small fibrous roots of plants and trees.

Aure, *s.* a tenon that fits in a mortise; a cut or notch at the end of a stick, to keep a thing from slipping off.

Aurearea, *s.* a strong athletic person; see *taurearea.*

Aureure, *a.* spiral as an augur; involved in a curve as a rope. +

Aureva, *v. a.* to impose upon a person under the appearance of friendship.

Auri, *s.* young saplings of the *uru*, *ahia*, *mape*, and *vi* trees.

Auri, *s.* iron of all sorts.

Aurirerire, *s.* bosom friends.

Auriirii, *s.* the state of being deeply laden; see *tomo.*

Auriri, *s.* a disturbed state of mind produced by anger.

Auro, *s.* [Latin, *aurum*; ancient British, *aur*;] gold.

Auroro, *s.* a small fish of the *orie* kind.

Auru, *s.* the top ends of small twigs or branches; the end, extremity, or point of a thing.

Auru, *s.* the first setting in of the wind from any quarter; a slight, indistinct knowledge; what is merely superficial.
—*a.* slight, superficial.
Aurua, *s.* native thatch twice stitched; see *au* and *rua.*
Aurupae, *s* fugitives, or some of the enemy wrecked and driven on the reef in bad weather.
Aururu, *v. n.* to assemble; see *tairuru.*
Aururua, *s.* double buds, or points; also *aurupiti.*
Autâ, *s.* a sigh or groan.
Autâ, *v. n.* to sigh or groan through pain or grief.
Auta, *s.* the act of cutting the body of an enemy; a needle used in thatching.
Auta, *s.* the operation of supercission, not circumcision, as it has been wrongly called; see *teke.*
Autaa, *a.* temporary, as *fare autaa*, a temporary shed or hut put up on a journey for a night.
Autahu, *s.* small chips or pieces of wood to kindle fire with; *fig.*—the beginnings of strife.
Autahua, *s.* the company of priests.
Autai, *v. n.* to pass along in a canoe or a boat without landing.
Autai, *s.* a current caused by a great sea.
Autao, *s.* any thing on the point of which a cocoanut is grated.
Autao, *s.* a preparation of food for the king.
Autara, *v. a.* to sharpen the edge of a bamboo splinter for cutting with.
Autaraa, *s.* a species of spotted conch shell; see *bu.*
Autaraa, *s.* the name of a tree, the leaves are like those of the common oak, and the seed a sort of acorn; see *auaruroa.*
Autaraaivavao, *s.* an expression used in some of the old prayers; see *upu.*
Autari, *s.* a follower of another; see *utari.*
Autari, *v. n.* to be anxious to return to one's own country.
Autaripo, *v. n.* to whirl, or turn round rapidly.
Autariri, *s.* a person that forsakes his house through displeasure.
—*v. n.* to leave home in displeasure.
Autaritari, *v. a* & *v. n.* to follow another again and again; to be repeatedly anxious to return to one's country.
Autataino, *s.* a violent current that draws a canoe under water; see *arutataino.*
Aute, *s.* [*ute,*] the cloth plant, of which the best of the native garments are made. It is the Chinese mulberry, [*morus papyrifera.*]
Aute, *s.* the name of a small tree or shrub bearing scarlet flowers, but destitute of scent.
Autepohoa, *s.* an inferior sort of *aute*; *fig.*—a person of an indifferent character.
Autea, *s.* a species of the cavally fish.
Auti, *s.* the leaves of the *ti* plant; see *tau.*
Autia, *s.* a species of breadfruit.

Autia, *a* spoken of a kite, when it flies well.

Autina, *v. a.* to fasten or sew, applied to a canoe; to tie with sinnet; see *tautina.*

✓ Autina, *v. a.* to press to diligence; to keep a person to his task.

Autoi, *s* the name of a certain feast, and of the ceremonies of canoe builders.

Autia, *v n.* to swim on the back, as *auotua*

Autua, *s.* the act of sculling a canoe with the steer paddle.

Autui, *s.* fish sacrificed to the gods.

Auvaa, *s.* a fleet of canoes going together.

Auvaa, *s.* the young brood of the fish *fai* or stingray.

Auvaa, *s.* the wreck of a canoe or boat.

Auvaha, *s.* the mouth of a vessel.

Auvaha, *s.* the person who speaks for the king or chief.

Auvaha reo, *s.* an orator, or one that can speak well on any matter.

Auveo, *s.* a species of snail of a disagreeable smell.

Auvete, *s.* the name of a certain mode of fishing; see *tautai.*

Auveuveu, *s.* the name of a large flat fish.

Auviri, *a.* crooked or turned, applied to the foot

Ava, *s.* [*kava,*] the name of a plant common in most of the South Sea Islands, of which an intoxicating liquor is made.

Ava, *s* [*kava, awa,*] the juice, or liquor made of the *ava* plant; also all kinds of spirituous and intoxicating liquors.

Ava, *s.* [*awa,*] the fish called white salmon.

Ava, *s.* [*awa,*] an entrance into a harbour; an opening that will admit of ships and other vessels to approach the shore.

Avaa, *s* the space between the two sides of a *marae.*

Avaava, *s* a small opening in the coral reef.

Avaava, *s.* the tobacco plant, and what is made of it, formerly called *tiare ura* and *pata.*

Avaava, *a.* sour, acrid, bitter; also saltish.

Avaavaa, *s.* when applied to the ear, signifies eagerness to hear a report, or a wish to hear more.

Avaavaa, *s.* the roughness of the water when agitated by the wind.

—*a.* rough, as the water through the agitation of the wind.

Avaavairai, *s.* a wild species of the *ava* plant, very acrid, and not used.

Avae, *s.* the moon, also a lunar month.

Avae, *s.* [*wawae, vaevae,*] the foot or leg.

Avae, *s* a part of a ship, boat, or canoe, just above the keel.

Avae, *s.* a species of the sugar cane; see *to.*

Avaefafao, *s* the right foot put in the posture of defence in the wrestling matches of Tahiti.

Avaefaurua, *s.* the feet regularly placed as those of soldiers in marching.

Avaehiihii, *v. n.* to press on, or go forward: to walk well, and frequent

Avaemaoro, *v. n.* to stride along, but cautiously.

Avaeparai, *s.* a distinction of *tatau* among the *arioi* fraternity. The *avaeparai* was the highest class, having all the marks completed.

Avaereia, *a.* speedy, with long strides; from *reia*, a bird with long legs.

Avaereva, *s.* a person on the move, or about going.

Avaeriirii, *v. a.* to go repeatedly with some vile design.

Avaerupe, *s.* a certain knot put on a rope, like that of a line tied to the foot of the bird *rupe*.

Avaetahi, *s.* the name of a species of banana.

Avaetere, *s.* a forward foot, an imprudent step.

Avaetutuee, *s.* a stranger from another country, who is not interested in the welfare of the place of his residence.

Avaevae, *s.* the name of a game or play.

Avaevae, *a.* light, clear, white.

Avaha, *s.* the name of a certain voracious eel.

Avahapiti, *s.* a spear with two prongs.

Avai, *s.* the name of a large timber tree; see *apape.*

Avao, *s.* the name of a small tree or shrub, said to bear poisonous berries.

Avao, *s.* the name of a fresh water fish, a species of *oopu.*

Avapuhi, *s.* [*awapuhi,*] the name of an odoriferous plant, used for giving a pleasant scent to a native cloth called *puhi ara.*

Avari, *v. n.* to be in a convalescent state as a sick person.

Avari, *v. n.* to be revoked, or abolished, as the restriction called *rahui.*

Avarivari, *v. n.* to be a little recovered from sickness, yet not well.

Avarivari, *v. n.* to swag as a thin plank.

—*a.* swagging as a thin piece of timber.

Avaro, *s* the name of a tree of hard wood.

Avaro, *s.* the name of a god.

Avaro, *s.* a calabash, a cocoanut water bottle.

Avaro, *s.* the name of a cutaneous disease in which the skin is spotted.

Avaru, *a.* [*awalu, avalu, awaru,*] eight.

Avatamanu, *s.* the *ava* plant in a withering or dying state.

Avatamanu, *v. n.* to bend down as a plant in a dying state; to bow down as a person weak through sickness.

Avatea, [*awakea, oatea,*] midday, noon.

Avatua, *s.* sea sickness.

Avatufâ, *s.* calm hot weather, which is deadly to fish about the coral reefs.

—*v. n.* to be killed, as fish by low water and hot weather.

Avaturatura, *s.* the name of an useful medicinal plant.

Avau, *s.* scolding, reproof, clamour; also the person that scolds or reproves.

—*v. a.* to scold, reprove; use ill language.

—*a.* scolding, clamourous.

Ava'u, *a.* a contraction of *avaru*, eight.

Avauvau, *v. a.* to scold or reprove repeatedly; also *auaua* and *araaravau*.
Avauvau, *s.* the name of a small fish, a species of the *pahua* shell fish.
Ave, *s.* the strand of a rope, string of a sling.
Ave, *s.* the train or tail of a comet, or of a shooting star or meteor.
Aveaau, *s.* an offering taken to the *marae* by new comers on their first arrival.
Aveave, *s* the long feelers of the *fee* or cuttle fish; a tassel or ornament appended to a bow; the tail or train of a gown.
Aveavefetii, *s.* the several branches of a family.
Aveaverau, *s.* a speech that has many bearings.
Avei, *s.* a cutaneous disease.
Avei, *s.* the name of a fierce fresh water eel.
Avei, *s.* the name of a species of bread fruit with a rough skin.
Ave, *s.* a division or section, formerly applied to the prayers used in the *marae*, some of which had eight or ten sections. [*etaeta*.
Avei, *s.* a fathom; see *rea* and
Avei, *a.* well formed, strong.
Aveia, *s.* a mark to steer by when at sea, the sun by day, and moon and stars by night; a mariner's compass.
Aveia, *s.* an example, directory, or guide to go by.
Aveitaaiore, *s.* the long feelers of the cuttle fish, by means of which, it is said, it sometimes entangles and catches a mouse or a rat
Aveivei, *a.* strong, and well formed.
Avera, *s.* a season of the year when there is a small crop of bread-fruit.
Avera, *v. n.* to be burnt or scorched by the sun or fire, as in the dry season.
—*a.* burnt up, scorched or dried up.
Averavera, *v. n.* to be scorched repeatedly, or in many places.
Avere, *s.* the gums; the inside covering of the eye; the black edge of an oyster.
Avere, *v. a.* to caulk a vessel.
Averevere, *a.* empty, applied to the bowels.
Avero, *s.* the name of a sort of fish-hook.
Averua, *s.* two lines or ropes put together; two lines or trains of canoes.
Avetoru, *s.* three strands of a rope.
—*a.* three stranded, as a rope.
Aveu, *s.* a species of large water crab; see *upai*.
Avî, *s.* the grating noise of any thing; a thing that shrinks, or slips off when laid hold on.
Avî, *a.* creaking.
Avî, *v. a.* to grind the teeth, to show the teeth as one dog to another; see *feu*
Aviava, *s.* the small branches or stalks of *ava*.
Aviavi, *a.* slim, slender; also ill shaped as a piece of timber; ill grown.
Aviavia, *a.* withered, unripe.
Avii, *s.* the beginning or first part.
Avii, *v. a.* to gnash with the teeth. [plant.
Avini, *s.* a species of the *ava*

Aviri, *s.* a number of birds tied together, and called *aviri manu.*

Aviri, *v. a.* to twist cocoa-nut leaves to serve as a fishing net; see *raoere.*

Aviri, *v. n.* to join together in a company.

Aviri, *v. n.* to abound in fruit as certain trees, such as the *vi* and bread-fruit.

Aviri, *a.* fruitful as certain trees.

Aviti, *s.* a fish-hook made of the pearl oyster shell.

Avititaapiha, *s.* a pearl oyster fish-hook that is worn and laid aside.

Avivaviva, *v. n.* to make a noise with the mouth in eating.

Avivi, *a.* food not sufficiently cooked.

Aviu, *s.* the sound of a stick cutting the air; a whispering noise.

Aviuviu, *v. n.* to make an indistinct noise, and that repeatedly.

D

THE D is a letter often pronounced by the Tahitians, they confound it with the *t*, and cannot distinguish the sound of the one from that of the other, as is also the case in regard to the *b* and *p*, and in some of the islands the case is exactly the same as to the hard *g* and the *k*. No word perhaps, purely Tahitian, begins with *d* uniformly, yet on account of foreign words such as the following, it is proper to retain it.

Dara, *s.* [*dala, dollar,*] a Spanish dollar. The divisions of the dollar are as follows:—*afa dara*, that is 50 cents or two quarters; *tuata dara*, 25 cents; *rea*, a real, or the eighth of a dollar.

Dekato, *s.* [Greek, *dekatos,*] tythe, or the tenth.

Demoni, *s* [Gr. *daimon,*] a demon. The notion the natives had of their *tii* [*tigi*] seems to correspond in several particulars to that of the ancients about their demons.

Denari, *s.* [Latin, *denarius,*] the Roman penny.

Diabolo, *s.* [Gr. *diabolos,*] the devil.

Diakono, *s.* [Gr. *diakonos,*] a deacon.

Diluvi, *s.* [Lat. *diluvium,*] the deluge, applied to Noah's flood.

E

THE E is a letter that frequently occurs in Tahitian; it has one uniform vowel sound, viz. that of the English *e* in the words *met*, *men*, *den*, &c., which is never changed, but it is sometimes lengthened, and marked thus ê with a circumflex.

E, *the indefinite article*, as a or an, *e taata*, a man, *e fare*, a house, *e raau*, a tree.

E, *a prefix to adverbs and adjectives* when future, the *a* being the sign of the past, as *aore*, past, *e ore*, future; *a toru*, past, *e toru*, future.

E, *a sign of the vocative case*, being generally placed both before and after the noun, as *E Meha e*, O Meha, *E te Atua e*, O God; but though this is usual in the familiar style, yet in the solemn language of prayer, when addressing the true God, the last *e* should be omitted, or pronounced very short.

E, *a.* different, as *mea e*, a different thing; *taata e*, a different man, or a stranger; *huru e*, a different, or a strange likeness.

E, *a.* far, or distant, as *tei uta e*, far in the interior; *tei nia e*, far above, or very high; *tei raro e*, far below, or very low.

E, *adv.* away, away from, *haere e*, go away.

E, *v. auxiliary*, answering generally to the English auxiliaries would, could, should, ought, may, can, will, and shall. The *e* seems always future; though not always with a reference to present time, yet in reference to a time understood in the sentence.

E, *prep.* by, as *hamani hia e ana*, done by him; *parau hia e au*, spoken by me.

E. *after a verb*, signifying before, or long before, something mentioned, or understood; as *ua parau e hia na tava parau ra.* that word was spoken long before.

E, *v. n.* to swell, or tumify, *ua e ia*, it is swollen.

E, *v. n.* to be incommoded by wet, as a house or a room when water comes in, or rises from beneath.

E, *adv.* yea, yes, of assent, consent, or of affirmation.

E, *conj.* and, as *fenua e te tai*, the land and the sea; *rui e te ao*, day and night; also a disjunction, as *teie e tera*, this or that.

Ea, *s.* a road or pathway, a ladder; see *ara.*

Ea, *s.* salvation, health, liberty, escape; also a saviour or deliverer; see *faaea.*

Ea, *v. n.* to be in health, to be enjoying health or liberty; to be restored to health or liberty.

Ea, *a.* healed, saved, escaped, delivered.

Ea, *s.* a disease of the mouth, aphtha or thrush.

Ea, *interj.* of surprise or wonder, *ea!*

Eaea, *s.* a crust or scab on the wound of a fighting cock.

Eaea, *v. n.* to escape, and that repeatedly.

Eaea, *v. n* to be short breathed as one that had over loaded his stomach.

Eaha, *adv.* [*eaa,*] how? why? used interrogatively, as *eaha e ora'i?* how can (he) be saved? *eaha e ore ai?* why not?

Eaha, *pron.* what? *eaha ia?* what is that? or what is it? *eaha atu?* what more, or beside? *eaha iho a?* what else?

Eaha, *interj* what! *eaha! aore taa raa!* what! is there no remedy! all hopeless!

Eahu'u, *s* a priest belonging to the *marae*; a leader in the dance.

Eahitu, *s.* a woman supposed

to go with child beyond the usual period.

Eara, *v. a.* to watch, to be vigilant; also a word of caution, beware, take good heed.

Eatia, *s.* a road or path; see *ea.*

Eatipi, *s.* a by-path.

Eatu, *s.* the old word for a road; see *eatia.*

Ee, *a.* strange, as *taata ee*, strangers; the two e's mark the plurality.

Ee, *s.* a saw.

Ee, *s.* the axilla; also the second in a combat.

Ee, *v. a.* to draw the *fara* leaves to and fro, against a post, to prepare them for thatching; and from this action came the word *ee* for a saw, and also as a *v. a.* for sawing.

Ee, *v. a.* to clap the hands by way of amusement.

Ee, *v. n.* to mount a horse; to get on board a canoe, boat, or ship; to ground, as a ship on a shallow place.

—*a.* grounded, as a ship; *pahi ee*, grounded ship.

Ee, *adv. or v. aux.* as in *ee oia*, it was it, *ee aita*, it was not.

Eeao, *s.* a passenger who forces himself into a company proceeding by a water or land conveyance, not on foot.

Eena, *s.* a kind of native food, a sort of pudding.

Eene, *adv.* of enquiry or negation, as *e ene?* is it not? *e ene*, it is not; see *e ere.*

E ere, *adv.* of enquiry or negation; see *e ene.*

Eeri, *interj.* an exclamation made in the diversion of swimming in the surf, on meeting with a large hollow wave.

Eero, *v. n.* to ascend, as the moon after it has arisen; see *paata.*

Eetuouta, *s.* one intending to be a passenger; see *eeao.*

Eeva, *v. n.* to ascend, as the moon and stars; see *eero.*

Eha, *s.* the barbs, feelers, or antennæ that are attached to the heads of some fishes.

Ehaeha, *a.* ill savoured, as food kept too long.

Ehia, *adv.* how many? what number? *ehia* when speaking of things, but of persons *toohia*; in the past the *a* is prefixed as *ahia? ehia* is the future.

Ehoa, *s.* a friend, companion, partner; see *taio*; it is also used as a common term of address to either male or female.

E hoa ino, *s.* is a familiar term of address from one friend to another, but does not seem suitable in solemn discourse.

Eho'ma, *s. pl.* friends; a contraction of *ehoa ma*, viz. *ehoa*, friend, and *ma*, the party with him; a respectful term of address, as Sirs.

Ehu, *a.* red, or of sandy colour, as the hair; discoloured, as water by reddish earth; muddy, as disturbed water.

Ehu, *v. n.* to be devastated as in time of war.

Ehu, *a.* devastated, as *fenua ehu*, devastated country.

—*s.* devastation.

Ehuehu, *v. n.* to be transiently agitated either with fear or pleasure.

Ehuehu, *s* a transient agitation.
Ei, *prep.* for, *ei parau raa*, for a conversation; *ei rapaau mai*, for or to be a medicine; *ei ora*, to be for health or salvation; *ei hara*, to be a crime, or for a crime.
Ei, *v. n.* let it be, as a wish or command, *ei mea rahi*, let it be a large thing.
Ei, *adv.* as *ei reira*, then or there, at that time or place, mentioned or understood; *ei hea?* where? at what place? *ei roto*, within, *ei rapae*, without, *ei nia*, above.
Eiâ, *s.* a theft, a thief.
—*v. a.* to steal.
Eiaha, *v. anomalous*, do not, desist, used imperatively; see *auaa.*
Eiaha, *adv.* no, not so, *eiaha roa*, not at all, by no means.
Eiatea, *s.* the largest of the *paaihere* fish; a war term.
Eie, *pron.* this; see *teie.*
Eieie, *v. n.* to be in a state of consternation from the news of war or the coming of strangers.
Eieiere, *s* a mode of fishing
Eieiere, *s.* apprehension or agitation on account of expected evil.
—*v. n* to be in agitation.
Eie nei, *pron.* this or there; see *teie nei.*
Eima, *adv.* no, not, will not, shall not, (future); see *aima.*
Eimo, *s.* the young spawn of the fish *paauara.*
Eina, *s.* a sort of pudding.
Einaa, *s* the female attendants of the queen or chief woman, principally young girls.
Einaa, *s.* the small fry of the fresh water fish called *oopu*; at the proper season of the year they are caught by baskets full at the mouths of the rivers.
Einamoa, *s.* mildew, mouldiness of cloth, &c.
—*a.* mouldy, mildewed.
Eipa, *adv.* no, not, (future;) see *aima.*
Eipo, *s.* a darling child; a favorite article of property; see *maimoa.*
Eipa, *s.* a cup or dish; see *aipu, aua.*
Eira, *s.* a mole or natural spot on the skin.
Eita, *adv.* no, not, will not, (future); see *aita.*
Eito, *s.* equality.
—*a.* equal; see *faito.*
Eitoa, *s.* the bruised or injured part of a fruit or an animal.
—*a.* bruised, injured as fruit, &c.
Ekalesia, *s.* [Greek,] a church or congregation of God's people.
Enaena, *adv.* quickly, expeditiously.
Ene, *v. a.* to splice, mend, or repair a net, mat, or a rope.
Ene, *s.* a mender of ropes or nets.
Ene, *v. n.* to approach near or too near.
Eneene, *s* the rolls of fat on the neck of a fat person; the parts that hang down under the neck of a beast.
Eneene, *a* strong, urgent, pressing; *hinaaro eneene*, a pressing or urgent desire
Enemi, *s.* [Eng.] enemy.
Eore, *adv.* no, not, will not, shall not, (future.)

Epa, *s.* a small enclosure sacred to the infant king; also an enclosure for the use of dancers.
Episekopo, *s.* [G. *Episkopos,*] an overseer or bishop.
Episetole, *s.* [Gr. Epistole,] an epistle or letter.
Epiti, *s.* a couple.
—*a.* two in counting.
Era, *pron.* that; see *tera.*
Ere, *v. n.* [*ngere, nele,*] to be disappointed, not obtaining something sought, desired, or expected.
Ere, *s.* the person that is disappointed.
Ereavae, *s.* a sort of wicker work basket used for catching small fish.
Ereere, *a.* [*eleele,*] black; also dark or blue.
Ereerefenua, *s.* according to Tahitian tradition, the spirits of the dead that used to appear in old time before the commencement of a destructive war.
Ereere tape moana, *a.* dark, as the colour of the sea where the deep water commences.
Erehuru, *s.* the state of being encumbered.
—*a.* encumbered.
Erepuahoe, *s.* the mass of the people, populace.
Erepuru, *s.* a company going compactly together on the road.
Erepuru, *v. a.* to take care of those that remain at the conclusion of a battle, by taking them to a place of safety, &c.
Erevae, *s.* the name of a basket; see *ereavae.*
Eri, *v. a.* to undermine.
—*s.* underminer.
Eritamai, *s.* a war term signifying that the people of a country are ruining themselves.
Ero, *s.* a kind of sauce; see *taiero.*
Ero, *s.* a word used in calling pigs, *ero, ero.*
Erohi, *v. imp.* a word of excitement, as be vigilant, be active, be watchful.
Eru, *v. a.* to scoop or scrape up the earth; to scratch, as a fowl; see *heru.*
Etaeta, *a.* hard, strong, firm; also obstinate.
Etahi, *a.* one in counting; see *atahi* and *tahi.*
Etahi, *an article,* used in the same way as the French article of unity, *un* or *une*; see *hoe* and *tehoe.*
Ete, *s.* [*kete,*] the name of a small basket; also a small bag or pocket.
—*v. n.* to flinch.
Eteete, *v. n.* to be shocked, disgusted, shamed.
Etene, *s.* [Greek, *Ethnikos,*] a heathen.
Eterauaha, *s.* a sort of net basket, formerly employed to hold the *too* or image of a god—*fig.* a clever, well informed man.
Etu, *v. a.* [*eku,*] to root, as a pig.
Etu, *s.* a rooter, or the thing that turns up the earth.
—*a.* rooting, *e mea etu,* a rooting thing.
Etuautu, *s.* an intruding passenger in a canoe, boat, or a ship.
Eu, *s.* a batch of any kind of baked food.
Eu, *v. a.* to bake any kind of food.

Eu, *a.* baked, dressed or done in an oven.

Euai, *v. n.* to flinch; give way in battle.

Eue, *interj.* a call or exclamation of the *arioi.*

Euea, *s.* the young leaves of the *pandanus* or *fara,* used for making mats.

Euea, *s.* a batch of food for the use of visitors.

Euea, *a.* strong, powerful by muscular strength.

Eueu, *v. a.* to bake food repeatedly, and generally in small quantities.

Eueu, *v. n.* to move, or stir, as an infant under its sleeping cloth.

Euhari, *s.* [Gr. *Eucharistia,*] the ordinance of the Lord's Supper, or holy communion.

Euhe, *s.* [Gr. *Euche,*] a vow.

Eumaa, *s.* a baker, cook, or dresser of food.

Eunuha, *s.* [Gr. *Eunouchas,*] an eunuch.

Evanelia, *s.* [Gr. *Euangelion,*] the Gospel, or good tidings.

Eve, *s.* the secundines of a beast.

Evehoe, *s.* twins; see *machaa.*

Eveeve, *s.* raggedness.
—*a.* torn, ragged.

F

THE letter F frequently occurs in Tahitian, it is discarded in some of the Polynesian dialects, and the *h* is substituted; others discard the *h* altogether, but in Tahitian both are used, and in some instances are mutually interchanged, as in the *causative prefix faa* and *haa.*

Fa, *s.* a butt or mark at which a shot is aimed, or to which a spear is thrown.

Fa, *s.* the stalk of some large leaves such as *taro,* plantain, and also the cocoanut.

Fa, *s.* a perpendicular branching cloud viewed as an omen. *fig.* the butt of ill will, or a person that is an object of hatred; also the ground of contention in war.

Fa, *v. n.* to appear, come in sight.

Fa, *interj.* a word used in calling hogs.

Faa, *s.* a valley; a low place among the hills.

Faa, a *causative prefix,* common to most, if not all the Polynesian dialects; in the Tahitian it is *faa* or *haa,* and in some instances *ta;* but in other dialects *faka, haka, aku,* and *hoo.* It is prefixed to nouns, adjectives, and verbs neuter, by means of which they are turned into verbs active.

Faaaa, *v. a.* to teaze or provoke to anger.

Faaaa, *v. a.* to kindle fire, to make it burn well; to cause food to be well cooked.

Faaaano, *v. a.* to make broad, to cause extension.

Faaaau, *s.* a person that commits suicide.

Faaaau, *v. n.* to commit suicide; to endanger life voluntarily.

Faaae, *v. a.* to assist a person to climb.

Faaaea, *v. a.* to make a curve.

Faaaeae, *v. n.* to be in the act of dying.

Faaaereere, *v. a.* to shake, to agitate.

Faaahaaha, *v. n.* to boast, brag; make an ostentatious display.

Faaahehe, *v. a.* to make a rustling noise.

Faaahoa, *v. a.* to present the first fruit of a garden or field to the king or principal chief.
—*s.* the thing so presented.

Faaahoahoa, *v. a.* to trouble.
— *a.* annoying, causing trouble.

Faaahu, *v. a.* to clothe, put on clothes.

Faaahua, *v. a.* to make and to place a piece of wood called *ahua*, which see.

Faaai, *v. a.* to feed, nurse; see *ai.*

Faaai, *v. a.* to cause animals to copulate.

Faaai, *v. a* to parry, or fend off a thrust or a blow.

Faaai, *s.* a fosterer, a nurse, a feeder.

Faaai, *s.* an ornament put in the ear; see *poe.*

Faaai, *a.* foster, feeding, as *metua faaai*, a nursing father.

Faaaiai, *v. n.* to spare one's self.

Faaaiere, *v. n.* to be forward in proposing an undertaking, and backward in performing or joining to effect it.

Faaami, *v. a.* to make a person wink or start.

Faaamiami, *v. a.* to make a person wink or start repeatedly; to cause one person to dread another.

Faaamo, *v. a.* to make to flinch.

Faaamoamo, *v. a.* to make a person wink or flinch repeatedly.

Faaamu, *v. a.* to feed, supply with food.

Faaamuamu, *v. a.* to supply with little food; to feed repeatedly.

Faaanaane, *v. a.* to brighten, make shine; see *anaana.*

Faaaneane, *v. a.* to garnish; to clear; see *aneane.*

Faaani, *v. a.* to give or bestow freely on any one who asks.

Faaani, *s.* the act of giving, or squandering away in a thoughtless manner.

Faaano, *v. a.* to make desolate; see *ano.*
—*s.* that which makes desolate.

Faaanoano, *v. n.* to sit apart, to be apart, self exalted.

Faaa'o, *s.* an advocate or councillor.
—*v. a.* to counsel, to give advice or warning; see *a'o.*

Faaao, *v. n.* to be looking out with expectation.

Faaapi, *v. a.* to close, to shut up; see *api.*

Faaapiapi, *v. a.* to fill up, to encumber, as by crowding a place.

Faaapo, *v. a.* to make concave or hollow out.

Faaapo, *v. n.* to draw in the stomach.

Faaapu, *s.* a gardener, cultivator of the ground, a husbandman.

Faaapu, *v. a.* to cultivate the ground.
—*a.* belonging to husbandry.

Faaara, *v. a.* to awake, to arouse from sleep.

Faaara, *v. a.* to put a person on his guard, by warning or apprizing him of something.

Faaaraa, *v. a.* to lighten a canoe or vessel on the water that is over loaded.

Faaaraara, *v. a.* to arouse repeatedly from sleep, forgetfulness, or carelessness.
Faaaraara, *v. a.* to commence or make a beginning of any thing; see *araara.*
Faaaratai, *s.* a guide, conductor; see *aratai.*
—*v. a.* to guide or conduct.
Faaareare, *v. a.* to brighten.
Faaareare, *v. a.* to cause qualmishness.
Faaarere, *v. a.* to procure or cause an *arere* or messenger to be sent.
Faaariari, *v. a.* to make a display of one's property; to give the first present of food to the king, or to a new married couple.
Faaarii, *v. a.* to invest with royal authority.
Faaaro, *v.n.* to conceal; see *aro.*
Faaaroha, *s.* a keep-sake, a relic.
Faaaroha, *v. a.* to cause pity or compassion.
Faaarue, *v. a.* to cause a person or thing to be praised; see *arue.*
Faaaruerue, *v. a* to make a reverberating noise.
Faaata, *v. a.* to excite risibility.
Faaata, *a* droll, laughable, causing laughter.
Faaataata, *v. a.* to cause much or repeated laughter; see *ata.*
Faaâtaâta, *v. a.* to shock, disgust, raise aversion in a person; see *âtaâta.*
Faaâtaâta, *a.* disgusting, causing aversion.
Faaatea, *v. a.* to give place, make room; put further off; see *atea.*
Faaatete, *v. a.* to make a clashing or a cracking noise; see *atete.*
Faaatu, *v. a.* to place, and to keep common things apart from those that are sacred.
Faa atua, *v. a.* to deify; to constitute something to be a god; to acknowledge, serve, or act towards some person or thing as a god.
Faaatuatu, *v. a.* to keep common things apart from sacred ones; to keep or preserve old relics.
Faaatuatu, *v. a.* to make things neat and orderly, and keeping them so.
—*a.* keeping one's property in good order; carefully preserving old relics.
Faaau, *v. a.* to assist another to swim; to cause an article or thing to float by swimming with it.
Faaau, *v. a.* to fit or suit one thing to another; to regulate, set in order; make an agreement; see *au.*
Faaauau, *v. a.* to teach to swim.
Faaauau, *v. a.* to convey a sick person from one place to another for the sake of the air, &c.
Faaaumai, *v. a.* to produce an earnest desire or concern.
Faaauraa, *s.* an agreement; the time or place of an agreement; the meaning, import, or design of a thing.
Faaavari, *v. a.* to remove or abolish a restriction; see *rahui.*
Faaavari, *s.* the first fruit of a garden or plantation presented to the king, or the chief of the place; see *faaahoa.*
Faaavarivari, *v a.* to make pliant or flexible.

Faaea, *v. a.* to save, deliver, or to heal.
Faaea, *v. n.* to cease; to rest.
Faaeaea, *v. n.* to stop or rest frequently; to go on loiteringly.
Faaea raa, *s.* a resting place, [a resting time.
Faaee, *v. a.* to push up one's self against another; to put up, or hang up a thing.
Faaee, *v. a.* to convey anything by water.
Faaêho, *v. a* to set apart, appoint, separate.
Faaehu, *v. a.* to persuade others to engage in an undertaking, and afterwards desert them.
—*s.* a person that sets others about any work, and then leaves them.
Faaehu, *v. a.* to stir up or befoul water—*fig.* to stir up strife or commotion.
Faaehuehu, *v. a.* to stir up violently and repeatedly, either water or strife.
Faaene, *v. a.* to encroach, as on the border of land.
—*s.* an encroacher, encroachments.
Faaeneene, *v a.* to encroach repeatedly, or to do so gradually.
Faaere, *v a.* to disappoint, defeat the expectation of property, or of some thing that is desired.
Faaereavae, *v. a.* to make use of a basket called *ereavae.*
Faaerieri, *s.* a present of food given to a new made chief, or a new married couple; see *faaariari.*
Faaerieri, *v. a.* to give a present to a new made chief, or to a new married couple.
Faaeo, *v n.* to be so affected with grief or love as to lose the appetite.
Faaero, *s.* an abortive, applied to fruit, &c.
Faaero, *a* addled, rotten, applied to eggs.
Faaetaeta, *v. a* to make firm or strong, to oppose with vigour.
Faaetaeta, *v. n.* to be obstinate; to harden one's self; to be resolute.
Faaetaeta, *s.* a person who invigorates another; that which strengthens.
Faaeteete, *v. n.* to make much of one's self; to spare one's self in work by putting it upon others.
Faaeva, *v. n.* to be vain of dress; not putting the hand to work.
Faafaa, *s* the deep indented small vallies
Faafaaao, *v a.* to send a person to look out; see *faaao.*
Faafaaroo, *v. a.* to produce faith or obedience.
—*v. n.* to pretend to faith or obedience in order to gain some end.
Faafai, *v. a.* to conclude the prayers when officiating at the *marae.*
Faafai, *v. a.* to carry tales, publish secrets
—*a.* tale bearing, as *taata faafai*, a tale bearing man.
Faafaito, *v a.* to make equal; weigh, measure.
—*s.* a measurer of any thing; see *faito.*
Faafaha, *v. a.* to take the largest portion; to guard property.
Faafana, *a* taking the largest share for himself.

Faafanau, *v. a.* to support a woman in labour; to perform the duties of a midwife.

Faafano, *s.* the departure of the soul when a person dies.

Faafano, *v. a.* to go out as the spirit from one possessed; to depart as the supposed god from the inspired *taura* or prophet.

Faafao, *v. a.* to degrade, oppress, enslave.

Faafarava, *v. a.* to make to bend from the perpendicular; see *farava.*

Faafarerei, *v. a.* to procure a meeting.

Faafariu, *v. a.* to cause a person or a thing to turn round to an opposite position by any means—*fig.* to convert another; see *fariu.*

—*s.* the person, or means, by which any other person or thing is so turned.

Faafaro, *v. n.* to stoop or bend down.

—*a.* stooping or bending.

—*adv.* bendingly.

Faafatata, *v. a.* to bring near; see *fatata.*

Faafatata, *v. n.* to approach, to draw near. [see *fati.*

Faafati, *v. a.* to cause a break;

Faafati, *v. a.* a war term, to terrify a party to cause them to break up or flee away.

Faafaufaa, *v. a.* to make an undertaking profitable.

Faafaufau, *v. a.* to call or denominate a person or a thing base, filthy, disgusting.

Faafaufau, *v. n.* to affect disgust or abhorrence of a thing.

Faafaura, *v. a.* to put a tenon into a mortise.

Faafaura, *v. n.* to appear in sight; see *fa.*

Faafefe, *v. a.* to bend, or make any thing curved.

Faafene, *v. a.* to break up; see *faafati.*

Faafifi, *v. a.* to entangle; see *fifi;* to detain or prevent a person going to battle, or to a journey; to hinder or obstruct.

Faafifi, *s.* hinderance; the person that hinders.

Faah'aah'aa, *v. a.* to humble; to make low; see *haahaa.*

Faahaamâ, *v. a.* to put to shame, or make ashamed.

—*v. n.* to put on shame; to act as one abashed or shamed.

Faahaamâ, *s.* the person or circumstance that makes another ashamed.

Faahaehae, *v. a.* to provoke; see *faatihaehae.*

Faahaerea, *s.* conversation, mode of conduct.

Faahaereaatâ, *v. n.* to be tedious; to hold one's age well; to be long childless.

Faahâha, *v. a.* to turn off or aside. [to avoid a person.

Faahahao, *v. n.* to turn aside as

Faahahau, *v. n.* to turn aside; see *hahau.*

Faahahe, *v. a.* to get or procure *hahe,* a sort of cloth used for the gods; to use such cloth.

Faahahi, *v. a.* to cause an error or mistake.

Faahana, *v. n.* to magnify or exalt one's self.

Faahanahana, *v. a.* to give glory or dignity to another; see *hanahana.*

Faahaorea, *v. a.* to create alarm, cause perplexity.

Faahapa, *v. a* to cause an error or mistake; see *hopa.*

Faahapa, *v. a.* to convict, condemn.

—*s.* condemnation.

Faahape, *v. a.* to condemn, blame; cause error.

✝ Faahara, *v. a.* to commit sin or transgression.

Faaharamaau, *v. a.* to do or say something that causes disturbance, by setting others at variance.

—*a.* as *taata faaharamaau*, setting others at variance.

Faahau, *v. a.* to make peace; see *hau*; to watch, or act as a guard.

—*s.* a peace-maker; a watchman; a soldier.

Faahau, *v. a.* to cause inequality, or one thing to be greater, longer, or beyond another; see *hau.*

Faahauhau, *v. a.* to make repeated efforts for peace.

Faahauhau, *v. a.* to make uneven, as some things longer or higher than others.

Faahe, *v. a.* to condemn; accuse of error; see *he.*

—*v. a.* to cause error, to lead astray.

Faahee, *v. n.* to remove, or leave through some offence or displeasure.

Faahee, *v. a.* to cause an evacuation of the body by a purgative; see *hee.*

Faahee, *v. n.* to float or swim on a board, as the Tahitians do in a great surf of the sea in the pastime *horue.*

Faahêhê, *v a.* to cause alienation between friends or acquaintances.

—*a.* strange, distant, not familiar.

Faahei, *v. a.* to put a garland on the head.

Faahei, *v. a.* to catch fish in a net; see *hei.*

Faahei, *v. a.* to get or obtain some good or benefit.

Faaheia, the *passive* of *faahei*, to have met opportunely with some good or benefit.

Faaheimoe, *v. a.* to cause dreaming or visions during sleep; see *moe.*

Faaheipo, *v. a.* to accuse or charge falsely, knowing it to be so; *pl. faaheipoheipo.*

Faaheirui, the same as *faaheipo.*

Faaheitaoto, the same as *faaheimoe.*

Faahema, *s.* a deceiver; one that promises fair but does not perform.

—*v. a.* to deceive, impose upon a person; to tempt.

Faahemo, *v. a.* to out-do, excel; see *hemo.*

Faahemo, *v. a.* to break, or nullify an agreement.

—*s* a breaker of an agreement.

—*a.* addicted to break agreements.

Faahepo, *v. a.* to command, impel to action.

—*v. n.* to domineer, exert authority or power, to tyrannise over others.

Faahepohepo, *v. a.* to repeat commands as a master.

Faahere, *v. a.* to make use of a snare; see *here.*

Faaherehere, *v. a.* to spare, to favour.

Faahì, *s.* a pump, a syringe; see *hí.*

—*v. a.* to pump, to use a syringe; to make water to gush.

Faahia, *v.a.* to cause something that was standing, as a tree, a post, or a man, to fall down.
Faahiahia, *s.* the quality that causes a thing to be admired.
—*v. n.* to admire an agreeable object.
Faahiahia, *a.* admirable, agreeable, fine.
Faahinuhinu, *v. a.* to cause lustre or splendour; to make respected or honourable.
Faahipa, *v. n.* to turn aside; to assume supercilious airs.
Faahipo, *v. n.* to play the coxcomb, and affect what is not real.
Faahiti, *v. a.* to pronounce, to mention a thing.
Faahoa, *v. a.* to make a friend, procure a friend; see *hoa*; to take a partner in any concern; to adopt a companion; to associate another with one's self.
Faahohoa, *v. a.* to compare as to likeness; to esteem as bearing such a likeness.
—*v. a.* to pourtray or make a likeness of a person or of a thing.
Faahohoni, *s.* a vice, pair of pincers or nippers.
—*v. a.* to put in a vice, to pince or nip; to cause to bite; see *hohoni*.
Faahoi, *v. a.* to send back; to cause to return.
Faahope, *v. a.* to make an end, to finish; to take all.
Faahopea, *s.* the end or finis; the last one.
Faahopu, *v. a.* to bathe another in water.
Faahopue, *v. a.* to cause fermentation.
Faahopue, *s.* leaven, or any thing which causes fermentation; see *hopue; fig.* malice or ill-will.
—*v. n.* to ferment; to bear malice until it breaks out into some evil act.
Faahoro, *v. a.* to make another to run; to ride a horse and so make it run; to cause a thing to slide down; to use a certain mode of fishing.
Faahorohoro, *v. a.* to remove property from one place to another, as when people change their residence.
Faahoropapa, *v. a.* to lay a floor, put up a shelf, or fit up a bed place.
Faahotu, *v. a.* to produce fruitfulness in trees, &c.; see *hotu*.
Faahou, *v. a.* to renew; see *hou* and *api*.
Faahou, *adv.* again, done over again.
Faahouu, *v. a.* to abash, make ashamed.
Faahua, *v. a.* to assume the appearance of something not real, or appear to be acting what is not intended.
Faahuahua, *v. a.* to assume repeatedly the appearance of something not real.
Faahuahua, *v. a.* to beat, or reduce a thing to atoms.
Faahume, *v. a.* to tie up the girdle called *maro*.
Faahupehupe, *v. a.* to mar, make unsightly, disfigure; see *hupehupe*.
Faahurué, to transfigure, make of another likeness; see *hurué*.
Faahururu, *v. a.* to make use of the *hururu*, a play thing

for children; to drive away hogs, &c., by the noise of the *haruru*.

Faai, *v. a.* to fill any thing, or space; see *i*; to engross the whole of the conversation.

—*s.* that which filleth any vessel, cavity, or space; that which takes up the whole of the conversation.

Faaïe, *v. a.* to procure a sail, to put it up; see *ie*; to get a cloth mallet.

Faaieie, *v. n.* to act in a vain foppish manner.

—*s* a person that acts foppishly.

Faaiheihe, *v. a.* to decorate with ornaments.

Faaiho, *v. a.* to cause, or help a person to descend; to let down a thing.

—*s.* one that leads another down, or lets a thing down from an eminence.

Faaihō, *v. a.* to use prayers and ceremonies, as the priests did formerly, to procure the presence of a god in or with the image.

Faaihu, *v.a.* to strangle, drown, or smother.

—*s.* the person that strangles or drowns.

Faaihuihu, *v. a.* to repeat the act of smothering, drowning, or strangling any thing.

Faaii, *v. a.* the plural of to fill; to fill repeatedly.

—*s.* that which fills many vessels or cavities.

Faaita, *v. a.* to harden, to make stiff.

Faaite, *v. a.* to reconcile those who were at variance.

—*s.* one that reconciles, a reconciler.

Faaina, *s.* a grind-stone, a whetstone; any thing to sharpen a tool.

—*v.a.* to grind, whet, or sharpen a tool.

Faainaina atua, *s.* evil speech or blasphemy.

Faainati, *v. a.* to call out the names of the various *maraes*, &c., when peace was to be established.

Faainati, *v. a.* to appoint the under chiefs; to present or take food by means of the *inati* or under chiefs; to make use of the *inati* in presenting food, &c, through their hands.

Faaine, *v. a.* to encroach on another in any way.

—*s.* an encroacher, as to land and other things.

Faaineine, *v. a.* to make ready, prepare, or to cause preparation to be made.

Faaini, *v. a.* to make or procure an *ini*, that is a butt or mark to which darts or spears are thrown—*fig.* to go carefully about an affair so as to hit the true medium, which is the *ini*.

Faaino, *v. a.* to defame, to injure; also to hurt or spoil a thing.

—*s.* defamation, a defamer.

Faainoino, *v. a.* to give offence, to shew dislike or ill feeling towards an object.

Faaio, *s* cloth that is partly coloured red and partly white.

Faaioio, *v. a.* to make of various colours, and thereby to set off to advantage; see *ioio*.

Faaioio, *v. n.* to put on stillness,

or apparent serenity in the article of death, or when about to depart.

Faaipaea, *s.* that which may increase the number of a party, but not its efficiency; or the bulk of a thing, but not its value.

—*v. a.* to increase the number or bulk merely.

Faaipaupau, *v. a.* to deride, turn to scorn, provoke.

Faaipo, *s.* the name of a tree; also of a goddess.

Faaipoipo, *v. a.* to marry.

Faaipoipo raa, *s.* marriage.

Faairi, *v. a.* to cause a thing to be lodged or placed; to use or put up a board for any purpose; see *iri.*

Faaita, *v. n.* to distort the lips and chin; to make grimaces by way of contempt, or to excite laughter.

Faaitaita, *v. n.* to make repeated grimaces by way of contempt, or to produce laughter.

Faaite, *v. a.* to teach, make known, produce knowledge; see *ite.*

—*s.* a teacher, one that makes known or produces knowledge.

Faaiteite, *v. a.* to teach or make known repeatedly; to make repeated and partial discoveries; to make known or shew by small degrees.

Faaiti, *v. a.* to reduce, diminish in size; to lessen in rank or influence.

Faaitiiti, *v. a.* to diminish by little and little; to reduce by degrees; see *iti.*

Faa iti ma te apiapi, *s.* a little contracted valley—*fig.* the situation of one surrounded with difficulties.

Faaitoito, *v. a.* to excite to vigilance and watchfulness; often used imperatively, be vigilant, watchful, active.

—*v. n.* to be active and vigilant.

—*s* one that excites to vigilance.

Faamahu, *v. n.* to bear with patience.

—*a.* patient, forbearing.

—*s.* patience.

Faamaitai, *v. a.* to produce or make good, to praise; see *haamaitai.*

—*s.* praise, encomium; a praiser, that which produces amendment, or makes good; see *maitai.*

Faamatau, *v. a.* to terrify, to threaten, to produce fear; see *matau.*

—*s.* one that causes fear, or that which makes afraid.

—*v. n.* to put on fear, to act as one in fear, to affect to be afraid.

Faamate, *v. a.* to produce illness or death; to kill.

—*v. n.* to affect sickness; to commit suicide.

Faamaue, *v. a.* to cause flight; see *maue.*

Faamoana, *s.* a sort of cage of wicker work, used for catching fish. [see *nā.*

Faana, *v. a.* to pacify a child;

—*s.* a pacifier, one that pacifies.

Faanahonaho, *v. a.* to prepare, set in order; commonly applied to a table and what concerns eating; see *nahonaho.*

Faananau, *v. n.* to strive, as in difficult evacuation; or as a woman in travail; see *tītohi.*

Faananaue, *v.n.* to linger, hang behind; to withdraw.
Faanaonao, *v. a.* to decorate; see *naonao*.
Faanaunau, *s.* one that cooks food, and does other things with cleverness and neatness; the neatness or cleverness with which any thing is done.
—*a.* neat, clean, clever.
—*adv.* neatly, cleanly, cleverly.
Faanavai, *v.a.* to make up what is deficient; see *navai*.
Faanavanavai, *v. a.* to supply, or make up deficiencies.
Faanavenave, *v. a.* to procure delight or pleasure, cause delight.
—*s.* one that delights, or causes pleasure to another.
Faanee, *s.* a steersman in a boat or ship.
—*v. a.* to steer, as a helmsman or cockswain.
Faaneenee, *v. a.* to steer repeatedly, or in different directions.
Faanehenehe, *v. a.* to adorn, set in good and decent order; see *nehenehe*.
—*s.* one that decorates, or sets in decent order; that which adorns.
Faanenee, *v. a.* the dual of to steer; see *nee*.
Faania, *v. a.* to turn over, applied to any thing in cooking; see *nia*.
Faanihinihi, *v. a.* the old word for to decorate.
Faanoa, *v. a.* to profane, make common.
Faanoho, *v. a.* to cause to sit or abide; to place.
Faanoho, *s.* one who places things or persons in their proper places; one who fixes another in his land.
Faanono, *v. a.* to procure *nono*, to dye with *nono*.
Faanonoa, *v. a.* to spurn with disgust, applied to husbands and wives that have an aversion to each other; see *nonoa*.
Faanonoue, *v.n.* to linger, hang behind.
Faanoo, *v. a.* to put a *noo*, or square stern to a canoe.
Faanua, *s.* a sluggard.
Faanuanua, *v. n.* to be indolent, sparing one's self.
Faanuu, *v. a.* to procure, or gather a *nuu* or fleet.
Faanuu, *v. n.* to slide, or move towards another place.
Faaô, *v. n.* to enter, as into a room, or any other place.
Faaô, *v. a.* to have, or take a present as an introduction; to cause or procure an introduction.
Faao, *v. n.* to look out.
Faaoao, *v.n.* to look out repeatedly as with expectation.
—*s.* a looker out, one that looks out repeatedly.
Faaoaoa, *v. n.* to rejoice.
—*v. a.* to cause joy.
Faaoeoe, *v. a.* to sharpen to a point, as a dart or spear; see *oeoe*.
Faaoha, *v. a.* to cause to lean or bend; see *oha*.
—*v. n.* to go bending, as a person through age; to come down, as a bird on its roost.
Faaohipa, *v.a.* to procure work; to cause work to be done.
Faaoho, *v. a.* to use a stick or rod in a certain mode of fishing.

Faaohu, *v. a* to cause any thing to turn as a wheel.

Faaohu, *v. a.* to put up earth in ridges.

Faaohu, *v. a.* to tie up leaves in small bundles.

Faaohu, *s.* one that turns any thing, as a wheel; the handle by which any thing is turned round.

Faaoi, *v. a.* to grind, whet, or sharpen, as a tool; to bring any thing to a sharp point.

—*s.* one that grinds, whets, or sharpens any tool; one that brings to a sharp point; a grind stone, or whet stone; see *faaina.*

Faaoioi, *v. a.* to make brisk; to hasten.

Faaoma, *v. a.* to make way for water.

Faaonaona, *v. a.* to cut the hair in a peculiar manner.

Faaoo, *v. n.* to leave a space between two ridges when thatching a native house.

Faaoohu, *v. a.* to wrap food in leaves, in order to be baked in a native oven.

Faaooo, *v. a.* to provoke, to stir up another's displeasure; see *ooo.*

—*s.* a person that provokes; any thing or circumstance that provokes.

Faaoopa, *v. a.* to upset, or turn a thing over.

—*s.* one who upsets or turns over a canoe, &c.; see *oopa.*

Faaoopi, *v. a.* to shut or close, such as the leaves of a book; see *oopi.*

Faaopea, *v. a.* to place things cross ways, as a pile of fire-wood.

Faaopeapea, *v. a.* to put things cross ways repeatedly.

Faaopupu, *v. a.* to raise a blister; from *opupu*, a bladder.

—*s.* that which causes a blister; a blistering plaster.

Faaopupu, *v. a.* to put up a small sail to a canoe or a boat.

Faaora, *v. a.* to save, heal, deliver; to bless; see *faaea* and *ora.*

—*s.* a Saviour, healer, deliverer, redeemer.

Faaorare, *v. a.* to disturb, cause mischief by evil reports, &c.

Faaore, *v. a.* to annul laws or customs; to forgive, or do away the punishment of a crime; to annihilate; see *ore.*

—*s.* the person or thing which disannuls, or causes any thing to be done away.

Faaoreore, *v. a.* to do away repeatedly, or gradually.

Faaori, *v. a.* to cause or procure a dance; to procure or employ a dancer.

Faaoro, *v. n.* to abstain from food through grief, or some other cause.

Faaoro, *v. a.* to procure, or make use of the sweet scented *oro*; see *oro.*

Faaoroa, *v. a.* to make a feast; to cause the observance of some feast or ceremony; see *oroa.*

—*v. a.* since the reception of Christianity, the ordinances of Baptism and the Lord's Supper are called *Oroa*; and *faaoroa* is to appoint and observe either of them.

Faaoroaia, *v. a.* to cause grief or sorrow.

Faaoromai, *s.* patience, forbearance.
—*v. n.* to be patient; to bear with patience; see *haamahu*.
—*a.* patient, forbearing; calm under sufferings.

Faaorooro, *v. a.* to make use of the rasps called *orooro*.

Faaorui, *v. a.* to cause the failure of good.

Faaote, *v. a.* to suckle, give suck as a mother.

Faaoti, *v. a.* to finish, or complete a thing; also, to leave off for the present.
—*s.* a finisher, or one that brings to an end, see *oti*.

Faaoto, *v. a.* to cause weeping, sorrow, or grief; to sound any sort of instrument; the *oto* is the sound or noise of a thing.
—*s.* one that causes weeping, crying, or grief of mind; one that sounds any sort of instrument; see *tai*.

Faaotooto, *v. a.* to produce repeated weeping or grief of mind; to sound an instrument repeatedly.

Faapaari, *v. a.* to cause maturity or ripeness; to make wise, cunning, skilful.
—*s.* one that causes or brings to maturity; one that instructs, makes wise, or cunning.

Faapeapea, *v. a.* to teaze, perplex; see *peapea*.

Faapitaataa, *v. a.* to cause the loosening, cracking, or splitting of the kernel in the cocoanut shell; see *pitaataa*.

Faapoaupu, *v. a.* to destroy any of one's family by means of sorcery.

Faapuora, *v. a.* to take a person or thing to a place of safety; to remove a sick person from place to place for the sake of the restoration of health; see *haapuora*.
—*v. n.* to go to a refuge or place of safety.

Faapurara, *v. a.* to scatter, spread abroad.

Faapurero, *v. n.* to appear unexpectedly, as a person concealed.

Faapuroro, *v. n.* to issue out suddenly, as a person concealed in a thicket.

Faaraa, *v. a.* to consecrate; see *haamoa*.

Faarahi, *v. a.* to enlarge, to magnify any thing.

Faarairai, *v. a.* to make thin, or slender.

Faarao, *v. a.* to lay rollers, as in drawing up a boat or acnoe; to lay sticks under any thing for it to rest upon, or in order to haul it up.

Faaraoa, *v. a* to cause choking by swallowing fish bones.

Faaraoa, *v. n.* to endeavour to vomit up any thing with which one is choking; see *raoa*.

Faaraorao, *v. a.* to make use of rollers repeatedly, or of many rollers.

Faaraorao, *a.* fly attracting, applied to meat, or any thing that brings flies together.

Faarapu, *v. a.* to stir, or cause to mix well, any liquid or pulp.

Faarapurapu, *v. a.* to stir gradually, or repeatedly, any sort of liquid or pulp.

Faararua, *v. a.* to put up two sails; see *rarua*.

Faarare, *s.* a ramrod.

Faarare, *v. a.* to stir or mix up the food called *popoi.*

Faararerare, *v. a.* to stir or mix up *popoi* repeatedly.

Faarari, *v. a.* to wet any thing; see *rari.*

—*s.* any thing or garment used as a protection against wet; a great coat is *ahu faarariua.*

Faarata, *v. a.* to tame, to make a person or a thing familiar; see *rata.*

Faarau, *s.* a piece of net work at the butt end of a fishing rod, on which the natives hook the pearl fish-hook; also the *oma*, a small fish with which a hook for catching the fish *aahi* is baited.

Faarau, *s.* the spring of a lock, or any other steel spring.

—*v. a.* to make hundreds, or count by hundreds; see *rau;* to put a spring to a lock; to fix a bait to a pearl hook, &c.

Faaraurau, *s.* the name of a certain feast and ceremony used in abolishing a restriction.

Faaravai, *v. a.* to supply a deficiency.

Faaravaravai, *v. a.* to supply various deficiencies, or supply a deficiency repeatedly.

Faarearea, *v. a.* to wheedle, or flatter a person.

Faareeree, *v. a.* to apportion, or furnish equal parts for a feast; to furnish equal parts in any general contribution.

Faarefa, *v. a.* to make a motion to dazzle the eyes.

Faarefarefa, *v. n.* to roll the eyes about repeatedly.

Faarei, *s.* a mode of using a fishing net.

Faareirei, *v. a.* to use the net, or catch fish in the *faarei* manner.

Faareirei, *v. n.* to stretch, as a person lifting himself up.

Faarepu, *v. a.* to stir up anger or commotion.

—*s.* one that causes strife.

Faareureu, *v. n.* to make merry or to be joyful; also to be liberal with food, &c.

Faariaria, *v. a.* to shock, to disgust.

—*v. n.* to shew, or affect disgust.

Faarirerire, *v. a.* to applaud or exalt a person or a thing; to boast.

—*s.* bombast, boasting; a boaster.

Faario, *v. a.* to raise a fishing net in various places, that persons may take the fish.

Faariri, *v. a.* to provoke to anger; see *riri.*

—*v. n.* to work up one's self to a state of anger; to put on the appearance of anger.

Faaroa, *v. a.* to lengthen, see *haamaoro.*

—*v. n.* to prolong, to delay.

Faaroo, *s.* [*fakarongo, vakarongo, akarongo,*] faith or belief; obedience.

—*v. a.* to believe; to act in obedience.

Faaroo, *v. n.* to hear; see *roo* and *roroo.*

—*a.* obedient, hearing.

Faarooroo, *v. n.* to listen or hear repeatedly.

Faaroroa, *v. a.* to lengthen repeatedly.

—*v. n.* to prolong, or delay from time to time.

Faaroroo, *v. n.* the dual of *faaroo*, to hear or listen.

—*a.* quick of hearing.

Faarori, *v. a.* to move, shake, or pull a thing from side to side in order to make it loose.
—*s* a person that moves or shakes a thing, or that which shakes a thing.

Faarorirori, *v a.* to move or shake repeatedly.

Faarou, *v. a.* to use a *rou* or crook in order to reach fruit, &c.

Faarourou, *v. n.* to be still, wait in silence.

Faarû, *v. a.* to cause haste; see *ru*.

Faarua, *s.* the boisterous N. or N. E. wind; see *haaputi*.

Faaruai, *v. a.* to give a vomit, cause vomiting [vomiting
—*s.* an emetic, that which causes

Faarue, *v. a.* [*fakaruke, akaruke,*] to cast away, forsake; to leave off.

Faaruoi, *v. n.* to feign illness and inability. [*oromai*.

Faarumai, *s.* the same as *faa-*

Faarumaruma, *v. n.* to make one's self appear gloomy, austere, forbidding; see *rumaruma*.

Faaruru, *v. a.* to brave danger, encounter difficulties.

Faarûrû, *v. n* to cause a self trembling, as formerly in the case of the pretended prophets or *taura*.

Faarurua, *s* a shelter or defence.
—*v. n.* to take shelter.

Faaruu, *v. a.* to use a certain mode of fishing.

Faaruuruu, *v a.* to prepare for a battle, as the warriors used to do by wrapping about their bodies

Faataa. *v. a.* [*wakataka, akataka,*] to part, disjoin, or set aside; also to throw, or roll down from a precipice.

Faataaê, *v. a.* to put far off, to separate entirely.

Faataataa, *v. a.* to separate or put away obstacles; to make distinct parts or parties; also to shift from one place to another.

Faatae, *v. a.* to go quite to, or reach quite out to any thing, as to fruit at the extremity of a branch; to excite to go, to set a going; to take a person or thing to a *marae*. [any thing.
—*s.* the person who excites to

Faataeaau, *v. a.* to excite the desire of the heart for any thing.
—*s.* that which excites desire after any thing.

Faataeae, *v. a.* to make, or profess to be a brother or brethren.

Faatahataha, *v. n.* to cast a side glance at something disagreeable; to turn aside to avoid a person.

Faatahinu, *v. a.* to anoint, cause the anointing of a person.

Faatahoa, *v. a.* to weary, or teaze in any way.
—*v. n.* to trouble one's self; to be in want of patience, so as to be a self troubler; see *tahoa*.

Faatahua, *v. a.* to constitute or employ a priest; to employ an artizan to teach a person any art or trade.

Faatai, *v. a.* to make one grieve or weep; see *faaoto*.

Faataia, *v. a.* to discourage, cause heaviness or grief; see *taia*.

Faatiapapau, *v. a.* to play tricks to frighten people, as if there was a ghost; see *tupapau.*

Faatiapiti, *v. n.* to blow from two different quarters, as the wind in certain places.

—*v. n.* to contend, as two parties.

Faatiara, *v. a.* to bear up to the wind, as a canoe.

Faatiatia, *v. a.* to discourse, converse together, reason together; also to relate a conversation.

Faatiatia, *v. a.* to quiet a child, by carrying, tossing, or diverting it in some way or other.

Faatiatia, *v n.* to be withholding a person's share or right.

Faatietie, *v. a.* to boast, glory, eulogize.

—*s* a boaster.

Faatihae, *v. a.* to provoke a dog or other beast; to insult the mourners in the *heva.*

Faatihaehae, *v. a.* to insult or provoke repeatedly.

Faatiho, *v a.* to speak degradingly and contemptuously of the property of another, that he may be disgusted, and disregard it.

Faatihotiho, *v. a.* to excite repeatedly the disgust of a person in regard to his house or property, so that he may disregard it.

Faatii, *v. a.* to cause one to be disappointed in something he wished or expected.

Faatimo, *v. a.* to make use of a stone called *timo* in a game or play of that name.

Faatina, *v. a.* to propose or appoint marriage connexions, as parents often do.

Faatina, *v. a.* to pledge or challenge in eating, drinking, or giving of presents; to cram or fill up with food, to surfeit.

Faatio, *v. a* to use contemptuous language, to dare.

Faatiopa, *v. a.* to turn a thing on its side.

Faatiotio, *v a.* to dare, make little of repeatedly.

Faatiotioo, *v. a.* to excite to anger by daring and contemptuous language.

Faatipaupau, *v. a.* to vex, excite to jealousy or envy.

Faatirava, *v. a.* to lay beams horizontally.

Faatiri, *a.* prolific, as a female of the human or brute species.

—*s.* seed, progeny of any kind.

Faatitapou, *v. a.* to put a thing bottom upwards.

Faatitarava, *v. a.* to place things horizontally side by side.

Faatitiahemo, *v. a.* to use exertions to excel another in work, &c.

Faatitiaifaro, *v a.* to straighten what is crooked in several places; to rectify what is wrong in several respects.

Faatitiaua, *v. a.* to seek to excel another.

Faatitina, *v. a.* to exert over much, to attempt to do too much.

Faatito, *v. a.* to cause cocks, dogs, he goats, &c, to fight; see *tito.*

Faatito, *v. a.* to urge a person to procure property for another.

Faatitô, *s.* a funnel.

—*v. a.* to fill or pour liquid into a vessel; see *titô*

Faatitomoa, *s.* a person that promotes cock-fighting.

Faatitotito, *v. a.* to excite cocks, &c., to fight.

Faatô, *v a.* to fill, or pour into a cask or bottle; to cast any kind of metal.

Faato, *v. a.* to put shoots of the *ava* plant in a hole, with wet leaves, in order to cause them to grow, and then take them for planting.

Faatoa, *v. a.* to cast a stone called *toa*, as a confirmation of something settled.

Faatoa, *v n.* to crow together.

Faatoa, *v. a.* to make courageous or warlike; also to excite to mischief.

Faatoa, *v. n.* to settle at the bottom, applied to a fish that has been hooked.

Faatoatoa, *v. a.* to be very brave.

Faatoatoa, *v. a.* to make exertions too soon after sickness.

Faatoe, *v. a.* to leave some, spare a remainder.

Faatohe, *v. a.* to make the first part of a net or basket.

Faatohu, *v. a.* to point at a person or thing by the finger; see *tohu*.

Faatohutohu, *v. a.* to point repeatedly.

Faatoi, *s* the name of a feast made by parents, on removing certain restrictions that regarded their children; a family feast.

Faatomo, *v. a.* to load a canoe, boat, or ship.

—*v. a.* to cause a ship or other vessel to sink in the water; see *tomo*.

Faatomo, *v. a.* to cause an entrance into a house or other place; to cause the first entrance or public opening of a place of worship.

Faatomotomo, *v. a.* to heap one thing upon another in a vessel, or in putting a burden upon a person so as to over load him.

Faatono, *v. a.* to send a messenger; to cause one to be sent; see *tono*.

Faatootoo, *v. a.* to make use of a staff; see *tootoo*.

Faatoro, *v. a.* to trace, to follow the footsteps of a thief.

Faatoro, *v. a.* to stretch out the hand or foot.

Faatoro, *v. a.* to lead, or go before, as a canoe in a fishing party; to solicit the making of native cloth, as the chiefs often do; to trace a report.

—*s.* one that searches out a thing.

Faatoro hara, *v. a.* to trace the evidences of a crime.

Faatoroa, *v. a.* to invest with office; see *toroa*.

Faatoropaaa, *v. a.* to trace, as the root of the yam through all the intricacies of the vines coming from it—*fig* to find out causes by their effects

Faatorotoro, *v a.* to trace, or search out with perseverance; to stretch out repeatedly.

Faatoto, *v. n* to be in a rage to such a degree as to alter the countenance.

Faatôtô, *v. a.* to enclose a *hue* or calabash in a sort of net.

Faatotoa, *v. n.* to lag, or hang behind, as a warrior; to be shy of another, avoiding his company.

Faatu, *v. a.* to raise up, put in an erect posture; also to support, assist; see *faatia.*

Faatuatua, *v. n.* to frown; see *tuatua.*

Faatupu, *v. a.* to cause any thing to grow, happen, or come to pass, see *tupu.*

Faatupua, *v. n.* to be silent, grave, serious.

—*a.* reserved; also sullen.

—*s* reservedness, sullenness.

Faatupui, *s.* the remaining one of a family or race, who is to keep it from extinction by becoming the root of a future progeny.

Faatuputupuatau, *a.* of long forbearance or endurance, yet will break out. A figurative expression taken from the sea among the breakers, where it may appear smooth for a while, yet will break out suddenly.

Faatuou, *v. n.* to nod, or give a sign.

Faatura, *v. a.* to honor, exalt, shew respect.

Faaturai, *v. a* to push, throw down by pushing.

Faturatura, *v. a.* to honor continually or repeatedly.

Faaturatura, *v. n.* to assume consequence.

Faatureirei, *v n* to be carelessly, or by way of daring, putting one's self in a dangerous place.

—*v. a.* to place a thing in a slippery, insecure, or dangerous position.

Faaturi, *s.* prostitution, adultery, or fornication.

—*v. a.* to commit adultery or fornication; but most commonly the term is applied to prostitution for hire.

Faaturi, *v. n.* to pretend deafness; see *turi.*

Faaturituri, *v. n.* to turn a deaf ear repeatedly; to pretend deafness, or that what is said is not intelligible.

Faaturu, *v. a.* to prop, put up a *turu* or support; see *turu.*

Faaturui, *v. n.* to lean against, or upon a thing.

Faaturui rua, *v. n.* to stand or lean between two; to halt between two opinions.

Faaturuma, *v. a.* to be silent, to appear thoughtful and serious.

Faaturuturu, *v. a.* to prop up repeatedly.

Faaturuturui, *v. n.* to go a lounging from place to place.

Faatutu, *v. a.* to fish with two nets, a large and a small one.

·Faatûtû, *v. a.* to dandle a child; see *faatiatia.*

Faatutû, *v. n.* to stand on equal terms, applied to antagonists.

Faaû, *v. n.* to be resolute, facing all sorts of weather.

Faauana, *v. a.* to use exertion, make a strong effort; see *uana.*

Faauaua, *v. a.* to command imperiously and incessantly.

Faauaua, *v. a.* to make stiff or tough.

Faaue, *v. a.* to order, bid, command

—*s.* an order or bidding.

Faaueue, *v. a.* to order, or excite to action repeatedly.

Faauiui, *v. n.* to perceive or hear indistinctly.

Faaunauna, *s.* an ornament, decoration.

Faaunauna, *v. a.* to decorate or adorn.

Faaupaparia, *v. n.* to turn a deaf ear to a request.

Faauru, *s.* a pilot, one that brings in a vessel.

—*v. a.* to conduct a vessel into an anchoring place; see *uru.*

Faauruai, *v. n.* to have a slight impression, desire, or excitement.

Faaurutuaau, *v. a.* to cause a canoe or a vessel to go on a reef at all risks, either through violence of the weather, or ignorance of an harbour.

Faauta, *v. a.* to convey by water from one place to another; see *uta.*

Faauteute, *v. a.* to make a thing red; see *uteute.*

Faautu, *v n.* to make grimaces, distort the lips.

Faautunui, *v. n.* to pout, look sullen, make thick lips.

Faauturea, *v. n.* to be sullen, refusing to eat through displeasure, or fear of a superior.

Faautuutu, *v. a.* to repulse an offer, refuse through displeasure.

Faautuutu, *v. a.* to do a thing with effect.

Faauu, *v. n.* to be resolute in accomplishing what a person designed, in the face of danger and difficulties.

Faauuru, *s.* the name of a plaything that makes a noise, from which the name is taken.

Faea, *s.* duplicity, feigned appearance.

Faeatai, *s.* a swarm of fish which come in their season, swarms of flies, multitude of people, or abundance of food at a particular time.

Faefae, *a.* unsettled, dilatory, making false pretences.

Faeo, *s.* the name of a game among children.

Faeo, *v. n* to have an unsatisfied desire for a particular kind of food.

Faepa, *s.* the name of a prayer, or some part of the ceremonies in investing a chief with his office.

Faeno, *a.* dwarfish, or of low stature.

Faepaepa, *s.* a ceremony used in investing the king or principal chief with his office.

Faere, *s.* a large and prominent belly.

Faeva, *a.* alienated.

Fafa, *v. n.* to feel, or touch with the hand; to try the disposition or inclination of a person.

Fafa, *s.* the stem of *taro,* plantain, or cocoanut branch.

Fafaanunui, *v. n.* to appear to one's imagination.

Fafai, *v. a.* to confess or divulge (dual number.)

Fafai, *v. a.* to moderate a great evil, to stay injurious proceedings; to crush peaceably any affair that is likely to produce mischief.

Fafai, *s.* a thicket of bushes on the land, or an assemblage of coral in the sea.

Fafao, *v. a.* to put into a receptacle, as food into a basket, the arm into a sleeve, &c.

—*a.* having entrance, or capacity of receiving, such as a garment put on, that is called *ahu fafao.*

Fafarofaro, *v. n.* to go bendingly forward.

Fafaru, *s.* the name of a vessel in which a certain sauce or food is kept.

Fafau, *v. a.* to tie together, as an adze to its helve—*fig.* to make a contract, or firm agreement, or covenant.

Fatauraro, *v. a.* to go about stirring up mischief or sedition.

Fâi, *v. a.* to confess, reveal, divulge.

Fai, *v. a.* to deceive by fair speech and apparent friendship.

Fai, *s.* the skate, or sting ray fish, of which there are many varieties.

Fai, *s.* a certain Tahitian curse or imprecation.

Fai, *s.* the name of a part of the offering which the priests used to eat in the *marae.*

Fai, *s.* the name of a game played by children.

—*v. a* to play the *fai.*

Faia, *s.* the name of a fish.

Faiaia, *s* the dead bodies obtained in war, and taken to a *marae*, were called *haia*, but after the prayers were performed *faiaia.*

Faiere, *s.* any creature newly delivered of its young.

Faifai, *s.* the name of a large timber tree.

Faifai, *v. a.* to gather or pluck fruit.

Faifai, *v a.* to conciliate.

Faifaiâ, *a.* bulky, large in size or quantity; plenteous.

Faifaiapo, *s.* a dream, or ominous sleep.

Faiite, *v a.* to reconcile those who were at variance.

Faino, *v. n.* to equal, to balance, to be even.

Faipuu, *s.* the name of a tree with odoriferous leaves which are used in the *monoi.*

Faira, *s.* [Eng. *file,*] steel, file, or rasp.

Faira, *a.* [Eng. *file,*] hard, niggardly.

Fairaro, *s.* a part of the sacrifice in the *marae.*

Fairu, *v. a.* to befoul a person in contempt.

Faita, *v. n.* to make grimaces.

Faite, *v. n.* to be equal; see *faino.*

—*s.* an equal, or that which is equal.

Faito, *a.* equal in any sense; see *faafaito.*

—*v. n.* to be equal, balance alike.

Faito, *s.* a measure, balance, scales.

—*v. a.* to measure, balance, weigh.

Fana, *s.* a bow of the archer.

Fanâ, *s.* the yard of a ship.

Fanae, *s.* the time soon after midnight, when the tide begins to ebb.

Fana horo aoao, *s.* a bow difficult to bend—*fig.* an ill tempered person, difficult to manage.

Fanao, *s.* delight, pleasure, boast, glory.

—*v. n.* to glory, boast, take pleasure in.

Fanau, *v. n* to be born.

—*v. a.* to bring forth.

—*a.* birth, as *arii fanau*, chief by birth.

Fanaua, *s.* what is brought forth; the young of any animal, man, beast, bird, or fish, as also all insects.

Fanau raa, *s.* the time or place of birth.

Fanaueve, *v. n* to be exhausted and weakened by bringing forth young repeatedly.

Fane, *v. n.* to break; see *fati* and *fene.*

Fanefane, *v. n.* to break repeatedly, or in many places; see *fatifati.*

Faniu, *s.* the thick end of the cocoanut branch that adheres to the tree; see *niu.*

Fano, *v. n.* to sail; see *tere.*

Fanu, *a.* few, some; when applied to persons *too* is commonly prefixed, as *too fanu*, some persons.

Fao, *s.* [*wao,*] a nail or chisel.

—*v. a.* to make holes with a *fao.*

Fao, *a.* lank, lean, as a fish after spawning.

Fao, *s.* a person that speaks through the nose, a snuffler.

Fao, *a.* enslaved, brought under subjection, and hard usage.

Fao, *s.* the weakest out of a litter of pigs.

Fao, *s* the dedication of a new *marae* or a house; see *hao.*

Faoa, *s.* a stone adze; see *haoa.*

Faoafaatu, *v. a.* to re-establish the *marae*, or the possession of land, by certain prayers, &c.

Faoaoà, *a.* stony, rugged

Faoatumarae, *s.* an upright stone in the *marae*, against which the priest leaned while praying.

Faofao, *s.* the dropsy; see *ofao.*

Faofao, *a.* empty, applied to the stomach

Fara, *s.* [*fala, hala, ha'a,*] the pandanus or palmetto: there are various species, as *fara aaoo, fara puoo, fara omao,* &c.

Farafara, *s.* an eel.

Farafara, *s.* a species of mountain plantain.

Fara motu, *s.* an antagonist with no one to balk him.

Farapai, *s.* a reciprocal strife or contest.

Fara papaa, *s.* the pine apple, from the resemblance of the leaves to the *fara.*

Farapepe, *s.* a running plant that grows in the mountains and rocks, whose fibrous roots are called *ieie,* which see.

Farapata, *s.* an adept in any thing.

Farara, *v. n.* to spring up, as the wind; to be in a slanting position.

—*adv.* aslant, obliquely.

—*s* the slant position of any thing.

Farau, *s.* a shed for a boat or canoe.

Farauru, *s.* a species of the pandanus of good foliage.

—*a.* rich in foliage—*fig* gaudy in dress.

Fare, *s.* [*hare, fa'e, fale, hale,*] a house.

Fareauta, *s.* a temporary shed.

Fareauti, *s* a shed covered with *ti* leaves.

Fareahu, *s.* a tent.

Farefare, *a* hollow, as the stomach for want of food.

Farefare, *v. n.* to overhang, as a rock, or as a curling wave before it breaks.

Farefare matai, *s* a sort of tent for the image of a god.

Farefare rau uru raau, *s.* the name of a certain ceremony or exhibition of the persons of the *pori*, in order to see which was the fattest and best looking.

Farehaa, *s.* a shelter for refugees among bushes or rocks; also a shed in which to beat the native cloth, &c.

Farehaupape, *s.* a house with gable ends. [ends not oval.

Farehauparu, *s.* a house with

Farenatinati, *s.* an inaccessible house, such as those of the wizzards were said to be.

Fareohu, *s.* a small moveable round house, used for sheltering things.

Fareorai, *s.* distress occasioned by war, famine, or tempest.

Farepora, *s.* a small neatly thatched house put on board the large double canoes of the Paumotu.

Farepotaa, *s.* an oval house.

Farepotee, *s.* the same.

Fareranape, *s.* an umbrella, from *fare* a house, and *rauape*, the leaf of the *ape*, and used for the same purpose.

Farerei, *v. a.* to meet.

Farero, *s.* the branchiug coral.

Farero, *s.* any sort of screw.

Faretoau, *s.* a sponge.

Faretupapau, *s.* a house for the dead.

Fareturuma, *s.* an out house to keep lumber in; also one occupied by a *tii*.

Fareu'a, *s.* the shell of the *maava* fish, which the crab *u'a* sometimes enters.

Fareureu, *v. a.* to arrange food neatly for a meal.

Fareutu, *s.* a sort of watch-house at the side of a camp.

Farii, *s.* a vessel, a receptacle of any kind.

—*v. n.* to contain, as a vessel.

—*v. n.* to receive, to admit, entertain.

Fariu, *v. n.* to turn to or from a thing or person.

Faro, *v. n.* to bend, stoop, or to hang down.

Faro, *v. n.* to be anxiously waiting or expecting.

Farofaro, *v. n.* to be bending; to be moving up and down, as a slender pole does when carried.

Farofaro, *v a.* to scoop out; to lade; to take by little and little.

Faru, *v. a.* to deflour virginity.

Fata, *s.* an altar; a scaffold put up for any purpose; a piece of wood to hang baskets of food, &c.

Fata, *v. a.* to pile up fire wood; to set the fire in order in the native oven.

Fatafata, *a.* open, not filled up or closed; careless, loose, indifferent, the opposite to vigourous and active.

Fatanu, *s.* a butt of plantain stalk, to which, as a mark, spears and darts are thrown.

Fatanu, *a.* settled, pre-meditated, as applied to war.

Fatarau, *s.* the common altar for sacrifices.

Fatarua, *s.* two (family) altars set up. [or place.

Fatata, *s.* nearness, as to time

Fatata, *a.* [*vaitata*, *tata*,] near, not far off.

—*adv* nearly, almost at hand.

Fati, *s.* a breach; see *ofati* and *fene*. [sound.

Fati, *a.* broken, not whole or

Fati, *v. n.* to break, as a stick; to break, as a wave of the sea; to disperse, as a company; to break up and flee, as an army; see *fene*, *afa*, *motu*.

Fatia, *v. a.* to place hot stones within an animal in cooking; also to heat water by putting hot stones into it.

Fatifati, *a.* bruised, broken in several places.

—*v. n.* to break repeatedly.

Fatifatiâ, *s.* a roll or fold of cloth that is not neatly folded.

Fatifatiaeve, *s* an immense roll of native cloth.

Fatifatiairi, *s.* a slight wound, skin deep;—*fig.* applied to a country subdued in war, while the chiefs and leading men are still alive.

Fatifatirara, *v. a.* to break off the branches while the body of the tree remains unhurt—*fig* to remove some evil effects, while the cause still remains.

Fatimanava, *s.* fear, arising from evil tidings.

Fatimauu, *s* impatience, eagerness of desire.

—*v. n.* to be impatient, to be eager to obtain something that is expected.

Fatino, *s.* a mode of fishing.

Fatino, *v. n.* to move slowly, as a cat watching its prey; to go slyly and slowly, as a thief, that he may secure his prey.

Fatipapa, *a.* thigh broken, or hurt.

Fatitô, *a.* the quality of breaking short.

—*v. n.* to break off short, as sugar cane.

Fatiue, *a.* broken, but held by fibres.

Fatiueue, *a.* broken, bent, but not parted, because of tough fibres—*fig.* unyielding, as a person that will still cleave to his purpose.

Fatu, [*Atu, Haku,*] Lord, master, owner.

Fatu, *s.* the gristly part of an oyster; the core of an abscess.

Fatu, *v. a.* to plat or braid; to weave.

Fatupehe, *s.* the maker of a song; see *pehe.*

Fatui, *s* some of the first fish caught in a new net, and presented to the gods, or to the king.

Faturei, *s.* the stones on the lower edge of a fishing net.

Fatu umu ti, *s.* the largest stones in a large native oven.

Fau, *s.* the same as the *purau* tree.

Faa, *s.* a sort of head dress. × fau

Fau, *s.* a god, as being head or above; a king or principal chief was formerly called *fau*, as being above others.

Faufaa, *s* gain, profit, advantage.

Fauhaa, *v. a.* to be busily engaged in work.

Fauhaea, *s.* the *fau* tree stripped or torn, which sometimes began a quarrel.

Faufau, *a.* vile, filthy, base, disgusting.

Faufaua, *v. a.* to make straight by bringing into a line.

Faufaurai, *interj* an exclamation of grief

Fauai, *s.* a darling son during his minority; some concluding ceremony at the time of marriage.

Fauaipa, *s.* some part of the ceremonies used in investing a principal chief with his authority

Faupa, *s.* a tough species of the *fau* tree.

Faupara moa, *s.* a head ornament of feathers.

Faupare, *s* the front of a house, an ornament put in an oblique direction.
Faupoo, *s* a hat, cap, or bonnet; see *taupoo*.
Faura, *v. n* to appear; see *fa*.
Fauraepa, *s* the name of certain prayers or ceremonies used at the *marae*
Fauroi i, *v. a.* to labour and toil incessantly.
Faurourou, *s* a darling or beloved child who engrosses the time and affection of the parent.
Fautaitai apurua, *s.* a feast kept by the parents of a married couple.
Fautarafare, *s.* the bend of the round part of a native house; also a quarrel on account of a *fau* or darling child.
Fautia, *s.* a medicinal plant.
Fautu, *s.* a plant of the hibiscus kind, *fautia.*
Fautua, *s.* some great work or labour.
Fauurumaa, *s.* a war cap.
Feaa, *v. n.* to cogitate, think, hesitate.
Feaaore, *a.* thoughtless, unconcerned.
Feaapiti, *v. n.* to halt between two opinions.
Feaarua, *v. n.* the same as *feaapiti*, to hesitate between two opinions.
Feaarua, *s.* double mindedness.
—*a.* double minded.
feau Faafeau, *v. n.* to doubt, hesitate.
Feai, *s.* strife, contention.
Feai, *v. n.* to meet, as two opposite seas; to clash, as opposite interests.
Feao, *s.* a jib sail; the stern of a canoe of a particular make.

Feau, *v. n.* to cogitate, think, and hesitate.
Fee, *s.* [*fege*, *feke*,] the cuttle fish.
Feefee, *s.* a disease common in the islands, a species of the *Elephantiasis*, but not answering the description commonly given in medical books.
Feetere, *s.* a cuttle fish that swims in different directions; *fig.* an unsettled person.
Feeti, *s.* the name of a southerly wind.
Feetietie, *s.* a cool southerly wind.
Feetono, *s.* a cuttle fish, remarkable for being tough—*fig.* an obstinate or an unyielding person.
Feetonotono, *s.* a tough cuttle fish.
Fêfé, *s* a pimple, or a small boil.
Fefe, *a.* crooked, bent; see *haafefe*.
Fefefefe, *a.* crooked, having many bends.
Fefeia, *v a.* to search, examine a discourse.
Fefena, *s.* a place in *Taruu* valley, and applied to the extremities of other vallies.
Fefeiu, *s.* a sort of sauce, or the vessel that holds it.
Fefetu, *v. a.* to roll, or fold up cloth.
—*s.* a fold of cloth.
Fefeu, *v. a.* to open, spread out, see *héheu*.
Fei, *s* the mountain plantain, of which there are many species, each of which has a distinct name.
Feia, *s.* people, party, company.

Feiai, *s.* some prayers or ceremonies accompanying a sacrifice in the *marae*.
—*v. a.* to perform certain ceremonies accompanied with prayers.
Feifeiapo, *s.* dreams or visions in the night.
Feii, *s.* envy, jealousy.
—*v. n.* to envy, grudge, be jealous.
—*a.* envious, jealous.
Feiuro, *v. a.* to prolong or lengthen out, as in doing work; to lengthen out a speech, or prayer.
Feirâ, *s.* a sail looming from a distance.
Feira, *v. a.* to examine, search diligently.
Feitara o te mao, *s.* one of the sea gods of Tahiti.
Feiutu, *a.* restless, as children.
Feiutu, *a.* envious, biting each other, as dogs.
—*v. a.* to bite each other, as envious dogs.
Fenae, *s.* the time towards morning; see *fanae*.
Fenafena, *a.* not sufficiently cooked. [see *fati*.
Fene, *s.* a breach, fracture;
—*v. n.* to break, as a stick; to dash, as the waves of the sea; to break up, as a company.
Fene, *a.* six in counting; see *ono*.
Fenefene, *a.* bruised, broken in several places, or at different times. [tude.
Fenefenea, *s.* weariness, lassi-
Feneî, *s.* the foulness of a vessel, house, &c.
—*a.* full, quite full.
Fenia, *s* a tree, the bark of which is used in dying.
Fenofeno, *a.* not sufficiently cooked.
Fenuû, *s.* the strand of a rope; the twisted cord of a net.
—*v. a.* to twist cords for net making.
Fenua, *s.* [Malay, *benua;* other dialects of the Polynesian, *enua*, *wenua*, *honua*, and *vanua*,] land, country; the earth.
Fenû motu, *s.* a broken strand, or twisted cord—*fig.* a forsaking friend; the remainder or relict of a family.
Feo, *s.* a species of coral that irritates the skin when touched.
Feo, *a.* irregular, as the surface of stony land; rough, as the sea; acrid, as the *ahifa* coral.
Feofeo, *a.* much, abundant, great in quantity.
Feori, *v. n.* to forsake or change their haunt, as fish do in certain seasons; to wander, as an idle person.
—*s.* a rambler, a person of changeable habits.
Feoro, *v. a.* to investigate or examine a discourse.
Fera, *a.* indistinct, as the vision of a sleepy or intoxicated person; wry, as the eye by disease.
Ferafera, *v. a.* to remove wrinkles from cloth.
Feraorao, *s.* the break of day; the time when there is light enough to see flies flying.
Fefei, *s.* an indecent mode of exhibiting the person in a Tahitian dance, applied to both sexes.
—*v. a.* to exhibit, disclose, unfold.

Feri, *s.* a sort of *poe* or pudding made of various ingredients.

Fero, *v a.* to lace up, tie, or fasten with sinnet.

Feruri, *v. n.* to ponder, reason, muse, consult.

Feruri, *s* a cogitator, cogitation; a judge..

Feruriruri, *v. n.* to think, reason repeatedly, examine in the mind, and judge.

Fetafetau, *v a.* to quarrel, or combat in pairs.

Fetau, *v. a.* to wrestle, or combat, as two cocks.

Fetee, *v.n.* to burst out, through pressure, as the contents of a bag.

Feteetee, *v. n* to burst out repeatedly, as the contents of a bag or wrapper.

Fetia, *s* a star; seee *fetu.*

Fetia ave, *s.* a star with a train, a comet.

Fetiapoipoi, *s.* the morning star, commonly Venus, sometimes Jupiter.

Fetiaura, *s.* the red star, the planet Mars

Fetia taiao, *s.* the morning star.

Fetii, *s.* a family; the relations of a person.

Fetii, *v. a.* to tie or bind.

—*s.* a binding or knot.

Fetiitii, *v. a.* to bind or tie several things together.

Fetiti, *v. n.* to gush or burst out through pressure.

Fetofeto, *s.* the motions of anger in the mind.

—*v. n.* to feel passion and rage rising in the mind; to be disturbed by angry feeling.

Fetoitoi, *v. n.* to rage, as the waves of the sea when agitated by strong wind; to be agitated by the risings of anger.

Fetu, *s.* [*etu, wetu,*] a star; see *fetia*

Fetuave, *s* a comet.

Fetu, *v. a.* to roll, or fold up; see *tufetu.*

Fetua, *v. n.* to roll in succession, as the waves of the sea.

Fetuaruru, *v. a.* a war term, implying to act with union and strength, like persons making up a *ruru* or bale of folded cloth. a figurative expression.

Fetue, *s.* the star fish.

Fetue, *a.* exhausted, as land which has been often planted.

Fetufetu, *v. n* to roll one upon another, applied to the waves of the sea.

Fetufetuaruru, *v. a.* a technical war term, implying to act with union, as the pieces of cloth are united in a *ruru.*

Fetufeturuni, *v. a* a term of like import with *fetufetuaruru.*

Fetui, *s.* the time about midnight.

Fetui, *v. a.* to string together, as beads.

Fetuna, *v. n.* to be agitated, or moved, applied to the sea, or to the mind.

Feturanunui, *s.* a hero, or great warrior.

Fetu verovero, *s.* a twinkling star—*fig.* a lover of war.

Feu, *v. n.* to growl, as a dog; snarl, grumble.

—*v. n.* to snort, breathe short through the nose.

Feufeu, *a.* growling, surly, unfriendly.

Feufeu, *v n.* to snort repeatedly.

Feufeu, *v. a.* to shake a garment, table cloth, &c.

Feui, *v. n.* to consider, seek by calling to remembrance.

Feume, *s* envy, malice, settled hatred between persons; see *feii.*

Feure, *v. n.* to rekindle, as fire that was nearly extinct; to appear, as the red streaks in the morning sky; to be renewed in remembrance.

Feuraura, *s.* the red streaks of the morning sky; also a company of men coming in succession.

Feuti, *v. n.* to bear ill-will to a person.

Feutu, *v. n.* to be ill disposed or envious towards a neighbour.

Fifi, *a.* entangled, enslaved; intricate.

—*v. n.* to be involved in difficulties.

Fifi, *s.* a chain; also intricacy.

Fifififi, *a.* full of intricacies or entanglements.

Fifihoi, *s.* the vine of the plant *hoi.*

Fifiu, *a.* wild, shy, applied to an animal.

Firi, *v. a.* to plait, as sinnet, human hair, &c.

Firia, *s.* the name of a Tahitian month.

Firia, *s.* a sentence or agreement between different parties.

Firifiriaufau, *v. a.* to trace a person's ancestry.

Fitii, *s.* a family, relations of a person.

Fiu, *a.* tired, glutted with food; wearied.

Fumua, *s.* the fore fins of a turtle; see *humua.*

Fumuri, *s.* the fore fins of a turtle; see *humuri.*

H

THIS Letter or aspirate is of frequent use in Tahitian, though discarded entirely in some dialects of the Polynesian, and they substitute the *f* for it; but in Tahitian the *f* and *h* are interchangeable in many words, and particularly so in the causal prefixes *faa* and *haa.*

Ha, *s.* a prayer or incantation formerly used for the healing of a person poisoned by eating certain fishes, or of a person that was choked by eating fish bones.

Haa, *s.* a dwarf.

Haa, *s.* [*hanga, anga, hana,*] work of any kind.

Haa, *a prefix,* [*haka, faka, aka, waka, hoo,*] to verbs, nouns, and adjectives, by means of which they are generally turned into active verbs; see *faa.* In many instances *faa* and *haa* are used indiscriminately; in others it is customary to use one of them, as in *faaamu, faaora, faaani, &c.,* and not *haaamu, &c.;* and again *haamanao, haamehara, &c.,* and not *faamanao* In some few instances, the prefix *ta* is employed for the same purpose, as in *tahinu, tahana, taati, &c.*

Haa, *v. a.* to work, or operate any way; but lately both noun and verb have been most commonly applied to cloth making by the women, see *ohipa.*

Haaaruaru, *a.* infirm, not solid, applied to any soft pliant substance that is slippery or slimy.

Haaava, *s.* a species of bamboo.

Haaava, *s.* a good and suitable arrow for the bow; an old resident; a wise man.

Haae, *s.* the saliva from the mouth.

Haaeae, *a.* fullness, shortness of breath in consequence of eating too much.

Haaeae, *s.* the gasping of a person near death.

Haeho, *v. n.* to be in pain, on account of over-loading the stomach.

Haafao, *v. a.* to oppress.

Haafarara, *v. a.* to put a thing in a slanting direction; see *farara.*

Haafare, *v. a.* to house, to procure a house; to work at a house; see *haa.*

Haafarerei, *v. a.* to cause persons to meet together.

Haafata, *v. a.* to put up a scaffold, or a place to hang up baskets of food.

Haafatata, *v. n* to approach, draw near.

Haafefe, *v. a* to bend, to cause a curvature.

Haafetoitoi, *v. n.* to toss and work, as a rough sea.

Haafifi, *v a.* to ensnare, entangle; to involve or perplex a subject that was clear and easy before.

Haahaa, *s.* lowness, humility.

—*a.* low, humble.

Haahaha, *v a.* to turn a run of water into another channel.

Haahano, *s.* the departure of the god, or his forsaking the *taura* or pretended prophet.

Haahapa, *v. a.* to condemn; see *faahapa.*

Haahara, *v. a.* to give offence, cause an offence.

Haai, *v. n* to sleep with the face upwards, and the arms spread; to come, as a supposed ghost.

Haaî, *v. a.* to fill; see *î* and *faaî.*

Haaivi, *v. n.* to pretend to be a widow.

Haainâ, *s* shame, remorse.

—*v. n.* to be ashamed.

—*a.* shameful, indecent.

Haamaa, *v. a.* to get food, to take food; see *tamaa.*

Haamaamaa, *v. a.* to make one to appear foolish.

—*v. n.* to act the fool; to appear foolish.

Haamaau, *v. a.* to cause a blemish, to mar.

Haamaau, *v. n.* to be bashful in asking.

Haamaea, *v. n.* to be cross, peevish, as a child.

Haamaehe, *v. a.* to dry, or cause a thing to dry.

Haamaha, *v. a.* to appease; to pacify anger; to allay thirst or anger; see *maha.*

Haamahealiea, *v. a.* to cause fading; to make ashamed; see *mahеahea.*

Haamaheaitu, *v. a.* to cause offence; to cause trouble of mind; see *maheaitu.*

Haamahiti, *v. a.* to make mention of a thing; to start a subject

Haamahiti, *s* the person who begins or starts a subject; *see mahiti.*

Haamahitihiti, *v. a.* to start or mention a subject repeatedly, or in parts.

Haamahora, *v. a.* to open or expand a thing; to put up a neat fence in the front of a house, enclosing a court.

Haamahorahora, *v a* to open repeatedly and spread out; to open and explain a sub ject; see *mahora.*

Haamahu, *s.* patience, forbearance.

—*v. n.* to bear, sustain, endure.

Haamahue, *v. a.* to cause a thing to be developed or divulged; see *mahue.*

Haamahue, *v. a.* to heap up property, or things placed in a receptacle, such as a chest, so that it cannot be shut.

Haamahui, *v. a.* to develope, or bring a thing to light that was not known.

Haamahuta, *v. a.* to cause something to start, leap, or fly; see *mahuta.*

Haamaineine, *v a.* to tickle by gentle touching

Haamairi, *v. a.* to drop, let fall, leave behind

Haamaitai, *v. a* to make good, also to praise, laud, glorify; see *faamaitai.*

Haamama, *v. a.* to open the mouth, to gape; to be open, as a grave, or any hole.

—*s* the open or gaping state of any thing.

Haamàmâ, *v a.* to cause a thing to be light, or less heavy; to treat any thing or subject. slightly, with indifference, and without force.

Haamamae, *v. a.* to inflict pain.

Haamamu, *v. a.* to blunt, or turn the edge of a tool; to rebut an argument or charge, so as to cause it to return upon the person that brought it.

Haamana, *v. a.* to empower, make powerful, bestow authority or power; see *mana.*

—*s* he that gives authority or power to another.

Haamanao, *v. n.* to think, remember, or call to mind some thing known before.

Haamanaonao, *v. a.* to alarm, cause anxiety.

—*s.* work that causes anxiety.

Haamanii, *v. a.* to spill, or shed, as any liquid, or other things.

Haamanina, *v. a.* to make level or smooth; to soothe or assuage.

Haamanino, *v. a.* to cause calmness of the sea, or of the mind.

—*v. n.* to become calm, by the wind and sea decreasing.

Haamanua, *v n.* to put on consequence, by holding back, and not shewing promptness.

Haamaoro, *v. a.* to lengthen; to cause delay.

Haamarari, *v. a.* to clear a piece of ground, either by removing what grows upon it, or by treading down

—*v. n.* to disperse, as a company.

Haamarirau, *a.* slow, inactive, indolent.

Haamaruhi, *v. a.* to make soft, easy, pliable; to soften down asperity, to moderate; to induce an obstinate person to reason and moderation.

Haamata, *v. a.* to commence any thing.

Haamatara, *v. a.* to untie, set at liberty.
Haamataratara, *v. a.* to set free, untie repeatedly; also to slacken or loosen without untying. [accustom.
Haamataro, *v. a.* to inure or
Haamatarotaro, *v. a.* to accustom repeatedly, or by degrees.
Haamatau, *v. a.* the old word for to accustom.
Haamatau, *v. a.* to threaten, alarm, put in fear.
Haamatautau, *v. a.* to cause fear, by threatening, or repeated alarm.
Haamate, *v. a.* to cause death; see *mate;* to kill, cause illness; also to feign illness.
Haamatea, *v. n.* to be disappointed in food expected.
Haamati, *v. a.* to use the *mati* berries in dying scarlet.
Haamatia, *v. a.* to promote the growth of plants; to promote health.
Haamatie, *v. a.* to promote growth, as *haamatia.*
Haamau, *v. a.* to establish, or fix a thing.
Haamâua, *v. a.* to waste, spend without profit.
Haamaua, *v. a.* to call another ignorant.
—*v. n.* to put on, or pretend ignorance.
Haamaue, *v. a.* to cause to fly.
Haamauiui, *v. a.* to inflict, or cause pain.
Haamaumau, *v. a.* to hold, continue to hold; to impress repeatedly, and by degrees, any subject on the mind; see *tamaumau.*
—*v. a.* to make fast in a temporary manner.
Haamaumau orero, *v. a.* to repeat old grievances, or prevent them from being forgotten; to fix, or give a temporary permanence to a report.
Haamauruuru, *v. a.* to give pleasure or satisfaction.
Haamehara, *v. n.* to remember, recollect.
Haamene, *v. a.* to give rotundity to a thing.
Haamenemene, *v. a.* to repeat the action of making a thing round.
Haamere, *v. a.* to undervalue the goodness of a thing in buying.
Haameremere, *v. a.* to undervalue repeatedly.
Haamio, *v. a.* to make a thing wrinkled.
Haamiomio, *v. a.* to cause a thing to have many wrinkles, or to be often wrinkled.
Haamitioo, *v. a.* to search thoroughly, and with perseverance.
Haamoa, *v. a.* to make sacred; see *moa.*
Haamoamoa, *v. a.* to observe the former customs as to sacred places and persons, restrictions regarding food, &c.
Haamoahua, *s.* the companion or friend of the *Oromatua.*
Haamoe, *v. a.* to lose, forget; see *moe.*
Haamoeapaapa, *s.* a fixed, persevering desire.
Haamoemoe, *v. a.* to make lonesome.
—*v. n.* to yield one's self to lonesomeness.
Haamomomo, *v. a.* to break a thing to shivers.
Haamomomomo, *v. a.* to break

repeatedly any brittle thing to shivers.

Haamomoua, *v. a.* to be careful of one's property.

Haamono, *v. a.* to stop a gap; to fill a vacuity; to stop a running fluid.

Haamore, *v. a.* to make one bare, destitue, without ornament or support.

Haamore, *v. a.* to make any one ashamed by degrading him in the presence of others, stripping him of his clothes or ornaments, depriving him of property or office.

Haamoremore, *v. a.* the repetition of the act, or to *haamore* repeatedly.

Haamori, *s.* the worship of a Deity.

—*v. a.* to worship a Deity, to perform religious services; see *pure.*

Haamou, *v. a.* to consume, annihilate, extirpate.

Haamû, *v. a.* to pelt, throw a stone—*fig.* to throw out a hasty charge against another.

Haamure, *v. a.* to shorten, cut short.

Haamute, *v. a.* same as *haamure.*

Haana, *s.* certain garments of priests or warriors; armour of a warrior.

Haaoruoru, *a.* slimy, slippery.

Haapa, *v. a.* to begin an attack, to seize a person.

Haapa, *v. a.* to use a certain ceremony in taking an office from another; to send up a *pauma* or paper kite.

Haapaa, *s.* a sort of dark native cloth.

—*v. a.* to dye the cloth called *haapaa.*

Haapaaavae, *s.* a certain ceremony.

Haapaari, *v. a* to make mature, or wise; to put a restriction on fruit, &c.

Haapaau, *v. a.* to wear or produce the coarse cloth called *paau.*

Haapae, *v. a.* to put off, lay aside; to divorce.

Haapahi, *v. a.* to vex, harrass, or weary a person.

—*v. n.* to be peevish, as a child.

Haapahu, *v. a.* to stop, or dam up, applied to water; to retain, or keep back what ought to be spoken.

Haapahure, *s.* a person who provokes one he is not able to overcome.

Haapai, *v. a* to wet the stone pestle used in preparing some sorts of food.

Haapai, *v. n.* to be active and bold; to go aside.

Haapaia, *v. a.* to smooth, as in finishing some kinds of work; to make slippery, applied to a road.

—*v. a.* to deceive by flattering words.

Haapaia, *v. a.* to make up, or finish a meal; to satiate with food; see *paia.*

Haapaipai, *v. n.* to go from place to place.

—*v. a.* to remove things to different places.

Haapao, *v. a.* to regard, notice, take heed, obey.

Haapao atâ, *a.* heedless, regardless, disobedient.

Haapao ohie, *a.* the opposite to *haapao atâ,* viz.;—heedful, obedient, ready to regard or notice.

—*s.* obedience; see *faaroo.*

Haapaopao, *v. a.* to mark repeatedly; much used in a bad sense, viz. to mark for revenge.

Haapaopao, *v. a.* to make brownish or dark, a term used by those who dye the native cloth.

Haapao raa, *s* a direction, rule, copy, mark.

Haapao taiata, *a.* regardless; the same as *haapao atâ.*

—*s.* this modern word seems to be understood in a more extensive sense than the old word *haapao atâ*, the noun generally signifying a person given to all kinds of vices and evil doings.

Haapaoto, *v. a.* to provoke to anger by laughing, &c.

Haapâpâ, *s.* a ceremony by which a restriction is removed; see *rahui.*

Haapapa, *v. a.* to pile one thing upon another; to relate and give an orderly account of facts.

—*v. n.* to stay, waiting for a person.

Haapapû, *v. a.* to make level or flat; to make a complete, thorough work of any thing.

Haapara, *v. a.* to cause fruit to ripen; see *para.*

Haaparahurahu, *v. a* to widen or make broad

Haapararî, *v. a.* to break, or cause to break, such as potter's vessels; see *pararí.*

Haapatiitii, *v. a.* to make flat, or level.

—*s.* an instrument that makes flat, such as a mangle.

Haapau, *v. a.* to consume, devour, exhaust; to cause any thing to be consumed.

Haapaupau, *v. a.* to mock, treat with ridicule. [*ipaupau.*

—*s.* one that insults, see *faa-*

Haapê, *v a.* to cause mellowness or ripeness of fruit, such as the banana; to cause rottenness.

Haapea, *v. n.* to be joining together, applied to the ends of rafters.

Haapeapea, *v. a.* to trouble, harrass, perplex

Haapee, *v. a.* to make a thing to ascend.

Haapee, *s* a sort of long basket; see *haapora.*

Haapee, *v. a.* to sacrifice, put a sacrifice of hogs, fish, fowls, &c., on the altar.

Haapeepee, *v. n.* to be expeditious, to hasten

—*v. a* to make another to be nimble; to cause haste.

Haapehao, *v. n.* to turn a little aside, as a canoe or boat.

Haapeti, *v. n.* to be sparing in eating, as when a person is preparing to go to sea.

Haapetipeti, *v. n.* to eat sparingly.

—*v. a.* to do a thing partially.

Haapi, *v. a.* to feed, with a view to good appearance; see *haapori.*

Haapihaa, *v. a.* to make to boil, or to bubble up

Hapihaa, *v. a.* to rinse or cleanse in water.

Haapihae, *v. a.* to tear or cause a rent.

Haapihae, *v. a.* to cause vomiting.

Haapihee, *v. a* to cause purging.

Haapii, *v. a.* to teach or instruct; to learn

—*s* a teacher or instructor.

Haapii aaoa, *s.* a young cock just beginning to crow

Haapii parau, *s* a term formerly used for such as embraced Christianity; a disciple, a learner.

Haapiipii, *v. a.* to deride one's person; to undervalue a thing.

Haapii ture, *s.* a lawyer, a teacher ef law.

Haapio, *v a.* to make crooked; see *pio.*

Haapiopio, *v. a.* to make crooked repeatedly, or in many places.

—*s.* one who makes crooked, or difficult what was not so before.

Haapipi, *v. a.* to make a disciple.

Haapitaataa, *v. a.* to separate the kernel from the shell of a nut.

Haapiti, *s.* the north-east wind; see *faarua.*

Haapito, *v. a.* to degrade, undervalue a thing.

Haapitopito, *v. a.* to undervalue repeatedly.

Haapitumu, *s.* a species of the plantain—*fig.* an idle fellow, who is useless.

Haapoi, *v. a.* to join one piece of timber to another; see *poi.*

—*v. a.* to put a covering on a thing.

Haapopo, *v. a* to lessen one's self, or endeavour to take as little room as possible.

Haapoopoo, *v. a.* to make deep, applied to a pit.

Haapopôu, *v. a.* to admire, make much of a thing or person; to have much delight in another.

—*s* one that makes much of a person, or of a thing.

Haapora, *s.* a sort of a long basket.

Haaporahau, *s.* a promoter of peace.

Haapori, *v. a.* to make fat and delicate, by eating and keeping out of the sun; see *pori.*

Haaporia, *v. a.* to make fat, see *poria.*

Haapororı, *v. n.* to fast; see *pororı.*

Haaporutu, *v. n.* to stun by loud speaking.

Haapou, *v. a.* to cause a person to descend.

Haapou, *v. a.* to set up posts for a house or fence.

Haapu, *v. n.* to take refuge; to go from place to place for the sake of health.

Haapua, *s.* a place built to decoy fish

Haapuahaha, *v. a.* to make a bundle or bale of cloth to appear larger; see *puahaha.*

Haapuai, *v. n.* to put out from the mouth.

Haapuai, *v. a.* to exert or put forth strength.

Haapuaiai, *v. a.* to cause a current of air.

—*s.* that which causes a current of air, or refreshment by air.

Haapupu, *v. a.* to class, make into parties.

Haapûpû, *v. a.* to cause to pierce through.

—*s.* that which causes to go through.

Haapue, *v. a.* to keep together, to gather together.

Haapuêa, *v. n.* to go for health or safety.

Haapuhaha, *v. a.* to make a deceptive bale of cloth.

Haapuo, *s.* a basket used for catching small fish.

Haapuoho, *v. n.* to appear, just come in sight.

Haapuora, *v. n.* to go in quest of health or safety.

Haapura, *v. a.* to make sparks to fly.

Haapuraa, *s.* a refuge, a place of safety.

Haapurara, *s.* a disperser, one that scatters abroad.

—*v a.* to scatter, spread abroad; see *faapurara* and *purara.*

Haapurupuru, *v. a.* to attend and minister to a person.

Haaputa, *v. a.* to pierce, make an aperture.

Haaputaputa, *v. a.* to make many holes, pierce repeatedly.

Haaputè, *v. a.* to use a bag, make a pocket.

Haaputii, *v. a.* to put the hair in tufts.

Haaputu, *v. a.* to collect, gather together.

Haaputu, *s.* the name of a fish that is often poisonous.

Haaputuputu, *v. a* to gather or collect repeatedly; to collect in a body close together.

Haapututairua, *v. a.* to gather in pairs.

Haapuu, *v. a.* to make a hump; cause to swell out.

Haarari, *v. a.* to wet clothes, or any thing that belongs to another.

—*v. n.* to be in the rain or wet.

Haari, *s.* a general name for the cocoa tree and fruit, in all the varieties; see *niu.*

Haaro, *v. a.* to scoop, to lade; see *paaro.*

—*s.* a scoop, or ladle.

Haaruroruro, *v. a.* to take different parts in a Tahitian song.

Haatiapiti, *s.* two winds blowing from opposite quarters.

Haatitiaihaio, *v. a.* to make straight.

Haatitiharotia, *v. a.* to make straight, or upright.

Haatororiro, *v. n.* to humble one's self.

Haatumu, *v. a.* to lay a foundation; see *faatumu.*

Haatupu, *v. a.* to cause growth, promote increase.

Haatupua, *v. n.* to be silent, grave, serious.

Haatupua, *s.* an enchanter, one whose skill is supposed to save him from the power of sorcery; see *faatupua.*

Haaturama, *v. a.* to get torches for fishing, &c.

Haaturuma, *v. n.* to be silent, sad, or serious.

Haaupeupe, *v. a.* to do a thing slovenly.

Haaupoupo, *v. a.* to act carelessly and slovenly.

Haaututea, *s.* a lazy, worthless person.

Haavâ, *s.* a judge.

—*v. a.* to examine the ground of a charge; to pass a judicial sentence.

Haavaa, *v. a.* to use, or procure a canoe.

Haavahavaha, *v. a.* to cause a person or thing to be despised or undervalued.

Haavai, *v. n.* to decline from former vigour or usefulness.

Haavaovao, *v. n.* to make one's self light; to tread lightly.

Haavâ raa, *s.* a judgment seat; the judgment place or time.

Haavare, *s.* a lie, deception, falsehood of any kind.

—*v. n.* to lie, deceive, impose.

—*a.* lying, false, deceitful.

Haavarevare, *v. n.* to lie or deceive repeatedly.

Haavarevare, *a.* ropy, or viscous, as fruit.

Haavari, *s.* a sort of food consisting of hog's blood and fat baked together.

Haavari, *v. a.* to soil with mire or dirt.

Haavaro, *v. n.* to sit or remain in one's own place.

—*s.* a loop.

Haavauvau, *v. a.* to procure, or cause something to be spread out for other things to be spread or placed on it.

Haavavao, *v. a.* to cause, or procure an interposer to act between contending parties; to cause interposition.

Haaveevee, *a.* ripe, in a mature state, applied to the bread-fruit.

Haaveuveu, *v. a.* to produce disgust; see *veuveu.*

Haaveve, *v. a.* to make poor, destitute; see *veve.*

Haavevo, *v. a.* to produce a confused noise of voices.

Haavi, *v. a.* to cow, daunt, depress, subdue.

Haaviivii, *v. a.* to pollute, defile; see *viivii.*

Haavini, *v. n.* to make a smacking noise in eating.

Haavinivini, *v. n.* to repeat often the noise in eating, to which the islanders are accustomed.

Haaviri, *v. a.* to mix together two or more ingredients.

Haaviti, *v. a.* to cause a thing to be well finished.

Haavivi, *v. a.* to daunt or cow repeatedly.

Haavivo, *v. a.* to get or employ a *vivo* or the native flute; see *vivo.*

Haavivo, *v. n.* to give a turn to a discourse or subject to answer one's purpose.

Hae, *s.* jealousy; wildness of beasts.

—*v. n.* to be jealous, as men and women.

—*a.* jealous; wild, as beasts; enraged.

Hae, *interj.* an exclamation of excitement to some action, commonly some violent action, such as seizing upon a man or beast.

Hâê, *interj.* an exclamation of wonder.

Hae, *s.* saliva.

—*v. n.* to water, as the mouth of a man or beast, but most commonly applied to the saliva dropping from the mouth of a dog at the sight of food.

Hae, *s.* an imagined ghost, or the spirit of a drowned person.

Haea, *a.* torn, rent.

Haea, *s.* deceitfulness, duplicity.

Haeaea, *s.* the white, or sappy part of a tree, in distinction from *tomara,* the heart.

Haeaea, *adv.* inefficiently; *rave haeaea,* to do a thing not to the purpose.

Haeamata, *s.* an introductory invocation of a god that he might open his eyes and attend.

Haeamati, *s.* prayers and ceremonies on the first using of a new fishing net; also an offering of a human sacrifice before an intended war.

Haehae, *v. a.* to tear any thing; to break an agreement; to separate or break off, as an acquaintance.

Haeoro, *s.* a tree, the leaves of which are used for the sweet scented oil called *monoi.*

Haepiri, s. a plant, used also for the native *monoi.*

Haere, v. n. [*haele, hele, aere, here,*] to go or come, determined by the adverbs *atu, atura, mai* and *maira,* and also *ae.*

—*a* going, walking, or journeying, as *taata haere,* a walking or journeying man.

Haerea, s. walk, deportment, conversation.

Haerearii, v. n. to go by little and little.

Haereohiohio, v. n. to go as a spy, or a thief.

Haereominomino, v. n. to wander, go about.

Haereeora, s. a trance.

Haereoruirui, v. n. to go softly, as a person in fear.

Haereotaratara, v. n. to go from place to place without settling.

Haererihiti, v. n. to go by sudden starts.

Haeretia, v. n. to move or go direct to a place or thing; to go with uprightness.

Hâhâ, s. the name of a diversion or play.

Haha, s. a loud laugh.

Haha, v n. to strut, go proudly.

Haha, *adv.* obliquely, not direct.

Hahaa, a. laborious, diligent in work, as *taata hahaa,* a laborious man.

Hahaanunui, v. n. to rove about, [wander.

Hahaanunui, v. n. to imagine, or dream of the appearance of an absent person.

Hahaatea, s. a species of sea crab that is very poisonous.

Hahae, v. a. to rend or tear; see *haehae.*

Hahaere, v. n. to walk or move from place to place.

Hahaha, a. rude, unpolished.

Hahahau, v n. to turn aside; see *faahahau.*

Hahai, a. diseased, afflicted.

Hahano, a. awful, dreadful; see *hanohano.*

Hahape, a. wild, as a beast; not familiar, applied to a person.

Hahara, s an evil imprecation.

Hahara, v. a. to split or divide a thing into two equal parts, as a fish or pig divided by the back bone.

Haharavea, a. stained, polluted.

Haharavee, a. stained or polluted, as a bloody garment.

Haharavii, a. defiled with sores, &c.

Haharu, v. a. to seize repeatedly by violence.

Hahataurua, s. the remaining food of a feast.

Hahatea, s. a species of the plant *ava.*

Hahau, v. n. to go aslant, or beat in, as the rain driven by the wind into a house

Hahau, v. a. to make a search or enquiry.

Hahavai, a. arrogant, vain, pretending to courage and skill, but destitute of them.

Hahe, s. a sort of sacred cloth for the gods.

Hahe, a great in size, abundant in quantity.

Hahehahe, a. daring, fearless as a warrior.

Hahenuu, a. abundant, as food, property, &c.

Hahetu, v. a. to agree hastily to some proposal.

Hahi, v. n. to commit a mistake inadvertently.

Hahu, s. a razor, plane, scraper.

Hahu, *v. a* to shave, to plane boards, or scrape

Hahua, *s.* something that is great, such as a wo k that a person cannot complete.

Hai, *s.* a sort of plantain.

Haia, *s* a human sacrifice; also the bodies of those slain in war.

Haia, *s.* a prayer for a person poisoned with fish.

Haiarua, *s.* the slain of both parties after a battle.

Haihai, *a* small, diminutive.

Haihai, *v. a.* to bind up fast to secure.

Haihai, *v. a.* to support or sustain a person or thing.

Haii, *a.* long in coming to maturity.

Haii, *a.* cunning, well informed, hard, miserly.

Haio, *v. a.* to turn over to another's account; to charge an innocent person with that which did not belong to him.

Haio, *interj* of dislike, as be off! away with you!

Haioa, *s.* a species of plantain

Haiiiri, *a.* unsightly, ugly, filthy.

Haiviivi, *s.* toil, great labour.

Hamaau, *v. n* to go in disguise, assume a false appearance.

Hamama, *v. n* to gape or yawn; to be open, as a pit

Hamani, *v. a.* [*hanga, anga, hana,*] to do, work, operate, or make any thing.

Hamariiau, *a.* slow, indolent.

Hamiama, *s* the name of three different nights of the Tahitian moon or month.

Hamû, *v a.* to cast a stone.

Hamu, *v. a.* to go to a feast whenever one occurs.

Hamu, *a.* gluttonous; see *aehamu*

Hamumu, *v. n.* to be burdensome to others by eating their food

Hamuti, *s.* a privy; a place of dirt and rubbish.

Hana, *a.* sad, sorrowful.

Hana, *v. n.* to be stiff and affected, as the eyes by long watching, smoke, the sun, water, &c.

Hanahana, *s.* splendour, glory, awfulness. [awful.
—*a.* glorious, magnificent,

Hanahiti, *s.* a person of the *hiti* or border; one of inferior note; see *hitiapa.*

Hanana, *s* a wanderer, not a resident.

Hananu, *v. n.* flowing, or rolling on, as the sea towards the land; see *pananu.*

Hanehanea, *s.* fatigue, weariness. [*fanea.*
—*v. n.* to be weary; see *fane-*

Hania, *s.* the top, or upper covering of a thing.

Hanihani, *v. a.* to caress or fondle.

Hanihanirea, *v a.* to fondle with a design to deceive.

Hanohano, *a.* dreadful, awful.

Hao, *s.* a prayer and ceremonies formerly used at the dedication of a new house, or of a canoe.

Hao, *v. a.* to encircle, as fishermen in bringing both ends of a fishing net together.

Hao, *v. a.* to dress the hair by cutting, combing, &c.

Hao, *s.* a technical term for a certain manœuvre in war.

Haoa, *s.* a hard stone, of which formerly adzes were made.

Haoa, *s* an adze or hatchet, from the name formerly given to the stone ones.
Haoa, *s.* a stone taken from an old *marae*, to commence a new one in another place.
Haoahao, *s.* an ill grown, ill favoured person.
Haoahao, *a.* unsettled, as the wind, changing suddenly and blowing from different quarters.
Haono, *v. n* to swell up or overflow, as water
Haoaoa, *a.* rugged, full of stones.
Haora, *a.* unpleasant, applied to the smell of certain things.
Haorea, *v. n.* to be hindered, perplexed by company, &c.
—*v. n.* to be affected by some ill report, a severe reproof, or something unexpected.
Haoro, *a.* dilatory, hanging behind.
Haoromatiti, *s.* one that unexpectedly joins a party.
Hapa, *s.* a deviation from a rule; a missing of a mark; error, sin, crime; see *hara.*
Hapaa, *s.* a sort of strong native cloth
Hapahapa, *a.* irregular, crooked.
Hape, *a.* crooked, turning in, applied to the feet.
Hape, *s.* the caterpillar; see *he.*
Hape, *s.* an error, a mistake, sin; see *hapa.*
Hape, *a.* unequal, irregular, wrong.
Hapehape, *a.* wrong, unequal, irregular in many places.
Hapepa, *s.* the palsy.
Hapepa, *v n.* to heave, or move up and down, as the thatch of a Tahitian house when moved by a strong wind.
Hapepapepa, *v. n.* to move repeatedly, or flap, as a sail.
Hapi, *a.* pregnant; see *hopu.*
Hapoi, *v. a.* to carry or convey; see *hopoi.*
Hapono, *v. a* to send a thing, not a person.
Haponoпoa, *s.* the thing sent or conveyed.
Hapu, *v. n.* [*hapui,*] to be in a state of pregnancy.
—*a.* pregnant, applied to females in general.
Hara, *s.* sin, transgression, crime, guilt.
Hara, *a.* unequal, not hiting the mark; see *hapa.*
—*v. n.* to be unequal, to be deviating from a line or rule; to be in a transgression.
Harahara, *v. a.* to split in pieces, as the carcase of a fish, or of a fowl.
Haraharaini, *v. a.* to begin with little things, and proceed to greater.
Haraharau, *s.* extreme loquacity; also the doctrine and customs of the *mamaia*, a religious sect.
—*a.* loquacious. talking idly.
Haraharavea, *a.* defiled, polluted with blood.
Haraharavee, *a.* besmeared, polluted.
Haraini, *adv.* slightly, loosely, carelessly.
Haratavai, *s* a species of bamboo that is remarkably sharp when split
Haratô, *a.* acrid, exciting pain.
Haraurau, *s.* a sort of wild *taro* or *ape*,—*fig.* a worthless fellow.
Haro, *v. a.* to smooth back the hair; to pull the *raoere* or

leaves tied together to catch fish; see *raoere*.

Haro, *v. n.* to skim along in flying, and wheel about, as a bird.

Haro, *v. a.* to print, or spread the scarlet dye on the Tahitian cloth called *ahu haro*.

Haro, *s.* the name of a certain mark printed on the skin in tattooing.

Haroa, *s.* a draught of fishes, what is caught in drawing a fishing net.

Haroa, *s.* one side or party.

Haroaroa, *v. n* to discern, perceive by the eye or the mind.

—*a.* distant, deep.

Harotea, *s.* a certain mark of the *arioi* in tattooing.

Haru, *v. a* to rob; seize by violence; to catch.

—*s.* a robber; one that seizes by violence.

Haruapo, *s.* a party of warriors that lie in wait till night, and when their enemies are asleep fall on them.

Haruapu, *v a.* to rush on all together to seize or catch a thing.

Haruharu, *v. a.* to seize repeatedly.

Harura, *s.* a person of an intelligent mind.

Haruru, *s* sound; noise, as of the sea, thunder, &c.

—*v. n.* to make a roaring or a thundering noise, applied to various things.

Hatatu, *v. n.* to be moving or shaking, as a slender plank when held by the middle.

Hatiapiti, *a.* abundant, plenteous; see *hatupiti*.

Hatuma, *s.* abundance, plenty.

—*a.* abundant, in large quantities.

Hatumatuma, *a.* abundant large.

Hatupiti, *a.* of great bulk, much, plenty.

Hau, *s* the dew that falls at night.

Hau, *s.* peace, government, reign.

Hau, *a.* more, or beyond, in comparing adjectives, greater, larger, longer, &c.

Haua, *s.* scent of any kind.

—*v. n.* to emit an effluvia, good or bad.

Hauarii, *s.* a kingly government.

Hauato, *s.* an instrument used in thatching.

Hauhau, *v. a.* to take off the first chips in hollowing a tree.

Haumanahune, *s.* a government of the common people; a democracy.

Haumanava, *s* an early batch of food; a great feast previous to an exploit.

Haumani, *s.* weariness, fatigue, listlessness.

—*a.* weary, tiresome.

Haumaraatira, *s.* the state of a people living as tenants or tributaries.

Haumarù, *a.* cooling, grateful, refreshing.

Haumateata, *s.* a government in the hand of a chief by blood, or hereditary descent.

Haumatatia, *s.* the same as *haumaraatira*.

Haumoe, *s* the cold night breezes of the vallies.

Haune, *v. a.* to plait, as baskets, mats, &c.

Hauou, *s.* the same as the *purau* tree.

Haupà, *s.* a tree tough and hard.

Haupape, *s.* a house with square ends.

Hauparu, *s.* same as *haupape.*
—*a* having square ends, applied to a house.

Haupau, *v. a.* to toil, to work hard.

Hauparuparu, *v. a* to attend upon and minister to a person

Hauraa, *s* the sword fish.

Hauri, *a.* ill smelled, as some kinds of fish.

Hauriria, *v. n.* to be in fear or dread.

Hauriuri, *a.* deep, unfathomable, as the sea.

Hauruo, *a.* faded, decayed, as a person in ill health.

Hautai, *s.* weeping, lamentation for the dead.

Hautaua, *v. n.* to grieve for a relation or friend.

Hauti, *v. a.* to annoy, disturb by restless doings.
—*a.* restless, annoying, disturbing.

Hautia, *s* the same as *hauparu.*

Hautiuti, *v. n.* to be moving.

Hautiuti, *v. a.* to cause disturbance by repeated motions.

Hautua, *s.* great work, much toil.

Hava, *v. n.* to be dirtied, befouled.
—*a* dirty, filthy, defiled.

Havaeimatapê, *s.* an ugly kind of the star fish; an idle person.

Havahava, *a.* dirty, filthy; having been repeatedly befouled, as an infant.

He, *s.* an error or mistake; see *hape.*
—*a.* wrong, erroneous, mistaken.

He, *s.* a caterpillar; see *hape.*

Hea, *v. n.* to grieve for the dead, to lament for the dead, using various ceremonies.

Hea, *s* a disease of children, the same as the thrush, but *hea* is vaguely used of various inward disorders, but these are sometimes distinguished by the terms *hea tapu, hea roto, hea maeô, hea pitoôo.*

Hea, *adv.* of time and place, with various prefixes, as *ahea?* when? *nahea?* whence? by which way? or in what manner? *eihea?* where? *teihea?* at what place? *nohea?* from whence? or whence?

Heamaeô, *s* some internal disease, causing a person to loathe his food, or to eat improper things.

Heamaterahe, *s.* sickness produced by love.

Heaoromatua, *s.* sickness caused by an *Oromatua*, that is the supposed spirit of some dead relation.

Heapaa, *s.* sickness causing a red swelling of the skin.

Heapaipai, *s* same as *heapaa.*

Heapitoôo, *s.* a disease causing an enlargement of the navel of children.

Hearoto, *s* nearly the same as *heamaeô.*

Heatapu, *s* a disease affecting the skin, and causing small pustules to break out.

Heatauete, *s* a disease affecting the blood and humours, turning the skin yellow; the jaundice.

Heatopara, *s.* see *hearoto* and *heamaeô.*

Hebedoma, *s* [Gr. *hebdomas*,] a week.
Hee, *s.* a certain skin mark in tattooing.
Hee, *v. a.* to purge or evacuate the body; see *tahee.*
Hee, *v. n.* to be swimming in the surf, a Tahitian diversion; see *faahee* and *horue.*
Hee, *v. n* to be in a discharged or banished condition, as one turned out of his place; see *faahee.*
Hee, *interj.* of surprise, as *ahe! uhu!*
Heeauru, *v n.* to swim on the top of a rolling sea.
Heepue, *v n.* to sail before the wind; to run or flee before an enemy who is chasing.
Heepuenui, *v. n.* to set without a cloud, applied to the sun.
Heetumu, *v. a.* to agree upon, settle some affair.
Heetumu, *v. n.* to keep well at home.
Heeuri, *v. n.* to be in a green flourishing condition, as plants and trees, to flourish, as a country.
Hefa, *v. n.* to squint.
—*a.* squint; oblique, as the look of the eyes.
Hefahefa, *a.* dim; confused, as the eyes by the brightness of the sun.
Hehe, *a* shy, alienated, strange
Hehê, *v. n* to laugh by way of contempt.
Hehe, *v. n.* to cut the yam in slices, in order to plant the pieces.
Hehei, *s.* a mode of fishing.
Hehemi, *s.* a loud laugh.
Hehemi, *v. n.* to laugh in a loud manner.
Heheu, *v a.* to open, uncover; see *maheu.*
Hei, *s.* a wreath or garland of flowers.
Hei, *v. a.* to entangle and catch fish in a net.
—*v. n.* to be in a state of entanglement, as fish in a net.
Heihei, *v. a.* to entangle repeatedly.
Heihei, *s.* a garland of flowers.
Heiheia, *s.* some unexpected good.
Heima, *s* [Gr. *cheima*,] winter.
Heioa, *a.* black all over; variegated.
Heiomii, *v. a* to have the heads, or chiefs caught and destroyed, as in war.
Heiomii, *v n.* to be entangled, as fish by the heads.
Heipue, *a.* gathered, congregated, as people.
Heipuni, *v. n.* to be surrounded, entangled, or beset on every side; to be in the midst of difficulties.
Heitutu, *v. n.* to be beset with affairs, difficulties, &c.
Heiva, *s.* a dance, an assembly for dancing.
Hema, *v. n* to be deceived, imposed upon
Hemahema, *s.* the little fish called the nautilus.
Hemo, *v. n.* to be out-done in a contest; to slip off, as the handle of a tool; see *faahemo.*
Henehenea, *v. n.* to be heavy, weary, drowsy.
Hepo, *v n.* to be in confusion.
Hepohepo, *v. n* to be confounded, or in confusion, not knowing well what to do.
Here, *s.* a string, noose, or snare.

Here, *s.* a sort of food.
Here, *v. a.* to ensnare, entrap, or catch by a *lure.*
Here, *s.* a favourite, a beloved one.
—*a.* dear, beloved, favoured.
Herepoto, *s* an instant attack
Heretau, *s.* a rope or string for suspending things at some height.
Heretê, *interj.* an exclamation of the *arioi* and other dancers.
Hereti, *s.* some part of a ceremony used by the sorcerers.
Heri, *s.* a rope tied to the foot of a pig, fowl, &c.
—*v. a.* to tie a pig, bird, or fowl, by a string
Heri, *v. a.* to dig a hole, as a rat or a crab does.
Heru, *v. a.* to scratch, as a hen does.
Heruheru, *v. a* to scratch repeatedly, as a fowl; to rake up old grievances; see *paheru.*
Hetaheta, *v. n.* to be enraged by some provocation.
Hete, *s.* likeness; see *huru.*
Hetehete, *s.* hair, wool, feathers; see *hui uhuru.*
Hetoheto, *v. n.* to be disturbed by angry feelings.
Hetuhetu, *v. n.* to roll, as the waves on the shore; see *fetufetu.*
Heu, *v. a.* to throw off, as an infant its covering.
Heuheu, *v. a.* to throw off clothes repeatedly; to shake out; see *peupeu.*
Heva, *s.* mourning for the dead; the name of a foolish custom, see *parae*; a mourning dress.
Hevaheva, *s.* a person not himself through violent passion.
Hevatama, *s.* mourning for children.
Heve, *a.* acrid, leaving a painful heat.
Hì, *v. a.* to fish, to angle with hook and line.
—*v. n* to gush out, as water or any liquid,
—*s.* a flux, the bloody flux; see *toto ohí.*
Hia, *an affix* to verbs, denoting the passive form, as *hinaaro,* to love, *hinaarohia,* loved.
Hia, *s.* [*hinga, hina,*] a fall.
Hia, *v. n.* to fall, as a person or a tree that was standing; not to drop down from a height, for that *mairi* and *topa* are used.
Hia, *v. a.* to use friction to procure fire.
Hiaa, *s.* a quantity of fish caught at a time.
Hiaa, *v. n.* to be sunk deep in the water.
Hiaa, *v. a.* to steal, as thieves formerly used to do, after addressing a prayer to *Hiro* the god of thieves for success.
Hiaai, *v. n.* to desire food or drink; to long for something to eat or drink.
Hiaata, *a* perplexing.
Hiafaifai, *v. n.* to be desolate, having the inhabitants exterminated by war.
Hiai, *s.* extreme venery.
Hiaia, *s.* the name of a Tahitian month.
Hiamateoa, *v. n.* to exult, rejoice; see *oaoa.*
Hiamaea, *s.* a certain idolatrous ceremony observed in time of war; valuable property was collected and placed some where between the two

armies, and whatever party seized it, it was an evil omen to itself.

Hiamu, v. n. to have an appetite, or to long for food or drink; see *hiaai*.

Hiaoa, s. a malicious or spiteful rejoicing.

—v. n. to rejoice in another's distress.

Hiaoto, v. n. to be troubled by importunities.

Hiaou, v. n. to be teazed or perplexed.

Hiata, s. the branches, stalks, and leaves of plants and trees.

Hiatai, v. n. to be teazed by many calls and importunities; to be wearied with troublesome prospects.

Hiatumu, v. n. to fall, root and branches.

Hiaumiti, s. a longing desire for something not obtained.

—v. n. to long, as for an absent relation.

Hie, *interj.* of disgust or contempt, as be off!

Hie, a. indented, as some trees, such as the chestnut.

Hiehie, a. violent, furious, applied to the aspect of the countenance.

Hiemateoa, v. n. to exult; the same as *hiamateoa*.

Hiero, s. [Gr. *hieron*,] the temple; see *nao*.

Hihi, s. the rays of the sun.

Hihi, s the whiskers of a cat, mouse, or rat; also the two holes in a cocoanut that cannot be pierced.

Hihi, s. men fleeing or running from a battle.

Hihi, s. a small shell fish.

Hihihihi, s the quivering of the lips, and motion of the teeth by extreme cold.

—v. n to quiver or chatter, as the teeth through cold.

Hihimata, s. the hairs of the eye lashes.

Hihimoa, s the feathers on the back of a fowl's neck.

Hihioura, s. the feelers of the cray fish.

Hihipapa, s a species of periwinkle that cleaves to the rocks.

Hihipo, s. the giddiness occasioned by a violent blow.

Hihirauape, s. the caul of beasts.

Hihitai, s. salt water periwinkles.

Hihivai, s. fresh water periwinkles.

Hihira, v. n. to look askance.

Hihiroa, s. the long hair in the eye lash.

Hihiroa, s. two plants growing out of one cocoanut.

Hihiu, a wild, shy, not familiar.

Hii, v. a to dandle, nurse, take a child in the arms.

Hii, s a sort of basket to put fruit in for the queen or chief woman.

Hiiatua, s. a priest that carried a god.

Hiimoea, v. a. to finish work.

Hiirima, s. the first fruit for the king, principal chief, or favourite son.

Himene, s [from the English,] a hymn.

—v. a. to hymn or sing an hymn.

Himu, s. a sort of small basket.

Hina, s. the name of the first woman, according to a Tahitian tradition, the wife of *Ti*, and by some said to be still in the moon.

Hina, *s.* a species of a small spider.
Hina, *s.* seed, posterity; see *huaai.*
Hinaaro, *s.* [*inganaro, hinanao, inengaro,*] love, desire, affection, will, pleasure, choice.
—*v. a.* to love, desire, will; to choose.
Hinahina, *a* grey, applied to the hair.
Hinai, *s* a sort of basket.
Hinaimatai, *s* a sort of fishing basket or net.
Hinana, *s.* a sot by drinking *ava*; a common drunkard.
Hinano, *s.* the blossom of the pandanus.
Hinavare, *a* near ripe, applied to the bread-fruit.
Hinere, *s.* [from the English,] a pair of hinges.
Hinerere, *s.* progeny, offspring, descendants; beginning with great. or great great grand children; see *huaai.*
Hinu, *s.* oil, fat, or grease.
Hinua, *s.* shyness of one not used to company.
Hinuhinu, *s.* brightness, lustre, glory.
—*a* bright, glossy, glistering
Hinuinui, *v.n* to linger behind; come on slowly.
Hinureoe, *v. n.* to grow quickly, and decay as quickly, by a little disease.
Hinutere, *v n.* to grow quickly.
Hio, *v. n* to look, see, behold; see *nana.*
—*s.* a looking-glass.
Hio, *s* a whistle, or the native flute; see *vivo.*
—*v. n.* to whistle: to blow, as a person out of breath
Hioana, *a* circumspect, cautious when surrounded with dangers.
Hioapahi, *v.n* to look askance, to leer archly
Hiorapa, *v. n.* to look slyly.
Hioaruri, *v.n* to look wantonly.
Hioata, *s.* a looking glass.
Hioata, *v. n.* to observe other people's affairs.
Hiofenua, *s.* a spy-glass
Hiohio, *s.* a spy, a soothsayer.
Hiohio, *s.* a rope fixed at the extremity of the mast to hoist up colours, or an ornament.
Hiohio, *v. a.* to observe, notice the affairs of people.
Hiohio, *v. n.* to whistle; see *hio.*
Hioe, *a.* thin of hair through disease.
Hiomahana, *s.* a quadrant or sextant.
Hiomao, *v. a.* to scrutinize to find defects.
Hiopoa, *s.* an inspector, a close examiner.
—*v. a.* to examine, scrutinize, inspect; to point out small defects: to act as a busybody.
Hipa, *s* self conceit or admiration.
—*a.* conceited, proud
Hipa, *s.* the sharp point of a sail.
Hipahipa, *v n* to display pride repeatedly.
Hipo, *s* [Gr. *hippos,*] a horse or mare.
Hipohipo, *s.* a disease that causes giddiness.
Hipu, *s* a children's game.
—*v. a* to pierce.
Hira, *s* bashfulness in the presence of a superior, or of many together.
Hirahira, *s* scrupulousness; the fear of eating sacred food,

or what the sorcerers have prayed over; some regard, or fear of others. [speech.
Hiraraiararau, *s.* banter in
Hirere, *v. n.* to fall, as water over a precipice.
Hiri, *s* a strong native cloth.
Hiri, *s.* the bark or tan used to colour and preserve the native cloth called *hiri*
Hiri, *v a* to dye or tan with the *hiri*.
Hirihirinai, *v. n.* to be perplexed on account of visitors; to be suspicious, to be in fear, or confusion.
Hiriiro, *v. n.* to pine away.
Hirinai, *v. n.* to be in fear or apprehensive of something distressing as likely to happen.
—*s.* painful apprehension.
Hirinai, *v. n.* to lean upon another as a sick child on the bosom of its parent; to sympathize.
Hirioa, *a.* groundless, ill-founded, as an idle report.
Hirioo, *v. n.* to whirl or turn about.
Hirioro, *adv.* deliberately, by slow degrees
Hiripoi, *v. n.* to faint, as through loss of blood.
Hirihiripoi, *v n* to be faint through a blow, or the loss of blood.
Hiripoi, *v. n.* to be in distress of mind.
Hiro, *s.* the god of thieves *Hiro* was a man who lived some ages ago, according to tradition, he was a famous voyager and robber. A rock in Huahine is called *Hiro's paddle*, and on the top of another rock is his *marae* He was deified after his death, and was reckoned the god and the patron of thieves
Hiro, *v. a.* to twist, or spin thread, or line; to exaggerate in speech
Hiroa, *s.* likeness, or idiocracy of a person.
Hiroeroe, *v. n.* to grow in a weak manner, as a plant oppressed by weeds.
Hirohiro, *s.* the first stone taken from the heap in the game called *timo raa*.
Hirohiro, *v. a.* to twist repeatedly, to spin. [stable.
Hirohirouri, *a.* changeable, un-
Hitahita, *a.* eager, impetuous.
—*s.* eagerness, impetuosity.
Hitahita, *adv.* hastily, eagerly, impatiently.
Hitahitaore, *s.* patience, temperance, self-restraint.
Hitaimaramara, *intj* of contempt.
Hitapere, *s.* a cascade.
—*v n* to come down violently, applied to the water of a cascade; see *hi* and *tapere*.
Hitau, *s.* a fisherman of the seasons
Hiti, *s.* an edge, border, extremity of a place, or thing.
Hiti, *s.* a play thing.
Hiti, *s.* a monster, or whatever is deformed at birth.
Hiti, *v. n.* to rise, applied to the sun, moon, and stars.
Hiti, *s* the revolution of time, as in the phrase *a tau a hiti noa 'tu.*
Hitia o te rà, *s* sun rising, the east.
Hitiapa, *s.* the inhabitant of border land.

Hitihiti, *s.* a sort of sand fly.

Hitimahuta, *v. n.* to start, to be moved by some sudden surprise; see *hiti* and *mahuta.*

Hitimaue, *v. n.* the same as *hitimahuta.*

Hitirere, *v. n.* to start, move suddenly, as by surprise; see *rere.*

Hito, *v. a.* to mock or deride; see *tahitohito.*

Hitoa, *a.* shrill, squeaking, applied to the human voice.

Hitu, *a.* [*fitu, itu,*] seven in counting.

Hiu, *s.* the tail of fishes.

Hiu, *a.* glutted, satiated; see *fiu;* also tired.

Hiuao, *a.* fleet, light, swift of foot.

Hiuniao, *v. a.* to scrutinize, find out blemishes.

Hiuniau, *a.* learned, skilled in various things.

Hiuta, *s.* the carved upper end of the ancient Tahitian masts.

Hiutia, *v. n.* to cut short, applied to speech.

—*a.* short, concise, as regards speech.

Hiutira, *s* a bunch of leaves used in the native dance.

Hiutira, *s* an intruder into a company.

Hiutira, *s.* a small altar for a god on board of a canoe; also a sort of temporary idol fitted up for a begging expedition.

Hiutoetoe, *a.* cold as water, applied also to the mind.

Hiva, *s.* a clan, the company in a canoe.

Hivahiva, *s.* abundance, a large quantity, or number.

Hivahivatau, *a.* abundant, plenteous

Hivarereata, *s.* agility, lightness of foot.

Ho, *intj.* a war shout, signifying joy or triumph.

Hoa, *a.* one in counting; see *hoe.*

Hoa, *s.* a fish of a red colour.

Hoa, *s.* a friend; see *taua* and *taio.*

Hoa, *v. n.* to flash as lightning; see *anapa.*

Hoa, *s.* a stick used for carrying things on the shoulder; see *mauhoa.*

Hoa, *s.* the head-ache; see *uiuhoa.*

Hoa, *v. a.* to grasp an antagonist, as a wrestler.

Hoa, *v. n.* to stand as an army.

Hoaa, *s.* a fine polish on wood, pearl shell, &c.

Hoaa, *s.* flavour, as that of a baked pig.

Hoahoa, *a.* teazing, perplexing; see *tahoa.*

Hoahoa, *s.* likeness, resemblance.

Hoahoauri, *a.* changeable, fickle.

Hoai, *a.* angry, indicating mischief, applied to the human countenance.

Hoaiavero, *s.* a friend in time of war or famine.

Hoani, *v a.* to tempt, coax, conciliate.

Hoaraatau, *s.* a ceremony in reviewing a fleet of war canoes.

Hoata, *s.* the name of a night of the Tahitian moon or month

Hoata, *v. n.* to jest, to speak to excite mirth.

Hoataata, *v. n.* to jest repeatedly.

Hoatae, *s.* a friend that is always willing.

Hoatau, *s* the office of him that indicated the confirmation of peace or war.

Hoatu, *v. a.* to give, the act proceeding from the person addressed; see *homai.*

Hôau, *a.* withered, stunted in growth; also cowed, abashed.

Hoavaa, *s.* the effect of agreeable news, or sounds on the ear; also agitation caused by some noise.

Hoè, *a.* or *article,* one as *hoa.* Sometimes it answers the indefinite article *a* with *te,* as *te hoe.*

Hoe, *s.* an oar or paddle, a helm of a ship.

—*v. a.* to row or paddle.

Hoefaatere, *s.* a rudder or steering oar.

Hoefatoa, *s.* a large long paddle used in distress.

Hoehapua, *s.* the same as *hoefatoa,* that is, a long oar or paddle to be used as a safe guard to a canoe at sea.

Hoehoe, *s* a mode of fishing, a thing to catch fish.

Hoehoe, *v. a.* to row or paddle repeatedly, or from place to place.

Hoehoe, *v. a.* to sharpen or clean the teeth of a wooden comb.

Hoene, *adv.* weakly, slenderly, as a plant choked by weeds; also delicately, effeminately, as a person not exposed to the sun, or weakly through illness

Hoetariai, *s.* an oar or paddle, as *hoehapua.*

Hofaa, *adv* carelessly.

Hofà, *v. a.* to clap the hands, as the dancers or *arioi.*

Hohe, *v. n.* to squint.

—*a.* squint, applied to the eye.

Hoho, *s.* the place just above the temple.

Hohoa, *s* an effigy, figure, form, likeness.

Hohoi, *v. n.* the dual of to return; see *hoi.*

Hohŏī, *v. a.* to kiss or touch noses as two persons.

Hohoio, *v. a.* to supplant, cause a person to be disappointed.

Hohoni, *v. a* to bite.

Hohonu, *a.* deep, profound.

Hohora, *v. n.* to open the hand with the palm upwards as a sign of agreement.

—*v. a.* to open what was shut or closed, to spread or lay out.

Hohore, *v. a.* to take off the skin of fruit, to peel off the bark of a tree; see *ihi.*

Hohori, *v. a.* to go about begging or demanding as the *arioi.*

Hohoro, *v. n.* the dual of to run.

Hohotu, *v. n.* the dual or plural of to bear.

Hoi, *s.* a root bearing a vine like the yam.

Hoi, *v. a.* [*hongi, honi,*] to kiss or touch noses.

Hoi, *v. n.* to smell.

Hoi, *v. n.* to return; see *faahoi.*

Hoi, *conj.* [*hoki, oki,*] also.

—*prep.* beside.

—*adv.* likewise.

Hoiamuri, *v. n.* to backslide, turn back.

Hoiha, *intj.* an exclamation of contempt of some order given.

Hoihoi, *a.* cross grained as timber, having scars or wounds, or pitted as with small pox

Hoimoimo, *v. n.* to shrink through cold, fear, or bashfulness.

Hoioio, *s.* diffidence, fear of a superior.

Hoiria, *a.* pettish, easily offended.

Homai, *v. a.* to give, being a request to a second person to give with the aspect towards the speaker; see *hoatu.*

Homee, *a.* reserved, irritable, illiberal.

Homimu, *v. n.* to be silenced, over-powered by speech, arguments, or fear of a superior.

Hona, *s.* copulation.

Honae, *a.* withered, faded as a cut branch.

Honae, *intj.* an exclamation of derision.

Honea, *a.* sharp, quick, applied to the voice.

Honi, *v. a.* to bite; see *hohoni.*

Honihoni, *v. a.* to gnaw, to bite by little and little.

Hono, *s.* a row of thatch about a fathom in breadth.

Hono, *s.* food taken by the *ava* drinkers after their drink.

Hono, *v. a.* to splice a rope, to join pieces of wood.

Honoa, *s.* an agreement, a plot, things joined.

Honoaparau, *s.* an agreement.

Honohono, *v n.* to be joined one after another in a continued line.

Honotua, *v. a.* to trace carefully to the origin.

Honu, *s.* [*fonu, ponu,*] the sea turtle.

Honu, *v. n.* to be glutted with over abundance.

Honuofai, *s* the land turtle or tortoise.

Hoo, *s.* [*hoko, hogo,*] price, exchange, equivalent.

—*v. a.* to buy or sell, exchange property.

Hoo raa, *s* market place, place or time of selling.

Hooura, *s* the blood from the head when struck with the shark's teeth, as formerly practised, in token of grief or affection.

Hoovai, *a* in law, as *metua hoovai*, father in law.

Hopara, *v. a.* to push away, resist; see *turai.*

Hope, *s.* the tail of a bird, the hair of a man tied behind.

—*v. n.* to be finished, ended, concluded.

Hopea, *s.* the end or extremity of a thing; the end or object of an action.

Hopeaore, *a.* endless; also useless, unprofitable.

Hopeataheore, *s.* great sayings or promises, but without fulfilment.

Hopepe, *s.* a species of the hedge-hog fish.

Hoperemu, *s.* the lower part of the spine.

Hopevini, *a.* of a dark colour like the tail of a *vini*, applied to the sea.

Hopii, *s.* the falling sickness, [epilepsy.

Hopiipii, *v. n.* to be cramped as the foot or arm; to be struck motionless by sudden fear.

Hopiri, *v n.* to sit closely, to sit in one place through fear.

Hopoi, *v. a.* to carry or convey a burden.
Hopoia, *s* the thing carried or conveyed.
Hopohopoi, *v. a.* to carry or convey repeatedly, or by little and little.
Hopu, *s* to dive under water; also to bathe.
Hopu, *s.* a certain prayer at the end of a ceremony.
Hopu, *v. a.* to sue for peace, to cut short a prayer as was done sometimes in the *marae.*
Hopue, *s.* the dropsy.
Hopue, *v. n* to ferment; see *faahopue.*
Hopuhopu, *v. n.* to dive repeatedly.
Hopuhopu a ruro, *v. n.* just to dip and out again, like the action of the bird *ruro.*
Hopuna, *s.* deep as a pool or fountain.
Hopupu, *s.* a species of the *totara.*
Hopûpû, *v n* to inflate or cause the mouth to swell.
Hopuu, *s.* the name of a fine native cloth, very white.
Hora, *s.* [Latin, *hora,*] an hour.
Hora, *s.* a poisonous plant.
Hora, *v. a* to use the *hora* to poison fish.
Horâ, *v. a.* to stretch out the hand in liberality.
Horahora, *v. a.* to spread out a garment, a mat, &c.
Horahora, *s.* the platform or, deck of a *Paumotu pahi* or canoe.
Horahora, *a.* disagreeable, acrid, or bitter in taste.
Horahora i te tau, *v. a.* to put each thing separate, to distinguish things
Hore, *v. a.* to peel—*horea,* peeled.
Hori, *s.* riot, wild or loose mirth, a rioter, player.
—*v n* to riot, dance, wander about.
Horihori, *v. n* to riot repeatedly.
Horiri, *v. n.* to be cold, seized with shivering.
Horiri, *v. n.* to be troubled, agitated in mind by fear or consternation.
Horo, *v. n.* to run—*hohoro,* dual of to run.
Horo, *s.* a piece of a mountain or hill that slips down to the vallies by reason of much rain.
Horoa, *a.* generous, liberal.
Horoa, *v. a* to give or bestow some good.
—*s.* the gift that is given.
Horoaino, *a.* ungenerous, illiberal.
Horoapuu, *v. n* to run, rush, or make a sudden push.
Horoapuu, *a.* brisk, or contrary to delay.
Horoatoitua, *a.* liberal in word, but not in actions.
Horofeto, *v. n.* to be choked with swallowing large quantities of dry food without drink.
Horohoro, *adv.* quickly, expeditiously.
Horohoroi, *v. a.* to wash repeatedly, or in different places.
Horohororere, *v. n.* to be perplexed, not knowing what to do.
Horoi, *v. a.* to wash or cleanse.
Horoiatoto, *s.* a man for a sacrifice.
Horomaanuu, *a.* bloated; gluttonous.

Horomaarai, *a.* the same as *horomaanuu.*

Horomii, *v. n.* to swallow; see *momi.*

Horomiri, *v. a.* to examine with fondness; to stroke or fondle.

Horopae, *s.* the gang way of a canoe.

Horopae, *v. n.* to go by the edge or extremity.

Horopoipoi, *s.* the morning star, commonly Venus, but sometimes Jupiter.

Horopuupuu, *v. n.* to swallow eagerly without mastication.

Hororiri, *v. n.* to go or run away in anger; also to go head over heels.

Horotaetae, *v. n.* to go naked; to be destitute.

Horotoroto, *v. n.* to weep, or grieve, so that the tears run down.

Horu, *s.* the opening of the cranium in infants.

Horu, *s.* a disease.

Horue, *s.* an amusement in which persons slide on the side of a hill, or swim on a board in the surf of the sea; see *faahee.*

Horuhoru. *v. n.* to be agitated, troubled in mind.

Horuru, *s.* a head ornament; the plaited hair of a person deceased, kept in remembrance of him.

Horuru, *v. n.* to be drunk with *ava*, &c.

Hota, *s.* cough, cold; see *mare.*

—*v. n.* to cough.

Hotahota, *v. n* to cough often.

Hotae, *v.n* to talk in one's sleep.

Hotaratara, *v. n.* to be affected with fear or dread, so that the hair stand erect; see *ponu.*

Hotate, *s.* a fever or ague attended with wasting, a disease common in the islands.

Hotato, *intj.* an exclamation of contempt, such as pshaw!

Hotê, *a.* strait, confined; crammed so as not to admit more.

Hotè, *a.* short, small, diminutive in stature.

Hotehote, *a.* small in quantity; also men of low birth, or diminutive in stature.

Hoto, *s.* a sort of spear; see *ihe.*

Hotohoto, *a.* passionate, raging; see *fetofeto.*

Hotu, *v. n.* to bear fruit, as a tree; to kindle, as anger; to swell, applied to the sea.

Hotua, *s.* force, power, bravery, perseverance in work, forbearance.

Hotuoi, *s.* the second rank, or that behind the front rank in an army; see *aroviri.*

Hotuapo, *s.* a sudden, and unexpected attack, in the night time; a secret counsel.

Hotuhotu, *v. n.* the kindling of anger, and that often.

Hotumata, *s.* the act of attacking or seizing suddenly.

Hoturoto, *s.* one that is greatly esteemed by another.

Hotutau, *s.* a season bearing tree or plant, such as bears only once in a year.

Hotûtû, *a.* flatulent.

Hotuumu, *s.* a rich soil.

Hou, *s.* sweat.

—*v. n.* to perspire or sweat.

Hou, *s.* an auger or gimblet.

—*v. a.* to bore with an auger.

Hou, *a.* new, late.

—*adv.* lately, recently.

Houa, *v. n.* to be in a state of perspiration.

Houhou, *s.* a disease of the head, or back of the neck.
Houhou, *a.* well done or baked, as *taro,* and other things in a native oven.
Houhou, *v. a.* to irritate by provoking words.
Houu, *a.* sullen, sulky, subdued or in fear.
Houvaru, *s.* a pit formed by the sinking of the earth or by digging.
Hovanavana, *s.* the rising of anger in the mind.
Hu, *s.* wind emitted from the rectum.
Hua, *s.* an atom, a grain of sand, a particle, the thread of a garment.
Hua, *s.* a pattern, as *hua vaa,* pattern of a canoe.
Hua, *s.* the testicles of animals.
Hua, *s.* the name of a rank among the *arioi.*
Hua, *s.* the string of a bow; also a spray of the sea.
Hua, *s.* the aged, the infirm, women and children put in a place of safety in time of war.
Huà. *a.* congealed, coagulated.
Hua, *adv.* very, very much, completely, fully.
Huaa, *s.* family, lineage, ancestry.
Huaaau, *s.* a species of rupture.
Huaaeho, *s.* the down on the *aeho* or reed.
Huaahi, *s.* a spark of fire.
Huaai, *s.* seed, progeny.
Huaarua, *a.* of two parentages.
Huaaute, *s.* the down on the *aute* plant.
Huahua, *s.* pimples on the skin.
Huahua, *v. n.* to be reduced to atoms, pulverized.
Huahua, *intj.* an obscene exclamation.
Huahuamatoa, *s* an hermaphrodite.
Huai, *v. a.* to open or uncover a native oven, or any thing buried in the earth.
Huaira, *a.* intrepid, of great power or force, as a wild beast.
Huaimario, *a.* untimely in birth, applied to infants.
Huairio, *s.* abortive, as *huaimario.*
Huamanu, *s.* a bunch of red feathers taken to an artificer when a canoe was to be built.
Huamiri, *s.* small particles, the act of making small as practised by embalmers; see *miri.*
Huamoa, *s.* an unfledged chicken.
Huanane, *v. a.* to mix up well certain articles of food.
Huanane, *v. n.* to be all in confusion, applied to a company of people.
Huapareva, *s.* an egg of the bird *pareva,* often found on some floating rubbish in the sea; *fig.* a person of a mean origin or parentage.
Huapipi, *s.* the youth called *pori,* who were fed for some time to make them fair and delicate.
Huarauau, *s.* saw dust, or that caused by worms.
Huaraau, *s.* land got by conquest; see *aua.*
Huarama, *s.* the particles that fall from a torch.
Huararo, *s.* the name of a species of *taro.*
Huare, *s* spittle, saliva.
Huarepau, *s.* a scold.

Huarepo, *s.* a warrior; called also *huarero*.

Huarau, *s* the name of a flower.

Huaieru, *s* the seed of *mamau* or cabbage tree.

Huaparau, *s.* fragments of speech.

Huâri, *s.* a person of a despicable birth.

Huaroro, *s.* a species of a small gourd, used for bottles to hold sweet scented oil.

Huaroto, *s.* a species of plantain.

Huâru, *s.* the watery part of an over ripe fruit, the white froth of the sea.

Huaruri, *s.* a mode of holding the spear in the exercise of *taraaû.*

Huata, *s.* a second small crop of bread-fruit.

Huatau, *s.* a strong north wind.

Huatô, *s.* the down on the top of the sugar cane.

Huaupu, *s.* fragments of ancient Tahitian prayers.

Hue. *s* a gourd or calabash, to hold water, &c.

Hue, *s.* a cask, keg, or bottle; see *paero.*

Hue, *s.* a chequered sea fish that is exceedingly poisonous, those that eat it generally die quickly, except they can vomit it up. From a likeness to the skin of this fish English cheque is called *nihue.*

Hue, *v. a.* to throw up into a heap; to overthrow and cast out useless things.

Hue, *s.* a restriction on food; see *rahui.*

Hueaere, *s* a gourd that fills a place with leaves, but does not bear.

Hueavai, *a.* profuse, prodigal, improvident; also pompous, affecting greatness.

Huehue, *s.* a fish; also a small gourd.

Huehue, *a.* distended, applied to a swollen stomach.

Huehue, *v. n* to be in terror or amazement.

Huerepoa, *s.* one that is prosperous in fishing.

Huerereue, *s* a small fly;—*fig.* an idle wandering person.

Huero, *s.* seeds of trees and plants, eggs of birds, fishes, lizards, &c.; also progeny.

Huero moa, *s.* hen's eggs.

Hufaa, *s.* the thigh of any creature.

Hufaapapai, *s.* an incendiary, a breeder of contention; one that strikes his thigh in defiance of his enemy.

Huhe, *v. n.* to be exhausted as in working.

Huho, *s.* the grunt of a wild hog with a snap at what disturbs him, a word in imitation of the sound.

Huhô, *intj* a word of rejoicing used by victors; also a word of excitement when a number of men are engaged in pulling a tree or a canoe.

Huhu, *s* a species of wild bee; called also *tane taroto.*

Huhu, *s* the sliding door or window shutter; the string of a bag.

—*v. a* to slide a door, or the shutter of a window; to draw the string of a bag so as to close its mouth; to brail up a sail.

Huhua, *s.* the top of a mountain; see *tahuhua.*

Huhue, *v. a.* the dual of *hue*, to throw or heap up.

Huhui, *v. a.* to fix wash boards on the sides of a canoe, to prevent the sea from washing in.

Huhuna, *v. a.* to hide or conceal repeatedly.

Huhupara, *a.* shorn of its leaves as a deciduous tree, such as the *ii* and *atae*, whose leaves fall yearly.

Huhupara, *v. a.* to cleanse a new born infant.

Huhura, *v. n.* to run, make speed.

Huhure, *v. a.* to gather both fruit and branches together through carelessness.

Huhuti, *v. a.* to pluck feathers, hair, grass, &c., and that repeatedly; see *huti.*

Hui, a *plural* or *collective* particle prefixed to various nouns, as *hui arii*, the royal party or family; *hui raatira*, the inferior chiefs collectively; *hui tupuna*, ancestors; *hui metua*, parents; *hui hoa*, friends, &c.

Hui, *v. a.* to pierce, lance, or prick.

Hui, *v. a.* to make a long side stroke with a sword or a club.

Hui, *v. n.* to throb, as a vein or artery.

Hui, *s.* a cocoanut emptied of its milk.

Hui, *v. a.* to eat forbidden food slyly.

Hui, *v. a.* to skip a rope.

Huia, *s.* the suckers of the *pia* plant; a parent with his descendants.

Huiaere, *s.* see *hueaere.*

Huihui, *s* throbbings, or twitchings in the flesh.

—*v n* to be throbbing as an artery.

Huihui, *a.* highly polished, handsome.

Huihuimama, *s.* a calm, when no wind stirs

Huihuimanu, *s* a flock of birds.

Huihuimatau, *v. a* to polish the pearl fish-hook.

Huihuimoria, *a.* elegant, unsoiled, pretty.

Huioa, *s.* the name of a bird; also a company prettily attired.

Huirere, *v. a* to do a thing at random, to report at random.

Huità, *s.* consternation as from a blow.

—*v. a.* to strike a side stroke; also *hità.*

Huitarava, *s.* three noted stars of Orion.

Huitoto, *v. a* to bleed; also to open an abscess.

Huitoto, *s.* the act of destroying an infant in the womb; called also *huitamaru.*

Humâ, *s* a species of crab.

Huma, *s.* the children, infirm, and decrepit of a land that suffers by war.

Humae, *v. a.* to disclose, make known.

Humaha, *s* the thigh; see *hufaa.*

Humahuma, *a.* abundant, plenteous.

Humahuma, *s* vast abundance.

Hume, *v. a* to put the strip of cloth called maro about the loins, and between the legs.

Humi, *s.* a seal, or sea calf.

Humii, *a* hard, niggardly; see *homee.*

Humu, *s* a secret plot of murder, &c.

Huna, *v. a.* to hide or conceal a thing.

Hunà, *v. a.* the same as *huna.*

Hunahuna, *v. a.* to hide or conceal artfully, and also repeatedly.

Hunahunaai, *s.* the act of concealing the names of the true proprietors of lands.

Hune. *s.* the core of bread fruit

Hunehune, *s.* the itch, or a cutaneous disorder resembling the itch.

Huniu, *s.* the cocoanut blossom; also something to represent a slain enemy when the body could not be produced

Hunô, *intj* an exclamation of derision.

Hunéa, *s* a son or daughter-in law.

Huoi, *s* a stranger, a wanderer, or a straggler from a fleet of war canoes.

Huoro. *s* the seed of any tree or plant; see *huero.*

Huororo, *s* a small gourd; see *huaroro.*

Hupapi, *s.* the name of a dance, or of a certain mot on in the native dance.

Hupê, *s.* the mucous of the nose.

Hupe. *s* a part of the mourner's head dress.

Hupe. *s.* the dew that falls in the night.

Hupe, *s* the land wind that blows in the morning from off the land, see *hau.*

Hupevao, *s* the night dew in the vallies.

Hupehupe, *a.* shabby, ugly, ill favoured.

Hura, *s* a native dance or play.

Hura, *v. n.* to exult with joy; see *hia matcoa.*

Hurâ, *v. n.* to be impelled by impetuous desire.

Hurahuiâtai, *s.* the act of settling a thing speedily by combat.

Huraiti, *s.* a player, or skilful dancer.

Hûrê, *v. n.* to be glutted with food; see *honu.*

Hurepaapaa, *s.* utter extinction or extirpation.

Huri, *v. a.* to turn over, to roll as a cask.

Huriâvero, *v. n* to be overturned by a storm.

Huriâô, *s.* food prepared by the cultivators of land, to be presented to their chief, out of their first fruits.

Huriaroa, *v. n.* to turn away the front or face; to be estranged in affection and refuse civilities.

Huriea, *v. n* to deliberate, weigh affairs as in a council of war and peace.

Hurifau, *s.* a person that remains unhurt in the midst of a battle.

Hurifenua, *s* a disturber of the peace of a country by acts of sedition.

Hurifenua, *s* the name given to a very tempestuous wind.

Hurihuri, *v. a* to turn over repeatedly.

Hurihurifenua, *v n.* to deliberate or turn over in the mind the political affairs of the country

Hurihurifenua, *s.* a very strong tempestuous wind, or a hurricane.

Hurihurițiaraa, *s* a consultation about the affairs of the country, such as peace or war

Hurihurituraa, *s* the same as *hurihurituraa*, a meeting for political affairs

Hurire, *v. a.* to turn over the victory; see *re*.

Huritaere, *v a.* to turn over keel upward; see *taere*—*fig.* to over-turn the Government.

Huritumu, *v a.* to over-throw from the foundation.

Hurô, *intj* an exclamation of joy, huzza!

Huru, *s.* likeness, resemblance of a thing.

Huru, *s.* the bones of the *totara* fish.

Hurufenua, *s.* a landscape; appearance of a country.

Huruhuru, *s.* [*fulufulu*, Malay *bulu*,] hair, wool, feathers; see *hetehete*.

Hurui, *v. a.* to make the skirts of a garment to hang down.

Hurumau, *a.* of one likeness, bearing his age well.

Hurupà, *v. n.* to be in consternation by an ill report.

Hurupà, *s.* a thicket.

Hurupatautai, *v. n.* to sham sleep to prevent the joining of a night fishing party.

Hururau, *a.* manifold, of many likenesses

Hururima, *s* a large portion taken unfairly.

Hururû, *v. n* to be in a hurry.

Hurutoi, *s* the fringes of the sinnet tied to the handle of the native hatchet.

Hurutoi, *v n* to be convalescent

Hurutoi, *s* a company of mechanics; also a bundle of adzes.

Hutehute, *a.* mean in rank, of low birth.

Huti, *v a* to pluck, as feathers, hair, grass, weeds, &c.

Huti, *v. a.* to pull or draw a fishing line. hoist up a flag.

Huti, *v. n* to breathe, or draw the breath.

Hutiavere, *a* glutinous, adhesive as certain substances

Hutiavere, *v. n.* to move the lips in a certain way in making grimaces; see *faita*.

Hutihuti, *v. a.* to pluck, pull, or draw repeatedly

Hutitoro, *s.* a mode of fishing.

Hutitoro, *v. n.* to be pressing in asking or demanding.

Huto, *s.* anger, displeasure; see *fetofeto*.

Hutu, *s.* the *Barringtonia*; its fruit is a large nut of the shape of a heart, and the kernel is used for intoxicating fishes.

Hutu, *s.* the heart of animals, of the same shape as the *hutu* nut.

Hutu, *v. n* to send up spray as the sea before a ship.

Hutuhutu, *v n.* to be growing up, as anger or rage in the mind.

Hutupanutai, *s.* a drifted *hutu* nut thrown ashore by the sea—*fig.* a contemptuous designation for a stranger, or one that has neither friends nor relations, house nor home.

Hutureva, *s.* a species of the *hutu* with smaller leaves and nuts, which are of a different shape, and said to be poisonous.

I

IS the third Tahitian vowel, and commonly pronounced as the English *i* in the words *bid*, *pin*, *sin*; but when circumflexed thus î, as in the words *magazine*, *marine*.

I, when prefixed, or going before verbs, is a sign of the past tense.

I, *prep.* before nouns in the oblique cases, when they are preceded by *a te*, as *i te mea*, otherwise it should be *ia*.

I, *v. n* to speak, but the word is obsolete.

I, *prep.* at, for, in, as *i reira*, at that place or time, *i te mea*, for such a thing, *i te fare*, in the house.

I, *v. a.* to pick out, choose, select.

I, *v. a.* to prepare bread fruit for the *mahi*.

Ia, *s* [*ika*, Malay *ikan*,] fish of any kind.

Ia, *v. a.* to pitch, daub, or paint.

Ia, *adv.* when, in the past time, as *ia oe i parahi i taua fare ra*, when thou didst dwell in such a house

Ia, *adv.* when, future, and pronounced a little different, *ia haere au*, when I go

Ia, *conj.* if, as *ia ore ia tae mai*, if he comes not.

Ia, *prep.* [*kia*, *ki*,] by, with, for, to, and so preceding all nouns and pronouns, but sometimes the *a* is dropped.

Ia, *v aux* by way of wish or supplication, as *ia tae mai*, may it come; *ia ora*, may (it) live.

Ia, *pron.* pronounced in two syllables, that, or it, as *eaha ia ?* what is that? *e mea ia*, it is such a thing; *eita ia e tae*, he or it will not go.

Ia, *v. n.* or of *being*, pronounced in two syllables, am, is, or are.

Iaa, *s* a sort of food used in time of scarcity.

Iaararoa, *s.* a fish, a present of fish taken to a chief.

Ia ea, *v* expressing a wish for health; see *ia ora*.

Ia ea na, *v.* of praying for, or wishing health and all good to the person addressed, as *Ia ora na*.

Iaha, *adv.* not, do not; see *eiaha*, *auaa*.

Iaia, *pron.* a compound of *ia prep.* to, with, by, and *ia pron.* formerly used at Tahiti, and still in other dialects, to him, by him, with him, as *eita vau e parau iaia*, I will not speak to him.

Iaia, *s.* a piece of coral used to rasp an *umete*.

Ia'na, *pron* a compound of the *prep. ia*, and *ana*, the third person singular, him or it, signifying to him, by him, with him, her, or it.

Ia oe, *pron.* thee, to thee, by thee, with thee.

Iato, *s.* [*iako*,] the transverse beams which connect the out-rigger to a canoe.

Iatoai, *s.* the second class of the inferior chiefs.

Iatomoe, *s.* the centre division of a fleet.

Ia'u, *pron* me, to me, by me, with me.

Ia vai, *pron. inter.* to whom? by whom? with whom?

Ie, *s.* a boat or ship's sail of any sort.

Ie, *s.* the mallet used for beating cloth.

Ieie, *s.* the fibrous roots of the plant *farapepe*, used for tying fences, making baskets, &c.

Ieieere, *s* consternation on account of some unexpected event of a disastrous nature.

Iha, *s.* anger, high displeasure.
—*v. n.* to be much displeased.

Ihaiha, *v. n.* to be panting because of oppression by heat

Ihaiha, *a.* disagreeable, offensive in smell.

Ihara, *s.* the name of a rough instrument of music, struck with sticks; commonly a piece of bamboo open on one side.

Ihata, *s.* a box, cage, or scaffold; see *pafata.*

Ihe, *s.* a dart or spear; see *hoto.*

Iheihe, *a* neat, elegant; also ill savoured; see *ihaiha.*

Iheihere, *v. n.* to wander idly from place to place

Ihi, *s.* skill, wisdom, dexterity.
—*a.* skilful, wise, dextrous.

Ihi, *s* [*ifi, ibi, ii,*] the horse chestnut; see *rata.*

Ihiamoea, *s.* property collected to induce the god *Oro* to be propitious to the party when engaged in war; and in case of such property being seized by the opposite party, it was judged an omen of that party's destruction.

Ihiihi, *s.* skill, economy, good order; also a preparation to meet difficulties.

Ihihi, *a.* cunning, knowing, crafty.

Ihihi, *a.* of slow growth, as a child.

Ihiorea, *s.* discretion, prudence.
—*a* discreet, prudent.

Ihipapa, *v a.* the act of raising up the large flat stones in the sea with which to build a marae—*fig.* the act of banishing a family.

Ihipapa, *v. a.* to demolish, extirpate root and branch.

Ihipeetue, *v. a.* to demolish, as *ihipapa.*

Ihipiro, *a.* crafty, illiberal; also not noticing a person.

Ihipiro, *a.* stumpy, short, of ill growth.

Ihirea, *s.* trouble, perplexity, consternation, fear.
—*v. n.* to be troubled, to be in confusion.

Ihitai, *s.* a mariner, one skilful at sea.

Ihitumu, *v. a.* to overthrow, demolish from the foundation; see *taihi.*
—*v. n.* to be in a state of demolition.

Iho, *pron.* self, an affix to pronouns, as *vau iho, oe iho, oia iho, &c*, myself, thyself, himself, &c.

Iho, an *affix* to adverbs and prepositions, *i o iho, i onei iho, reira iho, nia iho, raro iho, pihai iho, &c*; see those words, it denotes sameness or proximity.

Iho, *s.* the essence or nature of a thing or person.

Iho, *v n.* to descend, or come down from an eminence; see *pou.*

Iho, *v n.* applied to a person coming to himself, or recovering his intellectual faculties.

Ihoa, *s.* a great collection or heap of property.

Ihoarii, *s* the dignity and office of a king or principal chief.

Ihoaiitepa, *s.* a god of the *arioi* company.

Ihoiho, *s* the manes or remains of the dead.

Ihoihoa, *s.* the same as *ihoiho*, the ghosts of the dead which were supposed often to visit the living, especially relations, and to inflict illness and death.

Ihona, *adv.* a compound of *iho* and *na*, signifying lately, or close to the person addressed

Ihonei, *adv.* compound of *iho*, self, or proximate, and *nei*, here, lately at this place, just now.

Ihoihoatupu, *s.* the living relatives of a dead person.

Ihomaamaa, *s.* a fool; also foolishness.

Ihoneneva, *s.* the same as *ihomaamaa.*

Ihopohe, *s.* mortality.

Ihora, *adv.* a compound of *iho*, self, and *ra*, and added to verbs signifies proximity of the action to the person or thing, the time or place connected with the preceding verb.

Ihotaata, *s.* the person himself with regard to something sacred.

Ihotatau, *s.* reckoning of descent, genealogy.

Ihotoi, *s.* the name of a ceremony and prayer of a canoe builder in cutting a tree for a new canoe.

Ihotupu, *s* the native of a place; one of the aborigines.

—*a.* indigenous, not foreign

Ihu, *s.* the nose, snout, bill of a bird; the fore part of a canoe is called also *ihu vaa.*

Ihu, *v. n.* to work in the sea, as the fore part of a canoe in a high sea.

Ihu, *v. n.* to be lost, or going at random among trees and bushes, not knowing the road.

Ihuihu, *v. n.* to be choked or smothered.

—*a.* choking, smothering.

Ihumamea, *s.* the beginning of an affair.

Ihumanu, *s.* a fowler, a searcher for birds.

Ihupaa, *s* a disease of the nose.

Iia, *s.* the name of a piece in the side of a canoe.

Ii, *a.* the plural of *i* full

Iihi, *s.* the name of a red fish, of which there are several species.

Iihi, *a.* of a red, or reddish colour.

Iii, *a* sleepless, not having the eyes closed in sleep.

Iimi, *v. a.* the dual, or the past of *imi*, to search.

Iina, *a* straight, full, plump; without irregularities.

Iino, *a.* the plural of bad or ill.

Iiore, *s* a species of blubber-like fish.

Iiri, *a.* thick, stiff, applied to paste.

Iiru, *a.* thick, adhesive.

Iita, *v. n.* to harden or be hardened; see *faaita.*

Iita, *a.* stiffened, as body or mind; obdurate.

Iita, *s.* the tetanus or locked jaw.

Iite, *v. a.* the dual of *ite* to know or perceive; also the past or perfect of *ite* to know.

Iitu, *v. a* to pinch or squeeze with the fingers.

Iiti, *s.* slight twitchings before labour pains.

Iivi, *s* a hog which a feeder detains for himself—*fig.* one that loiters, or hangs behind, is called *iivi faatautau.*

Imi, *v. a.* to search, seek, look for a thing: enquire.

Imioro. *s* a person that seeks and gathers the small herbs of which the little ornament called *oro* consists.

Imiroa, *s.* one of the jury on a trial; also those who act as constables.

Imo, *s.* the young of he *paauara* fish.

Ina, *s.* the edge of a tool; see *faaina.*

Ina, *s.* the name of a small shell fish with sharp prickles.

Ina, *a.* sharp, keen, as the edge of a tool.

Ina, *v a.* to make straight what was crooked.

Inaa, *s* the small fry of fish; see *einaa.*

Inai, *s.* any thing to eat with bread or vegetables, such as pork, fish, or fowl; also bread or vegetables to accompany flesh.

Inaina, *s.* the water of child birth.

Inaina, *v. a* to take off the hair of a pig by scalding, or by singing over the fire.

Inanai, *s.* meat with bread, or bread with meat.

Ineine, *v. n.* to be ready, or in a state of preparation.

Ini, *s.* the upper part of a butt or mark at wh ch spears are thrown.

Iniini, *s* fragments, leavings of food.

Ino, *s* [*kino, kikino,*] evil of any kind; badness, vileness.

Ino, *a.* bad, evil, wicked, base, vile, sinful.

Ino, *a.* a modern familiar term used in addressing friends or relations, as *paino,* father, *pateaino,* mother, *e hoa ino,* a familiar friend. A term of endearment.

Ino, *adv.* badly, wickedly.

Inoino, *s.* vexation, displeasure, grief of mind.

—*v. n* to be vexed, displeased, grieved.

Inu, *s* drink of any kind.

—*v n.* to drink

Io, *s* a single hair of the head, called *io rouru*

Io, *s* a division of the inhabitants of Moorea; those on one side of the island are called *Te io i nia,* and those on the other *Te io i raro.*

Io, *s* [*kigo,*] flesh, or the muscular part without the fat; also the substance of any fruit.

Io, *adv.* there in that place; it is compounded with *nei* and *na,* as *io nei,* here in this place, *io na,* yonder at a distance, or where the person addressed may be at the time.

Io, *prep* with, as *io na,* with him, *io'u,* with me.

Io or Oio, *s.* the name of a sea bird, from its cry.

Ioa, *s.* [*inoa, inoa,*] a name.

Ioio, *s.* the name of a fish remarkable for many bones.

Ioio, *v n.* to make a noise as little children; to chirp as chickens or birds.

Ioio, *a* handsome, brilliant, of good quality as cloth; variegated.

Ioie. *s.* [*kioie, kioe,*] the native rat or mouse.

Iore, *s.* a piece of wood in the stern of a canoe.

Iorepapaa, *s.* a rabbit; any large foreign rat.

Ipai, *v. a.* to peel or to take off the rind of the *ii.*
Ipo, *s* a lump of bread-fruit, *mahi,* or dough.
Ipo, *s* a darling, one made much of.
Ipo, *v. a.* to make a lump of *mahi,* or dough.
Ira, *s.* a mole or mark on the skin.
Irairavai, *a.* weak, inefficient, ignorant
Irava, *s.* a strip, streak or layer, a stratum; also lately used for a verse or stanza.
Iravarava, *s.* the plural of *irava,* stripes, streaks
Ire, *s.* a species of shark.
Ireire, *s.* some small parts or particles.
Iri, *s.* skin, bark, peeling; also leaves of the palmeto.
Iri, *s.* a board or plank; see *puru.*
Iri, *v. n.* to lodge, or be stuck in a thing or place.
Iria, *a.* morose, sour, passionate, ill natured.
Iriaa, *s.* the skin peeling off a person after being sun burnt; dryness of the skin from exposure to a strong breeze.
Iriaava, *s* a cut or crack in the rind of ripe fruit.
Iriaeo, *s* a species of nettle.
Iriaeo, *s.* the name of a fish.
Iriafafa, *s.* a thing of hardy growth, long in coming to maturity.
Iriamore, *s* the bark of the *purau* tree; also a mode of fighting without encumbrance.
Iriamuna, *s.* a door way; see *umuna.*
Irianu, *s.* a person not affected by cold, nor drowsiness.
Irianuanu, *s* the name of a certain idolatrous prayer; also internal wretchedness
Iriaohe, *a.* imperfect, as a gourd or calabash.
Iriaputa, *s.* a door way or window; see *uputa.*
Iriatai, *s* the surface of the sea, or the place where the sea and sky appear to meet, hence the expression *tei te iriatai te mahana,* the sun is gone to the *iriatai* when it is setting.
Iriavae, *s.* the name of a little fish.
Irifaani, *v. n.* to be running into danger; also to be insulting.
Irifaavi, *v. n.* the same as *irifaani.*
Irihaa, *s.* consternation on account of some disaster, such as the fall of a warrior.
—*v. n.* to be amazed, or in a consternation.
Irihea, *s.* fear, consternation, as *irihaa.*
Irihoa, *s.* sudden anger.
—*v. n.* to rise suddenly, as anger in the mind.
Iriiri, *s* small stones, pebbles, gravel, grit.
—*a.* gritty, gravelly, lumpy as some kind of food; irregular as certain works.
Iriirià, *s.* the name of a cutaneous disease, in which the skin is full of red blotches; the prickly heat.
Irimahere, *s.* some great man; an only and favourite son, when dead, or slain in war, was called *irimahere.*
Irimatoru, *a.* able to endure all weathers.
Iriô, *s* a rind gall in trees.
Iripa, *a.* petulant, saucy.

Iripa, *s.* petulance, sauciness.
Iripaia, *a.* smooth, fair skin
Iripo, *s.* a vortex or whirlpool.
Iripoa, *s.* the same as *iripo.*
Iriraumai, *a.* unable to bear cold weather.
Iritaahu, *s.* one that never puts off his clothes.
Iriti, *v. a.* to open, to draw out; to translate.
Iriti, *v. n.* to have spasms, or be convulsed.
Iritia, *v. n.* to be struck with sudden death.
Iritihoro, *v. a.* to take and run, as a thief.
Irititû, *s.* sudden death.
—*v.n.* to die by a sudden stroke; see *tairitu.* [see *tua.*
Iro, *s.* [*ilo,*] a maggot, a worm;
Iruri, *s.* the name of a sort of food; see *arure.*
Iruri, *s.* a species of native food.
Itae, *s.* the name of a bird of the pigeon kind.
Itaporo, *s.* the small fruit at the extremity of a bunch of plantains.
Itari, *s.* the stem of fruits; that of a cocoanut branch or plantain leaf; see *atari.*
Itarifara, *s.* the stem of the *pandanus* fruit—*fig.* the powerful hand of a wrestler.
Itatae, *s.* the name of a bird.
Ite, *s.* [*kite,*] knowledge, understanding, perception.
—*v. a.* to know, understand, perceive.
Ite, *v. a.* to accept, receive a person favourably.
Itea, *the passive of the verb ite,* [*kitea,*] known, understood; also found, perceived
Itehia, commonly the *passive* of *ite,* to know, accept, received, accepted; but sometimes the same as *itea.*
Itere, *s.* the tail of most kinds of fishes; but that of the stingray is called *aero.*
Itere, *s.* the fag end of a piece of cloth.
Iteretunatore, *a.* full fleshed, smooth, slippery as the eel's tail.
Iti, *a.* [*ngiti,*] small, little, slender
Itiiti, *a.* little, very little or small, diminished.
Itiiti, *s.* pain, indicating the approaching labour of a female.
Itiiti, *v. a.* to take off the husk of the cocoanut, generally done with the teeth.
Ito, *s.* vigilance, activity.
Ito, *v. a.* to smooth, or polish; to finish.
Itoito, *s.* vigilance, energy, activity.
—*v. n.* to be watchful, active, vigilant.
Itoito, *a.* stimulating, arousing.
Iu, *s.* a rasp or file of any sort, formerly a piece of shark skin.
—*v. a.* to file or rasp.
Iu, *s* a million; according to the late king Pomare II, the ancient numeration of Tahiti was as follows;—10 times 10 make one *rau* or a hundred, 10 *rau* one *mano,* 10 *mano* one *manotini,* 10 *manotini* one *rehu,* 10 *rehu* one *iu,* that is 1.000,000; but when they counted by couples, as sometimes they did, in that case the *rehu* was 200,000, and the *iu* 2,000,000.
Iuiu, *adv* soundly, deeply, applied to sleep; *topaiuiu te taoto,* to sleep soundly.

Iva, *a.* nine in counting.
Ivaiva, *a.* dark, dismal, as *po ivaiva*, a dark or dismal night.
Ivi, *s.* [*iwi,*] a bone of any sort.
Ivi, *s.* a widow.
—*a.* widow, as *vahine ivi*, a widow woman.
Ivi, *s.* one that falls in battle; the body of the *ivi* was taken to the *marae* as an offering.
Ivi, *s.* a place of ghosts, in or about the mount Mehani in Raiatea.
Ivi e, *intj.* an exclamation of a warrior when his opponent fell in battle.
Ivioro, *a* wary, deliberate, applied to speech.
Ivitiaio, *s.* the spine of any animal.
Ivituamoo, *s.* the spine, as *ivitiaio.*
Ivitiamoo, *s.* the same as *ivituamoo.*

M

IN Tahitian retains its uniform power, and is never exchanged for another letter.

Ma, *conj* and. It is an ancient Polynesian conjunction, retained in several dialects, and in Tahitian in counting, as *ahuru ma rima*, ten and five.
Ma, *a.* clean, not soiled or polluted.
Ma, *prep.* with, as *ma te opahi*, with an axe.
Ma, *s.* a mark in a target, a butt or mark.
Ma, *s.* company, as *o mea ma*, such a one and company.
Maa, used sometimes as an *article*, as *maa taata rahi*, a big man.
Maa, *s* food, provisions of any kind.
Maa, *s.* a sling to throw stones, formerly used in war.
—*v. a.* to sling stones.
Maa, *a.* small, a little part or quantity.
Maa, *a* cloven, divided, applied to many things.
Maa aaa, *s.* the root or stock of the plantain, used for food in time of scarcity.
Maamaa, *s.* a fool, an idiot; also a vain thoughtless person.
—*a.* foolish, vain, useless.
Maamaa, *s.* the seed of the *ofeo* tree.
Maamaa i raau, *s.* a fool, a heedless fellow.
Maamaa i tai, *s.* a species of the star fish.
Maaro, *a.* fresh, sweet, as water without brackishness.
Maaroaro, *v. n.* to be confounded or ashamed.
Maau, *s* blemish, injury, damage, hurt.
—*v. n.* to be injured, or damaged.
—*a* injured, damaged; also vile, slandered by accusation.
Maava, *s.* a shell fish.
Mae, *a* thin, lean, applied to animals when decaying or falling away; withered, fermented, soft or decaying, as fruit over ripe.
Mae, *v. n.* to be abashed or confounded on account of some charge or accusation, or unpleasant occurrence.
Mae, *s.* a species of the *poreho* or tyger shell fish
Maea, *s* the white or sappy part of trees—*fig.* a worthless person.

Maee, *s.* warped or twisted, as timber exposed to the sun

Maee, *v. n.* to be manageable, or moveable.

—*a.* manageable, moveable; see *maoi.*

Maehaa, *s*, twins at a birth; see *piriati.*

Maehae, *s.* a spear or lance.

Maehe, *a* dry, withered, scorched by the sun.

Maei, *v. n.* to gush out as water; to issue out as smoke.

Maemae, *a.* soft, ripe, as plantains or other fruit; over ripe as fruit; tending to dis solution as flesh or fish.

Maemae, *a.* cloudy, frowning as the sky, or countenance.

Maenuenu, *a.* disordered, confused, dishevelled as the human hair, or palmeto thatch.

Maenuenu, *v. n.* to be sick at stomach, to be disordered in mind on account of something disagreeable.

—*a.* surfeiting, loathsome.

Maeô, *s.* a wasting disease of children.

—*a.* dwarfish, of stunted growth through ill health.

Maeoeo, *s.* insatiated desire; a constant longing after some kind of food.

Maere, *v. n.* to wonder; to be surprised, astonished.

Maere, *a.* tedious, prolix.

—*adv.* tediously; minutely, as *ui maere,* enquire minutely.

Maero, *v. n.* to feel an itching sensation of the skin.

Maero, *a.* itching.

Maete, *v. n.* to crumble or fall in pieces.

Maeva, *s.* a mode of attack in war, when all engaged at once.

Maevaeva, *v. n.* to be shaking in the wind as a flag; to be dishevelled; see *marevareva.*

Mafaifai, *v. a.* to gather or pluck off fruit, or leaves.

Mafatu, *s.* the heart; see *hutu.*

Mafera, *v. a.* to take advantage of a person of the other sex when asleep.

Mafera, *v. a.* to fish for the *aahi* at night.

Maha, *v. n.* to be satiated as to food or drink; to be appeased in a case of anger; to have the desire satisfied.

Maha, *a.* a modern word for four in counting; see *aeha.*

Mahae, *a.* torn, rent; see *hahae.*

—, the *past* and *passive* of the verb *hahae,* to rend.

Mahaha, *s.* a person that is great in words only.

Mahaha, *a.* slothful, dilatory.

Mahainui, *s.* the name of a tree that is used medicinally.

—*a.* soothing, mollifying in quality, applied to speech; in allusion to the property of the tree *mahainui.*

Mahame, *s.* the name of a tree.

Mahamui, *v. n.* to part from through disaffection, and join another party.

Mahamehamea, *a.* sacred, as the person, house, food, &c., of a principal chief.

Mahana, *s.* the sun; also a day; see *rā.*

Mahanafirifirirau, *s.* a day of perplexity.

Mahanahana, *a.* hot, warm; see *vei avera.*

Mahanaioiô, *s.* a hot sunny day.

Mahanoo, *s.* a day remarkably hot; also *mahana paaroto* is a hot scorching day.

Mahana toahu, *s* a sultry day, no air stirring.

Mahara, *a.* clear or vacant; see *atea.*

Mahara, *v. n.* to recollect, see *haamehara.*

Maharoharo, *v. n.* to cease, applied to anger, or to a desire when extinct.

Mahatea, *v. n.* to be wearied of a thing.

Mahavero, *v. a.* to dart a reed in a certain play.

Mahavivo, *s.* a key; see *taviri.*

—*v. a.* to lock or unlock by turning a key; also to turn or twist.

—*v.n.* to be turning or twisting.

Mahea, *v. n.* to fade; to fail, applied to desire; to be pale through fear; to cease, applied to rain.

Maheahea, *a.* fading, pale, squalid.

—*v. n.* to turn pale, to fade, to be destitute.

Mâhealtu, *s.* mental trouble, concern of mind.

—*v. n.* to be troubled in mind, affected, or offended.

Mahei, *a.* full, applied to a fishing basket or net.

Maheirava, *s.* the last beating pulse.

—*v. n.* to beat, as the last pulses of an expiring person.

Mahemo, *v. n.* to slip out, as a handle from a tool; to pass, as time; to fall behind.

—*s.* the thing that slips off, an abortive.

Mahemohemo, *v. n.* to slip off repeatedly.

—*a.* apt to slip repeatedly

Mahere, *v n.* to become, to change to some other state or condition.

Maheu, the *past* and *passive* of *heheu,* to open or uncover; see *heheu.*

Maheu, *v. n.* to be coming into notice, or be knowable; but the regular passive of *heheu* is made thus: *heheu,* to uncover, *heheu hia,* uncovered. *Maheu* is applied neuterly to something coming to be known.

Maheuheu, *v. n.* to be dishevelled, as the human hair; to be blown into disorder by the wind, as the thatch of a native house; thrown into disorder as bed clothes.

Mahi, *s.* [*mai,*] a sour paste made of fermented bread-fruit, and preserved for food in time of scarcity; see *tioo.*

Mahia, *adv. of time,* and the general idea is shortly, speedily, quickly, as in *mahia na, mahia aera,* but it is difficult to find an exactly corresponding word. It is often preceded by a negative, as *aita mahia,* not long.

Mahie, *v. n.* to grow up as seeds; see *tupu.*

Mahihi, *v n.* to grow up irregularly, as seeds scattered by the wind; to be wandering about, as one that has no settled habitation.

Mahihi, *v.n.* to slip off before the time, as the young of beasts; to fall off, as abortive fruit.

Mahihi, *adv.* aslant, obliquely, as *puta mahihi,* pierced aslant, or in an oblique direction.

Mahimahi, *s.* the dorado or true dolphin of the moderns

Mahimahi, *a.* sharp faced.

Mahimao, *s.* a large pit with a collection of the sour paste called *mahi.*

Mahina, *s.* the name of a clan or tribe, but the moon in some other dialects.

Mahine, *s.* a daughter; see *tamahine.*

Mahiohio, *v. n.* to whistle; to make noise as the wind in blowing among reeds, lines, &c.

Mahiohio, *v. n.* to go to stool; a bye-word.

Mahita, *a.* hasty, passionate, soon angry.

Mahiti, *v. n.* to be soon angry; see *mahita.*

Mahiti, *v. n.* to be started, or mentioned as a subject brought to view, or hearing.

Mahiti, *v. n.* the *past* of *iriti,* to be drawn, pulled, or be opened, brought up; the regular passive of *iriti* to open, is *iritihia,* opened.

Mahitihiti, *a.* apt to fly up, applied to the out-rigger of a canoe.

—*v. a.* to pluck or pull up, such as weeds; to pluck repeatedly (in the past.)

Mahoahoa, *s.* a violent headache; see *hoa.*

Mahoahoa, *v. n.* to be disturbed by noise.

Mahoahoa, *v. n.* to be surfeited, cloyed.

Mahoararo, *v. n.* to be sounding low, as thunder towards the horizon.

Mahaha, *v. n.* to be weak, diseased, or ineffective, and so easily overcome in time of war; to be dilatory in accomplishing any work.

Mahoi, *s.* the essence, or soul of a god.

Mahoi, *v. n.* to light upon, or come by chance.

Mahomahoâ, *a.* inert, sluggish, loitering.

Mahora, *s.* a low fence enclosing the court yard; the space between the fence and the house.

Mahora, *s.* a small island or islet; a modern name that took its rise, apparently, from the circumstance of the late king Pomare II having his *mahora,* or court, on the small island *Motuuta,* in Papeete Bay.

Mahora, *v. n.* to appear fine and clear, as the sky after cloudy and dark weather.

Mahora, *v n.* to be spread out as cloth, or any thing opened and spread, see *haamahora.*

—*v. n.* to be opened, unravelled, as a subject.

Mahora, *a.* even, level, smooth, fair and open.

Mahorahora, *v. n.* to be opened, expanded repeatedly.

Mahorahora, *a.* open, level, cleared, as land.

Mahore, *v. n.* to be peeling off in scales, as the skin of a person after being sun burnt.

Mahori, *s* the name of a species of plantain.

Mahoru, *v. n.* to be satisfied or comforted.

Mahoru, *v. n.* to be reduced to calmness as the weather after a storm; to cease, be quiet, as those that had a quarrel.

Mahu, *s.* a mist or fog on the hills; a low cloud.

Mahu, *v. n.* to be in a contented

state of mind, to endure; see *haumahu*.

Mahu, *a.* meek, not irritable, see *mamahu*

Mahu, *v. n.* to be growing, springing up, as the seed that had been sown.

Mahu, *s.* the name of a mess of food of grated taro, &c.

Mahu, *v. n.* to cease or stop; see *mono;* to be quenched as thirst, satisfied as desire.

Mahuatoa, *s.* a war weapon; a stick in the hand of a chief at a meeting for consultation.

Mahue, *v. n.* to be pushed up, as the earth by the shooting and growth of some plants, such as the *patara*.

Mahue, *v. n.* to be in terror or dismay in some dismal place, such as that of the dead.

Mahue, *v. n.* to have an extraordinary appetite, as the women who were supposed to be possessed with a *Tii* or evil spirit.

Mahuehue, *v. n.* to be amazed repeatedly; to have an extraordinary appetite frequently.

Mahui, *v. n.* to break forth, or be coming to light, as a crime, or some secret that was concealed. [discover.

Mahui, *v. a.* to perceive, or

Mahuihui, *v. n.* to be coming to light by little and little, as something that was unknown.

Mahuie, *s.* the name of a person, who of old had fire in constant keeping; see *aoaomaiaiu*.

Mahuinia, *v. n.* to be springing altogether, as seeds that had been sown; to rise up at once as warriors.

Mahuinia, *s* the northern-most of the Magellanic clouds.

Mahuiraro, *s.* the southernmost of the Magellanic clouds.

Mahumahû, *a.* ugly, slovenly, ill favoured.

—*v. n.* to be slothful, careless, and indifferent, except his own interest is concerned

Mahura, *v. n.* to be detected, brought to light; or rather to be coming to light as a secret.

Mahuru, *s.* a little sucking child.

Mahuruhurua, *v. n.* to become vile, be debased.

Mahuta, *v. n.* to leap, to fly; see *maue, rere*.

Mahutahuta, *v. n.* to leap, or frisk about.

Mahuti, *v. a.* to draw out, or up.

Mahuti, *v. n.* to slip off.

Mai, *s.* disease, sickness; any bodily disorder.

Mai, *prep.* [pronounced short] with, as *mai te oe i te rima*, with a sword in hand; see *ma*.

Mai, *prep.* towards the speaker in opposition to *tu*, or *atu*, as *a parau mai oe ia'u*, speak thou to me, or towards me, *a parau atu ia'na*, speak to him or towards him; see *atu*.

Mai, *prep.* from, as *mai hea mai oe?* whence art thou, from what place?

Mai, *v n.* to be found, a play term used by children.

Mai, *v n* to gush out, as smoke through apertures not sufficiently closed.

Mâi, *a.* watery, withered, applied to taro, yam, &c., when injured by the sun or dry weather.

Maia, *s.* a midwife.

Maiaa, *s.* a sow, cow, hen, or the dam of any animal.

Maiai, *s.* the name of a timber tree.

Maiai, *s.* the first fruits of the season, which was taken to the king or principal chief.

Maiai, *a.* fulsome, flattering, as *parau maiai*, a fulsome speech.

Maiao, *s.* the foot, or leg, generally used of birds, beasts, and insects; see *avae.*

Maiere, *v. n.* to wonder, ponder, be struck with surprise.

Maiere, *adv.* deliberately, wary as in questioning.

Maehe, *a* dry; see *maro.*

Maiha, *adv.* through, as *ua puta maiha*, pierced through.

Maihe, *adv.* diligently, fully, thoroughly.

Maihea, *adv.* whence? from what place?

Maihi, *s.* a canoe sharp at both ends.

Maihi, *v. n.* to fall or slip off untimely as the abortives of brutes

Maiii, *v. n* to go irregularly, as an arrow from a bow; to turn aside by a different road.

Maimai, *s.* a scrofulous person, one full of disease.

—*a.* diseased, full of bodily complaints.

Maimai, *intj.* a call to pigs, fowls, &c.

Maimi, *v a.* to search carefully; see *imi.*

Maimoa, *s* a toy, pet, favourite; a play thing.

Maina, *adv.* from mai, towards a person, and *na*, denoting the place spoken of, or understood as at a distance.

Mainaina, *s.* pain of mind, or anguish caused by anger or displeasure.

—*v. n.* to feel anger or displeasure.

—*a.* cutting, galling, causing pain, as by an insulting speech.

Maine, *adv.* slowly, circumspectly.

Mainei, *adv.* from *mai*, towards the speaker, and *nei*, this place. [*maineine.*

Maineine, *a* ticklish; see *haa-*

Maineine, *v n.* to feel displeasure, as *mainaina.*

Mainu, *v. n.* to drift away; see *manu.*

Maiore, *s.* a modern name for the bread fruit tree and its fruit; see *uru.*

Maira, *adv.* a compound of *mai*, towards the speaker, and *ra*, signifying distance of place or time.

Maire, *s.* a species of good bread fruit.

Maire, *s.* a sweet scented fern.

Mairefatiatia, *s* clouds at the edge of the horizon.

Mairefatutu, *s.* the same as *mairefatiatia.*

Mairi, *v. n.* to fall or drop down from a high place; to fall behind; to fall asleep; to be dropped or disused as a custom; see *topa* and *haamairi.*

Mairifarara, *v. a.* to excite disturbance.

Mairihaa, *v. a.* to drop work.

Mairihia, the *passive* of *mairi*, fallen upon.

Mairimoto, *s* a fall by a blow; see *moto.*

Mairitaue, *v. n.* to fall off suddenly, wholly. no obstacle being in the way.

Mairo, *s.* the name of a game among children

Mairohe, *s.* an unsatiable desire for some kind of food.

Mairohe, *s.* sickness caused by ungratified desire.

Maitai, *s.* [*maitaki, meitaki,*] goodness, holiness, blessedness, all kinds of happiness.
—*a.* good, holy, happy, blessed.

Maitai, *v. n.* to be well in any sense.

Maitai, *adv.* carefully, rightly, properly.

Maitatai. plural *adj* good when applied to more than one.

Maitaunu, *s.* a chronic disease, a disease of long continuance.

Maitaupo, *s.* some disease of the back or shoulders; something that causes a person to be ashamed or shun observation.

Maite, *adv.* slowly, thorougly, circumspectly.

Maiti, *v. a.* to select or choose.

Maitihe, *s.* sneezing.
—*v. n.* to sneeze.

Maitiorero, *v. a.* to discuss, debate a subject; to consider a subject deliberately.

Maitiparau, *v a.* much the same as *maitiorero*.

Maito. *s.* the name of a small black fish.

Maitu, *s.* the name of one of the nights of the Tahitian moon or month.

Maiuu, *s.* a talon, a claw; the nails of the fingers, or of the toes.

Mama, *v. n.* to drop or leak as the thatch of a house.

Mama, *v. a.* to chew, or masticate food.

Mama. *a.* open as the mouth; see *hamama*.

Mâmâ, *a.* light, not heavy.

Mamà, *v. a.* to close a ceremony or prayer.

Mamaa, *v. a.* the dual or plural of *maa*, to sling stones.

Mamaa, *v. a.* to strike with a club above and below, as if at a person's head and legs, used in the exercise of arms called *tiaraau*.

Mamae, *s.* pain or anguish of body or mind.
—*v. n.* to be in pain or anguish.
—*a.* painful, as *mai mamae*, a painful disease.

Mamâe, *a.* sacred.

Mamahu, *a.* affable, gentle, easy.

Mamahu, *s.* the name of a sort of pudding.

Mamii, *a.* slothful, dilatory; see *mahaha*.

Mamaià, *s.* abortive fruit that falls from the trees.

Mamaià, *s.* a name used as an appellation of a party formed some time ago at Tahiti, and afterwards in the neighbouring islands, who professed to improve upon the received Religion, and to be given to extraordinary prayer; they discarded some of the essentials of Christianity, and were immoral in their conduct.

Mamamehai, *s.* a leak forward or a head, as in a canoe; —*fig.* some fault in the Government, or among those at the head of affairs.

Mamao, *s.* some offerings or first fruits taken to the gods.

Mamaorero, *s* the concluding speech at a public meeting.

Mamaoroaroa, *a* destitute of inhabitants, as the country, by war or disease.

Mamaoroaioa, *s.* continued solicitous expectation
Mamara, *s* a species of plantain.
Mamara, *s* a species of oyster that is often poisonous.
Mamara, *a.* bitter and saltish, as the taste of salt water.
—*v. n.* to have bitterness, applied to the mouth in reproving repeatedly a heedless person.
Mamaru, *a.* easy of access, as a lewd woman
Mamatai, *s.* the star fish.
Mamatea, *s.* the sappy part of wood.
Mamau, *s.* the name of a certain plant or tree.
Mamau, *v. a.* to shake by the hand.
Mamau, *v a.* to take hold, detain, the plural of *mau*
Mamau, *v. n.* to have abundance in possession.
Mamaue, *v. n.* the dual of *maue*, to fly.
Mamauniho. *v. a.* to hold each other by the beak, as cocks sometimes do in fighting.
Mamea, *s.* the name of a ferocious sea eel
Mamea, *s* a warrior. The name is borrowed from the ferocious eel called *mamea.*
Mamea mata tahuri ore, *s.* a dauntless warrior that fears no danger.
Mami, *s* the ripe fruits of the chestnut tree.
Mamia, *v. n.* to be burnt, as food over baked
Mamo, *s.* the name of a very small fish
Mamo, *s.* race, lineage, progeny. The word is obsolete in Tahiti, but retained in other dialects; see *huaai*
Mamû, *s* silence, taciturnity
—*v n* to be silent, mute, not complaining
—*a* silent.
Mamu, *s.* the name of a species of soft stone
Mana, *s* power, might, influence.
—*a* powerful, mighty, affluent.
—*v. n* to be in power, possess influence.
Mânà, *s.* [Heb.] the food of the Israelites in the wilderness
Manaa, *a* manageable, moveable, portable
—*v. n* to be able to do or manage a thing; but according to Tahitian idiom, the thing is mentioned as manageable or otherwise, as *manaa ia ia'u*, it is manageable by me.
Manaanaa, *v n.* to be moveable or attainable.
Manaha, *s.* the name of a house sacred to *Oro.*
Manânâ, *a* vagrant, unabiding, wandering
Manao. *s* thought, idea, meaning, conception.
—*v n.* to think, muse, reflect.
Mànaonao, *v. n.* to exercise anxious thoughts
Manatu *s* profit, advantage; see *faufaa.*
Manauà, *a* improvident, inconsiderate
Manava, *s.* the belly, stomach, interior man.
Manava, *intj.* an exclamation of welcome to strangers or visitors, *Manava! a haere mai*, you are welcome! come here.
Manavafafati, *s* anguish, bitterness of soul through distress grief, or anger.

Manavafati, v. n. to be in bitterness or grief of mind

Manavaheahea, v. n. to be affected so as not to eat.

Manavahoi, s. the early crop of bread fruit, about October; but the season of abundance at Tahiti commonly commences about the latter end of December.

Manavahuhui, v. n. to be so affected as not to be able to eat

Manavanava, v. n. to think, ponder.

Manavarû, s an eager desire after a thing.
—v n. to be eagerly desirous.

Manavataahia, v. n. to void the excrements through fear.

Manavatopa, v n. the same as *manavataahia*.

Mane, s. a part of the net used for the *operu* fish.

Manee, a. moveable, portable; see *manaa*.
—v. n to be able to move or manage.

Manehenehe, s. a cutaneous disorder.

Manehenehe, v. n. to be affected with uneasiness of body or mind; to sympathize with the distress of others

Maneva, a. foolish, giddy; see *neneva*.

Mania, s. a calm, no wind stirring.

Mania, a. serene, unruffled, applied to the mind.

Mania, a. blunt, pointless, without an edge.
—v n to be set on an edge, as the teeth by eating sour fruit.

Maniania, s. disturbance by any any kind of noise.

Maniania, v. n. to be disturbed by noise.
—intj an exclamation, hush! silence.

Maniao, s. the foot or toes; see *maiao*.

Maniaro, v. n. to be sick at stomach.
—a. sick, qualmish; sea sick.

Maniaro, a. sick at stomach, qualmish.

Maniataeahaa, s. a smooth calm sea.

Maniatiputaputa, s. a calm in some places, while others near are rough.

Maniatooue, s. a calm, when the sea appears as smooth as glass.

Manihi, v. n. to slip or slide as in climbing a smooth tree.

Manihinihi, s. uneasiness; see *manehenehe*.
—v. n. to be heavy, to feel lassitude, as in the commencement of a disease.
—v. n. to feel uneasiness of mind; to sympathize with the distress of others.

Manihini, s. guests, visitors; see *manuhiri*.

Manii v. n. to overflow, or be spilling.

Maniinii, v. n to be spilling repeatedly, or in several different places.

Maninaniao, s. the toes of the feet.

Manina, a. plain, smooth, level.

Manini, s. the name of a small fish.

Maniniatore, v. n. to be abating, declining.

Manino, a. calm, smooth.

Maniuru, s. the back part of the head.

Mano, *a.* thousand, or 10 *rau* counted singly, when counted by couples 2,000.
Mano, *a.* many indifferently.
—*v. n.* to be numerous; see *rau*, *raverahi*.
Manona, *s.* some word of provocation.
Manoni, *a.* manageable, portable; see *manaa*.
Manononi, *a.* moveable, portable; see *manee*.
Manono, *s.* the name of a tree.
Manono, *s.* a powerful, energetic man.
Manu, *s.* a general name for all sorts of birds, fowls, or winged insects; also sometimes an animal of any kind.
Manu, *s.* a short cross seat in a canoe.
Manu, *s.* a scout, a spy in time of war.
—*v. n.* to act as a scout, or a spy.
Mànu, *v. n.* to float, to be afloat; to go adrift.
Manuà, *v. n* to be surly, uncivil, soon angry.
Manuaiaihaa, *s.* any thing that eats human excrements; a woman that fishes on the reef; also a butterfly.
Manuanu, *a.* loathsome, surfeiting.
—*v. n.* to be sick, qualmish.
Manufaite, *s.* a pledge or token of agreement between hostile parties; token of a truce in time of war.
Manufiri, *s.* a guest or visitor; see *manihini*.
Manuhi, *v. n.* to slip off as the handle of a tool; see *mahemo*, to be easy of extraction, as weeds, &c.
Manuhini, *s.* a visitor or guest.
Manuhiri, *s.* a visitor, one entertained.
Manuhoa, *s.* a bunch of red feathers tied to the long finger of the right hand of a person deceased, to prevent the god from eating his soul or spirit in the *po*.
Manuhou, *s.* a ceremony used in token of a truce between hostile parties; see *manufaite*.
Manuia, *v n.* to be prosperous, or successful in some project; to obtain what a person sought, or wished for.
Manunanu, *s.* worms, insects, creeping things. [see *niho*.
Manumanu, *s.* the tooth-ache;
Manunu, *s.* lassitude, weariness from great exertion.
—*v. n.* to feel weariness of body in consequence of toil or disease.
Manuoroo, *s.* a multitude collected together at some feast, or to observe some ceremony; see *auhoe*.
Manuoroo, *s.* the company of fishermen belonging to the canoes that go out to catch the albicore, bonetto, dolphin, &c.
Manupaari, *s.* a familiar term for a wise or prudent person.
Manureia, *s.* a person of a roving disposition; see *iheihere*.
Manuteaa, *s.* the name of a god, which was reported at times to inspire the bird call d *areva*.
Manutipao, *s.* a person of a fickle or unsteady disposition.
Manutoroa, *s.* the figure of a bird which was an appendage of some *maraes*.

Manuu, *v. n* to move forward a little; see *nuu*.

Mao, *s.* the name of a tree, the bark of which is used in dying native cloth.

Mao, *v. n.* to cease, applied to rain; to become fair, as a rainy day.

Mao, *s.* [*mango, mano,*] the shark, of which there are several species.

Maoa, *a.* ripe, applied to breadfruit; see *para.*

Maoa, *v. n.* to be sufficiently baked, applied to food.

Maoa, *v. a.* to throw a spear; push or pierce; to lift up the hand.

Maoae, *s.* the east, or rather north-east trade wind.

Maoaemataê, *v. n.* to be estranged in affection.

Maoaeomumu, *v. n.* to be in anxiety whether the wind would allow an entrance into a place of shelter.

Maoaereoiti, *s.* a little favourable breeze.

Maoaetaiva, *v. n.* to be estranged from a friend.

Maoaeterehuna, *v. n.* to go off without taking leave; see *poroi.*

Maoaetererua, *v. n.* to go off clandestinely, as a wife leaving her husband.

Maoafà, *s.* the name of a diversion in which spears are thrown at a mark; see *fa.*

Maoaoa, *s.* shame, confusion.
—*v. n.* to be ashamed, confounded.

Maoaoa, *v. n.* to be wearied by travelling.

Maoaoa auahi, *s* the glare or flame of fire.

Maoaoa, *a.* light, frothy, as speech; unsteady.

Maohe, *a.* pretty, handsome.

Maoheohe, *a.* neat, in good order.

Maohi, *a.* common, native, not foreign.

Maohuaiape, *s.* a species of large shark;—*fig.* an ungovernable person.

Maoi, *a.* attainable, moveable; see *maunaa.*

Maoi, *v. n.* to be bent under, as the leg or foot in falling suddenly.

Maoia, *s.* a sprain, or stretch of the ligaments of the foot or hand.

Maoia, *s.* lameness in walking, from a strain of the ancle or foot;—*fig.* a hurt by some fault.

Maoioi, *v. n.* to be moveable, bearable.

Maomao, *s.* a species of sea weed.

Maomaomatapiti, *s* the young of the shark;—*fig.* a young beginner in any thing.

Maona, *s.* a wrestler.

Maonaania, *s* a wrestler who makes for, and seizes the head of his antagonist.

Maona aiani, *s.* a self confident boasting wrestler.

Maona mehai, *s.* one skilled in wrestling.

Maora, *v. n.* to calumniate or accuse falsely.

Maore, *s.* a species of breadfruit.

Maori, *a.* indigenous, not foreign; see *maohi.*

Maori, *adv.* except, save that.

Maori, *adv.* well then, let it be so, *oia maori.*

Maori, *a.* well, welcome.

Maoro, *a.* long, the opposite to *mure*; long or tall, applied to a person.

Maotarera, *s.* a very ravenous species of shark;—*fig.* a gluttonous person.

Maotarera, *a.* abundant.

Maoti, *adv.* as *maoti*

Maoti, *s.* an after comer, intruder by speech.

Maotihau, *s.* one who aims at stirring up strife.

Maou, *v n.* to disturb the peace.

Maoû, *v. n.* to rustle.

Mape, *s* the chestnut tree and fruit; see *rata.*

Mape, *s.* the kidneys of any animal.

Mapu, *s.* a whistle or native flute.

Mapu, *s* palpitation of the heart through running or carrying a burden.

Mapu, *v. n.* to blow as a person out of breath; to whistle, see *hio.*

Mapû, *s.* the desire of some thing.

Mapua, *s.* a species of water [mint

Mapuhi, *v.n.* to recover breath; to be revived after swooning.

Mapumapu, *s.* weariness, exhaustion.

—*v. n.* to be wearied, tired, out of breath.

Mapura, *s.* a species of white taro that grows wild in the mountains.

Mara, *s.* the name of a timber tree, one species of which is called *ahatea*

Mara, *s.* the old name for the *ava* plant.

Mara, *a.* hard, seasoned, as the heart of a tree, in distinction from the sappy parts; seasoned as calabashes, bamboos, &c, used for holding water, or oil.

Mara, *s* the name of a large fish, of which there are two species, with remarkably large scales, one is the *maratea*, which is often poisonous

Maraa, *a.* manageable, portable, see *manaa.*

Maraa, *v n* to bear, rise up, bear up; also to be bearable, manageable, attainable, see *manaa*, *manee*, *maoi.*

Maraai, *s.* [*mangarai*,] the south wind, or nearly from that point of the compass, but not exactly.

Maraamu, *s.* the modern word for southerly wind.

Maraaraa, *a.* heavy, but manageable, or moveable.

Marae, *s* the sacred place formerly used for worship, where stones were piled up, altars erected, sacrifices offered, prayers made, and sometimes the dead deposited.

Marae, *a* cleared of wood, weed, rubbish, as a garden, or the place of worship.

Maraea, *s* red earth; see *araea.*

Maraefara, *s* a wise person, one well furnished with the knowledge of things.

Maraehaava, *s* the same as *maraefara*, see *atitipau.*

Maraia, *s* a sort of dark native cloth.

Maraia, *s.* a negro or black man.

—*a* black, or darkish colour.

Marai noa, *a.* of good appearance, of good quality.

Marama, *s.* the moon, a month; see *aiae*

Maramafaaipa, *s* the moon standing erect as to its horns; *fig* a person keeping his appointments.

Maramara, *a* bitter, acrid or acid

Maramaramara, *s* the light.

— *a.* light, not dark or obscure.

Maramaroa, *s.* a long period of time.

Maraô, *a.* light, frothy, applied to speech.

Maraorao, *s.* the break of day; see *aahiata.*

Marapo, *s.* the false rough appearance of the sea at night.

Marara, *s* the flying fish; see *tipa.*

Marara, *a.* dispersed, scattered abroad.

Marare, *s.* the horse chestnut; see *rata.*

Marari, *v. n.* to be cleared; to be made flat or level, as a piece of ground where the grass is trodden down; to fall back or retreat, as a vanquished army.

Mararo, *s* the name of a large tree which grows in the mountains.

Mararo, *a* of ill or ugly growth.

Marau, *a.* old, worn out, fading, applied to garments and other things.

Marau, *s.* the name of a small fish.

Maraurau, *v. n.* to be worn out, or in a fading state; also to be accustomed.

Maraurau, *s* the name of a fish.

Marauri, *s.* the blackish *mara* tree. [*mara* tree.

Maravahie, *s* an old worn out

Mare, *s* the old word for cough, but in consequence of the king Tu taking the name of Po-*mare*, the word was changed to *hota.*

Mare, *v. n.* to cough.

Mare, *v. a.* to throw the water over the head in bathing.

Marea, *s* the yolk of an egg.

Marea, *s.* the name of a fish of the parrot kind

Marearea, *a* decaying, ill-looking, sickly.

Marehurehu, *s.* the dusk of the evening.

Marei, *s* a snare.

—*v. a.* to entrap or ensnare.

Mareiao, *a.* light, trifling; not steady.

Maremare, *a* sparkling, as the salt water at night.

Marereiao, *a.* light, trifling; see *mareiao.*

Mareva, *s.* a fleet of canoes with visitors, bringing presents from one island to another.

Mareva, *v. n.* to pass on, or go by.

Mareva, *v. n.* to be capable of carrying or conveying, as a canoe or other vessel.

Marevareva, *v. n.* to appear transiently at a distance, so that a person has just a glimpse; to be fickle, moving to and fro.

Marie, *a* indigenous; see *anoano marie.*

Marie, *adv* slowly, deliberately; see *maite.*

Marie, *v n* to be silent.

Mario, *v. n.* to be gone; to be enfeebled; to be retrograde.

Mâriri, *s.* [*makariri,*] cold, see *toitoe.*

Mâriri, v. n. to be cold shivering through cold.
—a. cold, see *anu, toetoe.*
Maririmatatahuna, s. a disorder that festers, and increases inwardly.
Mariripureao, s. a fisherman who promises, but performs not.
Mariripuiepo, s. a fisherman who performs what he promises.
Mariue, s. a certain idolatrous prayer and ceremony; see *tuumariua.*
Mariua vaa, v. n. to be sunk, as a canoe by the sea breaking over it; to be in a broken state, as a community.
Maro, s. a narrow piece of cloth worn by men instead of breeches; see *tihere.*
Marô, a. dry, not wet or damp.
Mârô, a. obstinate, perverse; also persevering.
—s. obstinacy, perverseness.
Maroa, s. the name of a fish.
Maroa, s. a male child, in opposition to *mahine*, a female child.
Maroa, s. the upper moulding in the edge of a canoe.
Maroahiihii, s. the name of a ceremony.
Maroao, s. the near approach of day.
Maroapi, s. a quilted *maro*
Maroapu, s. a wide girdle; see *tihere.*
Marôapu, s. an empty cocoanut,—*fig.* an empty frivolous person.
—a. empty, as the dry shell of a cocoanut.
Maroati, *adv.* promptly, readily.
Marohi, a. dry: also withered.
Maroia, s. indifference, listlessness
—*adv.* indifferently, without interest.
Maromaroa, a. dilatory, slow, unapt.
Marorarora, s. shame, bashfulness.
—v.n. to be abashed or ashamed.
Marotai, s an offering after a voyage, rather to deprecate future evil, than as a thanksgiving.
Marotaiapuu, s. a contention made by conquered parties to recover their names.
Mârôtarahoi, a. obstinate, selfwilled, a proverbial expression, from obstinacy at head quarters.
Maro û, s a wet or damp girdle.
Maru, s. a devotee to a particular god.
Maru, s shade, shadow, covert of a tree, rock, &c.
Marû, a. soft, gentle, easy; also affable.
—v. n. to be gentle, easy, affable.
Marua, v. n. to crumble, moulder, as a wall.
Maruao. s. day spring, dawn, or near approach of day.
Maruarua, s. a ditch, or water course; a place that is uneven, being turned up by hogs.
Maruea. a. feeble, inefficient.
Maruhi, s a name given to a fish when soft in the shell, or when taken out of it.
Maruhi, a soft, downy, soft, as light earth when dug up.
Maruhi, v. n. to be dead, or in a state of death, as a corpse.

Maiumana, *s.* the grand appearance of one in office.
Marumaru, *a* shady, free from the glare of light.
Marumaru, *v.n* to be low, near setting, applied to the sun, when the air begins to cool.
Marumaruao, *s* the faint morning light.
Marumarupo. *s.* the shade, or obscurity of night.
Maruruanahu, *s.* a steady inoffensive person.
—*a.* silent, not loquacious.
Maruuruu, *v n.* to be calmed, eased, pacified.
Mata, *s.* the face of any creature.
Mata, *s* the eye.
Mâta, *s* the first beginning of any thing; the edge of a tool.
—*v. a.* to begin any thing; see *haamata.*
Mataa, *s* light, life, happiness, deliverance from trouble.
Mataa, *adv.* dearly, thoroughly.
Mataamoamo, *s.* an eye given to winking.
Mataaoaoa, *s.* a thin narrow face.
Mataara, *s.* a vigilant, watchful eye.
Mataaraara, *s.* a shining or bright eye, a staring eye.
Mataare, *s* waves, head or top of waves.
Mataatao, *s* black clouds rising in the horizon like columns, formerly looked upon as a sign of war.
Mataatoa, *s.* an eye looking aside.
Mataê, *s* a stranger, strangeness, alienation.
—*a.* strange, alienated.
Matae, *v. n* to be teazed or vexed by being disregarded.
Mataeiraa, *s.* the subjects of a chief: a certain tribe, clan, or sub division of the inhabitants.
Mataetae, *a.* obstinate, hard to deal with.
Mataetae, *v n* to be discouraged by want of success in counselling, reproving, or some undertaking.
Matafaro, *s* the act of looking steadfastly on a person while he is eating, as a dog will.
Matafeofeo, *s* a frowning face.
Matahahe, *a.* fierce, applied to a warrior.
Matahahi, *v. n.* to look so as to have no distinct knowledge of a person or thing.
Matahataha, *a.* open, unobstructed, as a place.
—*v. n* to be in a clear, unobstructed state.
Matahefa, *s.* a squinting eye.
Matahefahefa, *s* a proud look, a squinting look
Matahehe. *s.* a shy, alienated face, or look.
Matahiapo, *s* [*hiapo,*] the first born
Matahio, *s.* a beggar, one that looks about in order to ask or beg
—*v n* to ask or beg for food, property. &c.
Matahihira, *s* an angry eye that will not notice his enemy.
Matahiti, *s* a year.
Matahiti, *s* some incantation or charm.
Matahiti *s.* an angry staring eye.
Matahohe, *s.* a squinting eye.
Matahoihoi, *s* a face with scars, or pock-marked.

Matahuira, *s.* a sullen gloomy countenance.
Matahurahura, *s.* the first beginning of a crop of bread-fruit.
Matahurahura, *v. n.* to ask in a careless manner.
Matai, *s.* [*matangi*, *matani*, *makani*, *tangi*,] wind, air.
Mataî, *s.* skilfulness, dexterity.
—*a.* skilful, knowing.
—*adv.* skilfully.
Mâtai, *s.* presents given to visitors. [*otai*, which see
Matai, *s.* the same as *atai* and
Mataifaaino aau, *s.* wind threatening a storm.
Mataihaaputu, *s.* the south wind seen blowing from a distance, by its effects.
Mataihoriri, *s.* a cold, chilling wind. [tenance.
Mataioio, *s.* a pleasant coun-
Mataioa, *s.* a pleasant breeze.
Mataipupu ee, *s.* wind blowing from different quarters.
Matairofai, *s.* a squall, or wind with a shower.
Matairorofai, *s.* a squall.
Mataitai, *v. n.* [*matagitagi*,] to look, examine, satisfy curiosity.
Mataitaiaheva, *v. a.* to contend, as slingers of stones in time of war, while neither party had been conquered.
Mataitaiaheva, *v. a.* to solicit vehemently for property, while the other party refuses.
Mataituurua, *s.* the same as *mataipupu ee.*
Matamarû, *s.* a gentle, affable countenance.
Matamata, *v. a* to stop up chinks or fissures in a canoe or boat.
Matamala, *s.* the front in a place of defence.
Matamata, *s.* a second or after crop of fruit.
Matamatâ, *s.* shame, or a bashful countenance
Matamataiore, *s.* the name of a game for children.
Matamataiore, *v a.* to peep, so as to watch the motions of another.
Matamatataua, *s.* an endless strife, or war.
Matamau, *s.* a beggar, one that asks food, &c.
—*v. a.* to beg, ask for food, or property.
Matamehai, *s.* the first, what is fore-most.
—*a.* first, fore-most.
Matamoamoa, *s.* a thin, narrow face.
Matamoe, *s.* a stranger.
Matamoe, *a.* unacquainted, unused to a place.
Matamoe, *v. n.* to be drowsy, from *mata*, eye, and *moe*, sleep.
Matamomoa, *s.* a thin face; used in derision.
Mâtâmua, *s.* the first, the beginning.
—*a.* first, fore-most.
Matana, *v. a.* to begin; see *haamata.* [army.
Mataniau, *s.* one side of an
Mata ô, *s.* a sharp pointed stick used for digging.
Mataofefa, *s* a proud, or high look
Matapapa, *s.* a southerly wind with clouds and rain.
Mataparapu, *s.* a violent, outrageous wind.
Matapio, *s.* reserve, restriction of kindness.

Matapo. *s* a blind eye, a blind person.
—*a.* blind; also ignorant.
Matapoopoo, *s.* a hollow, one with hollow eyes.
—*a.* hollow eyed.
Matapouri, *v. n.* to be faint through hunger.
Matapu, *a.* courageous, intrepid.
—*adv.* courageously.
Matapuna, *s.* a small spring of water; also a bog or marsh.
Matapuna, *a.* prolific, see *puna.*
Matara, *v. n.* to be untied, unloosened, disentangled.
Matara, *v. n.* to be forgiven a crime.
Matara raa, *s.* a loosening, untying, disentangling.
Matara raa hara, *s.* forgiveness of sin.
Mataratara, *v. n.* to be untied, or loosened repeatedly, or in different places.
Matarefa, *s.* an eye looking awry.
Matarefa, *a.* drowsy, heavy with sleep.
Matarii, *s.* [*Matariki,*] the Pleiades.
Matarii, *s.* a year or season, reckoning by the appearance of *Matarii* or *Pleiades.*
Mataro, *v. n.* to be used or accustomed to a thing.
Mataroa, *v. n.* to be anxious, expecting something that is desired.
—*s.* solicitude, anxiety, hope.
—*a.* anxious, desirous.
Matarua, *s.* a person of two sides or parties
Matarui, *s.* a blind person, a blind eye.
—*a.* blind; also ignorant.
Matatahea, *s.* an eye that looks aside.
Matatahuri, *s* the same as *matatahea.*
Matâtâ, *s.* weariness.
—*a.* weary, laborious.
Matatea, *s.* a pale face through fear or sickness.
—*a* pale, as being sick or in fear; also uncovered, standing at a distance.
Matatu, *s.* a gloomy face.
Matatua, *v. n.* to be estranged.
Matatuatua, *s.* a frowning face, or eye; a rough unhandsome face.
Matatui, *s.* the first fish obtained in a new net, formerly given to the gods; also the first slain in battle.
Matatutu, *s.* a surfeit.
Matatuu, *s.* the name of a war song.
Matauiui, *s.* a person with a handsome face.
Matau, *s.* [*mataku, matagu,*] fear, dread.
—*v. n.* to fear; to be in terror, or dread.
Mâtau, *v. n.* to be accustomed, or used to a thing.
Matau, *s.* a fish-hook.
Matauaru, *s.* a mode of ordering the onset of a battle.
Mataunati, *s.* a sort of fish-hook.
Mataura, *s.* a fiery face or countenance.
Matautau, *a.* fearful, dreadful.
—*v. n.* to have repeated sensations of fear.
Matautau, *v. n.* to accustom, or practise repeatedly, as *mataiotaro.*
Matautau, *v. n.* to be scrupulous.
—*adv.* carefully.
Matavavivavi, *s.* an unsteady countenance while conversing.

Mate, *s.* [Malay, *mate*,] death, illness, hurt, injury The word is universal.

—*v. n.* to die, to be ill, sick, or hurt. [when ill.

Matea, *v. n.* to be pale, as

Mateaî, *v. n.* to be longing, as for fish, &c.

Mateatea, *v. n.* to be pale in the face through fear or illness.

Mateatea, *v. n.* to be pleased with immodest scenes.

Matehainu, *s.* the traditionary name of a person that was famous for climbing trees and rocks.

Mateono, *s.* a strong affectionate desire.

—*v. n.* to exercise love, compassion, &c.

Matere, *v. n.* to be able to go, as an invalid.

Matere ore, *a.* immoveable, not able to move.

Mati, *s.* the name of a tree, and its berries, which were used with the *tou* leaves to dye scarlet; also from its bark nets are made.

Matia, *s.* an old cocoanut in a state of vegetation.

Matia, *s.* the fry of some small fishes.

Matia, *v. n* to grow, or spring up, as plants; to recover strength after illness.

Matiaa, *s.* the mother, or dam among animals.

Matiaaivi, *s.* the dam of animals; a lean sow that has had young ones; see *mutuaivi.*

Matiatia, *s.* the name of a certain mode of fishing.

Matiatia, *v. n* to be recovering a little after illness.

Matie, *s.* the name of a species of matted grass.

Matie, *v. n.* to grow; see *tupu.*

Matiemate, *s.* the name of a religious ceremony.

Matipi, *a.* flat and round, applied to a stone.

—*v. n.* to skim along the water, as a stone that has been thrown; to roll.

Matira, *s.* part of a fishing rod.

Matirahi, *v. n.* to be longing for fish, &c.

Matitaue, *s.* one of another clan or party.

Matiti, *s.* a pendant.

Matiti, *v. n.* to grow, as a plant.

Matitipara, *s* an ornament made of ripe leaves, on the mast of a canoe.

Matitititi, *v. n.* to spread out, as the rays of the sun soon after rising.

Mato, *s.* a rock, a craggy rock or precipice.

Matoapo, *s.* a craggy rock projecting out.

Matoe, *s.* a crack or split.

—*v. n.* to crack or split, as wood in the sun.

Matomato, *a.* rocky, full of craggy rocks or precipices.

Matomato, *v n.* to be bashful, shy, with a degree of awe or fear.

Matopahu, *s.* a steep sided rock.

Matotafare, *s.* a rock that overhangs, and forms a cavern.

Matotoreva, *s.* a rock that has a protuberance to which to fasten a rope.

Matoru, *v. n.* to be inured to hardship.

Matoru, *a.* thirteen in counting, as *ahuru matoru.*

Matoru, *a.* thick, full fleshed.

Matorutoru, *v. n.* to be subdued or overcome in a contest; to give way or retreat.

Matotiti, *s.* what grows in the rocks.

Matotiti, *a.* handsome.

Matou, *pronoun plural*, first person, we three or more, excluding those addressed.

Matua, *a.* vigorous, strong.

Matua, *a.* hard, fixed, habituated, of long standing; chronic as to disease.

—*v. n.* to become chronic; to be settled.

Matuaô, *s.* care of domestic affairs; sagacity.

Matuao, *a.* parsimonious, frugal.

Matuapapa, *v. n.* to be piled up; reckoned in order, as a lineage.

Matuatua, *a.* ancient, placed in order, as in reckoning lineage.

Matuatua, *v. n.* to be vigorous, as an elderly person; to be settled, habituated to some place or practice.

Matuhituhi, *a.* cloying, satiating.

Matuauu, *a.* age worn, time worn.

Matutu, *v. n.* to search, examine, consider.

Matutua, *a.* of an ancient date.

Mau, *a.* true, real, not false.

Mau, *a prefix to plural nouns*, as *mau taata*, men, *mau mea*, things, the word marks a plurality

Mau, *v. n* to retain or hold any thing, as *mau i te parau a te Atua*, make a profession of Christianity.

Mau, *v a.* to seize, take hold of a thing.

Mau, *intj.* an exclamation, hold! *ia mau!* take hold!

Mau, *a.* many; see *mano* and *rau.*

Maua, *pron.* *dual*, including the speaker and a person spoke of or understood, we two.

Maua, *a* ignorant, clumsy, unskilful

—*s.* an ignorant person, ignorance.

Maua, *s.* [*maunga, mauna,*] a mountain; see *moua.*

Màua, *s.* waste, wastefulness; see *haamâua.*

—*v. n.* to be lavish or wasteful.

Maua, *s* an old cocoanut tree; see *maui.*

Mauaea, *s.* a refuge.

Mauaea, *a.* appeased, satisfied, applied to hunger.

Mauaua, *a.* aged, beginning to fade or decay.

Maue, *v n.* to fly, as a bird; see *mahuta.*

—*v. n.* to start, leap, or jump.

Maueue, *v. n.* to be joyful, or much pleased.

—*s* pleasure, joy, gladness.

Maueue, *a.* grateful, satisfactory.

Maufaainaina, *s.* rage, anger, fierce anger.

Mauhaa, *s* the handle of a tool; stalk of fruit.

Mauhaa tamai, *s.* arms, implements of war

Mauhi, *a.* soft, downy.

Mauhonoa, *s.* an understanding or agreement between different parties.

Mauhonoa, *v. n.* to be abruptly joined together.

Maui, *s.* an old cocoanut tree that is nearly bare, and has ceased bearing; see *maua.*

Maui, *s.* the name of some religious ceremony.

Mâui, *s.* the name of a certain prophet, or wise man, mentioned in Tahitian traditions *

Maui, *v. n.* to be in a pet, or fit of anger, on account of disappointment in food, &c.

Mauifaatere, *s.* the name of a sacrifice offered to the gods before a voyage.

Mauitifai, *s.* a certain sacrifice or *oroa* performed hastily.

Mauiui, *s* pain, anguish, grief; see *mamae.*

—*v. n.* to be in pain, to be sore.

Maumau, *intj.* an exclamation of triumph; see *aitoa.*

Maumau i te hau e, *intj.* of envious triumph.

Maumauorero, *v. n.* to keep talking, or telling a tale.

Mauna, *s.* a carved piece of wood in the *marae.*

Mauna, *v. a.* to divulge a secret.

Maunauna, *v. n.* to be in a bare state; to be exposed.

Maunauna, *a.* rough, as cloth or leather.

Maunu, *s.* bait for fish; see *aramu.*

Maunu, *s.* the name of a sacred net named in some old tales.

Maunu, *a* bare, without leaves, hair, feathers, &c.

Maunu, *s.* ten fathoms in measure; see *umi.*

Maunu, *v. n.* to be peeled, made bare.

Maunu, *s.* fish newly obtained

Maunu atoa, *s* a wind that blows, and lulls again.

Maupihaa, *s.* the name of an island to the west of the Society Islands.

Maurau, *s.* a range of leaves tied together to catch fish.

Maure, *a.* shorn, as a tree of its leaves and branches.

Maureure, *s.* shame, dismay, on being too late for the ceremonies of an *oroa* or sacrifice.

—*v. n.* to be abashed, ashamed.

Maureure, *a.* clumsy, unskilful.

Mauri, *s.* a ghost, or departed spirit.

Mauri, *s.* a bunch of feathers formerly tied to the head of a person when near death.

Mauriuri, *s.* a singing noise in the ear.

—*v n.* to chirp as a cricket.

Mauroa, *s.* the tropic bird.

Mauru, *v. n.* to be shedding, or falling, as the hair.

—*a.* bare, shorn.

Mauruuru, *a.* agreeable, pleasing, satisfactory.

—*s.* pleasure, delight, satisfaction.

—*v. n.* to be pleased, satisfied, delighted.

Mautori, *v. n.* to withhold; to keep steadfastly; to make much of a thing.

Mauu, *a.* wet, damp.

Mavae, *s.* a fissure, crack, or split.

Mavaevae, *s* the same as *mavae.*

—*v. n.* to be split, or divided into parties.

Mavaevae, *a.* open, separated.

Mave, *v. n.* to be flowing, as hair in the wind.

Mavete, *a.* open, as a door; unfolded, as a garment.

---

* Mâui was a Priest, but afterwards deified, he being at one time engaged at the *marae*, and the sun getting low while his work was unfinished, he laid hold of the *hihi*, or sun rays, and stopped his course for some time.

Mea, *s.* a thing, a person, any thing mentioned.

Mea, *subst. pron. o mea,* such a one, when the person is not named, *ia mea,* by, with, or to such a one.

Mea, *v. a.* to do, a word used as a convenient substitute instead of naming the action.

Meâ, *v. n.* to be red, as the skin after eating fish that is poisonous, or very stale.

—*s.* the redness of the skin when affected by eating stale or poisonous fish.

Mee, *v. n.* to shrink or be warped, as green timber.

—*a.* shrunk, warped, as timber by the sun.

Mee, *a.* manageable; see *manaa, manee.*

Meha, *s.* the name of a small bird.

Meha, *s.* the name of a small black fish with dangerous thorns on the tail.

Mehai, *a.* first in order as to time or place.

Mehameha, *v. n.* to be terrified, frightened.

—*a.* frightful, terrifying.

Mehani, *s.* the name of a mountain in Raiatea, where the ghosts of the dead were said to go.

Mehara, *v. n.* to think, or remember.

Mehau, *s.* [Malay, *haua* or *hawa,*] the wind.

Meho, *s.* the name of a bird.

Meho, *v. n.* to be hiding, or seeking a refuge among the bushes, as fugitives in war time.

Mehoi, *s.* the substance of an image representing a god; the power and dignity of a god.

Mehomehoura, *s.* a class of men of fine growth.

Mei, *a.* full stuffed, as a bag.

Meia, *s.* the banana, of which there are several species and names.

Meia pare mai, *s.* a young banana used for sacrifice.

Meii, *s.* the fat of meat distinguished from the lean, called *i'o.*

Memee, *a.* shrunk, twisted, as timber in the sun.

Memeha, *v. n.* to recoil, to withdraw, as a warrior his spear.

Memeha, *s.* the name of a fish; see *meha.*

Memeru, *s.* the name of an ugly fish; an ill-grown ugly person.

Memu, *a.* swollen, applied to the lips.

Memu, *v. n.* to be silent; see *mamu.*

Memu, *a.* blunt, as a tool; see *haamemu.*

Memu, *v. n.* to be enlarged or magnified.

Memumemu, *a.* blunt, thick, enlarged.

Mena, *s.* a thing, the same as *mea.*

Menema, *s.* [Gr. *mnema,*] a monument, sepulchre.

Menemene, *a.* round, globular.

Meneû, *v. n.* to advance in quantity; to be aggravated.

Mere, *s.* the name of a star; see *hutarava.*

Mere, *s.* the affectionate grief of a parent.

Meremere, *v n.* to grieve on account of a child.

Mereû, *s.* the name of a game among children.

Meriue, *s.* a skipping rope used by children.
—*v. n.* to skip on a rope, a play of children.
Metia, *s* the modern word for a parent.
Metua, *s.* a parent, without determining the sex.
Metuaao, *s.* frugal, parsimonious.
Metuafaai, *s* a nursing parent.
Metuafaaamu, *s* the same as *metuafaai.*
Metuahoovai, *s* a parent in law.
Metuapuru, *s.* a parent that caresses his children.
Metua tane, *s* a father, or male parent.
Metuatanoa, *s.* the divider of the *ava.*
Metuatavai, *s.* a parent that adopts a child.
Metua vahine, *s.* a mother, or female parent.
Meu, *s.* the cry of a cat.
Meu, *a.* third in a certain game.
Meumeû, *a.* thick, as a board.
Meumeu, *v. n.* to be benumbed, or cramped.
Mihi, *s* grief, vexation, sorrow.
—*v. n.* to grieve, to be in sorrow or pain of mind.
Mihoorie, *s.* the name of a pleasant wind.
Mihumihu, *v. n.* to whisper; see *muhu.*
Miimii, *s* a grudge, an envy, a displeasure.
—*v. n.* to grudge, envy, murmur.
Mimi, *s* urine.
—*v. n.* to make urine.
Mimio, *a.* wrinkled, furrowed as the face, cloth, &c.
Miomio, *a.* wrinkled, as *mimio.*
Mira, *v. a.* to put pitch or gum on the ends of the Tahitian arrows; to polish clubs, spears, &c; to dress the head or hair with gum and oil.
Mire, *v. a.* the same as *mira.*
Miri, *v. a.* to embalm a corpse, as formerly practised in Tahiti.
Miri, *s.* [from the Eng. *mint,*] the horse mint.
Mirimiri, *v. a.* to handle and examine a thing.
Miro, *s.* [*milo,*] the *amae* tree; see *amae.*
Miro, *s.* an elderly looking person; a child of slow growth.
Miromiro, *a* belonging to an office, shewing an office.
Mirotumae, *v. a.* to exercise arms; see *tumiro.*
Mirotumarae, *s.* a thing of long standing, such as the *miro* tree standing in a *marae*; a true resident of a place; a hairy person.
Mitamita, *v. n.* to murmur, or scold to one's self.
Mitaro, *v. n* see *mataro, matau.*
Mitaromaroa, *v. n.* to be long accustomed to a thing.
Mitua, *s.* a parent; see *metua.*
Miti, *s* salt, salt water, sauce; see *tai.*
Miti, *v. a.* to lick, as a dog does.
Miti, *v. n* to smack the lips.
Miti, *s.* [from the Eng., Mr.] Master, Sir.
Mitiero, *s.* a sauce made of scraped cocoanut, shrimps, and salt water.
Mitimiti, *v. a.* to lick repeatedly, as a dog.
Moa, *s.* a fowl.
Mo'a, *a.* sacred, devoted to the gods; see *raa.*
Moa, *s.* the name of a species of fern.

Moa, *s.* a whirligig made of the *amae* seed.

Moa, *s.* a branch of *miro* leaves used in the *marae*.

Moafaatito, *s.* a fighting cock.

Moahururau, *s.* a fowl of many qualities ;—*fig.* an unsteady or fickle person.

Moa opapa, *s.* a fowl without a tail.

Moaofiri, *s.* the name of a plant; also a wild fowl.

Moapateatoto, *s.* a courageous cock ; a stern warrior.

Moapuruhi, *s.* a cowardly cock ; a cowardly warrior.

Moataratua, *s.* a cock with a long spur ;—*fig.* a bold warrior.

Moaraupia, *s.* a peculiarly coloured fowl.

Moana, *s.* the deep, or abyss ; the sea, or any deep water.

—*a.* deep, in opposition to shallow.

Moana afa, *s.* a sea that has deep gullies in the bottom.

Moanafaaaro, *s.* a place at sea where all land is lost sight of.

Moanafarere, *s.* the trackless deep.

Moana faoaoa, *s.* a troubled sea ; intestine commotions.

Moana faroaroa, *s.* a deep that is unfathomable.

Moana reva, *s.* the fathomless deep.

Moana tafarere, *s.* the same as *moana farere*.

Moana tere ore hia, *s.* an untried ocean ;—*fig.* a woman not known.

Moana haauriuri, *s.* the deep coloured sea.

Moana timatima, *s.* the black coloured sea.

Moana tumatuma, *s.* the same as *moana timatima*.

Moana topa tô, *s* a sudden abrupt depth.

Moana punao, *s.* a sea with gullies in the bottom.

Moapuapua, *s.* a sort of cap on the white shell first.

Moaraororaoro, *s.* a turkey, from its voice.

Moarava, *s* a peculiar coloured cockle.

Moarima, *s.* one finger hooked into another's finger.

Moataavae, *s.* a fowl tied by the leg.

Moatautini, *s.* a cock that beats all his opponents ; an undaunted warrior.

Moavari, *s.* a cock, the same as *moa oni*, a male fowl.

Moe, *s.* sleep ; see *taoto*.

—*v. n.* to sleep ; also to lie down.

Moe, *a.* lost ; see *riro*.

—*v. n.* to lose, forget ; see *haamoe*.

Moea, *s.* a mat to sleep on.

Moeahuru, *s.* the name of a certain wind.

Moeanae, *s.* anxious sleep.

Moeanaenae, *v. n.* to sleep with anxious thoughts.

Moeapa, *s.* a person seized by a warrior.

Moeapaa, *s.* the name of an idolatrous ceremony.

Moeapapa, *v. n.* to sit closely to any pursuit; to follow closely after a desired object

Moeapipiti, *s.* a mode of seizing a thing instantaneously.

Moearaaau, *s.* anxious sleep.

Moeauna, *v. n.* to ruminate as a person in bed, thinking on on various subjects.

Moeauna, *s.* a thoughtful sleep.

Moeihirea, *v. n.* to go to sleep under alarm and fear.

Moeiuiu, *s* a deep, sound sleep.
—*v. n.* to sleep soundly.
Moemoe, *s.* a species of native grass.
Moemoe, *a.* solitary, lonesome; also secret, as a place.
Moemoe, *s.* an ambush; see *taotooto.*
—*v. n.* to lie in ambush.
Moemoea, *s.* a dream; see *taoto, faaheimoe.*
—*v. n.* to dream; to wander, as the thoughts in a dream.
Moenanu, *v. n.* to talk in sleep.
Moeorau, *s.* anxious sleep.
Moeorio, *v. n.* to be in a reverie.
Moeorou, *v. n.* to be possessed of a strong desire after some good.
Moeoru, *v. n.* to sleep immoderately.
Moeparapara, *s.* a mode of seizing prey.
Moepo, *s.* the first embrace.
—*v. n.* to keep close together, as a new married couple.
Moerurua, *v. n.* to talk, or walk during sleep.
Moere, *s.* a fish-hook.
Moere, *s.* wind, cloudless sky.
—*a.* fine, cloudless.
Moererurua, *s.* wind with cloudless sky.
Moetuo, *v. n.* to sleep uneasily, longing for the morning.
Mohea, *a.* sickly, yellowish, or pale.
—*s.* yellowishness, sickliness.
—*v. n.* to be pale.
Mohemohe, *a.* dim, not clear, applied to a lamp.
—*v. n.* to be burning dimly, as a lamp.
Mohemohe, *v. n.* to be recovered a little from sickness.
Mohi, *v. n.* to be beclouded, made dim.
Mohi, *v. n.* to lie down in ambush.
Mohimohi, *s.* obscurity, indistinctness.
—*a.* obscure, indistinct
Mohimohi, *v. n.* to be dazzled, as the eyes by the sun; to be made dim, or have indistinct vision.
Mohina, *s.* a piece of wood chopped round and smooth.
Mohina, *s.* a glass or stone bottle.
Mohoi, *v n.* to be happening by chance.
Moi, *s.* the heart of a tree; see *popo.*
Moi, *s* the name of a fish.
Moiheha, *s.* stoppage in the nostrils
Moihi, *s.* a fibrous black substance that grows in bogs.
Moiho, *s* a lamp wick, a piece of cloth twisted, and oiled for a torch.
Moimoi, *a.* aged, stricken in years.
—*s* aged, principal, steady old men.
Moini, *s.* a sort of basket; see *oini.*
Moiri, *s.* the name of a famous legendary hog killed by *Hiro*, according to tradition.
Moiriiri, *v. n.* to swallow without mastication.
Moitaa, *s.* the joint on which the lower jaw hinges to the upper.
Momea, *s.* the name of a species of fern
Momi, *s* the name of a species of eel.
Momi, *v. a.* to swallow; see *horomii.*
Momoa, *s* the ankle joint; the knuckles.

Momoa, *v. a.* to espouse, or contract marriage.
Momoa, *v. a* to make sacred, put under a restriction.
Momoa. *a* long and narrow, applied to the face.
Momomo, *v. a.* to smash, to break to shivers.
Momona, *a* sweet, delicious.
Mona, *a.* sweet.
Monamona, *a* sweet; very sweet, as some food.
Moni, *s.* [Eng. *money.*] gold, silver, any coin, money
Moninipape, *s.* a whirlpool in a river.
—*v. n.* to feel drowsy after bathing.
Mono, *v. n.* to stop, or cease to run, as blood, water, &c.
Mono, *v. n.* to be in the room or place of another.
—*v a.* to substitute, or fill up vacancies.
Monoi, *s.* the sweet scented oil used by the natives.
Monomono, *v. n.* to be stopping or ceasing from flowing, applied to a fluid.
Monomono, *v. a.* to fill several vacancies.
Moo, *s.* [*moko,*] a lizard, of which there are many species
Moo, *s.* the spine, or spinal marrow; see *tuamoo*
Moo, *s.* taro shoots, or strips for planting.
Moohono, *s.* a backbone without proper joints.
Moohono, *a.* strong.
Mooi, *a.* manageable · see *maoi*
Moomu, *s.* the heart of the cocoanut tree.
Moopiro, *s.* a disease that affects the posteriors
Moopô, *v. n.* to be lost, or be extinct, as a family; to be erased, or lost.
Moorà. *s* the wild duck.
Mooi à papaa, *s.* a foreign duck.
Moorà ao, *s* a goose or gander; geese.
Moore, *s.* the same as *moorà.*
Mootaifare, *s.* a lizard that cries in the house, which cry is said to be a sign of wind.
Mootua, *s* a grand child.
Moôtua, *s* a great grand child.
Mootuaio, *s.* the spinal marrow.
Mootuatini, *s.* a great great grand child
Mootuatinitini, *s* a very distant progeny indefinitely known.
Mootuatuarau, *s* the same as *mootuatini.*
Moraurau, *s.* the abatement of anger after a dispute.
More, *s.* the bark of the *purau* tree, of which ropes and mats are made;—*fig.* a warrior that goes without his accoutrements.
More, *a.* short, black, and ugly, applied to children's teeth.
More, *v. n* to droop or fall, as *pia* leaves when ripe.
Morehu, *s.* the name of a certain wind.
Morehurehu, *a.* dark, not well heated, applied to the stones in a Tahitian oven.
Morehutariaroa, *s.* a wind said to be produced by the god *Teroro*, which carried all before it.
Morei, *s.* the cork of a bottle; see *orei.*
Moreiau, *s.* the name of a prayer used when investing a king, or principal chief, with authority.
Moremore, *a.* smooth, without branches, as a tree; even, without protuberances; also hairless.

Mori, *s* cocoanut oil; oil in general; a lamp.

Moria, *s.* the name of a certain religious ceremony performed by the Priests at the *marae*, with prayers and offerings, on the restoration of a person that had been dangerously ill.

Morimori, *s.* the prayers, &c, after the restoration of a sick person.

Morohi, *v n.* to fall to the ground, or come to nothing, as plans or schemes; to be forgotten, or be extinct.

Morohirohi, *v. n.* to cease by little and little, applied to a disturbance.

Moroitâ, *v. n.* to be struck dead as it were by fear, as when a person was seized by an enemy.

Motaifaa, *s.* a butt or mark to throw at.

Motaifai, *s.* a mark made of the tail of the stingray, used as a butt to throw at

Motaitai, *v. a.* to attempt; to make a beginning, as two persons beginning to box or wrestle.

Motara, *s.* the name of a sort of basket.

Moti, *v. n.* to terminate, as the boundary of land, or a season of the year.

Motia, *s.* a boundary, termination, or limit.

Moto, *s.* hard or unfermented bread fruit put in a pit of *mahi*; see *mahi* and *tioo*.

Moto, *s.* a blow from the fist.

—*v. a.* to box, or strike with the fist.

Motoate, *s.* an acute pain in the stomach or liver.

Motoe, *a.* cold; see *anuanu* and *toetoe*.

Motoe, *v. a.* to crawl, as an earth worm.

Motoi, *v. a.* to join, or put one piece of timber against another; to make one thing to meet another.

Motoi, *v. a.* to rebut, or retort an argument; to give a present, or bribe, to gain an end.

Motoî, *s.* a float or raft of trees, with a mast, &c.

Motomoto, *v a.* to box or fight; to quarrel, as two persons.

Motoro, *v a.* to make use of some means to awake and entice a person out of the house, in the night, for base purposes.

Mototano, *s.* a well directed blow with the fist.

Motu, *s* a cut, breach, or rent.

Motu, *s* an island, a low island, in opposition to *fenua*, where there is high land.

Motu, *v n.* to be in a state of separation, as a tree cut, a piece of cloth torn, thread or cord broken asunder.

—*a* torn, broken, cut.

Motufarô, *s* patience in waiting for a thing.

—*v n* to be in a state of solicitous waiting, or suspense.

Motufenû, *v. n.* the same as *motufarô*

Motumotu, *a.* torn in many places; ragged, full of holes.

Motunene, *a* complete, finished as a journey, work, or engagement.

Motunene, *v n.* to be clean gone, as a party.

Motupari, *s* a boundary; a line of distinction between two parties.

Motupari, *v. a.* to break off acquaintance or connexion.

Motupo, *s.* a nightly theft.
Mototô, *a.* broken short off, as sugar cane.
Motutootoo, *a.* vanquished, overcome in war.
Motutu, *v. n* to be beset on every side.
Motuu, *s.* the name of a mountain shrub that bears a dark red berry, used for dying.
Motuu, *v. n.* to be stranded, as a rope; to be in a state of mental weariness through waiting, &c.
Motuu, *a.* wearied, exhausted.
Motuura, *s.* something very agreeable or pleasant.
Motuuruuru, *a.* roughly cut; see *uruuru.*
Motuutuu, *s.* cramp, or numbness of the limbs.
Motuutuu, *a.* cutting, piercing, applied to speech.
—*v. n.* to be in pain through weariness.
Môu, *s.* the coarse sword grass, of which there are several species, as *môu haari, môu raupo, môu rau hahae, môu rarotaa.*
Mou, *v. n.* to be consumed; to fail, vanish, or be done away; see *haamou.*
Mouraa, *s.* extirpation, extinction, abolishment.
Moua, *s* [*mounga, mouna, mauna,*] a mountain.
Mouea, *s.* a refuge; a skilful physician; also abundance of food, &c.
Moupaa, *s.* a sort of native cloth of a dark colour
Mu, *s.* the name of a fish, sometimes called snapper.
Mu, *s.* a buzz or confused noise.
—*v n.* to make a confused noise or din.
Mua, *a.* first, fore-most.
Mua, *prep.* before, the opposite of *muri,* behind.
Mua, *s.* the head quarters, residence of chiefs, sacred places.
Muaarai, *v. n.* to make a noise by confused talking.
Muemue, *a.* of a full size from top to bottom.
Muhu, *s.* noise, the din of talking; see *mu.*
—*v. n.* to make a noise or din.
Mui, *s.* a bundle of bread-fruit, &c., tied together.
—*v. a.* to tie up bundles of *uru,* cocoanuts, &c.
Mûmû, *v. a.* to make a confused noise, as of a number of persons talking together.
Muna, *s.* a name given to a basket used by the sorcerers; see *tahutahu.*
Muna, *v. n.* to be sparing in eating certain kinds of food.
Munaa, *s.* the name of a cutaneous disease.
Munaiho, *adv.* formerly; see *mutaaiho.*
Munamuna, *v. n.* to mutter, to whisper.
Muofai, *s.* a patient person; one who can bear insults.
—*v. n.* to bear up under trouble, or insult.
Muofare, *s.* the consecration of a new dwelling house.
Muohau, *s.* the commencement of peace.
Muoo, *s.* taro shoots used for planting; see *moo.*
Muoo, *s.* a branch presented at the *marae* on commencing the building of a new house.
Muoo, *v. n.* to be full of anger or displeasure.

Mura, *s.* [Gr. *myron*, Latin *myrrha*,] myrrh.
Muraa, *prep.* before, in former time.
—*adv.* formerly, anciently.
Muraaiho, *adv.* formerly, as *muraa.*
Muraro, *v. n.* to endeavour, to persuade; see *puraro.*
Mure, *a.* short, in opposition to *maoro*, long.
—*v. n.* to be short; to cease, come to an end.
Mureavae, *v. n.* to go off in a swoon.
Muremure, *a.* short, very short, applied to a member of the body.
—*v. n.* to leave off or cut very short, as work, discourse, &c.
Mure ore, *a.* endless, without a termination. [see *mua.*
Muri, *prep.* behind, afterwards;
Muri, *s.* the place behind occupied by the women.
Muri'ho, *adv.* & *prep.* behind, backward, but close by.
Muriahoe, *v. n.* to be falling behind, as in paddling a canoe, or rowing a boat.
Muriaito, *s.* a sort of paint of a red colour, obtained from the *aito* tree.
Muriaroha, *s.* a lingering affection for a person.
—*v. a.* to follow after a person in regard and affection.
Muriavai, *s.* the mouth of a river or brook, where it enters the sea.
Muriapape, *s.* the same as *muriavai.*
Murihere, *s.* affection, or regard for a person.
Mutaa aenei, *adv.* formerly, in time past.
Mutaaiho, *adv.* & *prep.* formerly, anciently, first.
Mutamuta, *v. n.* to mutter without speaking out.
—*s.* a muttering, commonly of discontent.
Mute, *v. n.* to cease, to break off.
Mutea avae, *v. n.* having all departed; to be all gone, as the people of a place.
Mutoi, *v. n.* to listen secretly to the conversation of people.
Mutu, *v. n.* to be gone, applied to persons passing along.

N

THIS Letter is used with uniformity in Tahitian, except perhaps in a few words, where it is exchanged with *r*, as *e ene*, *e ere*, *namu*, *ramu*, &c.

Na, *prep.* of, belonging to a person; see *no*, *ta.*
Na, *article*, used before most things, when two or three, or a small number is understood.
Na, *pron.* contraction of *ana*, third person singular.
Na, *an affix* to verbs in the past or perfect tense, as *i amu na vau*, I have eaten; also in the future, *ua amu na vau*, I shall have eaten.
Na, *prep.* by, for, by way of.
Na, *v. a.* to present, or to offer.
Na, *intj.* lo! see! behold!
Na, *adv.* of order, as *oia na*, he first; *o vau na*, I first; *teie na*, this first.
Na, *a word* of calling pigs, fowls, &c., *na, na.*
Na, *adv.* of place, denoting the local position of the person addressed, as being at a dis-

tance, as *ia oe na*, with thee, (at some distance)

Nà, *a.* quiet, applied to a child that has ceased crying.

—*v. n.* to be quiet or still; to cease crying; see *faanà.*

Naenae, *s* the place where children were nursed.

Nafea, *adv.* when? of time past, as *i nafea oe i haere mai ai?* when didst thou come here? It is preceded by an *i.*

Naha, *s.* a sort of native cistern made of leaves; a receptacle for some liquid.

Naha, *adv.* hitherto, yet, up to this time.

Nahà, *intj.* behold! preceded by an i, as *i nahà!* denoting wonder or surprise, or that the thing demands notice.

Nahavaivai, *s.* a receptacle, or cistern well supplied with water; also abundance.

Nahanaha, *a.* well arranged, in good order.

Nahe, *s.* the gigantic fern, the root of which is used for food in time of scarcity.

Nahea, *adv* how? by what way, or in what manner?

Nahea e, *adv.* long ago, long since.

Nahoa, *s.* a great concourse, company, troop.

Nahonaho, *a.* well regulated, in good order, as an assembly.

—*v. n.* to be in good order, as a table well prepared, and well supplied.

Nahû, *a.* the same as *nahonaho.*

Nahuihua, *s.* the name of a star.

Nahuitarava ia mere, *s.* the stars of Orion.

Nahunahû, *a.* plenteous, abundant, as food.

Nainai, *s.* a play actor; a performer in the various native games. [also deceitful.

Nainai, *a.* small, diminutive;

Naiô, *a.* very small, see *haihai.*

Naiô, *s.* a fork, or division between the two great branches of a tree.

Namatarua, *s.* the two remarkable stars near the Crossiers, used by the islanders as a directory when at sea.

Namihere, *s.* a name given to the young of the cavally fish.

Naminami, *a.* having an ill scent.

Namu, *s* a musquito, see *ramu.*

Namua, *s.* a leader, a forerunner.

Namua, *prep.* before, further, forward; see *mua.*

—*adv.* previously, in time past; already.

Namurea, *s.* agreeableness, applied to food; as to scent and taste.

—*a.* fragrant, savoury, as food.

Namuri, *prep.* behind, abaft, following behind.

Nana, *s.* a flock or herd; a gang or company of men.

Nânâ, *v. n.* to look, or view; to direct the eye to some object; see *hio.*

Na'na, *poss pron.* a contraction of *na* and *ana*, his, hers, or its. [*nahi.*

Nanahi, *s.* yesterday; see *ana-*

Nanai, *s* a row, a number of things ranged in a line.

Nanaihere, *s.* leaves, foliage; see *rau.*

Nanaihere, *s.* a long range of cocoanut leaves tied together for a sort of fishing net.

Nanaihere, *a* hundred, that is 10 *umi*, which is 100 when counted singly, otherwise 200

Nanamu, *s.* a species of Tahitian grass.

Nanao, *s* the marks printed on the skin; see *tatau.*

Nanao, *v. a.* to thrust, or introduce the hand or arm into any cavity, hole, or aperture; see *tinao*

Nanati, *v a.* to tie up, or bind together; see *nati.*

Nanati, *v. a.* to make use of enchantments, as formerly done by the sorcerers.

Nanatiaha, *s.* from *nati* to tie, and *aha*, sinnet, a person who used enchantments.

—*v. a* to use sorcery, or enchantments, with a view to the injury or death of some one.

Nanatinati, *v. a.* to tie repeatedly, or in different places, a bundle, &c.

Nanau, *v. n.* to long for, or wish earnestly for something.

Nane, *v. a.* to knead such as dough, *mahi*, *pia*, &c.

Nane, *v.n.* to be all in confusion

Nane, *v. a.* to accuse without a certain knowledge, to spread a false report.

Nanea, *a* capacious, producing, or containing much.

Nanehuavai, *a.* glutinous, viscous as paste.

Nanei, *v n.* to go from a place.

Nanematie, *s.* foolishness; see *neneva.*

Nani, *a.* rich, having great possessions.

Nania, *v. a.* to go over; to resist again.

Nanihi, *v.n.* to be in a complete, or well finished state.

Nanihi ore, *a.* unfinished, not complete, as work.

Nanimani, *a.* well furnished, as a house, nothing wanting.

Nano, *s.* force, or power, as of a spear when thrown, or of a ball from a musket.

Nano, *a* full; *ua nano*, it is full.

Nanonano, *a.* forcible, applied to speech.

Nanu, *s* the matter in the nostrils of a new born infant.

Nanu, *s.* envy, jealousy, or displeasure, on account of not being properly considered as to a share of food, &c

—*v. n.* to grudge or envy what another has. [see *pananu.*

Nanumiti, *s.* the flux of the sea;

Nanuvai, *s.* the increase, or swelling of water.

Nanua, *v. a.* to go over, or above a thing.

Nanue, *s.* the name of a fish.

Nanunanu, *s.* the substance in the nose of an infant.

Nanunanu, *v. n.* to be envious of another's possessions.

Nanunanu, *v. n.* to make a noise like a pigeon.

Nanupo, *v. n.* to be disappointed at not having been awoke to partake of a feast prepared in the night.

Nao, *adv.* thus, in this way or manner.

Nao, *s* [Gr. *naos*,] a temple.

Nao, *v. a.* to take up, as food, by little and little; to eat repeatedly, going and returning to the same food.

Nao, *s.* a sort of fly or insect.

Naoa, *s.* a method, way, or proceeding

Naoa, *v. n.* to be altered, as from a good to a bad appearance, as the face.

Naonao, *s.* a species of small fly infesting fermented bread-fruit.

Naonao, *s.* the musquito ; see *ramu.*

Naonao, *a.* adorned, embellished, painted.

Napau, *s.* the name of a mountain tree.

Nape, *s.* sinnet made of the husk of the cocoanut.

Nape, *s.* the name of a small fish ; see *aha.*

Napehea, *adv.* how ? in what way or manner ?

Napenape, *s.* activity, vigilance. (a sea term.)

—*v. n.* to be active, vigilant, brisk.

—*a.* brisk in managing a canoe, &c.

Napereia, *adv.* in that way, or manner.

Napo, *s.* yester night.

Napo, *s.* profit, advantage ; see *faufaa.*

Naponapo, *v.n.* to be prepared, or possessed of things, so as not to be nonplussed by an accident.

Napu, *v. n.* to be nonplussed, not knowing what to do ; see *rapu.*

Napu, *v. a.* to mix some things by pressing with, or in the hand.

—*v. n.* to be mixed or blended together.

Nararo, *v. n.* to submit or yield.

Narui, *s* last night, or yesternight ; see *napo.*

Natauihe, *s.* the name of a star.

Natautoru, *s.* the name of a constellation.

Nati, *s.* the name of a stick with loops to catch eels.

Nati, *s.* a class, or distinction of men, as *nati arii*, the class of superior chiefs ; *nati raatira*, the class of inferior chiefs.

Nati, *v. a.* to tie or bind with a cord ; see *nanati.*

Nati, *a.* fitting or setting close ; a waistcoat is called *ahu nati*, because it encloses the body.

Natimaa, *s.* the name of a star.

Natimoe, *s.* a family or kindred.

Natinati, *v. a.* to tie, or enclose tight, and that repeatedly ; to catch eels by the *nati.*

Natinatiaha, *s.* a sorcerer ; see *nanati aha.*

Natipato, *v. a.* to make a short work, as of destruction.

Nativaea, *s.* a division, or portion ; a company divided, as in going to war.

Nato, *s.* a small fresh water fish.

Natonato, *v. n.* to be well provided with necessary things.

Natu, *v. a.* to mash some substance by clenching the hand ; to pinch with the thumb and finger.

Natu, *s.* a scratch or mark of pinching.

Natu, *v. n.* to be brought into a dilemma, or some intricacy ; see *rapu* and *napu.*

Natuaea, *s* a deceptive or indistinct vision ; see *atiuaea.*

Natufaufau, *s* a sort of food prepared from bread-fruit and cocoanut.

Natunatu, *v. a.* to pinch, or press repeatedly, as a secret sign ; to mash or mix repeatedly some food, with the hand.

Natutari, *s* a sort of food ; see *natufaufau.*

Nau, *s.* the name of a species of medicinal grass used in certain disorders.

Nau, *poss. pron.* sometimes used instead of *na oe*, thine. It is used in other dialects, but less regular than the Tahitian *na oe*.

Na'u, *poss. pron* a contraction of *na au*, mine; or for me; by me sometimes.

Naua, *v. a.* to get or obtain; see *nona*.

Naua, *a.* sunk, applied to the eyes.

Nauanei, *a.* to-day, with reference to the past.

Naue, *v. n.* to leap from an eminence to the deep water, a Tahitian diversion.

Naue, *s.* a play term in some games of children.

Naueraa, *s.* a place from which boys and others divert themselves by leaping into the water.

Nauma, *v. a.* to get, to obtain; see *navpa*.

Naumai, *v. a.* to recite, or rehearse something that it may be known.

Naunau, *s.* a lingering wish or desire.

—*v. n.* to long, or desire.

Naunauaveve, *s.* want, destitution.

Naupa, *v. a.* to get, obtain, succeed; see *raupa*.

Naupata, *s.* the name of a tree.

Naupata, *s.* a thicket of brushwood; a thicket of branching coral in the sea.

Na vai, *pron inter.* whose? for whom? by whom?

Navai, *v. n.* to suffice, last, hold out; see *ravai*.

Navai raa, *s.* a sufficiency.

Nave, *v. n.* to be pleased, or delighted.

Navenave, *a.* pleasurable, delightful.

Navenave raa, *s.* pleasure, gaiety.

Neanea, *a.* that which is abundant, applied to property.

Nee, *s.* a journey, excursion; the company of those that go the journey.

Nee, *s.* some business; see *tere*.

Nee, *v. n.* to crawl, or creep, as insects; also to move, or sail, as a ship.

—*a.* swift of motion, as a vessel at sea.

Neenee, *s.* some disorder of the lower limbs.

Neenee, *v. n.* to crawl or move repeatedly; to sail or move repeatedly on the water.

Neeneeahe, *v. n.* to crawl or move as the *he* or caterpillar.

Neeneearo, *v. n.* to crawl as the *ro* or ant.

Neeneeatohe, *v. n.* to slide in a sitting posture.

Neeneetapuahi, *v. n.* to crawl by an oven of food.

Nehenehe, *a.* neat, beautiful, handsome.

Nehu, *s.* the name of a fish proverbially sweet.

Nehunehu, *s.* the young of the *nehu*.

Nei, *adv.* here, in this place; now, at this time.

Nei, *adv.* of enquiry, *nei?* what? how? dost thou hear? expecting an answer.

Neia, *par. pass.* pressed, crushed, impressed.

Neinei, *s.* the name of a species of banana.

Neinei, *v.a.* to press or squeeze; to oppress.

Nemonemo, *s.* a disagreeable odour or smell.

Nena, *a.* stretched tight, as a garment; remaining smooth, as water without a wave.

Nenamu, *a.* grey, or drab colour; see *ninamu.*

Nenao, *v. n.* to introduce the hand into an aperture; see *nanao.*

Nenei, *v. a.* to squeeze, to press; to print.

Nenei, *v. n.* to suppress, or refrain, applied to laughter.

Nenei raa parau, *s.* a printing press.

Nenene, *a.* agreeable, sweet, fragrant, as the pine-apple, *ti*, &c.

Neneva, *s.* a fool; foolishness; giddiness.

—*a.* foolish; unsteady; also giddy.

Nenevahoa, *s.* the name of a noted wild idiot.

Nenevauhi, *s.* foolishness, produced, as was supposed, by eating yams before the requisite ceremonies had been performed.

Nenu, *s.* a species of Tahitian apple.

Nenunenu, *a.* agreeable; well tasted, as fruit, *vi* apple, oranges, &c.

Neoneo, *a.* offensive in smell, as rotten fish.

—*s.* offensive smell, stink.

Nevaneva, *a.* wild, unsteady; wandering, applied to the eye.

Nia, *prep.* above; see *nua.*

Nia, *v. n.* done or roasted on one side, as bread fruit on the fire; when turned in order to roast the other side, it is *ua nia.*

Niaa, *s.* the name given to the cocoanut after the kernel is formed, it is then best to drink.

Niame, *a.* brown coloured, as a species of native cloth.

Niau, *s.* the leaf or branch of the cocoanut tree.

Nifa, *s.* the name of a spotted fish.

Nifanifa, *a.* spotted, variegated, as the colours of the *nifa* fish.

Nihinihi, *a.* handsome, neat; see *neheneha.*

Niho, *s.* [*nifo*, *nio*,] a tooth; also a horn.

Nihoafa, *s.* a broken tooth.

Nihomanumanu, *s.* the tooth-ache.

Nihomarae, *s.* stones placed in a certain way in the wall of a *marae.*

Nihoritarita, *s.* fierce anger.

Nimaha, *s.* the same as *niaa*, a young cocoanut.

Nina, *v. a.* to cover with earth or water; to heap up earth about the stems of plants; *fig.* to bury some unpleasant report.

Ninahi, *s.* yesterday; see *nanahi.*

Ninaimoa, *s.* mouldiness of cloth, &c.

—*a.* mouldy, discoloured.

Ninamu, *a.* brown, or grey colour, as of cloth.

Ninavai, *v. n.* to be covered with a flood.

Nini, *s.* the sutures of the cranium; also cracks in the earth.

Nini, *v. n.* to turn away to avoid a person.

Ninii, *v. a.* to pour out liquids, or other things.

Nimore, *s.* a species of fish blubber; the same as *uore*.

Ninita, *s.* the papaw tree and its fruit.

Ninito, *v. n.* to go round in a circle.

Ninito, *v. n.* to stretch as one waking out of sleep, or when feeling weariness.

Ninivaru, *v. n.* to circumambulate a piece or tract of land; to obtain land by conquest.

Nino, *v. a.* to spin or twist.

Ninoa, *s.* a delineation as of land; also a description of pedigree or relationship.

Ninoa, *s* an understanding between parties; also the characteristic sentiments of a party.

Nitiniti, *a.* niggardly, close-fisted.

Niu, *s.* a general name for the cocoanut tree.

Niu, *s.* a foundation; the first row of stones in a wall.

Niu, *s.* a native spear, being commonly made of the *niu* or cocoanut tree; also the side of a piece of timber well adzed.

Niu, *s.* the wake of a ship, boat, or canoe; the track of large fishes.

Niu, *v. n* to run as a canoe or boat, after the rowers had ceased rowing. (a sea term)

Niu, *v. n.* to excel, as a cock in fighting; applied also to a courageous warrior.

Niu, *s.* an appearance of the sky, taken as a sign of some unfavourable event.

Niufiti, *s.* the north east wind; also *niuhiti*.

Niumate, *s.* the name of a ceremony, and certain prayers, to procure the favour of the gods.

Niuniu, *s.* certain fibrous roots; also wire.

Niupahi, *s.* the distance a ship runs on a tack

Nivaniva, *a.* unsteady; see *nevaneva*.

No, *prep.* of, belonging to; about, concerning. The *no* and *na* denote the possessive case of nouns, but they are not used promiscuously. The *na* signifies the possession of food, arms, and a few other things; the *no* is more general.

No, *prep.* of, and from, *no Tahiti*, of Tahiti.

Noa, *a.* common, in opposition to *raa*, sacred.

Noa, *adv.* a word of frequent use, and implying some negative idea, as *tupu noa*, grew spontaneously, without being planted; *aroha noa*, to pity freely, or to have compassion without any deserving cause.

Noâ, or Noaa, *conj.* although, yet, notwithstanding, as *parau noaa tu vau, e ore e faaroo mai*, although I speak, they will not hear.

Noaa, *v. a.* to obtain, or get something.

Noanoa, *a.* fragrant, of a pleasant smell.

Noha, *s.* the name of a large bird.

Noha, *s.* a competent person.

Noha, *s.* sea biscuit, and formerly a name given to the pumpkin.

Noho, *v. n.* [*nofo, n'o,*] to sit, abide, dwell.

Noho, *s.* the hinder ranks of an army set in battle array, according to the manner of the South Sea Islanders.

Nahoahu, *s.* a name given to the *tamanu* trees before the *marae;* also to the Priest that officiated in the *marae.*

Nohoraa, *s.* a seat, chair, or stool; a dwelling place; the time or place of sitting, or of residing.

Nohotahua, *v. n.* to dwell, sit, or continue naked; to abide in the unmarried state.

Nohu, *s.* the name of a small sea fish, that has a most dangerous and poisonous thorn.

Noi, *s.* the knot of a tree.

Noi, *v. n.* outdone, cowed, silenced.

Noi, *a.* knotty, tough, durable; also obstinate.

Noi, *a.* mellow, fat; free from stones, applied to a piece of ground.

Nôi, *s.* a savage, wickedly designing person,

Noi, *v. n.* to be unable to get forward, as a boat or canoe rowing against the wind; to fall, as the paper kite on the breaking of the string; to hang back.

Noiati, *s.* the stringy texture of the *ati* tree;—*fig.* obstinacy in speech or debate.

Noinoi, *s.* the cross grain of wood.

Noinoi, *a.* [*nohinohi,*] small, diminutive.

No'na, *poss. pron.* from *no* and *ona*, his, hers, or its; for him, of him, her, or it.

Nonenone, *a.* abundant, plenteous.

Nono, *s.* the sour apple, and the tree that bears it.

Nonoha, *s.* a species of grass with which the Tahitians cover the top of their houses, and also the floor inside.

Nonoa, *v. a* to spurn each other, or one of the parties being disgusted spurns the other, applied commonly to husbands and wives.

Nonoi, *v. n.* the dual or plural of *noi*, to recoil or draw back.

Nonoia, *s.* the name of a tree; it is one of the ingredients in the *monoi*, or sweet oil.

Noninoni, *a.* very small; see *noinoi.*

Nonoue, *v. n.* to hang back, recoil.

Noo, *s.* the stern of a canoe.

No oe, *poss. pron.* thine, for thee, of thee.

Nôu, *poss. pron.* thine, sometimes, instead of *no oe*

No'u, *poss. pron.* contraction of *no au*, mine.

Nounou, *s.* desire, covetousness. —*v. a.* to covet, desire, lust after.

No vai, *pron.* whose? of whom; for whom? on account of whom? interrogatively.

Nua, *prep.* [*runa, runga, luna,*] above; see *nia.*

Nuanua, *s.* the name of a tree of hard texture.

Nui, *a.* great, large; see the modern word *rahi.*

Nuna, *s* the name of a tree that grows in the rocks.

Nuna, *a.* mixed, amalgamated.

Nunaa, *s.* nation, kindred, people.

Nunaa, *s.* speech; also property.

Nunaatini, *s.* a concourse of people that follows a chief.

Nunu, *s.* one delicately brought up, and of a quiet inoffensive disposition.

Nunui, *v. n.* to be great; see *nui.*

Nupa, *s.* a thicket that cannot be entered; a patch of coral in the sea that cannot be passed, or entered.

Nupaa, *a.* handsome externally, but internally hollowness and deformity.

Nupaa, *s.* a stout, powerful person; a fierce warrior; a person allied to the royal family.

Nupanupa, *a.* troubled, overcast with gloom as the sky; affected, as the mind with the gloomy aspect of affairs.

—*v. n.* to be gloomy and sad, as the sky before a storm, or the mind when distressed with the prospect of danger, or something disagreeable.

Nupanupa po, *s.* an agitation of mind in the night time, arising from the expectation of the arrival of a party of the enemy.

Nuu, *v. n.* to slide along, to glide; see *faanuu.*

Nuu, *s* [*nuku,*] a fleet of canoes; an army or host passing by land or water.

O

IS a vowel of frequent occurrence in Tahitian, and is generally pronounced as *o* in God, but when circumflexed, as *o* in hope.

O, an *article* prefixed to proper names when in the nominacase, *o Tahiti, o Pare, o Tahaa, o Tu,* &c.; also to pronouns, as *o vau, o oe, o oia, o taua, o maua, o raua, o matou,* &c.; and also sometimes to adjectives when used substantively, as *o uteute, o teatea,* &c.

O, *s.* a spade, a stick used by the Tahitians to dig with.

O, *s.* a present of entrance or introduction to a person, *hopoi i te o,* take a present.

O, *s.* an enclosure, or a garden, where things are cultivated.

O, *s.* provisions for a journey, or a voyage.

O, *s.* a stick used to strip off the husk of the cocoanut.

O, *v. a.* to enter into a place; to open by piercing.

O, *v. a.* to dig the ground; dig a hole or ditch; to take off the husk of the cocoanut.

O, *adv.* of place, either here, or there, as the particles *tu, atu, mai, nei, ae, i, tei,* and *e* may direct us; *i o, tei o,* yonder, at a distance; *i o nei,* here at this place; *i o ae,* a little aside; *i o tu,* farther off.

O, *adv.* yes, in answer to a call, *o mea,* such a one, he will answer *O,* yes

O, *prep.* of, belonging to; see *no, na, to, ta.*

O, *prep.* at, with, as *tei o mea ra,* with such a one; *teihea?* where? *tei o,* at such a place.

O, *intj.* signifying the thing mentioned is made light of; also an exclamation to quiet a child.

O, *a.* husked, stripped of its outer cover, applied to a cocoanut.

Oà, *s.* the name of an aquatic bird.

Oa, *s.* the ribs or timber of a boat or ship; the timber of a little house placed on a canoe and called *fare oa.* Such a house on a sacred canoe was described by Captain Cook as the ark of the covenant, but to which it had no relation.

Oà, *s.* the name of a god, seen only at night; it was said to be black, and was also called *Hivari.*

Oa, *v. a.* to paint black; to pitch or tar a vessel; to daub or besmear in an irregular manner.

Oa, *s.* joy, gladness; see *oaoa.* —*v. n.* to be glad or rejoice.

Oaatoa, *s* red streaks in the sky, looked upon as a sign of wind.

Oaha, *s.* the name of a shrub or tree with long leaves;—*fig.* a seditious person.

Oana, *s.* the holes in a cocoanut shell called the monkey's eyes.

Oao, *s.* the name of a shrub bearing red berries.

Oao, *s.* a cocoanut that has no water or kernel.

Oaoa, *s.* joy, gladness. —*v. n.* to rejoice.

Oaoa, *a.* narrow, the opposite to *aano* or *apu.*

Oaóa, *s.* a game or diversion where a person plays with the hand on his windpipe or throat.

Oaoaahi, *s.* the great blaze of a fire.

Oaoao, *s.* an old empty cocoanut.

Oapa, *v. n.* any thing lying in a corner.

Oare, *s.* the fry of some little fish.

Oarero, *s.* a compound of *o* a stick to dig with, and *arero,* the tongue; it means a tongue that digs up mischief; or the tongue wants not the hands.

Oata, *s.* the monkey's eyes on a cocoanut; the mouth or neck of a gourd; also the meshes of a fishing net.

Oe, *pron.* the second person singular, thou.

Oe, *s.* a bell.

Oe, *s.* a sword.

Oe, *s.* a mistake, or an error; see *he, hape.*

O'e, *s.* scarcity, famine.

Oea, *a.* handsome, as a man or woman.

Oeatoti, *v. a.* to strike a person forcibly to the ground; the word is derived from the manner in which the fish called *atoti* are driven from the rocks.

Oeahôu, *s.* a young comer; a young person just come to age.

Oeha, *s.* the mesh of a net.

Oehaeha, *v n.* to be surfeited by eating too much.

Oehamu, *v. a.* to feast, eat immoderately.

Oehapa, *s.* the name of a coarse native cloth.

Oehapa, *v. a.* to split a piece of wood, &c.

Oehau, *v. a.* to disturb the peace.

Oeô, *a.* irregular, as a limb affected by the *feefee* or elephantiasis. [slender.

Oeoe, *a.* sharp, pointed; also

Oeoeo, *s.* pride, haughtiness. —*a.* proud, self conceited.

Oere, *v. n.* to gad about in a wanton idle manner.

Oere, *a.* thin, meagre, applied to a person.

Ofà, *v. a.* to collect or amass together food, &c.

Ofaa, *s.* a thicket, impenetrable brushwood.

Ofaa, *v. n.* to nestle, or lie close in a nest, as a bird.

Ofaaraa, *s.* the nest of a bird; kennel of a dog.

Ofàfà, *a.* inclining to rottenness, applied to taro roots.

Ofàfà, *s.* an idle, useless person.

Ofafai, *s.* a stone, or stones.

Ofai, *s.* a general name for a stone as used at present in the Tahitian dialect. In some of the dialects *toka* is a stone, hence the Tahitian *to'a;* in others *moka*, which is near *toka;* others have *pahaku*, or *tatu*, and hence probably the Tahitian *patu* for a stone wall. [mals.

Ofai, *s.* the testes of male ani-

Ofaiarà, *s.* a very heavy and hard stone.

Ofaiaràriorio, *s.* a stone, with two others called *Ofai eirorio*, *Ofai maue raa*, which, according to a Tahitian tradition, formed the stations of departed souls, from whcih they fled to the *Mehani*, in Raiatea.

Ofaiata, *s.* a stone thrown by a vigorous slinger; also an early comer.

Ofaifai, *a.* stony, impassable because of stones.

Ofaiora, *s* a stone at Papeare in Moorea, to which departed souls fled, (according to tradition,) at the apparent death of the body, but from which they returned. This was the stone of life. There was also *ofai ora* and *ofai pohe* on the mountain Taataa in Tahiti.

Ofai pai aia, *s* a very slippery stone; also a term signifying war.

Ofaipohe, *s.* another stone at Papeare in Moorea. This was the stone of death, and souls that fled there perished, or never returned to life.

Ofao, *s.* the front warrior.

Ofao, *s.* a disease, a species of the dropsy.

Ofaotuna, *s* an eel's hole or hiding place.

Ofara, *v. n.* to roam about in quest of food.

Ofarafara, *v. n.* to roam or wander repeatedly.

Ofata, *s.* flatulency of the bowels.

Ofati, *s.* the rheumatism.

Ofati, *v. a.* to break a thing; see *ofene*. [the neck.

Ofatiaî, *s.* a disease that affects

Ofatifati, *v. a.* to break a thing repeatedly, or in many places.

Ofatitia, *s* a stroke of the sun, causing sudden death. [*coup de soleil.*]

Ofe, *s.* the bamboo cane; see *ohe.*

Ofê, *s.* the name of a fish about the size of a herring, caught in great numbers in the proper season; see *orare.*

Ofefa, *a.* proud, conceited.

Ofene, *s.* the rheumatism; see *ofati.*

—*v. a.* to break a thing, such as a stick.

Ofenefene, *v. a.* to break a thing repeatedly.

Ofenefene, *s.* the rheumatism, from its affecting a person repeatedly, or in different parts of the body.

Ofeo, *s.* the name of a tree.

Ofeo, *s.* a species of crab.

Ofeo, *s.* pain in the abdomen in consequence of eating after long fasting.

Ofeofeo, *v. n.* to backbite.

Ofera, *v. a.* to turn out the inside of the eyelids, or to pull the eyelids widely open; a custom of children.

Oferafera, *v. a.* to repeat the custom of *ofera.*

Ofiri, *s.* any thing that is like a screw.

Ofiri, *v. n.* to be turning, or changing different ways.

Ofirifiri, *a.* unstable, changeable.

Oha, *a.* leaning, not perpendicular.

Oha, *v. n.* to be stooping, as a person by age and decrepitude.

—*adv.* bendingly, stoopingly, applied to walking.

Ohaoha, *v. n.* to be bending, or stooping repeatedly.

Ohapa, *v. a.* to cleave or split any thing.

Ohapahapa, *v. a.* to cleave or split something repeatedly.

Oharahara, *v. a.* to split or divide into pieces.

Ohau, *s.* an incendiary, or breeder of strife.

Ohe, *s.* [*kofe, ofe,*] a bamboo cane; also a dart.

Ohee, *s* the name of a fish resembling a herring; called also *ofê* or *ofee,* and *orare.*

Ohe ia rire, *s.* a name given to a warrior.

Ohemoepiha, *s.* a dart preserved in a quiver;—*fig.* a man made much of, a choice fellow.

Oheohe, *s.* the name of a shrub or tree; also a plant.

Oherauao, *s.* a very light species of bamboo;—*fig.* a wandering, unsettled person.

Oheohe, *a.* without branches; see *moremore.*

Ohetaorato, *s.* a man famous for war.

Ohetapu, *s.* a dart that does not fly well, but disappoints the archer;—*fig.* a man that commences an enterprise, but fails in the accomplishment.

Ohetuna, *v.n.* to be confined, and having no means of escape.

Ohi, *s.* young plants or shoots, as of *meia, fei,* &c.

Ohi, *v. a.* to gather fragments; to glean, pick up firewood, or any small things.

Ohî, *s.* the dysentery; see *hí.*

Ohî, *v. n.* to gush out, as water, or any liquid.

Ohi, *s* a disease, red spots on the skin.

Ohie, *a.* easy of accomplishment; apt.

—*adv.* aptly, readily, easily.

Ohi, *s.* the head of a beast; see *afii, porahu.*

Ohîhî, *v. n.* to gush out repeatedly.

Ohimu, slander, backbiting.

—*v n.* to murmur, to backbite.

Ohimuhimu, *v. n.* to murmur, or backbite repeatedly.

Ohina, *a.* grey, of a greyish colour.

Ohinahina, *a.* grey, greyish.

Ohinuhinu, *s.* the name of a species of bread-fruit.

Ohiohio, *s.* an evil designing look; the wild look of a thief or mischievous person.

—*v. n.* to look about with an evil design; to look about, as a person near death.

Ohiohioa, *s.* giddiness, instability.

Ohipa, *s.* work, employment; see *haa.*

—*v. a.* to work, labour, toil.

Ohipaê, *v. n.* to turn aside, go in another direction.

Ohîpape, *s.* the rushing, or gushing out of water.

Ohîtapere, *s.* a cascade, or water fall.

Ohî teitei, *s.* a cascade from a great height.

Ohiti, *s.* a small species of the beetle.

Ohiti, *s.* a species of sand crab, very small.

Ohiti, *v. a.* to pluck off, or pluck out.

Ohitihiti, *v. a.* to pluck off, or out repeatedly.

Ohitimapeeare, *s.* the small crab called *ohiti*

Ohiti mata aia, *s* the same as *ohiti*, and which is said not to sleep;—*fig* a fisherman, a wakeful man; also a warrior.

Ohiti mata ora, *s* from *ohiti; fig.* a person always ready, always on his guard, who knows how to avoid danger, and keep his habitation from invasion.

Ohitimataura, *s.* the name of a medicinal plant.

Ohitiporaorao, *v. a.* to grasp so as to get hold of the whole; to examine an affair thoroughly.

Ohitiraaroa, *v. a* to bring up old and past grievances.

Ohiu, *v. a.* to dart the reed without striking the ground, in the game of *apere raa.*

Ohiuhiu faarua, *s.* the first light breeze of the north-west wind, when it is setting in.

Ohiuhiu pafaite, *s.* the same as *ohiuhiu faarua;* also the commencement of an easterly breeze.

Oho, *s.* the highest in growth among the mulberry plants; the man whose head is highest is called *aute oho;* the second born of a family is also called *aute oho.*

Oho, *s.* the first-fruit.

Oho, *s* the fore-most warrior in an engagement.

Ohope, *s.* the name of a sort of basket.

Ohorehore, *a.* bare, as the eyebrows without hair, or a thing skinned.

Ohoro, *a.* soft by fermentation, as *mahi*, or bread-fruit prepared for the *mahi* pit.

Ohôu, *s.* a new garden or enclosure.

Ohu, *s.* a cloud settled on the top of the mountains.

Ohu, *s.* a bank, or ridge of earth thrown up.

Ohu, *s.* a bundle of some food tied up, and baked in the native oven; see *puohu.*

Ohu, *v. n* to bend downwards, as a branch of a tree, to stoop, as an elderly person.

—Ohu, *v. n.* to twirl round, as a wheel

Ohua, *s.* the name of a fish found at the bottom of rocks; *fig* a man, who like the *ohua* fish, is difficult to be obtained.

Ohua, *v. a.* to divide, or share in small parts; to make small.

Ohueraai, *s.* a turbulent man that breeds mischief.

Ohumu, *v. n.* to whisper, murmur, backbite.

—*s.* murmuring, backbiting.

Ohumuhumu, *v. a.* to backbite repeatedly.

Ohure, *s.* the anus; see *hoperemu.*

Ohuietô, *s. prolapsis ani*; also the bloody flux.

Ohutia, *s.* a bundle of food wrapt up in leaves.

Ohutu, *s.* the same as *ohutia;* see *ohu.*

Oi, *v. a.* to knead, applied to dough, *mahi*, &c.

Oi, *v. a.* to mingle different substances, by working with the hand in a dish.

Oi, *v. n.* to turn, as in steering a boat; see *tioi.*

— Oi, *a.* sharp, as the edge of a tool; see *faaoi.*

Oi, *adv.* indeed, really; *e mea maitai oi ra*, a good thing really, or indeed.

Oi, *adv.* had like to be, nearly been, as *oi pohe matou i tua*, we were nearly, or likely to have been lost at sea; *oi ore ta tatou oi naupa*, we were nearly disappointed in obtaining.

Oi, *adv.* while, or whilst, *oi vai ae te ao*, whilst it is day.

Oi, *conj.* lest, for fear that, *e ara oi vare outou*, beware lest you be deceived.

Oia, *pron.* third person singular, he, she, or it.

Oia, *adv.* yea, yes, it is so; *oia ia*, it is that, or it, or even so, it is so; *oia hoi ia*, verily so, or it is so, or so it is.

Oiâ, *a* overflowing, as water; *vai oiâ*, overflowing water.

—*v. n.* to flow over its banks, applied to a river.

Oia, *v. n.* to go down head foremost through press of sail, applied to a canoe.

Oie, *s* the external coat of the banana stalk, used as a case to hold food, &c.

Oieie, *a.* thick, as the native cloth when in a state of preparation.

Oiha, *adv.* yes, it is so, spoken rather contemptuously.

Oihamu, *s.* a certain feast; see *faatoi, oehamu.*

Oihe, *s.* the name of a certain fish.

Oihe, *s.* a stick used for digging; see *o.*

Oihe, *s.* a modern name for the *Dracæna* or *ti* plant; see *ti.*

Oihi, *v. n.* to turn aside from the direction intended, as a nail while driving.

Oihi, *adv.* slightly, or just entering, applied to the piercing of a thing.

Oimo, *s.* the custom of mourning for the dead; shaved patches on the head, &c.

Oimo, *v. a.* to shave patches on the head in token of grief for the dead.

Oimoimo, *v. a.* to repeat the *oimo.*

Oimoimo, *a.* ruffled, dishevelled, as the hair.

Oimoimo, *v. n.* to be wet, or soaked with rain.

Oineine, *v. n.* to be in readiness or preparation.

Oineine, *v. n.* to start up, and recoil again; to flutter as a bird.

Oini, *s.* the name of a small basket; see *moini*

Oio, *s.* the name of a sea bird, from its voice *oio.*

Oio, *s.* the sharp nose of a canoe.

Oio, *s.* the name of a species of plantain.

— Oioi, *a.* rapid, swift.

—*adv.* quickly, briskly, as *haere oioi*, go quickly.

Oioio, *s* the name of a plantain; see *oio.*

Oire, *s.* [Heb. *or*, *oir*, *orim*,] a city, or town.

Oiri, *s.* a black spot in the heavens near the Crossiers.

Oiri, *s.* the garfish, of which there are several species, viz.; *oiri ua*, *oiri hiutea*, *oiri iautaro*, *oiri humu*, and *oiri-rauape.*

Oiri, *s.* an axe or adze tied to the handle with sinnet.

Oiri, *v. n.* to be in fear or alarm on account of approaching danger.

Oiri, *v. a.* to fasten an adze by tying it to the handle with sinnet.

Oiriputa tô, *s.* a man that has been overcome in war.

Oiti, *s.* a small contracted passage; a small place; a little corner.

Oitu, *s* a ladle like fishing net with a long handle.

Oito, *s* the hair of the head tied up. [the hair.

—*v. a* to tie up, or fillet up

Oitoito, *a.* curly, applied to the human hair.

Oivi, *s.* [*hoivi*,] the body of man or beast.

Oivi, *s.* the body of a god, so were the *taura* or pretended prophets called. The man was the *oivi*, called also *tiino*, possessed for the time by the god, and actuated by him.

Oma, *s.* an adze; see *toi.*

Oma, *a.* fallen, or sunk, as the cheeks when a person loses his teeth.

Omaha, *s.* urine; see *mimi.*

—*v. n.* to discharge the urine.

Omai, *s.* drink to wash down a person's food.

Omamao, *s.* the name of a singing bird about the size of a sparrow.

Omamao tari aua, *s.* a tale bearer; the figure is from the bird *omamao* carrying things from a garden to build its nest

Omao, *s.* the soft leaves of the *fara* tree.

Omaoma, *v. a.* to banter, deride, call ill names.

Omaoma, *v. n.* to make mouths in derision.

Omaoma, *a.* vile, contemptuous, as speech. [*mao.*

Omaomao, *s.* the same as *oma-*

Omaomao, *s.* a noisy, chattering person, like the bird *omaomao.*

Omaomaopuâfau, *s.* one species of the bird *omaomao* that has yellow feathers.
Omata, *s.* the meshes of a net; see *oana.*
Omatafes, *s.* the name of a species of reddish cocoanut.
Omene, *s.* the name of a mountain plantain.
Omene, *v. a.* to double a stiff rope, or break a stick.
Omene, *v. a.* to serve one's self, or take to one's self, to the exclusion of others, as in sharing food or property.
Omenemene, *v. a.* to roll up or coil a rope; to make a thing of a roundish shape.
—*a.* round, plump.
Omenomeno, *a* nauseous, disagreeable; filthy, nauseous, as some evil practices.
—*v n.* to be disgusted by filthy things.
Omeo, *s.* a painful itching between the toes, occasioned by walking bare-footed in dirty and wet weather.
Ometometo, *v. n.* to be disgusted with a person or a thing.
Omi, *s.* the name of a small rock fish.
Omii, *s.* the head of a beast, or fish; see *afii.*
Omiimii, *a.* curled, as the head of a man, or of a beast; but *oitoito* is commonly used of the human hair.
Omiimii, *v. n.* to be angry, snarling, or fretful.
Omino, *v. n.* to go round.
—*adv.* roundly, circuitously.
Omino, *v. a.* to disappoint a person of his portion in sharing food; see *omene.*
Ominomino, *a.* crooked, circuitous.
Ominomino, *a.* perverse.
Omiomi, *a.* curled, or wrinkled.
Omiomio, *a.* wrinkled; see *miomio*
Omira, *v. a.* to rub, and prepare the darts for the bow.
Omire, *v a.* the same as *omira;* see *mira.*
Omiri, *v. a.* to fondle over a person; to handle
Omirimiri, *v. a.* to examine repeatedly; see *mirimiri*
Omiritaa, *v. a.* to make much of a wife or children.
Omito, *s.* a grudge, or displeasure of mind.
Omitomito, *v. n* to indulge a grudge, or displeasure, on account of not possessing something that is desired.
Omo, *v. a* to introduce or put into, as food into a basket, property into a bag, &c.
Omoe, *adv.* secretly, unawares.
Omoi, *s.* a firebrand;—*fig.* an active man in warlike exploits.
Omoi, *s* the last part of a feast.
Omono, *v.a.* to put in; see *oomo.*
Omono, *v. a.* to substitute one for another; see *mono.*
Omore, *s* a war club.
Omoro, *s.* the same as *omore.*
Omoto, *s* a cocoanut in the last state before the ripe *opaa.*
Omotu, *s* the name of a basket.
Omotu, *s.* a burning coal.
Omotumotu, *a.* variegated, as a basket of various colours.
Omou, *s.* the top of a pine apple; the top of a plant, or the top leaves, and branches.
Omua, *s.* a head, or fore-most one; a leader.

Omuâhea, *s.* a disease that causes redness of skin.

Omuâhea, *s.* a person most forward in business, but afterwards falls short of expectation.

Omuaia, *s.* a person who, unsolicited, joins a party.

Omuatao, *s.* the pointed part towards the end of a Tahitian spear.

Omuhumuhu, *v. a.* to whisper to the disadvantage of a person behind his back; see *muhu.*

Omumu, *v. n.* to whisper, or make a low noise by speaking.

Omutamuta, *v. n.* to whisper, as *omumu.*

O'na, *poss. pron.* his, hers, its; *o* and *na.*

Ona, *s.* a little breeze of wind.

Ona, *adv.* yonder, or there; *o* and *na.*

Ona, *v. n.* to recur, as a thought, or sickness.

Onana, *s.* a species of prawn or shrimp.

Onaona, *s* whiskers.

Onaona, *a.* acrid, unpleasant.

—*a.* unpleasant, as speech; unceasing, as evil.

Onaona, *v. n.* to recur frequently, as thoughts; or to return, as sickness of the stomach.

Onaonao, *a* variegated, adorned.

One, *s.* sand, dust, earthy particles.

Onê, *v. n.* to wrestle; see *maona*

Oneenee, *v. n.* to creep slowly; see *nee.*

Oneeuretopa, *s.* extreme decrepitude, or extreme listlessness.

Onei, *adv.* here, at this place; see *o* and *nei.*

Oneone, *a.* sandy, gritty; not well mixed.

Onevaneva, *s.* giddiness, or dizziness of the head.

Oni, *s.* the male of beasts, birds, insects, fishes, &c.

Oni, *v. a.* to climb a tree without the cord or line usually employed

Onìania, *s* giddiness, the effect of disease or of drunkenness.

Onìania, *v. n.* to be stirring a little, as a soft breeze.

Onihi, *v. n* to withdraw from a person; to slide.

Onihi, *v. a.* to untie, to set loose.

Onihi, *v. n.* to glide; to wear away.

Oniho, *s.* the name of a disease resembling the chicken pox.

Onihoniho, *s.* the prickly heat.

Onihoniho, *a.* approaching to rottenness, as fruit lying on the ground, or wet with salt water.

Onihu, *s.* a prayer, or words used in planting the post of a house.

Onioni, *v. n.* to swell and boast, as a wrestler.

Onioni, *a.* lumpy, not reduced to proper pulp.

Onini, *s.* the first forming of the fruit or berries of some trees, after the blossom falls.

Oninorino, *a* uneven, not plain and smooth.

Onivaniva, *v. n.* to be dizzy, having a confused vision in consequence of sickness, or of a blow on the head.

Ono, *a.* number six in counting; see *fene.*

Ono, *s.* the name of a large savage fish.

Ono, *s.* an avenger of blood.

Ono, *v. a.* to fix one's affection on another person.

Ono, *v. a.* to exchange one thing for another; to join one piece to another.

Ono, *s.* a substitute; see *mono.*

Onoaraiava, *s.* an undaunted brave warrior.

Onohe, *s.* a person that dies merely of age.

—*v. n.* to pine from age, not disease; to pine away through grief, not bodily disorder.

Onohi, *v. n.* to crouch, slide down, or falling into a sitting posture.

Onohi, *s.* suicide; see *faaaau.*

—*v. n.* to commit self murder.

Onohinohi, *v. n.* to loiter, hang back through fear.

Onoono, *v. n.* to be urgent, pressing in desire.

—*adv.* urgently, pressingly, vehemently.

—*a.* anxious, pressing; also delightful.

Onoono, *v. a.* to endeavour to please and gain the affection of a person; to place the affection on a person; to make much of a person; see *mateono.*

Onounou, *s.* covetousness; see *nounou.*

—*v. n.* to covet, to wish for the possession of something not obtained, and regret the want of it.

Onunu, *v. n.* to retire.

Oo, *s.* a large hole; the hollow between two waves.

Oo, *v. n.* to sound, as water near boiling.

Oo, *v. n.* to cluck, as a hen; make noise, as a lizard.

Oo, *s* flatulency, or griping of the bowels.

Ooa, *s.* a creek of the sea, or of a river; a small turning of a valley between high lands.

Ooairaa, *v. a* to annoy persons while eating by digging up the dust near them.

Ooao, *s* the name of a large tree; the leaves and bark of which are used medicinally.

Ooaha, *s.* the name of a shrub.

Ooaha, *s.* a breeder of disturbance.

—*v. a.* to breed disturbance by evil speaking.

Ooea, *s.* the name of a bird; see *pareua.*

Oohioa, *s.* giddiness of the head.

—*v. n.* to be giddy or dizzy.

Oohu, *s* a wrapper of leaves with fish, &c., inside.

Ooi, *a.* sharp, as an edged tool.

Ooia, *a.* swift, as a current of water.

Ooiee, *s.* the same as *oie,* which see.

Ooina, *a.* rapid, swift, as a current.

—*adv.* impetuously, furiously.

Ooma, *s* the human heart; see *mafatu.*

Ooma, *s.* delight; propensity.

Oomahere, *s.* something delighted in, a darling.

Oomamanava, *s* some disorder of the stomach.

Oomi, *v. n.* to frown, to knit the brows.

Oomiomi. *v. n.* to frown repeatedly.

Oomiomi, *a.* crumbled, wrinkled.

Oomo, *v. a* to put in, introduce, such as the hand into a bag; see *tinao.*

Oomu, *v. a.* to bake food, such as *mahi* unkneaded, unprepared.

Oona, *a.* great, heinous, aggravated, as a crime; *hara oona*, aggravated sin; see *aana*.

Oona, *a* consuming, increasing, as a disorder.

Oona, *v. n* to predict or foretel.

Ooni, *a.* sterile, seedless, as male trees, flowers, &c.

Ooni, *a.* contentious, fearless, aggravating.

—*v. a.* to contend, banter, provoke.

Ooni, *v. n.* to intrude.

Oono, *v. n.* to be pressing, or urgent.

— Ooo, *s.* anger, displeasure, internal grief.

— —*v. n.* to be provoked, irritated, much displeased.

Ooo, *s.* a top, or whirligig.

Ooo, *s.* the burning rays of the sun when falling upon a person.

—*a.* burning, applied to the rays of the sun.

Ooo, *v. n.* to turn, as a top, whirligig, &c.

Ooo, *a.* cutting, as speech; sweet, luscious, as food.

Oopa, *s.* a narrow, confined place.

— Oopa, *v. n.* to turn as in bed; to lie on the side.

Oopape, *a.* cracked, as fruit over-ripe.

— Oopi, *v. a.* to shut, as the leaves of a book.

— Oopi, *a.* close, niggardly, as to food, &c.

Oopiriati, *v. a.* to collect the drops of gum from the bark of the *ati*; to gather ill and malicious reports

Oopu, *s.* the name of a small fresh water fish.

Oopu, *a.* dark or black, applied to beasts.

Oore, *a.* maimed, deformed, decrepit.

Oore, *v. n.* to fail, fade away, as the leaves of a tree; to fail or die away, as desire; to forsake, fall away.

Oori, *v. n.* to dance very frequently.

Ooro, *s* an ornament of sweet flowers.

Ooro, *v. n.* to snore during sleep.

Oore, *v. n.* to have pain in the bowels.

Ooroaia, *a.* sorrow, bitterness.

Ooroô, *v. n.* to stoop; to be abashed.

Ooru, *v. n.* to be swollen; to be puffed up with disease.

Ootea, *a.* light coloured, as a Tahitian.

Ooti, *v. a.* to cut with an instrument.

Ooure, *s.* the catkins of the bread-fruit.

Ooure, *s.* a small canoe in the form of the *uru* catkins.

Oouri, *a.* dark or black, as a Tahitian.

Oovau, *s.* the name of a tree; see *ooao*.

Oovea, *s.* the bird called *areva-reva*.

Oovi, *s.* a certain scrophulous disorder.

—*a.* affected with the *oovi* disorder.

Oovi, *s.* the name given to a niggardly person.

Opa, *s.* a wicked careless person that attends to no good.

Opa, *s.* a corner, as of a room.

Opa, *a.* wearied, as the limbs by a long walk.

Opa, *v. n.* to be wearied, fatigued, as a traveller.
Opa, *v. n.* to sail close to the wind.
Opa, *a.* on one side; leaning on one side.
—*v. n.* to be on one side; to lean greatly to one side, as a boat, canoe, or ship.
Opaa, *s.* a full ripe cocoanut, before it begins to grow.
Opae, *v. n.* to turn aside; go a little out of the course, or road.
—*v n.* to sail with a side wind; to drift to leeward.
Opaero, *a.* ill-favoured, ill-grown; also *maetioe*.
Opaetaria, *s.* a person that turns aside his ear, especially to the female sex.
—*v. n.* to turn aside to listen, so as not to attend to his proper business.
Opahi, *s.* an axe, commonly a large one.
Opahi, *s.* the scrophula affecting the neck.
Opahi mato, *s.* a felling axe.
Opahi peue, *s.* a broad axe.
Opai, *s.* a young pig, or other animal of a few months old.
Opai, *a.* unripe, as taro; see *ovaivai*.
Opai, *s.* the young banana before it bears large leaves; the young bamboo.
Opai, *s.* weariness, soreness, and weakness of the thighs, as from a long journey, or in the case of a pregnant woman.
Opai, *v. n.* to drift to leeward; see *opae*.
Opai, *v. n.* to turn aside a little; see *opae*.
Opaipai, *v. n.* to drift side ways.
Opaipai, *v. n* to have pain of the thighs and legs, as a weary traveller, &c.
Opana, *v. a.* to turn out a stone with a handspike, or an iron bar; to poke, or search for a thing with an instrument; to turn out a person from his possession; to rake out old grievances; see *pana*.
Opanapana, *v. a.* to poke, or use an instrument for *opāna*, and that repeatedly; see *panapana*.
Opani, *s.* a door, shutter, or cover; the close or conclusion of a subject.
—*v. a.* to shut a door, or window; to cover, or close a thing; to conclude a subject.
Opapa, *s.* the name of a species of crab.
Opapa, *s.* the name of a sort of lobster.
Opapa, *s.* a fowl that has lost its tail.
Opapa, *v. n.* to triumph over an opponent.
Opapa, *v. n.* to lie flat, or in a horizontal position.
Opapa tohe io ore, *s.* a very lean person.
Opâpâ, *s.* the name of a certain spotted cloth, also a bale.
Opape, *s.* a shower with a gust of wind.
Opape, *s* a species of shrimp or prawn.
Opape, *s* a current, see *ovai*.
Opata, *s* a spot or blot.
Opatapata, *a* spotted, chequered; also blotted with many blots.
Ope, *v. a.* to go and collect; bring all to one place.
Opê, *s.* abortive fruit; see *anpara*, *mamaia*.

Opea, *s* the name of a small black bird

Opea, *v. a* to lay things cross ways, such as fire-wood to dry. [as lattice work

—*a.* trellised, or put cross ways,

Opeapea, *v. a.* to put things cross ways repeatedly.

Openu, *a.* inclining to rotundity; see *omene.*

Openu, *v. a.* to amass food, &c., together.

Opeope, *v. a.* to collect together repeatedly

Opeope, *s.* leaves of plants and trees; see *rau.*

Opeope, *s* carcases, property, and things of all descriptions, which in the rage of war, had been thrown into the rivers, then carried to the sea, and afterwards thrown on shore again.

Opere, *s.* a portion, also the person that divided into portions.

—*v a.* to divide food, property, &c., into portions.

Operea, *s.* a division, or a share.

Opererua, *s.* a wind that allows of sailing in opposite directions.

Operu, *s.* the name of a fish resembling the herring, but smaller.

Operupai te aha, *s.* the *operu* that has often escaped the net;—*fig.* a man that escapes out of the hand of warriors.

Opetî, *s* a voice said to be heard in old times, either at midnight, or mid-day, crying, "I am destroyed," it was believed to be the departed soul of one slain in war, and a sign of approaching destructive war

Opi, *v a.* to shut or close up; see *oopi.*

Opî. *s.* the stranguary, or some affection of the urinary passages; also some stage of the venereal disorder.

Opi, *a* late, new, young; see *hou, api.*

Opihamatavai, *s* a watercourse.

Opio, *s.* an immensely large native oven or pit, in which after making a quantity of stones red hot by a strong fire. some thousands of bread-fruit are put, covered with leaves, hot stones, and earth; then left for two days, and afterwards the baked bread-fruit is taken out as it may be wanted for use.

—*v. a.* to make an *opio* oven; to bake fruit whole, skin and all, in a common oven, and leave it to soak for a night or more.

Opiopio, *adv.* rovingly, wanderingly. [confusion.

Opipiri, *s.* bashfulness, shame,

—*v n* to be bashful, ashamed, confounded; also to appear modest.

Opiri, *s.* a sluggish, inert, ill-grown person.

Opiri, *adv.* unsteadily, as *haere opiri*, go unsteadily.

Opiri, *v. a.* to collect the drops of gum called *piri.*

Opirioa, *a.* grand, as a place claiming awe and reverence.

Opirioa, *v. n* to be weak through want of food, or by sickness.

Opiripiri, *s* a species of bread-fruit with rough skin.

Opiripiri, *a* dribbling, as water out of the rocks

—*adv* dribblingly, sparingly.

Opiropiro, *a.* offensive in smell.

Opiti, *pron. dual*, you two; see *orua.*

Opiti, *v. a.* to roll a thing, such as a cask.

Opito, *s.* a vortex; hollow deep places in water.

Opitopito, *s.* little black knots in boards, or pieces of timber, the risings of anger.

Opoe, *v. n.* to be checked in growth, as trees in winter.

Opoepoe, *v. n.* having died, as the leaves of plants, &c.

Opohe, *v. n.* the same as *opoe.*

Oporo, *s.* the name of a Tahitian plant that bears berries resembling the *capsicum.*

Oporo, *s.* the various kinds of *capsicum* or *Cayenne* pepper.

Oporovainui, *s.* the name of a tree full of sap;—*fig.* a person not easily provoked.

Opoto, *s.* the name of a species of eel; a person without a settled abode.

Opu, *s.* [*kopu,*] the belly; also the mind.

—*s.* the belly like form of a thing.

Opu, *v. a.* to wash or cleanse, as fish from blood.

Opu, *v. n* to be just rising, applied to the sun.

Opua, *v. a.* to resolve, intend, appoint, settle before hand.

Opuaoao, *s.* the name of a banana.

Opuaraa, *s.* determination, appointment; the time or place of appointing.

Opuharura, *s.* a person that is well informed.

Opuhi, *s.* a sweet scented plant, called also *opui* and *puhiava.*

Opuhoa, *s.* the name of a fish with a large belly; a person with a noted large belly.

Opuhoa, *v. n.* to emit the intestines through the mouth, as some fish will when in extremity; to put out the tongue, as some people when in extreme fear.

Opumarama, *s.* an enlightened mind; one of a thoughtful mind, and retentive memory.

Opumoemoe ee, *s.* a stranger of another country or family, who is not to be trusted.

Opuopu, *v. a.* to wash; see *horoi.*

Opuparapara, *v a.* to eat till all is consumed.

Opupu, *s.* a bladder, a blister.

Opupu, *s.* a canoe with a sail in the form of a bladder; a small sail.

Opura, *s.* a good species of the Tahitian cultivated yam.

Opurapura, *v. n.* to be flashing obscurely, as fire.

Opure, *a.* spotted, applied to a fowl.

Opure, *s.* those that attended the ceremonies at the marae, though not priests by office.

Opurei, *s.* a meteor, commonly called a shooting star.

Oputahaotahaoa, *a.* rapacious, insatiable.

Oputauâ, *a.* fearful, cowardly; see *tavâ.*

Oputii, *s.* a very large belly like that of the *tii*, which was always made large.

Oputu, *s* the name of a bird; see *putu.*

Opuvera, *v. a.* to plant on the surface, not deep enough.

Ora, *s.* life, salvation, health; a Saviour, deliverer.

— Ora, *v. n* to live, to be healed, to be saved, or delivered.

— Ora, *a* live, or alive, in opposition to *poke*, dead.

Ora, *s* a wedge; the wrench used in fixing pieces of a canoe together.

—*v. a.* to wrench, or put tight together pieces of a canoe.

Oraa, *s* the noted tree called *aoa*; see *aoa*.

—*s.* cloth made of the bark of the *aoa* tree.

Oraa, *s.* any perplexing affair, or speech, in allusion to the intricate roots of the *oraa*.

Oraerae, *a.* shallow, as water; see *papau*.

Orai, *v. n* to flinch back; to evade a blow; to recede through fear, draw back.

Oraihoro, *s.* one that avoids danger, as war, or trouble; see *tapuhoro*.

Orairai, *v. n.* to flinch repeatedly from danger

Orairai, *a.* thin, slender in some places, hanging in wrinkles, as the skin of a lank person.

Oraora, *v. a.* to set close together, applied to pieces of a canoe when joined.

Oraora, *a.* cadaverous.

Orapa, *s.* any square thing; a square case bottle.

Oraparapa, *a.* having squares irregular, as the shape of some *mape* trees.

Orarai, *a.* thin, lean; see *pararai*

— Orare, *s* a modern name for the *ohee* fish.

— Orare, *s* that which provokes, or stirs up mischief.

—*v. a.* to provoke, stir up mischief.

Oravarava, *s.* a species of the cuttle fish.

Oravarava, *v. n.* to be rippled with the wind, as the sea after a calm.

Oravarava, *a.* tall and slender, as a person

—Ore, *adv.* the negative no, not; but most commonly it answers to the English affix *less*; as *matau*, to fear; *matau ore*, fearless; *haapao*, to regard; *haapao ore*, regardless.

Orê, *s* a modern name for the *oraa* tree.

Orea, *s.* the maiden plantain.

Orearea, *a.* yellowish, as the sea in some shallow places among the coral rocks, also a word of obscene signification.

Orei, *s.* a cork, stopple of a bottle, bung of a cask.

—*v. a.* to cork a bottle, bung a cask, &c.

Orei, *s.* the last of a crop of bread-fruit.

Oreore, *s.* the sharp teeth of the shark or *ono* fish.

Oreore, *s.* the name of three different nights of the Tahitian moon, viz; first *oreore*, middle *oreore*, and last *oreore*.

Oreore, *adv.* a reduplication of the negative *ore*, to express it forcibly, as no, not at all, or no never.

Orepe, *s.* a sharp edge, or top, as of a rock or hill.

Orero, *s* [*korero, olelo,*] language, speech, oration.

Orero, *s.* an orator, or public speaker.

—*v. n.* to speak, to address, make an oration.

Oreromoo, *v. n.* to muse, think seriously; to speak to one's self.

Oreronui, *s.* a man of long speech.

Orerorero, *v. n.* to speak repeatedly, as two persons in a dispute.

Oreroririi, *v. a.* to communicate something secretly, or with a low voice.

Orevareva, *a.* destitute of food, supplies, &c.

Ori, *s.* walking about, rambling.

Ori, *s.* a dance, a shaking; see *upa.*

—*v. n.* to dance, to shake; to ramble about.

Orie, *s.* the small fry of some fishes; a fugitive.

Orio, *s.* the apple of the eye.

Orio, *s.* small knots in wood.

Oriori, *v. n.* to gad about.

Oriori, *v. n.* to shake, or dance repeatedly.

Oriori, *a.* unsettled, rambling.

Oriori, *a.* small, used with *iti.*

Oriorio, *v. n.* to fade, wither, or shrivel, as a plant; to wither, as a person by old age.

Oriorio, *v. n.* to be abashed, to be in fear.

Orire, *a.* not sufficiently cooked, applied to food baked, roasted, &c.

Orivahea, *v. n.* to separate, as one party from another; see *faataa e.*

Oro, *s.* the god of war, the great national god of Tahiti, introduced there from Raiatea, &c.

Oro, *s.* the leaves of a little sweet scented plant.

Oro, *v. a.* to grate the *taro.*

Oroa, *s.* a feast connected with prayers and other religious observances. The *oroas* were of very frequent occurrence, and had names according to the nature of the ceremonies observed, and the persons concerned; such as *oroa arioi, oroa amoa, oroa faatoi, oroa oehamu, oroa taupiti maona, oroa faatito rau moa, oroa aperea, oroa faaneenee, &c.;* see the words *arioi, amoa, faatoi, oehamu, taupiti maona, &c &c.*

Oroaia, *s.* lingering affection of relations for absent friends; a longing to see them.

Oroaia, *s.* a concern of mind on account of some disastrous occurrence.

Oroaia, *v. n.* to feel an abiding affection for a relative or friend that is absent.

Oroapafata, *s.* a feast, in which the food is brought in a sort of case, or cage called *pafata,*

Oroaru, *s.* a deep hole in the ground where the earth has sunk; see *orovaru.*

Oroau, *s.* a sunken hole, a bog, or marshy hole;—*fig.* a voracious, greedy person.

Oroe, *s* the case out of which comes the blossom of the cocoanut

—*s.* a small canoe in the shape of the cocoanut *oroe;* also a whale boat, on account of its shape.

Oroea, *s.* the name of a tree; called also *toroea.*

Oroea, *a.* sick, low, dispirited.

—*v. n.* to be in a low, sickly

13 state; to be low spirited through grief.

Orofea, *s.* a glutton; see *orohea.*
Orofeto, *s.* the name of a fish of the stingray kind.
Orofeto, *v. n.* to be choking; to be unable to eat or swallow on account of alarm; not eatable, as some kinds of food.
Orohea, *s.* a person of a most voracious appetite.
Orohea, *s.* a warrior; one not satiated with fighting.
Orohea, *a.* populous, as a place of many inhabitants.
Orohenâ, *s.* the name of the highest mountain in Tahiti.
Orohenâ, *s.* the upper fin of fish.
Oroi, *v. n.* to be out of perpendicular, as a wall, or a house.
Oroi, *v. n.* to turn, as the wind to another quarter; to alter the course, as a ship.
Oroi, *a.* dark, dismal, as a place.
Oroi, *v. a* to inform, take leave; see *poroi.*
Oroio, *v. n.* to give one's self to grief and death; see *faaaau* and *onohi.*
Oromatua, *s.* the skull of a dead relative preserved, as was formerly the custom. It was wrapped up in cloth, and at certain times, (such as a case of sickness, &c.,) it was produced, when the priest made prayers to the *Oromatua*, in the *po* or night, for the restoration of the sick.
Oromatua, *s.* the ghosts of the dead, who were supposed to be transformed into a sort of inferior gods, but of a malevolent disposition, and therefore prayers were addressed to them to coax them from doing mischief.
Oromatua ai aru, *s.* a fierce *oromatua*, said to come from the *po* or other world, to kill and destroy the living.
Oromatua nihoniho roroa, *s.* the god, or semi god that came, as was supposed, to strangle and eat some surviving relations.
Orometua, *s.* an instructor of any sort, either of religion, or of any art, or trade.
Orometua, *s.* an example, copy, or pattern.
Oromi, *v. n* to disappear, or be lost sight of suddenly.
Oromoo, *s.* some disease; the thrush of children.
Oronau, *s* some unknown voice or shouting, supposed to be heard at different times as a sign of war.
Oronau, *s.* an uncommon consumer of food; a cannibal.
—*a.* ravenous, immoderately eager for food.
Orooro, *s.* an ornament of feathers used for religious purposes, and also worn by warriors.
Orooro, *v. a.* to rub a thing; to rub between the hands.
Orora, *s* the name of a small shell fish.
Orotava, *s.* a species of the cockle fish.
Orotefa, *a.* vain, proud, assuming consequence.
Orotemu, *s.* the name of a small fish.
Orotemu, *v. n.* to shrink away, withdraw from notice.
Oroto, *s.* inside, the place within.
Orotooto, *s.* the inmates of a house.

Orotou, *s.* the name of a mountain.
Oroua, *a.* decrepit through age.
Orouto, *a.* unripe, as fruit; not sufficiently done, as cooked food; dry, as a breast.
Orouto, *v. n.* to be choked through eating eagerly.
Orovaao, *s.* a caterpillar.
Orovaru, *s.* a sunken hole in the ground.
Orovì, *v n.* to be cowed, made timorous.
Oru, *s* a swelling.
—*v. n.* to swell; to grow big with rage; to rebound, as a ship in firing great guns.
Orua, *pron. dual*, you two, to the exclusion of others.
Oruhi, *s.* a certain crab when out of the shell.
Oruirui, *a.* feeble, languid, wanting firmness.
—*v. n* to be languid, void of exertion.
Orure, *v. a.* to provoke, stir up mischief.
Orurehau, *s.* a rebel, disturber of the peace.
—*v. a.* to disturb the peace, or government.
Ota, *s.* chaff, bran, refuse.
Ota, *a.* raw, as meat undressed.
Ota, *v. a.* to fell, or cut down a tree.
Otaa, *s* a ball, roll, or bundle, [as of cloth.
Otaa avaava, *s.* a quid, or chew of tobacco.
Otaetae, *s.* the tree *otae*
Otaha, *s.* the man of war bird.
Otahaati, *s.* an *otaha* perfectly black.
Otahaharorai, *s.* an *otaha* that flies very high.
Otahataaia, *s* a term used for a fisherman.
Otahaumauma, *s* an *otaha* with gills like a cock.
Otahi, *a.* one, also only.
Otai, *s.* the name of a fish.
Otai, *s* an engagement at sea.
Otaivaha, *v. a.* to exaggerate, to represent things greater and better than they are.
Otaota, *a.* lumpy, not reduced to a pulp.
Otapere, *s.* a hole that is large below and small above.
Otaratara, *s.* a wriggler, always moving and uneasy.
—*v. n.* to be always moving and uneasy.
Otaratara, *v. n.* to stand aloof from danger.
Otare, *s.* an orphan.
Otarepape, *s* a thick or watery cloud, with wind.
Otaro, *s.* a ball, or roll, as of cloth or paper.
—*v. a.* to roll up into a ball
Otatare, *s.* the name of a bird resembling the woodpecker.
Otate, *a.* abortive, as gourds, melons, &c.
Otau, *s.* the roots of the *oraa.*
Ote, *v. a.* to suck, or draw the breast.
Otea, *s.* the name of a species [of bread fruit.
Otea, *v n.* to walk with the legs wide apart.
Oteatea, *a.* whitish; see *teatea.*
Oteatea, *s.* the blossom of the plantain.
Oteatea, *v. n.* to lag behind, as a weary traveller.
Otefa, *v. n.* to be vainly admiring one's self.
Otemu, *s.* the name of a fish, which on being seen, recedes into a hole, so as to be lost.
—*v. n.* to recede, to shrink back from sight.

Otemu, *a.* unstable, not to be trusted.

Otemu, *adv.* hesitatingly, reluctantly.

Otemutemu, *v. n* to recede, to shrink back repeatedly.

Oteo, *a.* gaudy, showy in dress, &c.

Oteo, *v. n.* to shoot, or bud, as a plant.

Oteote, *s* little spots in the grain of wood

Oteote, *v. a* to suck repeatedly.

Oteote, *s.* some spots on the skin.

Oteoteo, *a.* proud, self conceited.

Oteretere, *v. n.* to move slowly, creep along.

Oteu, *s.* the name of one species of *taro.*

Oteu, *v. n.* to bud, or sprout, as a plant.

Oti, *v. a.* to cut, as with a knife.

—Oti, *v. n.* to be done or finished; see *faaoti.*

Otî, *v. n.* to recoil, as a gun or cannon after explosion.

Otî, *s* a fowl of variegated feathers

Otî, *s* the cry of the bird *otatare* over a person, which was supposed to be ominous of death.

Otia, *s.* a boundary, limit, or land mark.

Otia, *s.* the name of a large fish of the whale kind.

Otiapohue, *s.* the name of an idolatrous feast.

Otiataiê, *v. n.* to be in advance of others, as a ship, boat, or canoe; to be a-head, or first in advance.

Otiaverevere, *v. n.* to be in a straggling state, as the inhabitants of a place.

Otimo, *v. a.* to slander, speak ill of a person.

Otimotimo, *v. a* to slander a person repeatedly.

Otipi, *s.* the name of a fishing net.

Otipi, *v. n.* to go aside; see *ohipa e.*

Otiore, *s* the name of a gradation of *tatau* among the *arioi;* see *tatau.*

Otioti, *v. a.* to cut repeatedly with an instrument.

Otiotio, *s.* the name of a small fish.

—Oto, *s.* weeping, crying; the noise of the sea on the reef; the singing of birds, insects, &c.

—Oto, *s.* grief, sorrow; see *tai.* —*v. n.* to cry, weep, lament, grieve.

—Oto, *v. n.* to sound, as a bell, or instrument.

Oto, *v. a.* to condole; to congratulate.

Otohaa, *s.* condolence, on account of the death of a person, the departure of a friend, &c.

Otohe, *v. n.* to slide, to retreat.

Otohe, *v. a.* to make an excuse.

Otohe raa, *s.* an excuse, an apology.

Otohi, *s.* a modern name for the *mahi.*

Otore, *v a.* to embowel; see *atore.*

Otu, *s.* see *Tu*, the name of a god, and of the late king.

Otua, *v. n* to lie on the back

Otue, *s.* a promontary, or head land jutting into the sea.

Otue, *s* peaks or tops; the ends of the fingers, &c.

Otuhituhi, *a* of a greyish colour; see *ohinahina.*

Otui, *v. a.* to box; to push away a person or thing; to butt, thump, or ram

Otui, *v. a.* to join or amass together.

Otui, *v. n.* to beat, as the pulse of an artery.

Otuiate, *s.* an acute disease of the stomach or liver, attended with high pulsation.

Otuitui, *v. a.* to butt, thump, or ram repeatedly.

Otuitui, *v. n.* to stutter, or stammer in speaking; to be put in repeated motion, as a thing agitated, or as a report.

Otumutumu, *a.* short, stumpy, as the grass where cattle has been feeding.

Otutu, *a* ill savoured, such as the disagreeable smell of rotten *mahi*, &c

Otuu, *s.* a bird of the heron kind.

Ou, *v. a.* to pull off the bark of a young tree in a line parallel to the trunk whence it comes; to put the head of a person towards the ground.

O'u, *pron poss.* of the first person singular, my, mine, of mine; see *a'u*, *ta'v*, *to'u.*

Oua, *s* the fish called porpoise.

Oua, *v a.* to leap, bound, or jump

Ouma, *s* the breast or bosom.

Oumapao, *s* a climber of trees for bread-fruit, &c.

Oumu, *s* the sour paste called *mahi*, when ill worked, or when of a bad quality.

Ounu, *v. n.* to recede, or hang behind, retreat.

Ounuunu, *v. n.* to return, or retreat repeatedly.

Ouo, *s* a cocoanut, before the kernel forms.

Ouo, *s.* a score cut at the end of a log of timber for fastening a rope.

Oura, *s.* the prawn or shrimp.

Oura pape, *s.* a fresh water shrimp.

Oura tai, *s.* a salt water shrimp.

Ouraura, *a.* reddish, as the colour of a beast.

Oura vaero, *s* the craw-fish, or lobster.

Ouru, *s.* the name of a small tree that grows on the low islands.

Ouru, *s.* the end or point of a thing; see *auru.*

Outeute, *a.* reddish, or inclining to red; see *ouraura.*

Outou, *pron.* second person plural, you or ye, three or more.

Outu, *s* a promontary; see *otue.*

Ovae, *s.* a child that presents the feet at the birth.

Ovaha, *s.* a sort of a rock plant.

Ovai, *pron. relative*, who? used interrogatively.

Ovai, *s* a current of water; see *opape.*

Ovai, *s.* shrimps; see *opape.*

Ovaivai, *s* a sucking pig

Ovaie, *s* the name of a fish.

Ovarevare, *a.* scanty, as the belly of food, the land of inhabitants, &c.

Ovarivari, *s.* the name of a sea insect

Ovarivari, *v n* to be slack, as a rope that had been tight; or the belly after abstinence.

Ovarivari, *a.* empty, slack, sluggish, inactive.

Ovaro, *v. a.* to put the out side in of the bread-fruit leaf, when wrapping pieces of *mahi* for baking.

Ovaru, *s.* a garden or enclosure overrun with weeds.

Ovatavata, *s.* the name of a species of plantain.

Ovau, *pron. sing.* of the first person, I; see *vau.*

Ovava, *a.* careless, worthless, idle, as a vagrant.

Ovava, *s.* the name of a certain song; see *pehe.*

Ovea, *s.* the name of a small fish.

Oveo, *s.* the name of one kind of *taro.*

Oveoveo, *s.* taro, the same as *oveo.*

Oveoveo, *a.* clamorous, noisy, as a woman that is generally scolding.

Overe, *a.* slovenly, untidy; see *tofeto.*

Ovì, *a.* athletic, powerful; also hard, as food.

Oviri, *a.* wild, untamed.

Oviri, *v. a.* to give a turning motion to a cocoanut in throwingitdownfrom a tree, that it may not split.

Oviriviri, *s.* the name of a shrub bearing red berries.

Oviriviri, *s.* the cry of the bird *omaomao.*

Ovìvì, *v. n.* to be cast down, dispirited, brought into subjection by force or apprehension.

—*a.* cowardly, timorous.

P

IS a letter extensively used in Tahitian, and is pronounced as *p* in *put*; but is sometimes softened so as nearly to approach the sound of *b.*

Pa, *s.* a term of reverence answering to father, and commonly used by children in addressing their father, and common people their chief; see *patea.*

Pa, *s.* a fence or hedge; see [*patia.*

Pa, *s.* a small enclosed place sacred to the young king or chief; also such a place sacred to the use of the *upuupa* dancers.

Pa, *v. a.* to give, or bestow, see *horoa.*

Pà, *a.* barren, as a woman that had ceased to bear children.

Paa, *s.* the external crust of bread fruit, &c.

Paa, *s.* scales on the skin; the hoops of a cask.

Paaa, *v. n.* to grow to great maturity, as trees or plants that are not molested.

Paaa, *v. a.* to track by the tendrils of a vine, such as the yam, in order to find out the root.

Paaamotu, *s* a vine broken from its root;—*fig.* an agreement broken, or not regarded.

Paaara, *a.* dry, as a garment when dried in the sun.

Paae, *s.* some supposed crime punished by the gods; the punishment supposed to be inflicted; see *pahara.*

Paae, *v a.* to rake; to train or drag along.

Paaehere, *s* the cavally fish; see *paamuhere*.

Paaerepo, *s.* a rake.

Paaha, *s.* a little sinnet fastened to a wooden dish for the purpose of hanging it up; also a string fastened to a fed turtle.

Paahi, *v. a.* to scrape off the soft fleshy substance from the seeds of the pandanus when they are eaten.

Paahii, *s.* cloth for an infant, swaddling cloth.

Paahu, *v. a.* to dig the earth; see *utaru*.

Paahue, *s.* an iron, or wooden hoop.

Paaiea, *s.* the name of a small crab.

Paaiea, *a.* mature, grown to perfection, as a plant; well informed or skilled, applied to a person.

Paaiu, *v. n.* to rustle, as the wind; spring up, as a breeze of wind.

Paamea, *s.* the boneto fish.

Paamoa, *s.* the boneto, the same as *paamea*.

Paamuhere, *s.* the cavally fish; see *urua*.

Paana, *a.* strong, vigorous, healthy.

Paaoao, *a.* dwarfish, diminutive in size, diminished through illness; see *aao*.

Paaoroa, *v. p* gone, consumed; see *pau*.

Paapaa, *a.* scorched, dried up by heat; over done, as baked or roasted food.

Paapaamaehe, *a* dried up, dry.

Paapaamarô, *a.* dry, as land; dry land, in opposition to the sea, or to marshy ground.

Paara, *s.* certain sticks or staves used by the mourners for the dead; see *heva*

Paara, *v. a* to strike against a thing, as a paddle against the side of a canoe; to strike the canoe, as a signal

Paara, *v. a.* to try to trip each other, as boys in their game of walking on stilts.

Paarara, *s* the name of a fresh water eel.

Paare, *s.* sickness at stomach; sea sickness

Paareare, *a.* calm, when the water is without a ripple.

Paareare, *s.* sea sickness, sickness at stomach.

—Paari, *s.* wisdom, knowledge, skill, cunning.
—*a.* wise, knowing, skilful, cunning.

—Paari, *a.* mature, old, ripe; hard.

Paaro, *v. a.* to excavate, or hollow out, as in taking the kernel out of a cocoanut, or fish out of a shell.

Paarovai, *v. a.* to scoop the kernel out of a cocoanut while the water remains in it.

Paata, *v. n.* to come within view, as the moon in rising.

Paata, *v. a.* to excite merriment or laughter.

Paatahi, *a.* enveloped in one folding.

Paatahi, *a.* large, as the platted leaves of a native basket; also one sided, as water when running on one side of the channel

Paato, *v a.* to lop off the tops of plants, or leaves; to pick up some sorts of fruit.

Paatoa, *adv.* generally; also universally.

Paatoa, *a.* general, common; universal.

Paatoato, *v. a.* to lop off, or pluck leaves or fruit repeatedly.

Paau, *s.* the name of a coarse kind of native cloth.

Paau, *s.* a comb, see *pahere.*

Paau, *v a.* to skim off from the surface of a thing.

Paauara, *s.* the name of an excellent root like a potato, but has a vine like the yam.

Paauara, *s.* the name of a delicious small fish.

Paave, *v. a.* to suspend, or hang up; see *faauta.*

Paave, *v. a.* to carry, or convey on the back

Paave piripou, *s.* a suspender to keep up a pair of trousers.

Pae, *s* side, part, division, or dividend.

Pae, *s.* a block, stone, or any thing put under to fix and support the joists under a floor, sill, threshhold, &c

Pae, *s.* the uncastrated male of animals.

Pae, *v. n.* to drift, go to leeward, as a boat, ship, &c

Paea, *s.* an inferior species of bread-fruit.

Paea, *s.* a division set apart.

Paearua, *s.* of both sides.

Paeau, *s.* a side or division.

Paeavae, *s.* a foot stool; a place by the feet.

Paee, *v. a.* to skin off; to scrape, or take off what is on the surface.

Paehere, *s.* a darling.

Paenapu, *a.* dry, as by the sun. —*v n.* to dry, as by the sun

Paepiti, *s.* the same as *paearua,* also *paeapiti.*

Paeore, *s.* a species of *fara* or pandanus, the leaves of which are used for mats.

Paeore, *s.* the name of a fish.

Paepae, *s.* a pavement of stones; scaffolding for a building; a platform; the pavement of a *marae.*

Paepaea, *a* narrow, confined.

Paepaeahutae, *s.* an even pavement.

Paere, *s.* the name of a lean sort of fish.

Paere, *a.* lank, lean; *taata paere,* a lean man.

Paero, *s.* [from the Eng. *pail,*] a pail, bucket, or cask.

Paetaeta, *s.* the name of a bird.

Paetaaaitu, *s.* the name of a certain ceremony and prayers previous to war engagements.

Paetahi, *adv* partly, partially, in some degree.

Paete, *v. n.* to be made angry, to feel displeasure.

Paeteete, *adv.* tardily, inefficiently.

Paevahine, *s.* a man that pays extraordinary attention to the other sex; an effeminate man.

Pafai, *v. a.* to pluck, or break off fruit, flowers, &c.

Pafaifai, *v. a.* to pluck off fruit, &c., repeatedly.

Pafaite, *s* the north-west wind.

Pafao, *s.* a fish-hook, see *pifao.*

Pafao, *v. a.* to use certain enchantments.

Pafata, *s.* a cage, a box; see *afata.*

Pafataatuu, *s.* the name of a tree.

Pafeofeo, *a.* abundance, applied to food, &c.

Paha, *s.* a wild boar.
Paha, *adv.* perhaps, peradventure, may be.
Pahae, *v. a* to rend or tear, such as cloth, paper, &c.
Pahahae, *v. a.* to rend or tear; to cause divisions.
Pahahi, *s.* an error or mistake.
—*v. n.* to fall into an error or mistake.
Pahahoi, *adv.* yes surely, certainly so, so it is indeed.
Pahara, *s* judgment or punishment in consequence of some offence to the gods.
Paharahara, *s.* the same as *pahara.*
Paheahea, *adv.* inefficiently, ineffectually.
Pahee, *v. n.* to slide or slip, as the foot; to ebb or flow back, as the tide; see *pananu.*
Paheehee, *a.* slippery, as the road.
Paheheru, *v. a.* to search repeatedly.
Pahemo, *v. n.* to slip off; see *hemo, mahemo.*
Pahemohemo, *v. n.* to slip off repeatedly.
Paheo, *s.* a lazy lounging fellow that spends his time uselessly.
Paheo, *a* indulged, as a spoiled child.
Pahere, *s.* a comb; see *pahoro*
—*v. a.* to comb the head.
Pahere, *v. a.* to pare off the rind or outside of cold breadfruit that has been baked; to pare off the skin of the ?? apple, &c.
Paherehere a iri, *v. n.* to be but merely skin deep, spoken of a slight wound.
Paheri, *v. a.* to search, turn over things in searching.
Paheru, *v. a.* to scratch, as a hen; to dig and search for a thing; to make a thorough search.
Paheruateve, *v. a.* to amass food or property.
Paheruheru, *v. a.* to search again and again, to continue to search; also to pry into or examine the affairs of others.
Pahi, *s.* a ship, boat, or Paumotu canoe.
Pàhi, *s.* a spray of the sea.
Pàhi, *v. a.* to splash the water that it may wet a person.
Pahiha, *v. a* to miss aim, make a wrong step.
Pahii, *s.* an infant's cloth, or little mat.
Pahiihii, *s.* a certain mode of fishing.
Pahio, *s.* a lazy person; see *paheo.*
Pahipahi, *v. n* to be teazed, as by a froward child; see *haapahi.*
—*v. n* to be vexed with cares and anxieties.
Pahitafarau, *s.* a ship or boat that remains in its covered shed;—*fig.* a person that is seldom from home.
Pahiturere, *a.* startling, causing to startle.
—*v. n.* to startle, see *hitimaue.*
Pahô, *s.* first-fruit; see *oho.*
Pahô, *v. n.* to be first in advance, as before an army.
Pahoa, *s.* a bill hook.
Pahoa, *v. n.* to prepare the bark for the making of the native cloth.
Pahoa, *v. a* to demand something peremptorily, as with authority.

Pahaahoa, *v. a.* to demand repeatedly.

Pahoatia, *s* an angry saying, sudden burst of anger.

Pahano, *v, a.* to splice or join things together; to finish a work that another had commenced.

Pahonoa, *s.* that which had been joined together; the band, or that which binds

Pahonohono, *v. a.* to join things together repeatedly.

Pahore, *a. v.* to flay or skin, peel off the out ward covering; see *hohore*, to excoriate.

Pahoro, *s.* a comb see *pahere.*

Pahoro, *s* a painful swelling of the foot or hand.

Pahoro, *s.* a species of the parrot fist.

Pahoro, *v.a.* to comb the head, to rake ground.

Pahorohoro, *v. a* to be in pain as a glutton after over loading his stomach.

Pahou, *s.* the name of some disease of the head.

Pahou, *a.* young, new, late, see *hou.*

Pahou, *v. a.* to pierce or bore.

Pahu, *s.* *(Pa'u)* the drum, of which the Tahitians had several sorts used for diversion or worship of the gods

Pahu, *v.n.* to be dammed up as water, stopped or pent up as any liquid.

Pahu, *v. n.* to spatter up as soft mud when carelesly trod upon.

Pahua, *s.* a species of gigantic oyster.

Pahuhu, *v. n.* to draw a thing through the hand, as a wet rope, to press out the water.

Pahunena, *a.* full, as of food, property &c.

Pahure, *a* bald, without hair; without branches.

Pahure, *v. n.* to be excoriated as the skin.

Pahurehure, *v.n.* to be excoriated repeatedly.

Pahuri, *s.* the name of a mode of fishing, the name of a fishing net.

Pahuri, *v. a.* to turn over horizontally.

Pahuruhuru, *s.* a slovenly careless person.

Pahurutoea, *s.* the name of a very small fish.

Pahurutoeo, *s.* the name of a powerful fish that often breaks the fishing net; see *hiroa.*

'Pahute, *a.* abundant, plentiful.

Pahutini, *a.* full, congregated, as many people.

Pahutoere, *s.* the name of the long drum used in the marae.

Pai, *s.* the nipple of animals.

Pai, *s.* the rough skin caused by puncturing for marking the *tahu.*

Pa'i, *adv* surely, even so, see *pahahoi.*

Pai, *a.* dry, as a breast that has no milk.

Pai, *v. a* to wrap up carefully as fish in leaves to be baked.

Paia, *a.* slippery; smooth.

Paia, *s.* sodomy; see *aipai.*

Paia, *cong* because, on account of.

Paiaa, *s.* the roots, long and small of a tree or plant.

Paiare, *s.* a species of shark whose skin was used for drum heads.

Paiatai, *s.* the flying fish; see *marara.*

Paiatiare, *s* the name of a certain heathen custom or ceremony, when some restrictions, in regard of female children, were removed.

Paiatua, *s.* an idolatrous ceremony on the new decoration of the *too* or image of a god; see *too*.

Paie, *s.* abundle or wrapper containig a quantity of the tahitian fish sauce called taiero; see *mitiero*.

Paiere, *a.* clear as the sky; clear as a garden.

Paieti, *s. (Engl. piety)* piety, godliness.

Paifee, *s.* the stump of one of the feelers of the cuttle fish when it has been bitten off by another fish; see *fee*.

Paifee, *s.* the name of a species of bread fruit.

Paihi, *v. a.* to root out, extirpate; see *ihitumu*.

Paihu, *s* the name of a part of the nose; also a part of a canoe.

Paimi, *v.a.* to search, seek, see *maimi*

Paina, *s.* a crashing noise, a crashing like the breaking of a stick.

Painu, *v. n.* to go adrift; see *panu*.

Paino, *s* a familiar term of endearment used by a child in addressing his father; see *pa* and *patea*.

Paio, *v. a.* to arrange adjust a matter, or affair.

Paipai, *s.* the sea blubber.

Paipai, *v, a.* to drive a *tii* or demon out of a person supposed to be posessed.

Paipaiata, *a.* populous, full of inhabitants.

Paipaita taata, *s.* the nettle or stinging fish.

Paira, *s.* a mark or scar, as that of a warrior.

Pairia, *s.* sudden anger, see *iria*, *riri*.

Paita, *s.* great anger.

Paitaita, *v. n.* to be affected with great anger, to rage.

Paitaita, *v. n.* to be affected with cold, see *toetoe*.

Paiti, *s.* a term of endearment addressed to a father, see *pa* and *iti*.

Paiti, *v. a.* to snatch or pick up as the fish from a net, or drag of leaves; to gather small things.

Paiti, *a. n.* to think deliberately and examine.

Paiti iti, *v. n.* to think deliberately and repeatdly, examine with care; see *paio*, *feruri*.

Paito, *a.* vigilant, dexterous as a workman.

Paitoito, *a.* as *paito*, adroit, dexterous.

Paiuma, *v.n.* to climb or ascend; see *ae*.

Pamu, *s.(Angl.pump)* a pump, formaly *faahe*.

Pamu, *v. n.* to pump as in a ship.

Panu, *s.* a case or wrapper containing food.

Pana, *s.* the name of an amusement of children.

Pana, *v. a.* to search or feel for a thing by means of some instrument; to raise up a thing with a lever or bar; to move or turn over with a hand spike; to toss or kick a foot ball.

Panafara, *s.* the name of a species of bread fruit.

Panai, *s.* a ridge or stratum.

Panai, *v.n.* to stand in a line or row; see *nanai* to be straight.

Panane, *v. a.* to mix up, or stir some kind of food with a spoon or stick.

Pananenane, *v. a.* to stir up, or mix food repeatedly.

Pananu, *v. n.* to flow as the tide of the sea.

Panao, *v. a.* to introduce the hand into an opening, bag or basket; see *tinao.*

Panaonao, *v. a.* to introduce the hand repeatedly into a bag, basket, &c.

Panapana, *v. a.* to poke repeatedly.

Panave, *v. n.* to be in trouble, nsed ironically; see *navenave* which signifies pleasure.

Pane, *s.* the long lobes in some cases of the elephantiasis having divisions between them called pane; see *fatia.*

Pane, *s. (Latin panis)* bread a loaf.

Panehenehe, *s.* the first fish obtained in a net; the first person killed in a war.

Panena. *a.* spread out; stretched out smooth as native cloth; see *nena.*

Panepane, *v. n.* to have many lobes, as a *feefee leg.*

Pani, *s. (Engl. pan)* a kettle, pot, sauce-pan.

Pani, *v. a.* to close, or shut up a breach; see *papani.*

Pani, *v. a.* the upper shell of the *tete*; a sort of a hand bell made of pearl oyster shells, and beaten as a token of mourning for the dead.

Paniarua, *s.* a human sacrifice offered at the close of certain prayers and ceremonies.

Panina, *v. a.* to cover as with mould or earth.

Panino, *v. a.* to twist or spin; see *nino.*

Panipani, *v. a.* to close or shut up a breach; to rectify misunderstandings; to hide a thing.

Panitatui, *s.* the name of a certain heathen ceremony, relative to a deceased person, in order to prevent his spirit from returning to anoy the living.

Panitutui *s.* the name of a ceremony observed in order to purify a place defiled by the dead.

Paniuru, *s.* the highest part of the back of the neck.

Paniuru, *s.* a species of pipe clay.

Panoo, *s.* a board in the stern of a canoe.

Panoonoo, *s.* agitation of mind, aniety.

Panoonoo, *v. n.* to be anxious or uneasy in mind, as in time of war &c.

Panu, *v. n.* to go adrift.

Pao, *s.* a meteor, commonly called a shooting star.

Pao, *v. a.* to seize or snatch suddenly, as a dog does a piece of meat.

Pao, *s.* the name of a fish.

Pao, *v. a.* to dig, excavate or hollow out a piece of timber or a stone; to dig out a hollow place; to beat or bruise

the bark of a tree that the sap may run out.

Pao, *v. a.* to strike and lacerate the head with sharks teeth, as was formerly the custom of the women in token of grief, or affection.

Paoa, *s.* a mode of fishing; see *tautai*.

Paoa, *s.* the nostrils, called also apoo ihu.

Paoa, *s.* a hole or crevice applied to such places in the rocks as the foot might be placed in in climbing.

Paoaoa, *a.* narrow, as a piece of timber.

Paoaoa, *v. n.* to whine, or speak with a low tone of voice.

Paoaora, *s.* applied to a family when the different branches of it are all alive.

Paoapohe, *s.* a family that becomes extinct in its several branches.

Pahoe, *a.* neat

Paoho, *s.* a loud squalling laugh, as of one that wishes to be noticed.

Paoho, *s.* to go boldly in advance as a warrior; to leap as a fish inclosed in a net.

Paoi, *adv.* a contraction of *paha hoi*, surely, even so, so it is, indeed, certainly, see *paha*.

Paoo, *v. n.* to be consumed, expended, all gone.

Paoo, *s.* the bark of the *aute* or china mulberry tree when in a state of preparation for being pasted together; see *ahu*.

Paonoono, *v. n.* to sleep undisturbedly.

Paopao, *v. a.* to strike the head repeatedly with sharks teeth; to dig, hollow out with repeated strokes.

Paopao, *v.n.* to be bespattered, as with mud.

Paora, *v. n.* to be dried up as land through want of rain

Paora, *a.* dry, hard by reason of drought.

Paorae, *a.* strait, confined; see *paepaea*.

Paoratu mato, *s.* the name of a tree that grows in the rocks, the same as the *aeae*.

Paoroao, *v. n.* to be wasted by disease, see *nao*.

Paotaota, *a* parboiled, half boiled or roasted.

Paoti, *s* a pair of scissors, or nippers

Paoti, *v. a.* to cut or clip with scissors.

Paoto, *v. n* to be violently angry.

Paoto oto, *v n.* to be repeatedly angry

Paoutuiaio, *s.* the name of a little fish which manages cunningly to escape leaving others to be taken; *fig.* one that leads others into difficulties, but escapes himself.

Papa, *s* a board; a seat; a flat stone.

Papa, *s* a rock; a stratum of rock; the shoulder blade.

Papa, *v n.* to fly or crack as a stone in the fire.

Papa, *a.* flying, cracking, breaking as some stones that will not bear the fire

Papaa, *s* a series of facts or occurrences; a certain range or class of things, such as islands, countries &c.

Papaa, *s.* a foreigner, formerly applied to the inhabitants of the *Paumotu* islands before europeans visited them, but since to all foreigners; in some islands it is *papalangy.*

Papaa, *a.* foreign, not belonging to the place.

Papaa, *s.* the general name of crabs.

Papaaaha, *s.* a person of long standing in a place; an intelligent person.

Papaaaha, *s.* a fleet, or army preparing for war.

Papaafara, *s.* a person that never ceases talking and scolding; see *hvare paa.*

Papaate, *v. n.* to be whole, without crack or breach, as a board, slate &c., *fig.* to be in league together; to be complete in a branch of knowledge.

Papaatua etaeta, *s.* a species of crab with a very hard shell; *fig.* a relentless warrior.

Papaatua fare, *s.* a side or back part of a house.

Papaatuahonu, *s.* a sort of crab with a turtle back.

Papaatua rau, *s.* a heap or pile of many parts. *fig.* an accumulation of various crimes.

Papaa tuavaru, *s.* an accumulated heap.

Papae, *s.* the name of a fish.

Papae, *v. n.* to drive before the wind, as a ship.

Papae, *s.* a timorous person, a coward.

Papae, *v. a.* to use indirect means of seduction.

Papahi, *s.* the sun fish, formerly sacred to the gods.

Papahi, *s.* a fat animal, or man.

Papahia, *s.* the name of a stool or block on which fruits &c, are beaten into a pulp.

Papahia, *v. a.* to beat bread fruit, plantains &c, on the block papahia; to pound as in a mortar; also to break to shivers.

Papahoro, *s.* a board used for swimming in the surf in the native pastime of *horue.*

Papahoro, *s.* a bearer, such as carried the king on the shoulders.

Papahuaa, *v. a.* to trace genealogy; see *aufau.*

Papai, *v. a.* to strike, beat, chastise; see *tata.*

Papai, *v. a.* to write.

Papai, *v. a.* to recite a tale; see *ta.*

Papai, *v. a.* to mark the skin with the *tatau.*

Papai, *v. a.* to make, and use a net; see *upea.*

Papai, *v. a.* to make a fish hook, work at house building, making a canoe or a boat; to chop fire wood, &c.

Papai, *v. a.* to play as children in their game of papai raa pohue.

Papai, *s.* a species of plantain.

Papai, *s.* a rod, or weapon to strike with.

Papai au, *v. n.* to be wasted through disease.

Papai au, *a.* thin, lean; see *tutoivi.*

Papae, *s.* a wrapper for fish sauce, &c.

Papaina, *s.* a cracking sharp noise.

Papaina, *v. n.* to make a cracking noise, as in the breaking of a stick.

Papaiearo, *v. n.* to beset before.

Papaiotua, *v. a.* to beset behind.

Papaipauruvaa, *s.* a person that performed certain ceremonies on board a fleet of war canoes.

Papaitaputua, *s.* the name of a certain *tatau* on the back.

Papaitaputua, *a.* ill arranged, as a speech.

Papamare, *s.* the name of a certain play of children in the water.

Papamaehe, *a.* dry as the ground, grass, &c.

Papamaohe, *a.* dry.

Papamarô, *a.* the same as *papamaehe.*

Papanai, *a.* equal in size, rank, standing.

Papani, *v. a.* to stop up or shut; to silence.

Papanihinihi, *s.* plain, as land; of good likeness.

Papanihinihi, *s.* a large tahitian seat or stool.

Papanipari, *v. a.* to stop, or shut up repeatedly.

Papao, *s.* a sort of sling used for war, and made of the aute bark; see *maa.*

Papaonao, *s.* a multitude of people, birds, &c.

Papaora, *v. n.* to become hard as the dry ground.

Papaora, *s.* a cadaverous smell as of a dead body.

Papaora, *a.* ill smelling.

Papapae, *s.* a board that has drifted in the sea.

Papapanu, *s.* the same as papapae.

Papapapa, *s.* the name of a species of grass.

Papapapâ, *s.* the indications of puberty or manhood.

Papape, *s.* a squall of wind and rain.

Papapâ, *v. n.* to be consumed, as the food or fruit produced in one place.

Paparaharaha, *s.* a rock, the mother of earthly things according to tahitian tradition.

Paparauhaa, *s.* a broad flat board used by females in mat making.

Paparepo, *s.* a thick matted substance found in bags: see *moihi.*

Paparia, *s.* (*paringa*) the cheek; see *papauru.*

Paparia, *adv.* side ways, obliquely.

Papariahovai, *s.* an ill natured, ill designing person.

Papariataratara, *s.* one delighting in mischief.

Paparu, *s.* a species of bread fruit.

Paparu, *v. a.* a reduplication of the verb *paru* to feed, or throw food for hogs, fowls, &c.

Papataiore, *a.* slender, of graceful mien.

Papataua, *a.* drawling, tiresome as a speech.

Papatea, *s.* stones covered with a white crust of coralline matter, which are found on the shore.

Papatea, *s.* a person not marked by the *tatau*; also the title of some principal chiefs.

Papati, *s.* the name of a running plant.

Papati, *a.* diminutive, as the leaves of an ill grown tree.

Papatia, *s.* an upright post ; a straight cocoanut.

Papatuahonu, *s.* the shell on the back of the turtle.

Papatuetaeta, *s.* a long tottering person, yet of more strength than might be expected.

Papatuai, *s.* the same as papatuetaeta.

Papau, *s.* a shallow place.

Papau, *a.* shallow applied to water.

Papaupea, *s.* one length out of those lengths that compose a net.

Papaupea, *s.* a camp, a fleet, or army preparing for war.

Papaurae, *a.* shallow; see *papau.*

Papauri, *s.* a title given to inferiors.

Papauru, *s.* the cheek ; see *paparia*, the cheek or one side of a fishes head.

Papavaha, *s.* vain pomposity, emptiness, deceit.

Pape, *s.* water, see *vai* ; the juice of any thing.

Papepape, *s.* cotton; see *vavai.*

Papi, *v. n.* to speak hastily and disorderly.

Papi, *v. a.* to eat voraciously and hastily.

Papi, *v. a.* to sprinkle or splash the water at each other, as boys sometimes do in bathing.

Papi, *v. n.* to get on the shallows, as fish when driven.

Papo, s, the gum or hard juice of plants and trees.

Papo, *s.* the matter of a gathering or sore ; the mortified part.

Papu, *a.* sluggish, inert, cumbersome: see *topapu.*

Papô, *a.* plain, of an even surface.

—*adv.* thoroughly, completely, perfectly.

Papua, *s.* a green branch of a tree or plant,

Para, *a.* ripe, as fruit ; come to a head, as an abcess.

Para, *s.* a species of root eaten in times of scarcity.

Para, *s.* manure, dung, dirt, rotten vegetables.

Para, *s.* particles of food adhering to a vessel or to the hands.

Para, *s.* the white slime of a new born infant.

Paraa, *s.* the spot, or wound occasioned by a sling stone.

Parabole, *s.* *(greek parabole)* a parable.

Parae, *s.* the cap or head piece of the dress worn by the chief mourner in the tahitian *heva* ; also a cap worn by a warrior, a sort of wooden dish.

Paraerae, *a.* dimness of sight by the glare of the sun, fire, &c.

— *v. n.* to be dim through something glaring.

Parafatu, *s.* the name of a species of plantain.

Parafarero, *s.* a sort of bait for fish.

Paraha, *s.* the name of a broad flat fish.

Parahaputii, *s.* a species of the paraha fish, there are several, as paraha rau to, paraha petue, &c.

Parahaita, *v. n.* to be wearied as in searching for a thing ; to have the patience exhausted

Paraharahu, *s.* a fish, the same as paraha.

Parahi, *v. n.* to sit, dwell, abide, see *noho*.

Parahihufa, *v. n.* to be sustained, fed, nourished, supported, or caressed by another.

Parahirahi. *v. n.* to be transient, or abiding a little while only in a place.

Parahoro, *v. n.* to be fully ripe as plantains that are falling from the tree; to be sunken as a mahi pit that was too full.

Paraahu, *a.* broad, level; see *aano*.

Parahuhu, *v. a.* to draw a thing between the thumb and finger, as the tahitians do in emptying the intestines of pigs.

Parahurahu, *a.* broad; see *aano*.

Parai, *s.* the name of a fish.
— *s.* a species of yam.
— *v. a.* to daub, blot, obliterate.

Paraia, the liver of a beast.

Paraia ati, *s.* a warrior of courage and hardihood.

Paraioro, *a.* wearisome, as a speech without energy.
— *v. a.* to smooth.
— *v. n.* to evade by a smooth speech.

Paraoha, *v. n.* to hang down, as the leaves and branches of a tree newly planted.

Paraoro, *v. a.* to take the wrinkles out of cloth.

Paraparau, *v. n.* to converse, as two or more persons.

Paraparauraa, *s.* conversation.

Paraparai, *v. a.* to daub, besmear or blot repeatedly.

Parapau, *s.* a person that has lost his fame or consequence.

Parara, *v. a.* to singe or scorch over the fire.

Parara, *v. n.* to go off the mark; as an arrow shot.

Parara, *a.* ill adapted, unfit.
— *s.* a mode of fishing by driving the fish into crevices in order to catch them.

Pararai, *a.* thin, lean, wasted away.

Pararau, *v. n.* to converse in pairs.

Parare, *v. n.* to spread wide.
— *a.* broken, stammering, as speech,

Parari, *a.* broken, bruised; see *haaparari*.

Pararo, *s.* the name of a small flat blackish fish.

Parau, *s.* speech, manner, custom, conversation.
— *s.* a book, talk, report, saying, or word.

Parau, *v. n.* to speak, converse.

Parau, *v. a.* to declare, to advise.

Pârau, *s.* the shell of the pearl oyster.

Pârauoota, *s.* the black oyster shell.

Pârau tauara, *s.* a pearl oyster difficult to be obtained: any thing difficult of access, or hard to be obtained.

Pârauuouo, *s.* a white clear oyster shell.

Parau, *v. a.* to scratch; see *raurau*.

Paraurau, *v. a.* to scratch repeatedly.

Parauriirii, *s.* whispering, tale telling.
— *v. n.* to whisper, small talk and in a bad sense.

Parararu, *v. s.* the name of a garment worn by warriors, also a fowl that happens to have four long pendent feathers on each side of its tail.

Pare, *s.* a fort, castle, place of refuge.

Parehe, *s.* the name of a fish; see *tehu.*

Pareirei, *s.* a fishing net of a particular kind.

Paremo, *v. n.* to sink in the water, to be drowned.

Pereora, *s.* a place of refuge.

— *s.* to shelter, deliver or save.

Parepare, *v. n.* to pray or entreat a deity for favour.

— *v. a.* to defend or guard, as a warrior.

Parepare matua, *s.* a heathen prayer to the gods; also the act of defending a people or country.

Paretai, *s.* a place of refuge in the sea.

— *v. n.* to take refuge at sea.

Paretia, *s.* the same as *pareora.*

Pareu, *s.* a garment worn as a petticoat, round the loins of both sexes.

Pareu, *v. a.* to put on a *pareu.*

Pareuruvaa, *s.* a person that performed some ceremonies on board of a war canoe.

Pari, *v. a.* to accuse, blame, criminate.

Pari, *s.* the rocks or perpendicular cliffs by the sea side.

Pari, *v. a.* to square or shape a piece of timber.

Parima, *s.* a ceremony, or the dismissed of those who attended it.

Pârima, *v. a.* to discharge from attendance, to dismiss.

Paripari, *s.* a song about the transactions and qualities of a place.

Paripari, *v. v.* the spray breaking on the shore, or a canoe, &c.

Pariri, *v. n.* to be in a violent rage.

Paritarita, *s.* violent anger.

Paroe, *s.* a kind of wooden dish, an *umete.*

Paroere, *v, n.* to be dim through something glaring.

— *a,* dimness of sight through the glare of the sun, fire, &c.

Paroo, *a.* famous, either for good or bad.

— *v. n.* to be noted or famous; see *tuiroo.*

Paropii, *s.* the maker of ornaments.

Parora, *a.* sweet scented.

— *v. n.* to become tedious or dilatory; to attempt long without success.

Parorarora, *v. n.* to be delaying or protracting the time.

Parore, *v. a.* to trip a person, by shaking that on which he stands.

Parorerore, *v. a.* to trip a person repeatedly.

Paroto, *s.* a piece of wood fitted in a canoe.

Paru, *s.* the name of a fish.

— *s.* a species of *monoi,* or scented oil.

— *v. a.* to throw food in small pieces to hogs or fowls.

Parupape, *s.* a species of fine white native cloth; also white linen or calico.

Parupape, *s.* a white linen or calico shirt.

Paruparu, *a.* weak, feeble, bruised, broken or diseased.

Parupoa. *s.* a bait for fish, a bribe.

— *s.* a certain prayer formerly used by fishermen.

Pararaoa, *s.* a soft bait to catch the *raoa* fish.

Parure, *s.* a strong native cloth.

Parure, *v. a.* to beat into a pulp, as some kinds of food.

Paruru, *s.* a screen, a curtain; a shield.

— *v. a.* to defend, screen or shelter.

Parutotara, *s.* a small crop of bread fruit which is ripe in the *totara* season.

Parutu, *a.* gloomy & dark, applied to the sky.

Paruu, *v. a.* to repair a fence orhedge.

Pata, *s.* a scorpion, of which there are a few in Tahiti.

Pata, *s.* a spot.

Pata, *s.* an insect found in the thatch of houses, and whose noise in striking the thatch indicates war.

Pata, *s.* a cocoanut that was split whilst the priest prayed for success in fishing.

Pata, *v. a.* to strike, as the insect pata does with its tail; to snap with the finger and thumb upon any thing; to strike smartly with the finger.

Pataa, *s.* a drop of any thing, a particle.

Pataataa, *s.* a term used in some of the Tahitian *aai* or legendary tales.

Patahamu, *s.* a voracious eater, yet not to satiety.

Patahi, *s.* a dexterous mode of using the spear.

Pataitai, s. a small black fish found on the rocks.

Pataô, *a.* shy, as a fish that had been pierced.

Patapata, *v. a.* to strike repeatedly with the finger.

Patapatairite, *v. n.* to be consumed, finished, concluded.

Patapatahainia, *s.* a canoe that could not be hurt by the Atua mao, the shark god, called *tahainia*.

Patapo, *a.* prominent or projecting.

Patapoa, *s.* a native custom of striking the throat with the finger when speaking of food.

Patara, *s.* the name of a good edible root, which grows in the mountains.

Pataru, *v. a.* to dig the earth to make it level.

Patatâ, *a.* able, having skill sufficient substance, &c.

Patâtâ, *a.* slack.

Patatoa, *a.* crafty, subtle.

Patatu, *a.* bulky in size, or in quantity.

Patatuara, *a.* strolling, wandering without a home.

Patatue, *s.* soft, downy, as a bed.

Patatuera, *a.* skilled, able, dexterous.

Patau, *s.* the prompter, or leader of the song in the native diversions, or in dragging a tree, canoe, &c.

Patau, *v. a.* to lead the song in the native music.

Patatau, *v. n.* to repeat the patau over again.

Patē, *v. a.* to strike, as the clapper of a bell, flint and steel, &c.

Pate, *v. a.* to sound with lead and line.

Pate, *v. n.* to rebound in any direction.

Patea, *s.* a term of respect addressed to a mother or a woman of rank; see *pa.*

Patea, *s.* a species of bread-fruit.

Pateaino, *s.* a term of respect addressed by children to their mother, as paino, is to their father.

Pateatoto, *s.* a game or fighting cock: fig. a brave warrior.

Pataraupaa. *s.* a cowardly cock; fig. a coward.

Pateatea, *s.* a sort of native cloth.

Pateetee, *v. n.* the noise arising from the clattering of hard substances when jolted.

— *adv.* carelessly, listlessly, applied to actions.

Patehe, *v. a.* to castrate.

— *s.* a castrated brute.

Patehu, *s.* the same as tehu.

Patehutehu, *s.* the young of the fish tehu.

Patere, *s.* the same as patero.

Patere, *adv.* slightly, erroneously, as the slight piercing of a spear.

Patere, *v. a.* to push on to the heart of an engagement.

Pati, *s.* a rank of soldiers, people standing in a row, a range of mountains.

Pati, *v. n.* to leap or jump suddenly, to start.

Patia, *s.* a spear, or javelin.

Patia, *s.* a fence of upright sticks, see *pa.*

Patia, *v. a.* to stab or lance.

Patia, *v. a.* to let blood.

Patiamaa, *s.* a fork.

Patiatia, *v. a.* to pierce, lance, or stab repeatedly.

Patiatiairiamoa, *adv.* lightly, applied to an action.

Patii, *s.* the flat fish called flounder.

Patii, *s.* the name of a basket.

Patii, *a.* flat, pressed wide.

Patiitii, *a.* level, flat, wide.

Patiitinaiahi, *s.* a broad flounder; fig. a covetous person.

Patipatitea, *a.* great in number, large in quantity.

Patiri, *s.* thunder.

Patiri, *v. n.* to thunder.

Patirihoainîa, *s.* thunder over head.

Putirituiiraro, *s.* thunder at a distance.

Patitì, *v. n.* to spatter, as drops of water, to flounder, as fish in shallow water.

Patiti, *v. a.* to nail, or fasten.

Patito, *s.* a small fresh-water fish.

Patitotito, *v. a.* to nibble repeatedly, as fish at the bait.

Patô, *v. a.* to propel, or shoot forward.

Pato, *v. n.* to break the shell, as young chickens.

Patoa, *s.* the stopper in the shell *maava.*

Patoa, *s.* the name of a plant.

—*v. a.* to put an end to a religious ceremony, to rest and take refreshment, as a body of fishermen.

Patoi, *v. n.* to reply, rebut, put in an objection.

—*s.* objection, reply.

Patoitoi, *v. n.* to contradict repeatedly.

Patoo, *s.* the sprit of a sail.

— *v. a.* to force a canoe along shallow places by means of a long pole.

Patootoo *v. a.* to rap or knock at a door for admittance, to rap with the finger on a melon or cocoanut.

Patote, *a.* short, as shortly in time.

Patu, *s* a cocoanut used by way of divination by breaking the shell and casting it into the sea, accompanied with prayers offered by the priest, to know the fate of war or peace. Also a cocoanut used by fishermen with prayers, &c. that the gods might give them success in fishing.

Patu, *s.* a stone wall, perhaps from *poatu*, or *pofatu* or *pohaku*, a stone in the other dialects: the Malay for stone, is *batu*, or *patu*, and the Fijian, *vatu*.

Patu, *v. a.* to build with stone, as the wall of a marae.

Patu, *s.* a little wooden mallet.

Patu, *s.* a species of bread-fruit.

Patu, *s.* a subdivision of a district.

Patu, *v. a.* to repulse, or keep off, to push back.

Patu, *v. n.* to cease to flow, applied to the menses.

Pâtu, *v. a.* to nourish, or nurse a sick person.

Patue, *s.* a puff of wind before rain.

Patuatini, *s.* a fence within a fence sacred to the king.

Patuhamuri, *s.* the back part of the wall of the marae.

Patuhi, *a.* wearisome, or disgusting, applied to a speech.

Patui, *s.* the name of a fish, proverbial for its deafness.

Patunihi, *s.* the stern of a canoe or ship, the residence of the captain.

Patupatu, *v. a.* to repulse, or oppose repeatedly.

Patupiti, *s.* two divisions of a family; also one under two different chiefs.

Paturu, *s.* a prop, helper, supporter.

Paturu, *v. a.* to support, help.

Paturua, *s.* one that is under two chiefs.

Paturuturu, *v. a.* to help repeatedly.

Patutaata, *s.* a class, or rank of men.

Patutu, *s.* the class of fishermen.

Pau, *v. p.* consumed, expended. It is often joined to another passive verb, such as, pau te amuhia, it is consumed by eating, or having been eaten.

Pau, *v. n.* to be in a state of conquest, or expenditure.

—*a.* conquered.

—*s.* the white scurf in the hair of the head.

Pâu, *s.* a place of shallow water.

Pau, *s.* a woman who is prolific.

—*v. a.* to splash the water at one another, as children when bathing.

Paua, *s.* a coarse mat, or screen, of cocoanut leaves, as an ornament put under the eaves of the roof.

Pauaua, *a.* strong, athletic, gigantic.

Pauaua, *a.* advanced in years.'

Pauhia. *s.* the heap of slain after battle.

Pauhoro, *v. n.* to be destroyed by the earth sliding from a mountain

— *s.* those destroyed in running from battle.

Pauhuhu, *v. n* to be moth eaten.

Pauhunu, *v. n.* to be worm eaten as vestments.

Paui, *s.* a species of the pearl oyster shell.

Paûma, *s.* a paper or cloth kite.

Paumu, *v. n.* to retreat as an army.

Paunu, *s.* (Eng. pound) as in money or weight.

Pàuo, *s.* the name of a fresh water eel.

Paupauahoroa, *s.* an aquatic game of children.

Paupauteaho, *v. n.* to be out of breath.

Paura, *s.* the close of harvest & season of fish.

— *s* the time of scarcity.

— *s.* gunpowder (fom the Eng.)

Pàuraura, *s.* a species of native cloth.

Paurae, *a* shallow, applied to water.

Pauru, *v. a* to smack with the open hand

—*v. n* to splash with the spray of the sea

Pauri, *a.* black, or dark coloured, as feathers.

Pauraura, *v. a.* to smack repeatedly, see *Pauru*

Pauteute, *s.* native cloth.

Pâutu, *s* a part of the dress of the mourners for the dead.

Pauturu, *s* naked, poor, applied to a country.

Pàva, *s.* the name of a fish, the same as *pathere*

— *s* a ceremony and prayer to prevent further child bearing.

Pavaha, *s.* leavings, or remainders of food. *fig* an useless speech that has no propriety.

Pavahavaha, *v n.* to speak repeatedly and uselessly.

Pavai, *s* a puff of wind before a shower.

Pavare, *s.* mistaken security in time of war.

Pavera, *v. n* to be burning with anger in the mind.

Pe, *a.* decayed, rotten, also worn out.

— *a.* ripe, applied to plantains, and other fruit.

— *a* loose, moveable.

— *v. n.* to be disengaged; to be off; as ua pe te faa amu, the feast is over.

Pea, *s.* a stick laid crosswise; see *apea.*

— *v. n* to be perplexed.

Peapea, *s.* twigs, small branches; see *amaa.*

— *a.* troublesome, perplexing, vexatious.

— *v. n.* to be troubled, or teazed.

Pee, *a.* swift, or quick.

— *v. n.* to ascend as smoke, or a paper kite.

— *v. a.* to follow after a person.

Peea. *a.* narrow, confined, as pieces of land.

Peeau, *s.* a follower, or intimate companion.

Peehau, *s.* one that follows a chief to obtain some office.
Peenave, *s.* a cluster of fruit.
Peenevaneva, *v. a.* to fly irregularly, as an arrow.
Peepee, *v. n.* to be agile, nimble.
— *a* decent, pretty, as a horse.
Peeutari, *v. a.* to keep following; see *utari*.
Pehâ, *s.* a piece of any thing, such as the half of a bread-fruit.
Pehâa, *s.* a modern name for *mahi*.
Pehao, *v. n.* to pass away in an unexpected course.
Pehau, *s.* the fin of fish.
Pehe, *s.* a native song, or ditty.
— *v. n.* to repeat the pehe in the way of condolence.
Peheo, *s.* the name of a bird.
Pehepehe, *v. n.* to be delighted by something.
Pehepehea, *a.* ignorant, unskillful.
Pehepupite, *v. a* to sing alternately, as two persons, or parties.
Pehi, *v. a.* to cast a stone or some other substance.
Peho, *s.* a valley, the upper part of a valley, see *faa.*
— *s.* a corner.
Pehu, *s.* rubbish, such as grass, leaves, &c.
— *s* the name of a species of taro.
Pei. *s.* the name of an amusement in which stones, or limes, are thrown and caught.
— *s.* the name of a certain prayer.
— *s.* a ceremony formerly observed in the dedication of a house.
Peiari, *s.* a species of the shark.
Peiha, *s.* the throat fins of a fish.
Peihaha, *s* the same as peiha.
Peinae, *adv.* it may be, or perhaps.
Pena, *v n.* to bring up the rear, or weak part of an army, when in danger.
Penapena. *v. a.* to bring up, and shelter repeatedly, those that are behind in an army when retreating; also to cover and protect the helpless.
Pene, *s.* (anc. British pen, a head, a mark) a chapter.
Peneiae, *adv.* peradventure, it may be so. if so be
Penu, *s* (Engl. *pen,*) a pen to write with.
Penitaia, *s* (Engl. *pencil.*) a lead or slate pencil.
Penu, *s.* a stone pestle.
— *intj* an idolatrous exclamation, formerly used by the pretended prophets when asking for property. Penu! penu ai vaa
Peo, *prep.* by that way, or manner; see *nao.*
Pèo, *adv.* in this or that manner.
Pepe. *s.* a butterfly.
— *v. a.* to turn up a garment, shirt sleeve, &c.
Pêpê, *s.* sweet, ripe bread-fruit.
Pepee, *a.* flirty, unsteady, moving from place to place.
Pepehi, *v. a.* to bruise, but in some of the dialects to kill.
Pepeiaha, *s*, the jaw of a fish
Pepeiau; *s.* the ear, see *taria.*
Pepepepe, *v. a.* to put close round, as garments.
Peperehu, *s.* a dark coloured butterfly.

Peperehû, *v. n.* to burst as breadfruit over ripe, &c.
Peperu, *s.* a roll or bundle of cloth, &c.
— *v. a* to roll, or bundle up.
— *v. n.* to put about a vessel; a sea term.
— *s.* the jib of a vessel, ie pepera, jib sail.
Pepetu, *s.* the name of a fish.
Pera, *s.* the remains of a dead person, the human bones
Pera, *s.* filth and dirt, rubbish of a dunghill.
Pereaiai, *s.* the name of a fish.
Perearu, *s* a square, or gable ended house: see *haaparu,* and *haapepe.*
Pereau, *v. a.* to search for a thing; see *pareh ihu.*
Perehâ, *v. n.* to be wearied in unsuccessful search.
Perehahâ, *v. a.* to search, to feel, to grope in the dark.
Perehairi, *a.* slight, in a small degree.
Perehatâ, *v n.* to be wearied in searching.
Perehû, *v n.* to burst, as over ripe fruit.
Peroo, *s.* a plaything of children to turn in the wind made of cocoanut leaves; also a whirlgig made of the amae nut.
Pereoo, *s.* a wheel, coach, or chariot.
Perepetâ, *v. a.* to tie up carelessly and slovenly.
— *s.* a string or rope that fastens any thing.
Pereperetau, *v. n.* to be hanging down, as fruit on a tree that weighs down the branches.
Pererau, *s.* the wing of a fowl.
Peretau, *s.* a sort of basket, used by women in fishing.
Peretau, *v a* to carry a child, or other things, on the hip.
Peretei, *s.* the name of a small chirping cricket.
Peretete, *s.* a small insect of the grasshopper kind.
— *v. n.* to stumble, see *tururo.*
Peretia, *s.* a certain food made of the plantain root.
Peretiti, *s.* the name of a small sea fish.
Pereue, *s.* a coat.
— *s* the dew that falls in the night.
— *v. n.* to hang down the wings, as a sick fowl.
Peritome, *s.* (greek *peritome*) circumcision.
— *v. n* to circumcise.
Peiopero, *v. n* to be uselessly toiling from place to place.
Peru, *v. n.* to return or retreat as a warrior.
— *v. a* to repel a disease, to lap up a liquid.
Perue, *s.* the name of a bird.
Peruperu, *v. a.* to steer, applied to a canoe; to fold up in a good condition.
Petave, *s.* a bunch or cluster; see *peenave.*
Petea, *s* a long tailed paroquet.
Petepete, *v. a.* to snap on a thing with the finger nail.
Peti, *s.* the name of one kind of bread fruit.
Petipeti, *s.* finished, complete.
Petiti, *v. a.* to remove a stake.
Peu, *s.* a custom, habit, manner, fashion, ordinance, institution.
Peue, *s.* a mat, see *moea.*
— *a.* broad, applied to an axe, as opahi peue, a broad axe.

Peue, *s.* the name of a fish.
Pi, *s.* the custom of prohibiting the use of a word or syllable, which had become sacred by its having been adopted as the whole or part of the name of some chief, when another word or syllable was substituted in its place; as *rui* for *po.* and *hota* for *mare*, as these two words formed the name of the late king Pomare.
— *s.* young, or unripe, as fruit; immature.
— *a.* ignorant, unskilful.
— *v. n.* to be grown as the tusks of a boar.
Pia, *s.* a species of arrow root.
— *v. a.* to paste with the pia.
Piaa, *a.* fat and fleshy, as a barren sow
Piahi, *s* a learner, see *pipi.*
Piao, *s.* the dragon fly.
— *v. a* to make an incision in the bark of a bread fruit tree.
— *v. a.* to present red feathers, &c. to guard against a ghost.
Piaoao, *a* thin, lank, as a person reduced by sickness.
Piapia, *s.* the sweet gum in the blossom of the banana.
— *s* coagulated blood; female *lochia.*
Piareutahi, *s* a species of the pia or arrow root, of which there are also the au maire, rarotoa, &c.
Piarorea, *a.* lean, wasted.
Piaruai, *s.* the sweet potato, when too young for use.
Piataieve, *a* prolific, teeming with young.
Piavai, *s* the brains of brutes and fishes.
Piavai, *s* the case that covers the banana blossom.
Piaua, *s.* a certain method of fishing used by women.
Piavere, *a.* mouldy.
Pieê, *a* fat, applied to barren sows, cows, &c.
Piee, *v. a.* to purge; see *pihee.*
Piehi, *v. a.* to spread the hot stones in a native oven, and to extinguish the fire.
Pieiei, *v n.* to be full of cracks and fissures
Piere, *s.* a native preserve of dried banana.
Pifao, *s.* a hook, a fishing hook, see *matau.*
— *s* a destructive incantation as was formerly supposed to — have taken place.
— *v. a.* to perform the ceremony of the pifao.
Piha, *s.* a box, a chest; also a room.
— *a.* having a room, or rooms, as fare piha, a house with rooms.
Pihâ, *s.* the name of a small fish.
Pihaa, *v. n.* to boil as water; to bubble up as the water of a spring.
— *v. a.* to rinse or cleanse.
Pihae, *v. a* to rend or tear.
— *s.* a current of wind.
— *v n.* to vomit; see *ruai.*
Pihaehae, *s.* a light breeze, the first stirrings of the air.
— *v. n.* to belch up wind.
— *v. a* to tear repeatedly.
Pihahahe, *s* the name of one kind of plantain.
Pihahoe, *s.* the froth caused by an oar or a paddle.
Pihaiho, *prep.* by the side of, near to.

Pihaitiiho, *prep.* a little way off
Pihapapairaaparau, *s.* a writing desk.
Pihau, *v. a.* to rend, or tear; see *pihae.*
Pihaune, *s.* a chest with drawers.
Pihee, *s.* diarrhoea, laxity of the bowels.
— *v. n* to purge.
Pihi, *s.* the name of a shell fish
Pii, *s.* an ornament of black feathers; see *oroio.*
— *v. n* to be learned; see *haapii.*
— *v a.* to call upon a person or a thing.
— *v. n.* to shout, to raise up the voice.
Piia, s. a species of breadfruit.
— *v. n.* to be exhausted, dried up, applied to water, to be expended, applied to food.
— *a.* extinct, extirpated, applied to men.
Piifare, *s.* a cat, see *uri.*
Piipiia, *s.* the name of one kind of bread fruit, see *piia.*
Piirou, *s.* the apertures or passages in the rocks and mountains, at the upper parts of the valley.
— the rudiments of speech or of knowledge.
Piitii, *v. n* to become scarce, as food, fruit, &c.
Pinai, *s.* echo.
— *v. n* to echo.
Pinainai, *v n.* to echo repeatedly.
Pinainai, *s* ill smelled, as a dirty garment.
Pine, *s.* the name of a tree.
Pine, *s.* (from Eng. *pin*) a pin or skewer.
Pine, *s.* the name of a barbarous custom of beating and ill treating the bodies of the slain in battle.
Pinea, *v. n* to be scarce, applied to food, to be consumed, or exhausted, as water, &c.
Pinepine, *adv.* often, repeatedly.
Pio. *a.* (piko) crooked, wrong in a moral sense.
— *v. n* to be wrong; to be crooked or bent.
Pioa, *s.* the crevices among rocks; also the rudiments of speech or knowledge.
Piohe, *s.* a person of influence in the government.
Pioi, *s* great anger lodged in the mind
Piopio, *s.* having many bendings. or crooked places.
Pipi, *s* a disciple, a learner, or pupil.
— *s* pease, beans, &c.
Pipi *v a.* to sprinkle with water, or other liquid.
Pipiha, *v. n.* to be pierced through.
Pipii, *v. a.* to be cramped or contracted, as the limbs, to be folded in a circle as a dog's tail.
Pipii, *a.* covetous, niggardly.
— *v. n* to be illiberal.
— *s.* a name given to two stars that appear nearly joining.
Pipitio, *s.* the name of a little fish.
Piraatai, *s* the name of a certain upu or prayer.
Pirae, *s.* the name of a bird.
Pirahi, *v. n.* to sit or dwell; see *noho.*
— *s.* the name of a species of

food, also bundles of food tied up.

Pirao. *v. n.* to be destroyed, as fish in bad water.

Pirara, *s.* the fish called skip-jack.

Pirarorea, *s.* a long thin person; see *piavao*

Pirau, *s.* the pus, or matter of a sore.

Piri, *s.* a wonder, a curiosity, a puzzle.

— *a.* narrow, confined.

— *a.* adhesive, glutinous.

— *v. n.* to adhere, to stick to a thing.

— *v. n.* to be squeezed, or confined close.

Piria, *s,* the groin, see *tapa.*

Piriapu, *s.* an enigma, or puzzle.

Piriarii, s. one that adheres to the king.

Piriati, *s.* a twin; see *pirirua.*

Pirifetau, *s.* a stranger or alien; an outer branch, not rising out of the proper trunk.

— *v. n.* to be nearly separated or broken off.

Pirihaô, *a.* narrow, strait.

— *v. n.* to be contracted or made strait.

Piriita, *v. n.* to be closed, or made to close as the mouth.

Pirimomano, *v. n.* to be in a virgin state.

Pirioi, *s.* a cripple, a lame person.

— *a.* lame, or crippled.

Piripiri, *s.* a species of grass, bearing a troublesome bur; also a foreign plant, called by some cowhage, introduced to Tahiti, from Norfolk Island, in 1800.

Piripiritoheroa, *s.* the name of a native shrub, very difficult to root out.

Piripou, *s.* a pair of trowsers, or breeches.

Pirirua, *s.* a twin; see *maehaa.*

Pirita, *s.* the root ieie; also a basket made of it.

Piritaa, *s.* a relation by consanguinity, or by affinity.

Piritia, *s.* the name of a fish.

— *s.* a piece of cloth worn by the dancers in the heiva.

— *s.* a cartridge box.

Pirititau, *s.* a thing ardently sought after.

Piro, *s.* filth, uncleanness.

— *a.* worn, or soiled, applied to a garment.

— *a.* ill savoured.

Piroa, *intj.* an exclamation of contempt.

Piropiro, *a.* offensive, as a person's breath, or other things of a bad scent.

Pirorau, *s.* the long range of leaves, used in fishing, when they begin to decay.

Pirovaha, *s.* the name of a little fish; see *nape.*

Pita, *v. n.* to tempt, or tantalize, as in using the tiger shell in fishing for the cuttle fish.

Pitâ, *v. n.* to be swagging, as a heavy pole, when carried on the shoulder.

Pitaa, *v. n.* to separate, applied to the kernel of a dry cocoanut.

Pitaataa, *v. n.* to have small cracks or fissures in timber, caused by the sun and weather, &c.

Pitao, *a.* blackish, or discoloured, as mahi, cloth, &c.

Pitaotao, *a.* discoloured in

many places; black and dark, applied to the sky.
— *a.* ill looking, as a sick person.
Pitapita, *v. n.* to be swagging repeatedly as a pole.
Pitau, *s.* a meteor.
Piti, *a.* two in numbering, rua is the old word.
Pitipitiô, *s.* the name of a crab.
— *s.* the name of a running plant, bearing hard red seeds, like beans.
Pitipititohe, *s.* the line of separation where the human anus is.
Pito, *s.* the navel; the navel string
— *v. a.* to link one arm into that of another person.
Pitoa, *a.* having discoloured spots, commonly applied to ripe bread fruit.
Pitoatoa, *a.* having many discoloured spots, as bread fruit which has fallen from the trees.
Pitofifi, *s.* an entangled navel string, it was reckoned ominous, and the child was expected to turn out either a brave warrior or a mischievous person.
Pitohaare, *s.* a diseased navel string; *fig.* a worthless person.
Pitohiti, *s.* a protruded navel.
Pitohoe, *s.* persons of one fraternity.
Pitoi, *s.* a bruise in bread fruit, or other fruit.
Pitoitoi, *a.* full of bruised places, as bread fruit.
Pitopito, *s.* a button.
Pitoroâi, *s* the name of a medicinal plant.
Pitoraoere, *s.* the two extreme ends of a range of leaves used for fishing the ouma.
Pitoroa, *s.* a long winded person.
Pitotafifi, *s.* the same as pitofifi, which see.
Pitotai, *s* one not affected with cold; also an able warrior.
— *s.* an army; unconquered land.
Pitotaaitetua, *s* a decrepit person.
Pitoumi, *s.* the same as pitoroa.
Piu, *v. a.* to pull a fishing line.
Piuu, *s.* the muscle shell fish.
Pivai, *s.* the smallest pig in a litter.
— *s.* the brains of animals in general, except those of men, which are called roro.
— *s.* the name of a bird, or of a god, to which anoa is added, as pivai anoa.
Pivaiarii, *s.* the name of a certain ceremony, when a chief was invested with his government, and at which a human sacrifice was offered.
Po, *s.* night, see *rui* and *arui.*
— *s* the unknown world, or hades; the place of punishment in the other world.
— *s.* antiquity, unknown, ancient date.
Poa, *s.* the scales of fish.
— *s.* the mouth and throat; see *arapoa.*
— *s.* a dent, or mark, in the surface of any thing.
— *a.* dented, marked with a dent.

Poai, s. the dry or winter season of Tahiti.
— s. a coil of rope or line.
— s. the fishing tackle of boats.
Poaiaia, *intj.* alas! welcome! see *poino.*
Poairunai, s. some supposed place in the po, or other world.
Poanuu, s. the name of a heathen prayer.
Poara, a. wakeful, watchful.
— v. n. to be watching at night.
— v. a. to smite, slap the face, box the ears.
Poarai, s. the name of a prayer, the same as *poanuu.*
Poaruara, s. a troublesome anxious night.
Poaruarua, s. the same as poaruara.
Poe, s. a pearl, also beads.
— s. a species of food made by mixing fruits or baked roots, as pia, taro, &c.
Poea, s. the dirty scum of stagnant water.
Poematauiui, s. a fine clean pearl; *fig.* a handsome person.
Poepoea, s. an ill grown yam.
Poepoepuaa, s. a mark on a pig dedicated to a god.
Poère, s. a night of disappointment, a word used by fishermen.
Poere, s. to soil or defile.
Pofaafaa, v. a. to seek with diligence and perseverance.
Pofai, v. n. to gather, or pluck fruit, or leaves.
Pofaifai, v. a. to gather, or pluck repeatedly.
Pofatuaoao, s. the name of a small tree of hard wood.
Pofatumataoneone, s. the name of an idolatrous feast and ceremony: see *teputahi.*
Pohara, *intj.* of lamentation, wo! alas!
Pohe, s. death; also hurt, injury, sickness, see *mate.*
— v. n. to die, to be ill, or diseased, to be hurt.
— v. n. to be foiled in an argument; see *mate.*
— v. n. to perish, or to be punished for ever.
— v. n. to be affected with jealousy.
Pohehae, s. jealousy, see *matehae.*
Poheoe, s death by famine, or hunger.
Pohiihii, s. the name of a certain prayer.
Pohiri, s. young shoots rising from the main stem.
Pohu, v. n. to be entering deep, as the yam in growing.
Pohue, s. the name of a species of convolvulus.
— s. advantage, management.
Pohutu, v. n. to be fed to satiety; to be worked to weariness.
Poi, s. a season, the time of birth or death.
— v. a. to join one thing to another; to add to a thing in length or bulk; also to ingraft.
— v. n. to be in a covered state; see *haapoi.*
— v. a. to fasten, or tie fast, such as the out rigger of a canoe.
— *adv.* surely, even so, see *paha hoi,* and *pai.*
Poia, s. hunger; see *pårori.*
Pôia, a. dark as the sky: *raipoia,* a dark, or gloomy sky.

Poia, *v. n.* to be hungry, or feeling hunger.
Poihâ, *a.* thirsty.
— *v. n.* to feel thirsty.
— *s.* thirst.
Poihaa, *s* a species of the ava —plant.
Poihere, *v. a.* to administer to a person's comfort and necessities
Poiheretue, *s.* a well grown athletic person.
Poihu, *s* weariness or disgust.
— *v. n* to be wearied, or disgusted.
Poina, *v. n.* to forget; see *moina.*
Poini, *s.* the name of a basket; see *moini.*
Poinipeho, *s.* a basket with corners.
Poiniuri, *s.* a large sort of basket.
Poino, *s* an ill natured, ill behaved fellow.
— *intj.* an exclamation of sorrow, as wo! alas!
Poiouma, *s.* the place between the breasts.
Poipoi, *s.* (*pongipongi, poniponi,*) the morning.
Poiri, *s*, darkness; see *pouri.*
— *a.* dark, obscure.
Poito, *s.* pieces of wood or cork, used in the upper side of a fishing net.
— *s.* the buoy of an anchor.
Poitopa. *s.* a man that has a large projecting belly.
Poivaiva, *s.* the dusk of evening; see *ahiahi.*
Poivehi, *s.* a strong, gigantic person.
Pomairiavai, *s.* an ill tempered person; ill nature.
Pomaoao, *a.* superficial, insignificant; applied to a speech.
Pona, *s.* a knot, a tie, or binding.
— *s.* a joint of the finger or toe.
Ponaivi, *s.* the joint, or joining of the bones.
Ponao, *s.* a thimble; a razor case.
— *s.* a padlock.
Ponapona, *a.* knotty, having joints, as the sugar cane or bamboo.
Ponaponao, *s.* insatiable appetite.
Ponataamoo. *s.* the joints of the back bone.
Ponaturi, *s.* the knee joint.
Ponia, *s* the young, imperfect nut, just forming on the coconut tree.
— *s.* the hair of the head, when standing up by fright.
Pono, *a.* right or straight; see *tia*, but this word is more used in other dialects.
— *v. a* to direct straight forward, as in sailing to some place.
Ponopono auta, *v. a* to direct the course from one headland to another.
Ponotia, *v. a.* to make a direct course to a place.
Pononiairauai a Taaroa, *s.* blindness, great darkness.
Poo, *v. a.* to slap with the open hand on a person's own breast, as the wrestlers used to do in giving challenge.
Pooa, *v n.* to be washing away, applied to the land when diminishing by the wash of the sea or rivers.

Poohu, *s.* an inlet or strait; see *roia.*

Poopoo. *a.* deep as a hole; sunken, depressed.

— *v. n.* to be sunken, or fallen low.

— *s.* the name of a childrens' play.

Poopaotati, *s.* the name of an indecent dance.

Popohu, *s.* the upper part of the *fa*, or mark, at which the reeds are shot; see *iti.*

Pôpô, *v. a.* to clap hands, as fishermen sometimes do; to pat slightly with the hand.

Popo, *s.* the core or matter of a sore, see *papo.*

Popoa. *s.* an indented place in a breadfruit.

Popoi, *v. a.* to clap the hand as in surprise.

— *v. n.* to beckon with the hand.

— *s.* a sort of soft pudding made of plaintain, &c.

Popoo, *v. n.* to be hollow, indented, sunken.

Popone, *s.* a craving desire after a thing.

— *a.* covetous, eagerly desirous.

— *v. a.* to covet a thing eagerly.

Popotaia, *v. a.* to conduct such as might escape in a sea engagement.

— *s.* the handle of a basket; *fig.* one who takes great care of children.

Popoti, *s.* the general name for the beetle kind of which there are various species, but the most common is the Indian cockroach brought to the islands in various ships.

Popotifareturu, *s.* the name of a small crab.

Popotimiti, *s.* a kind of marine beetle.

Popoto, *a.* short; see *poto*; also the dual or plural of poto.

Popou, *s.* admiration, fondness, delight.

— *v. n.* to admire, to be delighted.

— *a.* admirable, agreeable; see *haapopou.*

Popounu, *v. n.* to be hasty, or in a hurry to be gone.

— *s* joy.

Popoure, *s* the catkins of the breadfruit tree.

Popouru, *s.* the young branches of the breadfruit tree, when stripped of the bark.

Porahu, *s.* the head of a beast, and by way of contempt, the head of a man, or the skull of the dead.

Porao *s.* a spot, speck, or soil, on any clean substance.

Poraorao, *s* a spot, or blemish.

— *v. n* to be spotted, or having blemishes.

— *v. n* to remove the porao or speck; see *ahiti poraorao.*

Poreariea, *s.* a joyful, pleasant, night.

Poreho, *s* the tiger shell, of which there are many species, such as amara, airahe, &c.

Porehu, *a.* dusky, dark, as the evening.

Porehuruhu, *v. n.* to grow dusky, or dark.

Poti, *s.* the bulk, or size, as that of a man, or a tree.

— *s.* certain persons of both sexes, but chiefly women, who pampered their bodies, to become fat and fair; see *haapori.*

Poiia, *a.* fat, fleshy, in good condition, as a man, or beast.

Poro, *s.* a crier, or herald.

— *v. a.* to cry, proclaim, or publish, as the messenger of the king, or as the priests did.

— *s.* the heel, or elbow.

— *s.* the handle of a tool, such as a knife, or chisel; the end of a ridge pole.

Poroaa, *s.* a wheel, or something circular.

Porohinere, *s.* the name of a star.

Poroi, *s* a charge, direction given; a saying.

— *v. a* to take leave, or bid farewell; also to inform.

Poroihiva, *s.* the name of a sweet scented tree.

Poropa, *s.* a large and unsightly collection of food intended for visitors.

Porori, *s.* hunger; see *poia.*

— *v. n.* to be hungry.

Porori, *s* the roots of the ava plant.

Pororû, *v. n.* to be deeply grown in the earth, as the roots of the yam; to be deep or obscure, as a subject of discourse.

— *a.* obscure, as a dark corner.

Porotaa, *s* a wheel; a block with a shive for a rope; any thing that will turn as a wheel.

Porotata, *s.* a block and shive, such as sailors use.

Poru-naru-maru, *s.* a dark and dismal night.

Porutu, *a.* loud, clamorous, applied to a voice.

— *v. n.* to be speaking very loud.

Poruturutu, *v. n.* to be vociferating in a loud and clamorous manner.

Poruuruu, *v. a.* to rally, reinvigorate; to raise from dejection, to comfort.

— *s.* the person that rallies, reinvigorates, revives, restores.

Pota, *s.* any vegetable, such as cabbage, taro leaves, &c, that are eaten as greens.

Potaa, *a.* oval, or circular, as a house.

Potao, *a.* dark, or blackish, as a sick person.

Potaotao, *s.* a very black or dark night.

Potaro, *s* a ball or round thing, such as a ball of thread or cotton.

Potaua. *s.* a friend who has ceased to show kindness.

Potee, *a.* circular, or oval; see *potaa.*

Potea, *s.* a piece of sinnet put in the ear of a pig, to mark it as devoted to a god; also the white part of a fowl's ear.

Potehetehe, *s* the notch cut in the end of a tree in order to fasten a rope to it; also a notch cut in a stick on which to carry any thing on the shoulder, to prevent the articles slipping off.

— *v. a.* to make such a notch or score.

Poti, *s.* (from Eng. *boat*) a boat; see *pahi*

— *s.* a dark or red coloured taro.

Potii, *s.* (*potiki*) a girl; see *tamahine*.

Potiitarire, *s* the name of a certain god who was invoked by sorcerers.

— *s.* a handsome person.

Potiitiriaria, *s.* the name of an article made of feathers, and which was put up to deter the demon or god from doing mischief, in the time of a dance, or play.

Potiiitini, *s* a dark night.

— *s.* an indefinitely large number.

Potipoti, *s.* a beetle, cock roach, but commonly applied to small beetles.

Potiti, *v. n.* to become small to sight by distance.

— *a.* diminutive, small; languid.

Potiu, *s.* the first formation of the cocoanut.

Poto, *a* short; see *mure*.

Potopoto, *a.* short, shortish; see *muremure*; commonly applied to a plurality.

Potuaruu, *s.* a log of wood on which were formed *Tii* images on its whole length, and which was set up as the guardian of the rahui, or restriction, &c.

Potupopau, *s* the name of a certain feast and ceremonies performed on account of the dead.

Pou, *s.* a post or pillar; also a log of wood.

— *v. n.* to descend from a high place.

— *s* the name given to the colon or large gut.

Poumuuna, *v. n.* to dive head foremost into the water.

Pouohu, *s.* a ditch.

Pouohure, *s.* the rectum.

Pouri, *s.* (*pouli*, *poui*) darkness, obscurity.

— *a.* dark, obscure; see *poiri*.

Poutia, *s.* a species of mountain plantain.

Poutu, *s.* to throw a stone directly upwards.

— *a.* erect in position, as a straight tree.

Pouturi, *a.* deaf, deaf as a post, feigned deaf.

Pu, *s.* a conch shell; a trumpet.

— *a.* young, as fruit.

— *s.* the conclusion of a thing.

— *s.* the middle or centre.

— *s.* a cluster of small trees, shrubs, or grass. This is *pu aihere.*

— *s.* the head of the fee, or cuttle fish.

— *s.* the bottom of a cascade.

— *s.* the interior of a country.

— *v. n.* to be obtained, as the object of one's desire; to be gratified; to be completed, or terminated, as the upaupa, or play, ua *pu* te upaupa, the upaupa is terminated.

Pua, *s.* (*buna*, *bunga*, Malay *bunga*) the coral rock.

— *s.* a disease accompanied with a swelling and an abcess.

— *s* the name of a tree bearing fragrant yellow flowers; see *hauou*. The blossom of that tree.

— *s.* a shrub bearing yellow berries, which is used as a medicine.

— *s.* the head of the Dolphin fish.

— *s.* soap of any kind.

Pua, *v. a.* to wash with soap; to rub or scour with a piece of coral.

Pua, *s.* the person that scours or washes.

Puà, *v. n.* to blossom, as reeds, bamboos, &c.

— *s.* the blossom of reeds, sugar cane, &c.

Puaa, *s.* *(puaka)* the general name for the swine species; and, perhaps the name will apply to all the larger animals that have hoofs, whether cloven or not, and that the term *uri* may be applied to all other quadrupeds that have claws, except the mouse, rat, &c.

Puaa, *v. n.* to be enlarged, as the abdomen, either in health or by disease.

Puàà, *a.* mouldy, as food. — *s.* mould.

Puaaaipapati, *s.* a hog that eats the running plant called *papati*, *fig* one who is attached to his residence.

Puaafatoi, *s.* a feast, and ceremony, when the members of a family eat together for the first time, children having been considered sacred, and having eaten apart.

Puaahaapàpà, *s.* a hog roasted for the queen; a small sucking pig which was taken before the marae, and presented to the god at the conclusion of the ceremonies attending the investment of the king with royal authority; also a ceremony which was performed when the restrictions were taken off a child, so that he might eat with his parents.

Puaahorofenua, *s.* a horse; see *hipo*.

Puaahuaira, *s.* an undaunted, fierce, and athletic, person.

Puaamamoe, *s.* a sheep; see *mamoe*.

Puaaniho, *s.* the goat species; also a hog with large tusks.

Puaaoehamu, *s.* the name of a certain feast among relations, when much gluttony and riot was usualy indulged in.

Puaarai, *s.* white clouds.

Puaaraufau, *s.* the name of an arioi feast and ceremony.

Puaaroiroi, *s.* a hog that was baked to feed females, which at other times was to them forbidden food.

Puaatafetii, *s.* a family feast.

Puaataipito, *s.* the same as *puaatafetii*, it was a feast for the family and relations only.

Puae, *s.* the centre division of a fleet of canoes where the principal persons used to be, and when one was killed there, it was reckoned an ill omen, and the rest were discouraged.

Puaea, *s* indistinctness of vision, as of a person just about swooning.

— *a.* dim, indistinct.

Puafaatere, *s.* a disease in which a number of abscesses succeed each other in various parts of the body.

Puafao, *v. n.* to press on vigorously, as two armies, to fight.

Puafafao, *s.* a mode of attack in war.

Puafau, *s* the yellow blossom of the *fau* or purau tree, see *purau*
— *s* the yellow fat in the head of the cuttle fish, in crabs, &c.
Puahaha, *s*. the bulky, puffed appearance of a person, or a thing.
— *a*. bulky, large in show only, as a bundle of cloth puffed out, or a person dressed to make a shew.
— *adv*. slovenly.
Puahea, *v. n* to come up without obtaining what was sought, as a diver; to diverge or fly aside from the mark, as an arrow.
— *a*. divergent, apt to fly aside.
— *s* obliquity, deviation.
Puaheetoa, *s*. the name of a certain boisterous wind, also the pua tree stripped of its leaves or blossoms.
Puahema, *s*. a mode of using a club in the exercise called *tiaraau*.
— *v. a*. to deceive by stratagem.
Puahi, *a*. hot, heated, as herbs for medicine.
Puahoho, *s*. a whirl wind; the wind or whistle of a stone from a sling, or a shot from a gun.
Puahuaru, *s*. a species of soft coral used for rubbing and smoothing a cocoanut cup.
Puai, *s*. muscular and physical strength or force.
— *a*. strong, forcible; see *uana*.
Puaiai, *s*. refreshment by air; see *toahu*.
— *v. n* to be refreshed by cool air.
— *a* refreshing as cool air.
— *v. n*. to be in an alarm; see *puauau*.
Puaihere, *s*. a bush.
Puaioio, *s*. a handsome blossom; a handsome person.
Puaioru, *s*. the name of a fragrant medicinal herb.
Puaitu, *v. a*. to be in a state of dread or fear.
— *a*. timorous.
Puamatapipiu, *s*. the blossom of the pua whose edges curl.
Puanuanu, *v. n*. to be chilled; to be dejected in mind; see *anuanu*; to grieve or be sorowful.
Puao, *s*. a cartridge of powder; any small wrapper, or thing rolled up, as paper, cloth, &c.
— *v. a*. to make cartridges; to wrap or roll up small things.
Puapipi, *s*. the blossom of the wild pea; *fig*. a winding, intricate, speech.
Puapua, *s*. the blossoms of sugar cane reeds, and of bamboos.
Puaraitu, *s*. a provocation.
— *v. a*. to provoke.
— *s*. the name of a tree that grows in the mountains, and produces red blossoms.
Puaraumata, *s*. the name of an excellent fish of great strength, that usually breaks the fishing net. *fig*. an intrepid warrior that breaks through; also a simile from the *pua* blossom to signify a handsome person.
Puaraumataura, *s*. a daring warrior.

Puarautahi, *s.* the name of a tree and its blossom.

Puare, *s.* the name of a small shellfish.

Puareaie, *s.* qualmishness of stomach.

— *v. n.* to be drunk, to be agitated with fear.

Puaru, *s.* a new born infant, a strangled infant.

Puaruaiu, *s.* fear, agitation of mind

— *v. n.* to be agitated, as the bowels; to be agitated as the mind, see *puauau.*

Puata, *a.* not compact, loose, not tight and firm; easily imposed upon

— *s* looseness, incompactness.

Puataruru *s.* the fragrant blossoms of the pua tree.

Puatau, *s.* an early flowering pua tree.

Puatauere, *s.* the title of a certain native song.

Puatauma, *s.* the name of a shrub with large prickly leaves, which hook in the clothes of passengers; *fig.* a person who draws or pulls another by the clothes

Puaterori, *s.* the head of the sea dog, which is gathered up as a frill, and to which a frill is often compared.

Puau, *v. n* to be in agitation as the bowels; to be agitated, applied to the mind.

Puautau. *v. n.* to be agitated repeatedly.

— *v. n.* to run as a current.

— *s.* a rapid current in a stream of water.

Puauahi, *s.* the middle of the fire.

Puauia, *s.* the red blossom of the puarata.

Puauru, *s.* a steady warrior who delights in war.

Puavaovao, *s.* the name of a fragrant tree.

Puaveoveo, *s.* the same as puataruru.

Puavere. *s.* the name of a tree.

— *s.* mildew; a sort of beard that grows in the cold damp cracks of the earth; a sort of mushroom.

— *s* small sticks of the purau used for a cage.

— *a.* mildewed, mouldy, as food, &c.

Puaverevere, *s.* cobwebs of every sort, gauze; any thin web.

Puavihi. *s.* a stick held with the shoulders shrugged up, in in the exercise of arms, called *tiuraau.*

Puaviri, *v a.* to defend one's self, or ward off a blow, in the haraau.

Puaviriviri, *v. a* to act repeatedly on the defensive in the tiaraau.

— *s.* the pua tree when producing abundance of blossoms; any tree that bears abundantly, such as uru, &c.

— *a.* highly decorated; see *viruiri.*

Pue. *s.* a heap or hillock of earth, as pue umara.

Pue, *v. a* to heap up earth or mould, in order to plant any thing in it.

— *a.* denoting a plurality, as pue taata, men, usually two in number; pue arii, the royal party, or principal chiefs; pue raatira, the inferior chiefs collectively; pue mea, a collection of things. Vai pue, is a collection of water from many streams, or a flood.

— *v. n.* to be brought together, or to be collected, as goods, or various things; see *haapue*. Ua pue te vahie, the fuel is collected,

Puea, *s.* a heap, or collection.

Puehu, *v. n.* & *p.* to be blown by the wind; to be scattered or driven away; to be dispersed, as a conquered party in war.

Puehuehu, *v. n.* to be dispersed repeatedly, or in many places.

— *a.* pompous, showy, with great pomp.

— *adv.* pompously.

Pueraa, *s.* a collection, magazine or treasury; also the time and place when things are collected.

Puere, *a.* mouldy, mildewed, see *puavere*.

Puero, *s.* a species of breadfruit.

Pueu, *s.* the white species of the ahia apple, or jumbo (the Eugenia Mallacensis.)

— *s.* the name of a small blade fish.

— *v.* to break roughly, applied to the waves; to be surrounded with danger.

Pueueu, *s.* the name of a marine substance used for rubbing and smoothing wooden vessels.

— *s.* a rag; the ragged end of a rope.

— *a.* ragged, rough; cross grained, as timber.

Pufà, *s.* a disease of the sole of the foot where matter is formed, which, if evacuated by a small puncture, is soon healed.

— *a.* scorched or burnt up by the sun or fire.

— *v. n.* to be overcome with heat; to be exhausted by the pains of childbirth.

Pufafaru, *s.* a calabash that contains a sort of food called *fafaru*, which see.

Pufao, *s.* a disease of a cancerous nature; see *ufao*.

— *s.* an instrument to make holes, used by canoe builders.

Pufara, *s.* a camp for a temporary residence.

— *v. a.* to encamp or set up temporary houses.

Pufara tahitihiti, *s.* a shifting camp.

Pufarefare, *s.* hollowness, or emptiness, as of a bag, or of the stomach.

— *s.* a breaking wave of the sea, such as bends over, hangs, and then breaks.

— *a.* hollow, as the stomach; or as a wave before it breaks.

Pufanua, *s.* the placenta, also pufenua.

Pufeto, *v. a.* to be suffocated, as with food, grief, or sudden alarm.

Puha, *s.* the same as pufa, which see.

Puhâ, *v. n.* to blow, as the honu, whale, &c.

Puhaharu, *s.* the same as pufafaru.

Puhapa, *s.* a camp; see *pufara* and *tiahapa*.

— *v. a.* to encamp.

Puhatato, *s.* the blossom of

the taro; also a whistle made of it.

Puheto, *v. n.* the same as pufeto.

Puhi, *s.* an eel, commonly a sea eel.

Puhia, *v. n.* & *p.* to be shot, to be blown away or to be driven, as by the wind.

Puhiairoto, *s.* the name of a species of eel; *fig.* a secret underminer, a snake in the grass.

Puhiaru, *s.* the mist arising from the wash of the sea on the reef.

Puhiava, *s.* the name of a sweet scented plant, see *opuhi* and *aropuhi.*

Puhipata, *s.* the name of a sea eel.

Puhipuhi, *s.* a pair of bellows.

— *v. n.* to blow out of the mouth; to blow as with a pair of bellows

— *v. a.* to fan the fire with a broad leaf.

Puhipuhi avaava, *s.* a tobacco pipe.

— *v. a.* to smoke tobacco.

Puhipuhiai, *s.* the white leaves, or cabbage of the cocoanut tree.

Puhireieieie, *s.* the name of an eel.

Puhori, *s.* a dancing party that goes from place to place with drum and flutes, in order to get cloth, &c.

Puhota, *v. n.* to be choked; see *pufeto.*

Puhura, *v. a.* to waste wantonly, to squander.

Puhurahura, *v. a.* to waste, or squander away goods repeatedly.

Puihauhau, *v. n* to blow gently, as a small breeze.

Puipui, *v. a.* to spread the pitch on the end of an arrow.

Puipuiai, *s.* a very thin and white substance near the heart, or cabbage part of the cocoanut tree.

Puipuirima, *s.* the name of a war song

— *s.* the scales of the maratea fish put on the arm of an archer, to prevent excoriation by the bow string.

Puita, *s* coldness, shivering by reason of cold.

Puitaao, *s.* a relic; one that remains of a family, and becomes the heir.

Puitao. *s.* arrow root of a bluish colour; also white cloth made blue in getting up.

Puitaita, *v. n* to cringe, as from cold, &c.

Puiti, *a* little, small, as the remainder of a work; few in a party.

Pumaha, *a.* scorched, dried for want of moisture and through heat of the sun or fire; see *pufa.*

Pumahu, *s* mould, mildew.

— *a.* mouldy, mildewed.

Pumahana, *a.* luke warm, as water.

Pumatai, *s.* the source of the wind, or the quarter from which it blows.

Pumiriraira, *s.* the fragrance of sweet smelling herbs.

Puna, *a.* prolific, as a female.

Puna, *s.* some particular haunt of fish, where the fishermen go to look for them.

Punaairi, *a.* of speedy growth,

or bulk, as a person; see *tupuarn.*

Punae, *s.* the name of a bird.

Punahere, *s.* probably this is a word imported, (*punahele.*) a coconnut that adheres long to the tree; a woman that takes care of her children, and will not let them leave her; a beast that keeps close to its young; a plant to which the young ones adhere.

Punaho, *s.* a feast for all the kindred

— *v. a.* to plait or weave some sorts of baskets.

— *v. n.* to sit down together till some purpose is accomplished.

— *a.* in good order; see *nahonaho.*

Punahonaho, *a* well ordered.

Punahu, *s.* a cutaneous disease.

Punaja, *s.* the haunt of fishes; *ia puna* is the first fish in the season, caught at such a place.

Punaneuneu, *s.* the name of a web footed bird.

Punano, *s* a person that keeps back apart.

— *a.* concealed, kept back clandestinely.

— *v. n.* to conceal or keep back a part.

Punaonao, *s* one that takes out something from a bag, or a basket of food; see *tinao.*

— *v. a.* to take out of a bag, or basket.

— *a.* taken out as food or property.

Punapunaô, *s.* a person greedy, or ravenous of food and other things.

Punapunaô, *a* greedy, ravenous, slovenly.

Punapuparau, *v n* to be prolific, very fruitful.

Punarua, *s* a man with two wives, or a woman with two husbands.

Punâu, *s.* a certain amusement in the water.

Punau, *v. n* to be slightly divulged, or discovered

Punaunau, *a* discovered, come to light, as a thing that was hidden or concealed

Puni, *v. a* to be enclosed, see *haapuni.*

Puna, *s.* a place of refuge, shelter, or safety, a harbour for fish, or hiding place of any animal.

— *s* a child's diversion, hide and whoop.

Punipuni, *v n* to hide, or conceal one's self.

Punipuniarea, *s.* a game of children, hide and seek.

Punu, *s.* (from Engl *spoon*) a spoon or ladle.

Punua, *s.* the name of a tahitian god who was said to preside over the rocks and precipices.

Puo, *s.* the pith. heart of a tree, the marrow of a bone, &c.

— *s.* an ulcer, or old sore, a cancerous sore.

— *s.* the appearance of land in the horizon.

— *v. n* to blow, applied to the wind

Puoa, *s* the name of a game in which a breadfruit is suspended from a branch of a tree, and at which darts are thrown.

Puoeoe, *s.* a fish gig with many sharp prongs of bamboo.

Puohi, *v. a.* to gather together, as old people gather up a few sticks; see *ohi.*

Puohu. *s.* a bundle, a wrapper of fish or other food enclosed in leaves

— *v n.* to make bundles, or wrap in leaves.

Puoi, *s.* a piece to join to another piece; a person that joins pieces together.

— *v. n.* to join pieces together.

— *a.* pieced, joined.

Puomaea, *s.* the heart of the meia, or banana stalk.

Puomahu, *s* the name of the place where evil spirits were said to reside.

Puono, *v. a.* to strengthen a party, as in time of war.

Puonoaro, *s.* the party that goes to strengthen those in front of the battle.

Puonoono, *s.* strong desire that cannot be restrained

Puooi, *a* fierce, vehement, as fire burning.

— *v. n.* to come suddenly.

Puopu. *v a.* to bathe the person, applied to women.

Puooura, *s.* a basket to catch shrimps.

Puora, *s* a pool of water in the bed of a river, when the stream is dried up; also a surviving parent, who remains the support of a married child who may be injured.

Puoraiaha, *s.* the conch shell made fit to use as a trumpet

Puori, *s.* a wanderer; an idle person that rambles about

— *a* idle, rambling; see *ori*.

Puoio, *v a.* to cleanse the inside of a calabash, or of a bottle, by means of gravel and water.

Puorooro, *v. a.* to wash or bathe repeatedly.

Puoiori, *s* the hollow inside of the *bich le mer*, through which it was said the spirits of men passed into the *po*, or night.

Puoiofaitau, *s.* the sacred *pu* or trumpet used at the marae.

Puoroa, *s.* the name of a certain basket used by those who pretended to conjuration.

Puotihi, *s* the inside of a *tihi* which was generally of an inferior sort of cloth; also the person that wore the *tihi*.

Puoura, *s* a reed used in the *raapere*.

Pupa, *s* a cold shivering in the commencement of a disease.

— *v. n.* to be shivering, as in a fit of the ague.

— *v. n* to be flapping, as the sails of a ship when there is a calm; and pupapupa is the repetition of it.

— *v. n* to be desiring the other sex.

Pupà *s* a tuft of feathers on the top of the mast used in the Tahitian sailing canoes.

— *s* the blossom of certain trees that grows in bunches, or tufts, as the tamanu, ahia, vi, &c.

Pupàtai, *s.* sudden consternation or alarm, on account of an *tii*, or person fallen in war.

Pupapii, *s.* the name of an ornament made of feathers for the head or breast

Pupara, *adv.* heedlessly, rashly, unthinkingly, applied to the going or action of a number together, whether of men or of animals.

Pupataute, *v. n.* to be divested of sacredness, as the priests were after performing certain ceremonies in the marae.

Pupepu, *s.* a sort of thin net like garment, not worn by any decent person.

Pupo. *v. a.* to strike one hand on the other in fishing for the opera.

Pupu, *s.* a company, party, or a class.

Pupu, *v. n.* to present one's person or property.

Pupu, *v. a.* to invest with an office.

— *s.* a general name for a class of shells of which there are many varieties.

Pupuaaoa, *s.* the flapping of a cock's wings at the time of crowing; early attempts at sexual intercourse.

Pupufatifati, *s* a broken shell, *fig* an old warrior.

Pupuhanihani, *s.* a company of loose women, who lay in wait to ensnare and seduce.

Pupuhi, *s.* a musket, or gun.

— *v. a* to shoot with a gun.

— to blow the fire, blow out a candle.

Pupuhifenua, *s.* a great gun or cannon.

Pupuhitereumu, *s* a pistol.

Pupuhivaharahi, *s.* a musketoon.

Pupuni, *v. n.* to hide one's self, to take shelter behind another.

Pupupu, *s.* a small couch shell.

Pupupu, *s.* a species of coral.

Pupure, *s.* the leprosy, or native disease resembling it, also the person affected.

Pupure, *a.* affected with the pupure.

Pupure, *v. n.* to pray frequently.

— *s.* frequent prayer.

Pupuru, *a.* rough, unbending, stiff.

Pupuru, *a.* thick, as a mixture with liquid.

Puputa, *s.* a species of mountain plaintain.

— *v.* hollow, and rotten inside, as a tree.

Puputauhani, *s.* a company of loose fellows that are fondling over each other with some base design; a party that will withdraw suddenly to avoid the suspicion of having committed a crime.

Pupuvaha, *s.* food to break the fast; a gargle.

— *v. n* to gargle the mouth, or wash it with a little water.

— *v. n.* to be going about as a talebearer.

Pura, *s.* a spark of fire; a flash of light or fire.

v. n. to flash, or blaze; to —sparkle, as the luminous particles in the sea.

— *a.* blazing, applied to fire.

15 Pûra, *s.* a fearless warrior.

— *v. n.* to be fearless, undaunted.

Puraau, *v. a.* to fight or wage war in consequence of a toraa or wrestling match.

Purae, *v. a.* to defend by fencing.

Purafea, *s.* sudden fear or alarm.
— *v. n.* to rise suddenly, as alarm; to be squeamish.

Puraha, *v. n.* to hold out the hands as in expectation of receiving something.

Purahu, *s* a bunch of leaves tied up, and set on a long pole, as a mark of restriction in that place, see *rahui.*

Purahui, *s.* a restriction put on hogs, fruit, or fish, by the king or chief.

Purai, *s.* a shoal of fishes.

Purara, *s.* dispersion, the state of being dispersed.
— *v. n.* to be dispersed or scattered.
— *a.* dispersed.

Purarea, *s.* sallowness, a sickly appearance.
— *a.* sallow; sickly.
— *v. a.* to be pale through fear.

Puraro, *s.* an underhand blow among boxers.
— *v. a* to catch the aahi fish, with the hook and line.
— *v. n.* to press forward, as a number of fish enclosed in a net.

Puraiohuna, *s.* some concealed action, as in giving property, or in using some stratagem.

Puraroraro, *v. a.* to repeat the act of puraro.

Puraiua, *a.* of equal strength, as two parties at variance, neither giving way.

Purau, *s.* the name of a tree, (*hibiscus tiliaceus*) the purau is also called *fao*, of which there are several varieties, and it is useful for many purposes.
— *s.* a fine garment made of the purau bark.

Puraurea, *v. n.* to be pale through fear.
— *a* pale, sallow.

Purautia, *s* the name of a disease, the jaundice.
— *a.* pale, sallow, sickly.

Purauti, *s.* a bunch of ti leaves used by a warrior.
— *s* a war song; see *rauti.*

Purauti, *s.* a well sounding nasal flute.

Purautaaivi, *s.* the purau that grows among the ridges of the mountains; *fig.* a stout athletic person.

Purautuitui, *s.* a thing done ineffectually; the term is from the native mode of clearing the ground by setting fire to the purau trees, while standing.

Pure. *s.* (*bule, bue, pule*) a prayer, worship.

Pure, *v. a.* to pray, to worship God, see *haumori.*

Purefa, *s* a piece of coarsely carved wood placed in the stem of a canoe.
— *s.* shoots of the plantain.
— *v. n.* to be seen as in issuing from a thicket; to be dazzled with flashes of light.
— *a.* open, as leaves.
— *v. n.* to be opening.

Purefarefa, *v. n.* to be dazzled repeatedly.

Purefaietoa, *s.* prayers and ceremonies performed at the seaside on account of sick persons.

Purehu, *s.* protrusion, the act of bursting forth.

— *v. n.* to protrude or burst forth
— *a.* protruding.

Purehua, *s.* a species of large moth.

Purehurehu, *v. n.* to burst forth repeatedly.

Pureohiohi, *s.* detached parts, as of a prayer, or of a discourse, a hasty sketch, an outline.

Purepâpâ, *s.* prayers made in the marae, by three, four, or more priests in success on.
— *s.* the name of a ceremony attended with prayers, and killing and offering up of a number of hogs, previous to the sailing of a fleet.

Purepure. *a.* spotted, chequered, of diverse colours

Purepureheiva, *s.* the appearance of a mourner for the dead, see *heiva.*

Purepureohiohi, *a.* marked, or stained; stained with bright colours.

Purera, *v. n.* to disperse, see *puiara.*
— *a.* dispersed; separated.

Purere, *v. a.* to eat food without waiting for the whole party to assemble.

Pureio, *s* utterance, eloquence, an orator.
— *a.* eloquent.
— *v. n* to straggle away from a company; to be straggling.

Pureroreroro, *v. n.* to continue to straggle in small parties.

Pureru, *s.* the name of a species of breadfruit.

Pureva, *v. n.* to be on the eve of going; to go quickly, as the clouds.
— *a* spoiled, useless, as pia or arrow-root, which through some defect, does not settle, but is poured out with the water.

Purevareva, *v. n* to be moving quickly and in succession, as the clouds of the sky.

Purevare, *s.* a sort of fish sperm that floats on the water; see *aano.*

Puri, *a.* angry, violent, and overbearing; also discoloured.

Purima, *s.* the hands put together and used as a trumpet; see *pu.*

Purimeamea, *s.* a sacred place; the houses of a company of warriors; the back part of the house of a principal person.
— *a* angry, using abusive language.

Purinuhumatua, *s* a garment that had been used by a priest; see *nunuhau.*

Purora, *a.* deceitful

Puroro, *s.* a disease of the brain.
— *v a.* to emit words out of the mouth, or water from a spring.

Puroto, *s.* the pu, or ball, such as is used in the game opoia; *fig.* the person who is the life and spirit of any undertaking.

Purotu, *s.* a comely, fair person.
— *a.* fair, comely, of good appearance.

Purotuaiai, *a.* fair, beautiful, neatly done.

Purotuhara, *a.* pleasing, as *purotuaiai.*

Purou, *v. a.* to cover the face and head.

Puru, *s* a board, see *papa* and *iri*.

— *s.* the husk of the cocoanut shell.

Purua, *s.* a father or mother-in-law.

Puruhi, *s* the name of a tree; *fig.* a cowardly cock, or faint hearted warrior.

— *a.* cowardly, see *taiā*.

Purumu, *s.* (from the English *broom*) a brush or broom, also the public road.

Puruoroоro, *a* strong, ardent, expression of desire.

Pururarao, *s* intensity of desire, strength of affection.

Purutaa, *v. a.* to help together as a body; to hang together; to assist, deliver, or rescue each other.

— *s.* a person that assists or supports those with whom he is connected.

Purutahuna, *s.* one that conceals a part of the truth.

Purutatau, *s.* some object that a person wishes to obtain.

— *v. a.* to be using means to obtain an object that is much desired.

Purutia, *s.* a sojourner, a temporary resident.

Puta, *s* an aperture or hole; a wound from some piercing instrument.

— *v. n.* to be pierced, wounded, or cut.

— *v. n.* to be cut, pierced, or deeply affected, as applied to the mind.

Putaai, *a.* well compacted, well put together; also well united when applied to persons.

Putaanuanu, *a* pierced with cold.

Putae, *s.* the name of a small tree or shrub, with fragrant leaves, used for monoi

— *s.* the name of a ceremony when conch shells are blown.

Putahi, *a* applied to a dog that has one spot on one of his ears, all the rest being white; also to mourners in the *heiva*, who had one side of one colour, and the other different.

— *v. n* to be united, as the young ones to the old; to come together to one place, as a family, or a party; to be united in one party.

Pu'ai, *v. a.* to pull, or drag along the ground.

Putairua, *s* one who belongs to two parties and will side with either as it suits him.

Putapu, *a.* pierced, applied to the mind when strongly affected by a certain speech.

Putaputa, *a.* sharp pointed, piercing; also full of holes or apertures; thinned, as the ranks of an army by desertion.

— *v. n.* to be thinned as the ranks of an army, or lessened by desertions

Putara, *s.* a species of univalve shell that has points.

Putaraia, *s.* made round and smooth like a shell

Putaratara, *s* any thing out of which a number of points issue, such as the sea egg, &c.

— *a.* prickly, thorny, having many points of thorns.

Putari, *s* the name of a conch shell.

Putaria, *s.* the centre of the ear; see *taria.*

Putarotaro, *s.* a certain idolatrous prayer for the sick

Putaurua, *s.* the name of a feast, or of a certain part of it; see *taurua.*

Putê, *s.* a bag of any kind; a pocket.

Putea, *a.* fair, whitish, comparatively fair, as the skin of the white ahia.

Puteetee, *a.* irregular in growth, as a cocoanut, or a gourd.

Putehetehe, *a.* or *adv.* loosely tied, slovenly, disorderly, applied to dress, badly tied as a bundle; and the opposite, putehetehe ore, is neat, orderly, becoming, well tied.

Putehutehu, *v. n.* to break up or scatter, as a company.

Puteputê, s. the name of a plantain of a small production.

— *a. fig.* small, diminutive.

Putete, *s* a bag enclosed in a small net, in which it is suspended.

Putihi, *s.* the large or centre piece in a tihi.

Putii, *s.* the name of a bird.

— *s.* food, so called from its being tied up

— *v. a.* to put the hair in tresses.

— *s.* hair tied in one or two bunches on the head, see *tope.*

Putii, *s.* an orphan; one without succour, also a clump of ti; see *ti.*

Putihiocoe, *s.* a part of the head dress of a priest, or of a dancer

Putiirua, *s.* the hair tied in two bunches on the head

Putiitaaie, *s.* a person that dressed his head in a singular manner, and went among the chiefs to stir them up to go to war.

Putiitii, *a.* having many holes, as a garment, or a piece of cloth, which had been gathered up and tied in bunches.

Putitii, *v, a.* to tie repeatedly in several places.

Puto, *s.* a cluster of sugar cane.

Putô *v. a.* to drag or pull a thing; also putô is applied to the leading of a beast, but the leading of a man is aratai.

Putoa, *s.* the name of a bird; also of a shell.

— *v. n.* to assemble together, as those who had been scattered by war.

Putoa. *s* a piece of coral.

— *v. a.* to encamp on all sides.

Putoetoe, *a.* cold, comfortless in mind.

Putohe, *s.* something held in reserve

Putohetohe, *v a.* to reserve property in different places, or at different times.

Putoi, *v. n.* to cringe, and hug one's self up, as the natives do when cold or wet; to sit closely, as persons under some shelter, when overtaken by a shower.

Putoitoi. *v. n.* the plural of putoi, to cringe repeatedly, or take shelter from rain.

Putorea, *s.* the name of a medicinal plant, that grows in marshes, and is also called *aou*, and *pitorea*.

Putorotoro, *a.* strange, having been long absent.

Putotoro, *a.* strange, not frequent in visits; the words putorotoro, putotoro, and putorotorohia, are used as exclamations, when visited by a person who seldom calls.

Putorotea, *s.* the name of a small tree of hard wood, called also *torotea*.

Putoru, *s.* a spear with three prongs; also a rope of three strands.

Putoto, *s.* blood, coagulated blood.

— *a.* bloody, bloodshot.

Putotototo, *a.* bloody, with many coagulations.

Putu, *s.* the name of a bird.

— *v. n.* to clap the hands.

— *s.* a perfumer, or one that makes sweet scented things.

— *v. a.* to collect spices or fragrant herbs for the sweet monoi.

Putua, *a.* thick, applied to liquids; coagulated.

Putua, *v. n.* to be drawn out of its course, as a ship.

Putuputu, *a.* gathered; close together, the opposite to varavara, or thinly scattered.

— *v. n.* to gather together, to assemble.

Pututu, *s* the body or company of fishermen.

Puu, *s.* a ball, protuberance, prominence.

Puuaraea, *s.* a prominent part of a hill of red earth.

Puunena, *v. n.* to be choked or suffocated with food.

Puunono, *s.* a tumour, or hard swelling; a disease of the posteriors.

Puumirimiria, *adv.* speedily, expeditiously, as a work soon dispatched.

Puupuu, *s.* a species of breadfruit.

Puupuu, *a.* rough, uneven, irregular; also agitated, as the sea.

Puuru, *s.* a man's portion of land, or inheritance, containing *uru*, or breadfruit.

Puvaavaa, *s.* a ribbon, frill, flounce, or bow of cloth, a leaf, or flower, gathered up in folds, or plaits.

Puveuveu, *s.* a rag.

— *a.* ragged.

Puvahaiti, *a.* inaudible, applied to the voice.

Puvaharahi, *a.* loud, audible, as a strong voice.

Puvaharau, *s.* a person that often changes his voice or speech; instability of mind.

— *a.* unstable, changeable.

Puvahi, *s.* a method of fishing at night with torches: also the peculiar colour of the hair of a dog.

Puvatavata, *a.* ill joined, loosely united.

Puvauvau, *s.* bashfulness, trepidation.

— *v. n.* to be bashful, or abashed.

Puvero, *s.* a species of breadfruit.

Puveromanu, *s.* a method of catching birds.

Puveromatahipahiipa, *s.* a sort of fish hook.

Puveroruaroa, *s.* a term used by fishermen relative to certain kinds of fish hooks.

R

IS a letter of frequent occurrence in tahitian, but in some of the other dialects it is either dropped or exchanged for *l*, and in some few tahitian words it is exchanged with *n*, as namu, ramu, and rapu, napu, &c.

Râ, *s.* (*la, a,*) the sun; also a day; see *mahana.*

Ra, *adv.* of time or place, implying distance with reference to either, as, te parau ra, which according to circumstances, signifies either, he is speaking *there*, at such a place, or was *then* speaking.

Ra, an *affix* to the words atu, iho, and mai; thus atu*ra*, iho*ra*, and mai*ra*, with relation to either time or place.

Râ, *s.* an ornament in the marae; see *unu.*

Râ, *conj.* but, as for, vau râ, as for me, outou râ, but you. It is pronounced with emphasis; see *area.*

Raa, *s.* the name of one of the chief tahitian gods.

Raa, *following verbs* converts them into participial nouns, as *parau* to speak. *parau raa*, the time or place of speaking; *apoo*, to meet, *apooraa*, meeting.

Râa, *a.* sacred, consecrated, devoted to a sacred purpose.

Raai, *s.* the name of a fish.

— *s.* a mode of attack in war.

— *v. n.* to be equal, or an equivalent in things purchased or exchanged.

— *s.* the line that passes through the upper and low-meshes of a fishing net; see *arahi.*

Raanu, *v. a.* to collect, or amass a large quantity of provisions.

Raanuu, *s.* a large collection of food for visitors.

Raaraa, *a.* sacred, as the residence of the gods.

Raatira, *s.* (*rangatira*, Malay *Raja*, or *Radja*,) a chief; the general title of the inferior chiefs; see *iatóai.*

— *s.* an officer on board a ship; see *tapena.*

Raau, *s.* (*rakau*,) a tree, wood, timber of any kind; any thing made of wood.

— *s.* plants, herbs; also medicines.

Raaurapaaumai, *s.* a medicine of any kind, because all tahitian medicines were herbs of one kind or other.

Rae, *s.* (Malay, *dae* or *rae*,) the forehead.

Raea, *v. n.* to be heated by exertion.

Raehiehie, *s.* a fierce front, a furious person.

13 Raehoa, *s.* the head ache; see *uruhoa.*

Raemoamoa, *s.* a prominent sharp forehead.

Rafirifiri, *a.* inconstant.

Raha, *a.* downy, hairy.

Raharaha, *v. n.* to be covered with down or loose hair.

— *v. n.* to be all attention to a person speaking.

Rahau, s. a peaceful day, or time; see *hau.*

Rahi, *s.* a wedge for splitting wood.

Rahi, *a.* large, great in quantity, or number.

Rahi, *s.* the whole, the gross number; also sometimes when *te* is prefixed, *te rahi*, the greatest part.

Rahi, *v. n.* to become great.

Rahi, *v. a.* to pinch or squeeze the throat; to arrange the bark for making the native cloth.

Rahihii, *a.* splendid, brilliant, as a company of people on a feast day.

Rahirahi, *a.* small; unequal, thin and wide.

Rahirahia, *s.* the temples.

Rahirahirimaarioi, *s.* dexterity, or dispatch in business.

Rahiri, *s.* the root of the ava plant.

Rahiri, *s* a bunch of cocoanut leaves presented to the king or chief, before the commencement of a dance.

Raho, *s.* the female pudenda.

Rahonui, *s.* a name given to a species of spider; see *tutuirahonui.*

Rahohaari, *s.* the name of an indecent dance, in which both sexes were perfectly naked.

Rahu, *s.* a certain prayer, or incantation used in laying a restriction on fruit, &c.

Rahui, *s.* a prohibition or restriction laid on hogs, fruit, &c. by the king, or chief.

Rahui, *v. a.* to lay on such a rahui; in several of the islands it is called *tapu.*

Rahuipotuaraa, *s.* the great or universal restriction by the chiefs.

Rahumate, *s.* a sorcerer, one that was supposed to be able to destroy by sorcery.

Rahune, *s.* the season of plenty; see *auhune.*

Rahuara, *s.* a deliverer; a benevolent person.

— *v. a.* to do good, feed the hungry, &c.

Rahupohe, *s.* a sorcerer; see *rahumate.*

Rahurahu, *v. n.* to eat sacred or forbidden things.

— *a.* sacred, forbidden; see *tapu.*

Rahutaria, *s.* the ceremony of presenting the ear of a pig in offering to the gods.

— *a.* heedless, indifferent.

— *v. n.* to listen with indifference.

Rai, *s.* (*rangi, langi,* Malay *langit,*) the sky; also heaven; see *ao* and *reva.*

Rai, *s.* the highest chief, or king; see *arii.*

Rai, *s.* a fish not easily taken; *fig.* one swift of foot.

Raiarii, *s.* a certain appearance in the clouds which was reckoned ominous.

Raiatea, *s.* a clear, fine, open sky.

Raifa, *s* the name of a native song.

Raimaemae, *s.* a dark lowering sky.

Raimareva, *a.* tall; vast in size or quantity.

Râine, *v. n.* to be in readiness, as a fleet of canoes about to sail.

— *v. n.* to be at rest, as the sea after a storm.

Raineaoa, *s.* the young blossoms of the cocoanut tree.

Raineatua, *s.* the cocoanut blossom presented to the god Oro.

Raineraatira, *s.* the cocoanut blossom presented by the chiefs on the restoration of peace.

Raipoia, *s.* a dark cloudy sky.

Raipoia, *v. n.* to be cloudy and dark; *fig.* to be gloomy through displeasure.

Rairai, *a.* thin, as cloth, boards, &c; also, thin, lean, as animals.

Rairaia, *a.* bulky, plenteous; see *faifaia.*

Raitu, *s.* a god, see *atua.*

— *s.* a term used for a darling child.

Raituataa, *v. n.* to be exceedingly great or vast.

Raituatua, *s.* a dark, rainy or gloomy day.

Raituatini, *s.* the highest heaven.

Raituatoru, *s.* the third heaven.

Raitupu, *s.* the name of a certain prayer.

Raitupuora, *s.* the imperishable sky.

Raiutiuti, *s.* a silvery mottled sky.

Raivahatete, *s.* a fish that is eager for his prey; a person eager of talking.

Rama, *s.* (*lama, ama,*) a torch used by fishermen.

— *s.* (from Engl. ram,) a ram.

Râmâ, *s.* a wicked stratagem; a deception.

— *v. a.* to deceive by false pretences.

Ramu, *s.* a musquito; see *namu.*

— *s.* the spirituous liquor called rum.

Ranunu, *s.* a noted warrior, a a powerful man.

Ranuu, *s.* provisions, property, &c.

Ra'o, *s.* (*rango, ao,*) a fly.

— *s.* something planted in the ground by way of enchantment.

— *s.* a block, or roller, under a boat or a canoe; sleepers under a floor.

— *s.* a fleet at sea.

— *s.* a native cloth presented to a visitor.

Raoa, *s.* the name of a fish with a large head.

— *v. n.* to be choked with food, fish bones, &c.

Raoere, *s.* the leaves used as a fishing net.

Raorao, *a.* ill savoured, filthy, breeding flies.

Raororauro, *s.* *a* turkey; see *moa.*

Rapa, *s.* the blade or paddle of an oar.

— *s.* a slab of stone or wood.

Rapaau, *s.* a medicine; see *raau.*

— *v. a.* to administer medicine.

— *v. a.* to cure or preserve, as by salting.

Rapae, *prep.* and *adv.* out, outside; without; see *vaho.*

Rapaeau, *adv.* without, outside, externally.

Rapafaturuinoa. *v. n.* to be unstable, movable at pleasure.

Rapahua, *s.* cumbersome, invalids in time of war.

Raparapa, *a.* square, as a part of a house.

— *a.* dirty; defiled by some uncleanness, also defiled with crime.

Rapatanuhia, *s.* the steady inhabitants of a place.

Rape, *s.* the wall plate of a house; see *arapai.*
Rapu, *s.* earth or dirt.
Rapu, *v. a.* to stir or mix together; see *tarapu.*
— *v. n.* to be in confusion.
— *v. a.* to squeeze, pinch, or scratch.
Rapufaufau, *s* the name of a sort of food.
Rara, *v. n.* to run; see *horo.*
— *s.* (*lala*) a branch; see *amaa.*
— *v. a.* to scorch over or on the fire.
— *v. a.* to melt or warm the pitch over the bottom of a boat, &c.
Raraa, *v. a.* to plat mats, or garments; to weave.
Rarafarapanu, *s.* a branch of the pandanus carried away by the sea, *fig.* a vagrant.
Rarara, *s.* scurf of the head.
Rarahi, *a.* great, the plural of rahi.
Rarai, *s.* an imprecation, or a curse.
Rarararauri, *v. n.* to be sunburnt; see *tuaraina.*
Rarau, *v. a.* to scratch repeatedly; see *raurau.*
Raravaru, *s.* the old native *pahi* or canoe with many sails, called eight *rara*, or branches, answering to the eight divisions of Moorea, Raiatea, &c.
Rare, *s.* the name of a species of breadfruit.
— *a.* soft, mature, as fruit; also rotten, decayed; see *tahuti.*
Rareau, *adv.* outside; see *vaho.*
Rari, *a.* wet, moist.
Rari, *v. n.* to be in a wet or moist state.
Rarirari, *v. n.* to be wet repeatedly, or in several places
Raririi, *v. n.* to be diminished, or becoming less and less.
Raro, *prep.* below, underneath; see *nia.*
Raro, *adv.* towards the west or sun-set, the east is reckoned *nia*, or above, and the west *raro* or below, in speaking of places.
Raroraroae, *a.* low, of very mean extraction.
Raru, *a.* ripe, as fruit; over ripe, when applied to the breadfruit.
— *s.* the name of a very small beetle.
Rarua, *s.* the strength, or undecayed vigour of any thing.
Raruraru, *s.* the name of a fish.
— *s.* the bends of a canoe or boat.
Rata, *a.* tame, docile; familiar.
Râtâ, *s.* the tahitian chestnut tree and fruit.
Rata, *s.* the kidneys.
Rataa, *s.* a day of meeting.
Ratere, *s.* travellers; persons of a newly arrived party, who are on a journey.
— *v. n.* to be in readiness for a journey.
Ratiitii, *s* handsomeness, elegance.
Rato, *v. a.* to drag or pull; see *to* and *puto.*
Ratou, *pron.* 3*d. person plur.* they, three or more persons.
Ratuarira, *s.* a place afar off.
Ratunuu, *s.* the sun when half above, and half below the horizon.

Rau, *s.* the leaf of any tree or plant.

Rau, *a.* one hundred; see *nanahere*, when the natives count by couples, it is 200.

— *a.* many, indefinitely; see *mano.*

Raua, *pron.* 3*d. person dual.* they, two persons.

Rauâ, *s.* a worthless vagrant.

'Raûa, *s.* a rainy day; see *ua.*

Rauaha, *a.* over baked, applied to animal food.

Rauai, *s* the banana stem bruised and put into the bottom of the native oven, to keep the food from burning.

Rauai, *s.* an offering to the goddess Toimata, when the first fruits of a garden or field were used.

Rauaia, *s.* the banana leaf used as a wrapper for food.

Raumaro, *s.* a narrow strip of land.

Rauape, *s.* the a-pe leaf used as an umbrella.

Rauapevai, s. the a-pe leaf with water in it used for bathing a new born babe, when an *upu*, or prayer was said.

— *s.* an a-pe leaf and water used for washing a god; it was so called though no water was used.

Rauaua, *s.* young breadfruit plants growing from the roots of the old ones.

— *s.* a banana made tough by the sun.

Rauava, *s.* the miro or amae leaves used in the marae for various sacred purposes.

Rauepa, *s.* the name of a certain idolatrous prayer said before the commencement of an upaupa or prayer.

Rauepa, *s.* a prayer before going to fish with the tira; see *tira.*

Raufaina, *s.* a stranger of no rank.

Raufara, *s.* the leaves of the pandanus which are used for thatching the native houses.

Raufarapapa, *s.* the leaves of a species of the pandanus noted for a cracking noise in burning, *fig* a noisy talkative person.

Raufau, *s.* the leaf or leaves of the fau or *purau*, laid down in decent order instead of a table cloth.

Raufauaano, *s.* the profusion and prodigality of the great, a figure taken from the broad *fau* leaves.

Rauhairi, *a.* faded; as a tree or plant; *fig.* one who has lost his dignity or office.

Rauhuru, *s.* the banana leaf in its dried state.

Rauhuruore, *a* void of leaves; without incumbrance.

Rauhurupe, *s.* an old banana; *fig.* an old decrepit person; a grand father.

Rauhutu, *s.* a *hutu* leaf; *fig.* an insignificant person.

Rauma, *v. a.* to obtain.

Raumae, *s.* the name of a species of breadfruit.

Raumai, *v n.* to be fair after rain; to cease raining.

Raumaire, *s.* the leaf of the breadfruit called *maire; fig.* the wife of a chief when of low rank.

— *s.* a figurative expression for

a person of only delegated authority.

Raumanu, *s.* the fish, where the birds congregate over some part of the sea; also the fish, caught at the end of the season.

Raumatavehi, *s.* the name of a feast and ceremony, used in making a profaned place sacred again; see *tapurehu.*

Raumatea, *v. n.* to be alarmed, made pale by evil tidings.

Raumati, *v. n.* to cease from rain, hold fair, applied to the weather.

Raumea, *s.* the gills of fish; see *aumea.*

Raumotu, *s.* a breach in a rank; the loss of a head warrior.

Rauone, *s.* free from stones, pebbles, &c. as the sandy beach.

Rauone, *s.* a part of a body where no bones are felt.

Rauopi, *s.* a leaf that is closing.

Rauoro, *s.* the leaves of the pandanus.

Rauoropapaa, *s.* the pine-apple; see *fara.*

Raupa, *v. a.* to obtain; see *naupa* & *roaa.*

Raupaa, *s.* an old withered leaf; the oldest leaves on a plant; the first, or lowest on the stem.

Raupape, *s.* the bruised stem of the banana.

Raupea, *s.* wages, an equivalent, compensation.

— *v. a.* to hire, pay wages; to barter.

Raupoi, *s.* the horizontal piece of wood, which caps the breadfruit or other fences; called also *aupoi*; see *poi* & *aumoa.*

Raura, *v. n.* te take that which is another's in order to save one's own,

Raurau, *v. a.* to scratch; see *raurau.*

Raurauuonu, *s.* the sharp extreme edges of a turtle shell.

Rauraua, *a.* profit, benefit; also possession, part, portion.

Rauraua, *s.* young breadfruit shoots that grow from the roots of the old tree.

Rauraumoo, *s.* a species of crab; *fig.* a person of low extraction.

Raurauo'e. *v. n.* to be in a state of scarcity, applied to the land or country.

Rautahi, *s.* a species of the pia or arrow-root.

Rautanunu, *s.* weariness from exertion.

— *v. n.* to be weary, or tired.

Rauti, *s.* the leaf of the *ti* plant; a war song.

Rauti, *v. n.* to excite to courage and bravery, as in time of war; to cause a party to retire.

Rautupu, *s.* the first grown leaf of the cocoanut tree.

Rauutu, *s.* the foremost in any kind of work; in war, in a race, in a journey; the first in bearing, applied to fruit trees

Rauvahivaha, *s.* falsehood, deception.

— *v. a.* to deceive, to effect by false pretences.

Rauvaravara, s the name of a species of breadfruit.
Rava, *a.* dark, or brownish.
Ravaai, *s* a fisherman.
— *v. a.* to fish.
Ravahine, *s.* the name of a noted deceiver; *fig.* falsehood; deception under fair pretences.
— *v. a.* to deceive by smooth words, and false pretences.
Ravai, *s.* the name of a part of the native pahi.
— *v. n.* to suffice, to be adequate to the end designed.
Ravarava, *a.* tall, slender, and handsome.
Ravaravai, *v. n.* to be sufficient for many.
Ravatua, *v. a.* to carry the omori or war club with the point behind; to fold the hands on the back and walk about.
Rave, *v. a.* to receive.
— *v. a.* to take, to do, to undertake, advise, &c.
— *v. a.* to seize or lay hold of a thing.
— *s.* work, operation, occurrence.
Ravea, *s.* a plan, scheme, operation, instrument, set means of doing a thing.
Raveauru, *v. a.* to do a thing slightly, to take hold of a thing slightly, or very superficially.
Ravehirioro, *v. a.* to do a thing tardily, or ineffectually.
Raverahi, *a.* many in number, much in quantity.
— *adv.* much, or in a great degree.
Raverave, *s.* one that attends upon another.
— *v. a*, to serve, or attend as a servant.
Raveita, *v. a.* to seize violently, applied to a disease.
Re, *s.* a prize gained by conquest, or competition.
Rea, *s.* the yolk of an egg.
— *s.* (*lea*, *renga*, Malay, *halea*,) ginger, turmeric.
— *s.* a fathom; sometimes used for *umi*, or ten fathoms; see *elaeta*.
— used in composition with aore, or aita, as an *adverb.* aita*rea.* seldom, rarely, or not much.
— *s.* (Spanish *real*) the eighth of a dollar.
Reaaro, *s.* turmeric.
Reamahu *a.* darkish, yellow in colour.
Reamoeruru, *s.* a species of ginger.
Reamotutau, *s.* the turmeric whose leaves perish the first in the season.
Rearea, *s.* (*rengarenga*) yellow in colour.
— *s.* joy, gayety, mirth.
— *v. n.* to be gay, or joyful; see *oaoa*.
— *adv.* gaily, joyously.
— *v. a.* to tow a thing in the water.
Reareaao, *s.* the yellowishness of the sky at the approach of the sun.
Rearerea, *v. a.* to lift up a thing by putting the hand underneath.
Reatataupoo, *s.* the blossom knobs of the ginger.
Reauraura, *s.* the ginger or *rea moeruru.*
Refa, *s.* the name of a species of native cloth.

— *s.* certain prints or marks on cloth.

— *s.* the dovetails joined in the corners of boxes.

— *s.* heaviness, drowsiness.

— *v. n.* to leer, cast a side look.

Refarefa, *a.* chequered, as some kinds of native cloth are.

— *v. n* to be sleepy, drowsy.

Rehe, *s.* the name of a fish; see *tehu.*

— *s.* two armies in presence of each other; or any two things near, but not touching.

Reherehetohe, *s.* the same as *pitipititohe.*

Rehirehia, *v. p.* handled and apportioned, it is applied to food.

Rehiti, *s.* a rash person that ventures into danger unnecessarily.

— *s.* a small portion of land.

Reho, *s.* a tiger shell, cut for the purpore of scraping the rind of the breadfruit.

— *v. a* to scrape the rind of breadfruit, &c.

Rehovahaiti, *s.* a figure from the tiger shell scraper, a person that by whispering breeds mischief between friends.

Rehovaharahi, *s.* a clamorous, noisy person.

Rehovava, *s.* a clamorous noisy woman.

Rehu, *s.* ashes, any fine pulverized powder.

Rehu, *v. a.* to level the earth for the floor of a house.

Rehuahimaa, *s.* ashes of an oven.

Rehuamaunu, *s.* the name of a certain feast for the company of fishermen.

Rehuauahi, *s* ashes of a hearth.

Rehufenua, *s.* a haze or mist over the land.

Rehurehu, *s.* the dusk, or darkness of the evening.

Rehutatau, *s.* powdered charcoal used for marking the skin; see *tatau.*

Rei, *s.* the back part of the neck.

Reia, *v. a.* to take, or seize food, &c, without reserve.

— *s.* a stranger from another place that goes about the country.

— *a.* dried up, or wasted away, as water in the dry season.

Reiamauroa, *s.* the name of a bird; *fig.* a person that is uncommonly swift of foot.

Reiamoari, *s.* some great calamity or distress.

Reihiti, *s.* a rash, or adventurous person in battle.

— *a.* rash, obstinate; not hearkening to advice.

Reimua, *s.* the forepart of a canoe; the bows of a ship.

Reimuri, *s.* the stern of a canoe.

Reina, *v. n.* to obtain, accomplish; see *roaa.*

Reinai, *a.* to be in readiness; see *ineine.*

Reioa, *s.* the stern of a large native canoe.

Reiofaaapiaifare, *s.* a figure head, or wooden image attached (according to a tahitian tale) to the head of Hiro's pahi, or large canoe, called Hohoio; see *Hiro.*

Reipahi, *s* the figure head of a ship.

Reipee, *s.* a species of native cloth.

Reipu, *s.* a sort of native cloth.

— *s* a person with a crooked back; see *tuapu.*

Reira, *adv.* of time and place, answering to *then* of time—*there* of place.

Reiraatira, *s.* the captain's cabin in a ship.

Reirei, *a.* thin, slender; see *rairai.*

— *v. n.* to waste through disease.

- *a.* unstable, unsettled.

Reme, *s.* a torch; see *rama.*

Rēō, s. voice, speech, language; a word.

— *s.* a tune, as of a hymn or song.

Reoauau, *s.* a stammering speech, or voice.

Reohe, *s.* a voice.

Reohitoa, *s.* a domineering voice.

Reomaere, *s* a voice of wonder or surprise.

Reomarû, *s* a soft agreeable voice; also a deep bass toned voice in singing.

Reomoanamona, *s* a fawning or jocular voice.

Reomona, *s.* a fawning, enticing voice.

Reoreo, *s.* hilarity; any action or speech that excites laughter.

—*s.* empty, and vain boasting.

— *v. n.* to be vainly boasting; see *tecteo.*

Reoriirii, *s* some secret whisperings, and evil speaking.

Reovava, *s.* an indistinct, unintelligible voice.

Repa, *s.* the thin edges of a flat fish.

Reparepa, *s* the skirts, or edges of a garment.

Repe, *s.* the comb of a fowl.

— *s* the fin on the back of the shark.

— *s.* the projections that grow in a singular manner on the trunk of the tuscarpis edulis, or native chesnut tree

— *s* the piece on which the ends of the rafters rest in a native house; a sort of projection.

Reperehe, *s.* the division of the posteriors; see *pitipititohe,* and *reherehetohe.*

Repo, *s.* (*lepo*) earth, dirt, mould, dust, or filth.

Repoa, *a.* dirty, soiled.

— *v n.* to be made dirty, muddy; or to be soiled.

Repua, *s* a large company, as in the feast called taupiti.

Repuahoe. *s.* the mats of the people; see *repua.*

Repu, *v. n.* to roll, or have a great motion, as a ship.

Repurepu, *v. n.* to roll repeatedly; to shake in the wind, as a sail.

Reiarerauri, *s* blackness of the skin, as that of fishermen caused by the sun and salt water.

Rerau, *v a.* to obtain the *re,* or prize of competition several times over; see *re* and *rau.*

Rerau, *s* a person that obtains the *re* repeatedly.

Rere, *v. a.* to fly or leap, see *marere* and *mahuta.*

Rereatua. *s.* the fly'ng of a god, it was applied to a running meteor in the sky, and was thought to be a god coming down.

Rereatua, *s* a person running between two armies to endeavour to make peace.

Rerehiri, *v. n.* to be surfeited, or sick at stomach.

Rerehiri, *v. n.* te be in a state of perplexity.

Rerehue, *intj* an exclamation used by children when diving in the water.

Rerei, *s.* a technical expression used by fishermen for the third draught of fishes in a new net; the first is called *tiopahu*, the second *tiahou*.

— *v. n* to waste away through sickness; to be lank and thin, as a sick person.

Rereiere, *s.* the name of a shell fish.

Rereioa, *s.* a dream, the wandering of the mind during sleep.

— *v. n* to dream; to be wandering during sleep; also to be alarmed by dreaming.

Reremauri, *s.* the flying of the *mauri* or spirit.

— *v. n.* to be in a great consternation so that no heat or spirit is left.

Rererere, *v. n.* to twitch; to be in motion, through rage or dread.

Rereue, *v. n.* to leap from an eminence into the water.

Rero, *s.* the name of a little poisonous fish.

Reroa, *s.* a long figure head of a canoe.

Reru, *a.* discoloured and muddy, applied to water.

— *v. n* to be muddy, and discoloured.

Retini, *s.* one that obtained many a *re*, or prize.

Reureu, *adv.* comfortably, undisturbedly; it is applied to visitors who are accommodated in a place.

— *v. a.* to bake or stew certain ingredients among vegetables.

Reureua, *s.* profit, advantage; see *faufaa*.

Reureuamoa, *s* the name ef a heathen goddess; see *vahine*.

— *s* the name of a tree; see *amoa*.

Reva, *s.* the firmament, or expanse of heaven.

— *s.* the abyss, or unknown deep, see *moanareva*; any unknown depth; see *hohonu*.

— *s.* the name of a tree, a species of the *hutu*, or *Barringtonia*.

— *a.* inexhaustible, as water from a cavern.

— *v. n.* to depart, go or come, to journey.

Revahahae, *s.* a little red flag, used at the birth, death, or sickness, of a child.

Revapihaarau, *s.* a body of water, into which many springs empty themselves.

Revareva, *v. n* to be flying, as many flags.

— *s.* the thin cabbage, or pellicles in the top part of the cocoanut-tree.

Ri, *v. n* to hang or suspend; see *tai*.

— *v. n.* to lodge, as a tree, or branch, in the branches of another.

Ria, *s* a vision in sleep, a phantom.

Riai, *v. n.* to be discouraged, or seized with fear, as a small party, in meeting a large company of warriors.
Riaria, *s.* horror, detestation, also disgust.
— *a* detestable, shocking, disgusting.
— *v. n.* to be shocked, or disgusted.
Rita, *a.* a scar of any sort.
Riha, *s* a nit, the eggs of a louse.
Rii, *a. pl.* small, little, young, used plurally.
Riirii. *adv.* by little and little, applied to an action.
Riirifai, *s.* sickness of stomach when at sea; also confusion of mind on account of evil tidings.
Riiritua, *s.* the consternation of a party overcome in war, or by affliction.
Rima, *s.* (*lima, ima*) the hand, also the arm.
— *a* (*lima, ima*, Malay, and Malagasse, *lima*,) number five; see *arima, apae*
Rimaatau, *s.* the right hand; see *atau.*
Rimaatua, *s.* the right hand of God; but *fig.* some sudden disease supposed to be inflicted immediately by the hand of God; also strife and ill will between persons.
Rimaaui, s. the left hand.
Rimahana, *s.* a hand full of wickedness.
Rimahaa, *s.* a hand that snatches all that comes within reach; a greedy, dishonest person.
Rimahere, *s* a generous hand, or liberal person
Rimaio, *s* an open, liberal hand.
Rimaioore, *s* an illiberal hand.
Rimaivi, *s* a long, lean hand; *fig.* a person reduced to a skeleton.
Rimanui, *s.* a greedy hand; *fig.* an avaricious person.
Rimapâ, *s.* some sudden disease; as *rimaatua.*
— *s* violence, some violent act.
Rimapoa, *s.* a hand contracted with the *oovi.*
— *s.* a person that handles fearlessly any sore or disgusting thing.
Rimapuru, *s.* a hand soaked in water.
Rimapuu, *s.* an illiberal, ill-natured person.
Rimarii, *s.* the fingers.
Rimarimarii, *s.* the fingers; little fingers.
Rimarimatafai, *s.* the plant called buckshorn.
Rimaroa, *s.* the long or middle finger.
Rimatona, *s.* an illiberal person.
Rimatotoânunui, *s.* a person who knows how to pursue his own self interest.
Rimatuai, *s.* a greedy, avaricious person.
Rimaume, *s.* a person that knows how to draw others to his interest or party.
Riinu, *s.* a general name for moss.
Rimu, *s.* sponge; also sea weed.
Rimurima, *s.* the same as rimarimatafai.
Rio, *s.* the name of a piece of wood in a fishing canoe.
— *s.* the name of a tahitian god.
Rioa, *s* a deep bay, or creek, see *ooa.*

Riorio, *s.* the departed spirit of a person, but particularly the ghost of an infant.

— *v. n.* to be possessed by a *tii*, or departed spirit.

Ripâ, *v. n.* to be wasted with disease.

Ripoa, *s.* the name of a certain *oroa* or feast.

— *s.* a vortex made by the violent running and return of a current; see *au*.

Ripoamarae, s. the corner or joining of the marae wall.

Ripoavahine, *s.* the name of a certain idolatrous ceremony.

Riraa, *s.* a gallows; see *ri* and *raa*.

Rire, *s.* the yellow vi apple.

— *v. n.* to be in a state of fear.

Ririre, *s.* a term addressed by a boy to his *pauma*, or paper kite.

Riri, *s.* anger, displeasure, also sometimes offence, vengeance, spite.

— *v. n.* to be angry, displeased, offended.

Ririo, *v. n.* to be dried, or shrivelled up.

Ririri, *a.* angry, jealous.

— *v. n.* to be angry, as two or more persons.

Ririroa, *a.* implacable, not easily pacified.

Ririririri, *v. n.* to be angry repeatedly.

Riritua, *v. n.* to be in a consternation.

Ririu, *v. n.* to be perplexed, confounded.

Riro, *v. n.* to be lost; or missed; see *moe.*

Riro, *v. n.* to become another thing; to be converted to another use; see *mahere.*

— *v. n.* in the future, signifies, it will or may be.

Rita, *s.* a species of cocoanut, very small and sweet.

— *s.* the spasm or convulsive motion, in the disorder of locked jaw.

— *v. n.* to be biting or gnashing the teeth.

— *v. n.* to be violently convulsed.

Ritamata, *v. n.* to sparkle and move, like the eyes of a person in a rage.

Ritarita, *v. a.* to eat voraciously, and bite the tongue.

Rito, *s.* a prohibition; see *rahui.*

—*v. a.* to lay a restriction on certain things.

— *v. n.* to put forth young buds or leaves, as trees in the spring.

Ritotai, *s.* the advance guard of a fleet of war canoes.

Riu, *s.* bilge water, a leak.

— *a.* leaky, as a canoe, boat or ship.

— *v. n.* to be sufficiently roasted, as the side of a breadfruit before it is turned.

— *v. n.* to be filled, as the basket used by the fishermen of the albicore, &c.

— *s.* a backslider.

Riuriu, *v. n.* to be moving round.

Riuriutua, *v. n.* to be drawing back.

— *v. n.* to be in a state of consternation.

Rivariva, *s.* abundance, great plenty; also a large bulk.

Rivarivaitau, *a.* bulky; abundant.

Ro, *s.* an ant, of which there are many species; as *ro apoo nui*, *ro avae roroa*, &c.

Roa, *a.* (*loa*, *oa*) long in measure, time, distance.

— *a.* in comparing qualities, it signifies a greater or longer degree.

— *adv.* thoroughly, completely, entirely.

—an *emphatic par.* when joined to adverbs of negation it augments the emphasis, as aitaroa, not at all, by no means; e ore roa, never, at any future time, and still more emphatic, e ore ore *roa atu*, never, at no time whatever, the strongest assertion possible.

— *s.* a decayed breadfruit, or chesnut tree.

Roà, *s.* a small tree, the bark of which is used like hemp for cordage, nets, &c.

Roaa, *v. n.* to obtain; see *noaa.*

Roaae, *a.* in comparing *roa* long, *roa ae* a little longer.

Roaitiae, *adv.* presently, after a little while.

Roaroa, *a.* protracted, applied to time.

— *v. n.* to be dilatory, procrastinating.

Roaroaitiae, *adv.* presently, soon.

Roeroe, *s.* the case of the cocoanut blossom.

— *s.* the name of a large fish, like salmon.

Rofai, *s.* a sudden gust of wind.

Rofaifai, *s.* a strong gust of wind with a shower of rain.

Roha, *s.* heaviness.

Roha, *v. n* to stagger, as a man under a heavy load, or as a drunken man.

Roha, *a.* faint, wearied; see *opaipai.*

Rohe, *s.* the father of famine, called *Rohe upoo nui*, large headed *Rohe.*

Roherohe, *s.* little red animalcules bred in standing water.

— *s.* the very small roots of plants.

— *s.* proud flesh in a sore; a certain stage of the growth of gourds.

Roheirohea, *s.* plump, or prominent eyes

— *v. n.* to be plump, fat, protuberant.

Rohi, *v. a.* to stimulate another to exertion.

— *v. n.* to be alert, vigilant, wakeful.

Rohipehe, *s.* a maker of songs; see *pehe.*

Rohirohi, *s.* lassitude, weariness.

— *v. n.* to be weary, tired or fatigued.

Rohutu, *s.* the residence of departed souls in the *po.*

Rohutunamua, *s.* a certain division of the Tahitian *hades*, but not the best.

Rohutunoanoa, *s.* a superior place in the Tahitian *hades.*

Rohutu, *s.* the name of a fish.

Rohutu, *s.* a very large species of the earth worm; see *toe.*

Roi, *s.* a bed, a bedstead or couch.

Roi, *s.* the name of a blackish fish

Roiitemoemoeoravaa, *s.* a bed for a god.

Roimata, *s.* a tear.
Roine, *s.* a line used in fishing for the albicore, &c.
Roipe, *s* one that lives to eat and sleep.
Roipoa, s. a bed or sleeping place near the king.
— *v. n.* te be insinuating into the favour of the king or principal chief, for some sinister end.
— *v. n.* to seek diligently the accomplishment of some purpose.
Roiroi, *a.* calm, unruffled, as the sea or sky ; also tranquil, peaceable, as a country.
Roitau, *s* a principal place where the chiefs used to collect their presents of food, cloth, &c.
Roma, *v. n.* to shrink, become less, as water in a pond, oil in a lamp. &c.
— *v, n.* to fall, as a swelling.
Romaha, *s.* the plant *rod*, or *roaa.*
Romatane, *s.* the name of a stone set in a marae, and dressed with sweet scented flowers.
— *s.* the name of a priest or god, who had the power of admittting the spirits of the dead into *Rohutunoanoa*, and also of excluding them.
— *s.* the drummers or players, employed in the heiva, upaupa, &c.
Romiromi, *v. n.* to hide or conceal from approaching visitors.
Roo, *s.* fame. notoriety, either good or bad.
— *s* a report ; see *paroo*, and *tuiroo.*
Roohia, *v. n.* overtaken, to be overtaken, or come up with.
Rooroоa, *a* to have repeated re-—ports coming ; *tauroorooa*, a season of repeated reports.
Ropa, *v. n.* to be taken unaware ; to be suddenly seized, as by a disease, &c.
Ropa, *v. n.* to turn aside, as one shy of another.
Ropàpà, *a.* well shaped, as a man or thing.
Roparopa, *s.* the name of a fish.
— *a.* irregular.
Ropatabi, *s.* a sudden gust of wind, also a disease.
Ropu, *a.* the middle.
Ropu, *prep.* between two, betwixt.
Ropu, *prep.* through the midst.
Ropuee *s.* a violent gust of wind.
Rorai, s a curse or imprecation of evil on children
Rore, *s.* stilts used by boys in play.
— *s.* a vice, or wrench, used by canoe builders.
— *v. a.* to wrench, or pinch, to put into a vice.
— *s.* the undervaluation of a thing, the disparagement of a bargain.
— *v. a.* to depreciate, or undervalue a thing.
Rori, *s.* the sea slug, or what the Portuguese call *bich* or *bicho le mer*, (worm of the sea.) of which there are several varieties. The tahitians had a notion that the spirits of the dead entered into the *rori*, and afterwards passed to some other place.
Roriatepa, *s.* a species of the *rori*, the others are, rorihua-

rari, rorimaoro, tahetahe, papao, &c.

Rori, *v. a.* to wash or cleanse in water; see *tihu*.

— *v. n.* to become hard and tough, as fruit, &c.

Rorirori, *a* hard, tough; difficult to solve.

— *a.* difficult to open or unravel, as a matter or speech.

Roro, *s.* the brains of mankind, not of beasts.

Roroa, *a.* long, longish; see *roa* and *maoro*.

Rorofai, *s.* a gust of wind, with a shower of rain.

Rorou, *adv.* not constant; applied to work.

Roroi, *a.* leaning to one side, as a post.

Roroimafa, *s.* a person or thing of long standing and growth, but of little stature.

Roroma, *v. n.* to decrease or shrink gradually.

Roroo, *s.* the chanting of the prayers in the marae.

— *v. n.* to begin to chant the prayers, as the priests used to do in the marae.

Roropu, *prep.* between, in the middle.

Roroau, *adv.* of time future, presently; shortly.

Roroauitiore, *adv.* soon, or presently.

Rorotea, *s* a thick heavy rain.

Rorovau, *adv.* shortly in a little while.

Rorovauitiae, *adv.* in a short space of time.

Roru, *v. n.* to be in a lax state, as the skin in the dropsy.

— *a.* soft, sodden, as ill baked food.

— *v. n.* to be in subjection, as the people when submissive to the laws.

— *s* a sort of chorus, or repetition in a native song.

— *s.* a bruise, or hurt of the flesh.

Rôrû, *s.* a species of the tiger shell fish.

Rorua, *s.* a line made of the bark of the roa for catching the albicore; see *raine*.

Roruroru, *v. n.* to be very lax, or soft, as the flesh of a dropsical person.

— *v. n.* to be flexible, as a long elastic board.

— *a.* lax, flexible, not firm.

Rotahi, *s.* singleness of mind, oneness in respect of any object.

— *v. n.* to be aiming only at one thing.

Rotea, to be ready to fall, it is applied to rain.

Rotia, *v. n.* to be gone, as the people used to say of their gods, *ua rotia te atua*, the god is gone.

— *s.* the name of a fish.

— *s* a species of large cocoanut.

Roto, *s.* a lake or pond; a lagoon.

Roto, *prep.* in, inside, within; see *teiroto*.

Rotomanava, *s* delight, any thing particularly agreeable.

Rotomati, *s.* the red colour of the mati berries impressed on the native cloth, or on the skin, as the arioi used to do.

Rotopa, *s.* a small enclosed lake or pond

Rotopu, *prep.* in the midst.

Rotu, *s.* an expression used in a certain idolatrous prayer.

Rotu, *v. a.* to smite or strike.

Rotu, *s.* the heavy rain of one day's continuance.

Rou, *s.* a long pole with a crook, used in gathering breadfruit from high branches of the tree.

— *v. a.* to gather fruit with the rou.

Rouae, *adv.* of time to come, quickly, shortly.

Rouaeho, *s.* a crook of the *aeho* reed, used for nefarious purposes.

Roupea, *s.* a branch, such as that of the breadfruit tree; see *pouru*.

— *v. a.* to gather or entangle one crook in another.

Rourou, *s.* the gristle of the nose.

Rouru, *s* the hair of the head, not of other parts of the body; see *huruhuru*.

Rouruatafare, *s.* curled black hair.

Rouruehu, *s.* reddish or sandy hair.

Rourufatufatu, *s.* grisled hair.

Rouruofirifiri, *s.* the same as rourufatufatu.

Rouruoitoito, *s.* curled black or matted hair.

Rourupiipii, *s.* thick curled hair.

Rovauae, *adv*, presently; see *rouae*.

Rovauitiae, *adv.* see *rorovauitiae*.

Ru, *s.* the name of a god, or noted man of old, who spread out the sky as a curtain.

Ru, *s.* impatience, violent haste, or great hurry.

Ru, *v. a.* to transplant or remove a certain part of the marae.

Ru, *v. n.* to be in haste or great hurry.

Ru, *a.* hasty, hurried.

Rua, *s.* (*lua*, *ua*, Malay *qua*) a hole, pit, aperture.

—*a.* two; see piti.

—*s.* the name of a Tahitian god.

Ruaahâ, *s.* the place where fishermen fish for the aahi, &c.

Ruaaha, *s.* a certain thing or place in which the sorcerer pretended to confine his *tii* or demon, employed by him.

Ruaaia, *s.* the act of offering to a god a man killed in war, or a fish.

Ruahatu, *s.* the name of a noted sea-god.

Ruahere, *s.* a place often frequented.

Ruahine, *s.* the name of a goddess.

— *v. a.* to gather breadfruit with a long pole, without climbing.

Ruahineaimamau, *s.* a female ancestor of the third generation back, and who takes care of her posterity.

Ruahineaimainoino, *s.* a stingy old woman that would never invite another to partake of her food.

Ruahineaimaamua, *s.* a contemptible name given to an old woman, that fed the children of a chief, but secretly ate the food.

Ruahineaimauu, *s.* a term used in connection with a batch of food, baked at the removing of restrictions in using a new fishing net.

Ruahineamafatu, *s.* a female that is skilful in her various occupations.

Ruahinearutaruta, *s.* the goddess of tale bearing.

Ruahineauna, *s.* the goddess of solicitude.

Ruahinefaaipu, *s.* the goddess of plain speech.

Ruahinemetua, *s.* a decrepit —old woman.

Ruahinemoeuuru, *s.* the goddess of dreams.

Ruahinenihonihororoa, *s.* the goddess of strife, of cruelty, and murder.

Ruahinenihonihotetei, *s.* the same goddess of strife, called also Ruahinefirifiriaufau.

Ruahineorerorero, *s.* the goddess of oratory.

Ruahinepuonoono, *s.* the goddess of persevering desire.

Ruahinetahua, *s.* the goddess of arts and prayers.

Ruahinetamaumauauahi, *s.* a goddess that kept fire always burning.

Ruahinetamaumauorero, *s.* the goddess of tale bearing, and sowing strife.

Ruahinevanaanaa, *s.* the goddess of eloquence.

Ruai, *v. n.* to vomit; see *pihae.*

— *s.* the matter thrown up in vomiting.

Ruairoto, *s.* the act of stirring up mischief.

Ruairoto, *v. n.* to stir up mischief.

Ruamano, *s.* one that tells his tale in many places.

Ruamaoro, *s.* the summer solstice in December.

Ruamatai, *s.* the point from which the wind blows.

Ruanuu, *s. (ruanugu)* the name of a god.

Ruapoto, *s.* the winter solstice in June.

Ruapuna, *s.* a sea-god without nostrils, who could remain very long under water.

Ruaroa, *s.* the summer solstice, the same as ruamaoro.

Ruaroroirai, *s.* a breeder of contention.

Ruarua, *v. a.* to backbite, slander, or defame.

Ruau, *a.* old, stricken in years.

— *s.* an old man or woman.

Ruaupu, *s.* the matter taught at school.

Rudimena, *s.(Engl. rudiments)* elements, first principles.

Ruerue, *s.* a certain figure marked on the skin.

— *a.* ill savoured; see *haua ino.*

Rufa, *a.* worn out, applied to a garment.

Rufarufa, *a.* worn out, as cloth.

— *s.* a part of the sharks head; also something that takes the attention and delights a person.

Ruharuha, *s.* a part of the totara, or the sharks head, the same as rufarufa; also a cant word for much, or plenty.

Ruhe, *s.* the name of a little fresh water fish.

Ruheruhe, *s.* the fish ruhe; also a small matter, or thing.

Ruhi, *s.* sleepiness, drowsiness.

— *v. n.* to be sleepy or drowsy.

Ruhiruhia, *a.* aged.

— with *raa, s.* old age.

Rui, *s.* night; see *arui* and *po.*
Rui, *v. n.* to be dark or blind.
Ruma, *s.* gloom, as of the evening; sullenness.
Rumaa, *a.* covetous, grasping.
Rumai, *v. n.* to be hurried to ripeness, before the proper time, as bananas, &c.
Rumaruma, *s.* gloominess, sullenness.
— *v. n.* to be dark, gloomy, sullen.
Rumarumapo, *s.* the gloominess of the evening.
Rumi, *v. a.* to wring, as cloth that had been washed.
— *v. n.* to turn over, or upset, as a canoe.
— *v. a.* to press and rub the limbs when weary, or in pain; see *taurumi.*
— *v. n.* to turn aside the eyes from looking at a person through dislike; to make a secret sign with the eyes, or by wrinkling the forehead.
Rumihuna, *v. n.* to make a secret sign to one of the other sex; to make a sign for the concealment of something.
Rumirumi, *v. a.* to press and smooth the wrinkles of a garment, or a piece of cloth; also to press and rub the limbs repeatedly.
Rumia, *s.* according to a very ancient tradition, *Rumia* was something like an egg floating in the abyss, or expanse, out of which came the materials of heaven and earth.
Runanu, *v. n.* to desire food, &c. most greedily; see *ru,* and *nanu.*
Ruoi, *a.* aged; see *ruau.*
Rupa, *s.* a thicket of brushwood; a thicket of branching coral; see *hurupa.*
Rupe, *s.* the name of a large land bird, a species of pigeon.
Rupeha, *s.* a thick haze on the land.
Ruperupe, *a.* flourishing, luxuriant, as a plant, or a tree; *fig.* good, flourishing, or prosperous.
— *s.* a species of the *hoi* plant; see *hoi.*
Ruperupehu, *s.* a place that is unsightly, or unhealthy.
Rupo, *s.* the name of a little fish; see *ruhe.*
— *s.* a sort of ornamented matting, that is wrapt about the lower ends of rafters in some Tahitian houses.
Ruporupo, *s.* giddiness of the head, from disease, or drunkenness.
— *v. n.* to be giddy, reel or stagger.
Rura, *s.* one who dies from being too hasty.
Ruraeri, *v. a.* to do mischief; to waste wantonly.
Rurahiri, *v. n.* to be mischievous and restless, as a child, or an idle boy.
Rurao, *v. n.* to breed mischief, disturb the peace.
— *s.* disturbance, mischief.
Rure, *s.* a rough instrument of music; see *ihara.*
Ruree, *s.* a term used in a native song.
Rurepa, *s.* a company of wicked young persons that join together for vile purposes.
Rurerure, *adv.* applied to a cer-

tain manner of the voice of a female, when crying or lamenting.

Rureva, *s.* a species of mountain plaintain.

Ruri, *v. a* to shift or remove, applied to the shifting or removing of a burden from one shoulder to the other; see *taruri.*

Ruri, *v. a.* to distort words from their proper meaning.

Ruriapo, *s.* a dream; see *moemoe.*

— *v. n.* to revert in sleep to something a person had been transacting.

Rurie, *v. a.* to subvert, or turn a thing aside.

Rurimatahuna, *v. n.* to wink, or look slily at a person, used in a bad sense.

Rurimatahapa, *v. n.* to turn the eye wantonly, or wickedly.

Ruriruri, *v. a.* to remove a thing repeatedly.

Ruro, *s.* the name of a bird, formerly sacred to the gods.

Ruroruro, *s.* unsightly tubercles on the body.

Ruru, *s.* the name of a large aquatic bird, probably the same as the albatross.

— *s.* a roll, or bale of cloth.

— *s.* the name of a land bird; see *otatare.*

— *v. a.* to congregate.

— *v. n.* to be assembling together; see *tairuru.*

Rûrû, *v. n.* to tremble, shake.

Rurua, *s.* a shelter from the wind; a lull.

Rurua, *a.* sheltered, applied to a place, as vahi rurua, a place sheltered from the wind.

Rûiûamore, *v. n.* to be bound with *more*, or purau bark *fig.* to be badly fastened.

Ruruapaa, *s.* the name of a certain *upu* or prayer; *fig.* false security.

Ruruhere, *s.* the name of a prayer and ceremony in dressing up the *too* of a god.

Rurutamai, *s.* a sort of turban used by warriors in going to battle.

Rurutamau, *s.* a head dress of human hair.

Rurutaina, *s.* trembling, shaking.

— *v. n.* to tremble, shake, quake.

Ruruu, *v. n.* to tie, or bind.

Ruta, *v. n.* to be in a hurry; see *ru.*

Rutaruta, *s.* a violent hurry.

Rutu, *s.* the name of a mountain plantain.

— *s.* a drummer; see *pahu.*

— *v. a.* to beat the drum.

— *s.* a certain mode of fishing.

Ruu, *s.* a mode of fishing; see *faaruu.*

Ruuruu. *s.* a bond or bondage.

Ruuruu, *v. a.* to tie or bind.

Ruuruuiriamore, *v. a.* to bind with *more*, *fig.* to make an unsound agreement.

T

IS a letter of frequent occurrence in the Tahitian dialect, in the Hawaiian it is turned into *k*, and the Tahitians themselves generally exchange it with *d* without at all noticing the difference; neither can they perceive the difference between it and *k.*

Ta, *v. a.* to strike; also to write; see *papai.*

Ta, *prep.* of, or belonging to, applied to certain things, such as food, arms, speech, &c. while *to* is applied to other things.

Ta, *pron* that which, the thing what, or that.

Ta, *v. a.* to make the meshes of a net.

Ta, *v. a.* to repeat, or tell a tale; see *aai.*

Ta, *s.* the instrument used for marking the skin; see *tatau.*

Ta, *s.* a rope pendent from a tree, by means of which children swing; also a skipping rope.

Ta, *s.* the motion of a child in the womb, when the mother is startled by some affecting, or unexpected news.

— *v. n.* to move, as a child in the womb.

— *s.* the stalk of the banana that supports the fruit.

— a *causal prefix* to verbs of the same signification as the *faa* or *haa*, which see, as *ta*maa, *tahu*ri, *ta*mau, &c.

Taa, *s.* the chin, or jaw-bone; see *mottaa.*

— *s.* the circular piece under the rafters of a Tahitian house, which joins them together.

— *v. n.* to fall from a rock, or a high place.

— *v. n.* to remove, as a thing out of its place, to separate, or slip off, or aside.

— *v. n.* to be single or separate, as unmarried persons.

— *v. n.* to be dismissed; to be set apart, or aside.

— *a.* separate; single, unmarried.

— *a.* settled, or dismissed, as the subject of a discourse; also let go.

Taaa, *v. a.* to cut the roots in order to fell a tree; see *aa.*

— *v. a.* to make use of the *aahaari*, or the fibrous substance of the cocoanut, to catch fish.

Taaaeae, *v. n.* to be gasping for breath, as a dying person.

Taaau. *a.* to helve an axe or other instrument.

Taaê, *a.* wonderful, strange; extraordinary.

Taaaî, *s.* a neckcloth.

Taafare, *s.* the piece that joins the rafters together.

Taahi, *v. a.* to tread with the foot.

Taahi, *v. a.* to separate; put an army in order.

Taahiaufau, *v. a.* to treat with contempt any one's ancestry, or fraternity.

Taahihuaa, *v. a.* the same as taahiaufau.

Taahiouma, *v. a.* to tread on a person's breast; a figurative expression, signifying ingratitude, or injurious return for good.

Taahipuoa, *v. a.* to tread carelessly on things that ought not to be trodden upon.

Taahoa, *s.* the head ache; see *hoa.*

— *v. n.* to be affected with head ache.

— *a.* vexing, troublesome.

— *v. n.* to be teazed and vexed.

Taahu, *v. a.* to attire, to dress; see *faaahu.*

Taahuri, *v. a.* to turn over.

— *v. n.* to be turning over.

Taai, *s.* a ball of *pia* tied up.

— *v. a.* to tie, or bind a thing; see *ruruu.*

— *v. a.* to plot, form political schemes of mischief.

— *v. n.* to journey, or be travelling about the country.

Taaipu, *s.* a spoon, skimmer, or ladle.

— *v. a.* to skim, to lade; to take with a spoon.

Taairi, *s.* a skipping rope used by children.

— *v. a.* to skip over a rope, a play of children.

Taamanu, *s.* a mode of catching birds.

Taamarara, *s.* a mode of catching the marara, or flying fish.

Taamotu, *s.* a range of little islands.

Taamu, *v. n.* to travel about the country.

— *v. a.* to plot against a chief; see *taai.*

— *v. a.* to tie, or bind; see *taai.*

Taanini, *v. n.* to stagger, or reel.

— *v. n.* to drift to leeward, as a ship.

Taanoa, *s.* a single or unmarried person.

— *a.* single, or unmarried.

— *v. n.* to slip, or fall, or to be going down spontaneously, or without any external force.

Taape, *s.* the name of a little yellow fish.

Taapu, *s.* a scrofulous chin.

— *v. n.* to be affected by the scrofula, in the neck and chin.

Taapuni, *s.* a warrior that has many trophies.

Taaraa. *s.* the time or place of falling, or of separating; the explanation of a sentence, so as to let it rest.

Taaroa, *s.* (*Tangaroa, Tanaroa,*) the great god of the Polynesians in general, he was said to be the father of the gods, and creator of all things, yet was scarcely reckoned an object of worship.

Taaru, *v. n.* to yield, abate, give up.

Taata, *s.* (*tangata, kanata, anata, tamata,*) a man; a human person, male or female; mankind.

Taàta, *s.* when two or three are mentioned, the word is pronounced a little different, taàta, a couple of men.

— *v. a.* to prepare the bark for cloth making, by taking off the rough outside bark.

Taataarapoa, *s.* a glutton; see *arapoa.*

Taataê, *s.* a stranger, or foreigner.

Taataee, *s.* the plural of stranger, strangers.

Taatahia, *v. n.* peopled, made full of people.

Taataata, *s.* the human jawbone, over which certain prayers were said in the marae.

Taatahotuanui, *s.* a man of prodigious strength, either of body, or mind.

Taatanoi, *s.* an athletic man; a skiful person.

Taataorero, *s.* a herald, a crier, a public speaker.

Taatarimarima, *s.* a thief; see *eia.*

Taatatapu, *s.* a human sacrifice; see *tapu.*

Taatatea, *s.* an archer; see *tea.*

Taatatufaa, *s.* an heir; one that has an inheritance, or a portion.

Taatatupu, *s.* a neighbour; an acquaintance.

Taati, *v. a.* to join, or unite things together.

— *v. n.* to go about, encompass; see *taamu.*

Taau, *v. a.* to procure any thing by swimming.

— *a.* twenty, or ten couples; see *umi.*

Taauahi, *v. a.* to use or employ fire.

Taauri, *v. a.* to use iron; to iron clothes.

Taavae, *v. a.* to put feet to a bench or stool.

Taavai, *s.* a stone worn smooth and polished in the water; a person of good appearance.

Taave, *v. a.* to hang or suspend a thing by a string from the neck; to hang or strangle.

Taaviri, *v. n.* to turn, as a person in bed.

Taaviriviri, *v. n.* to turn repeatedly.

Tae, *v. n.* to arrive; to come to a place, to arrive at a thing, or an act.

Tae, *v. n.* to go or come with strong desire.

Taea, *s.* the name of a red coloured fish.

Taea, *v. p.* arrived, attained, reached unto.

Taeae, *s.* (*Taeake*) a brother, cousin, any near relation.

Taeafao, *a.* clownish, not of repute; such as used to be marked for sacrifices.

Taee, *a.* bulky; robust.

Taefeiaitu, *s.* a bird sacred to the god tane.

Taehae, *s.* a savage man, or beast.

Taehae, *a.* wild, savage, untamed; cruel.

Taematuu, *v. n.* to grieve.

Taeo, *a.* poisoned, as by fish, also drunk.

— *v. n.* to be in a poisoned or inebriated state.

Taepepa, *v. n.* to shake, or to be agitated.

Taere, *s.* the bottom of a canoe, the keel of a ship.

— *v. a.* to pull, or drag along.

— *adv.* slowly, loiteringly.

— *a.* lazy; drawling, applied to the voice.

Taerea, *s.* the tying that joins a fish hook to the line.

— *adv.* as eita e tae rea, to go seldom; see *rea.*

Taerete, *v. n.* to swing about as the skin of one that had been very fat.

Taereereta, *s.* a term used by children in play.

Taerehape, *s.* a cocoanut having only a part of the kernel.

Taerepa, *s.* pain in the legs and joints after a long walk.

Taero. *a.* poisoned; also drunk; poisonous.

— *v. n.* to be poisoned; to be drunk.

Taetea, *s.* some ailment, sore, or disorder.

Taetata, *s.* disorder, ailment or sore.

Taetaeae, *s.* brethren.

Taetae, *s.* sharp thorns or prickles on the tail of fishes.

Taetaehaamoa, *s* a custom observed after the birth of a child.

Taetaehaamoa, *s.* some slight disorder.

Taetaevao, *s.* an inhabitant of the interior, a clown, one not accustomed to society.

— *a.* wild ; also clownish.

Taevao, *s.* an inhabitant of the interior; one not accustomed to society.

— *a.* clownish.

Tafa, *a.* sonorous, loud sounding.

Tafâ, *adv.* lazily, inertly.

Tafaafaa, *a.* irresolute, slack, unsteady, careless.

Tafafa, *a.* simple, easy to be imposed upon.

Tafai, *s.* a piece, or patch.

— *v. a.* to piece, patch, or mend a thing.

— *s.* the name of a legendary tale concerning *Tafao.*

Tafairei, *s.* a figure head of a ship or canoe.

Tafara, *s.* a species of breadfruit.

— *v. n.* to use the fara fruit for ripening the banana.

Tafarau, *v. a.* to put a boat or a canoe under the shelter of house, called *farau.*

Tafare, *s.* a hollow, or cave like place in a rock.

— *s.* a hollow wave of the sea.

Tafarefare, *v. n.* to be in hollows, as the waves.

Tafati, *s.* a piece of wood with an elbow ; the hollow part of a piece of wood.

Tafaarere, *a.* deep, unfathomable.

Tafati, *a.* having the form of a pocket knife when opened, as an elbow, tipi tafati.

Tafatu, *s.* the name of a species of taro.

Tafeta, *s* the name of a certain prayer.

— *s.* a spot or stain.

Tafetafeta, *a.* stained, discoloured ; variegated, or having spots of divers colours.

Tafiri, *s.* the name of a running plaut used medicinally by the tahitians.

— *s.* a person. or thing, that causes entanglement and perplexity.

— *v. n.* to entangle, or obstruct.

Taha, *s.* a cocoanut bottle.

— *s.* a side ; see *pae.*

Tahaa, *a.* naked, without clothes or covering.

Tahaaoao, *s.* the side under the arm.

Tahaatau, *s.* the right side of a person.

Tahaaui, *s.* the left side.

Tahahu, *s* a skimmer or ladle.

— *v. a.* to skim, bale, or lade.

Tahaia, *s* warlike, valiant.

Tahamaui. *s.* the left side ; see *tahaaui.*

Tahana, *v. a.* to warm again ; to recook

Tahanahana, *v. a.* to warm food repeatedly.

Tahamare, *v. a.* to dip, bathe, or plunge.

— *v. n.* to be surfeited.

Tahamiti, *s.* a cocoanut sauce bottle.

Tahatafiaoaa, *v. n.* to be of an ill appearance.

Tahaote, *s.* a cocoanut the inside of which has been fermented to use as sauce.

Taharae, *a.* having the hair fallen off the forehead.

Taharafaatau, *s.* a lazy, worthless fellow.

Taharaino, *s.* an useless fellow.

Taharahara, *v. a.* to befoul, daub or smear.

— *s.* a name for the penis.

Taharua, *s.* one who can use both hands.

Taharuharu, *v. n.* to yield; see *taaru.*

Tahataa, *s.* the kernel when separated from the shell.

Tahataha, *v. n.* to be declining, as the sun in the afternoon.

— *v. n.* to be wandering, as the eye on account of some evil that is felt, or designed.

Tahatahaoto, *s.* a crooked piece of wood on the top of the mast of some native canoes.

Tahatai, *s.* the beach, or sea shore.

Tahatuara, *s.* an expression of contempt.

Tahau, *v. a.* to bleach native cloth in the morning dew.

Tahauhau, *v. a.* to bleach repeatedly in the dew.

Tahavahava, *v. n.* to befoul.

Tahe, *v. n.* to run, as any liquid; to melt.

— *v. a.* (*tauhae*) to steal; see *eia.*

Taheavai, *s.* the under part of a branch.

Tahee, *v. n.* to be purging; see *faatahee*, to purge.

Tahefa, *v. n.* to be squinting, or looking obliquely.

— *a.* slow, applied to the voice, *e reo tahefa* a slow, or drawling voice.

— *adv.* loiteringly, as in walking.

— *s.* a method of fishing.

Tahei, *s.* a handkerchief, or an upper garment.

— *v. a.* to cast a net for fish.

Taheimanu, *s.* a fowler; or bird catcher.

Tahema, *s.* an ornamental piece of cloth, worn by dancers; a handkerchief or neckcloth.

Tahemo, *v. a.* to untie, as a knot.

— *v. n.* to disannul, or make void an agreement; to break a covenant.

Tahemohemo, *v. a.* to untie, or undo repeatedly.

Tahere, *s.* a sort of girdle used by the islanders.

— *v. a.* to make use of a *here* or snare.

Taheta, *s.* the effect of mouldiness; see *tafeta.*

Tahetahe, *v. n.* to bleed; to run as any liquid; to be oozing or running without ceasing.

Tahetaheavai, *s.* the pith or heart of a tree.

— *s.* the under part of a branch.

— *s.* little rivulets or streams.

Tahetatufà, *s.* acrid streams running among the coral when the sea is low, and the sun is hot.

Tahi, *a.* one in counting; see *atahi, etahi.*

— *adv.* once, as haere tahi, go at once.

— *conj.* as if, as; tahi mea, as if it were.

Tahifa, *s.* a small double canoe.
Tahinu, *v. a.* to anoint with oil.
Tahiora, *s.* a call for mercy.
Tahipotia. *s.* a word of intreaty, a call for mercy.
Tahiri, *s.* a fan.
— *v. a.* to fan, to shake a fly-flap.
— *v. n.* to wag the tail, as a dog.
— *v. a.* to sweep by striking the ground or the floor of a house with a sort of broom.
Tahirihiri, *v. a.* to fan repeatedly.
— *v. n.* to wag the tail repeatedly, as a dog.
Tahirihiriarahu, *v. a.* to fan the embers; a figurative expression for calling to memory.
Tahiripaoa, *v. a.* to brush and wet a dry stone in the side of a brook, in order to get fry.
Tahiripaea, *v. n.* to clear a place, in order to play some game, such as the opere raa.
Tahiriraarehuahi, *s.* the name of an idolatrous feast and ceremony.
Tahitahi, *v. a.* to brush by striking with the hand.
— *v. a.* to weed, to wipe off, make ready, make room.
— *v. a.* to divide or separate; to disown, applied to relatives.
— *s.* an officer in public assemblies, to see that room is made, distances kept, &c.
Tahitahimata. *s.* the plumpness of the face by good feeding.
Tahitahimuriavai, *s.* the first running of the water in a channel after the dry season.
Tahitahipuaverevere, *s.* the same as tahitahimuriavai.
Tahitahiroupoonui, *s.* vigilance, activity, like that of the large headed ro or ant.
Tahitapu, *s.* a term relative to human sacrifices; see *tapu.*
Tahiti, *s.* the name of the largest island in the Georgian groupe, discovered by Wallis, in 1767.
— *v. a.* to transplant; to remove a thing from its original place.
Tahitia, *s.* a *word* of intreaty, asking mercy, pity, compassion.
— *v. a.* to shew or exercise mercy, &c.
Tahitifaaea, *s.* an unsteady roving person.
Tahitireoaero, *s.* Tahiti's twisting tongue.
Tahito, *a.* old, decayed—mai tahito mai, of old, or from ancient times.
— *adv.* formerly, anciently.
— *v. a.* to deride, mock, or laugh at a thing.
Tahitohito, *v. a.* to deride, or mock repeatedly.
— *s.* derision, mockery, scorn.
Tahoa, *s.* the head ache; see *hoa* and *uruhoa.*
— *v. n.* to be teazed, vexed, annoyed.
— *a.* vexatious, tiresome, annoying.
Tahoni, *v. n.* to retreat, (a war term).
— *v. a.* to come unawares to a deep place.
— *a.* steep, approaching to a perpendicular.
Tahono, *v. a.* to join pieces to-

gether; to lengthen, by joining another piece.

Tahoo, *s.* a recompense, reward, revenge.

— *v. a.* to recompense, to retaliate.

Tahopu, *v. n.* to fall at one's feet as a suppliant.

Tahora, *s.* a bank, such as by the side of a river.

Tahoro, *s.* a swing used by children.

— *s.* a game of children where they run round and round till giddy.

— *v. n.* to waddle, or walk unseemly.

— *v. a.* to swallow, without mastication, soft food, such as the Tahitian *popoi.*

Tahu, *v. a.* to kindle a fire.

— *v. a.* to use certain ceremonies of sorcery or conjuration; to act as a sorcerer.

Tahua, *s.* the floor of a house; the deck of a ship or boat.

— *s.* (*tahunga, tahuna*) an artificer, a mechanic.

— *v. n.* to deliberate, settle by consultation.

Tahuaati, *s.* a place chosen for fighting.

— *s.* a complete priest or artificer.

Tahuamana, *s.* one skilled in the art he professes.

Tahuamatarau, *s.* an artificer that follows what every one says, and spoils all.

Tahuaoti, *s.* a confined place for fighting.

Tahuaparare, *s.* an open place for a battle.

Tahuapure, *s.* a priest officiating at the marae.

Tahuaraamaa, *s.* an arrangement about food.

Tahuarauava, *s.* a principal part of the marae.

Tahuararaa, *v. a.* to arrange well beforehand.

Tahuhu, *s* the ridge pole of a native house.

— *s.* a certain portion of the warriors in a battle.

Tahuhua, *s.* the summit of the mountains.

Tahuinia, *s.* the windward side of an island.

Tahuna, *v. a.* to hide or conceal; see *huna.*

Tahuraa, *s.* the kindling of fire.

— *s.* enchantment; the art of the sorcerer.

Tahurahura, *v. a.* to do a thing slightly.

Tahurere, *v. a.* to pray to a deceased friend to inflict injury upon an enemy.

Tahuri, *v. n.* to turn over, as a canoe; see *huri.*

Tahuriaroa, *v. a* to be acting friendly in time of peace; but if war happen, to become an enemy.

— *v. n.* to be estranged from a person with whom formerly there was friendship.

Tahurihuri, *v. n.* to be repeatedly turning from side to side; to toss, as a ship at sea.

Tahutahu, *s* a sorcerer, or conjurer; see *tahu.*

Tahutu, *v. n.* to be in a tumult or disorder.

— *v. n.* to be blundering over any thing.

—*adv.* blunderingly, heedlessly.

Tahutumu, *s.* the name of a certain feast, prayer, and ceremonies.

—*s*. a name given to a scolding woman.

Tai, *s*. (*hai*, *taki*, *taha*,) the sea, salt, salt water.

— *s*. (*tungi*, Malay, *tangis*,) weeping, sorrow, a cry.

— *v. n.* to weep, cry, grieve, to be sorrowful.

— *v. n.* to sound as an instrument; see *oto*.

— *prep*. by, as taipiti, taitoru, by two, three, &c.

Taia, *s*. grief, sorrow, heaviness.

— *v. n.* to be grieving, sorrowing.

Tai'a, *s*. a fisherman.

Tai'a, *v. a.* to fish by angling or otherwise.

Taia, *v. a.* to smooth a garment or piece of cloth; to iron clothes.

Tâia, *v. n.* to swoon, or faint; see *hautaua*.

— *v. n.* to die, from the supposed effect of eating without giving to the neighbours..

— *v. n.* to be alarmed.

Taiaia, *v. n.* to weep for the *aia* or lost land, food, &c.

— *v. n.* to be extirpated as in war; consumed, or cleared off entirely.

Taiaha, *a*. heavy, weighty.

Taiao, *s*. the dawn or daybreak; see *aahiata*.

Taiapuu, *s*. one who avenges, or makes good a failure in wrestling, &c.

— *v. a.* to make good a failure in wrestling, &c.

Taiara, *s*. a road, tract, or way.

— *s*. the road or walk of a turtle, by observing of which he may be caught.

Taiarapaoa, *s*. a road in the rocks; sea *paoa*.

Taiariu, *s*. the part of a canoe where it is baled out.

Taiaro, *s*. the space between the shore and the coral reef; any thing that is easy of access.

Taiaru, *s*. a noisy talker, whose voice resembles the roaring of the sea.

Taiata, *s*. a vile, wicked, or profane person.

— *a*. lewd, wicked, profane.

Taiatâ, *a*. hard, difficult to accomplish; see *ata*.

Taiatea, *s*. a wide open sea.

— *a*. ill savoured.

Taiato, *s*, a person noted for debauchery.

Taiau, *s*. the name of a god, the father of Oro.

Taiere, *v. a.* to put in a crack, or hole in the ground, the cuttings of yam or ava, until they begin to grow.

Taero, *s*. a sauce made of scraped cocoanut, salt water, and shrimps; see *mitiero*.

Taifa, *v. n.* to be expended, or dying away, as the wind.

Taifaaaro, *s*. the wide sea, where the sight of all land is lost.

Taifaratato, *a*. abundant, plentiful, as provisions.

Taifee, *s*. the spittle of the *fee* or cuttle fish.

Taihaa, *s*. condolence; see *atahua*.

— *v. n.* to condole, or lament with another.

Taiharato, *s*. itchiness caused by salt water.

Taiharato, *s*. a calm place without a current; also acrid salt water among the reefs.

Taihauriuri, *s.* the black, deep, or bottomless sea.
Taihei, *v. n.* to be itching from salt water.
Taiho, *v. a.* to let a thing down from a high place.
Taihitoa, *v. a.* to take the whale.
— *s.* a startling voice.
Taihitumu, *v. a.* to overthrow, to rase from the foundation; see *ihitumu.*
Taihoe, *a.* one, or by one at a time.
Taihoro, *v. n.* to shift about, or change, as the roaring of the sea on the reefs.
Taihorahora, *s.* the sea, when the waves begin to swell.
Taihótu, *s.* a high, towering sea.
Taii, *a.* hard, solid, of good age, as timber.
— *a.* cunning, knowing, hard to deal with.
— *s.* the steam of perspiration.
Taii, *v. n.* to fill up, as rain in the mountains.
Taiifara, *a.* hard, as the fara or pandanus tree.
Taiimaha, *a.* heavy, ponderous; see *teiaha.*
Taiimairoto, *v. a.* to gather, heap up.
Taiimaivaho, *v. a.* to squander, throw away.
Taimamu, *v. n.* to be still, not stirring, as if dead.
Taimamau, *s.* irreconcileable anger.
Taimatuu. *v. a.* to make one sorrowful.
Taimara, *s.* the sea, when sacred on account of some chief.
Taimatau, *v. n.* to grieve on account of some disaster.
Taimaue, *s.* the wind about S. W.
Taimootua, *a.* having grand children.
Tainee, *v. n.* to be shifting, as the wind and sea.
— *v. n.* to crawl, creep.
Taini, *s.* the lower part of the belly.
Tainoa, *s*, the name of a creeping plant.
— *a.* red, or reddish in colour.
Taio, *s.* a friend; see *hoa* and *taua.*
— *v. a.* to count, to read; see *tatau.*
Taioeoe, *s.* the noise made by young children.
Taiotua, *s.* the sea outside the reef.
Taipe, *s.* a decrepit old person.
Taipito, *s.* the name of a feast and ceremony.
Taipoi, *v. n.* to be covered, as a batch of food in the native oven.
Taipu, *v. a.* to lade or bale with an *ipu* or cup.
Taipu, *v. n.* to be heavy in one's limbs, as an infirm person.
Taira, *s.* a rope or cord; see *taura.*
Tairahiri, *s.* the name of a fish.
Taire, *s.* the name of a fish; see *tauo.*
Tairi, *v. a.* to strike, to hit.
Tairifa, *s.* the name of a poisonous fish.
Tairiri, *v. a.* to shake and throw, as a fisherman does his fishing line.
— *v. n.* to shew opposition, dislike, or contempt of some things said or done, by shaking the head.

Tairiorio, *v. n.* to cry, or make a noise, as it was supposed the souls of young infants did.
Tairitea, *s.* a player in the Tahitian heiva, &c
Tairitia, *s.* a sudden stroke, commonly applied to sudden death.
Tairitu, *s.* the sudden stroke of death.
Tairo, *v. a.* to mark, point out, select.
— *a.* marked, selected.
Tairoiro, *s.* a soothsayer, or conjuror.
— *s.* revenge, malice, spite, retaliation.
— *v. a.* to take revenge, or retaliate.
— *v. a.* to foretell, as a prophet, or soothsayer.
Tairoroo, *s.* a certain prayer in the marae.
Tairoto, *s.* the sea in a lagoon.
Tairupo, *s.* a courageous cock, that will continue fighting; *fig.* a brave warrior.
Taita, *v. n.* to be displeased; to be stiff, or inflated with anger.
— *intj.* an exclamation used by players.
Taitapu, *s.* the order of restriction; see *tapu.*
Taitahi, *a.* one, any one, some one.
— *prep.* one by one, or by one.
Taitai, *a.* salt, saltish, brackish; also bitter.
— *v. a.* to fetch or bring something from another place.
Taitaie, *v. n.* to give place, make room by moving.
Taitaiaho, *s.* one who perseveres on his journey regardless of difficulties.
Taitea, *s.* the shallows near the shore where the sea is not dark.
Taivaha, *s.* a sea that exists in a man's mouth, or imagination.
Taivahatete, *s.* a sea that ceases not to break and roar.
Taiva, *v. n.* to desert, forsake.
— *a.* faithless, deserting, inconstant.
Taivaiva, *s.* the name of a poisonous fish.
Taivava, *s.* a wave that breaks at one corner, and then runs along to the opposite side.
Taivavao, *s.* a sea that is swelling and breaking on the reef, but between the reef and shore, it is calm and the rocks are uncovered.
Tama, *s* the name of a Tahitian god.
— *s.* a child, male or female.
Tamâ, *v. a.* to wash, cleanse, purify.
Tama'a, *s.* (*kamaa,*) shoes, sandals, clogs.
— *v. a.* to take food for a journey; see *maa.*
Tamahaea. *s.* a person of a roving disposition.
— *s.* a family that is disunited.
Tamahana, *v. a.* to soothe, comfort, encourage.
— *s.* one who comforts another.
Tamahanahana, *v. a.* to warm and comfort a person repeatedly.
Tamahere, *s.* a beloved child.
— *s.* a nurse that takes good care of children.
Tamahine, *s.* a daughter, or female *tama.*

Tamahu, *s.* the name of a warrior in time of war.
Tamai, *s.* war, dispute, quarrel, contention.
— *v. a.* to contend, quarrel, dispute, fight.
Tamaiti, *s.* a son; a little *tama.*
Tamaitiiti, *s.* a little son.
Tamamai, *v. a.* to war, quarrel. (*plural.*)
Tamanava, *s.* a wound near the navel.
— *a.* stunted in growth.
— *v. n.* to be heavy with sleep.
Tamanu, *s.* the name of a large timber tree, (the *Callophyllum*, see *ati.*
Tamanufarii, *s.* the name of a medicinal plant.
Tamaomao, *s.* the name of a species of grass.
Tamarii, *s.* (*tamariki*) children.
Tamariirii. *s.* little children.
Tamaroa, *s.* a boy, a male.
Tamaru, *s.* to shade, or shadow.
Tamarû, *v. a.* to chew the cud, &c.
Tamata, *v. a.* to try, to begin a thing.
— *v. a.* to taste a thing.
Tamau, *s.* tinder, on which to catch sparks of fire.
— *v. a.* to take hold, persevere.
— *v. n.* to keep in memory.
— *adv.* perseveringly, constantly.
Tamaumau, *v. a.* to hold, continue to hold.
— *v. n.* to persevere in talking, retaining in memory, &c.
Tamauo, *v. n.* to keep burning, as a firebrand for the night.
Tamene, *v. n.* to compress a thing to reduce its bulk.
Tamino, *v. n.* to turn, or go in a circle.
Taminomino, *s.* pain in the bowels; the colic.
Tamore, *s.* a medicinal plant, a sort of wild mint
Tamôu, *s.* a strainer, made of the mou grass
— *v. a.* to strain pia, cocoanut, &c.
Tamua, *s.* the first row of fruit in a plantain bunch.
Tamui, *s.* a key to a lock; see *taviri.*
— *v. a.* to lock, or turn a key.
— *v. a.* to twist, or bind leaves together for fishing.
Tamumu, *s.* a din, noise
— *v. n* to make a din or noise; to congregate.
— *s.* tokens of puberty.
Tamuri, *s.* the name of a Tahitian god.
— *s.* the name of a plant.
Tamuta, (Engl. *carpenter*) a carpenter.
Tamute, *v. a.* to cut short.
Tamutemute, *v. a.* to shorten repeatedly.
— *a* undetermined.
Tana, *s* the name of a red fish.
—*pron.* his, hers, its, pronounced short.
Ta'na, *pron.* contracted of *prep. ta* and *ana*; his, hers, its, of things where *a* and *na* are used, otherwise it would be *to'na.*
Tanai, *s.* a species of the root and vine called *hoi.*
— *a.* confined, straitened.
— *v. n.* to be confined, or straitened.
— *adv.* roundly, plumply.
Tane, *s* the name of one of the principal Tahitian gods.

Tane, *s.* the male of mankind.
— *s.* a husband; see *vahine.*
— *s.* a disorder of the skin.
Taneenee, *a.* great, abundant.
— *v. n.* to go carefully.
Tanemao, *s.* a cutaneous disease.
Taniau, *v. a.* to send to different persons a piece of *niau* or cocoanut leaf, as a summons to attend a meeting, or some work of the chief.
Tanina, *v. a.* to cover, or fill up a hole or pit; to fill up mould or earth.
Tanini, *s.* the opening or crack in a cocoanut shell.
Taninito, *v. n.* to go round and round.
Tanitea, *s.* a disease of the skin.
Tano, *v. a.* to aim or direct, as in pointing a gun at an object; *fig.* to direct the mind to an object.
Tanoho, *s.* a division of an army set in array.
— *v. a.* to set in array, (a war term).
Tanohunohu, *v. n.* to be lingering behind, so as to be overtaken, when defeated.
Tanoo, *s.* a steersman in a boat or canoe; *fig.* one that directs the affairs of government.
— *v. a.* to steer, to direct the course of a vessel.
Tanotano, *a.* fair, delicate.
Tanu, *v. a.* to plant herbs, trees, &c.
— *v. n.* to bury a man, or any thing else.
Tanuai, *s.* a cultivator of the ground.
Tanuinui, *v. a.* to increase a thing, to enlarge.
Tanuna, *v. a.* to set on fire, as rubbish.
— *v. a.* to lay waste the country in time of war.
— *s.* the name of an apparatus used to catch the fish called *vete.*
— *v. a.* to cover or overtop.
Tanutanu, *s.* a certain mode of fishing.
Tanuu, *v. n.* to slide, or go towards one side.
— *v. a.* to procure or form a *nuu*, or fleet.
Tanuunuu, *v. n.* to slide, repeatedly.
— *v. a.* to encamp leisurely from place to place.
Tao, *s.* a spear used in war.
— *s.* a stick carried on the shoulder, with a bundle on each end.
— *s.* a cleft in a rock or in a tree.
— *s.* the leaves and stones with which the inside of a pig is stuffed, when baked in the native oven.
— *a.* baked, boiled, cooked.
— *s.* (*takao, tekao*) a word, speech, or saying.
— *v. n.* (*takao*) to speak; see *parau.*
— *v. a.* to bid, command, address.
Tâô, *s.* a species of breadfruit.
Taoa, *s.* property, goods of any sort.
— *s.* the place under the bend of the knee.
— *s.* a fissure, a hollow in a rock.
— *v. n.* to fall head foremost.

Taoae, *s.* a play term, a large stone in the timo raa.

Taoahi, *v. a.* to bake hastily in the native oven.

Taoaoa. *adv.* lightly, sparingly; as, amu taoaoa, to eat sparingly.

Taoau, *s.* a stick or seat, with which to grate cocoanuts.

Taoha, *v. a.* to bend down, as a fruitful branch.

Taohe, *v. a.* to make use of an ohe, or bamboo, for water, or other purposes.

Taohaa, *s.* property, goods.

Taohi, *s.* a man that guides a fishing canoe at night, having a torch.

Taohia, *passive* of *tao*; bidden, spoken.

Taoi, *v. a.* to turn aside a thing, as the head of a canoe in steering; see *tioi.*

Taomatotuatua. *s.* the hollows of craggy rocks.

Taona, *v. imp.* imprecating evil to or on a person, the opposite of *ia ora na.*

Taoo, *s.* a chasm, or crack in the earth, or a rock; *fig.* a rupture in war time.

— *v. n.* to be cracked or divided.

Taooto, *v. n.* to sleep, as two persons; to sleep repeatedly, or excessively.

Taopaopa, *v. n.* to roll, or turn from side to side, as a ship at sea, see *tiopaopa.*

Taora, *v. a.* to throw a stone or other thing.

— *v. n.* to reflect, or make censuring remarks on a person.

Taoranono. *s.* an intrigue, signified by throwing *nono* apples; see *nono.*

Taoraora, *s.* the name of a method of fishing.

Taore. *v. n.* to be without protection; a war term.

Tauro, *s.* a long string of cocoanuts tied together.

— *v. a.* to string, or put together, a number of things.

— *s.* a sort of streamer, or ornament.

— *s.* a row or chain of small islands.

Taorooro, *v. n.* to move, make a noise; rumble; applied to the bowels, and to a cask with some liquid in it, when moved.

Taota, *v. a.* to taste a thing; see *tamata.*

— *s.* the name of a mess of food, made of cocoanut and *pia*; se *pia.*

Taotao, *s.* a piece of carved work in a canoe.

— *a.* great, extreme; applied to darkness, as pouri taotao, extreme darkness.

Taotaofaa, *v. n.* to be decreased, as work that is nearly finished.

Taotaohaa, *v. n.* the same as taotaofaa.

Taotaota, *v. n.* to try, or taste repeatedly.

Taotii, *s.* a sorcerer.

Taoto. *v. n.* to sleep, see *moe,*

— *v. n.* to lie down.

— *v. n.* to be cohabiting as man and wife.

Taoto, *s.* a dream; see *moemoe.*

Taotoiuiu, *v. n.* to sleep very soundly.

Taotohauti, *s.* a restless sleep.

Taotonenene, *v. n.* to sleep sweetly.

Taotooto. *v. n.* to have frequent dreams.
— *v. n.* to waylay, lie in ambush.
Taotoatoa, *v. n.* to be mad, to dream; also to be waylaid.
Taotorereio, *v. n.* to have the night mare.
Taouu, *v. a.* to bake the breadfruit whole with the skin on.
Taova. *s.* a crack or fissure; see *taoa.*
Taovavahi, *v. a.* to bake breadfruit having first split it.
Tapa, *s.* the groin.
Tàpâ, *s.* the name of a mode of fishing.
— *v. a.* to bake food over again; see *tahana.*
Tapae, *s.* a basket for catching small fish, to be used as a bait.
— *v. n.* to land; to call or touch at a place, as a traveller on his journey.
Tapahea, *a.* careless, inefficient.
Tapahi, *s.* a cleaver with which to split breadfruit.
— *s.* the diarrhoea, or flux.
— *v. n.* to split, or divide breadfruit, taro, &c.
Tapahipahi, *v. a.* to split, or cleave repeatedly.
— *a.* without energy, applied to a speech.
— *s.* a bloody flux; the flow of the menses.
Tapahipu, *v. a.* to cleave in the midst.
Tapahitutii, *adv.* confusedly; as when many stand together.
Tapahiuti, *adv.* confusedly, applied to speaking.
Tapaie, *v. n.* to wrap up food in plantain stalks.
Tapaihea, *a.* squalid, dirty, filthy.
Tapairu, *s.* a young woman that lives delicately.
— *s.* a young woman that is an attendant on a chief woman.
Tapanehi, *s.* a transient visitor, or stranger.
— *a.* oblique, sloping, gone aside.
— *v. n.* to slide; to go on all fours, as a child, or a decrepit person.
Tapanihi, *a.* sluggish, careless, inattentive.
— *adv.* carelessly, slovenly; inattentively.
— *a.* slight, as a woman, also scanty, applied to knowledge.
Tapao, *s.* a sign, mark; a figure.
— *v. a.* to mark, set a sign; to select or choose; to notice.
Tapaoo, *v. a.* to make up in a hurry; to pack up things untidily.
Tapaopao, *v. a.* to mark repeatedly.
Tapaopao, *v. a.* to notice for revenge, or retaliation; see *tipaopao.*
Tapapa, *v. a.* to pile up, as stones or boards.
— *v. a.* to fetch, or to send for a person.
Tapape, *v. a.* to water, to use water in any way.
— *v. a.* to make smooth; see *tavai.*
— *s.* a razor strap, used after a hone.
Tapara, *v. a.* to manure a piece of land; see *para.*
— *s.* the fruit of the pandanus,

used for the purpose of making the banana fruit mellow and soft, by burying them together in the ground

— *v. a.* to use the tapara for ripening the banana.

Taparaaua, *s.* any thing used for hardening and finishing a native cup; see *aua.*

Taparahi, *v. a.* to beat, strike, use violence towards a person, or any living thing; also to kill, murder.

— *s.* the person that uses violence, or kills another.

Taparamati, *v. a.* to besmear with the *mati*

Taparau, *s* formerly used for a pen to write with.

— *s.* a writer, or secretary; see *papai.*

— *s.* the name of a certain game of children, making marks in the sand, &c.

— *v. n* to converse or talk together.

Tapare, *s* a sign, a signal by a motion of the head or of the hand.

— *v. a.* to make a sign, to beckon with the hand, or, by waving a piece of cloth, to invite a person to approach.

Tapare, *v. a.* to make a shade; to cover from the light.

Taparu, *s.* flattery, insinuating persuasion; also the flatterer, or one that persuades.

— *v. a.* to flatter another; to use soft persuasion, but commonly used in a bad sense.

Taparini, *s.* the rage of jealousy.

Taparuuri, *v. n.* to fawn as a dog.

Taparuru, *s.* ungovernable anger, or rage.

Tapatai, *a* fearless of wind and sea, applied to a fisherman.

Tapatapahi, *s* a bloody flux; also the menses.

Tapatapahaha, —*s.* magnitude, great bulk.

Tapatapahitoere, *s.* the name of a children's play.

Tapatapariri, *s.* great rage or anger.

Tapataparuru, *v. n.* to be in a rage, highly displeased.

Tapatoa, *s* a strong southerly wind; *fig.* the impetuosity of victors in war, when carrying all before them.

Tapau, *s.* gum, pitch, rosin; *fig.* obstinacy

— *s* lead, or pewter, any metal that will melt.

Tapàu, *s.* a platted piece of cocoanut leaves used by the priests to direct their prayers, like the rosary of the Roman Catholics.

Tape, *s* a fragment, as of cloth, a piece less than a fathom in measuring.

— *s* a detached part of an army, placed to cover the retreat of the women, children, &c.

Tapê, *v. a.* to use means of ripening fruit, bananas, &c.

Tapea, *s* a ring, buckle; any band, or tying.

Tapea, *v. a.* to tie or bind, also to keep, detain.

Tapeanuanua, *s.* a portion of a rainbow.

Tapearo, *s* those that urge on the rear of an army.

Tapemoana, *s* the edge of the deep water.

Tapena, *s* a thing devoted to the gods, such as a pig,

when a piece of sinnet was tied in the ear.
— *v. a.* to prepare ominous hogs, in order to tell the end of an approaching war.
— *s.* (Engl. *captain*,) the captain of a ship.
Tapepe, *v. a.* to repair a thing; to join or add articles of property together.
— *v. n.* to be soliciting repeatedly for a thing.
— *v. a.* to patch or piece a sail, &c.
— *v. n.* to roll one over another, as the waves of the sea.
Tapepepepe, *v. a.* to repair repeatedly.
Tapere, *s.* a thing that may be easily untied.
— *a.* overhanging, or stretching out, as a rock, or the earth, when a hole is wide below, and narrow above.
Tapetape, *v. n.* to be declining, as the sun in the afternoon.
— *v. a.* to taste the scraped hoi; see *hoi.*
— *s.* the boundary of the deep and shallow places in the sea; see *tapemoana.*
Tapetepete, *a.* small, slight.
— *adv.* lightly, scantily.
Tapi, *v. a.* to try, attempt, endeavour; to press after an object.
Tapiatâ, *a.* hard, difficult to obtain.
Tapihoo, *v. a.* to make an exchange; see *hoo.*
Tapii, *s.* the name of a Tahitian god.
— *s.* the circle sometimes seen about the moon.
— *v. n.* to cling over, or upon a thing.
Tapio, *s.* the name of a fish.
Tapiipii, *v. a.* to put up the end of a rope.
Tapipi, *s.* a person that looks out for his own share.
— *v. a.* to serve one's self in the first place.
Tapineva, *v. n.* to be in a hopeless condition, as one on a piece of rock surrounded by the deep sea.
Tapiri, *v. a.* to unite, or join things together.
Tapirihuahua, *v. a.* to join together many fragments.
Tapiriahuruhuru, *v. a.* to join things clumsily.
Tapiripapanoa, *v. a.* to join two flat edges together.
Tapirihune, *v. a.* to join things leaving the butts under.
Tapiriomaο, *v. a.* to join by raising an angular edge on one plank, and sinking the angle on the other.
Tapitapi. *v. n.* to be in trouble, perplexed, not knowing what to do.
Tapoa, *s.* the first person destroyed by a sorcerer; also the first that a warrior killed in battle.
Tapoi, *s.* the cover of any thing.
— *v. a.* to cover, to hide, or conceal.
Tapoipoi, *v. a.* to cover repeatedly, to hide or conceal repeatedly.
Tapoapoamuriavaa, *s.* the small fry of fish that at a particular season come to the rivers.
Tapono, *s.* a knot, or tying.
— *v. a.* to knot, to tie together in knots.

Tapono, *s.* the shoulder; see *paufifi.*
— *s.* a subdivision of an army.
Taponopono, *v. a.* to knot; or tie many knots.
Taporo, *s.* the first row in a bunch of plantains.
— *s.* the lime tree, and its fruit.
Tapotu, *s.* a blow given with a club.
— *v. a.* to give a blow with a club or other weapon.
Tapotu, *v. n.* to roll in quick succession, one over another, as the waves of the sea.
Tapu, *s.* a restriction; the word is obsolete in Tahiti, though much used in some islands.
— *a.* sacred, devoted, but this sense is nearly obsolete in Tahiti, although retained in other dialects.
— *s.* an oath or a certain solemn engagement to perform, or not to perform certain things. This is called *parau mate tapu.*
— *v. a.* to bind one's self, or another person, with an oath to do, or not to do a thing; to adjure.
— *s.* a sacrifice to the god Oro, commonly a man killed for the purpose, but this tapu, or taputapu, was generally called ia or fish.
Tapû, *v. a.* to chop, or cut down.
— *s.* a piece that is cut off.
Tapuae, *s.* a footstep.
Tapuaehii, *s.* a person that was employed to kill a man for a sacrifice.
Tapuaehii, *s.* the foot that steps from its proper track to produce mischief.
Tapuaepiipii, *s.* a person that travelled about to produce mischief repeatedly.
Tapuahi, *s.* a place where food is usually cooked.
Tapuata, *s.* the name of a sacred house for the use of priests; also a prayer.
Tapupu, *v. a.* to chop or cut repeatedly.
Tapufaaea, *v. n.* to halt, or rest awhile.
Tapufaaite, *s.* a human sacrifice publicly presented to the god Oro.
— *v. a.* to take leave of the gods in departing from the marae.
Tapuni, *v. n.* to hide or conceal one's self.
Tapuohue, *v. a.* to forsake a thing on account of not receiving payment.
Tapunu, *v. a.* to make use of a spoon; see *punu.*
Taputehu, *v. a.* to consecrate a place.
Tapuiu, *v. a.* to moisten, to macerate.
— *v. a.* to use any thing in taking hold of a hot iron.
Tapurui, *s.* property given to the gods on account of a person's illness.
Tapuruoiri, *adv.* vigorously.
Tapuparahi, *v. n.* to halt and rest; see *tapufaaea.*
Tapure, *v. n.* to cause a thing to be spotted.
Tapureahuruhuru, *s.* the name of a bird with black and white spots or streaks.
— *s.* the name of a disorder.
— *a.* variegated, as the fish called ahuruhuru.
Tapurehu, *s.* the name of an

idolatrous prayer, feast, and ceremony.

Taputapu, *s.* the custard apple, (*ammona triloba.*)

Taputapuatea, *s.* the name of a public and principal heiva, where the human sacrifices were offered to Oro.

Taputea, *s.* the rainbow; see *anuanua.*

Taputô, *v. a.* to combat, to wrestle; see *to.*

Taputôraa, *s.* a wrestling time or place.

Taputua, *s.* a certain tatau, or skin mark.

Tara, *s.* the horn of any beast.

— *s.* a thorn, or sharp point; a cock's spur.

— *s.* the corner or end of a house.

— *s.* the name of an instrument used to catch eels.

— *s.* the name of a disorder.

— *s.* a certain mode of enchantment.

— *v. a.* to use enchantments.

— *v. a.* to untie; see *tatara.*

Tarâ, *s.* a remedy, some expedient used for deliverance, when in difficulty.

— *v. n.* to be recovered, and in a good condition, as the country in time of peace.

— *v. n.* to be saying a prayer, while the covering of a god was being untied.

Taraehara, *s.* an atonement for sin.

Taraena, *s.* a sort of unpalatable food.

Tarahao, *s.* a stranger of another country.

Tarahea, *a.* lean, meagre, as children; unsightly.

— *v. n.* to be in a forlorn condition.

— *v. n.* to be odious or obnoxious.

Tarahehea, *adv.* lightly, partially; fearfully.

Tarahiriri, *a.* the same as tarahea.

Tarahu, *s.* hire, wages; see *utua.*

— *v. a.* to hire or engage for a compensation.

Tarahuarau, *s.* the name of a sea bird; *fig.* a talkative noisy person.

Tarai, *v. a.* to chop, or adze a piece of timber.

Târai, *v. a.* to lay out a thing in the sun to dry; to expose things to the air and sun; see *tauai.*

Taraire, *v. n.* to be of long standing, applied to peace between hostile parties

Tarania, *s.* the fin on the back of a fish.

Taranihi, *s.* a fin, or thorn under the belly of a fish.

Taranihi, *adv.* superficially, slightly.

Tarao, *s.* the name of a fish, called also maraao, and mauriuri, when young, and afterwards, faeta, iaroa, and tonu.

Tarao, *v. a.* to put a rao, or roller under a canoe, boat, or tree.

— *v. a.* to use red feathers, and perform certain idolatrous ceremonies in time of war.

Taraore, *s.* the name of a plant; see *paeore,* a species of the fara or pandanus.

Tarapape, *a.* thin, diluted with water; see *taravai.*

— *v. n.* to be disheartened and become weak as water.

Tarape, *v. a.* to beckon, or make a sign for a person to approach.

Taraperape, *v. a.* to make signs repeatedly.

Tarapu, *v. a.* to stir or mix up ingredients.

Tarapurapu, *v. n.* to stir or mix up repeatedly.

Tarara, *s.* the name of a bird.

Tararaa. *s.* the name of a feast and ceremony.

Tarare, *v. a* to mix up as paste until it becomes soft; also to use means to promote ripeness.

— *s.* the matter used to promote ripeness.

Tararo, *s.* a person employed as a messenger between the sexes generally, but not always used in a bad sense; a pimp ,or bawd.

Tararo, *v. a.* to act as a pimp.

Taratane, *s.* a married woman.

Taratara, *a* prickly, thorny, ragged.

— *v. a.* to untie, disentangle; see *tatara.*

Taratarahuaa, *v. a.* to trace ancestry; see *aufau.*

Taratairamoa, *s.* the spurs of a cock.

Tarataratauaroha, *s.* the name of a medicinal plant.

Taratea, *s.* a person that has tke indications of age upon him.

Taratoa, *s.* the name of an idolatrous prayer.

— *s.* a house sacred to the gods, its consecration was called, pure taratoa.

Tarau,*s* the ends of a fishing net.

Taraurau, *v. a.* to scratch; see *raurau.*

Taraufau, *s.* the name of a certain preparation of fish in the time of heathenism.

Tarava, *s.* a streak, or stripe, a chasm in a rock.

— *v. n.* to lie horizontally; to be across a thing; see *faatarava.*

— *prep.* athwart, transverse; across.

Taravahine, *s.* a married man.

Taravai, *a.* liquid, diluted with water, thin as paste; see *tarapope.*

— *v. n.* to be discouraged by fear, the heart become weak as water.

Taravera, *s.* spots on the leaves of the fara.

Tare, s, phlegm.

Tareatea, *v. a.* to hide a thing.

Tarei, s. the only one remaining of a race.

— *v. n.* to be nearly all gone, applied to the fruit of a tree.

— *v. a.* te spread a net, in a certain method of fishing.

— *s.* the name of a fish.

Tarehu, *v. a.* to becloud, or cause an illusion of vision.

Tarehua, *v. n* to have the senses beclouded; to have a vision.

Tareirei, *v. n.* to stumble.

Tarepa, *v n.* to shake or flap, as a loose sail in the wind.

Tareparepa, *v. n.* to shake repeatedly, as a sail.

— *v. a.* to use a paddle or an oar in a slight manner.

Tarepau, *s.* a person that has gained or exhausted all the knowledge of his teacher.

Tarera, *s.* a large grown, but clumsy person.
Tarere, *s.* a swing used by children and others.
Tarereva, *s.* the hollow of an overhanging rock.
Tarerevaiore, *s.* emptiness of a vessel.
Tari. *s.* the stalk of fruit.
— *s.* a bunch of bananas, mountain plantains, &c.
— *s.* the clapper of a bell.
— *v. a.* to carry, or convey property.
Tarî, *v. a.* to hang or suspend; see *ri.*
Taria, *s.* (*taringa*, *talinga*, Malay, *talinga*,) the ear.
Tariaiore, *s.* a fungus like a mushroom.
Tariamaeo, *s.* an itching ear.
Tariamaopi, *s.* a shrivelled ear.
Tariaoopi, *s.* the same as tariamaopi.
Tariapuu, *s.* a thing that is a pet, or darling.
— *s.* a covetous person that is for grasping every thing for himself.
Tariaroo, *s.* a listening ear.
Tariaroroa, *s.* the same as tariaroo.
Tariaturi, *s.* a deaf ear; also the deaf.
Tariavava, *s.* an ear that hears indistinctly.
Tarihau, *s.* the populace, or lower rank of the people; see *arii*, *tafau*, *iatoa* and *raatira.*
Tarii, *s.* a sort of basket to catch fish; see *arairi.*
Tariirii, *v. a.* to undermine, or undo a thing.
Tariniho, *s.* the gums; see *niho.*
Tariopu, *s.* the tendons that unite the bowels.
Taripaa, *s.* the stalk of a cluster of cocoanuts, also the sheath of that stalk.
Taripaoo, *v. a.* to take away every thing within reach.
Tariparau, *s.* a talebearer.
— *s.* a drum; see *pahu.*
Taritari. *v. a.* to remove or carry goods repeatedly.
Taritoa, *s.* family, or personal gods.
— *s.* a certain amulet to protect a person from witchcraft, &c.
Tariu, *s.* the deep place at the bottom of a mountain; a ravine, or deeu narrow valley.
Taro, *s.* (*talo*, *tao*,) the root *arum esculentum*, of which there are many varieties.
Taroa, *v. a.* to lengthen a thing; see *faaroa.*
Taroi, *s.* a long heavy rain.
Taroria, *v. n.* to be twisted, as branches by the wind.
Tarotaro, *s.* a short prayer addressed to the gods.
— *v. n.* to be saying a short prayer to the gods.
— *s.* an introductory address to a god.
Taroto, *s.* a purgative medicine.
Tarou, *v. a.* to use a *rou* or crook in getting fruit from a tree.
Tarourou, *v. a.* to take hold repeatedly with a crook.
Taru, *s.* speech, address; a saying.
— *v. n.* to speak; see *tao* and *parau.*
Tarumau, *s.* a true saying.
Tarutaru, *v. n.* to converse, or speak repeatedly.
Tarue, *s.* appearance of rain.

Tarue, *adv* tardily; listlessly.

Taruerue, *adv.* to come leisurely, as a threatening storm.

— *a.* having indications of rain.

Tarui, *a.* black, as the sky, lowering.

Tarureva, *v. a* to fall behind, as a weak person travelling in company.

Taruri, *adv.* slightly, indistinctly, as faaroo taruri, to hear indistinctly.

Tata, *v. n.* to delay; applied to a journey.

—*v. a.* to strike, to beat.

Tatâ, *s.* a ladle or vessel to bale with.

— *v. a.* to lade; to bale a canoe, boat. &c.

Tataa, *v. n.* the dual of taa to be separate.

Tataahi, *v. a.* to tread under foot; see *taahi.*

Tatahi, *adv.* singly, one by one.

— *s.* the shore or beach; see *tahatai.*

— *v. a.* to clear away rubbish.

Tatahiata, *s.* the dawn of day; see *auhiata.*

Tatahuu, *s.* the cry of the *rupe* bird in the valley.

Tatai, *s.* the shore, the beach; see *tatahi.*

— *v. n.* to tack. (A sea term)

— *s.* the covering or matting, with which the ends of rafters in a Tahitian house are covered.

— *v. a.* to repair, as the thatch of a Tahitian house.

Tatâi, *v. a.* to expel, or cast out a demon.

— *v. n.* to rehearse, or recapitulate the particulars of an argument.

— *v. a.* to fasten a line along the rafters of a house; to draw a line.

Tataiore, *s.* a species of the *fee* or cuttle fish, which is said to stretch out its feelers when along the shores, and by that means to catch the rats, &c.

Tatamai, *v a* to war, fight, breed contention.

Tatanu, *s.* a gardener.

— *v. a.* to plant, as trees, &c

Tatao, *s.* the highest central part of a cocoanut tree.

Tataoa. *v. a.* to give property; also *faataoa.*

Tatara, *v. a* to untie, set free from entanglement; see *tatatara.*

— *s.* a species of breadfruit

Tatarahapa, *s.* change of mind, repentance.

— *v. n.* to repent, to be sorry for having done something.

Tatarahara, *s.* the same as tatarahapa, or repentance.

Tatarahea, *a.* of an ill look, meagre, or emaciated, as a sick person.

Tatarahiro, *v. a.* to unravel, untie; *fig.* to examine an affair thoroughly.

Tataraio, *v. n.* to be under the effects of sorcery.

Tataramoa, *s.* the name of a prickly shrub, having some resemblance to a thorn.

Tataraohu, *v. n.* to lean, or hang down, as withered branches; *fig.* to be defeated.

Tataraû, *a.* half baked, applied to food.

Tatari, *v. n.* to wait, to expect, to delay.

Tatariavea, *v. n.* to wait as in

watching the surf in order to land safely.
— *v. n.* to delay; to lag behind.
Tataripo, *v. n.* to be waiting, as on the point of death.
Tataripoi, *v. n.* to wait as a dying person; according to a notion of the Tahitians some wait their *poi*, or the night or day for dying.
Tataro, *v. n.* to be accustomed; see *taataro.*
Tataru, *v. a.* the dual of to speak; as *pararau.*
Tatatau, *s.* a person that marks the skin; also the operation of marking the skin.
Tatau, *s.* the marks or points on the human skin; not *tatoo,* as it has been called.
— *v. a.* to mark, or point on the skin.
— *s.* counting, numbering; see *taio.*
— *v. n.* to count, or number.
— *v. a.* to ask for, call out; to challenge.
Tatautau, *v. a.* to make use of the tautau, a method of fishing.
Tatauvavea, *v. n.* to wait till certain surges or waves have rolled over.
Tatea, *s.* the semen of animals.
Tati, *v. a.* to reject, resist, oppose.
— *v. a.* to taunt, insult.
Tatia, *s.* the name of a fish.
— *s.* a girdle; see *tatua.*
— *v. a.* to put on a girdle.
— *a.* abrupt.
Tatiapaura, *s.* a cartridge box.
Tatipi, *v. n.* to use a knife; see *tipi.*
Tatinana, *v. a.* to lay a foundation.
Tatiti, *v. a.* to point, or ornament a piece of native cloth with various figures.
Tatití, *s.* scorn, mockery, contempt.
Tatitia, *v. n.* to rise and fall as the waves of the sea.
Tatitohe, *v. a.* to use a pair of breeches or trowsers.
Tatoa, *s.* a species of eel.
— *adv.* wholly, entirely, not by parts.
Tatohe, *s.* a pair of breeches or trowsers.
Tatohi, *v. a.* to use a tohi, or chisel.
Tataino, *s.* a rebel, or treacherous person.
Tatou, *pron.* we, including the speaker, and the party addressed.
Tatua, *s.* a girdle; a cartridge box.
— *v. a.* to gird the loins.
Tatuaai. *s.* a girdle, made of pandanus leaves.
Tatuaovero, *s.* a pinching hunger.
Tatuatehea, *v. n.* to be worn with age.
Tatuatua, *s.* the state of being naked, when fighting.
Tatuavero, *s.* clothing for stormy weather.
Tatui. *v. a.* to strike through, as a dart
Taturi, *s.* the wax of the ear.
Taturituri, *v. n.* to pretend deafness repeatedly.
Tau. *s.* a season; see *anotau.*
— *s.* an anchor.
— *s.* a sunken rock under water.
— *v. a.* to invocate, to address in prayer.
— *v. n.* to perch, or light upon a branch, as a bird.

— *pron.* (pronounced short.) my, mine.

Tau, *poss. pron.* a contraction of *ta* and *na*, mine, spoken of food, &c ; see *a*, *ta*, and *na*.

Taua, *s.* a friend, companion ; see *hoa*, *tino*.

— *s.* (*kaui.*) the old word for war; see *tamai*.

Taua, *pron. dem.* that, or which, that was spoken or ûnderstood.

Tauâ, *s.* a coward, one without courage.

— *a.* cowardly.

Tauahara, *s.* a faithful friend.

Tauaitu, *s.* a friend of the aitu or god; a priest.

— *s.* prayer to a god.

Tauaave, *a.* slow, dilatory, hanging behind.

Tauaha, *inter. pron.* what, what is it?

Tauahi, *v. a.* to embrace; to caress.

Tauahiahi *v. a.* to embrace repeatedly; also to make much of a person.

Tauai, *v. a.* to spread out clothes, &c in the sun and air to dry; see *tauaiari*.

Tauama, *s.* a canoe with an outrigger.

Tauana, *s.* caves or holes in the rocks under water.

Tauanuanu, *s.* the cold season.

Tauaoa, *s.* the roots of the aoa tree, of which cloth is made.

Tauaparau, *v a* to tattle, repeat, or tell tales ; used as a proverb.

Tauarai, *s.* an interposer, *taua* and *arai*.

— *v. n.* to spread out things ; to expose to the sun and air.

Tauaraino, *s. dual*, two bad bridges upon a road.

Tauaro, *s.* the lower branches.

Tauaro, *s.* the fore part; the space between the reef and the shore.

Tauaru, *s.* a fast observed at times, connected with prayers, and ceremonies.

Tauarua, *s. dual*, two dangerous holes in the highway.

Tauaruru, *v. n.* to be heavy, listless, as a sick person.

Tauaruaruâ, *a.* perplexing, as the effects of ill fame.

Tauatea. *s.* the right side of a canoe, that opposite to the out-rigger.

— *s.* the part of the army that has the advantage ground.

— *v. n.* to be on the advantage ground.

Tauatiaororoa, *s.* the name of a certain idolatrous ceremony.

Tauataipito, *s.* a person professing friendship to serve his own ends.

Tauau. *s.* a bad time for fishing with a hook.

Tauaua, *v. n.* to tattle, make use of needless words.

Taue, *s.* a swing, suspended to a tree ; see *tarere*.

— *adv.* carelessly ; wholly, entirely ; also, with violence, not regarding consequences.

Tauene, *v. a.* to splice or repair a mat.

Taueneene, *v. a.* to repair repeatedly.

Tauere, *v. a.* to contend, oppose, drive, rebut.

Tauete, *s.* the oval end of a house.

— *s.* a noose or loop fastened to a mast to fix the sail to.

Taueue, *v. n* to be swinging to and fro; to be unsteady or tottering.
— *a.* moving, swinging. A hammock on board a ship is, roi taueue, or swinging bed.
Taufaremato, *v. n.* to be concerned.
Taufatata, *s* fruit on the nearest branches.
Tauhâ, *s.* the four stars called the crosier.
— *s.* a bundle of four cocoanuts, &c.
Tauhaa, *s.* property, see *taoa*.
Tauhani, *v. a.* to fondle, caress, as different sexes; applied to both man and beast.
Tauhanifaarearea, *v. a.* to caress, or fondle.
Tauhanihani, *v a.* to repeat caresses.
Tauhiro, *s.* a large stone used in the timo raa.
Tauhiroiti, *s.* the small stone used in the timo raa; also food marked before it is put into the oven.
Tauhoani, *v. a.* to entice by soft words.
— *s.* the meeting of different winds.
— *v. n.* to have a longing desire, or wish for an object.
Tauhorahora, *s.* the happy state of peace.
Taui, *s.* a price, purchase, compensation.
— *v. a.* to exchange property, to buy.
Tauia, *s.* the name of some disorder.
Taumaeretei, *v. n.* to walk on the hands; also to hop on one leg.
Taumamao, *v. n.* to be out of reach, as fruit.
Taumamau, *v. n.* to be keeping in one place, as a sick person.
Taumaha, *s.* a portion of food offered to the gods, or spirits of the dead.
— *s.* the crosier; see *tauha*.
Taumata. *s.* the Tahitian bonnet of cocoanut leaves.
— *s.* a hat or bonnet; see *taupoo*.
Taumatateatuatu, *s.* a head-dress of the gods.
Taumi, *s.* an ornamented breast plate.
— *s.* a ballast, or weight to press down.
v. a. to press down a thing by weight.
Taunena, *v. a.* to stretch out a garment, &c.
Tauorea, *s.* a ledge of rocks under water.
Taupe, *v. a.* to bow down, applied to the head.
Taupêpê, *a.* cumbersome.
Taupêpê, *v. a.* to spread out a wet cloth, &c.
Taupeupe, *v. n.* to bow down repeatedly, or a plurality bowing down.
Taupiti, *s.* a double canoe; see *taurua*.
— *s* a public feast.
Taupiri, *s.* the train of the paper kite.
Taupiritea, *s.* a player.
Taupitimaona, *s.* a wrestling match.
Taupitiroroa, *s.* an idolatrous ceremony, with an exhibition of obscenity.
Taupo, *s.* the name of a certain disease.

Taupoo, *s.* a hat, cap, bonnet, or head dress.

Taupoto, *s* a short distance.

Taupupu, *s.* hindersome, cumbersome.

— *a.* heavy, cumbered, burdened.

Taura, *s.* a rope, cord, twist, line, or thread.

Taura, *s.* a herd or flock; a number of pigs, cattle, or fowls that commonly keep together.

Taura, *s.* (*kaura, kaula.*) a pretended prophet, or some one inspired by some god or goddess.

Taurai, *v. a.* see *tauai*, and *tauari.*

Taurearea, *s.* the young, healthy, and vigorous of the people.

Tauri, *v. n.* to be intermixed, as a family in a house.

Taurihau, *s* the name of a medicinal plant.

Tauru, *v. a.* to fasten or secure a part of the sinnet, in lashing a canoe.

Taurua, *s.* the name of the planet Venus.

Taurua, *s.* the name of a public feast.

Taurua, *s.* a double canoe.

Taurumi, *v. n.* to rest a little, as rowers in a canoe.

— *v. a.* to press and rub with the hand the limbs of a weary or sick person.

Taurupoto, *s.* a short distance.

Taururoa, *s.* a long distance.

Taurumirumi, *v. a.* to repeat the act of *taurumi.*

— *v. a.* to balance, or counterpoise a canoe, when in a rough sea.

Tauruurutaiata, *a.* dark, obscure, as the speech of a person.

Tauta, *v. n* to land; see *uta.*

Tautaa, *s.* a double jaw or cheek bone.

Tautai, *s.* a certain mode of fishing, of which there are many names.

Tautai, *s.* what is caught in a fishing excursion.

Tautaiaahi, *s.* what is caught in fishing for the *aahi.*

Tautapa, *s.* a stick used by fishermen.

Tautau, *v. a.* to catch a certain fish in fresh water.

— *v. n.* to hang down.

Tautaumaau, *v. a.* to do some mischief to another.

Taute, *s.* a person not allowed to eat with men, because of his cooking for his wife.

Tautea, *v. a.* to spread abroad, as *Ru* is said to have done with the sky.

Tautea, *v. a.* to rescue, deliver.

Tauteta, *s.* an idle proud fellow, that will not work.

Tauteute, *v. a.* to make a thing red.

— *s.* a large collection of different kinds of food.

Tautia, *v. n.* to be in the rear.

Tautini, *s.* *dual*, two victories obtained in one game.

Tautoru, *s.* the name of a fish.

Tautoo, *v. a.* to seek earnestly what a person wishes.

— *v. n.* to endeavour to raise one's self, when sick.

Tautu, *v. a.* to bite or strike with the tusk, as a hog is apt to do.

Tautu, *s.* a swelling of the lips; see *utu.*

Tautumaere, *v. a.* to laugh at any thing that is strange.

Tauturu, *s.* a prop, help, assistance.

— *v. a.* to help, assist, support.

Tauupu, *s.* the loins.

Tauvaru, *s.* eight joined together; as subdivisions of canoes, or of districts.

Tauuaivai, *s.* the commotion made in the water by a person jumping into it.

Tauvauvau, *s.* grass to spread on the floor of a house; or leaves to spread for a feast.

Tava, *s.* the name of a large shell fish.

— *v. a.* to prepare the bark for cloth making.

Tavae, *s.* a sort of basket for catching fish.

— *s.* a species of paroquet.

Tavaha, *s.* a bridle, gag.

— *v. a.* to bridle, to gag.

Tavahi, *s.* the name of a star.

— *s.* the black part of a cocoanut cup.

Tavahipapamea, *s.* the name of a species of plantain.

Tavai, *v. a* to anoint the body with oil.

— *s.* adoption of another's child.

— *a.* adopted, tamaiti tavai, an adopted son; see *faalavai.*

— *v. a.* to make use of water; see *tapape.*

— *s.* a razor strop to smooth with.

Tavaimani, *v. n.* to sit still, when an enemy is approaching, having been deceived by reports of peace.

Tavaimanino. *s.* smooth speech, flattery.

Tavairea, *v n.* to be unable to eat food from the effects of medicine; also to be deceived by the hopes of a sick person's recovery.

Tavana, *s.* (Engl. *Governor*) the principal chief of a district.

— *a.* appropriated for fishing, as vaa tavana, a fishing canoe.

Tavare, *v. a.* to deceive; see *haavare.*

Tavari, *v. a.* to make soft and smooth, as pulp, mortar, &c.

Tavaru, *s.* a fleet of canoes bringing food for the king or principal chief. The name is from varu eight; a meeting of eight divisions or matâeinaas.

Tavaru, *s.* a meeting of different districts, for business and feasting.

Tavau, *s.* a contraction of tavaru.

Tavava, *s.* a crack, or splitting by the sun.

— *v. a.* to crack, or split, in the sun.

Tavavaa, *s.* a species of moth.

Tavere, *s.* a thing taken in tow, as a boat behind a ship.

— *v. a.* to tow, or drag a thing in the water.

Taverevere, *v. a.* to drag, or tow repeatedly.

Tavero, *s.* a long spear.

Tavevo, *s.* echo; see *pinai.*

— *v. n.* to echo.

Tavevovevo, *v. n.* to echo repeatedly; see *pinainai*; to be making a noise, as an assembly, that is at a distance, breaking up.

Tavi, *v. n.* to make a rustling

noise; to feel a strange sensation on hearing bad news.

Tavii, *s.* a hum, or a low noise among the people in an assembly.

Tavini, *s.* (Engl. *servant,*) a servant, or attendant.

Taviri, *s.* a key for a lock.

— *v. a.* to turn a key, to lock or unlock.

Taviri, *v. a.* to turn or twist, as in rope making.

Tavirihau, *v. n.* to be disregarding the dues of government.

Tavirimaa, *v. n.* to be niggardly, grudging to give a chief the food, &c, that was his due.

Taviritaoa, *v. n.* to be unwilling to pay just dues.

Taviriviri, *s.* the colic, griping pains; a sensation of twisting.

— *v. n.* to turn and twist one's self repeatedly; to have twisting pains in the bowels,

— *v. a.* to turn a thing round and round.

— *a.* a *turned* thing; as *puaataviriviri*, a turned pig, that is a *roasted* pig.

Tavovovovo, *s.* a rolling, distant sound.

— *v. n.* to be rolling, or reverberating, as the noise of distant thunder.

Te, *the definite article*, as te *taata*, *the* man.

— *v. aux.* answering commonly to am, art, is, or are in the present tense; as *te* papai nei au I *am* writing, *te* parau nei oe, thou art speaking; It is also used with *ra* to denote the imperfect tense, as *te* parau *ra* oia, he *was* then speaking.

Te, *relative pron.* who, which, and that, as o te parau, *that* speaks or he who speaks; O vai te parau? Who speaks? O mea te parau, such a one (is) he who speaks.

Tea, *s.* a beam, rafter, or a horizontal stick, to fasten an upright fence to.

— *s.* any piece of wood fastened crossways.

— *s.* an arrow shot from a bow; see *ohe.*

— *v. a,* to shoot an arrow.

— *a.* white; se *uouo.*

Teaai, *v. n.* to nibble at the food, and not eat it.

Teaamu, *a.* fretting, corroding.

Teahitutai, *s.* one that cooks very often; *fig.* a fiery angry person, difficult to please.

Teai, *s.* a game played by the fingers.

Teamanuu, *s.* one of two contending armies.

Teatea, *a.* white; see *uouo.*

Tefatefa, *v. a.* to look repeatedly at one's dress from conceit.

Tehe, *v. a.* to castrate animals; to slit the prepuce above; *supercision*; see *patehe.*

Tehea, *adv.* where? used only interrogatively,

Tehea, *pron.* which? tehea te toru? which is the third?

Tehetehepi, *s.* the attendants of the king or principal chief, seizing and cultivating land wherever they can find it.

Tehitia o te rā, *s.* the east, or sun rising.

Tehiti o te rā, *s.* the same as tehitia o te rā.

Tehoaiavero, *s.* a great warrior, one that is very zealous. and acts generally in a bad cause.

Tehoaiteraipiri, *s.* a man over zealous in a bad cause.

Tehu, *s.* the name of a good fish; see *parala*.

— *a.* rough, as the skin of animals.

— *s.* one that has a protuberance on his body.

— *s.* a person worsted in combat, or in argument.

Tehutehu, *a.* worsted, or defeated repeatedly, either in combat, or in argument.

— *a.* having protuberances.

Tei, *prep.* in, as, tei te fare, in the house.

— *v. aux.* as, was, or were, has, or have in the preter tense.

— *rel. pron.* that, who, or which, see *te*.

Teî. *v. n.* to hop on one leg.

Teiaha, *a.* heavy, ponderous, cumbersome.

Teiai, *v. a.* to fetch food.

Teie, *dem. pron.* this, in opposition to that.

Teienei, *dem. pron.* this, this here.

— *adv.* now, immediately; shortly.

Teihea, *adv.* where? see *tehea*.

Teimaha, *a.* heavy; see *teiaha*.

Teina, *s* a younger brother or sister.

Teitei, *a.* high, tall, exalted.

Teiteiraupaa, *s.* a large man, when overcome by a little one; a large quantity of food consumed by few men; a thing large in bulk, but of little substance.

Temahani, *s.* the name of a tree.

Temaharo, *s.* one of the Tahitian gods it is also worshipped in other groupes of islands.

Temehani, *s.* the name of a mountain of Raiatea, the supposed residence of departed souls.

Tena, *dem. pron.* that, in addressing a person at some distance; that by you.

Tenana. *dem. pron.* that by you; see *na*.

— *adv.* now, but at the place of the person addressed.

Tenania, *prep.* upon, over a thing.

Teni, *v. a.* to exalt another; to impart power or authority to another.

Teniteni, *v. a.* to exalt another repeatedly.

— *a.* high, exalted.

Teoteo, *s.* pride, loftiness, haughtiness.

— *a.* proud, lofty, conceited.

Tepaparaharaha, *s.* according to Tahitian tradition, this papa, or rock, was the foundation of all lands.

Tepatua, *s.* the middle part of each side of an oval Tahitian house.

Tera, *dem. pron.* that, that at a distance.

Teratera, *a* sacred, or what once belonged to the king.

Tere, *s* a journey or voyage.

— *s.* a travelling company.

— *s.* the object, or business a person has in view, when he takes a journey.

— *v. n.* to sail, as a ship or canoe; to slide, or move along; to spread out.

Terearii, *s* the errand or journey of the sovereign.

Terearu, *s.* a canoe passing through a rough sea.

Teretereaurua, *v. n.* to go by two and two.

Teretereora, *s.* the walk of a person just recovering from sickness

Teretereorie, *s.* the stumbling of an infant, when attempting to walk.

Teretiaau, *v. a* to seek a good place to anchor where the wind will allow of going out again.

Teretuao, *s.* a long absence from home, so that the fruit ripens during the period.

Teriteriuri, *v. n.* to follow, as one person another.

Teruteru, *s.* anger, arising from disappointment.

Tete, *s.* two shells struck together, as a token of mourning for the dead.

— *v. n.* to make a noise, as the beaten shells; to be noisy, as a great talker.

Têtê, *s.* the name of a small fish.

Tetea, *s.* a person who remains always in the shade, and thereby becomes white; also a phantom said to appear at a spring of water.

Tetei, *v. n.* to close the teeth, as a dying person; to shew above water, as the rocks at low water, or at the ebbing of the sea.

Tetooa, *s.* the side or edge of a thing.

Tetooaoterâ, *s.* the west where the sun sets.

Tetua, *s.* a girl or young woman; a title given to those of the chief families.

Teu, *s.* an attendant on the chief, or principal man.

Teu, *v. n.* to be naked, used contemptuously.

— *s.* a term applied to the menses.

Teuau, *s.* an attendant on a chief.

Teuteu, *s.* servants, attendants on a chief.

Teuteuarii, *s.* the king's attendants.

Teve, *s.* the name of a plant, and acrid root.

Ti, *s.* the name of a plant, that has a large and sweet root. (*Dracæna terminalis.*

— *prep.* in; see *tei.*

Tia, *s.* the bottom of the belly, or just below the navel.

— *a.* (*tika*) just; straight, fit, proper.

— *s.* the back; see *tua.*

— *s.* the wide open sea.

— *v. n.* to stand up.

— *v. n.* to abide, remain; to keep doing a thing.

— *v. n.* to have power, or ability to do a thing; *e tia* iana i te hamani, he *is* able to do it.

— *s.* an advocate, or intercessor.

— *adv.* of course, well, or it might be, as pohe tia, well it might die, being shot through.

Tiaa, *s.* a company of people.

— *s.* a flock or herd of sheep, goats, &c.

— *s.* a shoe, clog, or sandal; see *tamâ.*

Tiaà, *a.* lewd, obscene, without shame.

Tiaaio, *s.* the back bone; see *tuaio.*

Tiaati, *v. n.* to join together; see *tuati*.

Tiaau, *s.* a steward, superintendant; see *tuau*.

— *v. n.* to be waiting, as for wind or weather.

Tiahuru, *s.* work left unfinished until the material decays.

Tiafa, *s.* the bare reef at low water.

Tiafaa, *s.* rain and fog in the narrow valleys among the mountains.

Tiafati, *v. a.* to fold cloth or garments.

Tiafetu, *v. a.* the same as *tiafati*, and *tufetu*.

Tiahami, *v. n.* to be exhausted, as tilled land.

Tiahapa. *adv.* over and above, more than.

Tiahara, *adv.* the same as *tiahapa*, *tuhapa*, and *tuhara*.

Tiahau, *a.* wild, fierce, untamed.

— *s.* a fierce, savage man or beast.

Tiahê, *a.* thin, emaciated, applied to man or beast.

Tiahi, *v. a.* to expel, drive away.

Tiahoi, *a.* unyielding, obstinate.

— *intj.* of wonder, pleasure, or triumph.

Tiahono, *s.* a piece to fill up a breach, or to lengthen a thing.

— *v. a.* to lengthen by adding a piece.

Tiahorotia, *a.* straight, straight forward.

Tiahou, *s.* a novice; see *tuhou*.

— *a.* new, not tried; inexperienced.

— *s.* first fruit; the first fish caught in a new net.

Tiahu, *s.* a lazy and wicked person; see *tuahu*.

Tiai, *s.* a keeper; one that waits or watches.

— *v. a.* to keep, protect from harm.

— *v. n.* to wait, expect; stay for a thing.

Tíai, *v. a.* to commit adultery with many.

Tiaia, *v. a.* to strike the foot against a stone; to stumble by striking against something.

— *v. a.* to touch a thing.

Tiaimaheireva, *s.* a person apparently dead, yet there is a little breath remaining.

Tiamatarua, *s.* a man who watched two deep holes, in which pigs were confined according to ancient custom; or one who watched two divisions in time of war.

Tiaipaiava, *s* the name of a strong wind which closes up the openings in the reef; also one who catches fish near the small openings.

Tiaipihaa, *v. a.* to seek conquest in some of the native games.

Tiaipoi, *v. n.* to wait the *poi*, or proper period when one is to die.

Tiaire *s.* the candle-nut tree, and fruit.

Tiairepapaa, *s.* the *Palma Christi*.

Tiairi, *s.* the small pebbles of a pavement.

Tiairoa, *s.* the long keeping of a thing.

Tiaivavea, *v. n.* to wait the falling of a high wave in order to land; see *vavea*.

Tiamâ, *a.* free, not a slave, bondman, or prisoner.

Tiamâ, *v. n.* to be free, having liberty; see *faatiama.*

Tiamaha, *s.* the reef of rocks, covered at low water; see *tufa.*

— *s.* an indecent exposure of the person, by either male or female.

— *v. a.* to expose the person shamefully.

Tiamaaava, *s.* a disease of the bowels.

Tiamatapoopoo, *s.* a person with sunken or hollow eyes.

Tiamii, *v. n.* to grumble, or grudge.

Tiamimi, *s.* the name of a small poisonous crab.

Tiamo, *v. n.* to be not hurt, not giving way in a contest.

Tiamoina, *v. n* to be lost, as a bird caught by the ihu manu, or bird catcher; see *aromoina.*

Tiamu, *v. a.* to tie a rope; see *taamu.*

Tiamû, *a.* blunt, having the point broken off; see *tuima.*

Tianee, *s.* the name of a shell-fish.

Tiani, *s.* one who supports, or helps; a helper.

Tianoa, *s.* a mole, or mark on the skin.

— *s.* the name of a disorder.

Tianoo, *s.* an enchantment or curse.

Tiao, *s.* the sky when dark, but no parting clouds.

— *v. a.* to search, seek out; to throw a spear at a thing without piercing it.

— *v. n.* to be looking out.

Tiaoro, *v. a.* to call, to invoke; see *tuoro.*

Tiaou, to nod, to incline the head; see *tuou.*

Tiapai. *s.* a hammer or mallet; see *tupai.*

— *v. a.* to strike, beat, hammer.

Tiapana, *s.* a span; see *tupana.*

— *v. a.* to span, measure by the span.

Tiapapau, *s.* a corpse, a ghost; see *tupapau.*

Tiapuu, *s.* an arrow shot farther than the preceding one.

Tiapatapataô, *s* a person who is restless, or remaining but a short time in one place.

Tiapona, *s.* a knot tied on the garment of a native under the chin; see *tupona.*

Tiapuna, *s.* an ancestor, grandfather; see *tupuna.*

— *s.* an ornament in the stern of a canoe.

Tiaputa, *s.* a native garment.

Tiaraau, *s.* the native exercise of arms.

Tiaraaturuma, *s* a place used as a dunghill, or as a burying ground.

Tiapou, *v. n.* to expose the posteriors.

— *v. a.* to strike the posteriors, and expose them by way of contempt.

Tiapû, *a* humpbacked; see *tuapu.*

Tiarai, *v. a.* to push away; see *turai.*

Tiarama, *s* a torch, lamp, taper, or light.

— *v. a.* to guide with a torch; see *turama.*

Tiare, *s.* the name of a sweet scented flower.

— *s.* flowers or blossoms in general.

Tiareorei, *s.* the brink of a precipice.

Tiareirei, *v. n.* to grow without much earth; also to stand in an elevated place, without any thing to hold by.

Tiarepu, *v. a.* to stir, to agitate, to mix; see *turepu.*

Tiaria, *v. a.* to scorch; as by the sun.

Tiaro, *v. a.* to wash or cleanse the eye, a sore, &c.

Tiarua, *v. n.* to be both standing together.

Tiaruhi, *a.* tiresome, wearisome; sea *turuhi.*

Tiatà, *v. a.* to carry a child on the hips.

Tiatae, *s.* the excrements of animals.

Tiataeatua, *s.* the excrements of the gods; the name given to still born infants.

Tiataeauri, *s.* the rust of iron or other metals.

— *s.* a name recently given to such as have lost their character by being convicted of immoral practices, transgressing the laws. &c.

Tiataeiorehia, *a.* defiled by rat's dung.

Tiatareva, *v. a.* to splice with a long piece of wood

Tiatao, *s.* the name of a fish.

— *s.* the name of a long spear.

Tiataro, *s.* an anchor; see *tutau.*

— *v. a.* to cast anchor.

Tiatau, *s* an anchor; see *tutau.*

— *v. a.* to anchor, or cast anchor.

Tiatea, *s.* the name of a species of bread fruit.

Tiatia, *s.* a flea; see *tutua.*

— *v. n.* to get up a little, as a sick person.

— *v. a.* tô stimulate to action in time of war.

— *v. a.* to carry, or convey; see *tietie.*

Tiatiaaau, *s.* a species of small crab.

Tiatiahau, *s.* the conservators of peace, or of the government.

Tiatiaohe, *s.* the fetcher of arrows in the diversion of tiaraa, or archery.

Tiatiarahonui, *s.* a spider.

Tiatiavea, *s.* a messenger of the chiefs.

Tiatonu, *v. n.* to stare to gaze; to look steadfastly.

Tiatu, *s.* the name of a game in which children imitated the doings of the marae.

Tiatua, *s.* a flea; see *tutua.*

Tiaturi, *s.* the name of a fish; see *tuturi.*

— *s.* a stone in the marae, against which the priest leaned when officiating.

— *v. n.* to lean, or rest upon a thing; *fig.* to trust, put confidence in another, for help, or support.

Tiaturiraa, *s.* a resting place, or a place to rest upon; *fig.* a ground of trust or confidence.

Tiavâ, *s.* the top, tiaû, or head stone of a corner.

Tiavaru, *v. a.* to expel or banish a person.

Tiavero, *s.* the name of a part of a mourner's head dress; see *parae.*

Tie, *s.* the stalk of leaves and fruit; see *tari.*
— *v. a.* to remove or convey things.
Tiea, *s.* a stick or a club thrown at a thing.
— *v. a.* to throw such a stick, or piece of wood.
Tiee, *s.* a modern name for taro.
Tiehi, *v. a.* to expel, or drive away.
Tiei, *v. a.* to turn the face aside to look at a thing; to reach over and look.
Tieiei, *v. n.* to turn the face repeatedly and look.
Tiere, *s.* the name of an amusement.
Tierefaraoa, *v.* the name of a plant.
Tiete, *v. a.* to feed and nurse a chief woman after her accouchement.
Tietie, *s.* a conveyer of things.
— *v. a.* to carry or convey repeatedly.
Tifa, *a.* striped with various colours.
— *v. a.* to join things together, to dovetail.
Tifai, *s.* a patch, or fragment to patch with.
— *v. a.* to mend or patch a thing.
Tifatifa, *s.* the name of a king's canoe.
— *v. a.* to join things together.
Tifeirei, *s.* a carved image, or figure head of a ship; also a doll.
Tifeiro, *s.* the name of a household god.
Tifene, *v.n.* to be folding together, as a pocket knife, called tipi tifene.
Tifenefene. *v. n.* to be folding repeatedly.
Tifiti, *v. a.* to entangle; see *tafifi.*
Tihaa, *v. a.* to rinse in water, in order to cleanse; see *horoi.*
Tihae, *s.* a piece of the rainbow.
— *v. n.* to go, as a party before an army.
Tihana, *v. a.* to recook food.
Tihauhau, *v. a.* to beat sticks in order to keep time, as a dancer.
Tihere, *s.* a sort of girdle, worn by men, to cover their nakedness; see *tahere.*
Tihetihe, *s.* elevations in the bark of breadfruit trees.
Tihi, *s.* a sort of petticoat.
— *s.* a large quantity of cloth wrapped about the waist in old times, and afterwards given to visitors.
Tihirahi, *s.* a large corner stone in a marae.
Tihitihi, *a.* large, corpulent.
— *s.* small twigs or branches; see *peapea.*
Tihiuru, *s.* a large native shawl, stained about the border.
Tiho, *v. a.* to slander, speak evil of another.
Tihotiho, *v. a.* to slander a person repeatedly.
Tii, *s.* the name of the first man according to Tahitian tradition, and his wife's name was Hina.
Tii, *s.* (*tiki, tigi,*) an image; a demon or wicked spirit, a class of beings supposed to be different from men and gods.

— *v. a.* to fetch a thing; to go or come for a thing.

Tiifa, *s.* the upper part of a fishing hook.

Tiimotoe, *s.* the name of a destructive demon.

Tiinihororoa, *s.* an ugly image with long teeth; an evil demon destructive to men.

Tiipa, *a.* barren, applied to women.

Tiiahu, *s* one who fetches cloths.

Tiiruauna, *s.* the name of a wicked demon.

Tima, *s.* fair, clear, as the colour of a garment.

— *v. a.* to bale a canoe, or boat.

— *s.* a thing fastened to a long pole to bring down a bread-fruit.

Timaa, *s.* a shoe; see *tamaa.*

— *s.* a string fastened to the feet in order to climb a tree.

Timatima, *v. n.* to be well set, as colours or paint.

— *v. n.* to be lost in obscurity, as the land, when at a distance at sea.

Timo, *s.* the name of a play with stones.

— *v. a.* to play the timo.

Timene, *v. a.* to squeeze any thing together, or compress it so as to be of a roundish form.

Timoraa, *s.* an amusement.

Timotaro, *s.* the play of timo.

Timui, *s.* a key; see *taviri.*

— *v. a.* to lock, or turn a key.

Timutimu, *v. n.* to be obscured by distance.

Tinai, *v. a.* to extinguish a candle, or fire, to cause any thing to cease.

— *v. a* to separate water, so as to run in different currents or courses.

Tinaimataraa, *v. a.* to cause an enemy to return by imploring peace.

Tinana, *s.* a trunk; a source; a foundation.

Tinao, *v. a.* to put the hand into an aperture or cavity.

Tinao, *s.* a fire kept in old rotten wood, for purposes of smoking out musquitoes.

Tinatinai, *v. a.* to extinguish the large fires on the mountains.

— *v. a.* to search for small fish in fresh water.

— *v. a.* to cause some plan or project to be abandoned.

Tini, *v. a.* to exalt, or make a poor man a chief.

— *v. n.* to be feeling, though solitary, as if in company.

Tino, *s.* the body; see *oivi.*

— *s.* a name given to a pretended prophet, as if he were the *tino* or body of the god that inspired him; called also *oivi.*

Tinopapa, *s.* the human body.

Tinorua, *s.* the name of a demon or god.

Tinotinoatua, *s.* the body, or vehicle of a god.

Tinotinovahine, *s.* a woman pretending to be inspired.

Tio, *s.* a species of small oyster.

Tioa, *s.* a piece of timber, to raise the sides of a canoe.

Tioe, *v. a.* to cook food in haste, that it may be soon ready; also to close a debate hastily.

Tioi, *v. n.* to warp, or turn another way.

Tiomata, *v. a.* to stare, gaze at; a play of children.

Tioo, *s.* a modern name for the *mahi*, which see.

Tiopa, *v. n.* to turn over.

Tiopaopa, *v. n.* to roll, or turn over again and again.

Tiope, *s.* the leaves of plants, and trees.

— *s.* a sort of net of leaves to catch fish; see *raoere.*

Tiopeope, *s.* leaves, leaves repeatedly collected.

Tiori, *v. a.* to wink with one eye.

Tiotio, *s.* a protuberance on a limb affected with the elephantiasis.

Tiotioo, *v. n.* to be displeased or vexed; to have a resentful feeling.

— *a.* hot, as the weather.

Tiote, *v. n.* to be early in bearing fruit, as *tiote ohie.*

Tipa, *s.* a young flying fish; see *pararu.*

Tipâ, *s.* one of the Tahitian gods, who was said to preside over the healing art.

Tipaa, *v. a.* to bake, or rebake some sorts of food.

Tipae, *s.* the fish basket that is so called.

— *v. n.* to sit cross legged as a tailor.

— *v. a.* to land; to call at a place.

Tipaeama, *s.* a canoe with an outrigger.

Tipaeati, *s.* a double canoe.

Tipaeraa, *s.* the same as tipaeati.

Tipai, *s.* the sin of sodomy; see *aitipai.*

Tipana, *a.* great, vast; also numerous.

Tipao, *s* a mark; see *tapao.*

— *s.* a rule, measure, or scales to weigh with.

— *v. a.* to mark, select, to measure.

Tipaopao, *v. a.* to mark, or notice, in order to revenge.

Tipapa, *v. a.* to fetch a person; see *tapapa.*

— *v. n.* to lie down on the face and belly.

Tipâpâ, *s.* the roof of a house forming an obtuse angle.

Tipara, *s.* a sort of native cloth; see *tapara.*

— *v. a.* to borrow a thing; also to beg.

Tiparu, *v. a.* to flatter, entice, tempt; see *taparu.*

Tipatia, *s.* the *ti* plant, which has been planted, in opposition to that which grows wild.

Tipe, *s.* a sort of native cloth.

— *v. a.* to cause fruit, such as bananas, to ripen.

— *v. a.* to beg, or borrow.

Tipea, *s.* a band, ring, or buckler; see *tapea.*

Tipepe, *v. a.* to patch; see *tafai.*

— *s.* a piece or patch.

Tipi, *s.* a knife of any sort.

— *v. a.* to cut with a knife.

Tipiparamaa, *s.* a case-knife.

Tipipeni. *s.* a penknife.

Tipitafene, *s.* a pocket or clasp-knife.

Tipitohe, *s.* a pruning knife.

Tipitipi, *v. a* to cut repeatedly with a knife.

Tipo, *s.* the corner of a hole; the hollow of a wave.

— *s.* a roll of baked bread fruit, or of *mahi.*

Tipona, *s.* a knot; see *tapona.*
— *v. a.* to tie a knot.
Tipono, *v. a.* to send a thing; see *hapono.*
Tipoati, *s.* the hollow of a curling wave.
Tipu. *v. n.* to lie down on the side, bending the knees.
— *v. a.* to chop, or cut with an axe; see *tapu.*
Tipupu, *v. a.* to cut or chop repeatedly; see *tapupu.*
Tiputa, *s.* the name of a garment worn commonly by the islanders; see *tuputa, taputa.*
— *v. a.* to pierce, or make a hole in a thing.
Tiputaputa. *v. a.* to pierce or make holes repeatedly.
Tira, *s.* the mast of any sailing vessel.
— *s.* a fishing canoe fitted with a mast.
— *s.* a pole or stick put up in marae.
Tiraha, *v. n.* to lie down on the back.
— *adv.* over against, opposite.
Tirahaomama, *v. a.* to defame, speak evil of one, and that without foundation.
Tiraharaha, *v. n.* to lie down on the back as a sick person.
Tirao, *v. a.* to exhort to peace; — to excite to peace.
Tiraorao, *v. a.* to excite to peace repeatedly.
— *v. a.* to place two sticks across each other.
Tirara, *a.* all, no more remaining.
Tiratiamanava, *s.* the name of a part of the belly.
Tiratira, *v. a.* to put up a high house; to invest a person with authority.
Tiraurau, *v. a.* to bribe or use means to get favour.
Tireo, *s.* the first day of the moon, or first night.
— *s.* young suckers; the last of the progeny of a woman.
Tiri, *s.* a man that was an attendant on a god.
— *v. n.* to throw, or cast a small fishing net into the water.
Tiriaina, *s.* a place where the heads of the dead were presented to the gods.
— *s.* a shallow place where fish are caught.
Tiriapera, *s* a place where the bones of the dead, sacred cloth belonging to the chiefs, &c. were thrown to rot; a dunghill.
Tiriapu, *s.* fish which are taken out of their season.
Tiripuu, *s.* the protuberance where the branch is joined to the tree; *fig.* some evil after peace.
Tiriumu, *s.* a pistol.
Tirivara. *s.* a certain tempestuous wind; *fig.* a boisterous ungoverned passion.
Tiro, *v. a.* to mark, or select a thing; see *tapao.*
Tiroaroa, *v. n.* to stretch our at full length.
Tiromi, *s.* a bundle of small taro, scraped and baked together.
Tiromii, *v. a.* to hill up earth about a plant; to beat up taro to a thick paste.
Tiropapari, *v. n.* to be constipated.
Tiroria, *s.* an ill grown weakly person.

— *a.* shaken, disturbed. as a tree by the wind.

Tiioroa, *v. n.* to be sleeping with the legs stretched out.

Tiiotiro, *s.* a remainder.

— *a.* small, little.

Titae, *s.* a parent, a term of endearment used by a child for his father or mother.

Titaha, *a* circuitous, round about, as a road

— *adv* circuitously.

Titaimaorohea, *s.* a name that occurs in the legend about Turi.

— *a.* diminutive.

Titaporo, *s.* the smallest of the fruit in a bunch of plantains.

Titapu, *s* the jew's harp.

Titari, *v. a.* to draw out fish from a hole; to tempt or entice a person; to use means of provoking to war, &c.

Titau, *v. a.* to seek, ask, importune.

Titaua, *s.* one that has obtained nothing, as an unsuccessful fisherman.

Tite, *s.* the aute, or aute cloth; see *aute*.

Titea, *s.* a sprit for a sail.

Titea, *s.* the name of a children's game.

Titeamata, *s.* a pair of spectacles.

Titeamatahani, *s.* uxoriousness.

— *v. a.* to cast a look upon a person.

Titeamatatoto, *s.* a name given to a warrior.

Titeta, *s.* (Eng. teakettle) a kettle.

Titete, *s.* a name given to the native cloth, when in a certain state of preparation.

Titi, *s.* a nail, pin or peg, a stake.

— *s.* a bundle of cocoanuts containing five *mui*, of four cococoanuts each.

— *v. a.* to pin or peg, to fasten with nails, or with stakes in the ground; see *patiti*.

— *v. n.* to stick fast, as a mote in the eye

Titî, *s.* a captive in war, a slave; a refugee

Titia, *s.* short sticks used for fastening together the pieces of a canoe when building it.

— *v. n.* to drop, as water through the roof.

— *s.* the long beam on which the native women beat the bark for cloth making.

— *v. n.* to beat the bark for cloth making, on the beam *titia*.

— *v. a.* to kindle fire; see *tutui*.

— *s* a mode of catching the small fry, called oma, used for a bait.

Titiaifaro *a.* straight, not crooked.

Titiahoiotia, *a.* straight.

Titiaifarotia, *a.* the same as titiaifaro.

Titiaivai, *s* the name of a fresh water fish.

Titiaveravera, *v. a.* to be burned up or scorched by the sun and wind.

Titiaveravera, *v. n.* to be uncovered and dried, as the reefs in a hot day; *fig* to be desolated by war.

Titihopeore, *s.* the name of a bird.

Titihoria, *s.* a refugee, a wanderer.

Titimoopiro, *s.* the name of a disease.

Titio, *v. n.* to void excrements.

Titipatoa, *s.* the cap on the *maava* shell fish.

— *s.* the name of a medical plant.

Titipauru, *s.* a game among children, as hide and seek; see *tupaurupauru.*

Titiporo, *s.* the name of a game.

Titiri, *v. a.* to throw or fling off a thing.

Titiromatatia, *v. n.* to gaze, to look steadfastly, to cast a lustful look.

Titiripu, *v. a.* to cast in a bundle.

Tititao, *s.* the name of a game.

Tititi. *s.* pieces or wedges used in joining a canoe.

— *v. a.* to make use of wedges or pieces of wood for joining closely the parts of a canoe.

Títívahaora, *s.* a vain captive insensible to his circumstances.

Tito, *v. a.* to peck as a fowl; to fight, as cocks, dogs, goats, &c.

— *v. n.* to go softly on tiptoe, as a thief.

Titô, *s.* a funnel; see *faito.*

— *v. a.* to fill a vessel, such as a cask, bottle, &c.

Titoe, *s.* an instrument to make a groove; any kind of beading or grooving plane.

— *v. a.* to form any kind of grooves.

Titohe, *s.* a pair of breeches or trowsers.

Titohi, *s.* the throes of a female in labour.

Titohi, *v. a.* to be in pain, as a woman in labour.

Titohu, *v. n.* to point with the finger; see *tohu.*

Titoi, *s.* the intercourse of the sexes.

— *v. a.* to have intercourse, as the sexes; also to enact the vile sin of Onanism.

Titoo, *s.* a piece of wood or a pole by which to stretch out a sail.

— *v. a.* to stretch out a sail, &c.

— *v. n.* to stretch out an arm, foot, &c.

Titooraaavae, *s.* a footstep.

Titore, *v. a.* to split straw, grass, fara leaves, &c. for mats, or for the platting of hats, &c.

Titoro, *v. a.* to seek to trace thieves or stolen property; to put the hand to the mouth of a hole to catch a crab, &c.

— *v. a.* to intrigue, or have by secret means criminal intercourse with another's wife.

— *v. n.* to stretch out the arm; see *faatoro.*

Titoropaahoi, *v. a.* to heap upon a man the various crimes of his ancestors.

Titotai, *s.* a clever fisherman; see *ihitai.*

Tîtumarae, *s.* an indigenous person.

Titurí, *s.* an instrument to catch eels.

Tiu, *v. a.* to beg or demand property from house to house, as was formerly done by the chiefs and their servants.

Tiue, *s.* a mode of casting a fishing net.

Tiue, *v. a.* to cast a net; to throw a stone.

Tiupoorua, *s.* a ti root out of which grows two stems; *fig.* a person who has beside his wife, another secret one.

Tiutiu, *s.* a calabash to hold water.

— *s.* the germ of the cocoanut

Tivahipaparua, *s.* a species of banana.

Tivai, *v. a.* to anoint with oil; see *tivai*

Tivera, *v a.* to act with diligence and expedition.

— *adv.* vigorously, diligently, fully.

To, *s.* sugar cane; also sugar.

— *v. n.* to wrestle.

— *prep.* of, belonging to; see *ta, na, no.*

— *v. n.* to conceive, used of women only.

Toa, *s.* the hard iron wood, called also aito, the *casuarina.*

— *s.* a warrior, a valiant man.

— *a* courageous, valiant.

— *a.* mischievous, savage.

— *s.* (*toka*) a rock, a stone; coral rock.

— *conj.* also, likewise; see *atoa.*

— *adv.* entirely, all.

— s. large clots of blood.

Tôâ, *a.* self conceited, proud, see *oteo.*

Toaa, *s* the hard substance in the pulp of the bread fruit; the bruises, or bites of insects in the body of the fruit

— *a.* bruised, or having hard discoloured places, applied to bread fruit.

Toaaau, *s.* the rocky coral reef.

Toaati, *s.* a round mass of coral.

Toae, *s* an expression used by an orator in commencing his speech.

Toaauau, *s* a mass of coral over which the current runs.

Toafaaruru, *s* a mass of coral beset by eddies

Toafare, *s.* a house for barter, fare toa.

Toaheabe, *s* the ripples of the sea, produced by a gentle breeze.

Toahiti, *s* the name of the god of the valleys

Toaharahia, *s* the coral poisoned by the plant *hora.*

Toahu, *s* heat, sultriness.

— *a.* close, sultry, no air stirring.

Toahua, *s.* the fat lining the ribs of animals.

Toahuahu, *a.* hot, pungent, as the *capsicum.*

Toahue, *s.* the perspiration after eating.

Toahuri, *s* a strong wind that comes in gusts

Toahuripapa, *s* a strong tempestuous wind.

Toai, *v n.* to sit nearly erect.

Toamatapu, *s* intrepidity, courage.

— *a.* courageous, dauntless.

Toapu, *s* the same as toa ati.

Toaraa, *s.* a mass of coral rocks above water

Toarau, *s* a species of breadfruit

Toare, *s.* the name of a native drum.

— *v. n.* to be in commotion, as the sea, &c.

Toareare, *v. n.* to be ruffled,

and in repeated commotion, applied to the sea.
— *v. n.* to be sick at stomach.
Toaroto, *s.* a figurative expression for the king, or principal chief, when among his people.
Toaru, *a.* slack, loose, as the skin and flesh of a person that had been fat, loose as a rope untwisted; careless, or without energy.
Toaruaru, *a.* slack, dilatory, without energy.
— *v. n.* to be without energy in any thing.
Toatamarii, *s.* the *lochia*, clots of blood.
Toatapahi, *v. n.* to be destitute of fear.
Toatoa, *s.* a very offensive smell emitted from the sea.
— *v. n.* to be disgusted.
— *s.* small coral.
Toatoaarii, *s* a painful wound or stab.
Toatoapapu, *s.* surfeit, disgust of a pregnant woman.
Toaû, *v. n.* to be in the midst of warriors or people, as a chief; see *toaroto*
Toauau, *a.* badly prepared, as the hoi root.
— *s.* disturbance of mind, consternation, on account of bad tidings; see *puavau*
Toavauva, *a* sour, acid.
— *v. n.* to become sour.
Toe, *s.* an earthworm; also the worms that feed on the dead.
Toe, *v. n* to remain, or be left as a remainder; to be left out, not included.
Toea, *s* a remainder, residue, what was not included.
Toea, *s* an old person, see *ruau*.
Toeapoia, *s* a single bread fruit on the end of a branch that cannot be obtained.
Toehaeha, *a.* sourish, inclining to sourness.
Toehaumi, *a.* soft or damp, as by dew.
Toerau, *s.* a westerly, or northwesterly wind.
Toetoe, *s.* cold, coldness, chilliness
— *a.* cold; see *maariri.*
Toetoepahao, *s.* the name of a crab.
Tofea, *v. n.* to be surfeited; see *tahea.*
— *v. n.* to be over worked, as land that ceases to bear.
Tofaafaa, *s.* one who does his work lazily.
Tohe. *s.* the buttocks; the bottom of a vessel, the foundation of anything.
Tohea, *v. n.* to be surfeited, or crammed over much.
Toheami, *s.* a bottom very lean or shrunk.
Toheoioi, *s.* a person continually on the move.
Toheoo, *a.* enclosed in fat, as the hinder parts of a hog.
Tohepaparu, *s.* a heavy bottom, one that sits unconcerned, not assisting those that are near him.
Tohepu, *s.* a slender pointed conch shell.
Tohepuu, *s.* a buttock with an abscess.
Tohepe, *s.* a lazy fellow that crawls on his bottom.
Tohepeepee, *s.* one that is on the alert.
Tohepere, *s* a person whose buttocks were not tattooed.

Tohetiti, *s.* one to whom the game falls.

Tohetahe, *s.* the elements, or stamina of speech.

Tohetupou, *s.* the name of a species of breadfruit.

— *s.* the name of a medicinal plant.

Toheveri, *s.* the name of a large fish like the *aahi.*

— *s.* the name of a figure on the skin.

Tohi, *s.* a chisel; an instrument to cleave bread fruit.

— *v. a.* to use a chisel; to split bread fruit.

— *v. a.* to guard with a spear in fencing; see *tiarau.*

Tohimauriora, *s.* an idolatrous prayer.

Tohinu, *a.* calm, unruffled.

— *s.* calmness, smoothness.

Tohiahio, *s.* the name of an abcess.

Tohipu, *v. a.* to split bread fruit crossways.

Tohiuhiu, *s.* some misgivings, apprehensions.

Tohirepo, *s* a spade or shovel.

Tohitohi, *s.* a harpoon.

— *v. a.* to use a chisel.

Tohiumaio. *inj.* a word of salutation to a god, when beginning to inspire a person.

Tohora, *s.* a grampus, or whale.

Tohu, *s.* the name of a Tahitian shark god.

— *s.* a prophecy, or foretelling.

— *v. a.* to prophesy or foretell.

— *v. a.* to nod, make a significant sign with the head or eyes; also to point at a thing with the finger.

Tohua, *v. a* to give or share out in dribblets, while the one who shares keeps most for himself.

Tohua, *s.* small rain.

Tohuatea, *v. n.* to be in an imperfect state, as cocoanut sauce.

Tohuhe, *v. n* to be calmed or lulled a little, as the sea.

Tohureva, *s.* the going away of the grated pia with the water, not sinking in it; a superstitious notion that a person must not sneeze lest it go.

Tohutohu, *v. n.* to point at a thing repeatedly, or many pointing at once.

— *v. a.* to make tears to flow.

— *v. a.* to ask, solicit, or request a thing.

Tohuura, *s.* a piece of a rainbow; red clouds.

Toi, *s.* the name of a good timber tree.

— *s.* (*toki, togi,*) a hatchet or tomahawk.

Toiaha, *a.* heavy, ponderous; see *teiaha.*

Toiaraa, *s.* a lever.

— *v. a* to turn by a lever or handspike.

— *v. a.* to raise up a thing.

Toiau, *a.* heavy, burdened

— *v. n.* to be oppressed or burdened.

— *s* the name of a noted self invited guest.

— *v. a.* to use a lever.

Toieie, *s* confusion created by an alarm of war.

— *inj.* an exclamation of the arioi men.

— *adv.* at fingers' ends in wrestling, &c.

Toimaha, *a.* heavy, ponderous.

Toihaiha. *v. n.* to be overloaded by eating.

Toihau. *v. a.* to bleach in the dew.

Toimata, *s.* the name of a Tahitian goddess, by whom women were inspired.

Toimato, *s.* a stone adze; a fellihg axe.

Toimoerepo, *s.* a native of the place; an ingenious person.

Toimoetahora, *s.* the same as toimoerepo.

Toihoiho, *v. n.* to be declining, as the snn in the afternoon.

Toina, *v. n.* sought, fetched; see *toi.*

Toini, *s.* an ominous hog offered to the gods.

— *a.* well made, solid, substantial; a plump well grown man.

— *v. n.* to be light, as a drumhead; *fig.* to be swollen with rage.

Toipauru, *s.* an axe that stands ill on its helve.

Toipeue, *s.* a broad carpenter's axe.

Toiraufaino, *s.* an axe mentioned in the legend of Hiro.

Toiri, *v. a.* to collect in one place, cause to assemble; to drag a log, bark and all.

— *v. n.* to move in a body from place to place.

Toita, *a.* tight, well stretched; inflated.

— *a.* unripe, applied to fruit.

Toitamâ, *s.* an adze used for finishing work, or finally clearing and cleansing it.

— *v. a.* to extirpate, take off entirely.

Toivi, *s.* a widow; one without offspring.

Toma, *v. n.* to be in an extirpated state.

Tomaa. *v. n.* to be divided in mind or affection.

Tomara, *s.* the heart of a tree, without the sap.

— *v. a.* to season a bamboo, cocoanut cup, &c.; also to gloss, or polish with oil.

Tomea, *s.* redness of the skin, caused by eating stale fish, or by the sun.

Tomo, *v. a.* to enter, as at a door; to go into the vallies the first time in the season for mountain plantains.

— *v. n.* to be brought low, as a ship or boat heavily laden.

— *v. n.* to be sunken; to sink altogether, as a ship, boat, or canoe.

Tona, *s.* a wart or excrescence.

— *s.* a species of the venereal disease.

To'na, *pron. poss.* his, hers its; see *ta'na.*

Tona, *s.* niggardliness; see *horoaino.*

Tonahioe, *s.* the name of a disease in which the body wastes away gradually.

Tonatona, *a.* uneven, having a rough surface.

Tono, *v. a.* to send a messenger, a person, not a thing, for which *haapono* is used.

— *v. n.* to cause or excite a person to go.

Tonotono, *v. a.* to send repeatedly.

— *v. n.* to incline, to attend to a person or thing.

Tonu, *s.* the name of a fish that is often poisonous. It is of the tarao species, and commonly of a reddish colour, there are variations called tonufaraoa, tonuhamea, tonufaeta, &c.

Tonutonu, *a.* red, much sun burnt.

Too, *s.* a piece of wood forming the body of an idol.

— *s.* a pole to push a canoe along.

— *s.* the man at the head of a wandering dancing party.

— *s.* the largest of the fruit in a plaintain bunch.

— *v. a.* (*togo, toko,*) to pull, or drag along.

— a *prefix,* (*toko,*) to the number of persons (not things) mentioned, as toorua, tootoru, &c.

— *v. a.* to lay a restriction; see *rahui.*

— *v. n.* to vomit; see *ruai.*

Tooa, *s.* a certain ceremony among the *arioi.*

Tooaoterà, *s.* the west, or sun-setting.

Toofa, *s.* a chief next in rank to *aru.*

Toomaa, *s.* the forked branch of a tree; forked tail of a fish.

Tootoo, *v. n.* to vomit slightly.

— *v. a.* to push along a canoe with a pole.

— *s.* (*togotogo*) a staff or walking stick.

Toouuhi, *s.* the decayed *too* of a god taken out; *fig* a select party of warriors.

Topa, *v. n* to fall down straight, as a thing from an eminence; see *mairi.*

— *v. n.* to fall behind, as when in a company.

— *v. a.* to name a person or a thing.

— *s.* an abortion.

Topaapaa, *s* a disfigured, or an unhandsome face; an old face on young shoulders.

Topaatoa, *v. a* to add all together, all falling to work at once.

Topahaa, *v. a* to drop the work; to forsake utterly.

Topahura, *v. n.* to sit unconcerned, while others are acting.

— *a.* barren

Topamoto, *v. n* to fall from a blow of the fist; to be struck by some alarm.

Topamotoai, *s.* astonishment arising from ill news suddenly made known.

Topaoro, *a.* stunted, of long standing, but of diminutive growth.

Topapaa, *s.* maize, or Indian corn.

Topapu, *v. n.* to fall down, as drops of rain, when there is no wind.

— *v. n.* to be careless, void of energy; to be settled, dwelling at ease.

Topara, *a.* discoloured, as scorched leaves; discoloured, as water by a flood; having a withered appearance, as grass.

Toparere, *v. n.* to drop from a height.

— *v. n.* to be overtaken with sleep; to let fall; forget.

Toparuru, *v. a.* to frighten another.

— *s.* the fluttering of a bird that cannot fly.

Topata, *s.* a drop.

— *v. n* to drop, as rain, &c.

Topatai, *s.* a piece that forms,

the hind part of the keel of a canoe.

— *v. n.* to drop into the sea.

Topatairitê, *v. n.* to be soon done, or consumed.

Topatapata, *v. n.* to drop repeatedly, be dropping.

Topataparuru, *v. a.* to frighten another repeatedly.

Topatari, *v. n.* to fall, as a bunch, or cocoanut branch; see *tari.*

— *s.* a violent affliction of the mind, on being overtaken by some evil.

— *v. n.* to be in a hysteric or epileptic fit; to be, according to the native notion, under the powerful influence of some ghostly agent.

Topataûa, *s.* the name of a small fish found in inland places having no communication with the sea, and therefore supposed to drop with the rain, see *ua.*

Topataue. *v. a.* to fall from a height without being entangled.

Topatie, *v. n.* to be in a frantic state of mind.

Topato, *s.* the deep between two shallow places.

— *v. n.* to fall headlong.

Topatopau, *s.* the part of a pig's belly below the ribs on each side.

Topatopa, *v. n.* to fall by miscarriage or abortion.

Topatu, *v. n.* to fall in an erect posture.

Topaturi, *v. n.* to fall on the knees.

Topauru. *v. n.* to fall from a breadfruit tree; a frequent occurrence.

Tope, *s.* a tail, or lock of hair hanging behind.

Tope, *v. a.* to prune, cut off superfluous branches of a tree or plant; to chop off the ends of rafters, the eaves of a house, &c.

Topearo, *v. a.* to push forward.

— *v. n.* to rally, as an army.

Topetope, *v. n.* to prune, or cut repeatedly.

Topi, *s.* proneness to frequent pregnancy.

Topie, *s.* proneness to grow fat.

Tora, *a.* ill savoured.

Toraa, *s.* the time or place of conception; the time and place of wrestling.

Torahui, *s.* the act of laying a *rahui*; the person that lays the rahui or prohibition.

Torata, *adv.* slovenly, indecently.

Toratora, *s.* an offensive smell.

— *a.* of a lasting ill odour.

Tore, *s.* a part of a paper kite.

— *a.* striped, chequered, as cloth.

— *v. n.* to grow, as proud flesh in a sore.

Torea, *s.* the name of a bird.

— *s.* the name of a tune beaten on the cloth beam of the women.

Toreahuaore. *s.* a nimble light footed person.

Toreamatahere, *s.* a wary *torea* that has escaped a snare; *fig.* a wary person that cannot be imposed upon.

Toreataihee, *s.* a mode of attack in battle; also toreahueare.

Toreataioutu, *s.* a noisy mischief making person.

Toreataiouiu, *s.* a noisy mischief making person.

Toretahua, *s.* a place marked out and raised for the use of archers.

Toreto. *s.* the small eggs in a turtle.

Toretore, *v. n.* to be growing, as proud flesh in a sore.

— *v. n.* to be in streaks.

Toriirii, *a.* small, as drops of drizzling rain.

— *v. n.* to be falling in small drops.

Toro, *s.* the name of a species of banana.

— *s.* the name of a fishing net.

— *v. n.* to run or creep, as vines or roots of plants; to stretch out.

Toroa, *s.* business, office, occupation.

Toroa, *s.* the name of a marine bird.

Toroau, *s.* a very thin corpse.

Toroea, *s.* the name of a small tree, whose leaves resemble those of a coffee tree.

Toroire, *s.* the name of a pod bearing tree.

Toromaa, *v. n.* to be divided between two objects, as the mind, or affection.

Toromatatini, *s.* a fishing net.

Toromeho, *s.* the name of a sweet scented oil.

Toromiro, *s.* an offensive smell, as of a dead carcass.

— *s.* a name of the sacred tree *amae*; *fig.* a person of consideration.

Toroiriro, *v. n.* to be humbled or abashed before a superior; to humble one'self before a great man.

Tororû, *a.* plentiful, refreshing, applied to rain.

Torotea, *s.* the same as toroea.

— *s.* a full grown aute or paper mulberry.

Torotoro, *v. n.* to creep; see *toro.*

— *v. a.* to select, to pick out, to scrape together.

Torotoroiore, *s.* a piece of wood fastened to the lower ends of rafters in a Tahitian house.

Torotoromaa, *v. n.* to branch out, as the veins of the leg or arm.

Torotoroû, *s.* a lazy, inactive person.

Torotorouaua, *v. n.* to be distended, as the veins.

Toroû, *s* a lazy person, as torotoroû.

Toru, *a.* three; see *atoru*, *etoru*.

Tota, *intj.* an exclamation of derision.

Totara, *s.* the hedge hog fish.

Totaitai, *s.* an inferior sort of sugar cane.

Totamu, *v. a.* to caulk a boat, ship, &c.

Totaraupoonui, *s.* a peculiarly built canoe, the head not in proportion to the stern; *fig.* an injudicious mode of attack in war.

Tote, *s.* an apparatus for catching the cuttle fish.

— *v. a.* to fish for the cuttle-fish; to fasten by tying.

— *v. n.* to sound as a bell; to be in anger, to speak in confusion.

Toteatoti, *s.* a mode of fishing for the little atoti; an insignificant fish.

Totero, *s* small eggs of fowls, turtle, &c. also a contemptuous expression.

Toti, *a.* tied, secured, cemented; also bound by an agreement.

— *v. n.* to be double tied, as a bundle.

Totitotaa, *v. n.* to go from place to place to babble.

Toto, *s.* blood; also juice or sap of plants, &c.

Totô, *v. n.* to shake as a fisherman's line when the fish bite.

Tòtò, *s.* a net or bag for a calabash, in which it is carried about with water, &c.

Tôtô, *v. n.* to pant, as two fowls when fighting; to make a noise, as a hen when her nest is disturbed; to rap with a finger, or strike a drum with a finger.

Totoa, *v. a.* to do some mischief.

— *a.* mischievous, doing harm.

Totoe, *s.* a species of a crab.

— *s.* a piece of wood struck by a man, when removing the rahui.

— *s.* some supposed vengeance for a crime.

Totoee, *v. n.* to be not noticing a friend; also in speech, to wander from the subject.

Totoetai, *s.* the name of a crab.

Totohara, *s.* a visitation or punishment, supposed to be inflicted on account of some crime.

Totoie, *s.* a little game, or play of children.

Totomapû, *v. a.* to do some mischief or violence.

— *s.* the doer of some mischief; the same as *totoa.*

Tòtómato, *v. a.* to strike the ground when in pursuit of hidden property, that is supposed to be buried.

Totono. *v. a.* the dual of tono, to send.

Totoo, *v. a.* to distend.

Totoo, *v. a.* to enlarge a thing.

Totoorooro, *v. a.* to speak laconically; see *topatairite.*

Totopao, *s.* the blood obtained by striking the head with the shark's tooth; formerly a frequent custom of women in token of grief or affection.

Totoro, *s.* decrepitude.

— *v. n.* to be shrivelled, worn out by age.

— *v. n.* to creep, or move slowly.

— *v. a.* to trace by following a track, to trace a stalk or vine to the rest of a plant.

Totoroaena, *s.* decrepitude, old age.

— *a.* old, stricken in year's, worn with age.

Totoroaipo, *s.* the act of eating at home, being overtaken by darkness.

Totoriore, *s.* the same as *torotoroiore.*

Totoroporeho, *s.* a part of the instrument that is used to catch the cuttle fish.

Totorou, *s.* a work that will not be done.

Totorouto, *s.* a dancing tune beaten on the cloth beam by the women when making cloth.

Tototo, *s.* a species of broom, called also *atoto.*

Totova, *s.* mischief; the same as *totoa.*

Tou, *s.* the name of a tree, (the *cordia*).

To'u, *poss. pron.* my, mine; see *ta, to, na.*

Tou, *poss. pron.* thine, according to other dialects, but not much used at Tahiti, as *to'u*, mine, *to oe*, thine, *tona*, his, are the regular Tahitian *poss. pron.*

Touura, *a.* red, coloured by the sun.

Touri, *a.* darkish in colour.

Toutu, *a.* of a dark colour; see *uriuri*; marred, applied to the face.

Tovanuvanu, *s.* coldness; see *anuanu.*

Tu, *s* the name of a Tahitian god, as also formerly of the the king of Tahiti, so that the syllable *tu* became sacred, and was changed into *tia* in most words.

— *s.* an advocate, supporter, pleader for another; see *tia.*

— *v. n.* to stand erect; to be upright or straight.

— *v. n.* to fit, agree, to answer the purpose.

— *prep.* from; see *atu, atura*, or *tura.*

Tua, *s.* the back; the great open sea.

— *s.* a maggot; see *iro.*

— *s.* an upper flat stone of a wall; see *tuava.*

— *v. a.* to put on the upper stone of a wall.

— *v. a.* to cut; see *tapu.*

— *v. n.* to rest, or wait; see *tatari.*

— *s.* a company; see *tuaa.*

Tuaa, *a.* lewd, shameless, indecent, profane.

— *s.* a short sleep.

— *v. n.* to sleep a little.

Tuaaea, *s.* a sacred place.

Tuaana, *s.* (*tuakana*) an elder brother; also a senior relation.

Tuaane, *s.* a brother in relation to a sister.

Tuaaoa, *v. n.* to set in, applied to the wind.

Tuae, *v. a.* to make room; see *faaatea.*

Tuafati, *s.* a crick in the back.

Tuaha, *a.* full feathered, as a fowl able to fly.

Tuahee, *a*, lean, emaciated; see *tiahee*; also loose, as the coils of a rope.

Tuahine, *s.* a sister.

Tuahoro, *a.* strong, athletic.

Tuahu, *s.* a disease of the skin.

— *s.* a wharf, or quay.

— *s.* the name of a part of the marae.

— *v. a.* to fill up the earth about a plant; also to work wickedness.

Tuai, *v. n.* to wait, see *tiai*; to exercise patience.

— *s.* a small species of cockle.

— *a.* productive, as farinaceous plants.

— *v. n.* to lie on the back with the thighs extended; to move the thighs in dancing.

Tuaio, *s.* the back bone; the fleshy parts on each side of the back bone.

Tuaivi, *s.* the slope of a mountain ridge.

Tuamanuu, *s.* the same as *tuafati.*

Tuamata, *s.* the eyebrows.

Tuamoo, *s.* the spine.

Tuamoua, *s* a mountain ridge.

Tuani, *s.* a restorer, one who helps, or supports.

Tuaoao, *v. n.* to be practising as players.

Tuapa, *s.* a weakling in the ranks; a bird just beginning to fly.

Tuapau, *s.* great weariness, as by labour.

Tuapo, *s.* a dream; an unexpected favour.

Tuapu, *s.* a humpback.

— *a.* humpbacked.

Tuara, *s.* the sail of a vessel.

— *v. a.* to treat a person with contempt.

— *v. n.* to forage for food.

Tuara, *v. n.* to have weakness of the joints; to smite together, as the limbs, through weakness.

— *a.* unfit, unsuitable.

Tuaraaru, *v. n.* to be shaking through weakness.

Tuaruhuria, *v. n.* to move in a tremulous manner; to be aback, as a sail.

Tuaraina, *a.* sun burnt; discoloured by filth.

Tuararirii, *s.* small talk or conversation, commonly about evil things.

Tuarau, *s.* a bait used by fishermen in the canoe called *tira.*

Tuarehu, *a.* congregated, assembled.

— *v. n.* to be assembled, as a multitude.

Tuarii, *s.* a little trifling talk.

Tuariirii, *s.* the same as *tuarii,* and *tuararirii.*

Tuaroi, *s.* a bed, a place of sleeping; a place of rest or abode.

Tuaroaroa, *v. n.* to wait, to stay for; see *hapapa.*

Tuarorovau, *a.* unsettled, changeable as the wind.

Tuaru, *s.* a piece of wood on the ridge of a native house.

— *v. a.* to banish; see *tuvaru.*

Tuarua, *v. n.* to be ever returning, as a flood.

Tuata, *s.* the name of a stone adze.

— *v. a.* to spear fish by moonlight.

— *v. a.* to be gorged, or glutted with food.

Tuataata, *s.* the followers of a person.

Tuatahapa, *s.* a small effort to finish a work.

Tuatapapa, *v. n.* to trace in order of time various events and transactions.

Tuatapapa, *v. a.* to heap one thing upon another.

Tuatau, *a.* long, protracted, as the time of doing a thing.

Tuatea, *s.* the name of a species of yam.

Tuatea, *s.* a great rolling billow of the sea.

Tuateaea, *s.* a sacred place, such as the front of the marae, the back of the king, &c.

Tuateaehâ, *s.* the wide sea out of sight of land.

Tuati, *v. a.* to join, or close up, see *taati.*

Tuatii, *v. n.* to stand, as a *tii,* or image, in a senseless gaze or surprize.

Tuatoa, *v. n.* to be not diminished, to be in continuance.

Tuatoto, *s.* birth pains, the efforts of a woman in travail.

Tuatuâ, *s.* a word of address in prayer, used in the evening at a marae; in *Rarotonga* it signifies the same as *parau.*

Tuatua, *a.* rough, as the surface of a thing; also frowning; *matatuatua*, is a rough frowning face.

Tuatuaau, *s.* a secret robber and murderer.

— *v. a.* to rob and murder secretly.

Tuatuaautara, *v. n.* to stand aloof.

Tuatuai, *s.* a species of cockle.

— *s.* a large athletic person.

Tuatuaihu, *v. n.* to be bewildered as a traveller, after losing the road among the bushes.

Tuatuaohipa, *v. a.* to be overburdened with work.

Tuatuapoi, *s.* a swoon, or fainting fit.

— *v. n.* to swoon, or faint.

— *s.* a burdensome work.

Tuatuarau, *a.* multiplied, increased.

Tuatuarave, *intj.* signifying wonder at the greatness or strangeness of a thing.

Tuau, *s.* the name of a heathen prayer.

— *v. a.* to level or make plain and decent, as the gardener his ground.

— *v. a.* to ravage, or lay waste, as in war.

Tua'u, *v. n.* to banish, expel; — see *tuaru.*

Tuau'o, *s.* a powerful man, a heavy thing.

Tuaunahea, *v. n.* to be burnt by the sun.

Tuauri, *s.* the ancient people of the place; an old cunning priest.

Tuauru, *v. n.* to be overwhelmed with trouble.

Tuarua, *s.* a pillow.

Tuatuani, *s.* a person who seeks reconciliation with an enemy.

Tuava, *v. n.* to be wasted, as the body of a person by disease or famine.

Tuava, *s.* (*guava*) the guava tree and fruit, introduced to the islands in 1808.

Tuave, *s.* an unfinished story.

Tuavera, *s.* a species of breadfruit.

— *a.* burnt with the sun.

Tue, *s.* the core of the vi apple, kernel of the ahia, the body of a crab, star fish, &c.

— *v. a.* to impel, play at foot ball, kick with the foot; to strike against a thing.

Tuea, *s.* a hard vi apple that has no pulp.

Tuemata, *s* the eye brows.

Tuematafatiore, *s.* an eye that gazes steadily.

— *s.* the eyes of an adulterer.

Tuematamauru, *s.* a person with the hair of the eyebrows falling off, a sign of the venereal disease.

Tuere, *a.* loquacious, having words, but no doings.

Tuerehu, *s.* a great concourse of people.

Tueretahoraraa, *s.* a perfect calm.

Tueretahoroore, *s.* a knot in a net.

Tuete, *s.* the god of adultery and fornication.

Tuetue, *a.* thick, stout, as cloth; irregular, as cloth or boards.

— *v. n.* to withstand, oppose, rebut.

Tuetueavero, *s.* the first canoe that approaches the shore of an enemy.

Tueve, *v. a.* to press, or throng.

— *v. n.* to be first or foremost.

Tufa, *s.* the reef uncovered at low water.

— *v. n.* to be very loud, applied to the sea on the reefs; see *tiamaha.*

— *v. a.* to share, or divide portions.

— *v. a.* to spit; see *huare.*

Tufaa, *s.* a share, portion, division, heritage.

Tufafa, *a.* slack, inert, without vigour.

Tufara, *s.* the name of a large red fish.

— *s.* the name of a bird.

Tafarefare, *a.* empty, void of contents.

Tufatete, *adv.* lazily, slow in working.

Tufatufaee, *v. n.* to have each his share; to take each his course.

Tufera, *v. n.* to go obscenely exposed.

Tufera, *v. n.* to be indolent.

Tuferafera, *v. n.* to expose the person obscenely, and that repeatedly.

Tuferu, *v. a.* to scratch, as a hen.

Tufetu, *v. a.* to fold up; see *tiafetu.*

Tufetufetu, *v. a.* to fold a thing repeatedly.

Tufefeu, *v. n.* to be wrangling, promoting strife.

— *v. a.* to provoke by words or actions.

Tuha, *v. a.* to split, to divide; see *tufa.*

Tuhâ, *v. n.* to be something less than usual, as the flowing of the sea; to be low, as the water on the reefs; see *tufa, tiamaha.*

Tuhaa, *s.* a share; see *tufaa.*

Tuhatuha, *v. a.* to spit repeatedly.

Tuhatuhaee, *v. n.* the same as *tufatufaee.*

Tuhau, *s.* a visitor from another place.

Tuheru, *v. a.* the same as *tuferu.*

Tuhi, *s.* the name of a fish.

— *s.* an imprecation, or curse.

— *v. a.* to curse, to imprecate.

Tuhiauira, *v. a.* to charge rashly, and bluntly, without sufficient proof.

Tuhituhi, *v. a.* to curse repeatedly.

— *a.* cursing, given to cursing.

— *a.* cloying, luscious, over sweet.

— *v. n.* to be clogged, to be tired, or wearied of any thing.

Tuhou, *s.* a novice, a new comer; see *tiahou.*

— *s.* the first wetting of a fishing net.

— *a.* young, inexperienced.

Tuhuru, *s.* a young bird, when the feathers just begin to grow.

Tui, *s.* a disease of the ear.

— *v. a.* to pierce, make a hole or opening.

— *v. a.* to but, or impel; to strike with the head or horns, as a beast in fighting; to strike, smite with the hand.

— *s.* a part of a canoe.

— *s.* a certain prayer and ceremony on account of a deceased person, to prevent his soul returning and troubling the living; see *aiaru.*

— *s.* the hiccough.

— *s.* a section of a prayer, or song.
— *s.* a pestle; see *penu.*
— *s.* the name of a sort of spider.
— *v. n.* to spread, as a report; *ua tui te roo*, the fame is gone abroad.
— *v. n.* to be dividing, as midnight, which is called *tui* raa po.
— *v. a.* to beat or pound; see *otui.*
Tuia, *s.* a human sacrifice taken to the marae.
— *a.* lean, meagre; see *tiahê.*
Tuiaau, *s.* a warrior who seeks out his foe in every place.
— *s.* a fisherman who seeks fish in the holes in the reef.
Tuiaha, *s.* from *tui* to pierce, and *aha* sinnet; a hog marked with sinnet in token of dedication to the gods.
— *s.* a play term; the two first cocks that are put to fighting.
— *v. a.* to devote to the service of a god, by marking with *aha* or sinnet.
Tuiaroha, *v. n.* to faint through want of sustenance; se *matapouri.*
Tuiate, *s.* a disorder of the stomach.
Tuiau, *v. a.* to join hand in hand; to clasp hands, to hang on the arm.
— *v. n.* to be led, or drawn.
— *s.* a line that runs through the meshes of a Tahitian fishing net, to which are fastened the weights and buoys.
Tuiauorero, *v. a.* to wrest, or misinterpret a speech at a public meeting, &c.
Tuiee, *s.* a mode of attack by a wrestler.
Tuifara, *s.* a certain ceremony of the arioi.
— *s.* a violent blow with the fist.
Tuifaro, *v. n.* to be wearied in waiting.
Tuiharo, *s.* the same as *tuifaro.*
Tuiharoa, *v. n.* to be faint, as *tuiaroha.*
Tuihau, *s.* a visitor or guest.
Tuihê, *a.* thin, lank, meagre.
Tuihêhai, *s.* a wanton, or libidinous person.
Tuimua, *s.* a part of a canoe; *tuivaa.*
Tuiora, *v. a.* to set well with wedges and tyings, a term used by canoe builders.
Tuipaapaa, *v. a.* to finish, put an end to a work.
Tuiri, *s.* small stones, pebbles, gravel.
Tuiroo, *a.* famous, noted, warlike.
Tuiroro, *s.* a disease of the ear.
Tuita, *v. n.* to be fitted, or well joined together.
Tuitaa, *v. n.* to grind, as the jaws in anger.
Tuitaata. *s.* a barbarous ceremony performed at the conclusion of war, when peace was to be established. One of the slain was cut to pieces, and sent by messengers to the chiefs of the different divisions of the land, and this was *tuitaata.*
Tuitaora, *v. a.* to throw a stone.
Tuiteta, *v. a.* to cast the arm around, as a wrestler in the Tahitian wrestling matches.
— *v. a.* to take the first fruits to the gods and the king.
Tuitiua, *s.* the name of a fish.

Tuituiavera, *v. a.* to set fire to the mountains.
— *s.* the person that sets the mountain wilderness on fire; *fig.* a stirrer up of strife.
Tuituiaviso, *s.* a speech that causes strife.
Tuituiporo, *s.* a feast and ceremonies for canoe building.
Tuituitu, *v. a.* to burn a tree while standing.
Tuitupapau, *s.* a prayer, and certain ceremonies performed for the dead, that the spirit might not come to annoy the living.
Tuiupea, *s.* a stick used for convenience in carrying a large fishing net.
Tuma, *s.* a glutton, a gormandizer.
Tuma, *adv.* over and above, as *ehuru tumarua*, ten and two over or above.
Tumama, *s.* a root or foundation.
Tumami, *s.* certain motions in the native dance.
— *a.* having a large full kernel.
Tumaaha, *v. n.* to sit perfectly unconcerned in the midst of work, or of danger.
Tumaretei, *v. n.* to be turning or rolling over, to roll, as a wheel or hoop.
Tumaoaoa, *v. n.* to be ashamed, as a person not taken notice of.
Tumarorarora, *v. n.* to be ashamed, as *tumaoaoa.*
Tumata, *v. a.* to look at two persons fighting, without making any attempt to part them.
Tumata'a, *s.* the name of a renowned arioi.
Tumatapopoo, *s.* the name of a certain idolatrous feast and ceremony on account of the dead.
Tumatariri, *s.* an unfriendly countenance.
Tumatatea, *v. n.* to stand off at a distance, giving no help, only looking, while others are struggling with work, or some difficulty.
Tumatuma, *a.* vast, great in quantity; see *hatuma.*
Tumau, *s.* constipation.
Tumiro, *v. a.* to exercise in the use of arms.
Tumoa, *s.* ten fathoms; see *umi.*
Tumoarau, *s.* a fleet of canoes; see *papaupea*; the leaves used for catching fish; see *raoere.*
Tumu, *s.* root, origin, cause, foundation.
— *s.* the name of a certain bird.
Tumû, *a.* blunt, pointless; see *tiamu.*
— *v. n.* to be confounded.
Tumumu, *v. n.* to ring again, as some noise.
Tumureva, *s.* the name of a certain wind.
Tumutaua, *s.* lasting strife or contention.
Tumutumu, *s.* the red part of the bark of the *uru* tree.
— *v. n.* to distance, by receding from an object; to become small, as the object becomes distant.
Tumuna, *s.* a mountain plantain when half ripe.
Tuna, *s.* a fresh water eel; see *puhi.*
Tunahaavaro, *s.* a species of

the eel; *fig.* a restless person, whose speech and behaviour indicate malice.

Tunaofao, *s.* the same as *tunahaavaro*

Tunaoaro, *s.* the same as *haavaro.*

Tunapu, *s.* a fresh water eel that lives in very deep water.

Tunatoe, *s.* the remaining one, after all had been supplied

Tunatore, *s.* a species of salt water eel.

Tunoa, *s.* dark spots in the face.

Tunono, *s.* a game in which the nono apples are thrown by a sling.

Tunoo, *s.* a certain imprecation or curse.

— *s.* a certain ceremony used by the sorcerer, to cause a person's death.

— *v. a.* to practise the *tunoo.*

Tunu, *v. a.* to cook victuals by roasting or boiling.

— *a.* roasted or boiled, applied to food.

Tunupa, *a.* roasted in the skin, or roasted by being put on the fire.

Tunuvehi, *a.* roasted in a covering of leaves, &c.

Tuo, *v. n.* to bawl, or shout aloud.

Tuofao, *s.* such as go to the front of the battle.

Tuoi, *v. n.* to stumble through weakness.

Tuoivi, *a.* wasted, lean of flesh.

Tuoo, *v. n.* to sit sullen, from the absence of food, &c.

Tuoo, *a.* stunted, of slow growth.

Tuoou, *v. n.* to nod, as two persons to each other.

Tuoro, *s* a cry or call.

— *v. a.* to call upon a person; see *tiaoro.*

Tuoru, *s.* a sort of cloth, of which tiaputas are made.

Tuou, *v. n.* to beckon, or nod with the head.

Tuoufao, *s.* the same as *tuofao,* and *tuaifao.*

Tuouou, *v. n.* to beckon, nod, or make signs repeatedly.

— *s* a certain mode of catching fish.

Tuoura, *s.* the name of a species of yam.

— *a* red, reddish; beautifully attired.

Tuououvai, *s.* a puff of wind with rain.

Tupa, *s.* a land crab.

Tupâ, *v. a.* to hollow out, excavate or scoop.

Tupaata, *s.* laughter.

Tupâata, *v. n.* to laugh, to laugh to scorn.

Tupaetaurua, *s.* the ring that encircles a game.

Tupaha, *s.* a noisy talkative man.

Tupahono, *s.* a son who takes the place of his father as a warrior.

Tupai, *s.* a hammer, or mallet.

— *v. a.* to strike, hammer; beat, break a shell.

Tupao, *s.* holes in the rocks, where the fish take shelter to hide themselves.

— *v. a.* to chop unskilfully.

Tupaomhoroa, *s.* a long toothed person. Long teeth are reckoned by the Tahitians an unfavourable indication of the disposition of a person.

Tupaopao, *v. a.* to cut the hair in various figures.

Tupaopaoa, *s.* a steersman, a pilot.

Tupapa, *v. a.* to beg, teaze and take; to plunder; *v. a.* to collect together, to gather against a time of need.

— *a.* greedy, unsatiable.

Tupapaarau, *s.* things heaped on each other.

— *v a.* to heap one on another.

— *s.* a talebearer.

Tupapau, *s.* (*tupapaku*) a corpse.

— *s.* a ghost, or apparition, the supposed spirit of the dead; an old grievance raised from oblivion.

Tupapauraura, *a.* utterly consumed, wasted altogether, as by war.

Tuparu, *s.* a sort of pudding made of grated cocoanut, banana, &c. mixed together.

Tupatai, *s.* a fleet, sea forces arranged for a sea fight.

— *s.* a battle at sea.

Tupatapatao, *v. n.* to be on the move from place to place; to be unsettled as to residence.

Tupatupa, *a.* suspicious; having a dubious aspect.

— *v. n.* to surmise evil.

— *v. a* to excite to some evil.

Tupatupaahutoru, *s.* a crab from the crevices of a wall; *fig.* a person that crawls without shame into the presence of a chief, to teaze him by begging.

Tupatupatai, *v. a.* to strike repeatedly with the fist.

Tupaurupauru, *s.* the name of a play among children, hide and seek.

Tupautu, *s* an army going to fight on the land.

Tupautii, *s.* an ill favoured, ill grown person.

Tupe, *s.* a species of the cockle shell.

Tupeheva, *s.* the motions of the legs, &c. of the man who had the *parae*, which see.

Tupepu, *s.* the name of a species of thin native cloth; see *pupepu.*

Tupere, *s.* a shell of the cockle kind, that was worshipped in some of the islands, and said to be used by the gods in the po, to scrape the souls of men for food.

— *s.* (Engl. *gooseberry*) the cape gooseberry.

— *v. n.* to stumble, or trip in walking, to move, or roll, as a boat in the sea.

Tuperepere, *v. n.* to roll, or move repeatedly, as a vessel at sea; to stumble repeatedly.

Tuperetete, *v. n.* to be stumbling.

Tuperetii, *adv.* topsy turvy, head down, heels up.

Tuperetiti, *v. n.* the same as *tuperetete.*

Tupereua, *a.* random, heedless, without thought.

Tupetupe, *s.* a sort of fishing net.

— *s.* a word used by the priests in some of their idolatrous prayers.

— *adv.* loiteringly, behind all.

Tupoina, *v. n* to forget; see *aromoina.*

Tupotupo, *s.* a word of contempt addressed to the *parae* or *tupeheva.*

Tupou, *v. n.* to bow the head and show the posteriors towards a person, by way of contempt.

Tupu, *v. n.* to grow; to happen, to come to pass.

— *s.* the name of a plant.

— *s.* any thing that was used by a sorcerer to have access to a person, such as hair, spittle, &c.

Tupua, *s.* a charmer, one that could defend himself against the arts of a sorcerer.

— *s.* a lock of hair hanging behind.

— *s.* a lock of hair cut off from the head of a deceased person to keep in remembrance of him.

Tupuai, *s.* the crown of the head; the top of a mountain. The name of an island.

Tupuarii, *s.* a fine grown person.

Tupuhau, *s.* the highest in growth.

Tupumoea, *s.* a piece of a mat, by means of which the sorcerer worked destruction.

Tupuna, *s.* an ancestor, a grandfather.

Tuputino, *v. n.* to grow in bulk, but not otherwise.

Tuputu, *s.* a flock of birds.

— *s.* an ill founded report,

Tuputupu, *s.* a sort of mushroom.

— *s.* a red, dusty like mould, that grows on a stale bread fruit.

Tuputupua, *s.* a tii or demon.

— *s.* something vile, insignificant, ugly, or contemptible; also something extraordinary, large, or great.

Tura, *prep,* & *adv.* from; a contraction of *atu* and *ra,* which see.

Tura, *v. n.* to be exalted; to be invested with power, to have honour; see *faatura.*

Turaa, *s.* a cock fighter.

— *v. a.* to set cocks to fight.

Turaau, *s.* the manual exercise of the native arms.

— *s.* a fencer, one practised in the native exercise of arms; see *tiaraau.*

Turae, *v. a.* to resist; see *turai.*

Turahi, *v. a.* to caulk a vessel, boat, canoe, &c.

Turai, *v a.* to push from, resist, repulse.

Turaiarea, *v. n.* to be cut, or battered down, as the rea or turmeric in its season.

Turatura, *s.* the name of a medicinal plant.

— *a.* honoured, exalted.

Turau, *a.* prolific, as a fruit tree.

— *v. n.* to stand up, as a company together.

Ture, *s.* (*Heb. torah,* without the points *ture*) a law, rule of conduct; code of laws.

— *v. n.* to be exalted, honoured, see *tura.*

Tureia, *a.* conversant, communicative.

Tureiaore, *a.* not communicative, not moveable by entreaty.

Tureirei, *v. n.* to stand on the extreme end, or on a slippery place.

— *a.* unsettled, restless.

Turepu, *s* an agitator, disturber.

— *v. a.* to stir up, to cause disturbance.

Turepua, *s.* a crowd.

Tureru, *v. a.* to disturb; as *turepu.*

Turepurepu, *v. a.* to agitate repeatedly

Turerua, *v. n.* to be in peace, no agitation.

Turi, *s.* the name of an ancient hero of whom many tales were told.

— *s.* the knee; also a knee of timber in a boat or ship.

— *s.* deafness; a deaf person.

— *v. n* (*kuli, tuli,* Malay, *tuli*) to be deaf.

— *a.* deaf, not able to distinguish sounds.

Turimene, *s.* a disorder of the knee.

Turiopa, *s.* weakness of the knees, through weariness or disease.

Turiri, *v. n.* to be unsuitable, as not answering a purpose, applied to a piece of timber.

— *a.* inflexible, unmanageable.

Turituri, *s.* deafness by great noise.

Turoia, *a.* not able to move, as a bed ridden person.

Turora, *v. n.* to be weak through want of necessary food; to be in straits through deficiency of things.

Turori, *v. n.* to stagger, or stumble; to be unsteady.

Turorirori, *v. n.* to stagger or stumble repeatedly.

Turoto, *s.* comfort, contentment.

— *a.* comfortable, satisfying.

— *v. n.* to be comforted, or made contented.

Turou, *v. n.* to bow, incline the head; to be abashed, filled with shame.

s. a certain native curse.

— *v. a.* to curse in the turou manner.

Turu, *s.* a prop, side post of a house, any support or help, assistance; ea *turu*, a ladder.

— *v. a.* to prop, or render support in any way.

Turua, *v. n.* to stand equal on both sides; see *tu* and *rua.*

Turuarii, *s* the name of a certain feast and ceremony, when a human sacrifice was offered to *Oro*, and prayers made.

Turuhe, *s.* drowsiness, lethargy.

— *v. n.* to be drowsy; inclining to dullness.

Turui, *s.* a heap of stones; see *paepae.*

— *s.* a stone, or other thing, to lean against for support.

— *s.* the name of a feast and certain ceremonies.

— *v. n* to lean against a thing; see *tuturi.*

Turuiaparere, *s* an assistant who has gone away.

Turuiaparai, *s.* a prayer for the *paraitua*, as certain heathen ceremonies were called.

Turuma, *s.* a place in the outside of the back part of the native houses, where all refuse was cast, a sort of dunghill; but it was sacred, and no one ought to walk over it; see *tuuraa turuma.*

Turuora, *v. a.* to save alive in time of war.

Tururi, *v. n* to look aside, inattentively.

Tururû, *v. a.* to put off a thing as useless.
— *s.* a frightful noise by the mouth to astound another.
— *v. n.* to be put in fear by a startling noise.
— *s.* a friendly support or defence.
— *v. n.* to be helped by a taua or friend.
Turutootoo, *s.* (*turutogotogo*) a staff or a walking stick; see *tootoo.*
Turuturu, *s.* the side posts of a house.
— *v. a.* to help or assist repeatedly.
Tutà, *v. a.* to carry on the hip.
Tutaa, *s.* the name of a native pahi, or large canoe.
— *s.* a person noted for adultery.
Tutae, *s.* the excrements of any kind of animal.
Tutaeauri, *s.* the rust of iron, or any metal.
— *s.* a name given to those who have been convicted of breaking the laws.
Tutaee, *v. a.* to carry or convey under the arm and above the hip.
— *s.* the name of a ceremony for purifying from the pollution of the dead; burning for the dead, viz. the rubbish, &c., after the corpse was placed on a scaffold.
Tutaehautaua, *s.* the sudden impression made by the unexpected appearance of something formidable.
Tutaero, *s.* a blight of trees and plants, a disease of the bark, that generally kills them.
Tutàhoroa, *s.* the road by which the spirits of the dead were supposed to go to the *po.*
Tutai, *s.* red clouds on the horizon; also an expression in some of the heathenish prayers.
Tutaia, *s.* business; see *tere.*
Tutaimarohea, *s.* a small portion, an insufficient quantity.
Tutaimaroea, *s.* a small quantity, as *tutaimarohea.*
Tutaimaroiti, *s.* the same as *tutaimarohea.*
Tutairi, *v. n.* to appear and begone again presently.
Tutâivi, *v. n.* to carry the slain or wounded of the battle; from *tutà* to carry, and *ivi.*
Tutaivi, *s.* clouds as a sign of wind; see *tutai.*
Tutaora, *a.* reproachful, scurrilous.
— *v. a.* to reproach, defame.
Tutapa, *s.* an abscess in the groin; see *tapa.*
Tutaraai, *s.* a person that goes from place to place to eat what he can get.
Tutaraauaua, *s.* a species of cockroach.
Tutari, *v. n.* to lead or conduct; to move a bait backward and forward to induce an eel to come out of its hole; to tempt, entice.
Tutariharupuu, *s.* the person who calls the players to come to the game *haruraapuu.*
Tataritaripo, *v. a.* to conduct away in the night.
Tutau, *s.* an anchor; see *tiatau.*
— *v. a.* to cast anchor.
— *v. n.* to lie at anchor; te be

steeping or lying in soak in the water; to be sunk.

Tutautohe, *s.* laziness, inactivity.

— *v. n.* to lie at anchor, as it were sitting still, doing nothing.

Tutava, *v. a.* to pull the reverse way in order to go back with a boat.

— *s.* the branch that grows on the side of the trunk.

— *s.* the action of the male and female dogs in disengaging themselves.

Tutavae, *s* war with all its evil consequences.

Tute, *v. n.* to push away, force away; see *turai.*

Tutê, *a.* having indications of near ripeness, applied to plantains, and other fruits.

Tutei, *v. n.* to sit in a tottering unstable way; to slip or move from a place, to pass aside.

— *v. n.* to be enlarged through eating or disease, applied to the belly.

Tutei, *v. a.* to touch slightly.

Tuteraimarama, *s.* the name of the god of the *Meho*, or fugitives of the mountains.

Tutere, *s.* a party ready for journeying.

— *v. n.* to be consumed, as the inhabitants of a place; to be extirpated.

Tutetute, *v. a.* to push repeatedly; to push one against another.

Tutii, *s.* an ancestor; see *tupuna*; a person that would rest any where rather than at home.

— *s.* a carved image at the head of a canoe.

— *s.* a sort of scaffold on which the warriors stood in a sea-fight.

Tutiifaea, *s.* a person that does not regard his home.

Tutitahemoa, *s.* a name given to some of the inhabitants of Atehuru, on accouut of their niggardliness about fish.

Tutoa, *s* a fabled monster and cannibal, said to exist at Tahiti in old times.

Tutoee, *v. a.* to be stepping aside, to be doing the reverse of what is required.

Tutoi, *adv.* superficially, slightly; no proper foundation, as of an ill report.

Tutoia, *adv.* slightly, as *puta tutoia*, pierced or wounded slightly.

— *a.* fallen away from a full habit; see *tuahê.*

Tutoivi, *a.* lean, meagre.

Tutono, *v. a.* to send a messenger.

Tutonu, *s.* the name of a certain foolish game.

— *v. n.* to look steadfastly.

Tutoo, *s.* a lasting cough; the asthma.

— *v. a.* to pull, or drag along; see *puto.*

— *v. a.* to shove or push aside.

Tutou, *s.* the unexpected meeting of two hostile parties.

Tutu, *s.* the name of a tree.

— *s.* a short pole on the top of a fishing net.

— *s.* the name of a mode of fishing.

— *v. a.* to beat the layers of bark with the cloth mallet,

as the women do in cloth making.
— *v. a.* to cook food by means of hot stones.
— *v. a.* to strike or beat; to express the juice from the *mati* berries, in order to die a scarlet colour.
Tutua, *s.* the beam on which the women beat the bark for cloth making.
— *s.* a flea; see *tiatua.*
Tutuaaau, *s.* the name of a small crab on the coral reef.
Tutuahura, *s.* fishing for the *ahura* fish.
Tutuamuri, *s.* an agreeable easterly wind.
Tutuarahonui, *s.* the name of a large spider.
Tutuaroa, *v. n.* to be ashamed, or abashed.
Tutuautara, *v. n.* to be about beginning.
— *v. n.* to be not fixed or settled as to residence; to stand aloof, having the wish to go, but not the means.
Tutuê, *a.* unstable; having no proper root or foundation, on the mere surface.
Tutuha, *v. n.* to spit repeatedly; see *tuha.*
Tutuhaa, *v. a.* to beat the bark for cloth making.
Tutui, *v. a.* to kindle fire; to set fire to a thing.
— *s.* the *tiairi*, or candle nut tree and nuts; the *aleurites triloba* of the botanists.
Tutuifaraoa, *s.* the same as the *tiairi.*
Tutuifaruaa, *s.* the name of a running plant.
Tutuimaohi, *s.* the same as the candle nut.
Tutuiporo, *s.* the name of a feast.
Tutuiraihoa, *s.* the name of a heathenish prayer.
Tutuira, *s.* a name or word used in some of the old native songs.
Tutumatie, *v. n.* to stand up in a body; to commence an action.
Tutumihamiha, *v. a.* to destroy and waste all before them, as the Tahitian warriors did.
Tuturi, *s.* the name of a fish.
— *s.* a support to lean against; the stone against which the priest leaned in saying his prayers.
— *v. n.* to lean upon, or against a thing.
— *v. a.* to trust, or put confidence in a thing for support.
Tuturoropu. *s.* the midway; see *ropu.*
— *adv.* in the middle of the way.
Tuturu, *s.* a post, or prop for support.
— *v. a.* to prop or support.
Tuturu, *v. n.* to drop, as rain from the roof of a house.
— *s.* the fins of a shark.
Tuturumau, *v. a.* to place the foot so as to support one'self firmly.
Tuturumautaaiore, *s.* an unmoved foot; also a bawling noisy woman.
Tuturuo, *a.* sullen, regardless.
Tututahauri, *s.* a certain mode of standing among bow-men, (a term of archery).
Tututu, *s.* the sickening smell of provisions.
Tutututu, *s.* the smell of baked

hogs, and of other food, when in large quantities.

Tutuu, *s.* a bequest, legacy. or will; also counsel or advice left by a dying person with friends or relations.

Tutuuraa, *s.* the bestowment of a legacy.

Tu'u, *s* the name of a species of spider.

Tuu, *v. a.* (*tuku*) to let go; dismiss; to yield; also to deliver, to set free.

Tuua *post. par.* with the *adverb aita* or *aore*, as aita i *tuua*, did not let go, yielded not, or continued what is mentioned or understood.

Tuuati. *s.* the departure of the friends of a conquered party.

Tuumata, *s.* a spy.

Tuupiri, s. a puzzle, or enigma.

— *v. a.* to put an enigma, or a puzzle, to try a person's skill.

Tuuraamariua, *s.* the name of a certain heathen ceremony; see *mariua.*

Tuuraapahu, *s.* a part of some heathen ceremonies.

Tuuraaturuma, *s.* a place where the bodies of the dead were placed to be looked at.

Tuutuu *s.* a sort of spider.

Tuutuu, *v. a* to slacken or ease a rope, &c, to give in or yield; let go by little and little.

Tuutuuhua, *s.* a mode of attack with a war club.

Tuutuupiri, *v. n.* to give out puzzles.

Tuutuurea, *s.* a small body of messengers.

Tuutuuvea, *s.* a king's or chief's messenger.

Tuutuutautai, *s.* the frequent use of the fishing net.

Tuviriviri manu, *s.* a flock of birds; see *huihui*

U.

IS a letter of frequent occurrence in Tahitian, and is pronounced as the English *u* in the words *bull, full, &c.* and *oo* in *moon.*

U, *s.* the name for milk.

— *s.* the breasts of any thing that gives milk.

— *v. n.* to be damp, moist, or wet.

— *v. n.* to touch, as a boat or ship on the rocks.

— *v. a* to meet for encounter; to come face to face; to face danger.

— *v. n.* to prevail or conquer.

— *v. a.* to run against a thing.

— *s.* the name of a fish.

Ua, *s.* (*uha,* Malay *ujan.*) rain.

— *s.* a name given to the joining of the head to the body, the back of the neck.

— *v. n.* to grow, sprout, or spring up.

— *v. a.* to banish, expel, or drive away.

Uâ, *s.* a species of land crab.

Uâ, *v. n.* to scream; to bray, applied to the ass.

Ua, a *verb of being,* or a prefix to verbs and adjectives, affirming the present existence of the *quality,* or that the act existed, or had taken place, but implying a former absence of the act or quality affirmed.

Uaa, *v. n.* to open and distend, as a flower, or the buds of trees and plants.

— *v. a.* to divulge, tell, make known a thing.

Uai, *v. n.* to face about; to turn as a sick person.

Uama, *v. a.* to assuage, or lessen.

Uana, *a.* strong, forcible.

— *adv.* strongly, forcibly, vehemently.

Uanana, *adv.* vigorously; with renewed force.

Uanato, *s.* the remains of food at a feast.

— *v. n.* to be glutted with much food.

Uanau, *v. n.* to grieve; to emit a sound like a lizard.

Uao, *s.* the name of a bird.

Uara, s. the Hawaiian species of sweet potato; see *umara.*

Uaroa, *s.* a species of cane used by archers.

Uau, *s.* a part of the yam, which is next to the surface of the ground.

— *v. a.* to scrape off the skin or surface.

Uaua, *s.* a sinew, tendon, ligature; a vein.

— *a.* tough; also clammy, ropy, as gum, &c.

— *s.* the root called *paauara.*

Uauaai, *s.* a plant which grows in the mountains like the yam.

Uauariri, *s.* a violent ungovernable person.

Ue. *s.* the last struggling breath of an animal.

— *v. n.* to toss and move, as a dying person.

— *a.* strong, impetuous, as a wave of the sea.

Uenia, *s.* the name of a bird.

Uere, *s.* a sort of black Tahitian cloth.

Uererairai, *s.* a species of thin native cloth.

Ueue, *s.* a person or thing that shakes any thing; a sower of seeds, by shaking the hand.

— *v. a.* to sow seeds by shaking the hand.

— *a.* viscous, tough; *fig.* strong, hard.

Ufa, *s.* a female of brutes, birds, fishes, &c.

— *a.* a female in opposition to *oni*, a male; moa *ufa*, a female fowl.

— *s.* froth, foam; a bubble.

— *v. n.* to belch.

Ufafe, *s.* the name of a fish.

Ufao, *v. a.* to mortise, to dig or cut with a chisel.

— *v. n.* to be corroding; to be eating, as an ulcerous sore.

— *s.* an instrument for making holes.

Ufarufaru, *s.* a mode of fishing.

— *s.* a sort of ornamented cloth.

Ufatu, *s.* small lumps, pieces or fragments

— *a.* fine breeding, having the young of a good quality.

Ufatufatu, *a.* thick, stiff, as some pulpy mixture.

Ufaufa, *s.* the lungs of animals.

— *s.* froth, foam.

Ufaufamaori, *s.* a barren woman, a hermaphrodite

Ufaufamatoa, s. the same as *ufaufamaori.*

Ufaufatai, *s.* the froth of the sea.

Ufene, *v. n.* to be crammed, both cheeks being full.

— *v. a.* to press or squeeze; to wring, such as a washed garment, to press out the water.

— *a.* pinching, covetous, niggardly.

Ufenefene, *v. a.* to cram the mouth eagerly in eating; to show great greediness.

Ufenia, *a.* glossed over with a fine speech while the real thing is concealed.

Ufeu, *a.* much, abundant.

Ufeufeu, *a.* abundant in quantity.

Uha, *s.* a female of beasts, &c., see *ufa.*

Uha, *v. n.* te belch; as *ufa.*

Uhauha, *s.* lungs, froth, foam.

Uhe, *s.* a name given to the wind when blowing from a certain quarter.

Uhi *s. ufi, ui, ubi,* Malay, *ubi,* also Malagasse, *ubi,*) the general name of the yam.

— *s.* an instrument used in marking the skin.

— *s.* shoots or suckers of taro, plantains, &c.

— *s.* the name of a fish.

— *v. a.* to dip the hand or any other thing in water or any liquid; to rinse, or wash in water.

Uhiairi, *s.* a ceremony performed, when the navel string of a first born child was separated.

Uhipapa, *s.* a yam growing among the rocks, and so difficult to obtain; a steady warrior not easily mastered.

Uhu, *s.* the parrot fish of which there are several varieties.

Uhû, *intj.* of wonder, or sudden surprize.

Uhu, *s.* a sort of suppressed laugh.

Uhumama, *s.* a parrot fish caught by casting bread fruit to it from the mouth; *fig.* applied to some means used to deceive a person.

Ui, *s.* a single woman who never had a child.

Ui, *s.* an age, season, generation; see *tau.*

— *s.* a ringing noise in the ear.

— *s,* a grater, or rubber.

— *v. a.* to grate, to rub.

— *v. a.* to ask questions, to enquire.

— *s.* a catechism, or a set of questions.

— *a.* tough, unyielding, obstinate.

Uiau, *s.* the upper covering of a house, &c.; the finishing of a thing or of an affair.

Uihi, *s.* the whistling of any thing that cuts the air; also a light pleasant breeze.

Uihou, *s.* the young, or rising generation.

Uimatahoro, *s.* a young vigorous person.

Uini, *v. n.* to chirp, see *ioio.*

Uinia, *a.* superficial, slight, hasty.

Uioro, *v. a.* to grate, such as taro, potatoes, &c.

Uira, *s.* lightning.

— *v. n.* to lighten; see *anapa, hoa.*

Uiraa, *s.* catechising, questioning, the time or place of questioning.

Uirahoahoa, *s.* lightning round the edge of the horizon.

Uiramono, s. the frequent flashes of lightning in the evening, common about December.

Uiravaho, s. a mode of defence in the exercise of turaau.

— s. a person from another country.

— s. a sensation of excessive cold.

Uitari, v. a. to take the bunch of banana with the stem.

Uituamoa, s. strong men.

Uiui, s. the name of a disease of the skin.

— s. a company of women engaged in working cloth for a chief.

— s. a person that is skilful in work.

— a. delicate, affectedly nice as to food.

— s. a bundle of *mahi* or of *hoi*; see *hoi*.

— v. a. to rasp, rub, or file repeatedly.

— v. a. to ask questions repeatedly; see *ui*.

Uma, s. a private sign, such as a pinch.

— v. a. to make some secret sign, to pinch.

Umaa, s. business, office, occupation.

— s. a bundle of *mahi* or *hoi*; see *ipo*; a roll or bundle done up slovenly.

— s. a dress of cloth, such as the tihi.

Umaahiti, s. a man of two parties that cannot be trusted by either.

Umaairiiri, *adv.* carelessly, slovenly.

Umaamaa, s. a sort of native cloth.

Umaapiti, s. a person of two sides; see *umaahiti*.

Umaatapau, v. a. to be in confusion.

Umae, a. red, or reddish, applied to a hog.

Umamia, a. overbaked, as food.

Umamimami, v. n. to swallow down in haste.

Umaarua, s. the same as *umahiti*.

Umara, s. (*humara*, *uara*, *uala*,) sweet potatoes.

Umati, s. cloth made of the mati; or that is dyed scarlet.

Umauma, v. a. to pinch repeatedly; see *uma*.

Ume, s. the fish called leather jacket.

— v. a. to pull, draw, or drag a thing along.

— v. a. to draw by persuasion.

Umehani, v. a. to draw or persuade an associate.

Umeneû, v. n. to be stunned by a violent blow.

Umenoû, a. great in bulk or quantity.

Umeraro, v. n. to be submissive, obedient.

— v. a. to put in the sea a range of leaves to be used as a fishing net; see *raoere*.

— v. a. to communicate something slyly.

Umere, s. a saying of praise in behalf of a place, or of a party.

— v. n. to wonder, admire; to vaunt over a thing.

Umereraa, s. a ceremony or custom used formerly on reviewing a fleet of canoes.

Umete, s. a wooden dish used

for various purposes, but chiefly to hold food.

Umeume, *v. a.* to pull repeatedly.

Umiumi, *s.* (*kumikumi,*) the beard.

Umiumihahehahe, *s.* the white billows of the sea; an undaunted warrior.

— *s.* a person who has a young beard not come to maturity.

Umu, *s.* the native oven for baking food.

— *s.* an ornament to a canoe.

— *v. a.* to wring or press out any thing between the hands or fingers.

Umua, *v. a.* to form into round balls.

Umuhonu, *s.* an oven in which a turtle is baking; *fig.* something nice, delicate.

Umuhuti, s. an immense oven of *ti*; a large quantity.

Umuna, *s.* a door way; see *uputa.*

Umunaro, *v. n.* to be on the point of death.

Umuumu, *v. a.* to squeeze with the hands or fingers repeatedly.

— *s.* wrath, great displeasure.

Unâ, *s.* a cutaneous disorder.

— *adv.* following an interrogation or affirmation as, Eahara *una*? What can it be? Oia ra *una*, it is that, though doubted, or even so.

Unaefaratea, *v. n.* to be speaking enticing words.

— *s.* an unsettled person, one that cannot be depended upon.

Unahea, *v. n.* to be overworked in cooking fish.

Unahi, *v. a.* to scale a fish clean off the scales.

Unamata, *a.* fair faced, and that only.

Unania, *s.* the name of a stone god.

— *s.* an instrument used by the native surgeons.

Unauna, *s.* an ornament, a decoration; also splendour or glory.

— *a.* neat, decorated, ornamented; splendid, glorious.

— *s.* a party of women working for a chief; see *uiui.*

Unaunafaaura, *s.* a fair outward appearance, but not so internally

Unaunanohopapa, *s.* an image or *tii.*

— *s.* a chief arioi; also one that decorates himself and sits at rest; a lazy coxcomb.

Unaunapaa, *s.* a fair exterior, and that the only good quality.

Unaunanunui, *v. n.* to be fair outwardly only.

Unaunaraupaa, *s.* external good appearance.

Unaunaraununui, *s.* outward good appearance and that only.

Unaunatere, *s.* the honour of travelling in company with a chief, and that only.

Unaunatupapa, *s.* the prettiness of a tree that grows on a rock, but a blast of wind blows it down; *fig.* grandeur not well founded.

Unaunaa, *s.* some large work cast off.

Unaunau, *a.* when the word is preceded by a negative, as eita e *unaunau,* it signifies heedless, not caring for family, &c.

Unènê, *a.* bloated out with fatness.

— *v. n.* to be satiated.

Uneenee, *v. a.* to go humbly, and softly, to ask for food or property.

Unounoo, *a.* comely, fair, handsome.

Unu, *s.* a piece of carved wood put up in the marae on offering up a man.

— *s.* the crest on a cock's head; see *repe.*

— *v. n.* to pass as a season, or an age; to be over, or having ceased, as the wind.

Unuhi, *v. n.* to slip out; retire, or withdraw; to depart, as the soul at death.

— *v. a.* to draw out, as a knife from a case, a sword from a scabbard, &c.

— *v. n.* to swoon.

Unuhiarei, *v. n.* to be departing or going out.

Unuhifarere, *v. n.* to go off entirely, as at death.

Unuhitauritia, *s.* a sudden or instantaneous death.

Unuhitarere, *s.* the same as *unuhifarere.*

Unuma, *v. n.* to belong to a person in his own right.

Unumaa, *s.* the *unu* before the marae that has branches or divisions; *fig.* one of two parties, as *pueapiti.*

Unuunu, *s.* a restriction put to fishing on the coral reefs.

— *s.* an ornament in the marae.

— *a.* bloated, hanging in collops.

Uo, *a.* white; see *uouo.*

— *s.* the external skin of the banana, of which was made a covering for the pauma, or kite.

Uoa, *s.* the name of a certain restriction on food, &c.; see *rahui.*

— *s.* the brightness of noon; the clear shining of the moon; *fig.* a peaceable, placid, natural death.

— *a.* level; clear, without obstruction.

Uoahe, *s.* the sharp irregular edges of a split bamboo, which are dangerous.

Uomata, *s.* the ligatures attached to the eye.

Uoi, *v. n.* to be twisted or worked out of its proper position, as the edges that had been joined.

Uou, *s.* the name of a disease; also a sprain, or twist of the foot.

— *v. n.* to sink under a load, to be out of the due position; to be made to halt, to be abashed.

Uouo, *a.* white; see *teatea.*

Upa, *v. n.* to dance; see *ori.*

Upâ, *a.* enfeebled, as the arms of an archer.

Upua, *s.* the liver; see *paraia.*

— *s.* the name of a dark native cloth.

Upai, *s.* the name of an edible crab.

— *s.* a certain mode of fishing.

Upapariirii, *s.* cloth made of many layers of the aute bark.

Upaparu, *s.* the name of a small fish.

Uparu, *a.* yellowish, or of a cream colour.

Uparurôru, *s.* a hog that will soon repay its owner for its feeding.

Upaupa, *s.* the name of a mountain bird.

Upaupa, *s.* a play, diversion, music and dancing; any game or amusement. There are a great number of diversions that go under the name of *upaupa*, such as upaupa hura, upaupa mâû, upaupa mahamaha, upaupa otooto, upaupa pararaa, upaupa pehu pehu, upaupa poopootati, upaupa rohi pehe, upaupa tia raau, &c.

— *v. a.* to play the upaupa of any kind.

Upaupahura, *s.* the dance that was accompanied by the regular drum beating.

Upaupa, *s.* the noisy diversion of beating the bamboo called *ihara.*

Upaupatumuore, *s.* the name of a parasitic plant.

Upea, *s.* (*kupenga,*) a net, a fishing net.

Upeamatatiri, *s.* a net with small meshes.

Upehepehe, *s.* the name of a play; see *upaupa.*

Upêpê, *s.* collops of fat on the ribs.

Upepe, *v. a.* to add one thing to another as articles of property; see *tapepe.*

— *a.* wet, or moist as cloth.

Uperu, *s.* a small bundle of cloth; see *auperu.*

— *v. a.* to fold up, make a bundle.

Upepe, *s.* hanging collops that appear unsightly; see *fatifati.*

— *a.* filthy, unsightly.

Upoo, *s.* (*upoko, pao,*) the human head, the head of a party; see *afii, omii.*

Upooaha, *s.* an office.

Upooaura, *s.* the quietness of peace.

Upoofaito, *s.* a government of equal heads, that is, all on a level.

Upoomaa, *s.* one that makes it his business to seize what he can wherever he can find it.

Upoopua, *s.* a sort of turban used by warriors.

Upootia, *s.* a conqueror, one whose head is up.

Upootu, *s.* the same as *upootia.*

Upoupo, *a.* ugly, ill favoured; also dissatisfying.

Upu, *s.* a prayer.

— *s.* a set of prayers addressed to the gods by the priest and others; also a prayer addressed by the sorcerers to their *tiis* or demons, for some evil purpose.

— *v. n.* to repeat such an *upu* or prayer.

Uputa, *s.* (*upuka*) a doorway, entrance.

Uputara, *s.* a prayer or imprecation of a sorcerer to procure evil.

Ura, *s.* red feathers formerly sacred to the gods.

— *s.* a blaze, a flame of fire.

— *v. n.* to blaze, applied to fire.

— *a.* red; see *uteute.*

Uraaha, *s.* the name of an idolatrous ceremony, which was performed before engaging in war.

Uraepaepa, *s.* a name used by

the priest in performing the ceremonies of the *uhi airi.* Taking a young chief in his arms he would call out, "Uraepaepa! Urahiihii! Uramoemoe."

Uraepatetere, *s.* the name of an idolatrous prayer.

Urâêva, *s.* a restless person who can settle no where.

Uraeva, *a.* proud, haughty.

Uramarea, *s.* yellow feathers, used for the gods in the absence of red ones.

Uraraununui, *s.* a name given to the king.

Urarei, *a.* sorrowful, comfortless.

Urataetae, *s.* the name of a god that presided over all the upaupas, &c.

— *s.* the yellow feathers of the uupa.

Urateni, *s.* a chief person.

Urateo, *s.* a form of attack with the native club.

Uraura, *a.* red, of a reddish colour.

Ure. *s.* (*ue,*) the penis of all males.

Urea, *a.* yellow, yellowish with age.

Urepo, *s.* a native cloth coloured dark, by the mire of some bog; see *repo.*

Urepuaa, *a.* knotty, as the strand of a rope.

Urere, *s.* the name of a species of yam.

Ureure, *s.* a sort of fish called the sea snail.

— *s.* the destitute poor.

Ureuretiamoana, *s.* the water spout.

Ureuretumoana, *s.* the same as *ureuretiamoana.*

Uri, *s.* (*kuri, kuli, uli,*) a dog.

— *s.* the pilot fish.

— *a.* (*uli,*)discoloured; dark, or blackish.

— *v. n.* to be of a good and clear impression, as the leaf of a book.

Uriaiava, *s.* a seal or sea calf; see *kumí.*

Urie, *s.* the name of a fish, when well grown it is *uriuri.*

Urifa, *s.* the name of a fish.

— *s.* the rank smell of the sea beach.

Urio, *s.* the name of a little running vine.

— *s.* the name of a fish; see *urie.*

Uriiore, *s.* a cat; see *iore.*

Uripania, *s.* a good fighting dog.

Uripiifare, *s.* a cat; see *piifare.*

Uriti, *s.* the name of a bird.

— *s.* a stone thrown from a sling.

Uriuri, *s.* the full grown *urio* fish.

— *s.* the smell that attaches to a person that handles some kinds of fish.

Uru, *s.* (*ulu,*) the general name of the bread fruit tree and fruit (*arto carpus*); see *maiore.* There are at Tahiti between 20 and 30 species, and as many names.

— *s.* a thicket of wood; also of coral in the sea.

— *s.* the human skull; see *apu roro.*

— *v. a.* to level the stones in a native oven.

— *v. n.* to pass away, as a season.

— *v. n.* to enter. as a ship into a harbour.

Ûrû, *v. n.* to be inspired, as the pretended Tahitian prophets; to be under the influence of some uncommon feeling.

Urua, *s.* the cavally fish; see *urupiti, paehere.*

— *s.* the native pillow.

— *s.* the *too* or body of a god when wrapped up

Uruai, *v. a.* to take refuge under the wings of another.

Uruairaa, *s.* a place of shelter or rest.

Uruamataono, *s.* an intrepid, fast swimming fish; *fig,* a bold, dauntless warrior.

Uruana, *s.* a mass of coral in the sea; see *ana* to grate; *fig.* a dangerous place.

Uruaofefeu, *s.* a pillow for a god.

Uruauhune, *s.* the harvest, or the season of plenty of *uru,* about January.

Urufara, *s.* a grove of the pandanus.

Uruhi, *s.* a thicket that is not passable; a mass of branching coral in the sea.

— *s.* an ugly, scabby disease.

Uruhia, *v. p.* inspired; see *taúra.*

Uruhoa, *s.* a violent head ache; see *hoa.*

Urumatai, *s.* a sudden gust of wind.

Urunui, *s.* a large crop of bread fruit.

Urupa, *s.* a thicket; see *uruhi.*

— *s.* a violent wind; the calamities of war.

— *a.* of quick growth.

Urupae, *s.* a border, or that which is on the edge or side.

Urupaipai, *s.* a roasted breadfruit beaten soft between the hands; breadfruit prepared for what is called *poeveo.*

Urupani, *s.* an idolatrous prayer offered for a sick person.

Urapao, *s.* breadfruit injured by the operation of *pao,* or bruising the bark.

Urupiipii, *s.* destruction, calamity.

Urupiri, *s.* a close thicket.

Urupiti, *s.* the cavally fish; see *urua.*

Urupoo, *s.* the name of certain prints or tatau on the back of a person.

Urupu, *s.* the same as *urupiti.*

— *s.* young breadfruit; see *pu;* also large branches.

— *v. n.* to have a sight of the land when drawing near at sea.

Urupua, *s.* the patches of large and thick coral in the sea.

Urupuaa, *intj.* an exclamation to a person that is greedy to get another's food, though his own lies before him.

Urupuupuu, *s.* disturbances, commotion.

Urutia, *v. a.* to take off a restriction; see *rahui.*

Uruuru, *a.* rough, unsightly; also cross grained, as timber.

Uruuruava, *s.* a prayer before the marae, for the purpose of obtaining children.

Uruururauava, *s.* the same as *uruuruava.*

Uruvao, *s.* the trees or forests in the upper part of the valleys.

Uta, *s.* the shore, or land, in opposition to *tai,* the sea; the parts towards the interior.

Uta, *v. n.* to be carried or conveyed by water.
— *v. n.* to be suspended; see *faauta.*
— *v. a.* to carry, to take by water.
Utaa, *s.* the burden or load of a vessel.
— *s.* what is committed to the charge of a person, whether property or persons.
Utai, *v. n.* to be wet with salt water.
Utami, *s.* the name of an obscene dance of females.
— *v. n.* to dance obscenely.
Utamitami, *v. n.* to act the utami repeatedly.
Utari, *s.* to follow after a person.
Utaru, *s.* the same as *utari* and *peeutari.*
Utaru, *v. a.* to dig or grub up the ground; to soften the ground by digging, breaking up clods, &c.
Utarutaru, *v. a.* to dig the earth repeatedly.
Utatau, *s.* little yams that grow on the vines.
Utau, *s.* a nurse, a wet nurse.
— *v. a.* to nurse by giving suck.
Utautau, *s.* a sort of basket, or net for eels.
Utavitavi, *s.* a most obscene dance of males.
— *v. n.* to dance the *utavitavi.*
Utè, *s.* a song or ditty used by the natives.
— *v. a.* to sing the utê; to dance to the utê.
Ute, *a.* red; see *ura* and *uraura.*
Utehu, *a.* swollen, applied to the lips.
— *v. n.* to be affected with anger.
Utere, *v. a.* to rasp, or scrape off the skin of a bread fruit, &c.
Uteretere, *v. a.* to rasp, or scrape repeatedly.
Uteute, *a.* red, or scarlet coloured.
Utiuti, *s.* a motley sky, a sign of a calm.
Uto, *s.* a cocoanut in a state of vegetation.
Utoa, *v. a.* to take up water with a sponge.
Utoo, *v. n.* the same as above.
Utotia, *s.* a contemptuous name for a mean person.
Utou, *v. a.* to take up water with a cloth or sponge.
Utoutou, *v. a.* to stain cloth with mati; see *mati*; to besmear the face with scarlet colour.
Utu, *s.* the lip, bill of a bird, edge of a thing.
— *s.* the long snout of certain fishes.
— *s.* the hair from the head of a slain enemy, that was taken to the marae; the first person that fell at the commencement of hostilities.
— *s.* (*ugutu*, *kutu*, Malay, *kutu*,) a louse.
— *s.* a present to visitors, as a token of peace.
Utua, *s.* (*utu*) a reward, compensation, wages; the payment either of merit or demerit, penalty or reward.
Utuafare, *s.* a person's own home or house; also the family or household of a person.

Utuafarerau, *s.* a person of unsettled residence.
Utuahia, *v. p.* rewarded, recompensed.
Utuarau, *s.* manifold rewards or punishments.
Utuāura, *a.* a lazy person; also abstemious.
Utuaura, *a.* thin, lank.
Utuhi, *s.* the name of a heathenish prayer.
— *v. a.* to dip into the water; to rinse.
Utuitui, *v. a.* to thump with the hand, or butt with the elbow; to press under; see *atui*.
Utumehameha, *s.* grimaces of the lips.
Utupaa, *s.* a disease of the lips.
— *s.* the name of a certain ceremony and feast.
Utupeepee, *s.* perverse lips, the lips of a scold.
Utupehepehe, *s.* a woman that is an adept at the native *pehe* or song.
Uturairai, *s.* a scold, mischief-making lips.
Ututaa, *s.* forwardness, perverseness.
Ututu, *s.* an attendant on the sick.
— *v. a.* to attend and nurse the sick.
— *a.* powerful, strong, applied to the voice.
Uu, *s.* a species of the muscle shell fish; the shell used by the women in dressing their mats, splitting the leaves, &c.
— *s.* a disease of the limbs like the rheumatism.
— *v. n.* to be dauntless, intrepid.
Uuairao, *s.* a species of pigeon.
Uuao, *s.* a species of snail found on the leaves of the mountain plantain.
Uuene, *s.* one who supplies the place of another.
Uuhiva, *s.* barnacles, such as grow on ships and logs of wood, when long in the water.
Uui, *v. a.* to rub or polish a canoe, umete, &c.
Uumi, *v. a.* to strangle; to force a woman against her will, stopping her mouth, &c.
Uumu, *v. a.* to squeeze, as water out of a sponge, &c.
Uumu, *v. n.* to clench the fist.
Uuopiri, *v. a.* to take, with a muscle shell, drops of gum from wounded trees; such as the ati, uru, &c.
Uupa, *s.* a sort of pigeon.
Uupaparuru, *s.* one who assists another.
Uuratamafaarere, *s.* friendless orphans.
— *s.* a species of taro, of which the young shoots grow at a distance from the main root; *fig.* the first born of a family, because he was sacred, and *separated* from the rest.
Uuratamahere, *s.* a species of taro, the young shoots of which grow quite thick about the main root; *fig.* a parent with a numerous offspring; a king with many attached to him.
Uuru, *v. n.* to groan as in pain; to grunt.
Uutaina, *v. n.* to flow mightily, as a river, to rush on eagerly; to long or wish eagerly

for the possession of some chief.

Uutu, *s.* a word used by drunkards; uutu iti, a little more.

Uuvao, *s.* a snail; see *uuao.*

Uvao, *s.* the name of a fish, called also *aho, nape, pirovaha.*

Uvaravara, *s.* a thin sort of native cloth.

Uvavi, *s.* a deceiver, one who obtains food by deceitful stories.

Uvavia, *s.* unripe fruit, plantains, &c.; see *vavia.*

Uvavivavi, *s.* one who frequently practises deceit to obtain food.

Uverevere, *s.* the same as *uvaravara.*

Uvihi, *s.* a light whistling of the wind.

— *v. n.* to whistle, or sound as a light wind.

Uvira, *s.* lightning; see *uira.*

Uviravira, *s.* lightning, when frequent.

— *v. n.* to lighten; sea *anapa.*

V

BEGINS the following words, and has its usual power and sound.

Va, *s.* the space between the edges of the layers of thatch on the Tahitian houses.

— *s.* the rushing down of the rain that comes suddenly and is soon over.

Vaa, *s.* (*vaka, waka*; Fiji, *vanka,*) the native canoe.

Vaahara, *s.* a superior canoe, with one end a small bluff round.

Vaahiva, *s.* all the people within the prescribed limits of the Island, or district.

Vaamaihi, *s.* a small canoe made sharp at both ends.

Vaamataeinaa, *s.* a division of the land owners.

Vaamoemoe, *s.* a sacred canoe.

Vaatamai, *s.* a war canoe.

Vaatipaeama, *s.* a single canoe.

Vaatipaeati, *s.* a double canoe.

Vaati, *s.* affliction.

Vaavaevae, *s.* persons who go on foot during a journey, and do not use water conveyance.

Vae, *s.* the timbers of a boat or ship; the small rafters of a *fareoa,* or little house, made with a top like the cover of a wagon.

— *v. a.* to share out, or divide food, &c.

Vaea, *s.* a state of peace and plenty.

Vaehaa, *s.* a share or portion.

— *s.* a place; see *vahi.*

Vaere, *v. a.* to weed, to clear the ground.

Vaeremarae, *v. a.* to clear the marae, remove rubbish, and make the place decent.

Vaeremarae, *s.* the name of an idolatrous ceremony at the marae.

Vaero, *s.* the extremities, as feet, hands, &c. which in death are sometimes drawn up and darted down again suddenly.

Vaerua, *v. a.* to divide into two shares.

Vaevae, *s.* the leg and foot; see *avae.*

— *s.* the moon; moonlight; see *avae.*

— *v. a.* to divide repeatedly; see *vae.*

Vaevacaro, *s.* a division of an army.

— *s.* small drizzling rain.

Vaha, *s.* (*waha, vaa,*) the mouth.

Vahaava, *s.* the mouth of a harbour.

Vahaino, *s.* a person that puts all into consternation before he knows the truth of an occurrence.

Vahaioore, *s.* a mouth that boasteth great things, but performs nothing.

Vahaiti, *s.* a whisperer that breeds mischief.

Vahamana, *s.* a powerful pleader.

Vahamaniania, *s.* a clamorous person that speaks to little purpose.

Vahamariri, *s.* one that takes not the trouble to get his own food cooked, but lives upon others.

Vahamona, *s.* an idle talker to cause laughter; a sweet mouth to deceive.

Vahanavenave, *s.* a jocular person, or speech.

Vahapaari, *s.* a betrayer of secrets, one that tells all that he hears.

Vahapaari, *v. a.* to divulge secrets.

Vahapaoa, *s.* one that feels a disappointment.

Vahapape, *s.* a flattering mouth, a flatterer; also flattery, deceit.

— *v. a.* to use flattery to gain an end.

Vahapiropiro, *s.* a foul mouth, either as to breath or speech.

Vahapapâ, *s.* one that speaks indiscreetly.

Vahapapee, *s.* an angry person that has no control over his tongue.

Vaharau, *s* many spokesmen; a person that is inconsistent, speaking various ways.

Vaharua, *s.* a person of two mouths, who has two interests, and two ways of speaking, and cannot be trusted.

Vahataoa, *s.* one who gets property by means of his mouth, or speaking.

Vahautuutu, *s.* a person that speaks with energy.

Vahavaha, *s.* contempt, disregard.

— *v. a.* to esteem lightly; treat with contempt; despise.

Vahavai, *s.* a person of soft flattering speech; a flatterer; flattery; fawning.

— *v. n.* to use words of flattery.

Vahi, *s.* a place; a part or portion.

— *v. a.* to open, to split; see *afa.*

Vahia, *s.* a person that is an object of hatred and enmity, though he may not be an enemy.

Vahiavai, *s.* a disturber; sower of sedition.

— *v. a.* to break the waters; but used figuratively for commencing hostilities in the time of war.

Vahie, *s.* fuel, fire wood.

Vahieroa, *s.* the name of a god.

Vahine, *s* (*wahine, vaine, fifine,*) a woman.

Vahineravarava, *s.* a dark complexioned woman; also a tall handsome woman.
Vahinereureuamoa, *s.* the name of a goddess.
Vahinetaiata, *s.* a very vile, wanton woman; see *taiata*, *faaturi*.
Vahinetiai, *s.* a wanton woman.
Vahineuturairai, *s.* a scolding woman.
Vahiupoo, *s.* a violent head ache; see *hoa*.
Vaho, *adv.* & *prep.* out, outside, not inside; see *rapae*.
Vai, *pron.* who? as, *ovai?* who? *ia vai?* by whom? with whom? see *ovai*.
Vai, *v. n.* to be; to remain or abide.
— *v. a.* to place, to deposit.
Vai, *s.* (*wai*,) water; see the modern *pape*.
Vaiafa, *s.* the breaking of water, opening the flood gates; but *fig.* commencing hostilities, signified by the terms vai afa, vai amaha, vahi vai, and vahia vai.
Vaiaha, *s.* the same as *vaiafa*, *&c.*
Vaiaia, *a.* distant, applied to a relation.
Vaianui, *s.* the name of a medicinal plant.
Vaiata, *s.* the name of a species of taro.
— *s.* a morning bath; a phrase used by the arioi, who bathed early in the morning; see *ata*, *atahiata*.
Vaiatatia, *s.* living water; water that continues to run.
Vaiatea, *v. n.* to be distant; see *atea*.
Vaiateate, *s.* pure, clear water.
Vaieri, *s.* water that encroaches on the land, undermining some part of it.
Vaiehu, *v. n.* to be resolute in facing danger.
Vaieru, *s.* the same as *vaieri*.
Vaifaai, *s.* water that gathers from different quarters in the time of great rain.
Vaifau, *s.* a land newly cleared, a rich soil.
— *s.* a thing that is become natural or customary to a person.
Vaihaaoro, *s.* a place where there is an eddy.
Vaihanana, *s.* streams that leave their proper channels.
Vaihaono, *s.* implacability.
Vaiharo, *s.* the juice of fruits; also gravy of meat.
Vaihauri, *s.* water that smells disagreeably.
Vaihoe, *v. n.* to remain single or solitary.
Vaihapuna, *s.* a pool; a water spring.
Vaiiho, *v. a.* to lay, place, or put a thing in a certain place; to leave a thing in its place; to leave off; to let alone.
Vaiihoiho, *v. imp.* let it be, let it alone, let it remain, or abide where it is, or as it is.
Vaiihohia, *v. p.* left, placed, left remaining.
Vaimato, *s.* water from a rock.
Vaiohana, *s.* a species of taro.
Vaiooina, *s.* water that rushes violently in its course.
Vaiopiripiri, *s.* little streams among craggy rocks.
Vaiopuopu, *s.* scanty water not convenient for bathing.
Vaipa, *s.* food soon cooked;

also a small quantity for a large party.

Vaipararaau, *s.* a flood that brings down large trees.

Vaipihaa, *s.* water that bubbles up; spring water.

Vaipiharau, *s.* water that has many spring heads.

Vaipoea, *s.* bad water, with animalcules, &c.

Vaipuna, *s.* the same as *vaipihae.*

Vaipupu, *s.* small pools of water in the beds of rivers in the dry season.

Vaipurau, *s.* a species of white taro.

Vairaherahe, *s.* water full of animalcules.

Vairau, *s.* a warrior that has survived many battles.

— *s.* the place of a thing.

Vaireru, *s.* disturbed thick water.

Vaireva, *s.* a place encrusted over in a bog, but dangerous to tread upon.

Vairipo, *s.* a whirlpool, a vortex.

Vairoiroi, *s.* smooth water, unruffled by the wind; *fig.* profound peace.

Vairua, *s.* (*wairua, vaarua,*) the soul or spirit.

Vaitaeae, *s.* cousins, distant relations.

Vaitahu, *s.* a basket of fara leaves.

Vaitaitai, *s.* brackish water.

Vaitaoro, *s.* a coacoanut when nearly ripe.

Vaitapohe, *s.* water drained off, as of a fish pond; *fig.* warriors, such as the guard of the country.

Vaitavae, *s.* freshness caused by a journey, new clothes, &c.

Vaite, *s.* the soul or spirit; see *varua.*

Vaitonino, *s.* still water.

Vaitumu, *s.* water that has a good source.

Vaivai, *s.* the name of a native cloth.

Vaivai, *v. n.* to remain a little, abide a short interval.

Vaivaihaua, *s.* the name of a species of native cloth.

Vaiu, *s.* milk; also milk mixed with water.

Vaiuretehe, *s.* a disorder caused by the native custom of *tehe*, which see.

Vaivaitaurua, *s.* the name of a feast and ceremony of the arioi and other players; called also *vaivaitaupiti.*

Vana, *s.* the name of a small fish with rough and prickly skin; the sea egg.

— *s.* the name of a marine plant.

Vanaa, *s.* an orator, one fluent of words.

— *s.* an oration, see *orero*; counsel, advice.

Vanaanaa, *s.* eloquent speeches.

— *v. n.* to think with anxiety; see *mihimihi.*

Vanavana, *a.* rough, ragged, unpolished.

— *s.* a sensation felt when something disagreeable touches the body, as a worm crawling, &c.

Vane, *s.* an ornament made of feathers; also a fine mat usually given to the gods.

Vanevane, *s.* the toes; see *manimani.*

— *s.* red feathers fastened to

pieces of sinnet, and used for the gods.
— *a.* clear, as the air or sky.
Vao, *s.* the extremities of the inland valleys.
— *s.* a rustic or clown; see *taemo.*
Vaoa, *v. a.* to interpose, to separate contending parties.
Vaoataua, *s.* a peace maker.
Vaomaua, *s.* an ignorant person not used to society.
Vaoru, *s.* a thing on which the mind is set.
Varavara, *a.* thin, scattered, not close together.
Vare, *v. n.* to be deceived; see *haavare.*
— *s.* the matter of a diseased eye.
Varea, *v. n.* to be drowsy; overtaken with sleep.
Varepuai, *s.* the name of a fine thin cloth.
Vari, *s.* earth, mud, dirt, filth of any kind.
— *s.* blood discharged from the body.
— *v. n.* to be dirtied, befouled.
Varihia, *v. n.* to be smeared with mire or dirt.
Varo, *s.* a species of lobster.
— *s.* a sort of snare; a loop; see *haavaro.*
— *v. a.* to ensnare with the varo.
— *s.* the loop formed at the end of a rope.
Varovaro, *s.* the vibrations of sound on the ear, or of scents on the organ of smellings
— *s.* a voice heard without seeing the person.
Varu. *a.* (*valu, vau,*) eight in counting.
— *s.* the name of a fish.
— *v a.* to shave; to bark a tree; to scrape.
Varua, *s.* (*wairua, vairua, verua,* and also *vaitie*) the soul or spirit. The old Tahitian word seems to have been *vairua*, which is still retained in some islands.
Varuamaitai, *s.* the Holy Ghost, the Holy Spirit.
Varuaiore, *s.* not the ghost of a rat, as the words seem to signify, but the squeaking of rats and mice; and *fig.* the noise of childen and others, talking in sleep.
Vata, *s.* an opening, space or rent.
— *v. n.* to be separate, with a space between.
Vau, *pron.* first person singular, I.
— *a.* eight, see *varu, avaru.*
— *v. a.* to shave, to bark a tree.
Vaaau, *s.* a receptacle; see *vauvau.*
Vautiti, *s.* a mode of cutting the hair in various figures.
— *v. n.* to be burnt, as the mountains, when the grass is set on fire.
Vauvau, *s.* a receptacle; see *farii.*
— *v. a.* to spread grass or leaves on the ground; to grass the floors of native houses.
— *v. n.* to stand in readiness with a spear, waiting an antagonist.
Vava, *s.* a species of the locus'.
— *s.* a species of taro.
— *s.* an ominous hog; when put on the altar, the ears appeared as if listening; this was reckoned a bad omen.

— *s.* the sound or noise of wind and rain, or the agitation of water at a distance.
— *v. n.* to make a noise as rain, wind, or water.
— *a.* dumb, unable to speak plainly.
— *s.* a mute person.
Vavae, *v. n.* to make way, as a ship through the sea, or a person pushing through a crowd.
Vavahi, *v. a.* to split, to cleave or break a thing.
Vavahimatarua, *v. a.* to begin, as the wrestlers.
Vavai, *s.* the native cotton.
Vavaipapaa, *s.* the foreign cotton.
Vavao, *s.* an interposer between hostile parties.
— *v. a.* to interpose between contending parties; to separate combatants.
— *s.* a cocoanut that has no water in it; also *ovaovao.*
Vavara., *s.* a sort of chalky earth, or pipe clay, found in some places.
— *s.* a white substance found in the sea.
Vave, *adv.* soon, shortly, quickly, ere long.
Vavea, *s.* a high towering wave of the sea.
Vaverua, *v. a.* to contend, or war with equal violence, neither side gaining.
Vavevave, *adv.* quickly, nimbly; very soon.
Vavi, *a.* idle, unfounded, spoken of a tale.
— *adv.* unadvisedly, rashly, without sufficient foundation.
Vavia, *s.* young fruit, plantain, uru, &c.
— *a.* green, unripe, as bread-fruit, or mountain plantains.
Vavimânà, *s.* a proverbial expression from the name of a place in Raiatea, where the people were noted for speaking at random; unadvised speaking.
Vavivavi, *a.* clammy, viscous, glutinous.
— *s.* a person that is liberal, and ready to give.
Ve, *a prefix* to pronouns and adjectives, as *vetahi*, one, some one; *vetoofanu*, some, some few.
Vea, *s.* a messenger, see *arere.*
— *s.* a burning, conflagration; see *vera.*
— *v. n.* to burn, to be scalded or scorched.
Veavea, *s.* heat, as the sun, or from a fire.
Vehe, *v. a.* to divide, or separate.
Vehea, *v. p.* parted, separated.
— *s.* the thing that is parted or separated.
— *s.* a court, or place laid out decently, in the front of a native house; see *mahora.*
Veheraa, *s.* separation; parting, or partition.
— *v. n.* to be made hot.
Vehi, *s.* a case, sheath, or covering.
— *v. a.* to case, or cover a thing.
— *v. a.* to make a thing into a bundle, and tie it up.
Vehiiamoea, *s.* property taken to a god.
Vei, *a.* strong, well formed.
— *v. n.* to be deprived, brought low; to be extinct, as a family.

Veo, *s.* copper or brass.
— *s.* a species of taro.
— *s.* a sort of food.
Veoveo, *s.* an unpleasant smell, as of urine.
Venu, *s.* the threads that are woven into a mat.
Venua, *s.* land; see *fenua.*
Vera, *s.* fire, a general conflagration, as when a mountain is on fire.
— *v. n.* to be burnt, scalded, or scorched.
— *a.* hot, very warm, feverish.
— *a.* cooked, or hot, applied to food.
— *pron.* they, dual or plural.
Veravera, *a.* hot, very warm or hot.
Vere, *s.* oakum to caulk a vessel with.
Verevere, *a.* thin, gauze like; see *varavara.*
— *s.* the eye lids; and lately a name given to the female pudenda.
Vere, *s.* the centipede.
Veri, *s.* a sea insect.
Veriveria, *s.* a deep place; a place that is unsightly.
— *s.* great abundance of food, &c.
Veriverihiva, *a.* of various colours.
Vero, *s.* a storm or tempest; *fig.* great rage.
— *s.* part of the head dress of the *parae.*
— *v. a.* to dart, or throw a spear.
— *v. a.* to push off a canoe into the water.
—*v. n.* to raise up the hand and arm.
Verofa, *s.* a sort of dart; see *fa.*
Verohuri, *s.* a violent storm.
Veromatautaru, *s.* some great calamity.
Veroraafa, *s.* the name of a game in which darts are thrown at a mark.]
Verovero, *v. n.* to twinkle, as the stars.
Veru, *s.* gain, profit, advantage; see *faufaa.*
Verua, *s.* the soul or spirit; see *varua.*
Veruveru, *a.* stale, nasty, offensive in smell.
— *s.* profit, possessions; see *veru.*
— *s.* benefit, advantage.
Vetahi, *rel, pron.* one, some one; any one.
Vetahiê, *pron.* another, a different person.
Vete, *s.* the name of a fish remarkable for tumbling.
Vetea, *v. p.* separated, parted; untied.
Veu, *s.* downy hair; a woolly kind of hair; a sort of fringe on the border of a garment.
— *s.* the downy hair of a dog.
— *v. n.* to have a downy or shaggy border.
Veue. *s.* a stranger.
Veutupu, *s.* a neighbour; as *taatatupu.*
Veuveu, *s.* the fag-end; the untwisted end of a rope; the woolly surface of a thing.
— *a.* worthless, disgusting.
Veve, *a.* bare, poor, destitute, ragged, ill attired.
— *v. n.* to be in want, having no property.
Vevete, *v. a.* to separate, divide, lay open.
Vevetehia, *v. p.* opened, separated.

Vevo, *s.* echo; see *pinai.*
— *v. n.* to echo.
Vevovevo, *v. n.* to echo repeatedly.
Vi, *s.* the Tahitian yellow apple tree and fruit.
— *s.* a sound in the ear.
— *v. n.* to be subdued, brought under; to have a sound in the ear.
Vihî, *s.* a wrapper; see *vehí.*
Vihivihi, *s.* a mode of casting a stone from a sling.
Viivii, *s.* defilement, pollution.
Viivii, *a.* defiled, polluted; corrupt, impure.
— *s.* impurity, corruption.
Viiviitai, *s.* a light spray of the sea.
Vini, *s.* voluble, ready of speech.
Vini, *s.* the name of a small paroquet.
Vinipaura, *s.* a species of the *vini*, of which there are several varieties distinguished by colour, as *vinipauri, vinitea, vinitete, vinirehu*, and *vinipapaa.*
Vinitunupaa, *s.* roasted vini, but signifying something rare and delicious.
Vinivini, *v. n* to be smarting, as from the lash of a whip.
— *v. n.* to make a smacking noise in eating; see *haavini.*
— *v. n.* to speak with ease and volubility.
Vio, *a.* knotty, as the strands of a rope.
Viri, *s.* the front rank of an army.
— *v. a.* to lash up, to furl a sail; to roll some cloth round a corpse.
Viriaa, *v. n.* to withdraw; to separate and join another party; to be alienated.
Viriaro, *s.* the front of the battle.
Viriviri, *s.* an ornament of a native canoe, also an appendage of a marae.
Virua, *s.* the spirit, as *varua.*
Viruviru, *a.* neat, decent.
Viruvirua, *s.* the stamina of speech; also the relative affinities of persons.
Vita, *a.* tied, well tied, fast bound.
Vitahi, *pron.* some one; see *vetahi.*
Vitahie, *pron.* another.
Vitiviti, *a.* well set, clever, neat, well finished.
— *v. n.* to smack the tongue.
Viu, *a.* burnt, as food overdone, in roasting, frying, &c.
— *v. n.* to be scorched by the fire.
Vivi, *s.* a grasshopper.
— *s.* the beginning of a retreat of a party engaged in war.
— *s.* the spray of the sea.
Vivivivi, *v. n.* to chirp.
Vivo, *s.* the Tahitian nasal flute.
Vivovivo, *v. n.* see *vinivini.*

THE END.

TAHITI:
PRINTED AT THE LONDON MISSIONARY SOCIETY'S PRESS—1851.

APPENDIX.

CONTAINING A LIST OF FOREIGN WORDS USED IN THE TAHITIAN BIBLE, IN COMMERCE, ETC, WITH THE SOURCES FROM WHENCE THEY HAVE BEEN DERIVED.

N. B.—The small italic letters indicate the derivation: *gr.* Greek; *heb.* Hebrew; *eng.* English; *lat.* Latin, *fr.* French, &c: The dash following a word signifies that it is of the same derivation as the one preceding it.

A.

Abuso, *gr* an abyss.
Adama, *heb* a Sardine and Sardis.
Aeto, *gr* an eagle.
Afa, *eng* half.
Agemana, *heb* a caldron.
Ahei, — a bull rush.
Aheleme, — an amethyst.
Ahelima, — lign aloes.
Aileta sahara, — Aijelith sharah.
Aili, — the hart or hind.
Akaride, *gr* the locust.
Akera, *eng* an acre.
Alabata, — alabaster.
Alamuga, *heb* the almug tree.
Alamota, — alamoth
Ale, — an oak.
Alegoria, *gr* an allegory.
Aletasehita, *heb* Altaschith.
Aloe, — aloes.
Alona, *gr* a threshing floor.
Alope, — a fox.
Aluna, *heb* an oak.
Amene, — amen.
Anatema, *gr* anathema.
Anatole, --- East.
Aneke, *heb* a ferret.
Anephe, — the heron.
Aneto, *gr* anise.
Aposetolo, — an apostle.
Arabe, *heb* a locust.
Arenio, *gr* a lamb
Arezi, *heb* the cedar.
Ario, *gr* silver.
Arobe, *heb* a willow.
Arote, *gr* a plough.
Aruna, *heb* an ark, chest.
Aseka, — wounded testicles.
Asema, — a trespass offering.
Asepi, *eng* an asp.
Asini, *gr* an ass.
Auro, — gold.
Azazela, *heb* a scape goat.

B

Bakete, *eng* a bucket.
Bapetizo, *gr* baptise.
Barada, *heb* hail.
Basileia, *gr* a kingdom.
Bato, *heb* a bath, a measure.
Bedila, — tin
Behemota, — Behemoth.
Beka, — Bekah.
Beluni, — nuts.
Beme, *heb* cattle.
Berabeio, *gr* prize, crown.
Bereketa, *heb* carbuncle.
Berusi, — fir.
Boti, *eng* a boat
Bovi, *heb* an ox, oxen.
Buka, *eng* a book.

D.

Daba, *heb* a bear.

Dae, *heb* a vulture.
Darabana, — a goad.
Debure, — a bee.
Deheni, — millet.
Demoni, *gr* a devil.
Denari, — a penny.
Dia, — Jupiter.
Diabolo, — the devil.
Diakono, — a deacon.
Diluvi, *lat* deluge.
Dudaima, *heb* mandrakes.
Dukipata, — the lapwing.

E.

Ehideni, *gr* a viper.
Ekalesia, *gr* a church.
Enemi, *eng* an enemy.
Epaoidoi, *gr* magicians.
Epha, *heb* an ephah.
Ephoda, *heb* an ephod.
Episekopo, *gr* a bishop, overseer.
Episetole, — an epistle.
Etene, — heathen.
Euhari. — the Lord's Supper.
Euhe, *gr.* a vow.
Evanelia, — the Gospel.

F.

Fevera, *eng* fever.
Faraoa, — flour.
Feraipani, — frying pan.

G.

Geda, *heb* coriander.
Gehena, *gr* Hell.
Gima, *heb* a bull rush.
Gitita, — Gittith.
Goela, — kinsman.
Gopheri, — brimstone.
Gubi,— the great grasshopper.

H.

Hade, *gr* the grave, hell.
Hairesi, — division.
Halikedoni, — chalcedony.
Hamera, *eng* a hammer, also a blacksmith.
Hanere, *eng* a hundred.
Hapaina, — a glass tumbler.
Hatete, *eng* a jacket.
Hebere, *heb* a charmer.
Hebedoma, *gr.* a week.
Hedesa, *heb* a myrtle.
Helebe, *heb* cheese.
Helebena, *heb* Galbanum.
Heledu, — a weasel.
Heleni, *gr* Greek, Greece, a Grecian.
Hemera, *heb* pitch.
Herema, — a flat nose.
Herusoparasa, *gr* chrisophrasis.
Heruza, *heb* a threshing instrument.
Hesede, *heb* a stork.
Hesemala, — amber.
Hesene, — a breast plate.
Hetimi, — a signet.
Hezere, — courts.
Hezira, — leeks.
Hiero, *gr* a temple.
Himene, *eng* hymn, to sing.
Hina, *heb* a hin.
Hiona, *gr* snow.
Hipo, — a horse.
Hisopa, *heb* hyssop.
Homera — Homer.
Huakineto. *gr* Jacinth.
Huhe, *heb* a thorn.

I.

Ielema, *heb* a crystal.
Inesupha, — the great owl.
Inita, *eng* ink.
Ione, *heb* the ostrich, owl, and dove.
Isephe, — Jasper.
Iubili, *eng* Jubilee.

K.

Kadakasa, *heb* an agate.
Kade, — cassia.
Kafa, *eng* a calf.
Kamino, *heb* a furnace.
Kane, — a cane.
Kaphara, — camphor.
Kapharata, *gr* the mercy seat.
Karekema, *heb* saffron.

Kase, *heb* straw or stubble.
Kasema, — divination.
Kata, — a pelican.
Katara, *gr* to curse.
Kehe, *heb* the chameleon.
Keli, — pulse.
Kemeta, — a snail.
Keni, — lice.
Kephoda, — the bittern
Kera, — a partridge.
Keranio, *gr* Calvary.
Kerehe, *heb* crystal.
Kerite, — barley.
Kerubi, — cherubim.
Kesemuta, — Rye.
Kikeuna, — a gourd.
Kime, — the Pleiades.
Kinamo, — cinnamon.
Kinira, — a harp.
Kitana, — a coat.
Kiura, — a laver.
Koheleta, — Ecclesiastes.
Korebana, — corbon, a gift
Kubiti, *eng* a cubit.
Kumina, *heb* cummin.
Kuphi, — an ape.
Kusa, — an owl.
Kuse, — fetches.
Kuzion, — cassia.

L.

Lebene, *heb* the poplar.
Lemoni, *eng* lemon.
Leni — a line, chalk.
Leta, — a letter.
Lepera, — a leper.
Lesima, *heb* a figure.
Letae, — a lizard.
Leviatana, — leviathan.
Libano, — frankincense.
Lili. *eng* the lily.
Lino, *gr* flax.
Liona, *eng* a lion.
Loga, *heb* a log, a measure.
Logo, *gr* the word.
Lone *heb* wormwood.
Lota, *eng* a lock.
Luko, *gr* a wolf.
Luta, *heb* myrrh.

M.

Mahalata, *heb*. Mahaloth.
Mahalata leanota, *heb* Mahaluth leanathoth.
Mahula, *heb*. dances or pipes.
Malatete, *eng* molasses.
Mamoe, sheep.
Mamona, *gr* mammon.
Maschila, *heb* Maschil.
Maseli, — proverbs,
Medebara, — a wilderness
Mehete, — a censer.
Melahi, — an angel.
Meleni, *eng* a melon.
Meleti, a plate.
Meli, *gr* honey.
Menasehe, *heb* a chief musician.
Menehe, — a meat offering.
Menehesa, — an Enchanter.
Menora. — a weaver's beam.
Menure, — a candlestick.
Mera, — a dowry.
Mesia, — the Messiah.
Moili, — a robe.
Mule, a millstone.
Mura, *heb* myrrh.
Mutelabena, — Muthlabben.

N.

Nabala, *heb* Psalteries.
Nakata. — the scall.
Nao, *gr* Temple.
Naradi, *heb*. spikenard.
Natapha, — stacte.
Nazira, — a Nazarite.
Nehilota, — Nehiloth.
Nemera, — a leopard.
Nepheka, — an emerald
Nesa, — a hawk.
Neseka, — a drink offering.
Neseteia, *gr* a fasting or fast.
Niteia, *heb* nitre

O.

Ogura, *heb* a swallow.
Okabara. — the mouse.

Okereba, — a scorpion.
Olelepha, — a bat.
Olive, *eng* an olive.
Oluke, *heb* horseleech.
Olura, *gr* Rye.
Omera, *heb* an omer.
Oniani, *eng* an onion.
Ophali, *heb* emerods.
Ophereta, *heb* lead.
Ophi, *gr* a serpent.
Orabi, *heb* woof.
Orama, *gr* a vision.
Oramuna, *heb* the chesnut.
Oreba, — a raven.
Orebi, — a fly.
Osa, — a moth.
Osa, — Arcturus.
Ozeni, — the osprey.

P.

Pahi auahi, steam ship.
Paina, *eng* the pine.
Paieti, — piety.
Palake, *gr* a concubine.
Pane, *lat* Bread.
Pani, *eng* pan, pot.
Parabole, *gr* a parable.
Paradaiso. — Paradise.
Paritenia, — a virgin.
Pasa, *heb* the passover.
Penenima, — a ruby.
Peresa. — the ossiphage.
Peresibutero, *gr.* an elder.
Peritome, — circumcision
Peropheta, — *eng* a prophet
Perosephora, *gr.* an offering.
Petou, — a fan.
Pharemake, — a sorcerer, sorcery.
Pharisea, *eng* a Pharisee.
Pheradi, *heb.* a mule.
Phuli, — lentiles.
Poiephura, *gr* purple.
Poretiko, — porch.

R

Raite, *eng* rice.
Rana, *heb* the frog
Rase, — hemlock.
Reema, — the unicorn.
Reta, *eng* a razor.
Rehema, *heb.* the gier eagle.
Remuna, — the pomegranate.
Renanima, — the ostrich.
Retaina, — the Juniper.
Ribini, *eng* ribbon.
Ru, — a rule for measuring.

S.

Sabaka, *heb* the sackbut.
Sabati, *eng* the sabbath.
Sadukea, *gr* Sadducees.
Sairima, *heb* satyrs.
Salamo, *gr* Psalms.
Salu, *heb* the quail.
Saphana, — the coney.
Satani, *eng* Satan.
Satauro, *gr* the cross.
Sea, *heb* a measure.
Seba, --- the tortoise.
Sebu, --- the agate.
Sebela, --- an ear of corn.
Sehelata. --- onycha
Sehephate, --- consumption.
Sehipha, --- the cuckoo.
Sekadi, *heb* the almond.
Sekele. --- the shekel.
Sekene, --- the tabernacle.
Seleka, --- the cormorant.
Selese, --- instruments of music.
Seloma, *heb* the bald locust.
Semaradino, *gr* an emerald.
Semeio, *gr.* a sign.
Semisa, *heb* an adamant.
Sena, --- ivory.
Seninita, --- Shenninith.
Sepeta, *eng* sceptre.
Sephiphona, *heb* the adder or asp.
Seredona, --- an onyx.
Sesa, *heb* marble.
Sigaiona, --- shiggaion.
Sigionota, --- Shigeonoth.
Silo, --- shiloh.
Sinapi, *gr* mustard.

Sire, *heb* song.
Sitima, --- shittim.
Sitona, *gr* wheat.
Sosanina, *heb* Shoshannim.
Sukamino, *gr.* sycamore.
Suke, *gr* a fig.
Sumephonia, *heb* a dulcimer.
Sumi, — garlick.
Sunago, *gr* synagogue.
Sunadere, --- a council.
Supheri, *heb.* the cornet.
Suphete, — judgment.
Susena. --- a lily.

T.

Ta, *eng* Tar.
Tabena, *heb* stubble.
Tabereno, *gr* a tavern.
Taputae, *eng* turpentine.
Taime, *eng* time.
Taleni, *lat* a talent.
Tamara, *heb* the palm.
Tanesemata, --- the swan.
Taofe, *eng* coffee.
Taote, *eng* a doctor.
Tapetana, *eng* captain.
Tarati, *eng* a glass.
Tarisissa, *heb* a beryl.
Tausani, *eng* a thousand.
Tavana, --- governor.
Tahemesa, *heb* the night hawk.
Teki, --- a peacock.
Telona, *gr* a publican
Teni, *heb* the dragon or serpent.
Teraphima, *heb* Seraphim.
Tereze, --- the cypress.
Terume, --- a heave offering.
Tihota, *eng* sugar.
Tiripuna, *fr* tribunal.
Totini, *eng* stocking.
Titeta --- teakettle.
Tuata, *eng* a quarter.
Tumiama, *gr* incense.
Ture, *heb* law.
Tusia, *gr* an offering.
Tutama, *eng* cucumber.

U.

Uaitete, --- a waistcoat.
Uefa, --- a wafer.

V

Vinega, --- Vinegar.

Z.

Zabi, *heb* a roe.
Zebuo, --- a speckled bird.
Zepho, --- an adder, asp, or cockatrice.
Zephura, --- a sparrow.
Zeroe, --- the hornet.
Zizania. *gr* tares.
Zubi, *heb* an issue.

DAYS OF THE WEEK.

Tapati, *eng* Sabbath.
Monere, --- Monday.
Mahana piti, Tuesday.
Mahana toru, Wednesday.
Mahana maha, Thursday.
Faraire, *eng* Friday.
Mahana maa, Saturday.

MONTHS OF THE YEAR.

Ianuari, *eng* Januari.
Febuare, February.
Mati, March.
Eperera, April.
Me, May.
Iunu, June.
Atete, August.
Tetema, September.
Atopa, October.
Novema, November.
Ditema, December.

ERRATA.

PAGE.	COL.	LINE.	
2	2	6	read *maha* for *mahu*.
4	1	34	read *aararu* for *arararu*.
47	1	3	read *altar* for *alter*.
82	1	27	read *branching* for *brauching*.
83	2	18	read *Fau* for *Faa*.
84	1	40	read *Feafeau*, for *Faafeau*.
87	2	3	read *hind* for *fore*.
98	2	10	read *hapi* for *hapai*.
100	2	24	read *heamaterohe*, for *heamaterahe*.
123	2	43	read *mahanaoo* for *mahanoo*.
139	2	12	read *matirohi* for *matirahi*.
144	2	6	read *fish* for *first*
144	2	8	read *cock* for *cockle*.
161	1	1	read *beast* for *bea*.
181	1	21	read *fish* for *fist*.
182	1	25	read *ihitumu* for *ihituma*.
192	2	34	read *formerly feohi*, for *formaly faahe*.
195	1	9	read *peperu* for *pepera*.
195	1	22	read *perehahu* for *perehaha*.
196	1	35	read *lochia* for *lachia*.
199	1	8	read *rua* for *raa*.
201	2	17	read *poaatuamoo* for *ponataamoo*.
203	1	45	read *porumaruma* for *porumaramaruma*.
208	2	41	read *puhaharu* for *puhuharu*.
211	2	12	read *puoi oi oaitau* for *puororaitau*.
214	1	4	read *moth* for *snail*
217	1	15	read *torotea* for *toreteo*.
217	2	14	read *puuru* for *puura*.
218	2	17	read *iatoai* for *iatoa*.
220	1	15	read *faifaia* for *faifuia*.
226	2	43	read *maue* for *mane*
229	1	23	read *pauma* for *paunia*.
239	2	42	read *taetae* for *taetea*.
244	2	26	read *Tairo* for *Taero*.
249	1	24	read *taomatotuatua* for *taomatatuatua*.
249	2	23	read *taotao* for *taotoo*.
251	2	5	read *Topatapaiaha* for *tapatapiha*.
252	2	40	read *vai* for *vaa*.
264	1	7	read *paraha* for *parahe*.

269	2	41	read *Hina* for *Hira*.
270	2	8	read *hand* for *head*.
275	1	23	read *conceive* for *converse*.
275	2	25	read *toahuahu* for *toahuaha*.
275	2	19	read *hora* for *hara*.
277	1	3	read *tohetohe* for *tohitahe*.
288	2	22	read *raoere* for *rauere*.
294	1	19	read *turai* for *tarai*
296	1	23	read *Tuupiri* for *Taupiri*.
301	1	39	read *paeapiti* for *pueapiti*.
304	1	7	read *paaehere* for *paehere*.
309	1	15	read *rapae* for *rape*.
311	2	4	read *vaiite* for *vaitie*.
313	1	27	read *veri* for *vere*.

CPSIA information can be obtained
at www.ICGtesting.com
Printed in the USA
BVHW040521070222
628185BV00007B/111